SEE HOW THEY GROW:
INFANTS AND TODDLERS

Join us on the web at

EarlyChildEd.delmar.com

SEE HOW THEY GROW:
INFANTS AND TODDLERS

SUE MARTIN

JENNIFER BERKE

THOMSON

DELMAR LEARNING Australia Canada Mexico Singapore Spain United Kingdom United States

THOMSON

DELMAR LEARNING

See How They Grow: Infants and Toddlers

Sue Martin, Jennifer Berke

Vice President, Career Education SBU:
Dawn Gerrain

Managing Editor:
Robert L. Serenka, Jr.

Senior Acquisitions Editor:
Erin O'Connor

Editorial Assistant:
Stephanie Kelly

Product Manager:
Philip Mandl

Director of Production:
Wendy A. Troeger

Production Manager:
J.P. Henkel

Content Project Manager:
Amber Leith

Technology Project Manager:
Sandy Charette

Director of Marketing:
Wendy E. Mapstone

Channel Manager:
Kristin McNary

Cover Design:
Dolce Media

Composition:
Interactive Composition Corporation

Library of Congress
Cataloging-in-Publication Data

Martin, Sue.
   See how they grow : infants and toddlers /
Sue Martin, Jennifer Berke.
      p. cm.
Includes bibliographical references and index.
   ISBN-13: 978-1-4180-1922-8
   ISBN-10: 1-4180-1922-4
   1. Infants—Development.   2. Toddlers—
Development.   3. Child development.
I. Berke, Jennifer Eileen. II. Title.
   HQ774.M295 2007
   305.231--dc22

                              2006013105

NOTICE TO THE READER

Publisher does not warrant or guarantee any of the products described herein or perform any independent analysis in connection with any of the product information contained herein. Publisher does not assume, and expressly disclaims, any obligation to obtain and include information other than that provided to it by the manufacturer.

The reader is expressly warned to consider and adopt all safety precautions that might be indicated by the activities herein and to avoid all potential hazards. By following the instructions contained herein, the reader willingly assumes all risks in connection with such instructions.

The Publisher makes no representation or warranties of any kind, including but not limited to, the warranties of fitness for particular purpose or merchantability, nor are any such representations implied with respect to the material set forth herein, and the publisher takes no responsibility with respect to such material. The publisher shall not be liable for any special, consequential, or exemplary damages resulting, in whole or part, from the readers' use of, or reliance upon, this material.

The authors and Thomson Delmar Learning affirm that the Web site URLs referenced herein were accurate at the time of printing. However, due to the fluid nature of the Internet, we cannot guarantee their accuracy for the life of the edition.

Contents

CHAPTER 7
Me and You: Infants at 6 to 9 Months / 173

CHAPTER 8
Raring to Go: Infants at 9 to 12 Months / 199

CHAPTER 9
Becoming Toddlers: Children 12 to 18 Months / 227

CHAPTER 10
Feeling Around: Toddlers at 18 to 24 Months / 271

CHAPTER 11
Here and Now: Toddlers from 2 to 3 Years of Age / 301

Preface

BACKGROUND

Welcome to *See How They Grow*, a book that encourages the adoption of a responsive understanding of each child and invites the reader to develop the perspective that babies and young children are incredible human beings from the minute of birth. This book, originally published in Canada in 2003, offered such a unique perspective on the care and education of infants and toddlers, it was recommended that it be made available to the early childhood field in the United States.

PURPOSE

This text provides an overview of the growth and development of infants and toddlers from neonate up through the age of 3. Special emphasis is placed on the *phenomenological* approach of interacting with children throughout this time frame. In essence, this approach demands that caregivers create a mindset that leads to a more human and responsive understanding of each child. Instead of studying early childhood from the outside, this approach encourages all who interact with young children to try to get into the conscious world of the children, starting by recognizing their levels of alertness and reading their cues. This work involves becoming a sensitive observer and acquiring the skill of *being with* children, rather than *doing to* children. Combined with this approach is the scientific methodology garnered through the lens of child study. In merging these qualitatively different methods, readers will achieve a level of increased competence as they become reflective practitioners who work and interact with children and families in a more purposeful and meaningful style—a style that has responsiveness (responsivity) at its core.

Overall, the foundation of this book's approach is based on the acknowledgement that all children are competent and powerful learners and deserving of respect. Throughout the text, *teacher, caregiver, educarer, care provider, nurturer,* and other terms are used interchangeably, promoting the idea that the role of caring for and educating infants and toddlers is a seamless endeavor. Caring for educating, nurturing, and being with children are all of equal value and importance.

Research into what constitutes quality care is presented with particular stress on how to recognize and respond to individual, familial, and cultural differences. These elements are nested in developmentally appropriate practice, but special care has been taken to make teachers cognizant of the fact that development in our country is often filtered through the cultural lens of the Western world. Considering the increasing diversity of the population in the United States, it is imperative that we become aware of how culture, family beliefs, and traditions mediate our interpretation of child development.

You, the reader, have arrived at this point in time with numerous, but different, life experiences and skills. However, whatever your background, the overarching motivation that is required is an interest in learning about early childhood. As long as that initial interest exists, this book should offer you new perspectives and information. This text should be useful for:

- student early childhood educators—undergraduate and graduate
- practicing early childhood educators
- family child care providers
- infant and toddler specialists
- home visitors
- family educators
- resource teachers working with infants, toddlers, or 2-year-olds

It may also be of interest to individuals studying the philosophy of early care and education, child development, parenting skills, or family-life sciences.

SECTIONS AND FEATURES

The initial chapters describe the philosophy of the book, encourage readers to become action-researchers who begin formulating a philosophy of care and education for young children, explain various methods of observation and the importance of honing observational skills, provide a baseline of information on growth and development, discuss historical and recent contributions to the field of early childhood care and education, and describe the neonatal period in detail. Chapters 5 through 8 focus on development in three-month spans, Chapters 9 and 10 cover a six-month spans and Chapter 11 a one-year span. The breakdown in these age ranges allows an extensive examination of how children grow and change rapidly in all domains of development: physical, emotional, social, cognitive, and language. This approach was chosen purposefully so that students could tune into children and enter their life-world. Developmental variation and alerts, including those of exceptional children, are considered, as well as health and safety issues, potential signs of abuse and neglect, and the inclusion of families as partners in care. In addition, most chapters have topics of special interest that are considered in an in-depth manner.

Specifically, the textbook contains the following elements:

• Learning outcomes are listed at the beginning of each chapter so that the reader can see that specific goals are expected to be attained. These outcomes may be matched to course or program learning outcomes, competencies, or core body-of-knowledge goals, in accordance with the educational practice of an institution.

• This is followed by an account of a real life scenario, which offers the opportunity to think about one part of the information presented in the chapter.

• Chapter 1 challenges readers to examine their own values and beliefs in regard to the care and education of young children, describes the skills needed to become a reflective practitioner, briefly discusses some contributions to the history of the early care and education field, considers what constitutes developmentally appropriate practice, and begins to lay the foundation of philosophies for the care and education of infants and toddlers.

• Chapter 2 outlines the need for honing observation skills, since they are the foundation for best practices in early care and education. A variety of useful methods for observation and assessment are discussed. The phenomenological approach is more fully explained, and its intersection with current scientific approaches is examined.

• Chapter 3 provides an overview of growth and development supported by theories and research obtained from well-known and respected schools of thought, as well as from current research. The essential point of this chapter is to clarify the fact that there are many ways to interpret behavior. Findings from brain research, a recurring theme in this book, are examined, and some initiatives on behalf of young children and families are discussed.

After these introductory chapters, many text books would then focus on separate topics such as motor development, cognitive development, or guidance strategies, just to suggest a few. However, the authors chose to use a holistic approach to viewing children, and therefore merged these topics into an integrated whole. This was done with purposeful intent in order to encourage the reader to "see" the child as gaining these developmental aspects at the same time and needing responsive care, support, and guidance simultaneously. The child is holistic and so is the approach. Also, by thoroughly examining development in a deeper vein, the reader is forced to slow down his thinking. It is hoped that this enables the reader to more easily enter into the conscious world of the child.

Thus, in Chapters 4–11, the reader will encounter the following:

• The outlines of growth and behavioral changes that are likely to be observed through each of these stages of development: neonate; infants 6 weeks to 3 months; infants 3 to 6 months; infants 6 to 9 months; infants 9 to 12 months; toddlers 12 to 18 months; toddlers 18 to 24 months; and toddlers from 2 to 3 years. These overviews are not intended to be profiles of what *should* happen, only what might be observed. The text takes special care to avoid reinforcing the notion that there is a rigid timetable or schedule for development, and makes clear that children should not be measured against norms in a manner that finds any child intrinsically deficient or advanced. The emphasis is always on considering children competent!

• Developmental variations developmental alerts, and everyday health and safety factors are featured. As children change from infants to crawlers to walkers to runners, developmental variation and areas of concern may come to light. Also, increasing mobility brings new challenges for keeping children safe and healthy. These all require broader responsibilities on the part of care providers.

• The topics of abuse and neglect receive special focus. This is in keeping with the National Association for the Education of Young Children's effort to bring these topics to the forefront of care for young children. It is important that care providers understand that there are common strands of information about these sensitive and troubling subjects. The text also underscores the fact that manifestations of abuse and neglect are often related to the developmental stage of a child.

• Families as partners in education is another important topic that is featured. The child is not considered a separate entity, but part of a family and complex social system. Effective communication channels, which maximize the flow of information from home—to care facilities—back to home, are essential in order to ensure optimal development for children. Collaborating with families, as well as respecting familial values, beliefs, and cultures, is critical to the ongoing development of children. Strategies for creating and supporting communication and involvement are suggested.

• Each of these chapters has a section entitled "Getting in Tune," which sets the stage for responsivity, a core concept of this book that combines care and education, and enables the reader to appreciate how to individualize responsiveness.

• Each chapter has a summary of the main ideas presented in order to help the reader organize the material and check on comprehension of important points.

- A further reading section, useful videos, and helpful Web sites are listed at the end of each chapter.
- A glossary of key terms, a reference section, and an index are found at the end of the text.

FEATURES

Tools to help the reader translate the "theoretical" into the practical include:
- learning outcomes at the beginning of each chapter
- teaching descriptions from real life scenarios
- key terms
- highlighted anecdotes and additional information
- documentation through the use of photographs
- tables, figures, and boxes
- symbols to draw the reader's attention to specific topics
- Online Companion™

The changes from the original textbook include the following:
- New content relevant to the care and education of young children in the United States has been included in this edition.
- Research has been updated to include timely sources of information on various topics.
- Developmentally appropriate practice is aligned with a focus on best practice.
- Key Terms: You will find key terms defined on some of the pages of the text book. These are terms that the authors felt were essential to your understanding of the information. You will see these words written in **bold blue** type, and the definition of the term on the page.
- The Glossary contains the Key Terms, but also other educational terms that the reader may find helpful.
- There are highlighted sections throughout the book that contain personal comments or additional facts that may help the reader to better understand a concept by offering a real life perspective on a topic or supplementary information.
- More photographs are included than in the original textbook. The photos were taken in several child care centers and family child care homes. An attempt was made to include a more diverse population of children and providers. Sad to say, trying to find men involved in early care is never easy.
- Symbols used in this text book include:

    Developmental Alerts

Health Concerns and

    Online Companion

- The most significant change from the original textbook is the addition of the Online Companion. The Online Companion was created for the express purpose of engaging students in hands-on activities and research in order to help them expand their knowledge about child growth and development; additional early childhood topics; curriculum; guidance strategies; and other relevant issues. Including curriculum and guidance strategies in the Online Companion is a major shift from the original textbook. This was a necessary compromise, since there is always a space constraint for textbooks. A 60-page textbook lacks a certain appeal, so the decision was made to put some of the original textbook content into the companion.
- The Online Companion is comprised of sections that align with the textbook chapters or offer additional information:
  - Additional Support
  - Everyday Health and Safety
  - Getting in Tune with Infants, Toddlers, and Twos
  - Activities
  - Toys
  - Books

Each time you see the logo, the icon will direct you to a specific section of the Online Companion. If you utilize the **Additional Support** section, you will find that it expands on information covered in each chapter through the presentation of articles, Web links, or forms. For example, because learning to read cues from infants and toddlers is key to helping the adult meet the children where they are in any given moment, these cues are scrutinized in great detail, not only in the text but also in this tool, so that students feel prepared to begin their interactions with infants and toddlers on a solid footing. That is why in a number of chapters, the student will be directed to the Additional Support section to read information on interpreting facial expressions and body language. Here is the first suggestion to get you using this tool: Although this textbook starts with the neonate, we know that much happens to a child over the time frame encompassing from conception until the birth event. Go to the Additional Support section of your Online Companion and follow the links to discover some interesting information about the developing child.

The Everyday Health and Safety section allows the student to examine these specific topics at a more in-depth level. Each chapter lists which health topics are covered in this section.

The Getting in Tune section expands on the responsivity skills introduced in each chapter.

The **Activities** section serves two purposes. First, there are activities designed to enhance the reader's personal knowledge and skills. These include suggestions for hands-on inquiry, as well as Web sites for clarification of ideas or gaining a more-in-depth knowledge on a host of topics.

Second, there are activities designed for use with infants and toddlers. These are the curriculum and guidance ideas, and we urge you to use the Online Companion to investigate ways of supporting children's emerging skills. These are not "recipes" for activities, but rather suggestions of techniques to use to engage children. Since this combination of content and practicality clearly demonstrates that no separation exists between care and education, the pre-service teacher will ultimately comprehend that all aspects of interactions with infants and toddlers are critical to their overall development. Many of these activities, whether designed for the reader or for the dyad of reader–child, will help build a repertoire of ideas and skills that eventually should translate into an increased understanding of how to support and facilitate emerging skills in young children.

The **Toys** section contains lists of appropriate toys, which can be utilized with children at various stages of development.

The **Books** section contains titles of books to share with children and families in order to foster the acquisition of language and literacy.

PROFESSIONAL ENHANCEMENT SERIES

A new supplement to accompany this text is the Infants and Toddlers Professional Enhancement handbook for students. This resource, which is part of Thomson Delmar Learning's Early Childhood Education Professional Enhancement series, focuses on key topics of interest for future early childhood directors, teachers, and caregivers. Students will keep this informational supplement and use it for years to come in their early childhood professional development. This critical resource, along with all others in the Professional Enhancement series, provides students with similar tools, such as:

* Tips for getting off to a great start in a new environment
* Information about typical development patterns of children from birth through school age
* Suggestions for materials that promote development for children from infancy through the primary grades
* Tools to assist teachers in observing children and gathering data to help set appropriate goals for individual children
* Guides for planning appropriate classroom experiences and sample lesson plans
* Tips for introducing children to the joys of literacy
* Resources for teachers for professional development
* Case studies of relevant, realistic situations, as well as best practices for successfully navigating them
* Insight into issues and trends facing early childhood directors, educators, and teachers today

The Professional Enhancement series is intended for use by students in their first classrooms, as it is fully customizable, and there is ample space for users to make notes of their own experiences, successes, and suggestions for future lessons. The editors at Thomson Delmar Learning encourage and appreciate any feedback on this new venture. Go to www.earlychilded.delmar.com <http://www.earlychilded.delmar.com> and click on the "Professional Enhancement series feedback" link to let us know what you think.

Becoming a teacher is a process of continuing to grow, learn, reflect, and discover through experience. Having these resources may help tomorrow's teachers along their way.

CD-ROM

The CD-ROM, found in the back of the book, contains additional activities, exercises and checklists. Students are encouraged to explore the activities that have been created as an aid to reflect on and apply chapter concepts.

ACKNOWLEDGMENT

The first individual who must be acknowledged is the author of the original text, Sue Martin. I have never met or talked with Sue, but I felt an immediate connection to her, since some of my beliefs regarding early care and education resonated with ideas she presented in the text. I also perceived a common bond, since I had lived in Canada (Quebec) for the first eight years of my married life. My husband and all my children are Canadian citizens. I also appreciate a viewpoint that encourages those of us in the United States to look beyond our borders in order to seek a broader perspective on issues of infant and toddler care. Although I changed some of the original content, I hope that Sue's vision and voice still permeate the manuscript. It was, after all, her sensitive and loving treatment of this topic that guided my hand and thoughts in crafting the revision. Sue, your writing challenged me to dig deep and reflect, and I am grateful to you for all your hard work and effort. I do hope that you will find my effort sufficient.

No book is written in isolation, although at times it feels like a very solitary undertaking. This revision was a much larger endeavor than originally perceived, so the sheer amount of time devoted to it meant sacrifices had to be made. Those who felt the greatest effect were my family members. I am grateful for their understanding and support, especially that of my husband, Robert, who really lost a companion for 12 months. And how could I not acknowledge the contributions my four children have made to this book? Much of what I learned—and continue to learn—about very young children started with them. Metivia, Celeste, Jonathan, and Kayce—thank you for enabling me to obtain motherhood wisdom.

The children and families I have worked with throughout the years, whether in school settings or clinic settings, contributed to my understanding of how children grow and develop and how families evolve. My college students at Mercyhurst North East and Mercyhurst continue to help me experience the fascinating world of infants and toddlers as I set out on another journey of discovery in the Infant and Toddler course I teach each year. Every time there are fresh eyes to help me gain a new perspective on the very young child. These influences have to be acknowledged, since subtly, but irrevocably, they affect how I interpret the importance of being with children and families.

The contributions from the children, families, teachers, and staff of St. Benedicts, JCC Campus Children's Center, Findley Lake Early Childhood Center, and Family Health Services were immeasurable. They willingly gave of their time and accommodated, often on very short notice, my need to be in classrooms with children, as well as my requests for specific photographic shots.

Thank you to my dear friend and colleague, Renee Hanby, who took some beautiful and revealing photographs of children and adults, once again, usually on very short notice. Your sensitive touch is evident in this book.

Finally, my editor, Phil Mandl, who inherited me midway through a process I had never experienced before. Thank you for your input, suggestions, and guidance. It was greatly appreciated!

Jennifer Markulis Berke

To our reviewers, whose valuable comments and suggestions helped to shape the final text, we owe special thanks to:

Vicki Folds, Ed.D.
Palm Beach Community College
Parkland, FL

Patricia Dilko, MPA
Canada College
Redwood, CA

Jennifer Johnson, M.Ed.
Vance-Granville Community College
Henderson, NC

Dr. Margaret King, Ed.D.
Ohio University
Athens, OH

Elaine Boski-Wilkinson, M.Ed.
Collin County Community College
Plano, TX

About the Authors

JENNIFER BERKE received her undergraduate degree in elementary education from Syracuse University, and taught first grade for the Syracuse City School District for three years. There she served on the Experimental Pre-K Board for two years, the only first grade teacher in the district to be invited to do so. After moving to Boston, she taught in a multi-age classroom (first and second grade) for the Brookline School District. While living in Boston, she completed her Masters in Special Education with a concentration in Learning Disabilities from Boston State College.

Moving to Quebec, Canada, she became the Head Teacher at Ecole la Campagne, a bilingual parent cooperative preschool for children ages 2–6. Returning to New York State after eight years, she opened Rhymes, Rhythms, and Rainbows, a private preschool for children ages 3–5. She began her college teaching at this juncture, becoming an Adjunct Instructor at Jamestown Community College for ten years. She has also worked as a Cornell Cooperative Extension Agent, a Human Development Specialist for Family Health Services—a family practice medical setting—and as an Education Specialist for the Achievement Center, an agency providing services for children with identified needs, birth through 18, and their families. In this last position, she was honored to be charged with the responsibility of starting Findley Lake Early Childhood Center and guiding the program through the NAEYC accreditation process. She feels that this undertaking allowed her the opportunity to see best practices applied, because the Center celebrates the importance of the early years every single day. Play, child-directed activities, teachers as facilitators, involvement of families, appropriate and culturally sensitive approaches to learning, and the joy of childhood are just a few of the elements that make this a successful program and serve as a model for pre-service teachers and the community.

She completed her doctoral studies at the State University of New York at Buffalo with a concentration in Early Childhood, and since 2001 has been an Associate Professor at Mercyhurst North East and Chair of the Human Growth and Development Department. She remains passionate about the early childhood profession and hopes that her students catch some of that passion in order to remain committed to a field that sometimes seems to be under siege by individuals who often "'just don't get it.'"

She has served on the Board of the New York State Association for the Education of Young Children as Chairperson for Children and Families and as a member of the Nominating Committee. She is a Past President of Chautauqua County Association for the Education of Young Children, and chaired the local conference committee for ten years. Currently, she serves on the Northwest Regional Key Board (PA), which is responsible for the development of a comprehensive plan to help create a high-quality, accessible, and affordable system of early care and education for young children in Pennsylvania. She is also a member of the National Association for Early Childhood Teacher Educators (NAECTE).

She has written parenting columns in numerous magazines, and is a co-author of *See How They Grow: Infants and Toddlers* (2007), published by Thomson Delmar Learning.

SUE MARTIN received her teaching diploma at the Froebel Institute in London and then became an educator in Cambridge of children from birth to age eight. After further study in the social sciences, she began teaching at West Ham College, where she learned about the roots of child care in England and the deprivation associated with city life. Teaching at Harlow College in Essex, and Enfield College in London, offered the chance to better understand the learner as well as curriculum development. She became an examiner of the National Nursery Examination Board as well as an editor for a professional journal, *Nursery World*.

Moving to Canada provided her with the opportunity for college teaching in Toronto, where she became a Professor of Early Childhood Education. Her teaching career in Canada has now spanned eighteen years, during which she has seen significant changes in the politics of education, the widening demands put upon educators, and the pressures that learners experience. Sue enjoys engagement with her students and believes that true education involves a partnership and a shared pathway.

Sue completed her Masters Degree in Vermont, after which she undertook a secondment to the YMCA of Greater Toronto, where she set up in-service training for educators working directly with children. Sue was a member of the Board of the Association of Early Childhood Educators, Ontario (AECEO), and was elected to the Board of the Association for Childhood Education International (ACEI). She completed her doctoral work at State University of New York at Buffalo.

Sue has written numerous informal columns for parents in parenting magazines, and many professional articles for journals, including juried research pieces. She has made contributions to textbooks, including a chapter in: Isabel Doxey's (1990) *Child Care and Education: Canadian dimensions*, Nelson, a division of Thomson Canada Ltd., and has authored two text books: *Take a Look: observation and portfolio assessment in early childhood*, 4th edition (2006) Pearson Addison-Wesley, and *See How They Grow: Infants and Toddlers* (2003) Nelson, a division of Thomson Canada Ltd.

Sue's current project with Nelson is a collaborative effort with Dr. Patricia Corson, Ryerson University, Toronto, that re-conceptualizes guidance of young children. Its working title is "Intentional and Relationship-based Guidance in Early Childhood."

CHAPTER 1

All babies need love and nurturing. This caregiver cradles the baby close to her in order to nourish the feeling of trust.

Caregiving and Educating: Philosophy and Practice

LEARNING OUTCOMES

After reading and studying this chapter, you should be able to:

- discuss the core issues that contribute to the development of a philosophy of care and education
- articulate a philosophy of care for infants, toddlers, and two-year-olds
- determine the characteristics of high-quality programs for infants and toddlers
- identify the principles of effective caregiving, nurturance, guidance, and developmental support for infants, toddlers, and 2-year-olds

SCENE

A small group of early childhood education students discuss infant and toddler program philosophies in a seminar class.

"A few months ago I didn't think about philosophy very much—but I am happy to tell you that when a parent asked about the philosophy of the center where I am doing my placement, I could tell her the important points without even looking at its philosophy statement," said Karima, a second-year early childhood education (ECE) student.

The professor replied, "Well done. Your familiarity with the philosophy of the child care center is important for several reasons. It guides you in your work with the children. It enables you to coordinate your actions with others in meeting the needs of the children. It also helps you to communicate in a meaningful way with parents concerned about the care their children receive." Karima responded, "Thanks. I can see how philosophy makes a difference to what I do, but I couldn't write my own philosophy statement."

"You will, in time," the professor assured her. "But you'll keep changing your ideas as time goes by!"

THE GENESIS OF A PHILOSOPHY

By the time we are on the path to a professional role in working with young children, we have been exposed to a variety of philosophical approaches to care and education, even if we can't label each approach. Our own childhood has provided us with a framework for thinking about the **values** that underpin these approaches: We tend to compare later experiences with those of our own childhood.

Added to our experience as children is our adult learning in the values and philosophy of child care and education. Simply observing parents and other adults interacting with children exposes us to a variety of perspectives. Some of these perspectives are labeled—Montessori, Reggio Emilia, Waldorf, constructivist, cognitive, or self-directed. People true to these labels will have clearly defined values and principles of practice. Additionally, we may have studied the great philosophers, such as Plato, Rousseau, Kant, or Sartre. Familiarity with the insights of these philosophers helps us appreciate the values on which we base our programs. These might be profound values, such as belief in education as a process of social reform or in childhood as a distinct stage in human development.

No program or family can be value-free. We need to know what the values are, how they translate into practice, and how we might influence the shaping of values. We also need to learn how to determine a philosophical perspective by observing children, families, and programs.

This chapter will provide you with some ideas about developing your own philosophy of care and education for infants, toddlers, and 2-year-olds. Since you are most likely just entering your professional career as a caregiver and educator of young children, it is important to understand that the philosophy you are formulating is the genesis of a philosophy, or the beginning of a philosophy. As time goes by, you will continue to reformulate and refine your philosophy as you gain more knowledge and information regarding children and families. This type of process is exemplified by the following:

> Professional artists enhance their talents by a reflective study of the work of other artists. They strive to identify principles that will improve their craft and advance their field for others. An artful teacher who relies on raw ability alone may take years to become skillful and helpful to students. Another artful teacher who reads professional literature, experiments with and evaluates recommended materials and procedures . . . builds on natural talent to efficiently become a versatile and effective teacher. (Howard, Williams, & Lepper, 2005, p. 3)

You are encouraged to think critically, examine your own beliefs and values, and keep an open mind regarding different viewpoints about very young children. Ultimately, this may mean that you will disagree with some of the text's perspectives! However, it is hoped that because the overall approach is one of respecting children and families, you will not disagree with that concept, even if you might show respect in ways that are different than those discussed in the text. In addition, the style of the book is to offer research, theories, ideas, and experiences to help you develop your role as one offering responsive caregiving.

It is generally assumed that observing infants and toddlers, engaging in experiences with them, extending your knowledge base, and interpreting what you observe and experience will all contribute to developing your own **philosophy**. You cannot expect to have a clearly defined "carved in stone" philosophy at the end of this book, but you will be several steps closer to clarifying your own stance. In time, you may want to revisit some of the ideas found here to challenge and refresh your personal philosophy.

TRANSLATING VALUES INTO PRACTICE

As early childhood educators, it is important for us to be aware of our beliefs and values about children, families, and child care. Box 1.1 lists the kinds of things we need to think about in order to determine our values in the key areas of parents and families, societal expectations, personal knowledge/beliefs, and the caregiver role.

However, if we want our actions to be consistent with our values, we must do more than just be aware of our values. We need to work out what they mean in practice. If, for example, you

values

beliefs of a person or social group in which we have an emotional investment (either for or against)

The care and education of infants and toddlers requires an approach that demonstrates respect of children and families.

philosophy

the investigation of knowledge and being; the perspectives and values that underpin practice

BOX 1.1

EXAMINING YOUR BELIEFS AND VALUES

Listed below are items you should consider when examining your views about parents and families, social expectations, your personal knowledge and beliefs, and the practitioner's role.

Parents and Families

- how you perceive the parental role and parental choices
- the respect you have for young children and their families
- how you perceive the adult's role in parenting, caregiving, and educating infants and toddlers

Societal Expectations

- what society wants for its children
- how society values life and the rights of the child
- how society accommodates the diverse abilities of children
- what environments society considers appropriate for young children

Personal Knowledge/Beliefs

- what you believe about the child as a separate person (or part of a larger unit, such as a family or a society)
- how you view power and control or empowerment and freedom
- how you perceive the future
- how you understand the process of change through life
- what you believe about why children exist and the purpose of life
- how you understand the notion of personal reality and the nature of experience
- what you believe about equality and hierarchy
- what you understand about human biology, psychology, and other scientific or theoretical explanations of childhood
- what you understand about how children learn
- how you perceive success
- what you believe about human potential and how it can be achieved

Caregiver Role

- how you consider your own needs and goals as a professional
- how you enter into the life experience of the infant and toddler
- what you understand about the relationships between educators and families and how they can support very young children

value the right of families to make choices about their child, then you will have to find ways to support those choices. You might, for example, follow the family's instructions about the foods their child is to be fed, or enable the child to sleep because she was awake late at night. Some things you can do easily; others are more difficult. You find that one family's choice has an impact on the choice of another family. Reflect on the following:

In an infant room a family is concerned that their child's motor development is delayed. Every time the 9-month-old is placed on his stomach he starts to cry and scream. The family has requested that you ignore his cries and encourage him to start using his arm and trunk muscles to push himself up from the floor. However, another family has requested that their 8-week-old child have a very quiet environment for sleeping. The caregivers in this scenario have two conflicting requests. They realize that a screaming child may continually disturb the sleep of other children but, at the same time, not placing the child with delayed motor development on his stomach will certainly further impede his motor strength.

In situations like this you will probably never be able to meet everyone's needs. Solutions to these situations become even more difficult when clashes result from differences in values. Baptiste and Reyes (2005) contend that "the regular contact of families and their children's care/educators create increased opportunities for conflicts often due to different value systems" (p. 5).

Often these situations require a lot of soul-searching on the part of the caregiver, lengthy discussions with family members, and guidance from other colleagues. Another source of help that can be utilized by members of the early childhood profession is *The Code of Ethics*, which proposes a common basis for resolving situations that involve ethical decision-making and presents guidelines for responsible behavior.

Code of Ethics

a document that delineates a common basis for resolving situations that involve ethical decision-making and presents guidelines for responsible behavior

The **Code of Ethics** was developed by the National Association for the Education of Young Children (NAEYC). This organization was founded in 1926 and consists of nearly 100,000 members, including teachers, administrators, college personnel, students, and family members. Currently, it is the world's largest organization working on behalf of young children. Dedicated to improving the well-being of all young children, birth through age 8, the Association focuses particular attention on the quality of educational and developmental services for all children.

State organizations of educators, as well as educational groups in many countries, have also formulated their own codes relating to ethical behavior. All of these codes contain guidelines designed to help those involved in the early childhood profession reach decisions in a fair, just, and principled manner.

The Additional Support section in the Online Companion contains links to the Code of Ethics and the National Association for the Education of Young Children.

BEYOND INSTINCT

Some people who do not work with young children wonder why it is necessary to study for a job that they think relies on common sense and instinct. Many families, they argue, have no education in parenting and yet bring up children adequately; some home child care providers may have only a little training and seem to do well enough with the children in their care. Why, then, is a philosophy of caregiving and a knowledge of child development necessary?

Instinctive behavior can be useful, but it won't help in all situations. For example, our instincts might assist us in helping a child learn a new skill, but knowledge of the child's thinking patterns might help us do a better job. On the other hand, sometimes our instincts can help us out of difficult situations. For example, when a child is in distress, an adult might instinctively make the comforting sounds and movements that no textbook could teach.

Instinctive behavior on the part of the adult is a primitive mechanism for survival. But as educators we have much higher goals than survival. We need to articulate what we really want for children, and be clear about how we will attempt to achieve it. This is accomplished through a philosophy of practice that takes into account the needs of young children at each stage of development.

CHALLENGING ASSUMPTIONS AND FAMILIAR PERCEPTIONS ABOUT INFANTS AND TODDLERS

Let's take a few minutes to think about some of the ideas that we might already have about infants and toddlers. Here we are not trying to define a philosophy, just to challenge some of the assumptions that might lead us in the wrong direction. Critical thinking helps refine our philosophy and makes sure that we are reasonably free from automatically accepting familiar perceptions as correct. "If a teacher never questions the goals and values that guide his or her work, the context in which she or he teaches, or never examines his or her assumptions, then it is our belief that this individual is not engaged in reflective teaching" (Zeichner & Liston,

1996, p. 1). Some of the following ideas may have merit or they may have a "comfort of fit," meaning we have absorbed them into our frame of reference without examination just because they feel right. As professionals, we must critique all of our ideas. If we deem them worthwhile after analysis, then our decision to hold on to them is intentional.

As you read each of the following bulleted statements, consider whether you have thought these very words, or heard these words from family members or acquaintances. Think about the written responses under each statement and examine the arguments closely. **NOTE:** We are not advocating a right or wrong response, but rather encouraging you to utilize **reflection**. Often responses lie on a continuum of acceptability from "least" to "most." In other words, what would be the least beneficial or the most beneficial for children and families when all that is known from past and current years of theory and research in the field of early childhood is taken into account? This is often difficult, challenging, and repetitive work, but very necessary.

Figure 1.1 demonstrates the cyclical nature of reflection one must engage in as a teacher. You observe an event and connect it to such things as prior experiences, values, or assumptions. Your initial perception may be immediately impacted by numerous emotional and/or subconscious influences. However, your training and education, including what you know from theory, research, and pedagogy, must now be utilized during the evaluation step of reflective teaching. This will lead you to the final step as you make decisions regarding such things as learner needs, the setup of the environment, and interactions with family members, just to name a few. Through this reflective process you are able to keep making changes that align with what is currently known to be best practices in teaching. If you want to be the best possible teacher you can be, this is a process that never ends.

The way I was brought up—what was wrong with that?

The way each of us is brought up is often accepted as the "norm." We also tend to internalize the values associated with the practices of nurturing that we experienced. Childhood experience can lead to passive acceptance of a certain philosophical approach. The challenge for us as professionals is to question our assumptions and to become aware of and review everything that we do. With reflection and a thoughtful philosophical approach, our practice can improve significantly.

I was trained for the job—isn't that good enough?

Our values relating to child care are influenced by more than our own experiences: Professional training also contributes to a standardized view of what practice should be. All training and education reflects the values of the time and place in which it occurs. For example, the early

---

reflection

a learning method that engages an individual in a process of self-observation and self-examination

---

"Reflective teaching is a cyclical process, because once you start to implement changes, then the reflective and evaluative cycle begins again."

(Tice, J. retrieved May 6, 2005. © British Council 1 BBC Published July 2004)

Figure 1.1 Reflective Teaching

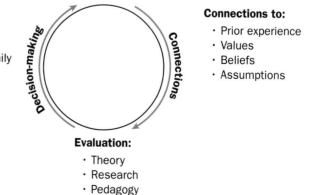

Event observed

Decision-making about:
- Learner needs
- Environment
- Interactions with family
- Adaptions

Decision-making

Connections

Connections to:
- Prior experience
- Values
- Beliefs
- Assumptions

Evaluation:
- Theory
- Research
- Pedagogy

childhood educators who studied in the 1950s will have a different mindset from those who studied in the 1980s or 1990s, or those who are studying now. Programs preparing adults to work with infants and toddlers reflect not only the current knowledge and research about children, but also differing values and societal influences.

Knowledge is increasing at a fast pace: It's difficult to keep up with current research or even to know what to believe. Although educators can help facilitate your learning, you will need to be open to new ideas, think critically, make up your own mind, and be prepared to challenge your own values. There is more than one way to approach most things; the care and education of infants is no exception. An unfamiliar child-rearing practice may have some merit, and something to teach us, although we shouldn't imitate it without reflection and examination of its applicability.

Isn't "child-centered" good?

One principle common to the philosophy of many child care centers is child-centeredness (putting the child at the center of practice). However, programs that claim to be child-centered may have different interpretations of the term, as evidenced by the following statements:

A program that is child-centered recognizes that childhood is precious and fleeting. As caregivers we need to be "in the moment" with children. This approach helps create memories that will sustain children for the rest of their lives.

- Child-centered means taking a "hands-off" approach indicating that young children play independently, and employ self-direction while the adults are rarely involved with the children's activity;
- Child-centered means that self-direction is encouraged but the adults follow the children's lead and are directly involved in the children's play;
- Child-centered means that "children have opportunities for real and meaningful input into the curriculum" (Ryan & Grieshaber, 2004, p. 50).

The term child-centered is often interchanged with child-led, child-negotiated, and even child-sensitive. How the term "child-centered" is interpreted makes a significant difference. If you use the term, be sure you define exactly what you mean by it. In general, however, you will need to think about the idea of self-direction as a part of child-centeredness.

More toys must make for a better program—mustn't they?

Providing infants and toddlers with toys and play material so that their learning potential can be realized has been the goal of many teachers who appreciate the fact that stimulation improves cognitive functioning. However, a focus on the child remains essential. Therefore, some teachers and parents now question an approach to stimulation that involves purchasing large numbers of toys, perhaps encouraging children to become mere consumers.

Young children need sensory play experiences. Is food a good choice for these experiences?

Twenty years ago, Holt (1985) stated, "We do not have to choose (yet) between survival and art, but we do need to examine how our teaching practices demonstrate our regard for the earth's resources and the people who rely on them" (p. 19). Since that time the issue of food as a play material has continued to be examined. Although many activities books continue to offer ideas that utilize food items [e.g., painting bread with food coloring, stringing macaroni to make necklaces, placing dried beans or rice in the sensory table, printing with fruit and vegetables], this topic deserves examination. Some researchers and authors (Derman-Sparks, 1989; Freeman & Swim, 2003; Jalongo & Stamp, 1997; Schirrmacher, 2005) argue that the use of food in art is inappropriate for several reasons:

- children may learn to take food for granted and not understand that it is a precious commodity that should not be wasted;
- the use of food for learning disregards and disrespects food's place in other cultures; and
- if children play with food, they may learn that it is acceptable to eat play materials.

Others (Eliason & Jenkins, 2002; Mayesky, 2005; York, 2003) give suggestions for using food in art activities that support the development of physical, social, emotional, and cognitive domains and provide necessary sensory play opportunities. What is your opinion when presented with these conflicting viewpoints?

▪▪ Development is divided into domains—has that changed?

Recently educators, researchers, and philosophers have been challenging some long-held beliefs about children's growth development and how the way we study these subjects shapes our thinking (Kilbride, 1997; Penn, 1999). For example, the concept of developmental domains, readily accepted by many, is really an artificial notion created as a way to provide more detailed information about particular aspects of development. Although domains of development are usually reviewed as parts of the whole, the concept of the whole is often overlooked, especially given the current atmosphere of *No Child Left Behind* (to be addressed later) and the downward push for academic accountability.

Clearly, holistic development focuses on "who the child is" rather than what the child can do in each developmental area. However, it must be acknowledged that hundreds of years of theory and research support the concept of developmental domains. Therefore, we should no more do away with the concept of developmental domains than throw out ideas such as Piaget's developmental stages, or Gesell's physical milestones. It is still essential to refer to developmental norms during the process of identifying the need for early intervention, as well as for making decisions regarding appropriate environments, curricula, and materials. The preamble in the *NAEYC Code of Ethical Conduct and Statement of Commitment* discusses the importance of using knowledge of child development, which would include domains and norms, when making decisions (NAEYC, 2005). However, we must understand that every child is a whole child despite behavior and characteristics that vary because of differences in developmental domains, temperament, learning style, gender, socioeconomic status, and culture, as well as many other factors. "Children are not deficient or at risk because they develop in unique directions" (Trawick-Smith, 2006, p. 9). This diversity makes them unique human beings.

What is the solution? An acceptable approach might be to combine the concept of the holistic view with the concept of domains. This method presents the child as a whole person, but also as one who can be viewed from a variety of different angles. Our thinking about fundamental concepts, such as developmental domains and the "norm" of developmental domains, also needs to expand to include the wide range of results which become increasingly more evident as we work with a growing number of children with diverse cultural backgrounds.

▪▪ Is developmentally appropriate practice still important?

Designing and delivering programs that are appropriate for the developmental level of the child seem like a logical way of programming. Bredekamp's (1987) original research and creation of what does, and does not, constitute developmentally appropriate practice (DAP) were influential in shaping how programs should be individually child-centered and suitable for the child's stage of development. The position statement offered guidelines for decision-making by early childhood practitioners. However, the publication of the first DAP document by the National Association for the Education of Young Children (NAEYC) was critiqued in such a way that it was found to be insufficiently inclusive from a cultural perspective—what was thought to be developmentally appropriate was actually limited to a monocultural point of view. Also the document suggested that education be guided largely by age-related characteristics, and was criticized by some because of its apparent limitations (Kessler & Swader, 1994; Lubeck, 1996; Mallory & New, 1994). Some practitioners mistakenly thought that the DAP document provided

---

sensory play

play that involves touching, smelling, tasting, hearing, or seeing individually or simultaneously

developmental domains

areas of individual growth and development, including the physical, intellectual, emotional, and social

holistic development

an approach to development that is based on a viewpoint which visualizes a wider concept of a child including history, relationships, experiences, culture, present status, health, gender, etc., as well as the interdependence of these parts

norms

the average performance of a large sample of children at designated ages

developmentally appropriate practice (DAP)

all aspects of children's programs and practices that are designed and implemented in ways that demonstrate that the needs of a group of children are met, that the different needs and developmental levels of individual students are considered and met, and that the needs of the family, including cultural and linguistic needs, are respected and included

a benchmark for ages and stages of development and used it to assess the development of children.

The 1987 document fostered much debate about early childhood education, both within and without the field, and did result in misunderstandings and misconceptions about the intent of DAP. Divisionary points included a lack of sensitivity to cultural and familial differences, concerns over the need for individualized practice, and the feeling that the document, as a North American creation, was not applicable in other contexts.

In 1997, Bredekamp and Copple expanded the scope of the original document to include answers to some of issues raised in the ongoing discourse. NAEYC recognized that it was critical to move "beyond the *either/or* polarizing debates in the early childhood field . . . to more *both/and* thinking that better reflects the complexity of the decisions inherent in the work of early childhood education" (Bredekamp & Copple, 1997, p. vi). Currently, developmentally appropriate practice intends that teachers' decisions be based upon knowledge about how children grow and learn, knowledge about individual children's needs and skills, and knowledge about the social, familial, cultural, and community context in which children live and learn.

It is evident from recent works (Elkind, 2005; Gallagher, 2005; Neuman & Roskos, 2005) that developmentally appropriate practice continues to need further explanation. Debate about this topic should continue because the document was not written in stone. It is intended to be revisited, reflected upon, and revised in order to accommodate new research and understanding regarding how children grow, develop, and learn. We must recognize that this framework for thinking, as well as other approaches, forms a significant part of our professional heritage and is a useful tool to help us along the path to new understandings.

▪▪ Is direct instruction wrong?

Developmentally appropriate practice is based on the idea of supporting emerging skills by providing suitable experiences that enhance development. Given time, materials, and space, children have always played; they don't usually need to be taught how to play. In fact, play, often an undervalued commodity in today's society, has been shown to contribute to the growth of all developmental domains. "Thousands of studies spanning decades have established incontrovertibly that creative play is a catalyst for social, emotional, moral, motoric, perceptual, intellectual, linguistic, and neurological development" (Olfman, 2005, p. 32). Undeniably

direct instruction

a method of teaching where the adult takes responsibility for structuring learning experiences; adult may use demonstration and other strategies

guided instruction

a method of instruction that includes strategies on a continuum ranging from less to more direction offered by the teacher

children learn much through play, but they also learn from **direct instruction**, or **guided instruction**, the preferred term, since the term direct instruction refers to one particular method of teaching. Vygotsky, a well-known theorist in the field of early childhood education, espoused the importance of guidance from others, whether it was from an adult or another peer. Today this type of instruction is often referred to as "scaffolding" and all learners benefit from this type of teaching. According to Piaget, another theorist, one type of knowledge that must be directly taught is social–conventional knowledge. This type of knowledge is culturally linked because what is deemed as important or acceptable for one culture may not have the same relevance for another. An example of social–conventional knowledge is color words. Red and rojo have the same meaning in different languages. In the English language it is agreed that the word is red, but in Spanish the same word is spelled and pronounced differently. The agreement is culturally linked and we teach English-speaking babies "red," while Spanish-speaking babies learn the word "rojo."

Parents and other adults have met with some success in instructing children. Research supports this; children do learn in structured environments. This might appear to contradict DAP, but it does not. Appropriate learning experiences can be mediated by adults, and they are most successful if the intervention is supplied at the right time developmentally and in a way that is mindful of the learning that has already occurred. Our philosophy doesn't have to be at either end of the structured-versus-unstructured continuum if we are well informed. DAP and guided (direct) instruction can be combined if we think this meets children's needs.

After thinking about these various issues, you might have shifted in your position—or you might hold on to what you thought at the beginning. What you also might realize is that you need to become better informed before you can define your own philosophy. The remaining chapters of this book should assist you, but remember that *See How They Grow* has its own stated philosophy. It is quite acceptable to disagree with the conclusions that are made here—but make sure that you have thought through your ideas and that you are basing your conclusions on sound research.

WHY DO WE NEED A PHILOSOPHY OF PRACTICE?

It is necessary to have a philosophy of care for infants and toddlers because we need a sense of direction and purpose in this work. Philosophy serves as a guide to practice. The philosophy should be based on the educated views and beliefs of all the people involved in the care of the children. When people are meeting the needs of children by working as a team, there must be a shared commitment and a common set of beliefs about how that commitment will be honored. Creating a well-thought-out and clearly written **philosophy statement** helps people to develop common understandings and to work together successfully. Most importantly, a philosophy statement can help educators consistently meet the needs of the children. If we can decide on a philosophy, then we can shape everything we do to the principles it contains.

philosophy statement

the critical analysis of fundamental assumptions or beliefs

COMPONENTS OF SEE HOW THEY GROW PHILOSOPHY

A. Historical Influences

Down through the ages, many individuals have contributed to a philosophy of care and education of young children. We do not have room here to list everyone or explain each person's contributions, but inspiration is drawn from the following individuals:*

Comenius	1592–1670	Czech
John Locke	1632–1734	British
Jean Jacques Rosseau	1712–1778	Swiss
Johann Heinrich Pestalozzi	1746–1827	Swiss
Friedrich Wilhelm August Froebel	1782–1852	German
Elizabeth Peabody	1804–1894	American
John Dewey	1859–1952	American
Rudolph Steiner	1861–1925	German
Maria Montessori	1870–1952	Italian

*It is worth noting that many of our historical influences are Western European. Currently, there is a much greater effort to acknowledge the contribution to early care and education from other countries and cultures.

Friedrich Froebel's philosophy inspired what has become known today as the Garden Analogy:

The Garden Analogy

The very young child is like a seed that is just beginning to sprout. Adults have the responsibility to protect this young life and nurture its growth, just as a gardener would tend to a plant. The environment in which the young life grows is the garden, over which the adult has stewardship. The style of garden management may vary, as do the young plants themselves, but each plant develops according to an inner direction that is shaped by encounters in the garden. Each adapts to the changing seasons as it gains knowledge and skills for life. As it develops, the plant changes, sometimes with rapid strides, but at other times in slower incremental stages, moving through to the next step in the cycle of life. Some days the plant will need greater support and will flourish if it receives it. Because each young plant may have different needs and patterns of behavior, the gardener should read each plant's cues and deliver the individual care required.

The garden analogy is rooted largely in the Froebelian principles of the Kindergarten (*Kinder* means children in German and *garten* means garden). Friedrich Froebel saw the child as developing in stages in the garden of life, and the adult as bearing responsibility for nurturing growth. This philosophy has been extended to embrace the need for individual nurturing; the garden image endures, providing us with a "back to nature" appreciation of the child as having special qualities in mind, spirit, and body. Ultimately the garden is only a part of the child's world, but it represents the part over which adults have responsibility and a small degree of control, if only to create the positive backdrop against which the child can thrive. From Froebel to new research in neuroscience, the garden analogy needs no reshaping: It fits 21st century cutting-edge science as well as it fit 20th century developmental theory and 19th century idealism.

Activity 1.1 on your Online Companion will help you learn about some of the important historical figures in the early childhood field.

B. Theoretical Influences

Many individuals have contributed to the understanding of how young children grow and develop. In later chapters of *See How They Grow* the contributions of Arnold Gesell, Jean Piaget, Erik Erikson, Sigmund Freud, B. F. Skinner, Lev Vygotsky, Loris Malaguzzi, Magda Gerber, Ron Lally, Urie Bronfrenbrenner, Alice Honig, and Howard Gardner will be acknowledged. These are some of the theorists and researchers who have contributed to the authors' understanding of the early childhood profession and have helped frame the philosophy upon which this book is based. This list is not exhaustive since there are many more researchers and educators who have contributed, and continue to contribute, to the early childhood field. Some theories conflict with one another, but because no one theory covers everything, it is important to carefully reflect on many theories and then choose elements that best meet the needs of a particular philosophical approach.

C. A Principle of Respect for Young Children

educare

the term that states there is no difference between care and education for young children since you accomplish both simultaneously

At the root of the philosophy of *See How They Grow* is a deep respect for each child. Magda Gerber (1998), a leader in the **educare** of infants and toddlers, did not invent respect for infants and toddlers, but she showed us how to respect them. With her sensitive approach of viewing experiences from the perspective of the baby, Gerber's attitude toward infants was refreshingly different. Avoiding sentimentality or the race to acquire skills early, Gerber respected the individual style and rhythm of each child. She mirrored the baby's pace and responded to its cues, in an effort to maximize communication and meet the needs of the baby. Gerber is a significant contributor to our understanding of early childhood care and education, and her principles are reflected in this book.

The Additional Support section of your Online Companion has a brief description of Magda Gerber's approach (Resources for Infant Educarers), as well links to information about the Program for Infants/Toddlers Caregivers (PITC), the High/Scope program for Infants and Toddlers, and Early Head Start.

Respect is an attitude as well as a set of behaviors. Very young children know without being told whether they are accepted and loved. Our every action speaks loudly to children about how we value them and how we value the task of caring. In turn, this contributes to children's sense of self-worth and shapes their perspective on the world.

Magda Gerber was trained at the Pickler Institute in Budapest, Hungary. According to her philosophy, the principle components of quality care for infants and toddlers are based upon responsive, reciprocal, and respectful relationships.

D. A Principle of Respect for Families

Another principle of the *See How They Grow* philosophy is maintaining and communicating respect for families. But that is easier to state in theory than to demonstrate in practice, especially when the families' views conflict with our own. Kilbride (1997) states that "families are our partners in the great enterprise of teaching and caring for children" (p. 21). Partnership requires a relationship of give-and-take.

Respect for families shows in most of the things that we do professionally, not only the things that parents see us do. Sometimes our attitude of respect may be challenged by parental views that are contrary to our own personal value system. Yet under no circumstances can our behavior indicate bias, favoritism, or personal preferences, nor can we shun those with whom we disagree. Even subtle behaviors can belie the respect that we must try to show. The professional role

BOX 1.2

RESPECT FOR INFANTS, TODDLERS, AND FAMILIES

- Tell the baby what you are about to do before you pick her up.
- Accommodate differing schedules for sleeping and feeding.
- Take time to tune in to the child's activity before you interrupt her with your ideas.
- Use developmentally appropriate guidance (e.g., do not ask a toddler to "use his words" when he has little language).
- Accept that crying tells you something and see that persistent crying is a repeated request, not a deliberate annoyance.
- When faced with a frustrated toddler, acknowledge his feelings before you try to distract him away from the frustration.
- Acknowledge that some children take longer than others to get used to new people and surroundings, and be prepared to spend the extra time nurturing a child who needs it.
- Have pictures and books that look like people from each child's culture.
- Show empathy for the child who is hurt, even if he seems to cry longer than you think the hurt warranted.
- Greet family members in their own language.
- Welcome families and siblings into the center.
- Ask the parent or family member about her or his day.
- Ensure that family members are included in the program wherever practical.
- Represent all types of diversity in the environment, particularly the ethnic mix of the children.
- Be tolerant of lifestyles that differ from your own.
- Support families that are undergoing stress, such as separation, culture shock, moving home, or caring for elderly relatives.
- Provide resources such as names and phone numbers for families in need of social services, religious supports, or referrals for assessments.
- Ask parents/families for their expertise.
- Use tact when telling families the truth when they ask how their child is doing.

requires deep sensitivity, based on knowledge and a readiness to admit our mistakes. Utilizing principles from Gerber's approach, Box 1.2 outlines some of the ways adults can show respect for young children and families.

E. A Concern for Health and Safety

Considerations of health and safety are essential components of the *See How They Grow* philosophy. The quality of care for children has to start with considerations for their health and safety. These issues need to be at the forefront of every facility and caregiver's endeavors. If health and safety are not guaranteed, nothing else really matters.

Health Concerns

According to Aronson, the author of *Healthy Young Children: A Manual for Programs* (2002), "The health component of a child care program must be carefully planned and carried out through comprehensive health policies and procedures developed from up-to-date information supplemented by use of community resources" (p. 1). Health policies in individual programs should, at a minimum, address:

- handwashing, recognized as the first line of defense against disease and infection
- tracking of immunizations
- tracking, reporting, and preventing of illnesses
- promotion of health practices with good nutrition
- oral, mental, and general health education, including physical fitness
- identification, treatment, and prevention of child abuse and neglect

Safety Concerns

Safety is another essential part of the adult's responsibility to the very young child. It requires an unceasing observation of the child and the child's environment. Because all elements of safety change according to the mobility, needs, and abilities of the child, the adult needs to understand child development principles in order to ensure physical and emotional security.

Safety is as much an attitude as a list of things to remember. Safe practice requires that the caregiver make wise choices about all items in the environment, observe continuously, intervene when necessary, be aware of developmental stages and appropriateness of activities, and avoid potential problems. A list of things to watch for can help safe practice, but vigilance in every part of every activity is the only way to avoid incidents. Each chapter of *See How They Grow* that deals with a particular age/stage of development indicates some potential hazards and how they can be addressed. The Additional Support section on your Online Companion contains links to a health and safety checklist that can be utilized to assess an infant and toddler child care center.

F. A Belief in Responsive Caregiving

responsive care

a philosophy of care, education, and nurturance that meets the changing needs of the developing infant and young child and is sensitive to the individual differences of each child

Responsive caregiving is an approach to meeting the child's needs that is mindful of how young children grow and develop and how the adult can support this process. Responsivity involves respect rather than power, nurturance rather than simply meeting physical needs, and reading the infant's cues rather than providing a set routine of care. Box 1.3 provides some guiding principles for responsive caregiving.

Infants and toddlers do not need the kind of planned curriculum that older children need, and they should not be exposed to a watered-down version of a curriculum designed for more mature children. Adult involvement is more important than any other element of "curriculum." The responsive adult becomes the curriculum. Adult observation and assessment should lead to responses that improve the child's experience of life, support the child's emotional well-being, show understanding of the individual child's temperamental style, adjust environments to maximize learning potential, reinforce the child's emotional attachments, provide social experiences that are appropriate and supported, aid in the acquisition of language and communication skills, and ascertain the child's specific and individual needs. Clearly, responsive caregiving requires sensitivity.

In Chapters 4 through 11, you will see how responsive caregiving can be offered in relation to the developing young child. As the child matures, the process remains the same, but the practicalities alter. This is why an understanding of development is as essential as being able to read the child's cues. Although practical responses should be linked to the development of the child,

---

BOX 1.3

GUIDING PRINCIPLES FOR RESPONSIVE CAREGIVING

The following are guiding principles for "being" and "doing" with infants, toddlers, and families.

1. Behavior is meaningful.
2. Everyone wants things to be better.
3. You are yourself and your role.
4. Don't just do something mindlessly—be there and pay attention.
5. Remember relationships.
6. Do unto others as you would have others do unto you.

Source: Pawl, J., & St. John, M. (1998). How you are is as important as what you do, In *Making a Positive Difference for Infants, Toddlers, and Their Families*. Washington, DC: Zero to Three, p. 7.

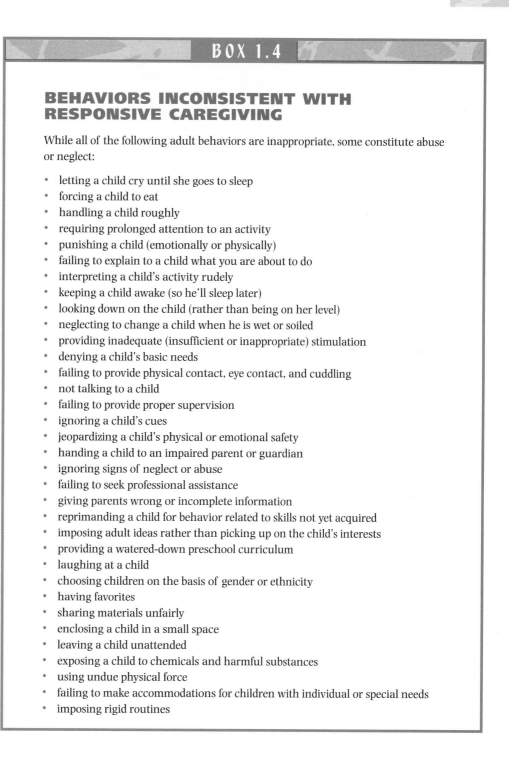

BOX 1.4

BEHAVIORS INCONSISTENT WITH RESPONSIVE CAREGIVING

While all of the following adult behaviors are inappropriate, some constitute abuse or neglect:

- letting a child cry until she goes to sleep
- forcing a child to eat
- handling a child roughly
- requiring prolonged attention to an activity
- punishing a child (emotionally or physically)
- failing to explain to a child what you are about to do
- interpreting a child's activity rudely
- keeping a child awake (so he'll sleep later)
- looking down on the child (rather than being on her level)
- neglecting to change a child when he is wet or soiled
- providing inadequate (insufficient or inappropriate) stimulation
- denying a child's basic needs
- failing to provide physical contact, eye contact, and cuddling
- not talking to a child
- failing to provide proper supervision
- ignoring a child's cues
- jeopardizing a child's physical or emotional safety
- handing a child to an impaired parent or guardian
- ignoring signs of neglect or abuse
- failing to seek professional assistance
- giving parents wrong or incomplete information
- reprimanding a child for behavior related to skills not yet acquired
- imposing adult ideas rather than picking up on the child's interests
- providing a watered-down preschool curriculum
- laughing at a child
- choosing children on the basis of gender or ethnicity
- having favorites
- sharing materials unfairly
- enclosing a child in a small space
- leaving a child unattended
- exposing a child to chemicals and harmful substances
- using undue physical force
- failing to make accommodations for children with individual or special needs
- imposing rigid routines

there are general standards for what is and what is not responsive caregiving. Box 1.4 lists some behaviors that are not consistent with responsive caregiving.

DETERMINING THE PHILOSOPHY OF A CENTER

Even as teachers of young children grapple with the creation of their own philosophy of caring and educating young children, so do child care facilities. In other business environments, the equivalent would be a company's mission, vision, and values statements. In the child care environment, the philosophy statement precipitates the formation of a plan of action, policies,

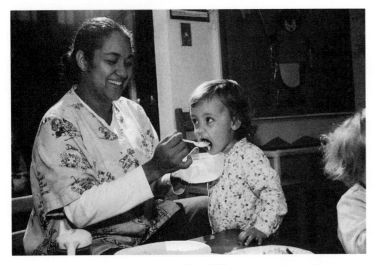

A care provider responds to the needs of this child.

best practices

ways of working (with children) that are accepted within the profession as exemplary

and indicators of **best practices** (characteristics of successful programs). As such, the philosophy statement provides the backdrop for the business of child care and acts as a reference point for all aspects of working with young children.

Personal and Center-Based Philosophies

Personal philosophies of infant and toddler caregiving and education are formed as you learn about, and work in, various child care settings. These experiences influence how you perceive your role and the ways in which children's needs can be met. You may encounter a child care center that demonstrates values you do not share and practices with which you do not feel comfortable. Part of your ongoing learning is to observe carefully and to ask questions about what you see and why certain practices are followed. Although staff members should be open to such questions, you will need to ask them appropriately and at the right time. Explanations may lead you to change your mind or become clearer about your own values and beliefs concerning practice. It is important to be respectful of the experience of center staff, whether or not you share their perspectives. Just as there are different ways of doing things "right" as a parent, there are different approaches to caregiving that might also be appropriate.

Only if there is an abuse of power, an experience of neglect, or the employment of a practice that harms the child should a philosophy be considered wrong. Read the comments about potential abuse later in the text before taking any action; it is not for you to judge—only to pass on your observations to the appropriate authorities for their action.

Terms Used in Philosophy Statements

Many child care centers and programs for very young children claim to have an eclectic philosophy and practice—that is, one drawing from many different philosophical and theoretical approaches. Typically you may encounter the following terms used to describe a philosophy: developmentally appropriate, sensory, play-based, developmental, discovery, child-directed, nurturing, primary caregiver, or social curriculum. In practice, most of these hint at a more responsive caregiving model than enriched, rigorous, structured, or educational models. Other terminology might alert you to the values of the program. Centers that speak of "guidance" rather than "discipline" may be more developmentally appropriate and nurturing since the term "discipline" has connotations of greater teacher direction and attempts to control children's behavior. "Pro-social skills" can be construed in various ways in practice: The term might mean an emphasis on positive role-modeling or an insistence that toddlers "share" things. Recently there have been aspirations to an "anti-violent" approach. The intent is to arm children with strategies for solving conflicts. Levin (2003) asserts that "in today's world, those who are concerned about the well-being of children have no choice but to use the best information and resources we have to help children deal with the violence they see and to help them learn nonviolent alternatives" (p. 7). This can be role-modeled and reinforced with young infants and toddlers.

Emphasis on one domain of development or another seems common in philosophy statements. You might see the terms "cognitively focused curriculum" or a "social–emotional focus" in their literature. Some programs promise an ideal that is unattainable or use rhetoric and fancy brochures designed to impress parents.

Terms such as "inclusion," "diversity," and "nature" may be used in a variety of ways in philosophy statements. Some programs that claim to be "inclusive" fail to live up to the term in any way other than including all children in activities. Programs claiming "diversity" might use the term to indicate an anti-bias perspective in the curriculum. The word "nature" or "natural" might indicate a setting with aesthetically pleasing use of light, wood, colors, fresh air, and textures, or a "scientific discovery" program. It might mean that only natural, not plastic, materials are used.

Some child care centers or private home child care settings are run by large companies, agents, or other associates who may share a philosophy, as well as administration. In these settings it is important to examine the central philosophy as well as the local or site-based philosophy and practice. Large organizations can find it difficult to ensure consistency of philosophy because so many individuals with differing views are working for the same employer. A center's reputation may be a guide, but to fully determine the philosophy of an infant and toddler program, you need to consider factors that point to quality of care.

Do not rush to judgment about a center's philosophy. When observing a center, it might be useful to consider the following points:

- Avoid judging what you see until you are sure you have all the information.
- There may be reasons why a child is handled a certain way or why the routine has been disrupted.
- Asking open questions may be helpful, but the center staff may be concentrating on meeting the children's needs, not yours.
- A center offering good quality care, whatever its philosophy, will find time for answering questions from students or parents, but that time may be after the program has finished for the day.
- Ask to read any information that the center has prepared about its own programs, including information available for new families and newsletters.

BEST PRACTICES

Indicators of Quality Care and Education

Earlier sections of this chapter have suggested some of the components of quality care and education. We need to expand this information by understanding the research that has been done to determine the characteristics of effective programs that deliver high-quality care and education. Research into **quality care indicators** for infants and toddlers highlights the following issues:

quality care indicators

in the early childhood field, these are generally agreed-upon measures which contribute to quality in caregiving

- *The ratio of children to adults.* Lower ratios tend to allow for better communication and attention and a better ability to meet children's needs.
- *The size of the group of children.* Smaller groups are more likely than larger groups to offer the context for appropriate nurturance and learning.
- *The education of the caregiver or educator.* Higher levels of education are equated with higher-quality care.
- *The amount of attention each child receives from an attentive adult.* The longer the attention, the better the experience for the child.
- *The communication style and methods used by the agency.* Open communication with families and multiple approaches to giving and receiving information are most effective.
- *Continuity of care.* When very young children consistently have the same caregiver, they are more likely to make and keep secure attachments.
- *Family involvement.* Where family involvement is high, there is likely to be a better outcome for the young child.
- *Remuneration.* The pay and benefits of the child care employee have an indirect, but clear, relationship to the overall quality of care that is offered.
- *The environment.* The adequacy of the physical environment and access to appropriate materials is associated with quality care and education.
- *The climate.* The emotional well-being of staff, children, and parents directly influences the quality of care and nurturance offered.
- *The administration.* Quality child care is financed, organized, and evaluated effectively and efficiently.

social context

every element of an
environment that influ-
ences an individual's
development, including
the people, institutions,
and values to which the
individual is exposed on
a daily basis

If current research makes it relatively easy to answer the question of what constitutes good care, it is more difficult to determine what actually constitutes a good program. The answer to the latter question will depend on what you are seeking and what fits with your beliefs about children's development. Programs with different philosophies can deliver equally good care. Activity 1.2 on your CD-ROM enables you to utilize these quality indicators in order to help you determine the philosophy of a center by encouraging you to observe its practices. There are also additional questions you can answer using words and phrases to characterize different elements of the program. At this point in your journey of learning about infant and toddler education and care, it would be beneficial for you become familiar with the principles and guidelines of NAEYC's Developmentally Appropriate Practice. The link to this important document is available in the Additional Support section of your Online Companion.

Developmentally Appropriate Practice

Since 1987, developmentally appropriate practice (DAP) has been a guiding force for quality in early childhood programs. With the broader definition of DAP that includes cultural and contextual perspectives (Bredekamp & Copple, 1997), many misconceptions were laid to rest. However, a debate still continues surrounding the usefulness of the practice.

For example, Roberts-Fiati (1997) is critical of DAP, suggesting that the practice is unhelpful because the context of each child's development differs. She believes that what is developmentally "appropriate" becomes the expectation for the development and, eventually, the means for assessing a child. However, DAP was never intended as an assessment method for children, but rather for programs. Clearly children's experiences need to be appropriate for their development, but the notion that particular behaviors are *always* expected at a particular age is a departure from the intention of DAP. For our purposes, DAP for infants and toddlers involves observing the development of each child and providing for all the young child's needs, according to that individual's developmental stages, whatever those might be.

Other concerns over DAP revolve mainly around the issue of cultural context, especially in countries where the populations are extremely diverse (Cannella, 2002). In the United States and Canada, classrooms may have numerous cultures, ethnicities, and languages represented, so it is a challenge for teachers to understand how to bridge the ever-widening gap. Anti-bias and multicultural approaches are two of the methods teachers are employing to ensure the inclusion of all children and families in their programs (Derman-Sparks & Phillips, 1997, Derman-Sparks & Ramsey, 2006; York, 2003).

We acknowledge the ongoing debate, but for the purposes of this textbook, DAP is considered essential to your understanding of what constitutes quality when providing care for young children. DAP is important for all young children, but especially for infants and toddlers, since they are at a stage of great dependence and vulnerability. It is crucial to provide tools and guidance to caregivers, thus enabling them to make decisions that are beneficial to children's care and education. DAP might be confusing, since it is really three separate things: a philosophy, a book, and a tool utilized in decision-making. However, we contend that it is a dependable framework for guiding our profession.

Social Contexts of Development

The **social context** for every child is unique and changing constantly. Each young child will experience the environment differently and interact with it individually. Every element of a child's environment influences that individual's development. Indeed, as Urie Bronfenbrenner (1979) says, human development happens as "a result of a person's exposure to and interaction with the environment" (p. 9).

Bronfenbrenner designed a model to illustrate the systems of the environment that are influential. These systems include the people, institutions, and values with which the child comes into contact. As caregivers, we are responsible for some parts of that social environment. Given its significant influence on the child, we must ensure that this environment is as positive as possible. To accomplish this, we must be able to appreciate how the child perceives the environment and adapts to it. This system will be more fully explained in Chapter 3.

Cultural Experience and Development

phenomenology

the systematic study of conscious experience; entering into the life-world of another person

The cultural style of caregiving influences the child's perception of the world, and this seems entirely desirable. The range of human experiences is part of what makes us different. As we will discuss at several points in the book, **phenomenology** is a school of thought in which people value the essence of the individual's human experience; they remind us that, although experience is essentially individual, the creation of the experience is shaped by the values and attitudes that surround the developing child.

Whether or not we live in a diverse community, we need to have some sensitivity to the wide variety of experiences of very young children. While there is wide cultural variation of experience, convincing evidence exists that almost all infants and toddlers go through the same stages of development in similar sequences.

However, Bernhard and Gonzalez-Mena (2000) carefully articulate the argument that our approach to understanding development needs to encompass a new, and perhaps more relevant, understanding of what comprises "normal" development and expectations. Although for years the profession has been guided by a generalized framework of development, "this particular, official construction of the child, however, may not coincide with parents' views of how children are, how they are supposed to be, and what they need" (Bernhard & Gonzalez-Mena, 2000, p. 253). That parental view is created through experiences drawn from culture, ethnicity, context, gender, class, education, values, traditions, and beliefs. Therefore, children may differ in their patterns of development for both ethno-cultural (ethnic origin and cultural experience) and individual reasons. One must be sensitive to possible cultural variations and not approach the issue with rigid expectations. There are many possible variations. (See Box 1.5.)

Also, Cannella (2002) warns against what is termed "globalized childhood" and states that "we have convinced ourselves that younger human beings are the same all over the world. We have ignored the variation in cultural values, the position of children in various cultures, and the power held by children" (p. 58). Although there may be a tendency to lump children together in a homogeneous grouping, DAP requires that we consider children as individuals. Further, the work being done in the schools of Reggio Emilia in Italy have compelled educators to view children as powerful creators of their knowledge. Since 1991, when these schools were identified as among the ten best schools in the world, the early childhood profession has sought to investigate the structures, attitudes, and approaches that underlie these remarkable programs

---

BOX 1.5

CULTURAL SHAPING OF DEVELOPMENT

An extended family in Seattle was characterized by its close-knit functioning, its high expectations for the four children, and the joy that the children gave their parents and grandparents. The grandparents, who were not born in the United States, had brought with them many of the ways of life from the old country. Many of these familiar values and practices were kept alive because the family lived among others of the same culture. Li Ming, the family's youngest child, was nearly two years old. She was dressed carefully and told not to spoil her nice clothes. Playing on her grandmother's knee, she learned songs in a language other than English. Li Ming learned quickly and pleased her family. She became familiar with the alphabet of the old country and acquired the socially acceptable behaviors of her family's and neighborhood's culture. She looked to the adults and older children to help her, so she didn't learn to tie her shoes or button her coat. When she started nursery school, Li Ming had not yet learned to feed herself or mastered any of the self-help skills that many other children had.

At nursery school Li Ming's development was recognized for what it was—culturally shaped. How could the teachers accommodate her developmental needs?

(Fu, Stremmel, & Hill, 2002; Gandini, Hill, Cadwell, & Schwall, 2005; Hendrick, 2004; Project Zero, 2001). Wurm (2005) notes that in "Reggio the child is viewed as strong, powerful, rich in potential, driven by the power of wanting to grow, and nurtured by adults who take this drive toward growth seriously" (p. 16). Informing yourself about the Reggio Emilia approach to care and education of children can enhance your ability to view all children as powerful learners who have a "hundred ways of knowing" (Edwards, Gandini, & Forman, 1998). The Additional Support section in your Online Companion has links to help you investigate the Reggio Emilia programs of Italy. This information might help you to reflect on your view of children.

Culturally Sensitive Programs

It is assumed that the reader is sympathetic to the idea that adults and children should be respectful to all people, but how each one of us expresses that belief could differ. For example, Western European culture values eye contact when talking. It is a sign of respect. However, in other cultures, direct eye contact is viewed as disrespectful. Think carefully about the positions you hold on a variety of issues. Examine the underlying beliefs you have and think carefully about the issues presented in this section.

Cultural sensitivity to families and children can be reflected in a variety of ways. Consider the following:

anti-bias curriculum

the curriculum and experience of the child that is designed and delivered in ways that address potential biases related to gender, race, culture, poverty, and other social issues

individual

a separate human being

- The use of an **anti-bias curriculum** is very appropriate. "Curriculum goals are to enable every child: to construct a knowledgeable, confident self-identity; to develop comfortable, empathetic, and just interaction with diversity; and to develop critical thinking and the skills for standing up for oneself and others in the face of injustice" (Derman-Sparks, 1989, p. ix).
- The core of good practices in this area is based on the attitudes and values that are held by all the adults in the child's life. How effectively and consistently are these attitudes and values transmitted in the choices made by the caregivers?
- When planning any activity or experience, consider how well it fits the **individual** in a cultural as well as a developmental sense.
- Visual information is significant to infants and toddlers, so images should include people with an ethnic or cultural similarity to each child.

culturally diverse

describes an environment that includes people of various cultures; an organization that welcomes people from different heritages; may also include individuals from various ethnic backgrounds, people of different religions, people from a range of geographic locations, people who speak different languages, and people living in different subcultures (groups within groups)

To ensure that our programs are culturally sensitive, we might wish to incorporate an anti-bias approach to our work. In recent years there have been some excellent resources available to help educators challenge their thinking and practices in relation to understanding and accommodating children, families, and co-workers of **culturally diverse** backgrounds. The seminal work of Derman-Sparks (1989) brought attention to the variety of potential bias and prejudice teachers may unwittingly be communicating to children. These include attitudes about ability, ageism, appearance, class, culture, ethnicity, family composition, gender, race, and sexuality. Consider the following:

Life in the United States is not fair for everyone. All kinds of discrimination keep individuals from having equal access to society's services and opportunities. Education is not neutral. Schools and child care centers are institutions, and as such, they are part of the social structure that discriminates against individuals. As part of the social structure, early childhood programs inadvertently teach white supremacy and perpetuate European-American, middle-class values. In the classroom, teachers pass on their values to children through their choice of bulletin board displays, toys, activities, celebrations, unit themes or projects, and through their interactions with the children and other adults. (York, 2003, p. xii)

This book's philosophy hopes that any of these biases are diffused within a respectful, caring, supportive, individually focused, nurturing, accepting environment. However, although we might want a perfect world, we cannot assume that all bias has been eliminated from aspects of our lives. We must examine all the possible attitudes and "isms" that might be communicated to children and families in order to ensure that a pro-diversity philosophy is incorporated into every part of our practice. Our reluctance to become proactive can easily be justified by misconceptions about what young children know about differences. It is difficult for some of us to believe that by age two many children are noticing physical differences including inabilities, gender differences, and even differences in food consumption and customs, but it is important that you begin to incorporate diversity into the environment, materials, and experiences.

How you decide to engage children in the discovery of differences will depend on the cultural makeup of the group. Obviously, familiar items that offer comfort and continuity should be part of the child's environment. In time, the child's world can enlarge to allow for discovery of new materials and different objects. Because the sensory perceptions of very young children are their primary means of discovering the world, this introduction to a larger world should be gradual, and should include items that are without bias and that support cultural values.

OTHER FACTORS

Child Care Settings

Child care takes place in a variety of settings—in the home environment, with parent, family, or nanny care; in full-day and part-time child care and drop-in centers; and in private home child care settings, or any combination of these. It is the quality and continuity of the caregiving experienced by the young child that is important, not where that care occurs. Any of these arrangements can meet the child's needs, depending on the skills of the caregivers involved.

Types of Child Care Services for Infants and Toddlers and Their Families

Group care is a widely used service for young children and parents. Within this category, there are private, nonprofit, government, workplace, laboratory school, or school-based services. These may have affiliations with churches, synagogues, temples, or other religious organizations. The programming may be age/stage-linked, multi-age, or intergenerational. Within the home, the infant or toddler may be cared for by one parent or both, or by a grandparent, qualified nanny, or family friend. Home child care can also be offered in someone else's home in either a licensed or unlicensed setting by a qualified professional or untrained home care provider.

In addition to child care centers, family resource programs might have drop-in facilities, toy libraries, playrooms, resource availability, infant massage workshops, discussion groups, therapies, classes for parents with their young children, and breast-feeding support. Family development centers are a relatively recent concept in the delivery of responsive programming. They may offer a wide variety of support and opportunities for children and families. Mental and physical health programs provide medical supports, interventions, and mental health resources. These can involve "well baby" clinics or be designed to support babies with medical conditions or special needs.

Need for Quality Child Care

Figure 1.2 displays the distribution of child care services for children three and under with employed mothers. This data demonstrates that in 2001, over 50 percent of children under three still received care in a setting that was family-linked. This care is sometimes referred to as kith and kin caregiving. Kith and kin care is defined as child care provided by family, friends, and neighbors. Kith refers to individuals who fill in as substitute family while the term kin refers to immediate family members or other relatives. This situation has both positive and negative connotations. The younger the child (under age three), the more likely they will benefit from care by a parent or a loving relative. However, many of these arrangements for care are unregulated. Questions remain about the health and safety conditions. Also, the quality of care is highly variable and may be linked to generational models of parenting behaviors, ranging on a continuum from poor to excellent, rather than on training or education.

Figure 1.2 Primary Child Care Arrangements for Children Under Age 3 with Employed Mothers

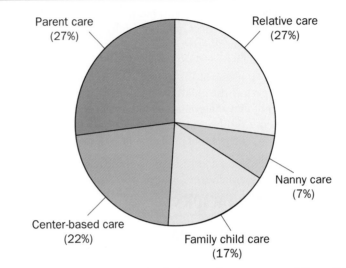

Source: Ehrle, J., Adams, G., & Tout, T. (2001). *Who's caring for our youngest children: Child care patterns of infants and toddlers.* Washington, DC: The Urban Institute, figure 1, p. 4. Reprinted with permission.

> "The quality dimension of child care is arguably as important as the quantity supplied because in many cases the alternative to high-quality child care is not home care, but lower-quality care."
>
> (Blau & Currie, 2003, 14)

Center care in the United States must be licensed according to state regulations. If the site receives federal funding, then it must also meet federal guidelines. Family child care homes can also be licensed by the state, although this remains a voluntary option to date, even though many states have laws that provide sanctions against unregulated care. Most states still do not prosecute individuals caring for children in unregulated homes and this remains a delicately balanced position as there is a great need for child care, especially for low-income and rural populations that often face limited options. In 2003, there were 116,409 centers licensed in the United States (Oser & Cohen, 2003) and in 2004, according to the National Association of Child Care Resource and Referral Agency, there were 300,032 regulated family child care homes.

The demand for more regulated spaces will continue to increase, since it is estimated that the number of working parents will continue to rise. In turn, the availability of facilities able to offer high-quality care remains elusive. Although 61 percent of all mothers with children three or under are part of the workforce (Oser & Cohen, 2003), the lack of quality care for infants and toddlers remains an impediment to employment.

In 2000 it was estimated that in the United States, over 6 million children under age 3 spent part or all of their day being cared for by someone other than their parents. Shonkoff, Phillips, and Keilty (2000) point out that second only to immediate family, child care is the context in which early development unfolds for many of our youngest citizens. Both the Abecedarian Study and the High/Scope Perry Preschool Project (Schweinhardt, 2005) have demonstrated that quality child care, especially for at-risk children, is beneficial when viewed on a long-term basis. Unfortunately, the reality of child care in the United States is explained in the following statement:

> . . . most child care [is] of mediocre quality. A high level of quality is extremely difficult for child care programs to attain when salaries are too low to attract well-qualified staff, state standards are too weak to ensure that staff has the necessary background for working with young children, and child-to-staff ratios are too high to provide children with individualized attention (Sonosky, 2004, p. 66).

In the end, the children who suffer most from the lack of quality child care are children who can be identified as at-risk because they are the least likely to receive high-quality care.

Many families find it difficult to afford child care, which can cost $4,000 to $10,000 per year—at least as much as college tuition at a public university. Yet one in four families with young children earns less than $25,000 a year, and a family with both parents working at

> "Poor families who paid for child care spent roughly three times more of their budget than non-poor families on child care (20 percent compared to 7 percent)."
>
> (Oser & Cohen, 2003, p. 58)

special needs (exceptional needs)

needs which have been identified as requiring help or intervention beyond the scope of ordinary adult interactions or normal classroom interactions and routines

the minimum wage earns only $21,400 a year. These low-income families struggle to afford child care on their limited budgets and are unlikely to receive any help from federal subsidies (Sonosky, 2004, p. 66).

These issues surrounding availability and affordability of child care are ones that have no easy solution. As a profession we would hope that families would choose child care based on the quality indicators. However, it is likely that many families have to make decisions about care based on the practical issues of cost, location, and hours of operation.

 What about child care services for Native Americans? Activity 1.3 in your Online Companion will help you discover the answer to this question.

Exceptional Needs and Early Intervention

This section addresses some of the issues related to infants' and toddlers' individual needs, and young children who have **special** or **exceptional needs.** We use either of the terms "special" or "exceptional" needs to refer to those children whose development is atypical—outside the range of what is typical for the majority of children at their stage. Some children may have diagnosed disabilities, but at this point, it is more fruitful to think of every young child as having different individual needs.

With training and support, caregivers can accommodate most children with special needs within a regular program for infants and toddlers. Caregivers may be concerned that they are not supported well enough to offer an inclusive program. However, the benefits for children and families are enormous. In brief, the benefits of inclusion are:

- emphasis on ability rather than disability
- better integration into society throughout the child's life
- increased family involvement throughout the program
- acceptance of developmental diversity among children, families, and society
- improved support for the holistic development of the child who has a special need
- higher-functioning peers as role models, play partners, and communicators
- emphasis on individual programming for all children within the program
- collaborative program planning with specialist supports

Early-intervention programs are those that support infants, toddlers, and their families when they are thought to be at risk. This category might include children in poverty, babies born prematurely, or parents who are drug- or alcohol-dependent or mentally ill. Erickson and Kurz-Riemer (1999) indicate that intervention must be broad-based, driven by family needs, and evaluated regularly.

Teaching Story

When Tyler was slow to walk, his mother thought it was because he was overweight. All of Tyler's peers could walk, but at 15 months he would sit placidly and make little attempt to crawl, much less walk. The educator at Tyler's child care center suggested that his mother make an appointment with her pediatrician to have her son examined. The doctor concluded that Tyler did not have a physical problem, but was mildly below average in intellectual functioning. Tyler needed extra cognitive stimulation, a moderately reduced diet, and some specific assistance and encouragement to walk. The educator and Tyler's parents provided all of these on a consistent basis. Without this early intervention, Tyler would not have achieved as much as he did. He was able to stay with his peers in the child care center and has sustained his place in the mainstream at elementary school.

early intervention

the practice of offering compensatory or other experiences to an infant or young child (birth to age five) and his family with the intention of ameliorating (making better) any deficit or at-risk condition, developing strategies for success, or addressing potential problems

By addressing needs and providing the resources that are most likely to lead to positive outcomes for the children, many child care programs are, in effect, offering **early intervention.** Specific programs build on family strengths and assist in parental decision-making skills. From the child's perspective, interventions are geared toward providing positive developmental outcomes, supporting emotional well-being, and offering protective mechanisms that address the risk factors. Shonkoff, Phillips, and Keilty (2000) confirm that "programs that combine child-focused educational activities with explicit attention to parent–child interaction patterns and relationship building appear to have the greatest success" (p. 11).

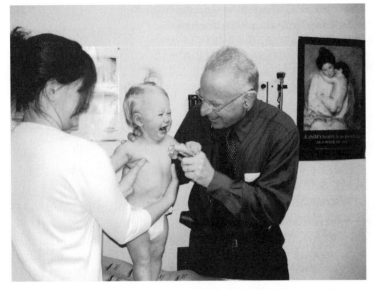

Often young children do not enjoy medical examinations, as evidenced by this photo. However, children's progress needs to be carefully monitored by families, care providers, and medical personnel.

Box 1.6 delineates the components of policy and practice in successful early-intervention programs. They should be considered when developing a philosophy of care and education for young children.

Early intervention, as the term implies, focuses on ensuring that the child's issues are considered and accommodated in the first days or months of life. The earlier the intervention, the more likely it is that there will be a positive result. Types of early intervention include supporting attachment behaviors, providing families with developmental information, assisting families in advocating for their child, and offering language support and play experiences. The interventions might be offered in the child's home, a clinical setting, a parenting center, or a child care center. Play therapists, early childhood educators, occupational therapists, psychologists, social workers, psychiatrists, speech-language pathologists, and pediatricians may work separately or in combination to deliver the intervention.

Basing our philosophy of care and education on sound research is important, especially in the area of meeting the needs of children with diverse developmental needs. If we appreciate the effectiveness of intervention programs, then we will endeavor to work with families to ensure the best possible outcome for their child. This might mean that an integral part of our program will be careful observation and identification of any concerns.

An exceptionality that often gets overlooked when this topic is discussed is giftedness, although it is often challenging to identify gifted individuals at this early stage of life. However, if a child is gifted, receiving the quality of care described in this book is most likely to fulfill many of his needs.

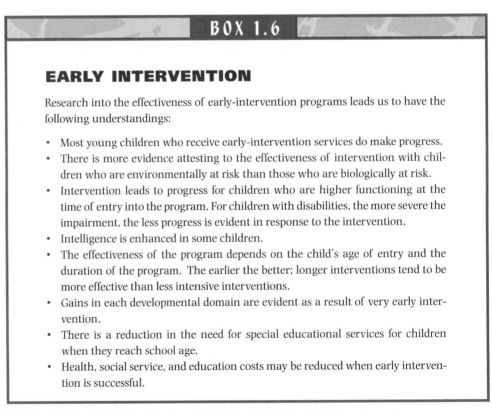

BOX 1.6

EARLY INTERVENTION

Research into the effectiveness of early-intervention programs leads us to have the following understandings:

- Most young children who receive early-intervention services do make progress.
- There is more evidence attesting to the effectiveness of intervention with children who are environmentally at risk than those who are biologically at risk.
- Intervention leads to progress for children who are higher functioning at the time of entry into the program. For children with disabilities, the more severe the impairment, the less progress is evident in response to the intervention.
- Intelligence is enhanced in some children.
- The effectiveness of the program depends on the child's age of entry and the duration of the program. The earlier the better; longer interventions tend to be more effective than less intensive interventions.
- Gains in each developmental domain are evident as a result of very early intervention.
- There is a reduction in the need for special educational services for children when they reach school age.
- Health, social service, and education costs may be reduced when early intervention is successful.

Determining the adult's role in caregiving can be one of the indicators of philosophy in practice. Here the adult models reading. He helps the infant hold a book and talks about the images. With guidance, the child can eventually learn to turn the pages by herself and hopefully gain a love of reading.

The philosophy you adopt on exceptionalities and inclusion will influence not only your interactions at the program you work in, but will also affect the way you view society as a whole. These are important issues to think about.

THE ROLE OF THE ADULT AS EDUCATOR AND CAREGIVER

Accepting responsibility for very young children places an educator in a privileged position. Unfortunately, many people think that working with young children is merely "babysitting" and that caregivers need neither education nor significant skills. The reality is that being an educator requires acquiring and applying knowledge from many areas, including biology, sociology, child development, observation and assessment, psychology, philosophy, curriculum design, health and safety, and responsive caregiving. In addition, the educator must be an excellent communicator, be able to articulate a clear philosophy of education and caregiving, and be able to provide a positive role model. The personal characteristics and attitudes that the educator must demonstrate include caring, responsiveness to needs, the ability to act swiftly to avert dangers, tolerance and understanding for challenging behaviors and situations, sensitivity to children's individual temperaments, respect for all families and children, and acceptance of a variety of different lifestyles and preferences among family members. In addition, educators must remain positive whatever the circumstances, keep information confidential, perform their roles as professionals, accommodate developmental differences, respond to a variety of social cues, and remain flexible in solving problems.

WRITING A PHILOSOPHY

See How You Grow draws inspiration from three separate models in formulating a philosophical framework: the research-based (responsive) approach, the practical (core competencies) approach, and the phenomenological (supportive guidance) approach. They are not presented as "right" or "wrong" ways of being in the lives of very young children. There are merits to each approach, and most programs for children draw on a variety of differing approaches to create what they think is best. Although the scientific approach—often called the "medical model"—has been critiqued as being insufficiently responsive, our modern version of responsive caregiving embraces current research. Thus, the scientific approach has developed over the years into something quite different from the medical model of the 1940s to 1970s, where cleanliness was considered the paramount virtue. For example, current scientific research emphasizes the development of the brain, and the application of the research leads us to acknowledge the role of attachments and relationships. We now know that the right side of the brain helps regulate emotions and that the quality of adult–child interactions affects the wiring of the brain, both positively and negatively. So "when a caregiver responds quickly and appropriately to a child's distress—rocking, speaking softly, meeting the child's gaze with a reassuring face—the child learns to expect the caregiver's support" (Gallagher, 2005, p. 17). These types of experiences strengthen connections in that part of the brain responsible for monitoring and regulating emotions. The child's brain learns to recognize a pattern of cause and effect. The eventual lesson learned—I'm unhappy; somebody cares; I am worthy. Obviously, data from brain research have reinforced what has been known intuitively: The child's emotional competence is affected in a positive way as the result of a responsive action by an adult. Therefore, science can help inform and improve our pedagogical practices.

The attributes from each approach are not meant to be comparable, since they evolved from different world views that cannot be easily categorized. These concepts—the research-based (responsive) approach, the practical (core competencies) approach, and the phenomenological (supportive guidance) approach—might challenge what we believe about the nature of how and what we need to be in the lives of children. However, if each characteristic is envisioned as equal in value, one is able to combine the strategies which work best in an overall pattern of quality caregiving.

The Additional Support section in your Online Companion fully outlines the three approaches to caregiving: the research-based (responsive) approach, the practical (core competencies) approach, and the phenomenological (supportive guidance) approach. This expanded version of the approaches offers many ideas for reflection.

How Might This Look in Real Life?

The staff, families, and community representatives came together to develop a common vision for the Rosegarden Infant and Toddler Center. First, they identified the following key characteristics that they felt were important to maintain in their philosophy and the day-to-day operation of the center:

Key Characteristics

- holistic support of children and families
- a human, research-based practical philosophy
- a balance of individual and collective rights/needs
- spontaneous and planned activities
- an environment that is hygienic and pleasant
- shared values, being flexible when necessary
- clear, simple policies
- cooperative staff group
- culturally and developmentally appropriate
- sympathetic and empathetic to individuals
- accepting and accommodating of diversity
- observation, assessment, and regular program evaluation
- responsive to individual children
- respectful of children and families
- warm and inviting, use of natural materials

After establishing their general philosophy, they utilized the three models—the researched-based approach, the practical approach, and the phenomenological approach—and crafted the particular approach that they felt best suited their unique needs. Figure 1.3 outlines how the Rosegarden Infant and Toddler Center combined elements from all three approaches. This will help them keep their goals clear as they work with architects, design the children's environments, and plan their program. They have articulated their intentions and now have their own model that will help keep them focused.

Although this section has only briefly touched on the role of the caregiver, hopefully the reader can begin to understand the complexity of the task. This is why early childhood educators need not only a sound preparatory education but also a variety of opportunities for mentored experience in working directly with infants and toddlers. This learning takes time and must be supported by those who have already gained competence.

Working with Very Young Children: Who Is the Right Person?

It is not enough to say that working with very young children requires patience and a fondness for children. These attributes may be essential, but they are only the beginning. Educational institutions and employers use a variety of tools to help them decide who should enter a program or be offered employment.

Across the United States, there is a wide variation in the preparatory programs offered for entry to work with very young children. Legislation varies enormously as to the level of preparation required. To some extent, the academic and practical preparation required of those who are to work with infants and toddlers indicates the values of that society. Potential for earned

REFLECT ON THIS QUOTE

"While cosmetologists must attend as much 2000 hours of training before they can get a license, 31 states allow teachers in a child care center to begin working with children before receiving any training in early childhood development."

(Sonosky, 2004, 66)

Figure 1.3 Adults in the Lives of Infants, Toddlers, and 2-Year-Olds

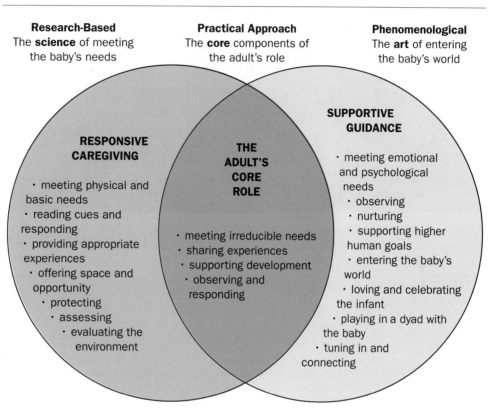

Research-Based
The **science** of meeting the baby's needs

Practical Approach
The **core** components of the adult's role

Phenomenological
The **art** of entering the baby's world

RESPONSIVE CAREGIVING

• meeting physical and basic needs
• reading cues and responding
• providing appropriate experiences
• offering space and opportunity
• protecting
• assessing
• evaluating the environment

THE ADULT'S CORE ROLE

• meeting irreducible needs
• sharing experiences
• supporting development
• observing and responding

SUPPORTIVE GUIDANCE

• meeting emotional and psychological needs
• observing
• nurturing
• supporting higher human goals
• entering the baby's world
• loving and celebrating the infant
• playing in a dyad with the baby
• tuning in and connecting

At the center of the adult's role is meeting the child's irreducible needs (see Brazelton & Greenspan, 2000). This includes being aware of meeting the most basic physical needs and entering into the child's world—combing the art and science of being in the life of the child.

income is also a factor. Typically, in the United States, most child care providers still do not earn a living wage. Many are forced to supplement their income through either a second job or dependence on additional revenue earned by other family members. This lack of financial compensation effects decisions about obtaining further training or an advanced degree. Efforts continue to be made on behalf of early childhood providers to ensure that compensation levels match responsibility levels. Other countries have adopted an approach that acknowledges the importance of early care providers. For example, Finland and some other European countries stress parental leave and demand high levels of preparation for caregivers and teachers of young children. These countries clearly value the importance of the early years, and are prepared to pay to maintain high standards.

Academic qualifications usually indicate that the holder of the diploma or degree will have certain competencies and will be able to demonstrate the appropriate knowledge, skills, and dispositions for a job in the field. However, academic qualifications alone are rarely reliable predictors of successful practice; additional personal qualities, motivations, and inner directions are also important factors. Working with infants and toddlers is specialized and stressful, and carries a high level of responsibility. Measuring the attributes required for such work is very difficult for employers because they appear to require subjective assessment.

College and university programs that articulate their program's learning outcomes offer some indication of the levels of knowledge, skills, and attitudes necessary for working with very young children. Some of these have been developed carefully, keeping in mind the needs of the community as well as the specific **competencies** required of the early childhood practitioner. Often the college or university catalog briefly outlines the competencies required for graduation or certification in a particular state. Sometimes

States require that students have a criminal records check and a child abuse clearance done before beginning practicum work. This is a necessary safeguard to exclude people who have been convicted of criminal offenses, especially those related to children. Also, most states now require anyone working with children on a regular basis to have a physical exam and a tuberculosis [tb] test upon initial volunteering (practicum) or employment and then every two years from that point on.

competencies

the level of observable functioning of the individual and/or the specified knowledge and skills that are to be acquired

Besides excellent academic training and practical skills, individuals who choose to work with infants and toddlers need qualities that may not be measured so easily, but are essential for fostering and maintaining responsive, respectful, and reciprocal relationships.

these competencies can also be found online from your college or university education Web site. Often these competencies align with accrediting educational organizations such as INTASC or NCATE.

Three organizations in the United States offer useful tools for assessing or documenting competencies: the National Association for the Education of Young Children (NAEYC), the Child Development Associate (CDA) national credentialing program at the Council for Professional Recognition, and ZERO TO THREE. (See the Additional Support section in your Online Companion for information on this documentation.) Canada, Australia, the United Kingdom, Jamaica, and many other countries have developed their own competency profiles, entry to practice standards, and training standards. Although (and because) they are articulated in different ways, it can be helpful and interesting to review them.

The competencies necessary for working with very young children are not all captured in formal statements, even though each competency document will try to capture the essence of what such work is about. Working with infants, toddlers, and 2-year-olds requires a genuine liking for children, not just a sentimental view of their "cuteness." It necessitates addressing your own needs because if you are not healthy and balanced, you cannot offer them what they need. Constant observation, knowing what to look for, and what to make of what you see is at the core of the work. It demands a sense of fun and a sense of the ridiculous. Seeing the world at the child's level is another part of the educator's abilities—without being condescending or patronizing. Educating involves anticipating what the children are about to do and then responding when they do the unexpected. Vast knowledge about children's development is necessary and it must be applied very quickly when the occasion arises. Communication and advocacy skills are an asset—applied so as to relate to the real context of children and families. Having respect for all people is vital even when they think differently or hold challenging beliefs. The early childhood practitioner must lead children to independence while sustaining a two-way attachment with them. Above all, practitioners need to honor the opportunity to be involved in the lives of other human beings. They must also "let go" when the time comes and accept that things don't always work out as they had hoped. Can all these things be measured? Not easily!

PRACTICAL EXPERIENCE FOR THE STUDENT EDUCATOR

Your Online Companion has a section entitled "Student Educator," which contains valuable information that can help you as you become involved in observing and working in practicum sites. It is recommended that you review this section before you begin any work at a child care facility. In addition to the information online, you always need to meet with the director and/or classroom teacher in order to familiarize yourself with the expectations and requirements of the site. Remember, once you walk through the front door of a child care facility, you are a representative of the early childhood profession and you must behave as a professional! Box 1.7 summarizes the essential components of the *See How They Grow* philosophy. As you read over this philosophy, reflect on all the different ideas you have encountered in Chapter 1. There is a *sample philosophy* in your Online Companion, which you can also use for reference. Use both the information in Box 1.7 and the *sample philosophy*

BOX 1.7

THE PHILOSOPHY OF *SEE HOW THEY GROW*

At the center of the philosophy of *See How They Grow* is the valuing of individual infants and toddlers for who they are, what they can do, and for the families they are based in. Each young child is an individual with diverse abilities, interests, and experiences. Children may be parented according to a range of values and beliefs, but each needs to be fully accepted and respected. Specifically, *See How They Grow* is based on the following beliefs:

- Babies are amazingly complex human beings.
- Babies and toddlers are competent and have incredible potential to make relationships, learn, and adapt.
- Parents are the most important adults in their children's lives.
- Parents are the caregivers' partners in supporting the needs of their young children.
- Respect for young children and their families is at the core of all aspects of practice.
- Safety and protection from harm are the first priorities of caregivers.
- Maintaining the infants' and toddlers' health and well-being is essential to caregiving strategies.
- Infants and toddlers are individuals in terms of their growth, rhythms, patterns of development, temperament styles, and needs.
- The study of infant and toddler development through observation, research, and application of theoretical models is essential for furthering understanding and meeting the needs of young children more effectively.
- The development of infants and toddlers is holistic, even though we may study its domains and issues separately.
- Infants and toddlers have the right to have all their basic physical and psychological needs met.
- Infants are born into cultural and familiar contexts, and their development must be viewed within those contexts.
- There are many ways of nurturing children, most of which should be openly accepted.
- Infants and toddlers of varying abilities, of differing appearances, from any culture or ethnic background, from any social or economic class, and from either gender are equally deserving of high-quality care and nurturance, although their needs may differ.
- Infants and toddlers must be in an environment that meets their needs for **attachment** and continuity of care.
- Observational, health, and contextual information should be kept up to date, and recorded and stored in a confidential manner.
- Guidance strategies used with infants and toddlers must support the individual developmental needs of the child.
- Adults act as mediators in many aspects of the young child's learning.
- Including children of all abilities is beneficial to all.
- It can be more important to "be" with children than to "do" with them.
- Abuse of young children stems from inappropriate power dynamics in adult–child relationships; how this abuse is demonstrated frequently relates to the child's developmental stage.
- Preparation for and evaluation of the caregiving role must be thorough and ongoing.
- Caregivers are responsible for their own health and well-being in the performance of their role.
- An infant or toddler's curriculum involves every aspects of the child's experience, both planned and unplanned.

 Activity 1.6 in the Online Companion encourages you to compare the written philosophies of different centers not only to each other and a sample center philosophy, but also to elements contained in your own philosophy of education and care for toddlers.

 as starting points to help you complete Part I of Activity 1.5 on your CD-ROM, the writing of a personal philosophy. Part II is a chart that contains each separate element of the *See How They Grow* philosophy so that you can track the information you learn while taking this course of study. This check sheet should help you elaborate on your philosophy as time goes by.

SUMMARY

A statement of philosophy contains the values and beliefs about children that drive all aspects of practice in a child care center. The philosophy must be carefully considered, discussed, and articulated so that it is understandable and becomes a living document that shapes all activity within an agency. Often long-held beliefs and assumptions must be reflected upon to ensure that there is a rationale for continuing to retain those ideas. A philosophy can draw from many different sources, including historical and theoretical components, principles of caregiving and education, concerns for the well-being of children and families, and rational beliefs.

Indicators of quality care and education have been identified. After health and safety issues, the top three include the *ratio of children to adults, the size of the group of children*, and *the education and training of the caregiver.* Understanding the *needs of groups of children*, the *unique needs of individual children*, and the *cultural context in which children live* are components of developmentally appropriate practices and help shape the decisions made on a daily basis.

The role of the caregiver and educator is impacted depending upon whether an individual adopts a research-based, practical, or phenomenological approach. In addition, the type of child care setting, the diversity of the student population, and the inclusion of children with identified needs can all impact the operation of a program, as well as its philosophy.

How a center arrives at the statement that contains its philosophy takes time and effort for both research and reflection. It will involve looking at beliefs about children, best practices, and examining current knowledge of child development, and seeking indicators of high-quality service delivery.

As students become practicing educators, they will continue on their path of lifelong learning. Maturity, experience, and reflective practice combine to allow the educator to be an increasingly responsive person delivering high-quality care and education.

DISCUSSION QUESTIONS

1. Where do your own beliefs about young children come from?
2. What would an ideal infant or toddler environment look like?
3. If parents and educators have differing views about children's needs and development, what compromise could be acceptable?
4. Looking at your society in general and the media in particular, what images of childhood are projected?
5. How do your beliefs about young children compare with society's view?

ADDITIONAL RESOURCES

Further Reading

American Academy of Pediatrics, American Public Health Association & National Resource Center for Health and Safety in Child Care. *Caring for our children: National health and safety performance standards* (2nd ed.). USA: American Academy of Pediatrics, American Public Health Association & National Resource Center for Health and Safety in Child Care.

Aronson, D. (Ed.). (2002). *Healthy young children: A manual for programs.* Washington, DC: NAEYC.

Brazelton, T. B., & Greenspan, S. I. (2000). *The irreducible needs of children: What every child must have to grow, learn and flourish.* Cambridge, MA: Perseus Press.

Bredekamp, S. & Copple, C. (Eds.). (1997). *Developmentally appropriate practice in early childhood programs* (Rev. ed.). Washington, DC: NAEYC.

Chandler, K. (2003). *Administering for quality: Canadian early childhood development programs.* Toronto: Prentice Hall.

David, M., & Appell, G. (1973). *LOCZY: An unusual approach to mothering.* (Lóczy ou le materage insolite, J. M. Clark, Trans.). Los Angeles: Resources for Infant Educators.

Derman-Sparks, L. (1989). *Anti-bias curriculum: Tools for empowering young children.* Washington, DC: NAEYC.

Doherty-Derkowski, G. (1995). *Quality matters: Excellence in early childhood programs.* Don Mills, ON: Addison-Wesley.

Doherty, G., & Friendly, M. (2002). *Making the best use of the You Bet I Care! data sets: Final report on a research forum.* Toronto: Childcare Resource & Research Unit.

Edwards, C., Gandini L., & Forman, G. (1998). *The hundred languages of children.* Norwood, NJ: Ablex Publishing Corporation.

Erickson, M., & Kurz-Riemer, K. (1999). *Infants, toddlers and families.* New York: Guilford Press.

Feeney, S., & Freeman, N. (1999). *Ethics and the early childhood educator: Using the NAEYC Code.* Washington, DC: NAEYC.

Gerber, M. (Ed.). (1987). *A manual for parents and professionals.* Los Angeles: Resources for Infant Educators.

Gestwicki, C. (1999). *Developmentally appropriate practice: Curriculum and development in early education* (2nd ed.) Clifton Park, NY: Thomson Delmar Learning.

Hewes, J. (1995). *Many ways to grow: Responding to cultural diversity in early childhood settings.* Edmonton, AB: Alberta Association for Young Children.

Ideas: Emotional Well-Being in Child Care. *Interaction.* Canadian Child Care Federation. George Brown College, Toronto.

Levin, D. E. (2003). *Teaching young children in violent times: Building a peaceable classroom* (2nd ed.). USA: Educators for Social Responsibility.

NICHD Early Child Care Research Network. (2002). Child Care Structure, Process Outcome: Direct and Indirect Effects of Child Care Quality on Young Children's Development. *Psychological Science 13*(3).

Phillips, D. A. (Ed.). (1988). *Quality in child care: What does the research tell us?* Washington, DC: NAEYC.

Shonkoff, J. P., & Phillips, D. A. (Eds.) (2000). *From neurons to neighborhoods: The science of early childhood development.* USA: National Academy Press.

Wardle, F. (2003). *Introduction to early childhood education: A multi-dimensional approach to child-centered care and learning.* Boston: Allyn & Bacon.

Useful Videos

Career Encounters: Early Childhood Education
  28-minute video

Caring for Our Children.
Six-video set, 30 minutes each, in conjunction with the American Academy of Pediatrics (Health and Safety Issues in Childcare)

Nurturing Growth: Child Growth and Development
  30-minute video

Tools for Teaching Developmentally Appropriate Practice: The Leading Edge in Early Childhood Education.
Four videos split into 5- to 12-minute segments—over 3 hours of video
Available from NAEYC. 1-800-424-2460 or www.naeyc.org/

Respectfully Yours: Magda Gerber's Approach to Professional Infant/Toddler Care. Available from the Program for Infants and Toddlers. http://www.pitc.org/ (58 minutes).

Useful Web Sites

Association for Childhood Education International (ACEI)
  www.acei.org
Children's Defense Fund
  www.childrensdefense.org
Division for Early Childhood of the Council for Exceptional Children
  www.dec.sped.org
Educarers: World of Infants
  www.educarer.com
National Association for the Education of Young Children (NAEYC)
  www.naeyc.org
National Association of Child Care Resource and Referral Agencies
  www.nacrra.org/
National Child Care Information Center
  www.nccid.org/
National Institute for Early Education Research (NIEER)
  www.nierr.org/
The Pikler Institute
  www.pikler.org/
Resources for Infant Educarers (RIE)
  www.rie.org/
Reggio Children—A Hundred Languages
  http://zerosei.comune.re.it/
ZERO TO THREE
  www.zerothree.org

CHAPTER 2

Getting in Focus: Observing Infants, Toddlers, and Twos

Following the child's lead means that we have to observe his behavior carefully and respond to *his* needs, not ours.

LEARNING OUTCOMES

After reading and studying this chapter, you should be able to:

- explain why it is important to observe and record pertinent information about the behavior of infants and toddlers
- identify the characteristics of effective observation strategies for infants and toddlers
- describe the use of developmental portfolios as authentic assessment tools for infants and toddlers
- develop a system for assessing the development of very young children that aligns with your philosophy of care and education

SCENE

A variety of learners, including early childhood students, hear the following in an elective course in art:

> "Ways of seeing are not just a matter of using your eyes," explained a university teacher. "It's not what your eyes see, but what your brain processes, and that's an issue related to your previous experience and beliefs." The teacher was addressing perception as it relates to appreciating art, but several listeners who were also early childhood education students felt that the notion applied to observing children, too.

Perception is a subject of interest to artists, philosophers, psychologists, medical professionals, and, of course, educators. The principles in each discipline are equally valid. Artists consider perception from an aesthetic perspective; philosophers approach it as a way of understanding values and beliefs. Psychologists study the role of the brain in perceptual functioning, and medical practitioners report new leaps forward in applications of perception in health care. Finally,

Figure 2.1 A Professional Cycle of Reflective Practice

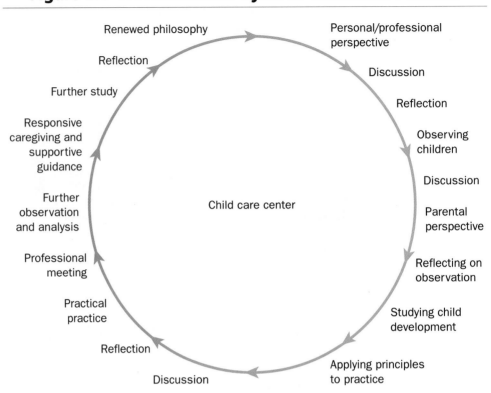

reflective practice

professional practice that includes regular evaluation of the program and one's effectiveness within it

educators examine perception and **reflective practice** when teaching methodologies of observation and recording. (See Figure 2.1.)

WHY OBSERVE?

"What's the point of learning all that stuff about observation methods? I can see, can't I?" asked a student at the start of my observational skills class. My response was "I'll ask you the same question at the end of the course." As it turned out, I did ask her the question as she handed in her last observation assignment. She replied, "Well, I didn't know before that the more I look, the more I see . . . and now I've learned something about child development. I know what to look for . . . The trouble is, the more I know about children, the more I know I need to learn about them . . . and as I observe more, I know I need to do more with the children."

That is the core of our challenge. We need to practice **observation** to learn about children. As we observe and study, we learn more about what to look for. We apply what we know about children and can then find improved ways of supporting them. An ongoing circle of action—that is, observing, interpreting, responding, and continuing to observe—will lead you to be a more effective caregiver for infants and toddlers.

Improved observation skills can help you:

observation

watching behavior and activities of children in a controlled, informed, educated, purposeful manner, often with specific goals, questions, or concerns in mind; usually involves recording data utilizing a variety of methods

- keep children safe
- increase your knowledge of child development
- assess the physical health of children
- learn to respond with sensitivity to children
- communicate with families
- develop methods to support and extend learning

- provide experiences that match the individual needs of each child
- assess development of children
- interpret what you see

This list only skims the surface of what you can gain from purposeful observation. Activity 2.1 in your Online Companion suggests a way to gather information about young children through observation.

WHAT TO OBSERVE

The more we observe, the better we respond; the more we know about developmental processes, the better we know what to look for. The essential pathway to knowing what to observe is practicing your observation skills and reviewing the effectiveness of the responses that you make, based on what you see. Increasing your experience with young children and studying developmental stages and theories allow you to appreciate the behavioral details that you might otherwise miss.

Having a Purpose

Focusing your attention, however well intentioned, is often inadequate and is different than purposeful observation. Focused attention might help you concentrate on a particular child, but it might not result in really learning very much more about her development, needs, or interests. We may be enjoying who we are looking at because we are enchanted by their incredible abilities. Often we are observing because we are responsible for the child's safety; we are ensuring that a child's curiosity does not lead to an accident or that a small baby does not roll off a change table onto the floor.

However, observing children for just these factors is not enough. We must intentionally be looking for additional information and signals from children, which can help us understand them to a much greater degree. Purposeful observation means that you plan on a daily basis to observe a child with intentional rationale. We may notice what interests the child or how his skills have increased. We may be looking for specific developmental information to assure us that everything is progressing well. Possibly we will notice behaviors that indicate something about the child's thinking abilities. Attachments to adults and relationships with other children can be observed; these can inform us about some emotional aspects of development. Listening to the child's early language can tell us about his expressive language skills. Watching responses to language can frequently let us know about the child's receptive language and what he understands. If we are trying to be in tune with the baby or toddler, then we observe the child to help us pick up his cues. Personality and temperamental styles are also observable and can help us to meet the child's needs for certain kinds of caregiving responses. Another reason for observing may be that there is cause for concern about a child's changing health status. For example, we may notice patterns of behavior that are different from the ones the child usually exhibits, or perhaps that his appearance has changed.

Ultimately, observation is the underpinning of good teaching. The ability to incorporate observation into the rhythm of the day is what can separate adequate teachers from excellent teachers. Consider the following:

We believe that observing creates an attitude of openness and wonder that allows you to know and understand the children you work with every day. Observing is essential to building trusting relationships with children and families that provide the foundation for a successful early childhood program. Only within the context of these trusting relationships can teachers promote children's development. Observing is so much more than a set of skills or another task to add to your already demanding schedule. . . . Suddenly observing is no longer something "out there" that you have to find time to do. Instead it becomes part of your everyday work. Watching, listening, reflecting, and relating are as important as anything else you do during the day, and this has implications for how you see your role as a teacher. (Jablon Dombro, & Dichtelmiller, 1999, pp. 6–7)

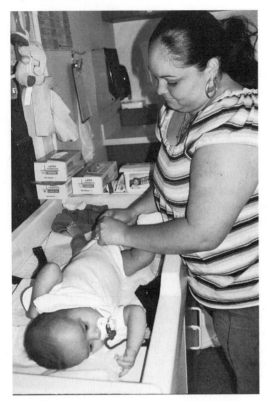

This daily care routine offers an opportunity for careful observation.

guidance strategies

techniques of discipline and instruction used in order to help children gain personal competence and self-discipline

participant observation

an observation made while the observer is engaged in activity or communication with the individual being observed

nonparticipant observation

an observation conducted from a distance without direct involvement in events or responsibility for what occurs

permission

the professional requirement to ask parents if it is acceptable to observe, record, or conduct an activity

Building Skills

Educators, caregivers, and parents can perform their roles more effectively if they build up their observation skills. They can create their **guidance strategies** and activity plans, enjoy the child's development more richly by entering into the child's world more meaningfully, and become better attuned to the child and thus more able to support her needs. Developing these skills requires a lot of practice, but it is both intriguing and satisfying.

How we see the young child depends on what we are looking for. What we know about developmental sequences, health, personality styles, and so on helps us to observe more usefully. Our perceptions of what we observe are far more significant than the actual visual information that we receive.

We learn about development from observing, and we observe more effectively by understanding the principles and patterns of development. This two-way process continues through our professional lives.

WHEN TO OBSERVE

No time of day is more important than another for observational purposes. Even the sleep times of infants and toddlers can provide you with interesting observations. Feeding, diaper-changing, bathing, and dressing times, as well as transitions and separations from the parents, are as significant as the times when the infant or toddler is playing or interacting with other people. Ensure that you informally observe all aspects of the young child's day. Also plan more organized systems for observation so that you can record sufficient information about all aspects of the child's day and all domains of the child's development. Although developmental domains can help you review all aspects of the child's development, you must remember that you are recording information about a whole human being. All children are deserving of respect, confidentiality, and an appreciation of their wholeness. Detailed information need not be cold and clinical; the purpose is to support the amazing, dynamic, and individual process of human development.

You can observe children while you are involved with their activity and while you are responsible for them. This is called **participant observation.** This can give you a feeling for what is happening, but it is impossible to record what is happening—unless you have a video camera catching your participation and children's behavior. **Nonparticipant observation** requires the observer to be free of direct responsibility or involvement with the children. There are advantages to being a nonparticipant because you can focus all your attention on your observation.

GETTING STARTED

Students are sometimes overwhelmed when they begin observing children and they have many questions:

- *How do I ask a family if I can observe their child?*
- *Do centers have permission agreements that cover me?*
- *What information can I share with families?*

Permission

Educators, caregivers, and students should always seek **permission** from the parents to observe, record information, or make evaluations about any child. Students who are learning about children, and acquiring skills in documentation, will need to seek and gain written permission from families before undertaking their work. Sometimes permission is granted by a family member on the original form on enrollment, but this cannot be assumed. As with any other research, permission should always be requested when it concerns human subjects—including children. If the permission is not up to date, it should be requested again.

When families enroll their children in a center, the observation and assessment processes should be discussed with them. This usually means that it becomes an accepted part of practice for educators to observe and record information about individual children. Families need to understand this and become active in participating in the observational protocols. It should be part of the interviewing process for families to sign a form giving their consent for appropriate observations to be recorded and stored. They should always be given reasonable access to any of this documentation.

Any data collected should not be discussed with family members until the student educator has checked with the cooperating teacher, director, or mentor. This means that any inference drawn from the observations must be checked before families see the material. Student educators must rely on the expertise of their mentors to advise them of what is appropriate to share with families. Like a doctor's diagnosis, professional opinions need to be reliable. Therefore, any comment that contains subjective opinions should never be shared with families.

A sample permission form is included in the Additional Support section on your Online Companion.

An Easy Way to Start

informal observation

casual or unrecorded observation

Informal observation should be the starting point for all interactions with young children and should guide all planning and responses. Observing and responding to very young children is an entirely natural activity. When a baby goes by, you are likely to turn to look. If the baby is in a stroller, you might pause for a few moments and peer at her while you make odd facial expressions. Given more time, you might talk to the baby in short sentences in a high-pitched voice while you try to maintain eye contact.

If the baby starts to get agitated, you may feel glad that you are not alone with her. Her cry may upset you. However, if you are left alone with the crying baby you might pick her up, rock her, or try singing a song, whether or not you have been exposed to many babies. Even people who are not familiar with infants are likely to do similar things. One reason for this is that babies have inborn mechanisms to ensure that their needs are met, and adults have instinctive behaviors relating to caring for the young of the species.

We are attracted to the faces of very young children (Morris, 1999) because they appeal to us, draw us toward them, and cause us to feel that we want to protect them. This may be nature's way of ensuring that they are cared for. When we watch young children, we can see their individual personalities and emerging skills, and then become more responsive to their needs. We respond both emotionally and practically. We provide comfort and reassurance, and ensure that no harm comes to the young child. We support the unfolding stages of the child's development. Both child and adult grow together: The toddler's mobility and activity get our attention and, protectively, we anticipate the dangers that are not understood by the toddler. Even without study, we have some insight into a toddler's thinking skills; this kind of knowledge replicates some of the wisdom of our ancestors, who were more ready to rely on practical skills, common sense, and instincts than most of us are today.

SELECTING OBSERVATION METHODS

As stated before, informal observation and intuitive responses will give you only limited knowledge about children. However, a variety of methods and techniques exist that can help teachers develop a more purposeful plan for observing children. The main categories of observational methods are outlined in Table 2.1.

There is a range of standard methods for observing children, and each method has a different use and purpose. Familiarizing yourself with the various methods can make the task of observation more efficient and markedly more effective. Narratives offer the opportunity for

Table 2.1 Observational Recording Methods for Infants and Toddlers

METHOD	DESCRIPTION	FEATURES
Narratives	Written accounts of behavior	Naturalistic descriptive recordings
1. Running records	Detailed records of everything the child says/does	Holistic view of development
2. Anecdotal records	Selected recording of behaviors/events that the adult considers pertinent	Efficient way to document pertinent behaviors
3. Diary records	Regular recordings detailing important developmental progressions, regressions, or activities	Identify individualized pattern of development
4. Specimen records	Very detailed, usually coded account of behaviors	Used by psychologists for close analysis
Samplings	Prepared formats used to determine occurrences of behavior	Identify behavior patterns
1. Time samplings	Behavior is described in a snapshot at predetermined time intervals	Patterns of play, sleep, etc., may be identified
2. Event samplings	A specific behavior is identified, defined, and charted	The duration, severity, causality, and frequency of the behavior may become evident
Checklists	Lists of behaviors that are checked off	Offers an overview of development
1. Prepared checklists	Valid and reliable listing of skills/behaviors, usually normative- and/or criterion-referenced	Can identify the child's developmental level and performance in relation to the norm
2. Self-designed checklists	Lists of skills/behaviors considered relevant to the caregiver	May offer indications of progress and overall development
Rating scales	A way of recording the degree to which a behavior, trait, or skill is demonstrated	Can offer a profile of individual temperament, skill levels, or development
1. Semantic differentials	Word opposites offer a way of indicating preferences or styles	These may offer a qualitative approach to identifying individual styles
2. Numerical scales	Numbers are used to indicate the degree to which a behavior is observable or a characteristic is thought applicable	Qualitative information may be helpful in detailing a personal profile
Charts	Pictorial or written data recorded on prepared sheets	Efficient way of recording personal functions and patterns
1. Daily log charts	Prepared charts indicating activity of the day	May provide an overview of the child's day, including feeding, diaper-changing, and play
2. Activity charts	Prepared charts to record interests, activities, play discovery, and learning	Offer an overview of the child's activity
3. Pictorial representations	Pie charts, bar graphs, diagrams, or other visual presentation of information	A way to make large amounts of data manageable and understandable
Media-Assisted	Electronic or technologically aided recording processes	Can provide ways of recording and storing large amounts of information about individual children, group functioning, and the program
1. Video recordings	Video camera is used to record individual skills, play sequences, and group activities	Provide detailed material for later analysis regarding play, communication, and other activities
2. Audio recordings	Tape recorder is used to record vocalizations, use of language, musical activities, singing, or any other sound	Useful for analysis of language development, rhythm, pitch, etc.
3. Photographs	Photographs are used to capture the changing bodies, size, skills, and the process and products of discovery	Provide visual documentation of development
4. Computer recordings	Used for storing information gleaned from traditional methods or as a direct process of documenting information	Provide storage and retrieval of data

This teacher utilizes a checklist to record information about children's development.

detailed "open-ended" recordings; samplings can help us to recognize behavior patterns; checklists can provide an overview of behavioral progress or evaluation of the environment; and rating scales help us to indicate the level of significance of various behaviors. You should familiarize yourself with these methods, using the information in Table 2.1 to identify their characteristics, purposes, strengths, and challenges.

The Additional Support section in your Online Companion has links to observation tools.

Recording Information

Not all observations are recorded. If they were, it would be impossible to do anything other than observe! However, recording observations is a very important part of the educator's role. Teachers must write things down because if they don't, within a very short time all the details of the event will be forgotten. Even if the method used is fairly open-ended, there must be a sense of purpose for the recording. It should be done as efficiently and effectively as possible and the information obtained used to enhance the child's life. A working knowledge of standard recording methods will allow you to choose the method that best suits your purposes. The following suggestions might be helpful:

1. Observations should always be recorded as soon as possible after they are made. Recording immediately after observation may help promote accuracy while avoiding the distraction of recording during observation.
2. Some methods require observing and recording simultaneously; this enables the observer to record small details that might otherwise be forgotten.
3. Due to personal perception, there will probably be some small differences between what actually happened and what you recorded.
4. If some time elapses between the observation and the recording, the likelihood of misrepresentation will be even greater.
5. Efficiency can be boosted if you use prepared observation sheets. These will help you focus on what you are seeing; they also cut down on writing time and can produce more readable results without the need for rewriting. However, make sure the prepared forms meet the needs of your particular group of children as well as the observational purpose.

Has this ever happened to you?

Why must we write things down?

I was having a very important dinner party at my home one weekend. I spent an hour making up the grocery list. I needed 22 different items, but some of them were only available at a store located 25 miles from my home. I ran to my car and raced to the market only to realize that I had left my list at home. I tried to remember what I needed and thought I had remembered everything. However, when I got home, I discovered that I had forgotten two essential items. I had to get back in my car and make another 50-mile round trip. Sometimes, you can't remember something unless you *write it down*.

Objectivity versus Subjectivity

It is important for all teachers to observe children with an objective eye. However, objectivity is tempered by a host of factors, such as:

- experiences with family, childhood, and friends;
- culture and heritage;
- beliefs and values;

Figure 2.2 Objectivity–Subjectivity Continuum

OBJECTIVITY	SUBJECTIVITY

- "absolute" truth
- certainty
- clear-cut decisions
- logical reasoning
- scientific processes
- thinking

- interpretations
- beliefs
- open-ended considerations
- intuition
- creative processes
- feelings

- level of training and education;
- temperament and learning style;
- personal factors such as health, finances, and emotional well-being; and
- biases and prejudices.

These are just some of the factors that can affect how you observe children and how you interpret what you observe.

Figure 2.2 shows a continuum, with objectivity and subjectivity at opposite poles. Most perceptions drawn from observational information are neither purely objective nor subjective; they lie on a continuum somewhere between the two. Objectivity in observation is usually considered desirable because it demands the rigor of science and logic. It helps the observer avoid judgments and assumptions. Observed information is purely visual and auditory data until our brains make some sense of the information. Perception involves the processing of visual and auditory data. However, under some circumstances, objectivity should be tempered with a degree of subjectivity, to allow for a more empathic and holistic understanding of the child being observed.

Dealing with Observer Bias

If two teachers observe the same child at the same time using the same method, the outcomes should be consistent. However, it often takes a lot of training for individuals to have agreement in their findings. This is because most observers have some sort of **bias**. Although you cannot always help your biases or know how they were formed, you must examine your perspective to see if some of your biases need to be reconsidered. When you begin to observe young children, you may find that it is hard to avoid some assumptions and even a few judgments that you didn't mean to make. Reviewing your recordings will help you eliminate comments that stem from such assumptions. It is particularly important to recognize the difference between a proven fact and an *interpretation* of the facts.

See Activity 2.2 on your CD-ROM to help you examine all the "baggage" you bring with you to the teaching experience.

ASSESSMENT

Most of our thinking necessarily involves making inferences or interpretations—we are all trying to make sense of our world. Observation and **assessment** are two distinct processes that require the separation of seeing and perceiving. Observation tries to avoid inferences and focuses on mere facts, while assessment involves making some sense of the facts, usually by comparing them to a norm, pattern, or theory to explain the observation.

Making Inferences

In the simplest terms, thinking is how we make sense of our world, and it often involves making interpretations or inferences. An **inference** is a deduction or an explanatory statement; in

---

> "The unexamined life is not worth living."
>
> Socrates

bias

any distorted perception of other people or social groups that is used to justify mistreatment; a preference, such as a visual preference

assessment

the process of gathering data (including observational information) from several sources using informal or standardized instruments and making deductions that explain behavior; child assessment is not based on a single measure

BOX 2.1

POSSIBLE CORRECT INFERENCES AND COMMON MISTAKES

A. Inferences That Might Be Correct

OBSERVATION	POSSIBLY CORRECT INFERENCES
A newborn baby turns her head when her cheek is stroked.	She is showing a rooting reflex.
A toddler shouts "no!"	The toddler wants autonomy.
An infant cries persistently and draws her legs up and down, extending her legs.	The infant is experiencing colic.
As he lies in his crib, a baby passes items from hand to hand.	He is showing an example of the proximodistal sequence of skill development, with physical control now extending to his arms and hands.
An infant of 9 months always rolls to the side when put into a sitting position.	The infant appears to have less back control than most infants her age.
A toddler swishes her hands in the bathtub and tries to pick up some bubbles on the surface of the water.	The toddler is in the sensorimotor stage of development.
At 12 months, the infant pulls himself to standing, cruises alongside a large box, and takes three steps toward the caregiver before falling to the floor.	The infant is demonstrating gross motor skills typical for his age.

B. Common Mistakes

OBSERVATION	POSSIBLY INCORRECT INFERENCES
The child is 30 months old.	The child is in the preoperational stage.
An infant plays in a solitary way.	The infant cannot play with others.
A toddler separates from a parent.	The toddler is securely attached.
A baby refuses his bottle.	The baby is sick.
A baby turns to the mother.	The baby's hearing is good.
The child does not follow simple instructions.	The child doesn't understand the instructions.
An infant responds to black-and-white images.	The infant prefers black-and-white images.
A toddler takes longer than his peers to become "toilet-trained."	The toddler is fixated on the anal stage.

inference

the process of drawing a conclusion from given evidence; to reach a decision by reasoning

other words, a conclusion. So, the goal of assessment is to be able to explain a child's behavior through inferences that are based on current understandings about child development. An inference might explain behavior using a theoretical explanation, such as inferring that a child is in the sensorimotor stage. Another way of explaining behavior is to match it to a normative profile, to see if the behavior indicates an age-level performance.

Doing this, we might infer that a particular child is using the two-word phrases typical of an 18-month-old toddler. Other explanations for behavior might factor in pieces of contextual information. We might infer that an infant's irritability is caused by a low-grade infection or that a toddler is becoming more comfortable with his mother leaving.

The inferences in part A of Box 2.1 are quite likely to be correct, but they need support. Support, or validation, is covered in the next section. Keep in mind that even if you establish support for an inference, it is possible that the inference might be incorrect. Part B of Box 2.1 shows some common inferences that might be incorrect. However, the risk of making a mistake shouldn't stop us from using critical thinking skills. It also means that teachers need to practice in order to improve observation skills, they have to continue to learn about child development, and they need to incorporate research findings into their knowledge base in order to strengthen their decision-making abilities.

Validating Your Inferences

An assessment involves making inferences, but it doesn't stop there. It also requires validation of those statements: We need to check to see if our inferences are correct. To be valid, the inferences must include reasons that are carefully considered and are supported in some way. It is best to validate inferences using reliable sources, such as books that offer well-researched information. You might use a normative reference, or apply a theory to validate your inference.

Validating inferences involves checking them through to see if they are likely to be correct. If the inferences that you make cannot be supported, they should not be stated—or they should be deleted. To make sure that your inferences can have support, or **validation**, you can try some of the following techniques:

- Ask other educators for their perceptions—do they *agree* with you?
- What *research* supports your inference or interpretation?
- Use *valid and reliable measures* (such as norms, if you think they are useful) as benchmarks for your inferences about a child's behavior.
- Match the behavior you have observed, and your inference related to it, with a recognized *theory* that offers a reasonable explanation.

Box 2.2 illustrates a running record (one method of observation) that includes both inferences and validations. The information written in *italics* is the information you could readily share with family members or other educators. There is a line drawn underneath the description of the facts of the event. The inferences and validations follow. These should not be shared with family members until agreement on the conclusions has been established. Please note that sources of support have been referenced—e.g., Ainsworth; Greenspan; etc. These supports lend credence and validity to the inferences.

It is important to realize that *validating your inferences does not mean that they have been proved.* Although supporting an inference does not prove it to be right, it does show that you have applied theory to practice and are, therefore, more likely to be right than if you did not attempt that process. If educators always went through this process and avoided making inferences that they couldn't validate, assessments would be much more reliable.

As you begin observing and recording children's behavior, you will probably find it difficult to record what you see, as well as make inferences or validate them. That ability comes gradually with experience and further study. However, don't let that overwhelm you. By the time you finish reading this textbook, you will know much more about children's development, theories, and relevant research. Your CD-ROM contains developmental profiles, or milestones. Utilize some of the reference materials and Web sites listed at the end of each chapter. Finally, just start observing children. In her work during the 1970s and 80s, Yetta Goodman coined the term "kidwatching," although the child studies in the 1930s had long established the importance of carefully observing children. "When observing through a kidwatching lens, beginner kidwatchers are always amazed by the intellectual curiosity and learning ingenuity of their students. They learn that while every child needs support in some areas, every child also has strengths (Owocki & Goodman, 2002, pg. xi). So become a kidwatcher and see how much you learn from watching.

Achieving a Balance

Don't try to write down everything, because observation then really loses its true purpose. "A profession that allows this to happen sacrifices one of the most joyful, engaging, and intellectually stimulating experiences readily available to teachers" (Curtis & Carter, 2000, p. xvi). Remember, the goal of observation is to learn about each and every child in your care. Spend most of your time with children watching them, and carefully choose the assessment forms you

> Never make a decision about a child based on one observation or assessment. In order to have the most reliable information about a child, you must repeat observations and assessments and then compare the data. You must also gather information from the child's family in order to "see" the child in the context of her experiences.

validation
being able to justify
or defend a statement

BOX 2.2

SAMPLE RUNNING RECORD OBSERVATION

The following is a short running record observation of Shaila (7 months) in an infant room in child care shortly before her mother leaves for work.

Running Record:

Shaila lies on the change table pushing downward with both her legs, kicking her mother's abdomen with both legs simultaneously. She does this repeatedly at the same time that both of her arms are swivelling outward with clenched fists. Her face is distorted, her eyes are almost closed and are somewhat watery. With reddened facial skin Shaila cries with a high-pitched sound, pausing only for quick gasps of air. Mom talks quietly as she removes her wet diaper. Gradually her legs cease their kicking and her arms continue to swivel outward, but they do so more slowly. The crying stops for a moment but starts again, this time more softly. Shaila's eyes open and settle on the gaze of her mother. Her coloring changes to a pink tone, although her eyes are still wet. Shaila changes her sound production to a gentle cooing, which is repeated by her mother. Now Shaila smiles weakly. She continues to gaze toward mother, but she sucks on the soother, which mother puts in her mouth.

Inference:

Shaila has an attachment to her mother.

Validation:

Ainsworth's attachment theory. There were indicators of Shaila's attachment to her mother. It was likely that Shaila's cry was an attempt to get attention because she was uncomfortable. There appeared to be some degree of trust that her mother would respond to her. She was able to be calmed by her mother and there was some taking turns in communicating. Shaila returned her mother's gaze and offered her a weak social smile. Ainsworth describes these behaviors as indicators of attachment; she researched the link between babies crying and mother's responses and saw greater attachment when the mother was responsive to the infant.

Inference:

Shaila's emotional development is typical for her age.

Validation:

Greenspan's research into emotional development and Allen and Marotz's developmental profiles. Shaila demonstrated a rhythm of initiating communications and responding that Greenspan describes as "falling in love" and "developing intentional communication." At 7 months, Shaila's development, in terms of her age and stage, falls between two stages of Greenspan's milestones. The behaviors that indicate that her emotional development is typical for her age include seeking attention, smiling when she is smiled at, gazing with interest, and seeking comfort. In addition, the Allen and Marotz profile for 4–8-month-old infants states that typically, at this time, infants establish a trust relationship if their needs are met consistently.

want to fill out. As a student, you need to learn how to use different observation tools, but try to obtain a balance between learning how to use the tools and learning how to watch children. When you have your own classroom, carefully design a system that allows you to systematically record observations on children, but do not have your head constantly buried in a form. If you do, you will miss out on much of the important stuff!

ASPECTS OF PROFESSIONAL OBSERVATION

When we observe infants and toddlers, there are several aspects to consider. First, we must conduct ourselves professionally and ethically. We must understand that we are bound by requirements of confidentiality and our professional Code of Ethics. Behavior that characterizes us as nosy or involves us in disussions about what we see or learn in caregiving facilities outside of professional boundaries cannot be condoned.

Confidentiality

The professional observer must have permission to observe and must respect the **confidentiality** of those being observed—making sure information is stored and shared discreetly. Confidentiality is needed to protect the privacy of children and their families. When you are writing observations, do so in a professional manner that observes confidentiality. Your recordings may assist your planning or some other part of your caregiving and educating. Whatever the reasons for making them, they should be shared with the parents and stored in a secure place.

Teamwork is essential in infant and toddler care. However, the need to communicate information within the team can breach confidentiality. Each member of the team needs to know the essential details of the child's health status, some contextual information about the child's family and background, and information from team members about recent occurrences. Along with the recorded observational information, this represents a lot of personal data.

Families have differing ideas about what constitutes privacy. Some might not want an observation chart that details their child's bowel movements. For others, this is no problem. The professional caregiver has to find ways to meet the needs of all families for privacy. Information about the child's family, health, and home must not be accessible, in any form, to anyone other than the family concerned and the professionals who are working with them.

Whatever the family's attitudes, it is always essential to protect all family information as confidential. For example, if you receive information about parents separating, this is not to be shared. If you have any observational information, this too must not be shared with anyone, unless permission has been granted.

Students sometimes face particular challenges with confidentiality issues. Sometimes caregivers are rightly reluctant to give students contextual information, even if it would help them to understand the child's behavior. If a child care agency is open to student fieldwork, it helps if it has a signed parent-release form that gives permission to students to access the information stored in files. If students are allowed access to this information, then they, too, must keep it absolutely confidential.

Authentic Assessment

Authentic assessment is a term educators use to describe a process of documenting children's growth and development over time, an assessment that considers each child in his or her own individual context, and is conducted in **naturalistic settings**—that is, in the child's normal, everyday environment. The documentation demonstrates what children are able to do and what they know and understand, not in a static manner (test score), but through ways that are meaningful to them and convey an image of the child as a powerful learner. Young children are especially sensitive to their surroundings, so keeping a normal pattern and schedule in a familiar environment will likely yield the most reliable information about them. Authentic assessment requires respect for the child and a "sympathetic understanding of the child" (Elkind, 1994). This type of assessment leads to the identification of the child's needs and connects to how the caregiver can respond to those needs. The data must be collected in an organized manner using methods that fit the purpose. The assessment should align with other parts of a philosophy and practice, such as curriculum and guidance, and it should involve collaborative teamwork that values critical thinking and the reflective process. Finally, in order for authentic assessment to be successful, caregivers must develop strong observation skills.

Objectivity

Most educators appear to value objectivity in observing and recording (the belief that there is a truth to what happened and that that truth must be sought). It is a good idea to start observing

These toddlers are exploring sticks, stones, and holes in a naturalistic setting.

with the idea of trying to be as factual as possible and recording only what you see. It is impossible to be entirely objective—and it may not be completely desirable. Human beings process information as they absorb it and, at times, subjective perceptions can be meaningful and useful. This does not mean that observers should be sloppy sentimentalists, but they might become increasingly reflective and honor their feeling responses as much as their factual ones. When trying to increase observational and recording skills, the aim of objectivity can serve the observer well, but as observers become more thoughtful and reflective about their recordings, subjective thoughts might provide further insight. As part of an authentic approach to assessment, one that is mindful of the child and how she is being assessed, both objective thought and subjective feeling responses can be valid—but the educator must be able to tell one from the other.

Remember that all the information you collect will need to be reviewed afterward so that you can consider what development is being demonstrated, what the individual needs might be, and how you can respond. Always separate the objectively recorded information from your analysis.

Participant and Nonparticipant Observation

Observations can be categorized as either participant or nonparticipant—that is, you are either involved in the situation with the child or you are standing apart, observing. Observing while participating is something that you should be doing all the time when working with young children. Nonparticipant observation leaves you free to see some details of behavior and interactions with others that you might miss if you were more directly involved. If you need to record information as well as observe, you may need to organize nonparticipant opportunities. Realistically, most adults working with young children do not get much nonparticipant time, so they need to establish ways to observe and then record soon after the action.

As stated before, most observations of very young children that are recorded are made in naturalistic settings. On very rare occasions, it may be necessary to set up testing-type situations so that you can observe particular skills or behaviors. These situations should be kept to a minimum, because they can be stressful for both the young child and the adult. It is more likely that an individual will perform well in situations that are without stress: play behaviors, social interactions, and cognitive skills may appear less well developed in structured scenarios. Do your observing when the child is comfortable and in her usual environment.

Portfolios

portfolio

a systematic collection of documentation on a child's growth and development, along with information on health, family background, and other relevant material

A single observation can be useful, but it cannot give a holistic picture of the very young child. Much of who the child is and how she behaves is shaped by her family and the culture in which she is nurtured. It is therefore very helpful to find out whatever you can to put the observations in a context. Families should be approached with the utmost respect and with the knowledge that they might decline access to the information. Explaining your goals to the families and building a trusting relationship with them is the key to success.

As illustrated in Figure 2.3, a **portfolio** is a systematic collection of documentation on a child's growth and development, along with information on health, family background, and

Figure 2.3 Child Portfolio

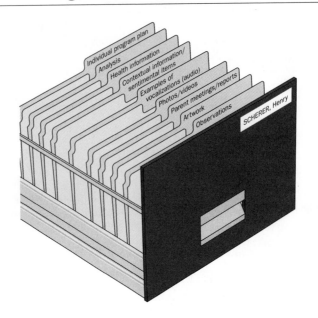

other relevant material. When combined, this information allows for the review of the child's development within the context of individual experience. As the child grows, the portfolio will include a variety of items made by the child, along with photographs and other memorabilia that document her life. Interspersed will be regular contributions from all the stakeholders in the child's life, updates, new observations, and ongoing assessments and individual plans. The first part of Activity 2.3 on your CD-ROM suggests items for a portfolio profile on a young child.

Documentation

Blending observation of the individual within the group and interpreting the significance of those observations is a method of documentation preferred by some professionals. This observational material might be shared with a group of parents and with other professionals, leading these adults to be responsive to the needs of the children as a group. "Documentation is the visible trace of process that children and teachers engage in during their investigations together. It provides a record of learning experiences in the classroom, reveals connections between events, and provides children, parents, and teachers with an opportunity to review and plan future experiences" (Fraser & Gestwicki, 2002, p. 129). Even with that description, the reader might get an impression that documentation is produced only at the conclusion of an activity or project. Although documentation does present learning in a visible format, the process involved in that learning is what is relevant. Documentation should be "an active and interactive vehicle through which a community of children and adults [share] the excitement of discovery and inquiry" (Fu, Stremmel, & Hill, 2002, p. 150).

Gray (2001, 2004) and Fu, Stremmel, and Hill (2002) describe how documentation has been used successfully in infant and toddler programs. Further examples of this approach can be seen in the Reggio Emilia programs for toddlers and older children. Educators record what they think is important about the children's activities and how they present an opportunity for demonstrating children's emerging skills. The documentation (observation/assessment/reflection) focuses not just on individual children but the whole group, because it can support learning for everyone. "Not only does the individual child learn how to learn, but the group becomes conscious of itself as a 'teaching place,' where the many languages are enriched, multiplied, refined, and generated, but also collide, 'contaminate,' and hybridize each other, and are renewed" (Giudici, Rinaldi, & Krechevsky, 2001, p. 83).

Documenting children's learning is an approach that is relatively new in the United States, and sometimes this method of documentation leaves itself open to accusations of subjectivity, lacking the validation of other methods. However, this type of assessment approach can be useful for experienced professionals who are already skilled at objective recording and the **analysis of observation** (inference and validation), and who have established a "comfort of fit" with being in the moment with children. [See Further Reading section for suggestions on the Reggio approach and documentation.]

analysis of observation

a method of documentation which separates observations into inference and validation sections and also includes specific references to theory, theorists, research, etc., in order to support conclusions

A PHENOMENOLOGICAL APPROACH TO THE STUDY OF INFANTS AND TODDLERS

In most studies of infants and toddlers, the child is a subject to be studied according to scientific methodology. This approach has given us significant knowledge about children and their development. Criticism of the scientific approach centers on its limitations in seeing and responding to the child with respect and humanity.

The **phenomenological approach**, rooted in phenomenological studies undertaken in the 19th century, looks at the child's "experience of being." Phenomenological studies try to get at what it's like to be, think like, and function as the child being studied. Phenomenologists consider the meaning of the experience of the child being studied. A phenomenologist considers the child's experience from the child's perspective and contributes an additional construction of meaning as an individual with her own experience meeting the child's experience. The new meaning is a crossover between the phenomenologist's perspective and the child's perspective. Table 2.2 offers a concise comparison between the phenomenological and scientific approaches to the study of infants and toddlers.

phenomenological approach

a philosophical approach to being and working with others that respects the consciousness of the other person and endeavors to enter into the person's life-world

When studying young children, the phenomenologist observes, interacts with, and "lives" side-by-side with the child. This might sound subjective when compared with the scientific method but phenomenologists would argue that subjective feeling and intuitive and interpretive responses are the keys to understanding. To accomplish their goal, phenomenologists must have an entirely nonjudgmental respect for their subject. Because the child's experience is an entirely personal and individual process, the phenomenologist meets this experience through her own eyes rather than through the distancing lenses of the scientist.

Table 2.2 A Comparison between Science and Phenomenology

APPROACH	SCIENCE	PHENOMENOLOGY
Focus	Behaviors	Lived experience
Attempts to explain	Forms, functions, and processes What and why	Living and being How
Methodologies	Experiments/controlled observation Analysis	Naturalistic observation Shared experience Reflection
Orientation	Objective	Subjective/intuitive
Values	"Hard" evidence	Holistic understanding
Uses	Contributes to fact-finding	Contributes to human understanding

Child care practice that is influenced by phenomenology is respectful, supportive, child-centered, and child-directed, with adults taking a role of observation and careful engagement with each child. You can begin to experience the phenomenological approach used when interacting with young children by undertaking the last exercise in Activity 2.3 on your CD-ROM.

DEVELOPMENTAL SCREENING AND ASSESSMENT

Caregivers can contribute to the formal assessments carried out by medical staff, health personnel, developmental specialists, and psychologists. The role of the parents and educators is to seek assistance if there are behavioral changes in or developmental concerns about a young child, or if other signs or symptoms cause concern. In most situations, families have the responsibility to approach these professionals, but the caregivers' observations can be very useful. The caregivers might tell the family members that they are concerned about the child. Alternatively, they might be the first to think there is a need for professional help and relay these thoughts to the caregivers.

Health and developmental screenings identify the need for further investigation. These are usually conducted by the child's pediatrician or other health professional, although developmental assessments are also carried out by professionals with special skills. Screenings may be part of regular checks, or they may be conducted because the educators or caregivers have identified a particular problem. Usually there is an opportunity to offer observations and to answer the questions of the assessor; family members, and caregivers if the family agrees, may attend a meeting for this purpose. The child's needs are more likely to be met by a team that includes parents, caregivers, other members of the family, and the health or developmental professional. Follow-up plans may be developed for the child that can be carried out cooperatively by the parents and caregivers. Some young children may need regular assessments and curriculum or special devices that are designed to meet their specific needs.

Functional Assessment Tools for Infants and Toddlers

We have discussed the informal methods used by care providers to collect information on children, as well as the use of formal tools when children who are at risk or who may have a suspected delay need to be assessed. However, standardized testing of young children is fraught with problems. Young children are not experienced test takers, they have limited capabilities to comprehend assessment cues such as verbal instructions or written instructions, they lack self-regulation ability, and they do not yet possess the higher-ordered thinking skills often required to respond correctly to the information presented (Meisels, 2001; Dichtelmiller & Ensier, 2004). These problems are only compounded when you are working with very young children. Also, many times standardized tools require extensive training in order to ensure that the results obtained are reliable.

Recently, there has been a growing interest in functional assessment tools focusing not so much on the tasks that children perform in their everyday lives (McAfee, Leong, & Bodrova, 2004) or the milestones reached, but rather looking at "each child's individual way of accomplishing certain functions or purposes" (Dichtelmiller & Ensier, 2004, p. 33). This approach helps care providers view children in a more holistic manner, rather than by a narrowly defined set of skills identified as expected accomplishments at certain ages. It is also an approach that respects a child's cultural experience, since culture mediates interactions with people and objects. Finally, this approach necessitates involvement of family members, since they know their child the best and can help interpret their child's behavior. Any assessment tool utilized with infants and toddlers must "include active participation of the child's family, information about the broad context in which the child and family live, varied methods of collecting assessment data, and intervention-relevant applications of assessment data" (Meisels, 2001, p. 10). Some of the tools developed to serve this purpose include the Infant–Toddler Developmental Assessment (IDA), the Transdisiplinary Play-Based Assessment (TPBA), The High/Scope COR for Infants and Toddlers, and the Ounce of Prevention Scale or Ounce

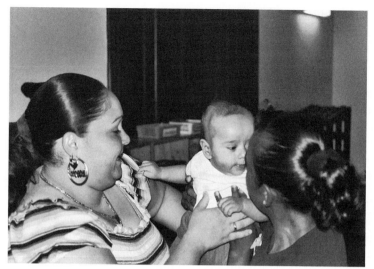

Ongoing communication is essential to ensure a "comfort of fit" for families, children, and providers. Here a teacher and family member take time to discuss the baby's day before Mom leaves for work.

Scale™. Of the four mentioned, the Ounce Scale has been specifically designed for practical use by care providers, not for exclusive use by professionals. A major goal of the Ounce Scale™ is to promote an ongoing and sustained conversation between the care provider and the family (Meisels, 2001). (See the Further Reading section at the end of this chapter for more information on this tool.)

RESPONDING TO ASSESSMENT RESULTS

There are many different ways of meeting the needs of very young children. The educator's task is to respond to the individual in the most appropriate manner. This section demonstrates some common ways caregivers respond to assessment information, whether based on their own observation or on the work of health and developmental professionals.

Communication with Families

Throughout the observation and assessment process, and on a daily basis, the educator should share information with parents and listen with sensitivity to parental observations, perceptions, and needs. The educator should work with families to find ways of helping their child that fit into their lifestyle and family needs.

Educators must treat families as partners in supporting their children. Although this seems obvious, parents are too frequently considered at the end of the assessment process rather than as an integral part of it. Assessment information should never be presented to families without ongoing consultation. In contrast to a summative assessment—that is, an assessment at the end of a set period of time—a formative, in-process assessment allows for ongoing communication and for quickly changing issues to receive the response they need.

Assessments may indicate the emergence of skills that can be encouraged or challenges that can be addressed. If families and educators both agree on the best strategies to support the child's development, then they are more likely to be successful. Consistency in approaches between home and school has clear advantages for the child.

However, educators may find themselves in a situation where family members are unable to grasp a potential health or developmental concern. They may, therefore, not understand the need for extra help for the infant or toddler and may refuse permission for such help. In such cases, the caregiver may find it helpful to talk to the center supervisor and licensing agency. If you do speak to anyone about the issue, you must treat the matter confidentially and not use the child's or family's name or identifying characteristics.

Resource Teachers and Special Educators

In some situations, resource teachers with specialized knowledge of children with special needs may assist the child one-on-one within the child care center. The special educator might be a regular visitor or an extra member of the caregiving team in the infant or toddler room.

As a team, the caregivers can work together and learn from one another to support the child. Developmental diversity can be accommodated within a child care center if the staff are willing and suitably prepared. This may mean that the specialized staff demonstrates particular strategies or techniques to the staff so that they become sufficiently skilled to provide nurturance, health support, and stimulation.

Early Intervention Programs

Individual Family Service Plan (IFSP)

a written plan developed by parents or guardians with input from a multidisciplinary team. The IFSP (1) addresses the family's strengths, needs, concerns, and priorities; (2) identifies support services available to meet those needs; and (3) empowers the family to meet the developmental needs of their infant or toddler with a disability

individual program plan

a curriculum or intervention plan created especially for one child on the basis of her assessed needs

facilitator

someone who makes progress easier; a person who makes it easier for learners to learn by attempting to discover what the learner is interested in knowing and determining the best way to make those experiences and information available to the learner

responsive care

a philosophy of care, education, and nurturance that meets the changing needs of the developing infant and young child and is sensitive to the individual differences of each child

There is extensive research which documents the successful and long-term effects of early intervention (Cook, Klein, & Tessler, 2004; Hooper & Umansky, 2004; Howard, Williams, & Lepper, 2005). If children are identified as being at risk or as having a developmental delay, the earlier services are started, the greater the likelihood of a positive outcome. Children from birth through age 3 qualifying for early intervention services have an **Individual Family Service Plan (IFSP)** written to meet their identified needs. The document is designed to meet learning goals in the communication, physical, social, emotional, cognitive, and adaptive domains. Since the intervention is with such young children, involvement of the families is crucial and input from them is required. In addition to the expected developmental outcomes for the child, the IFSP details family information, expected family outcomes, services that will be given, when and where the services will be offered, and steps for transitioning the child into another program. Since the rate of change is significant for children in this age group, the goals of the IFSP are revisited every six months. Sometimes caregivers are included in the ongoing therapies for identified children, so the family might discuss the IFSP with the caregiver, or the caregiver might be contacted by the agency coordinator or a particular therapist delivering services.

Creating an Individual Program Plan

In the United States a designed educational plan is most often thought of as the IFSP, or the IEP, Individual Educational Plan (children 3–5), and they are used only to assist those children with special health or developmental needs. However, after thorough observation and assessment, some care giving facilities are beginning to design an **individual program plan (IPP)** for all the children in their care. The IPP is a natural progression from the assessment, taking the process from what has been inferred to what will be done about it.

Although IPPs may be written in different formats, the intention is always the same. The IPP indicates what development is observed, how it can be supported, and what experiences will be provided to do this. Some IPPs formalize this information with clearly stated goals and objectives, but most take the form of a simple outline of current and emerging skills, a review of what needs to be done, and some ideas on how this will be achieved.

Authentic assessment approaches use IPPs that are updated regularly. It is usually preferable to support the child's emerging skills, rather than focus attention on what is anticipated to be the next stage. Accurate assessment is not dependent on a normative concept. Authentic program plans provide for more open-ended activities so that the child can operate successfully at her own level.

Remember, each child has her own internal time clock, which mediates the course and rate of her development. Pushing development is not appropriate. Instead, caregivers need to learn how to become **facilitators** of children's development. The normative patterns or milestones, although useful as guidelines, sometimes force adults to focus on whether a child has achieved a goal ahead of schedule, as if reaching that milestone "early" was somehow better. Think about the fact that the life expectancy for children who are currently infants and toddlers is probably 90. Why then do they have to achieve things "early"? Laying a strong foundation for future learning is what is important. When it comes to children's development, it is also wise to take the long view, not just the immediate view.

Responsive Caregiving

Infants and toddlers respond well to **responsive** caregivers who can read their cues and appreciate their stages of development. If educators observe and interpret carefully, they will be able to provide more appropriate responses than if they were to design activities before such individual observation.

Interpreting behaviors of children is a necessary part of responsive care. This child is utilizing a number of coordinated skills in order to engage in play.

Responsiveness is the heart of the educator's role. If the process of becoming more responsive is the intention of the educator, observation skills need to be practiced and finely tuned. If assessment is ongoing, responsiveness can be rapid. Daily observations allow the educator to notice subtle advances and changing needs and then to respond in a way that fits the individual.

DESIGNING ACTIVITIES AND EXPERIENCES

Planning Opportunities and Experiences for Learning

An important use of assessment information is for planning learning opportunities for children. Ideally, any plan should be based on the child's observed needs and interests. However, keep in mind that a "curriculum" for infants and toddlers looks very different than the curriculum you might implement for 4-year olds.

Regardless of where a child receives care, whether it is in her own home, a family child care home, or a child care center, the routines that make up daily life are at the heart of infant and toddler learning. These opportunities for learning are frequently overlooked by care providers because they often view them as mundane chores. These "chores" include the routines of feeding, dressing, diapering, toilet learning, handwashing, and sleeping. The opportunity for children to learn exists in all these routines. For example:

- The reciprocal interchange of sounds, facial expressions and body language allows an infant to participate in a communications dance.
- The close body contact while giving a baby a bottle enables her to learn about trust and relationships.
- The slow, gentle massage on a toddler's back while settling to sleep helps her learn to cope with a myriad of feelings.
- The sensory experience of water rushing through fingers and slippery soap is mediated by the motor and emotional parts of the brain and helps build cognitive concepts.

What seems simplistic and repetitive to the adult mind is viewed differently from a young child's perspective. Children change so rapidly, and so do their skills and abilities. Life for a 1-year-old is a constant barrage of changing landscapes. So do not dismiss the caregiving routines. They are rich with opportunities for learning.

That said, there are often points in the daily program when you will want to "design" some activities. Since educators work in a group setting, they must be prepared to offer a wide variety of activities and experiences that are open-ended and developmentally appropriate. It is important to note that such considerations are not an excuse for preplanning themes months in advance. This type of planning is not suitable for infants and toddlers.

The Additional Support section in your Online Companion contains some ideas for experiences for infants and toddlers.

It is essential to prepare sensory activities that can be enjoyed in a variety of ways. These types of experiences are pivotal to the development of a child's brain. Sensory experiences often translate into a four-letter word—"MESS." This is a critical point because children are having fewer and fewer opportunities to make messes. Families are often too exhausted and stressed to think of getting "down and dirty" with their children. Making playdough or mud pies is not high on their list of priorities. In addition, caregivers often do not want to have messes because they don't want to clean them up or their families do not want the children to get dirty. However, since it is well documented that children learn through their senses, we need to purposefully plan sensory experiences that consider the health and safety issues, but encourage children to plunge into a sensory smorgasbord. Figure 2.4 illustrates how sensory experiences (perception)

"It is more important for a baby to get into a position than to be in a position."

Magda Gerber's rationale for not pushing a child's physical development

Figure 2.4 How Sensory Experiences (Messes) Help a Child Increase Thinking Ability

SENSORY PERCEPTION (Often Messy)	MEDIATED BY	BUILDS CONCEPTS WHICH TRANSLATES INTO INCREASED THINKING ABILITY
• touch • taste • seeing • smell • hearing	• emotions • motor exploration	• better brain!!!!!

contribute to cognitive growth. When families realize that those dirty hands and clothes are actually positively affecting their child's brain growth (concept acquisition and thinking), they often are much more supportive of MESSES.

Activity 2.4 in your Online Companion suggests a variety of sensory experiences for you to try. They are appropriate for infants and toddlers, but you should always play with materials first before you introduce them to children.

Two other factors to consider when planning experiences are play and the freedom for exploration. All children learn best through play situations. Play is often misunderstood and undervalued in today's society. Play is the best use of time for children, and adults need to provide materials, space, and time for children to play. Adults also need to know how to encourage and support play in their classrooms. As children play, they also need the freedom to engage in exploration. This will involve the consideration of safety and health issues because ensuring that children are not injured is of prime importance. Infants explore by putting almost every object they grasp into their mouths. As soon as they can crawl, infants explore by covering every possible inch of open floor space, and by putting almost everything in their mouths. Toddlers begin to learn not to put *everything* in their mouths, but many objects still get there and, of course, toddlers toddle everywhere. This is followed by climbing and, shortly after, by running. You are fighting a losing battle if you attempt to keep toddlers from exploring. Read the story on the following page; then, when you visit your practicum sites, observe the types of opportunities provided for toddlers.

Toddlers enjoy a carefully planned sensory experience under the careful supervision of a teacher who is readily available to intercede or offer suggestions, if necessary. The teacher will use this opportunity to observe the children, individually and as a group.

Accessing Community Resources

Resources likely exist in the community that can help educators with their task of responding to observed development and assist them in understanding assessments that have been made by a professional team. Organizations that support and advocate for particular disability groups can be of particular help if understanding a diagnosed condition is necessary. Health practitioners, volunteers, information services, and college faculty can also be helpful. For print resources, try the local library, a specialist library, an Internet site, or a community resource center. Materials can be accessed from toy libraries, resource centers, libraries, special interest groups, specialist catalogue suppliers, or regular stores.

Making Referrals to Other Professionals

Educators must be competent in their role, and must also know when a situation requires knowledge outside their own skill set. Health care and social work are two of the professions most frequently contacted to assist both families and educators. Referrals are often facilitated by child care center staff, but they must be done with the full involvement and approval of the child's family.

Accommodating Diversity

To promote the emergence of a healthy self-concept, educators should ensure that infants and toddlers are in an environment that reflects their own physical appearance and includes culturally familiar objects.

To provide comfort and familiarity for the child, the educator must be aware of a great many issues pertaining to family lifestyle and cultural background. Caregivers should make sure that the center has a wide range of books, toys, decorations, and foods, so that all children can find things that are familiar and reflect their cultural experience. Communicating with parents must be done in a sensitive and inclusive manner. Observations of families and their interactions, as well as of the child, should help educators refine their cultural sensitivity and improve cross-cultural communication. Box 2.3 lists some methods of accommodating individual, family, and cultural differences.

Some additional considerations that may help caregivers deal with cultural differences are found in the Additional Support section in your Online Companion.

Guidance Strategies

The most important parts of program planning resulting from the educator's observations are the guidance strategies that are developed for the young child. These strategies may include identifying boundaries for behaviors, determining the adult's response to the child's patterns of action, planning the consequences of behaviors, and deciding the actions to encourage. Rather than disciplining the child, emphasize the reshaping of negative behaviors. Positive guidance strategies build from what the child does well and what is socially acceptable.

Infants and toddlers respond best if they experience consistent styles of guidance, nurturance, and adult interaction. Guidance strategies can be used to assist children in learning and to support them in their development. Specific strategies are based on the observational information that the educator has gathered. Sometimes educators will try out a way of guiding behavior and find that it was unsuccessful. Although it does not always result in success, this

Personal Story

In my job capacity, I visit many care facilities. Inevitably, what I find is that most toddler rooms have no equipment for the children to crawl under, over, into, on top of, or through.

Every fiber in a toddler's body is screaming, "MOVE!" and the expression "active learner" aptly describes toddlers.

These conditions are polar opposites, so is it any wonder that the toddler will listen to her inner voice, and not that of the teacher?

Climb they must and climb they do—on any piece of furniture or equipment that is available.

Most often it is tables and bookshelves.

This creates a situation where the teachers are constantly removing children from the furniture and telling them "No!"

The teachers get frustrated because the toddlers don't stop.

The lesson to be learned from this is that toddler rooms MUST encourage and make available equipment and activities to support large-muscle development.

Supporting children's needs instead of ignoring them seems an obvious choice, but frequently it does not occur.

BOX 2.3

RESPONDING TO INDIVIDUAL, FAMILY, AND CULTURAL DIFFERENCES

- Show respect for all families and children.
- Listen and wait patiently for comments and questions.
- Notice body language, but interpret it cautiously.
- Offer times and places for confidential discussions.
- Avoid confrontations by encouraging open communication.
- Be clear about what is a standard of practice and which program elements can be adjusted.
- Check your personal biases and avoid judgments.
- Use cross-cultural communication skills to assist shared meanings.
- Explain why parts of the program are offered in a particular way.
- Use informal opportunities to enhance parent education.
- Be prepared to learn from parents and children.
- Use questions from parents as a tool to evaluate the program's values and practices.
- Avoid making assumptions about specific cultures, or reinforcing stereotypes.
- Acknowledge profound beliefs, and do not attempt to change them.
- Use a variety of human and practical resources in supporting families.
- Be quick to apologize for your mistakes.
- Don't let differences paralyze your actions.
- Consider individual and collective needs and how you will meet them.

trial-and-error approach is quite suitable. Although there are some generally accepted guidance policies, individual interactions must be based on the communication and temperament styles of the children involved.

HEALTH CONCERNS

When the educator identifies changes in the infant or toddler's behavior or observes signs or symptoms of a health concern, then appropriate action must be taken. With very young infants, response must be particularly rapid because the child is extremely vulnerable. Daily baseline observations will give the educator a frame of reference for later observations. Some conditions require rapid response; others are less pressing. In all cases, families must be informed of an educator's health concerns. Educators must remember that they cannot diagnose an ailment or provide medical intervention. Family permission is required for every aspect of health care.

Responding to Potential Child Abuse

mandated reporters

those individuals who by law must report suspicion of child abuse to specific agencies

The primary role of caregivers is to ensure that children are healthy and that their needs are met. However, as **mandated reporters**, caregivers and teachers have a legal responsibility to contact a child protection agency when they have a reasonable suspicion that a child has been abused. As such, they need to be vigilant about noticing and documenting signs of abuse. In cases where abuse is suspected, they must follow the protocol of their child care center. In addition, they should write down all observations that indicate potential abuse.

It is important to note that caregivers do not conclude on their own that abuse has taken place. They simply report the indicators they have seen to a child protection agency. This can be done anonymously, or the child care center and caregiver may directly indicate their cause for concern. After a report is filed, any action taken is the responsibility of the child protection agency, not the caregiver or the center.

The Additional Support section in your Online Companion contains a position statement from NAEYC on child abuse prevention, as well as an overview on neglect.

SUMMARY

Observation is an essential part of the educator's role. It must be done continuously so that the children are always safely nurtured and supported in their development.

Educators need to use formal methods of observing and recording developmental information about infants and toddlers so that they can document important changes and respond to the children appropriately. Infants and toddlers must be observed and assessed in ways that capture their true competence and take into account contextual information. There are a variety of assessment techniques that can be utilized, including running records, anecdotal recordings, time sampling, checklists, rating scales, charts, and media-assisted tools.

Principles of observation include confidentiality, authentic assessment, making decisions about whether to be a participant or nonparticipant in the observation, documentation, and the creation of portfolios. Authentic assessments repeated over time result in the most valid and reliable information about children. The most effective way to do this is by creating a portfolio about each child. Families, who are our partners in providing care and education for each child, need to be involved in all aspects of the child's program, including making contributions to the observation and assessment process.

Naturalistic observation is an integral part of a child-centered philosophy. It can lead us to a better understanding of developmental processes and, most importantly, enable us to provide appropriate experiences and supportive guidance. However, care providers need to be aware of biases and prejudices they may have which subjectively influence their inferences about children's development. Utilizing an analysis of observation technique may help to achieve a more balanced interpretation of a child's development.

Information garnered through observation and assessment can be communicated to families through various methods. If there are concerns about the child's development, he can be referred to early intervention for further assessment. If a delay is detected, or the child is deemed to be at risk, an IFSP can be created for him. This information can also be used to provide responsive caregiving to the children and to design experiences to support their emerging skills and interests. Of special importance is the contribution of sensory experiences and play to the child's development, so caregivers need to ensure that these opportunities are available every day. Guidance strategies and cultural sensitivity can also be influenced by observation. These issues are important for ensuring that children's self-worth and self-esteem are enhanced as they live their lives in child care facilities.

Finally, as mandated reporters, child care providers are charged with the responsibility of monitoring the health and well-being of the children, including being vigilant about noticing and documenting any possible signs of child abuse or neglect.

DISCUSSION QUESTIONS

1. To what extent can you be unbiased about what you observe?

2. If you were to set up a new system for observation and record-keeping in an infant or toddler room, what would it include?

3. How might you encourage parents to share their observations of their child with you?

4. If you had some concerns about a 15-month-old child who was not yet walking or saying any words, what might you do?

5. From what you have read about the Reggio Emilia schools, would you say they have adopted a scientific approach or a phenomenological approach to the study of children? What evidence can you offer to support your belief?

ADDITIONAL RESOURCES

Further Reading

Allen, K. E., & Martoz, L. R.(2007). *By the ages: Behavior and development of children pre-birth through eight* (5th ed.). Clifton Park, NY: Thomson Delmar Learning.

Billman, J., & J. Sherman. (2003). *Observation and participation in early childhood settings: A practicum guide* (2nd ed.). Boston: Allyn & Bacon.

Brazelton, T. B. (1992). *Touchpoints the essential reference: Your child's emotional and behavioral development.*Reading, MA: Addison-Wesley.

Curtis, D., & Carter, M. (2000). *The art of awareness: How observation can transform your teaching.* St. Paul, MN: Redleaf Press.

Derman-Sparks, L. (1989). *Anti-bias curriculum: Tools for empowering young children.* Washington, DC: NAEYC

Dichtelmiller, M. L., & Ensier, L. Infant/toddler assessment: One program's experience. *Young Children,* 59(1), 30–33.

Dotsch, J. (1999). *Non-biased children's assessments.* Toronto: Bias-Free Early Childhood Services.

Edwards, C., Gandini, L., & Foreman, G. (1993). *The hundred languages of children: The Reggio Emilia approach to early childhood education.* Norwood, NJ: Ablex Publishing Corporation.

Fraser, S., & Gestwicki, C. (2002). *Authentic childhood: Exploring Reggio Emilia in the classroom* Clifton Park, NY: Delmar Thomson Learning.

Fu, V. R., Stremmel, A. J., & Hill, L. T. (2002). *Teaching and learning: Collaborative exploration of the Reggio Emilia approach.* Upper Saddle River, NJ: Merrill/Prentice Hall.

Gandini, L., & Edwards, C. P. (2001). *Bambini: The Italian approach of infant/toddler care.* New York: Teacher College Press.

Gober, S. (2002). *Six simple ways to assess young children.* Clifton Park, NY: Thomson Delmar Learning.

Gray, H. (2001). Initiation into documentation: A fishing trip with toddlers. *Young Children,* 56(6), 84–91.

Gray, H. (2004). "You go away and you come back": Supporting separations and reunions in an infant/toddler classroom. *Young Children,* 59(5), 100–107.

Greenman, J., & Stonehouse, A. (1996). *Prime times.* Beltsville, MD: Redleaf Press.

Howard, V. F., Williams, B. F., & Lepper, C. (2005). *Very young children with special needs: A formative approach for today's children.* Upper Saddle River, NJ: Merrill/Prentice Hall.

Jablon, J. R., Dombro, A. L., & Dichtelmiller, M. L. (1999). *The power of observation.* Washington, DC: Teaching Strategies.

Langford, R. (1999). *Checklist for quality inclusive education: A self-assessment tool and manual for early childhood settings.* Barrie, OH: Early Childhood Resource Teacher Network of Ontario.

Martin, S. (2003). *Take a look: Observation and portfolio assessment in early childhood* (3rd ed.). Don Mills, ON: Addison-Wesley.

Meisels, S. (2001). Fusing assessment and intervention: Changing parents' and providers' views of young children. *Zero to Three,* 21(4), 4–10.

Morris, D. (1995). *Illustrated babywatching.* London: Ebury Press.

Nilsen, B. A. (2005). *Week by week: Documenting the development of young children* (3 ed.). Clifton Park, NY: Thomson Delmar Learning.

Stonehouse, A. (Ed.). (1990). *Trusting toddlers.* St. Paul, MN: Toys n' Things Press.

Wortham, S. (2001). *Assessment in early childhood education* (3rd ed.). Upper Saddle River, NJ: Prentice Hall.

Wylie, S. (1999). *Observing young children: A guide for early childhood educators in Canada.* Toronto: Harcourt Brace.

Useful Videos

Child Care and Children with Special Needs.
  2-video set—23 minutes/30 minutes
Early Intervention: Natural Environments for Children
  28 minutes
Make a Difference: Report Child Abuse and Neglect.
  28 minutes
Windows on Learning: A Framework for Making Decisions
  20 minutes observation
  Available from NAEYC 1-800-424-2460 or www.naeyc.org
Observing Young Children: Learning to Look, Looking to Learn.
  30 minutes observation
Start Seeing Diversity: The Basic Guide to the Anti-Bias Classroom.
  Available from Redleaf Press 1-800-423-8309 or
  www.redleafpress.org
52 minutes—Although the ideas in this video focus on preschool-aged children, it is a good video to use in order to start thinking about the topic of bias and how to counter its effects.

Useful Web Sites

Born Learning Campaign
  www.bornlearning.org
Clearinghouse on Early Education and Parenting
  http://ceep.crc.uiuc.edu/ Click on Popular Topics
Frank Porter Graham Child Development Center
  www.fpg.unc.edu/
Individual Educational Plans
Individual Family Service Plans
  http://www.ericdigests.org/
In the search box, type in: Individual Educational Plan
  or Individual Family Service Plan
Magic of Everyday Moments
  www.zerotothree.org
Under the ZERO TO THREE programs,
scroll down to "The Magic of Everyday Moments Campaign"
March of Dimes
  www.marchofdimes.com
National Child Care Information Center
  www.nccic.org
National Network for Childcare
  http://www.nncc.org

CHAPTER 3

Infants demonstrate rapid growth and development in many different areas. Three months ago, this infant was not able to sit, nor could he grasp objects in his hands. Now he is able to crawl anywhere he wants and easily picks up objects. In another three months, it is likely he will be standing, perhaps attempting his first steps, as well as his first words.

Explaining Behavior: Understanding Growth and Development

LEARNING OUTCOMES

After reading and studying this chapter, you should be able to:

- describe the domains of development of infants and toddlers and how they interact in a holistic manner
- compare and contrast a range of schools of thought about infancy and toddlerhood
- apply principles of development to infants and toddlers
- discuss theoretical explanations for observed characteristics of the development of infants and toddlers
- respond to the needs of infants and toddlers

SCENE

"My Mom knows more about babies than anyone," said Kylie's mom. "She had eight of them!"

This statement underscores the belief and assumption that most of us have regarding the role that experience plays in learning about caring for children. It is also true that the way we were raised—which likely reflected our mothers' views of what children need at different stages of development and what was the expected "norm" at the time we were raised—is extremely important to our own understanding about how children develop and the context in which this should happen.

In the 1950s and early 60s, families and educators were taught that young children should always be cared for in the home by the mother. Our parents and grandparents were likely influenced by this thinking. Twenty years later, findings from the some of the first longitudinal studies on early childhood care and education in the United States [the North Carolina Abecedarian Study and the Ypsilanti/Perry Preschool Project] demonstrated that group care was an acceptable, indeed desirable way of nurturing young children. Our own beliefs have been molded by a combination of our traditions and the way societies shape knowledge.

See the Additional Support section in your Online Companion for more information on these important studies.

We know that a mother's firsthand experience, the values and beliefs held by a culture, the dominant scientific view, and a variety of other ways of knowing all contribute to our collective knowledge base about the development of young children. "Nonprofessionals" sometimes pour scorn on the jargon and "facts" presented by scientists, labeling such views "edu-babble." For their part, professionals sometimes believe that their knowledge is superior and represents a deeper understanding. As well, representatives from different cultures may find that their values clash with what professionals advocate. They may mistrust scientific "interference" in the way they raise their children. Faith in progress often leads people to believe that today's knowledge base must be better and more accurate than yesterday's. As educators, we must guard against all such certainties.

growth

increase in size of the individual; in infancy and early childhood it is typically assessed through measurement of height/length, weight, and head circumference; often growth can be easier to observe and measure than development

ossification

the process of converting cartilage to bone

calcification

the process of hardening, generally bone

myelination

the process where myelin is laid down on the nerves of the brain; when parts of the brain myelinate, it allows or improves the function of that area, such as movement or vision

development

the dynamic process of growth and change within an individual that occurs over time; also refers to an increase in complexity, a change that proceeds from the simple to the more complex

GROWTH AND DEVELOPMENT

"She's grown a lot" is a typical comment from an adult who has not seen a young child for even a short period of time. Usually the adult is commenting on how much physically bigger the child is, but with this growth comes increased capacity to do things.

The term **growth** relates only to the first element, the way the child is getting bigger. Growth means an increase in size, change in bodily proportions, and alteration of internal systems that account for that growth. These alterations include skeletal changes of **ossification** and **calcification** as the bones become stronger and harder. Muscular changes brought about by **myelination** allow for better coordination. Hormonal changes support the increase in size and bodily functioning, and changes in the central nervous system promote chemical and electrical communications within the body. All parts of the body undergo changes associated with growth. Most aspects of growth are measurable: Height, weight, and head circumference are the easiest to observe and measure.

The Additional Support section in your Online Companion contains a link to samples of the typical growth patterns of boys and girls in North America.

Infant and toddler development, like all aspects of human development, is in a constant state of complex change. **Development** is somewhat dependent upon growth, but the term relates more specifically to the increasing skills of the individual and the processes that enable the individual to adapt to life's experiences.

Development involves changes in complexity of functioning, and involves action, whether external or internal. Although external action is easier to observe than internal action, they are equally important. As infants develop, they increase their range of actions. Gradually, random actions become deliberate and then commonly become automatic responses that they do not have to think about.

INFANT AND TODDLER DEVELOPMENT

The Needs of Infants and Toddlers

Certain conditions must exist for an infant or very young child to grow and develop. Box 3.1 lists the needs and conditions required by children.

Although in this list the needs are separated, it is essential that the reader understand that the physical, psychological, and cognitive needs of a child are interrelated and interdependent.

BOX 3.1

physical needs

the individual's basic requirements—including food, clothing, and protection—without which the individual would fail to grow and develop

psychological needs

the conditions necessary for the development of a healthy psyche, soul, mind, or self—e.g., love

cognitive needs

requirements for intellectual functioning

optimal development

the best possible development; the realization of the child's potential

PHYSICAL NEEDS

- Food—nutritious and age-appropriate
- Shelter—protection from harm
- Warmth—suitable clothing
- Clean air and environment
- Preventative health and dental care
- Rest and activity—in requisite balance

PSYCHOLOGICAL NEEDS

- Physical contact
- Consistency of caregivers and enduring relationships
- Predictability of environment
- Encouragement
- Personal style and temperament type
- Respect
- Unconditional love
- Acceptance of individuality
- Appropriate guidance and support
- Positive role models
- Individual care and attention
- Resolution of emotional conflicts
- A sense of belonging to the family and group

COGNITIVE NEEDS

- Responses to their behavioral cues
- Sensory experiences
- Sensitivity to personal learning style
- Opportunity to explore, experiment, and pursue curiosity
- Adults who support learning
- Adults who provide language in a reciprocal relationship
- Appropriate toys and playthings
- Time, space, and opportunity to play
- Contrasts of experience
- Challenges that are achievable
- One-on-one attention

In addition, for **optimal development**—the best possible development and the realization of the infant or toddler's potential—the child needs:

- A positive and stimulating learning environment
- Harmonious parent and caregiver involvement
- High but attainable expectations
- Individualized and responsive programming
- A stress-controlled environment
- Emotional safety
- A primary caregiving model of child care
- Experiences that promote creative thought and problem-solving
- Clear parameters for behavior
- The demonstration of clear and consistent values
- Careful observation, assessment, and responses
- An aesthetically sensitive environment
- Acceptance of personal style

The list of needs is holistic in that it addresses each part of the child's development in a combined entity. There is also the concept of the child within the context of her community that needs to be considered—and it is a cultural context within which the child needs to function. Each of the needs relates to the child's environment, which is dependent upon both positive relationships and appropriate experiences. It is therefore necessary to understand that the adults in the life of the child—primarily families, but also professionals—are directly responsible for making sure these needs are met.

The idea of identifying the needs of individuals is not new, but there have been some recent attempts at refining them. Brazelton and Greenspan (2000) have combined their wisdom, born of experience with many very young children and their families, and developed a short list of what they call **irreducible needs**. These factors do not address the most obvious basic needs, but rather address "the fundamental building blocks for our higher-level emotional, social, and intellectual abilities" (Brazelton & Greenspan, 2000. p. xx). This is the list of the seven irreducible needs:

1. the need for ongoing nurturing relationships
2. the need for physical protection, safety, and regulation
3. the need for experiences tailored to individual differences
4. the need for developmentally appropriate experiences
5. the need for limit-setting, structure, and expectations
6. the need for stable, supportive communications and cultural continuity
7. the need to protect the future

In the "irreducible needs" model, Brazelton and Greenspan take the view that the professional practitioner's responsibilities include a multidisciplinary team of care providers. Ultimately, they see their concepts—starting with Brazelton's (1992) seminal work on the Touchpoints framework, which helped identify "periods during the first three years of life during which children's spurts in development result in pronounced disruption in the family system" (Brazelton & Greenspan, 2000, p. 184)—as being models that might influence the delivery of services for children, as well as provide a successful structure for supporting families with young children.

Developmental Domains

For purposes of understanding development more thoroughly, we sometimes divide the study into different **developmental domains**, or aspects of development. For example, we might isolate cognitive development or language skills. This is often an effective strategy for research and can lead to useful information, but it can also present us with a problem. After we look at development in segments, we need to put the interacting segments back together so that we can see that we are dealing with a whole human being. In other words, we need to utilize a **holistic response** with children.

Developmental domains are the categories or aspects of development that, together, make up the whole child. Experts in developmental studies use different categories depending upon their perspectives. "Physical," "cognitive," "social," "emotional," and "language development" constitute examples of separate domains.

Developmental domains can be studied by analyzing observable characteristics and indicators of change in each area. Also, theories that explain how this development occurs are extremely helpful for the educator. If we understand how a phenomenon occurs, we are more likely to be able to make informed decisions about what our role should be.

The Additional Support section of your Online Companion contains overviews of many of the developmental theories that are relevant to early childhood education.

Physical Development

Physical development concerns the changes in skill development of the body. It depends on growth, including observable increases in size, proportion, weight, and head circumference. These growth indicators are the ones most easily monitored by adults, and are tracked by medical personnel at clinics and health facilities. (See the Additional Support section in your Online Companion to view an example of a tracking sheet.)

irreducible needs

the child's basic and essential needs that must be met for healthy development

> If you want to figure out what a "curriculum" for infants and toddlers should be, you really do not have to search any further than the needs described in this section.

developmental domains

aspects of the individual's development— e.g., cognitive, social, emotional, physical

holistic response

any response to an individual that takes into account each interacting domain of the person's development

physical development

growth and change of the individual over time; involves the individual's body, gross motor skills (large body movement and mobility), and fine motor skills (small muscles such as hand control)

gross motor skills

learned behaviors involving the large muscles of the body—e.g., walking

fine motor skills

learned behaviors involving the small muscles of the body—e.g., the hands manipulating an object

habituation

the decrease in the response to a stimulus that occurs after repeated presentations of the stimulus—e.g., looking away from a mobile after continued stimulation

dishabituation

the increasse in responsiveness after stimulation changes

perception

taking in, processing, and interpreting sensory information, through one or more sensory channels

communication skills

the ability to share meaning with others; typically involves a shared language or signing system; includes ability to exchange ideas involving a sender and receiver of a message

baby signing

the use of hand signals, gestures, expressions, and body movements that have shared meaning

Physical development is driven by physiological changes in the body, particularly in the brain and nervous system. Without adequate nutrition and the satisfaction of all the basic needs, the very young child will not gain mastery of physical skills.

The two strands of physical development relate to increasing refinement of control of the large and small muscles of the body. **Gross motor skills** involve control of the large muscles of the body that allow sitting, crawling, walking, and so on. **Fine motor skills** concern the skill development of the smaller muscles that allow for hand control and coordination of hand and eye.

Perception and Sensory Development

Infants and toddlers learn through physical exploration of their world. They perform actions and take in information through their five senses: sight, hearing, touch, taste, and smell. Sensory information is processed, or perceived, according to what was previously absorbed. Infants have almost completely functioning senses, but lack experience; their processing of sensory information is limited because of their very limited understanding of what they are perceiving.

We can observe the interest infants and toddlers show in the things around them. We can see how items engage their interest, how they respond to a stimulus and then turn away from it when they tire of it. Observing **habituation** (a decline in interest) and **dishabituation** (a renewed level of interest in a stimulus) can be useful for educators trying to support learning by stimulating the senses.

Perception depends on the functioning of the senses and the processing of the information gained by the senses and sent to the brain. The degree to which each of the senses is ready to absorb information, the relative maturity of the nervous system carrying the information, and the readiness of the brain to sort, match, and process that data combine in a way that is extremely complex.

Communication and Language Development

Communication refers to interactions using visual and sound signals, and especially to the acquisition of language—the symbolic system of exchanging thoughts and feelings. **Communication skills** develop from babies' efforts to have their needs met. The central condition for communication skill development is attachment to the adult.

A wide variety of types of communication can be observed in infants and very young children. They may make sounds, expressions, and gestures. Some of these are deliberate attempts to communicate; others are cues that may be interpreted by an adult, thus beginning the dance of communication. Communication may be initiated by either the adult or the child. To fine-tune the communication process, the child needs to have plenty of opportunity to engage with an adult.

Advocates of **baby signing** believe that early communication enhanced by gesturing will expand the child's understanding by promoting neurological connections, which confers an intellectual advantage. These communication systems, designed to help babies share meanings before they can speak, have been gaining popularity. In addition to Garcia (2002), whose approach was based on work with individuals who had hearing losses, Acredolo, Goodwyn, and Abrams (2002), Briant (2004), and Anthony and Lindert (2005) have all published "how to" books on signing with children. These methods are all based on the American Sign Language (ASL) system used with deaf or hard-of-hearing children, but also have new methods that combine child-initiated and adult-initiated actions in a way that resembles spoken language. Regardless of the new found popularity and claims of increasing a baby's intelligence and making a child a better reader, it is important to keep in mind that no long-term quantitative studies have yet been conducted demonstrating any lasting benefits for early signing with children.

 See the Additional Support section in your Online Companion for more information on signing with infants and toddlers.

Language grows by expanding the dance of communication that is already established. **Language acquisition** depends on the child interacting with people and hearing language. Hart and Risely's (1995, 1999) critical work documented the differences in the amount of acquired language between children from different socioeconomic statuses. The findings

language acquisition

the process of becoming able to use a shared code or communication system involving rule-governed combinations of symbols

revealed that the important difference in language acquisition was in the *amount* of talking that occurred. Generally, all families used the same amount of language while dealing with routines of family life. However, the "optional talk," the talk utilized during play sessions, or while children and family members engaged in tasks in a parallel fashion, contributed to a significant increase in the sheer number of words the children heard:

> In other words, some families supplemented their routine interactions with their toddlers with freer, more playful conversations, and toddlers in these more talkative families were both hearing and practicing more varied and complex language. The children's increasing knowledge and communicative facility elicited increasingly complex and information-rich language from their conversation partners, and their learning tended to proceed at a rapid pace. (Bardige, 2005, p. 11)

Considering the complexity of the task, the very young child gains language skills remarkably quickly. As educators, we can facilitate that task if we know something about the process and stages of language acquisition. The adult assists the child to learn language by a scaffolding process (Bruner, 1983) involving sensitive responses to the infant's cues and assistance by providing necessary language structures and vocabulary.

Cognitive Development

cognitive development

changes in the individual over time that result from increased intellectual functioning; may be considered within a framework of stages; depends on interplay of heredity and experience; includes aspects of the mind, brain growth, and behavioral changes

Cognitive development concerns how the individual thinks and responds. Cognition depends on sensory input and perceptual processing. The study of this developmental domain centers on how young children come to understand the world they find themselves in, how they adapt to that world, and how they learn to represent it. According to Piaget, cognition is a complex process that depends on the following:

- Schema/Schemes
- Assimilation
- Accommodation
- Disequilibrium
- Equilibrium

The description in Box 3.2 is a very simple explanation of Piaget's theory. It is not a scientific or even an educational explanation. Hopefully, however, it will give you a better understanding of what these terms mean. In order to learn, humans must experience disequilibrium. Assimilation and accommodation are not opposite ends of a spectrum, but are complements in the learning process. Downtime for our brain is equilibrium, when all is right with the world. Newborns and infants are in states of disequilibrium much of their waking moments. That is one reason that overstimulation is not great for them. They need downtime in order to give themselves a break from all the assimilating and accommodating their brains are experiencing. Even toddlers are in a state of continual learning because they are always encountering the world in new ways as their knowledge and skills increase.

neural plasticity

the brain's ability to reorganize neural pathways based on new experiences

sensorimotor

the first stage of the individual's cognitive development; this stage has six substages

object permanence

the realization that objects continue to exist when they are out of sight

Think about This   Sometimes it is thought that the older we get, the less it seems we have to assimilate and accommodate. There is a familiar saying that reflects this sentiment—"You can't teach an old dog new tricks!" However, lifelong learning debunks that myth. Our brains will always be assimilating and accommodating information due to their **neural plasticity**, meaning their ability to reorganize neural pathways based on new experiences.

Early cognition occurs in a **sensorimotor** pattern (Piaget, 1952) that is restricted by the child's limited experience, egocentric perspective, memory, and thought capacity. Sensorimotor intelligence involves the young child coordinating physical actions and sensory information. The child creates schemes of understanding that can be considered preliminary concepts. These become increasingly refined with repeated action. During the sensorimotor stage, approximately the first two years of life, young children learn from imitation and hands-on experience. This allows them to perform actions deliberately, understand **object permanence** and some

---

BOX 3.2

PIAGET'S COGNITIVE THEORY

Schema (singular), Scheme (plural)—As each child learns, he creates a mental category, or schema. As a child adds to his experience, he groups similar concepts, or patterns, into the same part of the brain. [Our brain really is a pattern seeker.] If you think of the brain as being like a computer, then when you want to save information that would go into a particular file. For example, information about cats would go into the cat file, information about dogs into the dog file, and so on. Each file is a schema.

Assimilation—Now, when the child encounters information that is similar to a concept or pattern he has already saved, voila, he assimilates that information. He groups similar concepts together in the same file. Think of the word similar—assimilate.

Accommodation and Disequilibrium—When a child encounters information for which he has no schema (or file), his mind is out of balance temporarily. In Piagetian terms, this is known as disequilibrium. The child now has to accommodate his brain by creating a new schema (file) in which to place this information.

Equilibrium—The process of human adaptation to assimilate information or to no longer be in disequilibrium (accommodate information).

---

cause-and-effect

understanding that particular actions bring about (cause) particular reactions (effects)

symbolic thought

the representation of reality through the use of abstract concepts such as words and gestures; generally present in most children by the age of 18 months, when signs and symbols (usually in place of language) are used reliably to refer to concrete objects, events, and behaviors

zone of proximal development

behaviors that are on the edge of emergence; the gap between the child's actual performance when operating alone and the child's potential performance when assisted by more knowledgeable adults or children

cause-and-effect relationships, build some basic concepts, and begin to represent the world symbolically, eventually moving on to **symbolic thought**.

Although cognitive functions are internal, they can be glimpsed through children's behavior, particularly through the mistakes they make, and, with older toddlers, what they say. Cognitive processes can be challenging to understand because they require detailed observation, an understanding of theoretical explanations, and analysis of an individual child's behavior. Educators find studying cognitive processes extremely helpful in appreciating how the child sees the world and learns about it. Vygotsky (1934/1962) provided a model, called the **zone of proximal development** (see Figure 3.1), that describes the way that the adult can move

Figure 3.1   Zone of Proximal Development

Future Level of Knowledge

Current Level of Knowledge

Vygotsky believed that development was dependent on social interaction and that social learning actually leads to cognitive development. This phenomenon is called the "Zone of Proximal Development" and Vygotsky (1978) described it as "the distance between the actual development level as determined by independent problem-solving and the level of potential development as determined through problem-solving under adult guidance or in collaboration with more capable peers" (p. 86). What this means is that children can perform a task with adult or peer collaboration that they cannot achieve on their own. The Zone of Proximal Development bridges the gap between *what is known* and *what can be known*. According to Vygotsky's theory, the ZPD is where real learning occurs.

It is easier to observe physical skills than cognitive functioning. Here the child is attempting to fit a cube into a slot. He has grasped the cube, lifted it to the top slot, and dropped it toward the opening. The invisible cognitive process needed to perform this activity is extremely complex and not as easily assessed.

attachment

the positive emotional relationship that develops between two individuals—between adult and child

separation anxiety

distress shown because of the departure, or impending departure, of a person to whom the individual is attached

emotional development

changes in the individual over time that involve understanding the self and feelings, and regulating behavior; occurs in stages

self-awareness

having a sense of self as being distinct and separate from others

into the child's learning, identify what requires assistance, and provide supports so that the child can then perform tasks without adult help.

Emotional Development

Emotional development concerns children's increasing awareness and control of their feelings. Infants start life with a few basic emotions and develop others as they form social relationships. The most important aspect of infants' emotional development is rooted in the earliest relationships, the **attachments** they make with adults. There are observable stages of attachment (Bowlby, 1965) that are considered dependent upon sustained relationships with only a few adults. The term "bonding" is often used to describe the relationship a mother develops with her child shortly after birth while, according to Landy (2002), "Attachment is a system of behaviors that the infant or young child displays in order to establish proximity and contact with the caregiver. It is a child's tendency to seek this contact with a *specific person* and to do this when he is frightened, upset, tired, or ill" (p. 152). Figure 3.2 depicts the difference between bonding and attachment. Bonding lays the groundwork for attachment, and the importance of attachment cannot be underscored. It is the emotional tether upon which further emotional development hinges;

> Attachment is regarded by many psychologists as the seminal event in a person's emotional development—the primary source of a child's security, self-esteem, self-control, and social skills. Through this one incredibly intimate relationship, a baby learns how to identify her own feelings and how to read them in others. If the bond is healthy, . . . she will feel loved and accepted and begin to learn the value of affection and empathy. (Eliot, 1999, p. 307)

Attachments will always be challenged by separations from the adult. Very young infants may appear more interested in having their needs met than in who meets them. But older infants and toddlers will be more specifically attached and want particular adults to provide attention. Separation from these key adults can cause **separation anxiety**.

Children face a series of emotional tasks that provide challenges for each stage of development. Early **emotional development** tasks include:

- **self-awareness**, **self-recognition**, and **self-efficacy**, all of which contribute to **self-concept** and eventually **self-esteem**. "Infants develop their understanding of self and subsequently a self-concept through their social interactive experiences with others: how others respond to them" (Puckett & Black, 2005, p. 181). At the end of toddler period, most children have a basic self-awareness and self-recognition. For example, by age two and a half, most children can recognize themselves in a photograph and they can use language to identify specific characteristics about themselves such as their age or their gender. On the other hand, self-concept and self-esteem blossom gradually, and can be positively or negatively impacted depending on life experiences and interactions with peers and adults. Often what adults reflect back to children about their worth and competence directly impacts self-concept and self-esteem. This reflection can be sent through verbal and nonverbal messages, as well as through body language (Kostelnik, Whiren, Soderman, & Gregory, 2006).
- striving for independence, or becoming **autonomous** (Erikson, 1987), even while continuing to need emotional support
- **self-regulation**, or the ability to calm or otherwise control the self (Greenspan & Greenspan, 1994; Kostelnik et al., 2006).

Figure 3.2   Bonding and Attachment

Bonding one-direction: Mother to Child

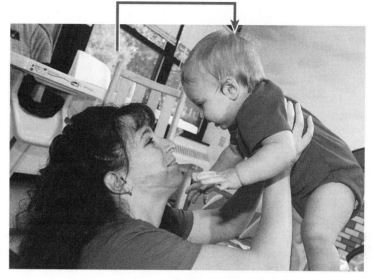

Attachment bi-directional: Mother to Child

Child to Mother

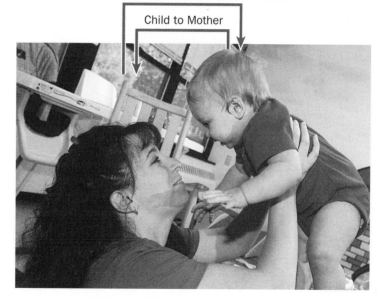

self-recognition

the ability to recognize your image in a mirror, reflection, or photograph, or through some other representation

self-efficacy

the feeling that one can act, do, and achieve success using one's own abilities

self-concept

the mental image, perception, or opinion that one has of oneself; in young children, self-concept evolves as they interact with the objects and people in their environment; often self-concept is affected by what is reflected back to individuals about their worth and capabilities from the significant people in their lives

self-esteem

one's overall sense of worth, competence, and control over life

autonomous

independent; self-directed; not controlled by others or by outside forces

self-regulation

the ability to control feelings and emotions, or the behavior that results from those emotions; the ability to modify or change behavior as a result of managing inner emotions

social referencing

the ability of a child to observe family members for clues to guide his own behavior

- intentional communication that gradually replaces crying
- **social referencing**, or the ability of the child to observe family members for clues to guide his own behavior
- developing skills in emotional thinking

Although emotions are inner feelings, they can be interpreted from the very young child's behavior, particularly from facial expressions, postures, and gestures. Emotional development is very challenging to support because it requires consistency and very sensitive responses to the infant and toddler. Goulet (2000), speaking in a video, explained that "caregivers who respond sensitively to the infant's emotional signals help to develop self-regulatory skills." Educators need to promote healthy attachments and ease separation difficulties. On a daily basis, they are confronted with emotional challenges. These are better handled when the educator understands their underlying cause.

social development

development of one's social capabilities, including identity, relationships with others, and understanding of one's place within a social environment

egocentricity

the state of seeing only from the individual's perspective; in infancy, an inability to think from the perspective of others

role-modeling

demonstrating appropriate actions and reactions through behavior; the set of actions associated with particular roles or jobs

solitary play

spontaneous activity involving only the individual, not involving others

parallel play

spontaneous activity occurring alongside other children, without sharing or cooperation; playing separately at the same activity at the same time and in the same space

moral development

the gradual increases and changes in understanding of right and wrong, and the acquisition of values; acceptance of socially acceptable behaviors and moral reasoning, and appreciating societal attitudes and beliefs; stages of moral judgment

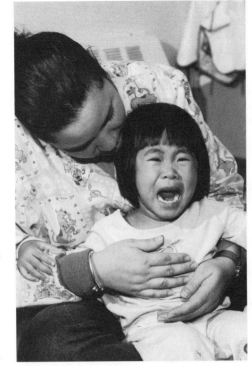

This toddler is still trying to understand many kinds of emotions. Self-regulation is not totally established. Her caregiver acknowledges her feelings while gently comforting her until control is regained.

However, it is wise to consider that conclusions about children's behavior also might be affected by cultural influences. An example of how our interpretations might be culturally mediated is described in Box 3.3. Culture is a complex issue, often overlapping with concepts such as race and ethnicity. Culture is a shared cognitive system of meaning, which is enhanced by values and beliefs. As educators, we must first understand that "shared meaning" does not imply that everyone interprets similar experiences in the same way. Culture dictates what the eyes, ears, and brain see and hear in very subtle and unique ways. One problem early childhood education faces is that for many years, we continued to interpret development in very implicit and universal trends, which, for us in the profession, implied truth. According to Coll and Magnuson (2000), "this detracts from our understanding of phenomena that are culturally bound [*and also prevents us from perceiving*] the influence of other social factors on development, thus affecting programming efforts on behalf of children and families" (p. 94). Make sure to read the short article in the Additional Support section of your Online Companion about cultural awareness.

Social Development

Social development concerns the infant or young child's identity, relationships with others, and understanding of his place within a social environment. Social development is shaped by the context of the child's experiences, but it must start with the child's understanding that he is a separate human being. The infant develops a concept of self through forming attachments to others. These attachments to adults and the opportunity to form relationships are essential for social development. But the capacity of very young children to relate to others is somewhat limited by their **egocentricity**—that is, their focus on themselves. Gaining skills to operate in social environments is significantly helped if the toddler has positive role models; much of the child's learning will come from observing adults and older children.

The social context of development forms the young child's social reality. The most effective social learning tools for toddlers are imitation and **role-modeling**; for younger babies, the social world consists of the adults and children to whom they have some attachment. The adult–child dyad is the center of the infant's social world; communication within it allows the baby's social skills to flourish.

An infant's social play consists largely of **solitary play** (Parten, 1932); the infant plays independently, without engaging with others. The egocentricity of young children does not allow them to see the perspectives of others. Gradually, children start to play alongside others in **parallel play**. Some pretend play may be observed in older toddlers, much of it imitating the adults they see.

The educator can help meet the social needs of infants and toddlers by appreciating the need for consistent care, relationship-building, positive role models, and appropriate conditions for social interactions.

Moral Development

Moral development concerns the child's ability to understand right and wrong and to function in a prosocial way—that is, in a manner that is socially positive (Eisenberg, 2003;

BOX 3.3

CULTURE FRAMES OUR INTERPRETATION OF BEHAVIOR

It is important to note that recent research has enhanced our awareness as to how culture impacts our perspectives. The views children develop about themselves occur within a framework that adults have constructed. Culture is not just an environmental factor, it is "an integrated pattern of human behavior that includes thoughts, communications, languages, practices, beliefs, values, customs, courtesies, rituals, manners of interacting, relationships, and expected behaviors of a racial, ethnic, religious, or social group. Culture is transmitted through succeeding generations and is dynamic" (Day & Parlakian, 2003, p. 2). Because culture shapes so many parts of a child's development, cultural contexts must be understood by educators. Without this understanding, it is impossible to interpret the child's behavior.

For example, "Westerners perceive children who are outgoing and eagerly explore new situations as demonstrating competence and having a positive self-concept, especially compared with children who do not appear to seek out and actively participate in these situations. In contrast, Eastern cultures place greater emphasis on maintaining harmonious, *interdependent* relationships" (Marshall, 2001, p. 19). As educators and Westerners, we may believe that children need to become independent or autonomous in order to be successful. However, other cultures do not view independence as being important, perhaps because they feel that it is much more valuable to understand the importance of depending upon each other.

Consequently, as care providers, we must broaden our perspectives in order to make everyone feel welcomed and respected. We must avoid making judgments about the beliefs of families whenever possible. Without respect and consistency of care, the very young child will end up confused.

Kostelnik et al., 2006). Prosocial behavior is the opposite of antisocial behavior because prosocial behavior is positive and benefits others, while antisocial behavior harms others and implies a disregard for other people's needs and rights (Honig, 1983).

Prosocial skills are seen in actions that benefit others, including

- sharing
- taking turns
- using socially acceptable language such as "please" and "thank you"
- cooperation
- empathy—being able to see and feel someone else's perspective
- altruism—acting unselfishly with no thought for personal benefit

Moral development depends upon both cognitive and social development because it requires an increasing understanding of people, things, and issues. Sometimes moral development is viewed as a process of social cognition. Although clear evidence of moral development can be seen in the toddler's gradual acquisition of pro-social skills, moral learning starts much earlier. Very young children internalize social views of their world when they observe role models. Because adults encourage some behaviors and discourage others, the very young child learns values and attitudes. What constitutes morality is largely externally driven through social learning, but there appears to be an inner drive that strives for justice, or fairness, in terms that relate to the child's ability to appreciate personal perspectives.

personality

the sum total of the enduring characteristics that differentiate one individual from another

temperament

the observable traits or patterns of behavior of an individual; the way the individual behaves

Personality Development

The study of **personality** development considers the temperament types of children and how they remain surprisingly constant through life. **Temperament** is considered the raw material of personality (Goldsmith, Lemery, Aksan, & Buss, 2000) and often is thought of as the

Young toddlers demonstrate the prosocial skills of sharing and taking turns as they paint cooperatively at an easel.

"how" of behavior, not the "why." Although the terms "personality" and "temperament" are sometimes used interchangeably, they are not the same. "Temperament refers more specifically to those emotional traits that are innate, carried into the world from the moment of birth, if not earlier. Temperament is thus considered a genetic trait . . . and remains fundamentally stable over the lives of most people" (Eliot, 1999, p. 316). Temperament contributes to personality, but personality is also shaped by one's life experiences and by the values, attitudes, and personalities of the primary caregivers (Sturm, 2004). Chess and Thomas (1996) are credited with the original classification of nine dimensions of temperament that affect the different styles of response individuals have to the environment (Thomas & Chess, 1977; Campos et al., 1983). The nine categories of components of temperament are:

1. activity level—the degree of energy in movement
2. rhythmicity—the regularity of eating, toileting, and sleeping
3. approach or withdrawal—the ease of approaching situations and people
4. adaptability—the ease of tolerating change in routines
5. threshold of responsiveness—the point at which there is a response
6. intensity of reaction—the degree to which there is a reaction to stimuli
7. quality of mood—the degree of affect (demonstration of emotion)
8. distractability—the ease of being distracted
9. attention span and persistence—the focus of attention or period spent focusing on an activity

shaken baby syndrome

a form of inflicted head trauma. Head injury, as a form of child abuse, can be caused by direct blows to the head, dropping or throwing the child, or shaking the child. This sudden whiplash motion can cause bleeding inside the head and increased pressure on the brain, causing the brain to pull apart, resulting in injury to the baby. The vast majority of incidents occur in infants who are younger than 1 year old

Never Shake a Baby!

In the majority of newborn infants, one of three temperament constellations can be observed. Each constellation is a cluster of several of the nine components. A simplified view of temperament categories places temperament in three rough groups: "the easy child," "the difficult child," and "the slow-to-warm-up child." See the Additional Support section of your Online Companion for more information on temperament, including how traits cluster (constellations), giving rise to the identification of these three categories.

A model of temperament applied in current research proposes two basic dimensions, which coexist and interact with each other (Sturm, 2004). Emotional and attentional reactivity comprise the first dimension, so what is considered is the intensity and substance of a child's reaction to internal and external stimuli. The second dimension focuses on a child's self-regulation skills, or how well he can manage or adapt his behavior to a particular situation. "As practitioners, we can benefit from this dual focus on reactivity and regulation when trying to make sense of a child's behavior" (Sturm, 2004, p. 6). In some ways, this simplifies the interpretation of temperament because the perspective is narrowed and more focused. We must remember, however, that definitions of temperament are mediated by cultural interpretation. For example, in Western cultures, a baby engaging in excessive crying might be labeled as a "difficult" child. In some instances this behavior might be a threat to the child's well-being, since **shaken baby syndrome** often occurs early in a baby's life and the perpetrators, in most cases, are almost always parents or caregivers, who shake the baby out of frustration or stress when the child is crying inconsolably. On the other hand, "members of economically disadvantaged societies interpret infant crying as advantageous to survival" (Blackwell, 2004, p. 41). See the Additional Support section of your Online Companion for more information on shaken baby syndrome.

Categorizing Information by Domain

 Now that you are familiar with the various developmental domains, you should proceed to Activity 3.1 on the CD-ROM, in order to categorize observed information about various domains.

The Whole Child

When we refer to the whole child, we are usually implying that we appreciate that the child is a human being who is an individual, and not just a subject who is splintered into developmental domains. Clearly, each domain overlaps and interrelates with the others. Consequently, it is important to study the interactions among all domains. For example, both language acquisition and emotional development have a social context. In addition, all the domains are, in one way or another, influenced by the child's physical status.

The Context of Development

Contextual factors can shape the process of development. Where the child is born and how the child is nurtured can make an enormous difference in how the child develops. Similarly, the culture in which the child is raised will influence motivation, encouragement, values, and many aspects of learning. Different backgrounds can also play a part in what language or languages are acquired; usually there is also an element of cultural learning embedded in learning a language. Poverty or affluence is likely to make a difference to the child's immediate environment, nutrition, and the meeting of needs. The child's family composition, lifestyle, level of education, and housing can also influence the very young child's development. The most important part of the very young child's context is not the quality of the physical environment, although that is a factor, but the quality of adult interaction and consistency of treatment. In a child care center, the contextual issue includes the quality of interactions between families and educators and the consistency of the child's treatment in the agency and the home.

Development within an Ecological System

Human development occurs within a social system. Infants' and toddlers' development may be driven by biological processes, but the possibility of realizing personal potential lies in the complex social network in which very young children find themselves.

We looked at Bronfenbrenner's work in Chapter 1, but we need to see his approach as being theoretical, as well as philosophical.

ecological system

the idea that human development occurs within and is influenced by complex social systems; involves concentric circles indicating differing social systems and levels

Bronfenbrenner (1979) offers a useful illustration of the interactions among the different aspects of an individual's social system, or what he calls the **ecological system**. As illustrated in Figure 3.3, this system consists of three concentric circles, with the child at the center. Bronfenbrenner labels these circles the microsystem, the exosystem, and the macrosystem. These represent, respectively, the layers of people, institutions, and values with which the individual interacts. Each person's ecological system is different, although there are similarities, particularly between family members. However, even two very young children growing up in the same family experience life from different perspectives. Because every child is born into a social structure and is influenced by the various aspects of this structure, understanding the actual *context* of a child's development helps us to appreciate the child's development patterns.

THEORIES OF DEVELOPMENT

The term *theory* tends to intimidate people when they start to study development. It need not be so difficult. A theory is just a model that helps us to understand what we observe. For example, we frequently make explanations for why a child is behaving in a particular way. This is a theory, an explanation for a phenomenon. Developmental theories attempt to explain what is occurring for an individual. Studying theories can be a challenge because there are so many of them and they often use complex terms. Ainsworth, Bandura, Bowlby, Bronfenbrenner, Bruner, Chomsky,

Figure 3.3

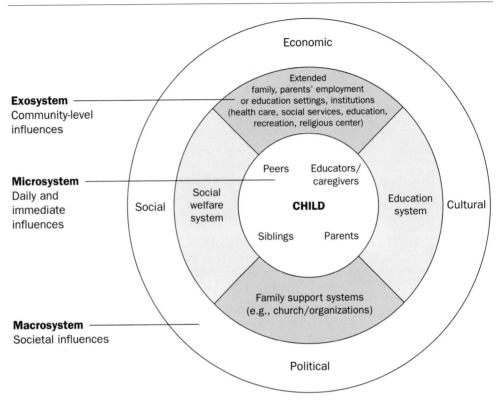

Source: Based on Bronfenbrenner, U. (1979). *The ecology of human development: Experiments by nature and design.* Cambridge, MA: Harvard University Press; and Petes, D., & Kontos, S. (1987). *Continuity and discontinuity of experience in child care.* Norwood, NJ: Ablex Publishing.

Erikson, Freud, Gardner, Izard, Kagan, Maslow, Piaget, and Vygotsky are a few of the important theorists who have offered significant models that attempt to explain young children's behavior. See the Additional Support section in your Online Companion for an overview of some of these theories.

Theorists arrive at their ideas through various methods of study. Most of the major theorists used approaches involving forms of observation. These included naturalistic observations and contrived observations in formal experiments. From these observations, explanations of development were hypothesized and then tested.

What we understand about children can be shaped by several important theoretical schools of thought about human cognition and behavior. People who follow different schools will observe an infant or toddler and see the same behavior but likely interpret it differently. Educators frequently pick and choose aspects from a number of schools rather than identify with one particular approach. They may explain one behavior with reference to a particular school but find that another behavior is best explained by a different school. We call this an **eclectic** approach—where we put together aspects of different schools. Most educators use an eclectic way of explaining behavior.

Applying Theory to What We Observe

Some of the theoretical models that are particularly useful to early childhood educators help explain the development that we observe every day. These theories tell us:

- why very young children repeat actions
- why young children need love as well as physical care
- how new skills are learned
- how infants make connections with an adult

eclectic (approach)

a philosophical approach to working with children that takes elements of various philosophies and combines them into a meaningful whole

The eclectic approach is like dining at a smorgasbord. You can partake from a wide variety of choices in order to satisfy your taste buds.

- what enables or drives toddlers to walk
- why newborns have reflexes that disappear
- why babies are interested in looking at visual contrasts
- when infants can understand symbols
- how language is learned
- why very young children have faces that attract attention
- why there can be difficulties for babies separating from adults
- when a toddler might learn to walk
- why toddlers are dependent on adults yet strive for independence
- how infants make sense of objects
- why babies look for lost items
- why toddlers seem self-centered

Maintaining a Questioning Attitude about Theories of Development

Theories will help you in your job of caring and educating. The results of someone else's detailed observing, recording, and hypothesizing may lead you to an understanding of a behavior that you might not have been able to think of on your own. Theoretical models are not always correct; moreover, they can be incorrectly applied. Use your common sense when testing the applicability of a theory, but don't dismiss a theory too quickly. Tread carefully through new concepts and test them out in ways that are harmless to the children. A theory may seem far-fetched at the start, but you might eventually find that it explains a behavior in a meaningful, if not obvious, way.

At the same time that you study child development theories, you should examine norms of behavior. Both of these areas will make more sense if you apply the knowledge to the infants or toddlers in your care. Theoretical explanations and **normative profiles** can work together to assist our understanding of infants and toddlers.

PRINCIPLES OF DEVELOPMENT

The **principles of development** are the pathways or **patterns of development** that have been observed by experts. Although most child development theorists agree that there is merit to each of the principles, each expert is likely to emphasize one principle over another.

Maturation

Maturation refers to a sequence of biological elements that reflect growth and development. The pattern of growth and sequence of skill acquisition for young children is largely determined before birth. Much of a child's developmental map is created by genetic information from the parents. Further developmental mapping may be determined by broader evolutionary processes. For example, the reflexes that are typical of a newborn infant appear and then disappear. They do this regardless of the genes from the parents. This is a pattern of development that may reflect the general need to survive, or it is perhaps an adaptation to the environment that was a necessity at an earlier time. Infants tend to follow a similar pattern of development in that they usually acquire skills in the same order. Yet individual schedules mean that children may acquire these skills earlier or later than their peers. For example, babies learn to sit before they learn to walk, but the ages at which they gain the skill of sitting or walking may be different. Some children gain more quickly in some domains and more slowly in others.

The above discussion may make it seem that we can do little about children's developmental achievements. However, the milestones can be achieved only if the child experiences conditions conducive to development. If children have insufficient food or love, they will not reach their potential in growth or any other area of development. So, while caregivers should know typical patterns of development, it is more important to provide the **optimal conditions** for growth and healthy development, described in Box 3.1.

---

normative profiles

charts and tables indicating the typical patterns of growth at designated ages of a particular population of children considered to represent the "norm"; often presented as percentiles

principles of development

the commonly agreed-upon ideas that explain human development—e.g., stage progression

patterns of development

the predictable stages and changes that are observable within each individual; may involve frequent progressions and some regressions; may be continuous or discontinuous

maturation

the biologically shaped, naturally unfolding course of growth and development

optimal conditions

the best possible situation; exemplary environment

In recent years, some educators have moved away from the use of developmental profiles or schedules, citing reasons such as cultural bias. Although these reasons seem valid, there is a danger in abandoning such profiles. Without them, we would have only limited understanding of developmental sequences and norms. Developmental profiles or schedules enable us to appreciate changes in the developmental process from a theoretical perspective.

The Human Life Cycle

life cycle

the natural and ongoing sequence of birth, life, and death; life-cycle theory proposed by Erikson

social clock

one of three clocks of life span development; the influence of culture and society

biological clock

one of three clocks of life span development—the influence of heredity and maturation

psychological clock

one of three clocks of life span development; the influence of inner needs and drives

stage

a period of time at which the individual demonstrates behavior associated with a labeled expectation—e.g., sensorimotor stage

healthy development

a desirable level of human development in which the individual becomes a fully functioning person

Infants and toddlers are at the start of their **life cycle**. Their experiences are likely to shape their later growth and development. Life-cycle theorists suggest that three clocks drive human development: the **social clock**, the **biological clock**, and the **psychological clock**. The social clock reflects the influences of expectation of society. The biological clock reflects the maturational process that drives developmental change. The psychological clock concerns the ability to think according to increasingly complex inner structures. Interaction between the clocks is what ultimately frames the uniqueness of each individual.

 See the Additional Support section in your Online Companion for more information on the interaction of these clocks.

Ages and Stages

The actual chronological age of a child provides a marker for adult expectations of the child. This is problematic for at least two reasons. First, people who make age-related remarks are often not familiar with "typical" development for that age. Second, age-related comments may label the child. These labels—slow, advanced, smart, and so on—can affect the future expectations that adults have of the child and that the child has of himself.

In contrast to chronological age, a **stage** is usually thought of as a set of behavioral indicators that, together, constitute an identified step in the development process. Stages are even less precise than ages in developmental terms. For example, infancy is considered to be a stage, but it is defined in different ways by different theorists. Despite these differences, stages can give us an idea about the typical sequence of developmental advances, help us understand why a child is behaving the way she is, help adults support the child to the next step, or stage, and help educators identify possible developmental difficulties.

Healthy Development

The term **healthy development** is being used more and more often by researchers to emphasize the need for positive development outcomes. Healthy development is not a perfect state, but it indicates that the child's process of development is progressing positively.

Health is a physical, emotional, and psychological process, and it requires careful planning and promotion. Pimento and Kernested (2000) indicate that, although attention is paid to the health care system, the most significant determinants of health are in fact social and economic. These include "income/social status, healthy child development, freedom from discrimination, and communication and life skills" (p. 7).

The American Academy of Pediatrics has also issued policy statements and guidelines that promote the adoption of attitudes and behaviors that recognize that health factors alone are not solely responsible for healthy developmental outcomes of children.

Individuality

Each child's experience of family, society, and culture is as individual as a fingerprint or DNA. Even the child's birth order in the family can contribute to her individual context. Although her experience may have many features in common with those of other family members, it is unique.

> You can predict the stage of development for a child, but you cannot easily predict how old the child will be when that particular stage of development occurs. In other words, *you can predict the stage, but not the age.*

BOX 3.4

DEVELOPMENTALLY APPROPRIATE PRACTICE IS BASED ON DEVELOPMENTAL PRINCIPLES

1. Domains of children's development—physical, social, emotional, and cognitive— are closely related. Development in one domain influences and is influenced by development in other areas.
2. Development occurs in a relatively orderly sequence, with later abilities, skills, and knowledge building on those already acquired.
3. Development proceeds at varying rates from child to child, as well as unevenly within different areas of each child's functioning.
4. Early experiences have both cumulative and delayed effects on individual children's development; optimal periods exist for certain types of development and learning.
5. Development proceeds in predictable directions toward greater complexity, organization, and internalization.
6. Development and learning occur in and are influenced by multiple social and cultural contexts.
7. Children are active learners, drawing on direct physical and social experience as well as culturally transmitted knowledge to construct their own understandings of the world around them.
8. Development and learning result from interaction of biological maturation and the environment, which includes both the physical and social worlds that children live in.
9. Play is an important vehicle for children's social, emotional, and cognitive development, as well as a reflection of their development.
10. Development advances when children have opportunities to practice newly acquired skills as well as when they experience a challenge just beyond the level of their present mastery.
11. Children demonstrate different modes of knowing and learning and different ways of representing what they know.
12. Children develop and learn best in the context of a community where they are safe and valued, their physical needs are met, and they feel psychologically secure.

Source: Excerpted, with permission, from the National Association for the Education of Young Children's position statement, "Developmentally Appropriate Practice in Early Childhood Programs Serving Children Birth through Age Eight." All rights reserved.

Core Principles that Support DAP

At this point it is important to acknowledge that NAEYC's position on developmentally appropriate practice is also based on knowledge about how children develop and learn. That knowledge has been accumulated over several centuries. At its core are twelve empirically based principles of child development and learning. They are delineated in Box 3.4. These principles should be reviewed periodically in order to help you remember that best practices in child care are supported by solid research, not by passing whims. For a complete explanation of these principles, see Bredekamp and Copple (1997) or follow the links provided in the Additional Support section of your Online Companion to examine these underlying principles of DAP.

ASPECTS OF DEVELOPMENT

This section reviews a number of different concepts which need to be considered when discussing development.

Developmental Norms

norms

the average performance of a large sample of children at designated ages

Earlier we discussed the philosophy of normative assessment; here we will look at where **norms** come from.

The study of development has been heavily dependent upon research that tells us what most children can do at a particular age. Arnold Gesell pioneered work in development by taking a sample of children and determining the average ages at which they demonstrated skills. More recently, researchers have tried to determine norms of development based on much wider samples of children. These profiles, including those by Allen and Marotz (2007) and Sheridan (2001), are used primarily for screening and assessment.

When used as criteria for evaluating a child's developmental progress, developmental norms can offer useful information. For assessment of infants or toddlers, they may provide a developmental profile of a child that leads to specific action or intervention. However, using norms is a limited process that is open to abuse. Critics have strongly condemned the overuse of normative assessments and have questioned their validity and reliability. Some think that norms should not be relied upon for measuring performances of children from different cultures, because their patterns of development may vary or their opportunities to develop skills may be somewhat different. Another complication centers on the sample of children from which the norm is derived. It could be too small or poorly representative of some cultural groups. For these reasons, we need to think seriously about what criteria we use for assessment. Norm referencing should, perhaps, be used only as one part of a much more comprehensive approach to assessment.

Despite these cautions, norms should not be dismissed because of the challenges they present. We need to ensure that the research sample is appropriate in size and representation. We also need to make sure that we use the norms as a yardstick for measurement rather than as an indication of failure. Normative tools can offer means for gathering some quantitative assessment information, data that are presented in numerical or otherwise measurable forms. Quantitative data involve measurable information, such as the child's height or how the child is performing at a particular age level. It is important to supplement such data with information specific to the child's context. With access to both normative and contextual information, we will have the most helpful combination.

Developmental Profiles

developmental profile

an overview of an individual's development that may include written components and examples that illustrate their level of performance, or a chart indicating average performance levels at each age group

The **developmental profile** is a complex listing of norms across all domains of development in a way that emphasizes the notion of "stage." A stage relates to a set of behaviors rather than single actions; together they indicate a general level of functioning. For example, a norm might indicate that at 6 months of age, an infant will hold items to her mouth. The stage approach sees this as just one of many behaviors that indicate that the infant is in the sensori-motor stage. The developmental profile acknowledges that the domains of development interact, and that there are deep structures underlying the observable characteristics of behavior.

The authors of stage profiles often present their structure of stages as progressive steps that may have some approximation to ages, but the focus is the stage rather than the age. Both Erikson and Piaget offer stage models that have significant usefulness to us as educators.

Some of these profiles of development have led people to think that if a child is not demonstrating the supposed "right" level of performance, there is something wrong. This is usually not the case. But the profiles can give us a good idea about what to expect in terms of the sequences and patterns of development for most children. They can assist us in making assessments that involve identification of atypical skill levels. Although these atypical levels should be noted, they do not necessarily mean there is anything troubling. It is always important to bear in mind that children have individual patterns. If you keep observing and responding to "where the child is now," you are likely to find that what you have observed was an individual quirk rather than a problem. If your continued observations suggest that the child's behavior is not what you might have expected, check your perceptions with normative profiles and with other professionals.

Developmental Progression

progression

steps forward in development

regression

steps backward in development

Another process that can be used to gauge skill acquisition uses the child's own pattern of change as markers for developmental **progression**. To assess a child's performance, the child's earlier skill performance level would be used as a point of reference for current assessment. Although this exercise is helpful to some extent, it tells us only what gains have been made, not whether the performance level is typical for the child's age. Sometimes **regressions** will also be evident; they are often part of ordinary development.

Continuity and Discontinuity

Development continues throughout childhood and beyond, but not always at the same rate. A period of accelerated progression may be followed by a plateau, during which time little change occurs. Educators and parents are likely to notice when a new skill is acquired rapidly, but they may not notice a period of slower development. The toddler who learns to use the toilet almost overnight provides a good example of rapid development.

continuity

the notion that the process of human growth and development follows a gradual progression

discontinuity

the notion that human growth and development follow a fluctuating pathway of progression and regression, rather than a gradual progression

Some domains of development appear to follow a continuous path of skill increase—**continuity**. Others may follow patterns of **discontinuity**. A toddler may swing between periods of intense effort to be independent and a reliance on an adult for some self-help skills, showing us that development may be accompanied by inner conflicts.

Directions of Development

The sequence of physical skill acquisition is similar in all children. The pattern involves increasing bodily control that starts at the top of the body and progresses downward (**cephalocaudal sequence**) and from the center of the body outward toward the extremities (**proximodistal sequence**). Thus, infants first learn to hold up their heads, then sit, stand, and walk, and so on.

cephalocaudal/ proximodistal sequences

the development of the body follows dual sequences simultaneously—from the head to foot and from the center of the body outward to the hands

Children may be ready to perform a skill, but they need time and opportunity to practice the action until mastery is achieved. This process of skill refinement continues for a long time after the core skill is demonstrated, and enables the child to perform actions more accurately and purposefully.

Figure 3.4

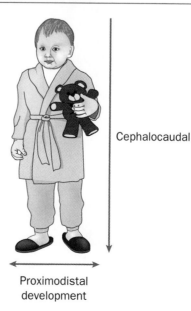

Cephalocaudal

Proximodistal development

Critical and Sensitive Periods

sensitive periods

the window of opportunity when the brain is most receptive to particular types of learning experiences

critical periods

the time when the child must be exposed to appropriate experiences for development to occur

Understanding the difference between the **sensitive periods** and **critical periods** identified by brain research is of crucial importance for care providers. In essence, these periods are benchmarks for opportune development and learning in the early years, although they are quantitatively and qualitatively different.

> When the effect of experience on the brain is particularly strong during a limited period in development, this period is referred to as a sensitive period. Such periods allow experience to instruct neural circuits to process or represent information in a way that is adaptive for the individual. When experience provides information that is essential for normal development and alters performance permanently, such sensitive periods are referred to as critical periods. (Knudsen, 2004, p. 1412)

Critical periods represent a narrow window of time during which a specific part of the human fetus or the individual is most susceptible to the absence of stimulation or to effects of environmental factors. They are the times in growth when certain input is essential for development. For example, many different opportunities for critical development occur during prenatal development (See Figure 3.5.). Week-by-week, cell formation and differentiation are responsible for creating numerous structures—fingers, toes, skin, bladder, spine—the list is endless. However, exposure to **teratogens**—substances that have the potential for damage during pregnancy—can have varying effects depending on time of exposure and the inherited genetic variations in women. An example of time of exposure is demonstrated by the drug thalidomide. Gable and Hunting (2001) explain that women who took the drug between the 38th and 46th days of pregnancy gave birth to infants with deformed arms, or no arms. Women who took the drug between the 40th and 46th days of pregnancy gave birth to infants with deformed legs or

teratogen

substances that have the potential for damage during pregnancy

Figure 3.5

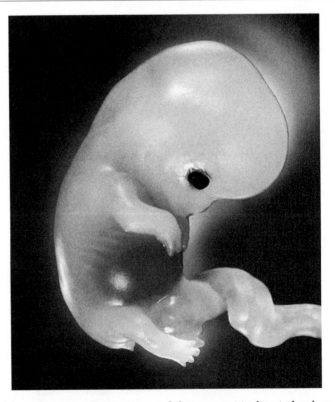

Cell division occurs rapidly in utero, and there are critical periods when a fetus is vulnerable to the presence of particular drugs or teratogens, or to the absence of required environmental elements such as good nutrition or oxygen.

no legs. Women who took the drug after the 50th day of pregnancy gave birth to babies with no birth defects or problems.

Critical periods also exist after a child is born. An infant who has very limited exposure to adults, and is therefore unable to make attachments, may have long-term, if not permanent, emotional difficulties. Meeting some basic needs for survival may seem to be enough for a child to develop satisfactorily, but research indicates that very young children need to have physical contact and love in their first months or they may be unable to grow and acquire skills. Spitz (1945) called this a **failure to thrive**, and captured harrowing film of infants and toddlers who were underdeveloped in every domain, despite apparent meeting of basic needs. More recently, follow-up with European and American families who adopted very young children from Romanian orphanages shows that families are contending with severely withdrawn older children. Although these children have been given love and nurturance since they were adopted, institutionalization for the first months of their lives did irreparable damage. Further adoption studies have highlighted difficulties in addressing developmental issues and providing meaningful compensation.

Another example involves the sense of sight. An infant must be exposed to light during the first six months of his life, otherwise the nerves leading from the eye to the visual cortex of the brain will slowly waste away and eventually the child will no longer have the ability to see since, ultimately, it is the brain that "sees."

Sensitive periods are the broad "windows of opportunity" (see Box. 3.5), or "prime times," for certain types of learning. "The term sensitive periods is preferred to critical periods because it implies less rigidity in the nature of the formative early experiences, their developmental timing, and their developmental outcomes" (Thompson, 2001, p. 85). Sensitive periods represent a more flexible and longer learning arc under which an individual can acquire skills such as language and vocabulary, and even develop emotional skills, including attachment and trust. However, if the opportunity is missed, there is always the possibility of gaining those skills later in life. The human brain's major function is to learn, so you can always learn to play a musical instrument or to speak a foreign language. It might take more time to acquire the skill, and you probably won't be playing at Carnegie Hall or speaking without an accent, but you can always learn at any point in your life.

Nevertheless, it is true that during the first three years of life, the brain experiences its most dramatic and dynamic connective growth, and it is in its most receptive state. The child is born ready to learn, with an almost insatiable curiosity, which can be either supported or thwarted. The effect on the neural wiring is significant and long-lasting. "We now know that the entire first three years of life represent an extraordinary window for learning virtually everything. . . . Among the most important windows of opportunity are those involving emotional and social development" (Ramey & Ramey, 1999, p. 14). Although we often think of the brain

failure to thrive

a condition where a seemingly healthy baby fails to grow and develop normally

Critical period
- begins and ends abruptly
- period beyond which a phenomenon will not appear

Sensitive period
- begins and ends gradually
- period of maximum sensitivity

BOX 3.5

WINDOWS OF OPPORTUNITY

TASK	WINDOW OF OPPORTUNITY
Emotional Attachment	Birth to 18 months
Movement Skills	Birth to 2 years
Language Development	Birth to 10 years
Music and Math Skills	1 year to 5 years
Visual Development	Birth to 4 years
Talking and Reading	Birth to 10 years
Learning Vocabulary	Birth to 3 years
Learning a Second Language	Birth to 10 years

in connection with cognitive functioning, Stephens (1999) asserts that brain development affects personality, temperament, social skills, the ability to regulate emotions, and the ability to function within the parameters of moral and ethical guidelines.

Sometimes, people have described sensitive periods as critical periods, thus endowing this time in the child's life with an almost unrealistic doom or gloom significance. This has resulted in some misunderstanding in the field of early childhood education. Bruer (2001) and Bailey and Symons (2001) caution against viewing sensitive periods as being critical and absolute. Perhaps it would be better to regard the early years as *crucial* to the design of the learning arc. Lifelong learning is always possible because of the neural plasticity of the brain, but it must be recognized that the breadth, depth, and strength of the initial foundation is what supports all future learning endeavors. "Lasting good effects are enhanced when supportive learning experiences start early, occur more often, and continue over many years. . . . There is no quick fix that will guarantee a rewarding and fulfilling life for any child. There is no short-term program which, if missed, will consign a child to the back of the pack" (Ramey & Ramey, 1999, p. 12). This statement offers a two fold cautionary tale:

- We need to pay attention to all children, but especially to those who are identified as at-risk; you cannot compensate for "too little, too late."
- Do not push children too early into academic learning; the old saying "slow and steady wins the race" is quite applicable here.

The implication for individuals who work with young children is that they need to be aware that brain research identifies birth through age 3 as a sensitive period for development and learning in all areas. If the philosophy of responsive care is practiced with all young children, then in all likelihood, their needs will be met fully.

Developmental "Catching Up"

catch up

the idea that, given certain remedial experiences, the child can resume a typical stage of development

typical development

human development that lies within the range of the norm or average

atypical development

patterns of human development that lie outside the range of the norm or average

The concept of the critical period can lead people to believe that nothing can be done for children whose development is delayed or for whom early experience was relatively poor. To a limited extent, it is possible to **catch up** in some areas of development. This is noticeable in infants and older children who have been hospitalized or institutionalized for a short period of time. Such children can reach the developmental level of their peers if their experience is not too long or traumatic. This may seem to contradict some of the things described above, but we are talking now about short periods of time spent in poor environments.

It is difficult to predict what amount of damage is done to a child whose learning experience is limited. It appears that temperament, emotional attachments, and compensatory experience may be deciding factors in the child's ultimate development.

Typical and Atypical Development

The concepts of **typical** and **atypical development** are contentious because of their judgmental tone. While it is crucial for adults working with very young children to appreciate the details of behavior of children at different ages and stages, care must be taken when such terms are used. They can lead to labeling and the lowering of expectations for the child about whom the statement is made.

Personal Story

During a workshop I was conducting on DAP, I spent 30 minutes debating the issue of learning with a member of the child care staff.

She was insistent that the children were only "learning" during the two-hour time slot that was designated as the "preschool" experience.

I could not help her to understand that you cannot separate education and care. These concepts are one and the same when you are with young children.

Children are born ready to learn.

The question always is, "What are they learning?"

There is a wide range of individual differences among young children that sometimes makes it difficult to distinguish between normal variations and maturational delays and other conditions that include temporary disorders and persistent impairments (Shonkoff & Phillips, 2000; Shonkoff, Phillips, & Keilty, 2000). Keep in mind that children have the ability to utilize multiple developmental pathways, rather than only one path labeled "normal." This interpretation helps to explain the unique competencies that children can develop in diverse cultural and familial contexts.

developmental diversity

evidence of a variety of developmental levels, abilities, and stages

Developmental diversity can include developmental delays or disabilities in the physical, social–emotional, communication, self-help, or cognitive areas, as well as special aptitudes, talents, and giftedness. There may be associated health concerns and particular stress on the child's family. For example, the child could have a condition that requires monitoring for medical interventions, such as cerebral palsy, seizure disorder, spinal chord injury, or asthma. A particular condition may not, in and of itself, be the cause of developmental challenges; the condition may create mobility, social, or other difficulties that, in turn, result in an interrelated developmental issue. Remember, a key principle of developmental and learning theory (see Box 3.4) is that all areas of development are interrelated, so that a delay in one area can affect a delay in another area. Box. 3. 6 describes how this is evidenced in the behavior of one child.

It should be remembered that there is very wide developmental variation within the population as a whole. The majority of children who are cared for in group settings can, and should, be supported in an inclusive child care environment and by skilled educators working collaboratively with the children's parents. Currently, there is little knowledge about the effects of

---

BOX 3.6

INTERACTION BETWEEN DEVELOPMENTAL DOMAINS

Principle 1. Domains of children's development—physical, social, emotional, and cognitive—are closely related. Development in one domain influences and is influenced by development in other areas.

Although the initial delay in the following example was identified as physical, the impact of the interrelatedness of developmental domains can begin to be understood as demonstrated by the following:

At age 1 Cassidy still has not starting crawling. Although she is sitting on her own, she seems unable to synchronize the movements required for crawling, such as pushing up to a crawling position and using reciprocal movements of hands and legs. Because she is stationary, the majority of objects and people in her environment have to be brought to her. This has the potential to impact her development in several ways. First, much of what a child learns about herself, especially early on, is dependent upon motor skills. Limited motor skills potentially mean limited experiences. The less feedback a child receives, the less described is her world. Other children Cassidy's age are beginning to learn a lot about cause and effect merely by encountering numerous "experiments" each day. Cause and effect is a great contributor to cognitive growth, especially in young children. Each experience either adds to accumulated knowledge, or creates a new learning opportunity. Second, by the age of 1 many children begin to demonstrate "onlooker" play behavior. Since Cassidy is unable to move, she can only observe the play behavior of other children within her range of site. This impacts her social development. Last, she continues to be dependent on other people in her environment to provide her with stimulation. This has the potential of affecting her emotionally, since it is difficult for her to begin to make her own way in the world or, in other words, achieve autonomy.

inclusion

integrating all children into a program, regardless of their ability levels or background

inclusion on typically developing toddlers enrolled in child care programs. However, Stahmer and Carter (2005) recently published results of a study examining parent perceptions of the benefits and limitations of their child's toddler program (inclusive or typical). Findings demonstrated that families were satisfied with the inclusion program and, in fact, they pointed to many benefits of inclusion.

ADDITIONAL DEVELOPMENTAL FACTORS

Nature and Nurture

Individual patterns of development occur whatever the circumstances of life. Identical twins may have the closest shared reality and a similar schedule for maturation, but even they have differing perspectives as they see each other and the rest of the world. The interaction of **nature and nurture** influences the pattern of each child's development, ensuring that development is truly individual.

nature/nurture (development)

the interaction of genetic inheritance and the life experience that contribute to making individuals who and what they are

Nature determines the individual's genetic map. Children inherit genes from their parents that set out the potential for each domain of development. Nurture is linked to the circumstances of individual life experience and helps determine whether the potential of an individual is achieved.

Whether or not the "nature versus nurture" debate remains pertinent is unknown. Some modern theorists believe the dual concepts to be redundant. If the truth lies in the combination of the two, the explanation for development is that it is a dynamic interaction between the biological potential of the individual and every aspect of that person's experience. Consideration of both forces appears to remain relevant while we grapple with understanding genetic inheritance and the changeable components of life experience.

Twin Studies

One way of studying whether components of development are determined more by nature or nurture is by comparing identical twins who have grown up separately with those who have been brought up together—twin studies. Of course, identical twins are not often raised separately, and it would be an ethical problem to split twins for the sake of an experiment. Galton (1875) was the first person to consider using twins to determine the outcome of the nature-versus-nurture debate. Since then, many researchers have conducted studies to see if particular attributes were determined by nature or nurture. When identical twins—that is, those who have the same genetic material—are reared apart, they still display some striking similarities. It has been found that various characteristics, as well as diseases, are heritable. Physical pattern of growth, personality attributes, and behavioral styles can all be heritable. In one study, male identical twins separated at birth met again in adulthood. They had chosen wives with the same names and similar looks, purchased similar models of car, lived in houses of similar style, and had numerous other similarities, including clothing and their choice of toiletries. Other than their fingerprints, there was little difference between them. Not all twin studies have offered such clear indication that attributes are heritable. There is agreement, though, that some characteristics and potentialities are genetically determined.

Motivation

Children's interests shape their learning. If they are motivated, their attention span is likely to be longer and they are more likely to attend to details. This principle is more obvious in older than younger children, but it is relevant to infants and toddlers.

Various elements interact in determining what might motivate a very young child. Some biological pre-wiring leads infants and toddlers to be interested in particular things at particular stages. For example, an infant is keenly interested in looking at faces or face-like patterns. Observing visual preferences tells us much about the child's interests. Differences in perceptual and cognitive functioning lead some children to pay more attention to some things than others.

Children who have a lower level of cognitive functioning are less likely to be curious and persist at a task.

Success in a particular area tends to be a strong reinforcer. Also, the infant or toddler is likely to want to be involved in an activity where there is some reward. Temperamental differences also play a part in motivating the child. Some toddlers will be more independent than others just because of their personal style. Older infants and toddlers can be motivated by their mothers to do things that they had refused to do alone (Kelley, Brownell, & Campbell, 2000). This could be because the relationship of trust allows the child to believe that the mother's request is all right. The adult's emotional responses can shape the child's interests. Approval or disapproval expressed on a parent's face may be enough to encourage or halt a child's interests.

But stronger still can be the young child's inner drive for control and **autonomy**. This motivator is difficult to influence, but it is not desirable to try to break the child's will to do something. Adult intervention needs to work with the intrinsic motivation, not in opposition to it.

Mutual Interactions

Development occurs in a reciprocal manner—that is, the infant's behavior influences the adult's as much as the adult's influences the child's. When we observe the interactions between adults and very young children—**mutual interactions**—we can see how much the child's behavior affects the adult's behavior and vice versa. This reciprocity allows for mutual attachments, complex relationships, a variety of learning experiences, two-way emotional comfort, and the creation of successful family and social groups.

Deprivation and Resilience

Deprivation refers to any condition in which the child's needs are not met in a serious or ongoing manner. It is not necessarily equated with poverty, although a family's limited financial resources can affect how well it provides the basic elements of life to children. Deprivation can involve physical, cognitive, or psychological damage, or a combination of these. Consequences of deprivation can be varied and are somewhat unpredictable.

Some children appear to be more **resilient** to deprivations than others, and are less affected for little apparent reason. Brookes and Goldstein (2001), as well as and Kosteck (2005), suggest that children's resiliency can be enhanced if they have external supports and internal mechanisms that act as protection from negative experiences. External protective factors include:

- families that are empathetic, communicate effectively, teach children to solve problems and make decisions, are able to cope with stress and repeated crises, utilize authoritative parenting style, and set realistic goals and expectations for children
- families and schools that work in collaborative, proactive, empathetic, and respectful partnerships; and
- communities and nations that support the family and see children as a shared and precious resource[1].

Internal protective factors, meaning what a child might possess, include such skills as:

- social competence (flexibility, empathy, caring);
- problem-solving ability (planning, decision-making, reasonable persistence; creative thinking);
- autonomy (self-awareness, sense of worthiness and competence, coping strategies); and
- an optimistic outlook.

autonomy

an inner drive to become independent and meet one's own needs; a sense of independence, self-government, or self-reliance

mutual interactions

two-way communication and actions that involve both individuals in meaningful exchanges

deprivation

the state in which essential experiences, basic needs, or relationships are denied, absent, or inaccessible

resilience

the idea that an individual can be prepared or strengthened to withstand and recover from negative circumstances

---

1. Source: Sparrow Lake Alliance, "Methods for Developing Resiliency in Children from Disadvantaged Populations," prepared for the National Forum on Health by Paul Steinhauser, March 31, 1996.

Although some personality types are more likely to have increased vulnerability, inner emotional resources are likely to ameliorate the effects of poor circumstances. However resilient the child is, her development is likely to be affected detrimentally if she is deprived of basic needs.

Readiness

readiness

the idea that there is a state of being when a child is ready to acquire a skill or experience something meaningful

developmental outcomes

increases in individual performance measured over a period of time; the results of a program or intervention that demonstrate its success or failure

Educators and families frequently talk about a young child's readiness. It might be readiness for weaning or for using a toilet. Whatever the skill, the notion of readiness assumes that because a child is competent in one area, he will automatically be "ready" for the next step. It may be a mistake to make this assumption, even if you are familiar with the child and with typical stages of development. Usually children will indicate readiness by demonstrating an emerging skill that is related to the task for which they might be ready. For example, if a toddler is ready to use a potty, he may indicate this by using appropriate actions and possibly some imitation of another child or adult.

Readiness is a concept used by some educators who believe that they can enhance the child's development by setting goals to achieve the next step. Readiness assessment is carried out in various settings, including child care centers. The most serious difficulty with readiness assessment is that there are very few ways of predicting the future abilities of children. Current performance is not always an indicator of future potential.

Researchers use the concept of **developmental outcomes** as measurable indicators of what children know and can do. There is a belief that achieving desired outcomes within a time frame or at the end of a period of education and nurturing is a useful predictor, or sign of readiness, for the next stage. This supposes that the developmental steps are achievable progressions and that gaining any one level indicates the potential for achieving the next. This is, to some extent, questionable. Wanting or not wanting to take the next step may be an issue. Also, as is the case with any type of skill acquisition, perhaps the optimal level or the maximum possible for that individual has already been reached! According to Grisham-Brown, Hemmeter, and Pretti-Frontczak (2005), "the important piece of this is ensuring that the outcomes, the teaching approaches for addressing the outcomes, and the processes that will be used to assess children's progress toward the outcomes are all developmentally appropriate" (p. 13).

RESEARCH AND INITIATIVES FOCUSING ON YOUNG CHILDREN

The following section discusses research endeavors and initiatives that are thought to be of significant value for anyone involved in the study of early childhood.

Child Care for Infants and Toddlers—A New Phenomenon

Children don't need to get ready for school; schools need to get ready for children!
In the early childhood profession, there is a strong belief that our job is not to get children "ready" for the next level of education. Our job is to focus on being with children in the present. Therefore, as educators, we need to ask—what do children need at their current level of development in order to help them build a strong foundation for future learning?

When compared to care for children preschool age to 12, services for infants and toddlers outside the home is still a relatively new phenomenon. "The topic of care for infants and toddlers cuts to the heart of conceptions of parental roles and responsibilities" (Phillips & Adams, 2001, p. 1). In 1975, only 34 percent of mothers with children under 3 were in the workforce, but by the year 2000, this figure had reached over 61 percent (Phillips & Adams, 2001). Figure 3.6 documents this trend.

It is obvious that the need for child care arrangements has grown at a rapid rate over the last 30 years. Families often are limited in child care choices by cost, physical location, and the hours of operation of child care facilities. Also, many child care centers still do not take infants, since the cost of care is much more expensive than for preschool children, and a business format requires a consideration of the bottom line. In addition to these factors, families recognize that children of different ages have varying developmental, response, and nurturing needs. The younger the child, the more one-on-one attention is necessary.

According to Ehrle, Adams, and Tout (2001), by the year 2000, infants and toddlers were more likely to be with relatives and in parent care than in center-based facilities. Among infants and toddlers, 27 percent were in relative care and another 27 percent in parent care, while smaller proportions were found in center-based care (22 percent) and family child care (17 percent). However, the use of center care for children under 3 nearly tripled in 20 years, from 8 percent in 1977 to 22 percent in 1997 (Phillips & Adams, 2001, p. 41). (See Figure 1.2 in Chapter 1).

Figure 3.6

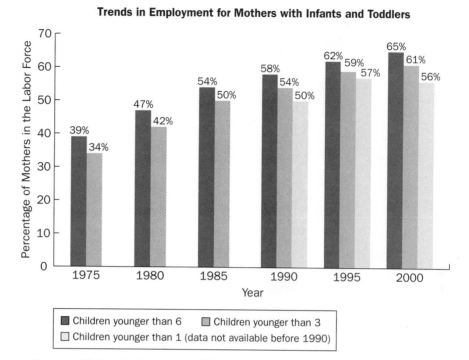

Trends in Employment for Mothers with Infants and Toddlers

Source: Bureau of Labor Statistics, unpublished tabulations. Reprinted with permission from *The Future of Children,* a publication of the David and Lucile Packard Foundation.

Even given that many more mothers are returning to the employment ranks, either through choice or economic necessity, it is still a difficult decision to make. As the statistics substantiate, many choose to leave their children with the other parent, or a relative, because it is comforting to feel that your child is being cared for by familiar individuals, and that, in most cases, the values and beliefs your child is exposed to are similar to those of your own. Also, there still remains an underlying belief in the United States that families should be solely responsible for the care and education of the very young.

See the Additional Support section in your Online Companion for more information on child care statistics.

Families make choices about employment and care for their children in a context that is shaped by public policies and colored by public opinion. Debates over whether the government should increase funding for child care or do more to help parents stay home with their children reflect tensions among strongly held ideas about family life, work, and the role of government. (Sylvester, 2001, p. 53)

A synthesis of public opinion polls about early caregiving, which focused on attitudinal positions regarding responsibility and involvement, revealed the following, according to Sylvester (2001):

- The American public believes that parents should be the primary influence in their children's lives, and that it is best if mothers can be home to care for the very young.
- The public also values family self-sufficiency and understands that low-income families may need child care assistance to balance child-rearing and employment responsibilities.
- However, skepticism about the appropriateness of government involvement in family life limits public support for proposals that the government act directly to provide or improve child care. (p. 53)

This pervasive attitude, in combination with costs, as well as comfort levels, has kept the numbers down in child care centers and programs and has made it difficult to study the effects of child care on our youngest children. Limited numbers result in less breadth and depth in studies and therefore often make "significance" in findings difficult. However, Phillips and Adams (2001) document that "early exposure to child care can foster a children's learning and enhance their lives, or it can leave them at risk for troubled relations. The outcome depends largely on the quality of the child care setting" (p. 35).

Initial Research on Childcare

Abecedarian Study

One of the longest-running studies that looked specifically at infant and toddler care in a center facility was the Abecedarian Study. The study began in 1971 and ran until 1985, although follow-up evaluation continues. Children (ages 3–6 months) from low-income families received full-time, high-quality educational intervention from infancy through age 5 years. This really was a unique undertaking, since center care for infants and toddlers was relatively nonexistent at that time. There were 111 children involved in the study: 57 children received quality child care services and the control group of 54 did not. The program's key components included appropriate adult–child ratios, ongoing professional development, salaries for staff based on the public school pay scale, and an individualized curriculum focusing on the social, emotional, and cognitive (especially language) domains. The curriculum was designed to enhance children's abilities through learning games.

Much has changed in the last thirty years in regard to infant and toddler care. Now, even very young children arrive at child care centers on a bus, not in the family car.

After three years, there was a significant difference in the average IQ between the two groups and, unlike many programs that began intervention at age 4, the effects of higher IQ between the two groups has held over the years. The children's progress was monitored by follow-up studies at age 12, 15, and 21. The major findings demonstrate that important and long-lasting benefits were associated with the high-quality early childhood program (Ramey, Campbell, & Blair, 1998).

The High/Scope Perry Preschool Project Study

Although the High/Scope Perry Preschool Project Study did not focus on infants and toddlers, it is a classic in the field of early childhood. From 1962 to 1967, subjects ranging in age from 3 to 4, were randomly divided between two groups. One group received a high-quality preschool program based on the High/Scope curriculum and philosophy while a control group received no preschool education. In the study's most recent follow-up, forty years later, 97 percent of the study's participants were interviewed. The data demonstrated that those who had received the preschool program were more likely to have graduated from high school, to have a job, had higher earnings, and had committed fewer crimes (Schweinhardt, 2005).

For more information on these and other landmarks studies, consult the Additional Support section of your Online Companion.

Other Studies

- *The Early Childhood Longitudinal Study, Birth Cohort (ECLS-B)* study is being conducted by The National Center for Education Statistics in the United States, the primary federal agency for collecting and analyzing data that are related to education both within the United States and from other nations. The ECLS-B selected a national sample of 10,221 children from the 4 million born in the year 2001. The study will provide national data on: children's status at birth and thereafter; children's transitions to nonparental care; early education programs; school experience; and growth and development through fifth grade. In addition, the study will also evaluate hypotheses regarding specific areas, including skills and abilities in various domains, the effect of early health care and status on later learning capabilities, a host of child care issues, and the impact of a father's participation in child-rearing on later learning.

- *The National Early Intervention Longitudinal Study (NEILS)* is a study following 3,338 children with disabilities, or at risk for disabilities, and their families from the initial point of entering the early intervention system into early elementary school. The questions being assessed are: Who are the children and families receiving services? What services are provided? What are the costs? What outcomes are experienced? How do outcomes vary?

- *The NICHD Study of Early Child Care (SECC)* is a comprehensive longitudinal study initiated by The National Institute of Child Health and Human Development (NICHD) in 1989 to answer the many questions about the relationship between child care experiences and children's developmental outcomes. In 1991, the study enrolled a very diverse sample of children, at 1 month of age, and their families in ten different locations across the United States. The NICHD SECC has a detailed study design that takes into account many variables, including characteristics of the child care and the family environment. Researchers are assessing children's development using multiple methods (trained observers, interviewers, questionnaires, and testing) and measuring social, emotional, intellectual, and language development, as well as behavioral problems and adjustment, and physical health. Researchers are measuring the children's development at frequent intervals from birth through adolescence. In 1991, the researchers enrolled 1,364 children in the study. Phase I of the study was conducted from 1991 to 1994, following the children from birth to age 3 years. Phase II of the study was conducted between 1995 and 2000 to follow the 1,226 children continuing to participate from age 3 through their second year in school. Phase III of the study was conducted between 2000 and 2005 to follow over 1,100 of the children through their seventh year in school. Phase IV, which is currently being conducted, will follow over 1,000 of the original families through age 15. (NICHD Web site—Summary)

- *What Grown-Ups Understand About Child Development: A National Benchmark Survey* is a landmark study of 3,000 American adults (including 1,066 parents of children aged newborn to 6) sponsored by Zero to Three and BRIO, and conducted by DYG, Inc., a recognized leader in the field of social and marketing research. In June and July of 2000, the survey assessed what the American public knew about early childhood development issues and government policy regarding children and child care. "The fundamental purpose of the survey was to measure the level of accurate knowledge American adults had about child development issues—with particular emphasis on the intellectual, emotional, and social development of children aged newborn to six" (DYG, Inc., 2000, p. 2).

Other Initiatives/Nonprofit Organizations

Early Head Start

In 1994, when Congress reauthorized the Head Start Act, it created Early Head Start [EHS]. This program is one of the federal government's most visible commitments of funds for low-income families with infants and toddlers. Its mission is to promote healthy prenatal outcomes for pregnant women, enhance the development of very young children, and promote healthy functioning in low-income families with infants and toddlers. The program has grown rapidly, from 68 programs in 1995 to 635 programs in 2001. By 2002, Early Head Start served 70,000 babies, toddlers, and pregnant women through 708 community-based programs, only 3 percent of the eligible population (Oser & Cohen, 2003). The EHS programs are administered by the Head Start Bureau, the regional offices of the Administration for Children and Families, and the American Indian/Alaska Native Programs Branch.

 See the Additional Support section in your Online Companion for a description of the National Evaluation of the EHS program, as well as an outline of the four guiding principles, or cornerstones, of program quality. These are available from *The Future of Children* publication.

No Child Left Behind is a well-known federally funded education reform act, but its focus is on older children. There is great controversy surrounding *NCLB* for a variety of reasons, including use of standardized tests with young children, accountability standards that are not equal or fair, lack of funding to complete the required tasks, and the undermining of the public education system. *NCLB* was one of the few education initiatives that received an increase in funding for 2005–2006. Compare that to funding for Early Head Start. Initially, 4 percent of Head Start funding went to EHS, but funding was not increased for 2005–2006. Given all that is known about the critical importance of the first three years of children's lives, it is unconscionable not to increase the funding for a program that could make a significant difference in the lives of many of our nation's children.

Child Care and the U.S. Military

Every day the U.S. Department of Defense (DoD) uses 297,451 diapers; prepares 594,902 servings of "liquid baby rations"; issues purchase orders for cribs, strollers, and rocking chairs; and sings thousands of lullaby "cadences." It was not always that way. The profile of the U.S. Armed Forces has changed from that of single members living in barracks to one of a diverse volunteer workforce with growing numbers of female service members, working spouses, and sole and dual military parents. Child care has become a workforce issue vital to U.S. Army, Navy, Air Force, and Marine families and to the military mission. The military child care program is truly a Cinderella story. At one time, it was known as the "ghetto of American child care," with unsafe and unsuitable facilities, weak standards that were sporadically enforced, staff who were poorly trained and compensated (with turnover rates at some centers as high as 300 percent), and a general lack of oversight and attention from military officials. In the past dozen years, however, military child care has achieved a remarkable turnaround. Today it is acclaimed as a model for the nation and described as the "gold standard for child care" (Lucas, 2001, p. 129).

NAEYC has accredited many child care sites located on military bases. The U.S. military made the simple decision that no one could afford quality child care, therefore it had to be subsidized. The child care model the military chose to create focused attention and resources on three cornerstones—quality, affordability, and availability—each documented in measurable outcomes. Currently, one-half of the children in military child care programs are under age 3, and the care they offers to infants and toddlers receives high marks for the cornerstone indicators. Campbell, Appelbaum, Martinson, and Martin (2000) state that "if a child care system as deficient as that confronting the military a decade ago could be turned around so dramatically—and by an institution as inherently conservative as the military—then surely similar success can be achieved in the civilian world" (p. 45) in order to expand access to high-quality, affordable child care to everyone. The lessons learned by the military in offering affordable, available, and quality child care were:

1. Do not be daunted by the task—the child care system can be improved.
2. Recognize the seriousness of the problem and acknowledge that inaction will have negative effects on both the workforce and the well-being of children.
3. Improve child care by enforcing standards, raising compensation levels for child care providers, and assisting the accreditation process.
4. Keep child care affordable through subsidies.
5. Expand the availability of child care.
6. Commit the resources necessary to get the job done.

A follow-up report conducted by the National Women's Law Center (Pomper, Blank, Campbell, & Schulman, 2005) has found that the military:

- continues to strengthen its accreditation system, now encouraging family child care providers to seek accreditation;
- has modestly improved fee scales for the lowest income families and has significantly expanded subsidies to family child care providers;
- has increased the number of slots available for child care and has plans to continue that expansion; and
- has dedicated more resources for specific appropriations for meeting the needs of child care for their personnel.

 See the Additional Support section in your Online Companion for more information on the military model for child care from *The Future of Children* publication, as well as information from the National Women's Law Center.

Healthy Start, Grow Smart

This effort was initiated by First Lady Laura Bush in order to help families learn about how important it is to read to their babies and to encourage children to play with books and

Of note is the fact that in 2003, "the national average wage for a full-time, full-year child care worker was $8.47 per hour, or $17, 610" (Pomper, Blank, Campbell, & Schulman, 2005, p. 13), while the entry level wage of a military caregiver in 2004 was between $9.34 and $13.24 per hour ($19, 483–$27, 635 annually).

As of this writing, Even Start had a proposed $25 million cut to its 2005–2006 funding year, although the Bush administration's budget had requested its elimination. It is interesting to note that at the same time the White House sponsored an initiative to help families understand the critical importance of reading and literacy (*Healthy Start, Grow Smart*), the Bush administration cut funding for a proven successful literacy program that has the potential to help lift families out of poverty.

develop essential skills before they enter school. Research on language acquisition and brain development shows that the groundwork for reading begins from the day a child is born (Neuman, Copple, & Bredekamp, 2000). The *Healthy Start, Grow Smart* magazine series provides activities designed to stimulate infant brain development and build skills that children will need once they start school. Ideas are included for fun, age-appropriate activities that focus on reading, language, and learning, and also include health and safety information for families. Printed in English and Spanish, the magazine is available every month for the first 12 months of a baby's life. Local family assistance clinics and state health and human services agencies are working to distribute the magazines to new mothers who might not otherwise have access to this vital information. However, the entire series is available on the Web site to anyone who is interested.

Even Start Family Literacy Program

Even Start Family Literacy Programs are school–community partnerships that attempt to break the cycle of poverty and illiteracy by integrating early childhood education, adult literacy, adult basic education, and parenting education into a unified approach that:

- enriches language development, extends learning, and supports educational success for children birth to age 7 and their parents;
- provides literacy services of sufficient hours and duration to make positive changes in a family;
- provides integrated services so children and their parents learn together to develop habits of lifelong learning; and
- supports families committed to education and to economic independence.

Reach Out and Read

Reach Out and Read (ROR) is a program that promotes early literacy by bringing new books and advice about the importance of reading aloud into the pediatric exam room. Doctors and nurses give new books to children at each well child visit from 6 months of age to 5 years, and accompany these books with developmentally appropriate advice to parents about reading aloud with their child. The ROR program model is based on research that shows a connection between the frequency of sharing books with babies, toddlers, and young children, and enhanced language development. Since 1989, ROR pediatricians have been prescribing books and reading aloud for their young patients, with a special focus on children growing up in poverty. ROR-trained doctors and nurses are currently promoting pediatric literacy at more than 2,400 hospitals, health centers, and private pediatric practices. A national, nonprofit literacy organization, Reach Out and Read is affiliated with the Department of Pediatrics, Boston Medical Center, Boston University School of Medicine.[2]

United Way Efforts

The United Way is a nonprofit organization that activates and coordinates community resources to make the greatest possible human impact. The mission of United Way is to improve people's lives by mobilizing the caring power of communities. For the past decade, the United Way has been involved with programs nationwide that help focus attention on the cognitive, emotional, and care needs of young children and the critical importance of mobilizing the energy and resources of families, communities, and decision makers toward achieving the goal of improved services and lives.

- The United Way's *Success By 6* is the nation's largest network of early childhood coalitions. The project helps business, government, and nonprofit sectors collaborate in new ways to give young children the best start in life. More than 350 *Success By 6* coalitions are currently helping communities and states focus on the issues that are relevant to early childhood development. Efforts help raise awareness of the needs in

2. Reprinted by permission by Reach Out and Read, Inc., and used and reproduced with the express written permission of Reach Out and Read, Inc.

local communities, which, in turn, often improves quality of and access to services. Another important goal is advocating for change in public policies, especially on issues involving early learning and child care.

Success By 6 Core Beliefs:

1. The period of life from birth to age 6 offers a crucial window of opportunity to establish a foundation for a child's future success.
2. Children birth to 6 depend on their parents and caregivers for early learning experiences that prepare them to succeed in school—and life.
3. It's up to all of us to create communities and systems that support young children, their early learning, and their families.

   • United Way's *Success By 6* has collaborated with the Ad Council and Civitas to promote *Born Learning,* a project that is termed a "public engagement" campaign. *Born Learning* provides "doable" action steps for parents and caregivers to help prepare young children for school. The activities have been designed to make learning fun, easy, and accomplished in everyday interactions.

The Additional Support section in your Online Companion highlights *Five Key Ideas for New Parents* identified by Born Learning.

Mind in the Making

Since the early 1990s, the Families and Work Institute has worked with many groups to increase public awareness of the importance of the early years. Although the general public is increasingly aware that children are born learning, there still is little agreement about what really constitutes learning. Through a partnership with New Screen Concepts, the Families and Work Institute is creating a national communications initiative on learning. They have been compiling the most compelling research on learning and on how children learn best, beginning with the early years. This research will be presented to the public through numerous channels of information, including radio PSAs in Spanish and English, television, video, educational materials for families and caregivers, and special information for college and university early childhood courses, just to name a few.

ZERO TO THREE

ZERO TO THREE, a nonprofit organization, defines its mission as follows: to promote the healthy development of the nation's infants and toddlers by supporting and strengthening families, communities, and those who work on their behalf. They are dedicated to advancing current knowledge; promoting beneficial policies and practices; communicating research and best practices to a wide variety of audiences; and providing training, technical assistance, and leadership development.[3]

Children's Defense Fund

The mission of the Children's Defense Fund is to Leave No Child Behind—a saying that sounds somewhat familiar, but has been used by CDF since its inception in 1973. It is a private, nonprofit organization supported by foundation and corporate grants, as well as individual donations. The vision of Leave No Child Behind is to ensure every child a *Healthy Start,* a *Head Start,* a *Fair Start,* a *Safe Start,* and a *Moral Start* in life, and successful passage to adulthood, with the help of caring families and communities. CDF provides a strong, effective voice for all the children of the United States who cannot vote, lobby, or speak for themselves. They pay particular attention to the needs of poor and minority children and those with disabilities. CDF educates the nation about the needs of children and encourages preventive investment before they get sick or into trouble, drop out of school, or suffer family breakdown. A yearly publication entitled *The State of America's Children* presents data on numerous issues that affect the lives of children and youth in the United States.[4]

---

3. Reprinted with permission from ZERO TO THREE.

4. Reprinted with permission from The Children's Defense Fund. Copyright 2005 Children's Defense Fund.

Can there be any doubt that these are minds in the making?

Brain Research

Over the last fifteen years, **neuroscience**, the study of the brain and behavior has contributed significantly to the field of early childhood education. The new information that neuroscience brings to early childhood development has influenced major findings in the United States, Canada, and the United Kingdom, with recommendations for new policies that reflect the importance of this period of life. In the past, practitioners would have to observe behaviors and infer what or how a baby was thinking. Now, technology that utilizes a brain scan (PET) allows us to "see" how the brain is functioning from the inside (Chugani, 1998). Research results confirm what those of us in the early childhood field have always known—that the first years of life are critical because they lay the foundation for all later learning. The evidence clearly underscores that there are large and long-lasting effects on the development of the brain, which are forged from the early life experiences and the child-rearing environment children encounter from the moment of birth (Bailey & Symons, 2001; National Scientific Council on the Developing Child, 2005; Ramey & Ramey, 2004; Shonkoff & Phillips, 2000; Shore, 2003). Some of the research has dramatically altered thinking about how the brain functions. Of special significance are the following crucial points:

neuroscience

interdisciplinary study of the brain and behavior

- Our brain is a social brain, and interactions with real people and real things are critical to its growth.
- Early interactions directly affect how the brain is wired and have a decisive impact on how people develop, learn, and regulate their emotions.
- The human brain has a remarkable capacity to change, and although the brain always learns, there are "windows of opportunities" or prime times for absorbing specific knowledge and skills.

These new advances in technology have increased our knowledge of the brain, including an improved understanding of the basic cell structure of the brain—neurons and neural pathways—as well as a better visualization of the tasks handled by specific areas of the brain, otherwise known as brain hemisphere specialization (Kolb & Whishaw, 2001; Schore, 2001). Most neurons are in place before a child is born, approximately 100 billion of them (Shore, 2003), while experience creates the conditions for the ever-increasing and dense synaptic connections. When a neural pathway is not utilized, it eventually gets pruned (or disconnected), so that inevitably that particular avenue of learning is no longer in existence. This happens over and over, since a human being cannot possibly maintain all neural pathways. Ramey and Ramey (2004), however, do point out that "children who learn more and who learn better are truly more intelligent and capable" (p. 8). This speaks once again to the importance of providing optimal conditions for care and education early in life. Much of the research has helped delineate the most favorable environmental conditions that support optimal development for a child's brain. Key findings include the following:

attachment

the positive emotional relationship that develops between two individuals—between adult and child

- breast milk/breast-feeding; the best food for optimal development
- healthy **attachment**: a strong, stable, and nurturing relationship with at least one adult that includes interaction, loving touch
- responsive care: care that responds to the child's needs and signals, establishes communication, and helps build a child's self-concept and self-esteem
- protection from harm: a childhood as free as possible from negative physical and mental stress; in other words, the opportunity to grow and flourish in a safe and healthy environment (Bertrand et al., 2001; McCormick Tribune Foundation, 1997).

These four components reinforce what we already appreciate about the psychological and irreducible needs of children. It is good to know that advances in science underscore the theories that have developed from other branches of child study. What is challenging is that there is little compromise in those four essential conditions for healthy brain development. As parents and professionals working in partnership for very young children, we need to ensure that these needs are met. According to the Families Work Institute, *Parent Action* (formerly the *I Am Your Child Campaign*), and the Canadian Child Care Federation, all of which reviewed the brain research findings, providing responsive care requires the caregiver, at a minimum, to:

- be warm, loving, and responsive in order to create conditions for attachment;
- watch for the child's own individual cues and signals and learn to anticipate when it is time for a cuddle, rest, or new activity;
- establish rituals and routines in order to create a stable and predictable environment;
- encourage safe exploration and play that will expose the child to new experiences and activities;
- watch for moments to extend the child's skills;
- recognize that each child is unique; and
- express affection and cheer specific accomplishments.

However, what has to be acknowledged is the reality that not all children live in environments which are conducive to optimal brain growth. We have learned what types of experiences can negatively impede the brain from growing to its full potential (Bailey & Symond, 2004; Bruer, 2004; Perry & Pollard, 1997; Shore, 2003). This would include such factors as poor environments, inadequate attachment figures, abuse and neglect, and poor learning experiences and environments. Research documents that **cortisol**, a stress hormone, is often released during these situations, and can negatively impact brain growth. A sustained release of too much stress hormone can lead to problems with memory and self-regulation (Bronson, 2000; Gallagher, 2005; Watamura, Donzella, Alwin, & Gunnar, 2003), destroy brain cells, and affect the formation of synaptic connections, or brain circuitry (Gunnar & Donzella, 2002; Louge, 2000).

cortisol

a hormone that is released by the body while experiencing stress. Research findings indicate that too much cortisol has the potential to negatively impact synapse development in the brain

However, research also documents that responsive and sensitive caregiving in quality environments can help reduce both the release and impact of stress hormones and, in fact, the relationships children have in the early years of their lives with their caregivers can have a significant effect on regulating stress hormone (National Scientific Council on the Developing Child, 2005). Children react differently to stress because they are unique individuals, but caregivers need to be mindful of the significance of creating an environment that provides a safe haven for children: a place where they can feel secure and cared about; a place where they can be independent, curious, and accepted. In addition, "research on cortisol and young children supports guidelines for developmentally appropriate practice in teaching to enhance development and learning" (Gallagher, 2005, p. 15), so providers need to ensure that best practices are adhered to in order to offset the negative effects of stress.

Dr. Bruce Perry, a leading researcher into the environment and its relationship to brain development, gives us additional substantive information for reflection. He and co-workers at the Child Trauma Program at Baylor College of Medicine have studied the impact of neglect and trauma on the neurobiology of over 1,000 abused and neglected children. In one study, 20 children who had been raised in globally understimulating environments—children who were rarely touched or spoken to and who had little opportunity to explore and experiment with toys—were examined with sophisticated new brain-imaging techniques and other measures of brain growth. The children were found to have brains that were physically 20–30 percent smaller than most children their age, and in over half the cases, parts of the children's brains appeared to have literally wasted away (Ounce of Prevention Fund, 1996). Dr. Perry believes that children are not resilient; they are malleable. He defines the term *resilient* as "marked by the ability to recover readily, as from misfortune" and *malleable* as "capable of being shaped, formed . . . or able to adjust to changing circumstances; adaptable" (Perry, 1997, p.124). Therefore, in the mature brain, adverse experiences can *influence*, but in the developing brain they actually *organize* the neural system. The first three years of life are not the only important period of life for development, but they are foundationally important. Perry (1997), citing contributions from other researchers, argues:

> We need to change our child-rearing practices. We need to change the malignant and destructive view that children are the property of their biological parents. Human beings evolved not as individuals, but as communities. Despite Western conceptualizations, the smallest functional biological unit of humankind is not the individual—it is the clan. No individual, no single parent–child dyad, no nuclear family could survive alone. We survived and evolved as clans—interdependent socially, emotionally, and biologically. Children *belong* to the community, they are *entrusted* to parents. American society, and its communities, have failed parents and children alike. We have not provided parents with the information and resources to optimize their children's potential and, when parents fail, we act too late and with impotence to protect and care for maltreated children. (p. 144)

What does all this mean for early childhood educators and families? In essence, it supports the belief that the quality of relationships with infants and toddlers is fundamentally important to their current and their future development. The scientific evidence only strengthens the argument for provision of the highest quality care for all children. The concept of responsive caregiving—which is central to this book—is also the required approach, according to the brain research findings. We need to learn to look for these cues more carefully, provide more appropriate experiences, follow the child's lead, and engage with each child in a positive, meaningful way.

As research continues, information about the myriad influences the brain has on our uniqueness and learning abilities will keep being discovered. Remember to review the information on critical and sensitive periods of brain development discussed earlier in the chapter, and use the Additional Support section in your Online Companion for more information on the brain.

The early childhood years are critical, but they also must be viewed in total context. Ultimately, positive developmental outcomes depend upon both the individual and the collective nurturance, strength, and wisdom of all who touch these precious lives.

This section has discussed only a very small number of efforts that are being made on behalf of children. Findings from studies, continuing research, and organizations focused on early childhood issues help add to the body of knowledge that we share about infants, toddlers, and families. What an inspiring time to be part of the early childhood profession!

WHAT COMES NEXT?

As you read and acquire more information, remember that information is not the same as knowledge; you need to make the information your own—construct your own understanding through combining information with experience.

Before moving on to the next chapters of the book, which outline specific growth and behavioral changes of infants and young children, pause to think about the material presented in the first three chapters, what you have learned from this material, and what you would like to learn next. Activity 3.2 on your CD-ROM provides the outline of a learning plan, which you should now take the time to complete.

SUMMARY

Chapter 3 began with a discussion of the physical (basic), psychological, and cognitive needs of children that are required in order to survive, as well as grow and develop. However, for optimal development, children need even more than these; They have irreducible needs, identified by Brazelton and Greenspan.

We frequently divide aspects of the child's development into domains, to make studying infants and toddlers more manageable. These are artificial constructs, but they enable us to look closely at a child's development. These domains interact dynamically, so that every child progresses in different ways. Without the concept of domains, we may see the child's holistic development more clearly, but we can be overwhelmed by how much is going on simultaneously. Special attention was paid to the physical, language, cognitive, emotional, social, and moral domains of development. The contributions of Piaget and Vygotsky to the understanding of some of these developmental areas were highlighted.

There are some principles that govern how development occurs. Appreciating these is particularly helpful because we can then understand what drives the developmental process. Research into infant and toddler behavior and biology has provided us with some understanding of how the process of development happens. However, the way that development is explained differs among different schools or traditions of thought. We need to become acquainted with very young children to learn about them, but we also need to apply some of the theories that are considered reliable, so that we can test their applicability. Comparing explanations of development can be confusing, but it assists the educator in understanding the infant and toddler's needs and how they can be met.

This chapter concludes with a discussion of some of the ongoing research, initiatives, and organizations that focus on early childhood issues. Of special interest to the early childhood profession are the brain research findings. They support the beliefs of our profession, but also demonstrate how crucial early experience is for the optimal development of children. This new information, along with years of other theory and research, only helps to strengthen our position in regard to the necessity of providing responsive and respectful care for young children.

A word of encouragement! The beginning student may be overwhelmed by the terminology used in this chapter: accommodation, assimilation, attachment, autonomy, bonding, cephalocaudal development, cortisol, developmental diversity, ecological system, failure to thrive, irreducible needs, maturation, mental schemes, myelination, normative profiles, object permanence, resilience, self-regulation, symbolic thought, temperament, and zone of proximal development. These are just some of the terms. Do not throw your hands up in despair. You will hear these terms used over and over again, not just in this course, but in many more to follow. Try to use the terminology and to connect it to the observations you make at your practicum sites. These connections will help you visualize the experience and make the terminology more meaningful.

DISCUSSION QUESTIONS

1. Consider your own development. If you categorized it according to domains, how much would this help you understand its complexities? Also, how much would it help you to appreciate "who you are"?

2. When you see toddlers playing with new sensory materials, how is their learning occurring?

3. Children's hunger, deprivation, and abandonment are disturbing. How might you predict the future for such children if you knew that, from today, they were going to receive appropriate nutrition, medical treatment, stimulation, and lots of love?

4. Research work leads us to better understand children's development. What ethical limits should there be on experimentation, observation, and other types of research?

5. What types of information from research about infants and toddlers might be helpful or interesting to you? How would you go about studying those issues?

ADDITIONAL RESOURCES

Further Reading

Bardige, B. (2005). *At a loss for words: How America is failing our children and what we can do about it.* USA: Temple University Press.

Beatty, N. (1992). *Heart start: The emotional foundations of school readiness.* Washington, DC: Zero to Three.

Berk, L. (2002). *Infants and children: Pre-natal through middle childhood.* Needham Heights, MA: Allyn & Bacon.

Bertrand, J., et al. (2001). *Nourish, nurture and neurodevelopment—Neurodevelopment research: Implications for caregiver practice.* Toronto: Canadian Child Care Federation.

Brazelton, T., & Greenspan, S. (2000). *The irreducible needs of children: What every child must have to grow, learn, and flourish.* Cambridge, MA: Perseus Publishing.

Carey, W. B., & McDevitt, S. C. (1995). *Coping with children's temperament: A guide for professionals.* USA: Basic Books.

Elkind, D. (2005). Early childhood amnesia: Reaffirming children's need for developmentally appropriate programs. *Young Children, 60*(4), 38–40.

Elliot, L. (1999). *What's going on in there? How the brain and mind develop in the first five years of life.* New York: Bantam Books.

Fabes, R., & Martin, C. (2003). *Exploring child development* (2nd ed.). Boston: Allyn & Bacon.

Fogel, A. (2001). *Infancy: Infant, family, and society* (4th ed.). St. Paul, MN: West.

Gallagher, K.C. (2005). Brain research and early childhood development: A primer for developmentally appropriate practice. *Young Children, 60*(4), 12–20.

Gopnik, A., Meltzoff, A. N., & Kuhl, P. K. (1999). *The scientist in the crib: What early learning tells us about the mind.* USA: Perennial.

Greenberg, P. (1991). *Character development: Encouraging self-esteem & self-discipline in infants, toddlers, & two-year olds.* Washington, DC: NAEYC.

Hart, B., & Risley, R. (1995). *Meaningful differences in the everyday experience of young American children.* Baltimore, MD: Paul H. Brookes Publishing Company.

Ramey, C. T., & Ramey, S. L (1999). *Right from the start: Building your child's foundation for life, Birth to 18 months.* USA: Goddard Press.

Shore, R. (2003). *Rethinking the brain: New insights into early development.* New York: Families and Work Institute.

Snow, C. W. (1998). *Infant development* (2nd ed.). Englewood Cliffs, NJ: Prentice Hall.

Useful Videos/CDs

Charting Growth: Assessment
   30 minutes
Cooing, Crying, Cuddling: Infant Brain Development.
   28 minutes
Laughing, Learning, Loving: Toddler Brain Development.
   28 minutes
NAEYC Accreditation: The Next Era.
   This is a toolkit with a PowerPoint Presentation
   Available from NAEYC 1-800-424-2460 or www.naeyc.org
The Secret Life of the Brain. Available from PBS
   http://www.pbs.org
   Click on Science and Nature, click on Health & Medicine, click on Secret Life of the Brain.
   This is a five-part video, but the first two are of special interest to those who care for infants and toddlers.

Useful Web Sites

The Consultative Group on Early Childhood Care and Development
   www.ecdgroup.com
All you need to know about psychology
   psychology.about.com
ECE Web Guide
   www.ecewebguide.com
The Human Early Learning Partnership (HELP)
   www.earlylearning.ubc.ca
Better Beginnings/Better Futures
   http://www.beststart.org
ERIC Clearinghouse on Elementary and Early Childhood Education
   ericeece.org
American Academy of Pediatrics
   www.aap.org
Child Care Information Exchange—Workshop on Brain Findings
   www.ccie.com
Children's Defense Fund
   http://www.childrensdefense.org
Early Childhood/Brain Development
   http://www.communitycollaboration.net
   Click on Enter, click on Health, Disability, Early Childhood and Brain Development and Human Biology, click on Early Childhood/Brain Development.
Even Start
   http://www.evenstart.org
Families and Work Institute—PowerPoint CD-ROM Presentation on Brain Development
   www.familiesandwork.org
Healthy Start, Grow Smart
   http://www.whitehouse.gov
   Click on Education, click on Healthy Start, click on Grow Smart.
Mind in the Making
   http://mindinthemaking.org
McCormick Tribune Foundation (*What Every Child Needs,* video, handouts)
   http://www.xnet.com
Parent Action—(Former *I Am Your Child Foundation,* videos, books, handouts)
   www.iamyourchild.org
Reach Out and Read
   http://www.reachoutandread.org
The Future of Children
   http://www.futureofchildren.org
ZERO TO THREE
   http://www.zerotothree.org

CHAPTER 4

New Beginnings: Newborn Infants

Off to a healthy start, this baby weighs in at 8 pounds 12.2 ounces. No longer do we view babies as helpless creatures. Instead, science and technology have enabled us to understand that babies are a lot more receptive and aware right from birth than we used to believe. All of their senses are active, even though some are in the early stages of development, and they are "primed" to learn from day one.

LEARNING OUTCOMES

After reading and studying this chapter, you should be able to:

- identify the observable characteristics of newborn infants
- explain the significance of newborn infant behaviors in a development context
- recognize and respond to the developmental diversity of neonates
- respond to the neonate's health, safety, and development with appropriate protection and caregiving
- discuss the need for research into infant abilities and how that may shape the caregiving strategies of parents and educators
- develop strategies to work with parents as partners in the care and education of their children

WHY DO WE NEED TO LEARN ABOUT NEWBORNS?

neonatal

the period of time around the birth of the infant—usually the first six weeks of life

neonate

the infant at birth and for the first few weeks of life

The period from the cutting of the umbilical cord through the first two, four, or even six weeks is the **neonatal** stage, sometimes referred to as the postpartum period. In this chapter we consider the newborn to be a **neonate** for approximately the first six weeks of life. The events of birth and early life experience lead us to have sensitivity for each baby. Understanding neonatal development helps us to set the stage for appreciating later progressions.

SCENE

A couple about to experience parenthood for the first time, discuss their concerns about the coming baby:

Conner explains his nervousness about having their first baby: "I'm the youngest child in my family and I've not really had the opportunity even to hold a baby, never mind look after one 24 hours a day." "That's not my worry," says his partner, Dahlia. "I just want the baby to be all right. I've read all those magazines about all the things that can go wrong. Just last night I saw on the box [television] a program about Siamese twins." Conner tries to reassure her, "The chances of that happening are so small we shouldn't even think about it." Then, "Let's try to think positively," Conner suggests.

Adults tend to have a few common reactions to newborn babies. "I'm afraid I'll drop her" or "He cries all the time" are perhaps the most frequently heard remarks. But how accurate are they? Newborns are, of course, **vulnerable** in a lot of ways, but they are probably more resilient than you might imagine. Think of the tough challenge they have gone through to be born. They can't be all that fragile. And although it may sometimes seem that they cry all the time, babies sleep for some of the night and during the day; even when they're awake there are times when they're not crying.

Wet and slippery when born, you might have thought that babies are always washed and dried before being handed to the parents. Not so; the **vernix**, a white waxy stuff covering the baby, may be left to dry and is likely to flake off. The baby may not look quite as you expected!

Many people think that babies can't do very much because they haven't had time to learn. Others know that they can show a wide range of automatic movements, called **reflexes**, including the ability to suck, grasp, and step.

The way the baby looks may cause you to wonder whether the newborn really belongs to the parents. Babies' skin tone and hair color may differ at first from those of their parents. Skin may be lighter in color or different in texture from that of the parents. In time the coloring will alter, and we are more likely to see a family resemblance.

You may notice that the infant's head seems oddly shaped—this is a result of the birth process. Depending upon whether newborns are premature, post-mature, or on time, their appearance is likely to be a little different. Perhaps you have noticed that average-sized babies have some roundness to their bodies because of their stored fat. Premature or low-birth-weight babies may be smaller, and they are also likely to be less filled out.

vulnerable

susceptible to physical or emotional injury, especially at an early age

vernix

a protective, creamy white, waxy substance that covers some of the skin of the newborn baby

reflex

an inborn, automatic response to stimulation

WHAT TO LOOK FOR

You may be wondering why you need to be aware of the development of newborns. Such young babies are rarely seen at child care centers. However, it is important to understand what unfolds after birth so that you can appreciate how rapid and complex development is. In addition, if you are not a parent already, it is likely that many of you may become one at some future time. This information will help you gain a realistic perspective on a neonate's behavior and characteristics.

Born into a Family

For most families, welcoming a new baby is a time of great joy and fulfillment. Parents may behave in ways not typical of their usual style. They will spend time with their babies and enjoy a sense of the miraculous when they look at them. However, some parents are slower than others at falling in love with their babies. Reasons for this may include hormonal changes and trouble adjusting to the enormous impact the new baby is having on their lifestyle. Once they have some time together to get to know each other, almost all babies find a way into the hearts of their mothers and fathers. Belsky and Kelly (1994) identified six abilities of parents that can help make the transition to parenthood a positive one. These include being able to: give up individual goals and work as a team; resolve differences about sharing tasks; handle stress successfully; understand that the good elements of a partnership will relate to different things after the baby; and communicate in ways that nurture their partnership.

BOX 4.1

A chief finding from **"What Grown-Ups Understand About Child Development: A National Benchmark Survey,"** sponsored in part by ZERO TO THREE, was that parents' knowledge about child development is limited. "They are more likely to seek information very early in their child's life (from birth to 8 months) than later . . . which suggests that it is important to get information on child development to new—and expectant—parents as early as possible" (Melmed, 1998, p. 245). An additional survey conducted in 2000 demonstrated that "while adults are well informed about many areas of child development there are significant information gaps—gaps that carry with them very real implications for how we raise and interact with our children in America today" (DYG, Inc., 2000, p. 4).

 Use the Additional Support section in your Online Companion to read about some of the startling findings of this study, including:

- 29 percent of all adults do not understand that brain development can be impacted very early on.
- 61 percent of parents of young children condone spanking as a regular form of punishment.
- 64 percent of all adults incorrectly believe that educational TV is beneficial to intellectual development.
- 44 percent of parents of young children incorrectly believe picking up a 3-month-old every time he cries will spoil a child (DYG, 2001).

Another factor to consider is that not only do parents have to refocus their goals and redefine their relationships after a child is born, they also actually perceive themselves differently (self-concept) because of the interactions they experience with a child as she grows and develops. Galinsky (1987) described six stages of parenthood that parallel a child's developmental stages. These stages reflect different tasks parents must accomplish as the dynamics of their family evolve. As caregivers, we must acknowledge that all families need to be supported as they make the transition to parenthood. If they are helped as they develop these necessary skills, they are more likely to become effective parents and meet the needs of their infants. Consult your Online Companion to review the six stages.

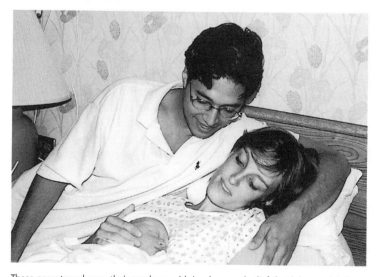

These parents welcome their newborn with joy, love, and relief that labor and delivery are over. Now the work of building a relationship awaits them. This newborn will be an active participant in helping shape his parents' reaction to him.

Growth and Physical Characteristics

At birth, infants are examined for an early assessment of their general health. The first assessment is likely to be the Apgar Scale, or Apgar Score (Apgar, 1953; Lamb, Bornstein, & Teti, 2002), which rates a baby's <u>A</u>ppearance (color), <u>P</u>ulse (heart rate), <u>G</u>rimace (reflex irritability or responsiveness), <u>A</u>ctivity (muscle tone), and <u>R</u>espiration (respiratory effort) with a number between zero and 2 (2 being the strongest rating). The numbers are totaled and a score of 10 is considered a perfect score. The assessment is conducted at 1 minute and at 5 minutes by the medical personnel. The 1-minute Apgar score helps the practitioner decide whether the baby needs immediate medical attention, and usually a baby with a score of 6 or under will receive some sort of medical intervention. The 5-minute Apgar score helps the medical personnel decide on the progression demonstrated by the child. At least 75 percent of babies receive scores of between 7 and 10 by the 5-minute interval (Lamb, Bornstein, & Teti, 2002). Further checks of these functions will continue, but in a less formalized way.

Size

At birth, the baby is, on average, about 18 to 21 inches long and weighs between 6.2 and 9.2 pounds. Boys tend to be little longer and heavier than girls, but the differences are small. Although a little weight is lost in the first few days, this is usually regained quickly.

The Neonate's Head

At birth, the neonatal baby's head is about one-quarter of the length of the body. As the baby develops, the proportion gradually changes: by adulthood the head is only one-eighth to one-tenth of the height of the body. The large head allows for greater development of the infant's brain than other parts of the body. Because the head likely was squeezed and molded during birth, it is probably somewhat pointed. Movement of the skull bones allows for a safe birth. Soon after birth, the head gains a more rounded appearance.

On the top of the head, the diamond-shaped anterior and posterior fontanels, or soft spots, are visible. There are four more **fontanels**, but they are harder to locate. While fontanels are less vulnerable than you might imagine, they do indicate parts of the brain that are not covered by the skull bones and take up to 18 months to fully close. These gradually close as the skull hardens.

fontanels

the soft spots, front (anterior) and back (posterior), on the infant's head, over which unconnected bones are lined with a protective material

The hair on the baby's head may be thick or fine, curly, or straight. Many babies are bald at birth, and some lose what hair they do have. After a few months, some babies may get a bald patch where they have been resting their heads, but this is not a long-term problem. Some babies also experience cradle cap, which is a crusting and scaling rash found on the scalps of many healthy babies. The sebaceous glands in their skin are hyper-activated often because of mom's hormones that crossed the placenta just before birth. These glands pump out a greasy substance that keeps the old skin cells attached as it dries. Generally, cradle cap does not need to be treated as long as it does not bother you or the baby. If treatment is necessary, the gentlest method is to simply rub a small amount of baby oil or olive oil onto the baby's scalp. After several minutes, the oil will soften and loosen the scales, and then they can be brushed away with a soft brush or a dry terry cloth washcloth.

lanugo

soft hair that covers the fetus and newborn and helps the vernix stick to the skin

Sometimes the infant's whole body is covered with soft hair, called **lanugo**. This usually results from a delayed fetal condition, and falls out in the first few weeks. It is no cause for concern unless the mother had been taking a steroid-type drug.

Skin and Temperature Regulation

The appearance of a newborn's skin correlates directly with the number of weeks' gestation the child is at birth. Premature babies often have very transparent looking skin, while babies born closer to term have less transparent skin. Babies of all races and ethnicities tend to have pinkish skin due to the fact that color from the red blood vessels shows through their thin layer of skin. For some children, it will take up to a year for their skin tone to develop. Between 30 and 40 percent of babies are born with **milia**, small white or yellow dots resembling pimples that usually disappear within a month's time. Other rashes, such as heat rash or urticaria, are caused by environmental conditions and allergies, so they call for careful observation and a quick response. Some children are born with birthmarks, but sometimes it is a few weeks before the marks are visible. Almost half of newborns develop a yellowish tinge to their skin a few days after birth. This may be jaundice, and for most babies it usually goes away within a relatively short period of time, although some children may require treatment with special lights.

milia

small white spots, mainly on the nose or the face, caused by blocked sebaceous glands; requires no treatment

Because babies cannot shiver or sweat, it is necessary to moderate room temperatures carefully and dress infants appropriately.

Bladder and Bowel Function

The neonate is not aware of passing urine. Only in time will the baby realize what causes the warm, wet sensation. Since a baby urinates every couple of hours, a conscientious caregiver might change the baby eight, ten, or twelve times a day. Diapers that take the wetness away from contact with the baby's skin make diaper-changing less urgent, but the commercials describing diapers that "keep baby dry" are not always to be trusted!

meconium

fetal fees, usually expelled after birth

One of the first diaper changes may be a surprise, because it will reveal **meconium**, a greenish-black substance that contains mucus, bile, and amniotic fluid. This is usually eliminated within 24 hours of birth. Later stools will be soft, yellowish, and inoffensive, particularly if the baby is breast-fed. Babies vary in their bowel movements. Observing the individual baby's usual pattern is useful; we can then identify any changes to that pattern that could indicate a potential problem.

Newborn babies' skin is sensitive, and will usually need some measures to prevent skin rash on the buttocks. Skin ointment should be applied only after the skin is cleaned. Otherwise, bacteria may be trapped underneath it. When adults dispense cream or ointment, they should not scoop it from the jar with their hands, because they could contaminate the contents. Instead, use a fresh spatula or disposable gloves to scoop a small amount and apply it carefully.

Cleanliness is essential in all parts of caregiving. Diaper-changing presents the greatest dangers. Thorough and regular handwashing is absolutely essential, and is the most effective way of reducing the spread of infection (Aronson, 2002).

The Newborn's Genitalia

Baby boys will typically have fully descended testicles, and their maleness will be obvious with a penis that functions for urination. Their genitals may look rather large and red, but this will correct itself without treatment. Some parents have their boys circumcised for religious or cultural reasons or because they believe it leads to better hygiene. Circumcision is controversial in terms of the pain endured by the baby and the procedure's supposed benefits.

Female babies will usually have pronounced labia, or genital folds, and a clitoris. They may have a white discharge from the vagina; it may even be slightly bloodstained because of hormonal changes. The breasts of newborn boys and girls may be a little fuller than you expected. Again, shifting hormonal levels are the cause, and this will normalize in a few days.

"If you ask experts at medical centers how often a child is born so noticeably atypical in terms of genitalia that a specialist in sex differentiation is called in, the number comes out to about 1 in 1,500 to 1 in 2,000 births. But a lot more people than that are born with subtler forms of sex anatomy variations, some of which won't show up until later in life" (courtesy of the Intersex Society of North America—www.isna.org). Sometimes, even after genetic tests have been conducted, there is still not a match of the appearance of the genitalia to the chromosomal identification. One of the first questions families usually ask immediately after birth is whether their child is a boy or a girl. If a doctor or mid-wife cannot tell a parent what sex their child is, it raises alarm bells in parents. The handling of such a situation requires much delicacy, and usually immediate intervention by specialists is required. "The birth of a child with ambiguous genitalia constitutes a social emergency. Because words spoken in the delivery room may have a lasting impact on parents and their relationship with their infant, it is important that no attempt be made to suggest a diagnosis or offer a gender assignment" (Kaye, 2000, p. 139).

To date, the treatment of intersex states still remains controversial. Much of the controversy revolves around early surgery and the possibility for complications of gender identification for the child at a later date. The ISNA is focused on changing the shame, secrecy, and unwanted genital surgeries for people born with an anatomy that someone decided is not standard for male or female. The following information is courtesy of the ISNA (www.insa.org):

- Intersexuality is primarily a problem of stigma and trauma, not gender.
- Parents' distress must not be treated by surgery on the child.
- Professional mental health care is essential.
- Honest, complete disclosure is good medicine.
- All children should be assigned as boy or girl, without early surgery.

These recommendations should be utilized when a family has to make decisions regarding their intersex child. It is worth noting that the American Academy of Pediatrics usually recommends that surgery be initiated before the child is 15 months old.

The Navel

The stump left on the baby's navel is the end of the umbilical cord, which was clamped and cut soon after birth. The stump needs little attention as long as it is kept clean and dry; it will usually fall away after 5–10 days.

Heart and Lungs

The newborn's heart weighs less than an ounce. Despite its small size, it can pump blood at a pulse rate from 140 to 180 beats per minute. Most babies breathe within a few moments of birth. Up to that time, the baby receives oxygen from the mother through the umbilical cord. The first breath is a reflex triggered by cold air. Breathing can be hindered if the lungs contain fluid. Sometimes babies have to have the fluid suctioned off to enable them to breathe easily.

Appeal to Adults

Babies are not always very attractive to anyone but their parents—indeed, some parents might even think that their offspring look a little weird, at first! After the first few days babies put on weight in ways that tend to make them more attractive. Some researchers (Brazelton, 1992; Morris, 1999) have suggested that the babies' appearance makes us want to pick them up and pay attention to them. We must keep in mind, that appearance is culturally monitored, meaning that culture tends to dictate what is meant by appealing. However, since newborns tend to have big heads, in comparison with the rest of their body, we tend to focus on such facial features as their eyes, cheeks, and foreheads. Their appearance and some of their behavior might be a built-in means of survival. For example, most adults have an emotional response when a baby wraps his small finger around their finger, and Kaplan (1978) explained that although the fat in the cheeks of babies helps them in sucking, those fat cheeks are often associated with babyhood and immaturity and may signal to adults the need for protection and care.

Responses

The type of delivery may influence the behavior you can observe in the newborn baby. An uncomplicated home birth may provide a calmer and quieter environment than would be possible in a noisy hospital. If the birth was a positive experience for the mother, the baby may also be calmer. However, it is hard to predict how the mother's labor will progress and exactly how that experience will affect her baby.

Reflexes

Reflexes are the inborn, automatic behaviors that show us that the baby is physically and intellectually healthy and that the nervous system is working well. Often physicians will check for these reflexes because they are indicators of normal development. Lack of some of these reflexes, or delayed appearance of reflexes, can be a red flag for a possible developmental delay. Some reflexes are survival reflexes, such as the cough-and-gag reflex and the breathing reflex. The sucking and swallowing reflexes gradually become more coordinated. Infants are able to blink and squint, and their pupils can dilate. These reflexes remain with us throughout our lifetime.

Reflexes particular to newborns are described in the following list:

- Moro reflex (startle)—If startled by a loud sound or a sudden body shift, the infant arches back, extends legs, throws arms outward, and then brings them toward the body.
- Palmar grasp—Spontaneous grasp on adult's finger when a finger is pressed against the infant's palm.
- Rooting reflex—Stroke the cheek toward corner of the child's mouth and the head turns to source of stimulation.
- Sucking reflex—If a finger is placed in an infant's mouth, rhythmic sucking will begin.
- Babinski's reflex—If the sole of the foot is stroked from the toes toward the heel, the toes will fan out and then curl as the foot twists in.
- Stepping reflex—If held under the arms with bare feet touching a flat surface, the infant will lift one foot after the other in a stepping movement.
- Tonic neck reflex—If the baby's head is turned to one side while lying on back, one arm extends to the side at eye level, the other arm is flexed, and the position resembles a "fencing" stance.
- Swimming reflex—If an infant is placed in water on his tummy, his legs and arms will move in a swimming motion.

Some reflexes appear gradually over the first few months of a child's life, and include:

- Landau reflex—When held in a horizontal prone position, the infant will lift her head and extend the neck and the trunk. When the neck is passively flexed, the whole body will flex.
- Reciprocal kicking (bicycling)—If the child is held out by an adult, he usually begins to kick his legs alternately.
- Parachute reflex—If an infant is held vertically in the air and then tilted towards the ground, her legs extend outward.

Figure 4.1 displays some reflexes that are present at and after birth.

All reflexes probably had a purpose at some point during human evolution, but the need for some may be less clear today. Without reflexive behaviors, it may be that later physical or cognitive skills would not develop. As deliberate bodily control increases, many of the reflexes disappear. They seem to serve their purpose and then go away.

By completing Activity 4.1 on your Online Companion, you will learn more about infant reflexes.

Senses

At birth, all five senses are in working order. The infant's sense of *touch* is well developed: she responds in different ways according to how she is touched or how she reacts to other tactile sensations, such as wind blowing in her face. Some babies do not like being touched as much as others, so the infant's cues must be heeded. Although **sensory stimulation** is important, the baby can be **overstimulated**. The neonate has sensitivity to pain, but it is thought that this is less in the first couple of days of life than later on. Newborn babies are unable to regulate their own temperature. However, they will respond to temperature changes.

As though programmed to like breast milk, newborns like the sweet *taste* of lactose in milk. They may also respond differently to salty, bitter, and sour tastes. Like their sense of taste, their sense of smell leads neonates to prefer the odor of a lactating—that is, milk-producing—mother. Newborns may make a face at or turn away from what they perceive as unpleasant smells, and they can sometimes locate the source of an odor.

Hearing is essential for much later skill development. The newborn can hear a range of sounds, and will prefer the sound of the mother to other sounds. Often neonates respond more positively to complex sounds than to single tones. They also respond more favorably to high-pitched, sing-song voices. This particular tone that adults use instinctively with infants is known as motherese or **parentese**. Babies' hearing ability enables them to hear their own sound production, which will ultimately allow them to learn language.

Vision is less well developed than the other senses in human neonates. They have some ability to see in color, but this is not yet well refined. Their focusing ability also takes time to develop. Babies try to focus on and scan objects in an effort to see them. Early focusing is possible if the object or person is close. The ideal focusing distance is about the space between an adult and a baby held in the adult's arms. Infants' eye movements are relatively slow and not very specific. Yet it will only take a few weeks for them to be able to see at a greater distance and with better coordination between both eyes. Their eyes will stop wandering as much. Significantly, they will be able to see in three dimensions, because of the coordination of the eye muscles for **binocular vision**. Within a month, newborns will fixate on an object or face and will scan it with eye movements that allow them to take in visual information. Another interesting fact is that children's eye color often takes about six months to stabilize. Some children may start out with blue eyes, which end up being green, and hazel eyes may gradually turn to brown eyes. The rule of thumb is that the color of the child's eyes is probably not permanent until at least 6 months of age.

Perception

There is a difference between taking in information from the senses and perceiving. What the young baby sees may be different from what we see, because we process the information differently. Adults have spent years experiencing what things look like, smell like, and so on, and can recognize things and people. Lack of experience means that the baby perceives differently.

sensory stimulation

auditory, olfactory, visual, taste, or touch information processed through one or more sense

overstimulation

a situation in which the infant or older individual is unable to process sensory information because it has become overwhelming

parentese

speech pattern used in talking with infants and young children; refers to either male or female and utilizes the elements found in motherese; the high-pitched, sing-song tone that adults use instinctively with infants

binocular vision

the capacity to coordinate the sensory input from both eyes; results in the ability to perceive depth

Figure 4.1 Reflexes At and After Birth

AT BIRTH

Moro reflex
(Startle reflex)

Palmar grasp reflex

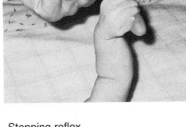

Tonic neck reflex

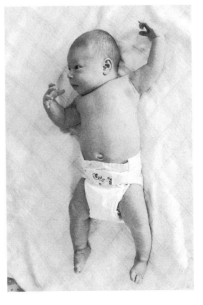

Rooting reflex

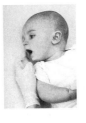

Stepping reflex

AFTER BIRTH

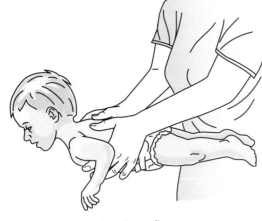

Landau reflex

Reciprocal kicking

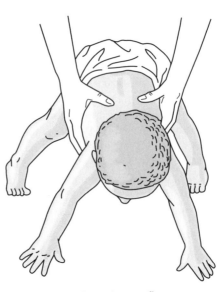

Parachute reflex

For most of the time that babies are awake and alert, more than one of their senses will be stimulated. They will hear while they see, for example, or feel something as they hear it. This kind of sensory information is called **multimodality**, because several senses are stimulated simultaneously. Infants have to learn to sort out all these bits of information in an attempt to understand what is happening. When presented with stimulation, the baby may briefly turn her head away and then re-engage by turning back. The child may have momentarily become familiar with the particular form of stimulation and may have tired of it, or the child may need a brief respite from the stimulation in order to allow her brain to "catch up." In either case, this type of behavior is known as **habituation**. This type of behavior enables caregivers to understand that significant neurological activity is occurring and that they may need to either slow the stimulation down in order to avoid overstimulation, or add some complexity to the stimulus in order to effectively engage the child's attention.

multimodal stimulation

stimulation of two or more senses simultaneously

habituation

the decrease in response to a stimulus that occurs after repeated presentations of the stimulus— e.g., looking away from a mobile after continued stimulation

Stimulation and Relaxation

Although sensory stimulation is necessary, it is important to recognize the baby's signs when she is telling you she has had enough. She will attempt to ignore information overload, but she does not have the ability to organize her thoughts or regulate her behavior. At birth, babies need little more stimulation than would come naturally from everyday interactions and domestic surroundings. Overstimulation does not produce babies who are more intelligent. Rather, over-stimulated babies may become irritable and confused. A common defense mechanism that infants employ against the rush of stimuli is sleep, a device that is used intermittently throughout a 24-hour period (Brazelton, 1992).

Another point of interest, and one that often causes disagreement among family members, is that babies can become used to sleeping with a noisy background. Therefore, environments do not need to be absolutely silent in order for babies to sleep. In fact, a baby who is used to a certain amount of sound may not be able to sleep in quieter places and may need music or white noise in order to settle into a sleep pattern.

Newborn Competence

Newborn babies' abilities are amazing. Recent experiments have shown that neonates have the ability to use all their senses and do sophisticated things like imitate a facial expression. For example, a baby can copy someone putting out his tongue by putting out her own. This behavior is remarkable—it may be reflexive, we don't know.

Numerous studies are currently being conducted into various functions of the neonatal brain. Theories about how babies are preprogrammed for various types of learning are likely to offer us some useful explanations for how learning happens. Most important for us as caregivers is to know that observable behaviors indicate significant advancements. These may help us to know what we should provide for babies to support their learning potential.

However, the field of infant research has its share of disagreements. For example, recent work that looked at the link between physical skills and neurological development has led some people to believe that it is a good idea to help the baby practice reflexive movements. The thinking is that practicing stepping would lead to earlier walking. Others think that there is no long-term benefit for the baby. The traditional perspective is that physical skills will happen when the child is ready, and that they should be supported at that time, not pushed prematurely. In the case of such disagreements, it may be best to let common sense prevail until we get really clear evidence.

Routines and Patterns

Each family deals with **routine** in different ways. Some parents think that infants should determine their own routines and eat and sleep when they like, but other parents prefer a more organized schedule. The problem is that the baby does not listen to the parents' requests for a full night's sleep. Establishing a routine is a gradual process whereby the infant's needs are met while the parents try to manipulate the timing. After about six weeks, most families have established a workable pattern, even if they manage it by sharing the care and the interruptions

routine

the regular and predictable sequence of mealtimes, sleep times, and activity during each day

during the night. You might observe parents suffering from a lack of sleep and feeling irritable as a result.

Sleep and Wakefulness

More easily observable than neurological activity are the infant's states of arousal or awareness. Although there has been much research on sleep in infants, yet there is still not an agreed-upon classification of the sleep/waking states in human infants—that is, active or rapid-eye-movement sleep (REM); quiet or non-REM sleep (NREM)—including its four stages; indeterminate sleep (IS); and wakefulness (Holzmann, et al., 1999; Storm and Reese, 2005). Much of the initial classification came from work conducted years ago. Wolff (1966) identified several stages of sleep and wakefulness:

- regular sleep that is calm and relaxed;
- irregular sleep that is jerky, with changing facial expressions;
- drowsiness that is seen with an unfocused stare or closed eyes;
- alert inactivity, where the baby is awake and curious;
- waking activity, where the baby has bursts of activity; and
- the state of crying.

Other observers describe these states more simply as uptime, downtime, trance, and sleep (Quilliam, 1994). Whichever model we use to help us interpret the infant's states, it is clear that there are many levels of awareness and receptiveness. We need to recognize these if we are to find the right way to respond. Any number of variable conditions can influence the infant's state. Noise, hunger, calming words, a pacifier, being swaddled, or being in a safety carrier in the back seat of the car can all make a difference. Moreover, babies differ in their patterns of wakefulness and sleep. Unhappily for some parents, most newborn babies do not appear to have a predictable pattern. After the parents become used to getting up several times a night, the baby will unexpectedly sleep through to morning; this will have the parents running in to see if everything is all right!

Crying

Crying is one behavior of infants that is particularly designed to reach the ears of adults. This is their way of communicating, but it might pose a challenge to a tired parent or to any caregiver when it doesn't seem to stop. Types and intensities of crying vary from infant to infant. Mothers may be able to identify their own baby's cries even when other babies are crying. This may be an evolutionary characteristic that supports attachment and survival. The cries are also heard by the adult in different ways, depending on circumstances—for instance, whether they have just fed the baby, or they themselves feel tired. All infants cry; typically, neonates cry for about two hours a day. This doesn't mean anything unusual is happening. At 6 weeks, crying may increase to about three hours a day (Shelov, 1993).

Families may think that the cries of their own babies are endless; the emotional tie between parent and child does not make the crying any easier to deal with. Between the second and fourth week, crying may increase because of **colic**, a condition that produces a high-pitched cry. Its real cause is not entirely understood, but it concerns the gastrointestinal tract. Indications of colic in a baby include clenched fists, extended or drawn-up legs, and extended periods of crying that do not respond to comforting.

Feeding

Newborn infants' feeding patterns will be as varied as their other patterns. Some babies are self-regulated and feed at predictable times. Other babies feed irregularly. In addition to variations in when and how often they feed, babies do not consume the same volume since some are breast-fed, while others are given formula.

There are many advantages to breast-feeding a baby. The infant receives antibodies in the breast milk. It is less expensive, requires no preparation, is at the correct temperature, and presents fewer hygiene problems than formula preparation. Breast milk is "designer" milk made especially to meet the human baby's nutritional needs. Research suggests there is lower incidence of sudden infant death syndrome (SIDS) among breast-fed babies. The hormones produced by breast-feeding help to cement the mother–child attachment. Even a short breast-feeding period is beneficial to the infant. The **colostrum**—that is, the pre-milk fluid—is rich in antibodies and provides essential nutrients.

colic

a condition in the newborn characterized by acute abdominal pain, knees drawn up to the chest, and a high-pitched cry

colostrum

the first fluid secreted by the mother's breasts soon after birth, before true milk comes through

A father enjoys the special moment of intimacy created while feeding his son.

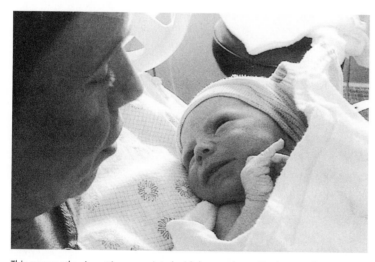

This new mother is getting acquainted with her newborn. She has set the stage for early bonding. This is the time for relationship building, leading to a secure attachment.

Another extremely important issue related to breast-feeding is one that has been discovered relatively recently; breast milk and breast-feeding are beneficial for brain development (Bouwstra et al, 2003; American Academy of Pediatrics, 2005). In fact, it is one of four major factors in ensuring healthy neurological development. Since breast milk contains specific proteins that promote brain development, breast-feeding could be viewed as the fourth trimester for a child's brain growth.

Although social attitudes about breast-feeding have changed, some people continue to view it in a negative way. They may feel that breast-feeding in public is unacceptable. There is a movement underfoot to counter that reaction (American Academy of Pediatrics, 2001b; Canahuati & de Suarez, 2001). Many health and professional organizations, such as the American Academy of Family Physicians and the American Dietetic Association, recognize the benefits of breast-feeding. The American Academy of Pediatrics promotes breast-feeding as a cultural norm and "adheres to the position that breast-feeding ensures the best possible health as well as developmental and psychosocial outcomes for the infant" (American Academy of Pediatrics, 2005, p. 506). Furthermore, the U.S. Department of Health & Human Service's Office on Women's Health (OWH), in cooperation with other federal agencies and health care professional organizations, has developed a comprehensive national breast-feeding policy entitled *HHS Blueprint for Action on Breastfeeding.* Funding will support an awareness campaign whose goal, by the year 2010, is to increase the number of mothers who breast-feed their babies following birth to 75 percent, to increase to 50 percent the number of children who continue to be breast-fed at 6 months of age, and to have a 25 percent breast-feeding rate at 1 year (American Academy of Pediatrics, 2001b).

We may often observe mothers establishing close relationships by breast-feeding their babies. Yet a similar quality of attachment can be observed with non-breast-feeding mothers and also between fathers and newborns. Formula-feeding parents who spend time cuddling their babies and tuning into them by watching, listening, and responding to their cues do form strong attachments. Much has been written about the psychological benefits of breast-feeding for the infant, and there is some evidence that indicates that breast-fed babies are better off in later life. However, caregivers need to respect the decision of the mother to breast-feed or formula-feed, and to offer any support they can to aid the mother in her decision.

bonding

the establishment of a close physical and emotional relationship (affectional tie) between an adult and a child in the early weeks after birth—usually between mother and child; bonding sets the stage for later attachment; Bowlby proposed that one key figure must create the bonding relationship

Attachment and Emotional Development

If the cutting of the umbilical cord was the first real separation of the baby and the mother, other aspects of attachment and separation occur in psychological as well as physical ways. Kaplan (1978) suggested that mending the "rupture" between mother and child is the major task of the "mother and newborn couple." Closeness and early **bonding**—making a stable relationship—are thought to have sensitive periods, such as the time immediately after birth. Many studies have shown the long-term advantages of making and sustaining these early relationships.

Klaus, Kennell, and Klaus (2000) insist that time needs to be made available for mother and child to connect with each other. It has been shown that mothers who have this time to bond are less likely to experience parenting problems months, and perhaps years, later. This bond is the beginning that allows the infant to reach his potential in the years ahead.

PARTICULAR NEEDS

The essential role of the adult in caring for newborn babies is to ensure that all their needs, both practical and emotional, are met. Newborns are not impressed with an expensively decorated room, but they respond well to comfort and feeding.

Basic needs include feeding, changing after urination or a bowel movement, shelter and a comfortable environment that provides protection, scrupulous hygiene, warmth and avoidance of extreme weather, suitable clothing that allows movement and growth, a balance between sensory stimulation and calming surroundings, and some degree of quiet and opportunity for making close relationships. Time and a calm, responsive caregiver are the best insurance that the needs of the newborn baby are being met.

Health Assessment

Newborns are at a very vulnerable stage of development, and have recently undergone one of the most traumatic events of their life, birthing. A variety of bodily functions need to be checked soon after birth, and will need to be watched until the baby is obviously stable and settled into a pattern of waking and sleeping, feeding and playing, being active and passive. Close observation is necessary for the first hours and days.

Protection from Infection

Although many babies are exposed to numerous people without incident, the possibility of exposure to life-threatening infection exists. Some parents are cautious, particularly with premature babies or those who have experienced difficulties, but others may not see the risk to a healthy newborn. The rise of bacteria such as streptococcus that are resistant to some antibiotic treatment presents an increasing risk to the newborn infant. Consequently, we must consider the issue of exposure to infection and appreciate that vulnerable newborns need to be protected. Their immune systems are immature, and they may be unable to fight infections that pose little risk to older children and adults.

Hygiene and Cleanliness

Hygiene is particularly important at this stage to maintain a high level of cleanliness. A sterile environment is not necessary, but caregivers must be scrupulous about cleanliness. The most significant thing that adults can do is to wash their hands frequently and appropriately (Aronson, 2002). Diaper-changing procedures should be carefully considered so that cross-infection is avoided. All baby equipment must be kept clean. Bleach solutions are the most effective sanitizing agents and should be used daily. Items that are in contact with the infant must be washed regularly; hot, soapy water and a rinse is usually all that is required.

NAEYC has recently issued new guidelines for cleaning and sanitizing frequencies in child care facilities, and these can be found in the Additional Support section of your Online Companion.

Bottles and all feeding equipment are breeding grounds for bacteria. These must be washed, rinsed, and sterilized in accordance with manufacturers' directions and stored where they cannot be contaminated. Because of the growth of microorganisms, used bottles should not be reheated. Microwave ovens should be avoided for warming milk: the milk continues to heat after the power is shut off (American Academy of Pediatrics, 2005), and microwaves may cause hot spots in the formula or cause steam to collect at the top of the bottle, which might scald the baby. According to some studies, microwaves might also damage the formula's composition. Microwave use may also be associated with careless re-warming of formula, presenting bacterial problems. Newborns must be protected from these hazards.

Physical Protection

Safety issues are particularly pertinent to the newborn. Because newborns are so small and unable to protect themselves by moving away from dangers, they are vulnerable to situations that would present little risk to older children. Careful observation, supervision, and involvement with the baby are necessary even after all potential dangers are removed.

Response to Cues

cues

any indicator or message sent (deliberately or not) by an infant or young child that is read and interpreted by an adult or older child; may include facial expressions, sound productions, gestures, and bodily movements

engagement

when an individual spends time paying attention to someone or something

disengagement

when the individual takes her attention away from a stimulus; may be deliberate or not

The mother, father, and other caregivers need to learn the infant's **cues**. Such learning often occurs through trial and error. From time to time, the mother may seem to know intuitively what the baby needs; at other times, it may be difficult to tune in, but persistence is essential. The cues cluster either around **engagement** behavior or behavior that signals the need for **disengagement**. Box 4.2 provides a list of some infant cues.

 The Additional Support section of your Online Companion has additional information on infant cues.

Quick responses to the baby's needs are essential for building relationships of trust. Newborns are not too particular about who meets their needs, as long as they are met. Although they can differentiate between people, and prefer those who are familiar, they can be calmed by the relaxed manner of a stranger's care. When infants send out messages to adults, they may persist until we understand them. However, adults cannot rely on the infant's persistence, and should always be alert to the cues the infant is giving.

BOX 4.2

DEFINITION OF INFANT CUES

I. Subtle **engagement** cues
   A. Alerting—Increased muscle tone of face, possibly with flushing to cheeks; eyes usually sparkle
   B. Brow raising—Elevating of eyebrows and formation of horizontal lines in forehead
   C. Feeding posture—Moderate abduction of the lower arms, forearm flexion, and fisted hands held palm inward
   D. Head raising—Elevation of head with eyes directed upward toward caregiver

II. Potent engagement cues
   A. Facing gaze—Looking at the parent's face
   B. Mutual gaze—Sustained eye-to-eye contact

III. Subtle **disengagement** cues
   A. Facial grimace—Combination of a frown, eye tightening, and upper lip raising
   B. Eyes clenched—Eyes tightly shut
   C. Gaze aversion—Eyes turned away from caregiver or object
   D. Diffuse body movements—Motor movement of arms and legs, usually tight or close in toward torso; movements can be jerky and give the impression that the infant is struggling
   E. Immobility—Can be either a positive or a disengagement cue; a stilling of movement of arms or legs, as if in anticipation of something to come
   F. Head lowering—Chin brought in toward chest; eyes usually lowered as well
   G. Hand to ear, neck, or behind neck

IV. Potent disengagement cues
   A. Crying (three types)
      1. Hunger or ordinary cry: somewhat low in volume, of short duration (1–2 seconds); rhythmical, with vocalization and 1–2-second pause, vocalization and 1–2-second pause, and so forth

(continues)

BOX 4.2 (Continued)

2. Angry cry: a far more forceful version of the hunger or ordinary cry; remains rhythmical
3. Pain cry: a vocalization of sudden onset, of long duration (approximately 7 seconds); loud, followed by audible expelling of air, gulping in air, repetition of above

B. Whining—A prolonged, high-pitched, somewhat nasal sound; not rhythmical, uttered by itself and repeated a few times in succession
C. Fussing—Staccato, short, low-pitched vocalizations; not rhythmical
D. Spitting—Spitting up small amounts of food, without gagging or forceful projection
E. Pulling away—Removing torso and/or head away from caregiver or object; that is, withdrawing and increasing distance from caregiver or object
F. Tray pound—Hitting the surface of highchair tray or tabletop with the palm of the hand
G. Lateral head shake—Turning head from side to side as if saying no

Adapted from partial list of Sumner and Spietz, in Erickson and Kurz-Reimer. G. Sumner and A. Spietz (1994), NCAST Caregiver/Parent–Child Interaction Feeding Manual (Seattle: NCAST Publications, University of Washington School of Nursing). For more information, contact NCAST, Box 35790, University of Washington, Seattle, WA, 98195-7920; fax:(206) 685-3285.

Supporting the Caregiver

Primary caregivers cannot offer high-quality care to newborns if their own needs are not adequately met. These needs include nutrition, sleep, and exercise, as well as time to do what makes them feel peaceful and whole. All of these contribute to the psychosocial health of the individual (Donatelle, 2004). Thus, as the backdrop to providing good care and responsiveness to infants, caregivers need to be proactive in ensuring that their own needs are met.

Mothers may need particular consideration. Their bodies have undergone the changes of pregnancy, labor, and birthing, and are experiencing hormonal changes; they are trying to adjust to a new role; and they now have multiple responsibilities during the day. These all have an impact on the way the mother is able to cope and to form attachments. The process is normal, but that does not mean it is easy. The mother may find that she needs practical assistance in domestic matters or a break from caregiving. Such assistance, outlined in Box 4.3, may prevent

BOX 4.3

A USEFUL STRATEGY FOR SHARING CARE: SUPPORTING NEW MOTHERS

New mothers do not automatically fall in love with their babies, although most feel some attachment from the time of their birth. Birthing is tiring, hormones are fluctuating, and the new addition to the family may alter the dynamics of the parental relationships. Enabling the mother to feel competent, reassuring her that it is perfectly normal to have feelings of ambivalence, and providing her with a little time to herself for sleep or a change of scenery can be very helpful. Educators can make comments about the mom's competence as they talk to the new baby: "Wow, how beautiful you are. Your mommy did a great job to make such a beautiful baby." Or in adult conversation it might be helpful to sit down for coffee and let the mom talk. Reassurance that other parents feel the same stressors and feel that they too are on an emotional roller coaster is supportive. Perhaps you can offer to extend baby care to enable mom to sleep, shop, or take time for herself.

some difficulties for both mother and baby. It may even protect the infant from the kind of neglect or abuse that can result from the mother's stress.

DEVELOPMENTAL VARIATION

Most babies are born healthy and without significant special needs. But variations in prenatal development mean that some babies face particular challenges. Some of the most significant variations of development happen because of length of gestation and the conditions for prenatal development. Many developmental variations stem from genetic inheritance, family patterns, exposure to teratogens such as chemicals or drugs, availability of prenatal care, the birth experience, or from other reasons we cannot determine.

The educator's task is to provide support to both the infant and the family as the baby is diagnosed and directed to necessary supports. Specifically the educator must:

1. observe and record pertinent behavior of the infant and be prepared to share that information
2. identify any developmental alerts with the assistance of the family
3. seek resources and direct the family to appropriate professionals (it is not the educator's job to intervene or refer the baby directly without permission from the family)
4. support the family through the processes of medical and other professional diagnoses and interventions
5. read the parent's cues and determine when and how to support the family
6. work collaboratively within the parenting and professional team to ensure that the child's needs are met
7. make appropriate accommodations to the program to meet family needs
8. set clear boundaries about her role, and what assistance is appropriate
9. nurture a close and supportive relationship while showing empathy for the family
10. avoid talking to others about any child or family

Prematurity and Low Birth Weight

placenta insufficiency

the situation where the placenta is unable to deliver the essential nutrients to the fetus for its growth, health, and development

Preterm babies and those who have low birth weights present particular challenges. A premature infant is one born before the 38th week of development. However, many preterm babies do not face significant developmental challenges. Low-birth-weight babies may have received insufficient nutrition before birth for a variety of reasons, including **placental insufficiency**. With medical intervention, many very tiny and extremely immature babies do survive. Yet this can present an immediate challenge for medical personnel and a long-term challenge for the parents and caregivers who will have responsibility for these children as they grow older. Delayed development may well remain evident when the child is in toddler and preschool child care and when the child goes to school (Harvey, O'Callaghan, & Mohay, 1999; Kessenich, 2003; Palta, Sadik-Badai, Evans, Weinstein, & McGuinness, 2000).

Respiration difficulties are the most common concern with small babies. They may also suffer vision problems, circulation difficulties, body-regulation concerns, and feeding and digestive problems. Generally, the smaller the preterm infant, the greater the likelihood of there being more significant problems.

Birth Defects/Congenital Conditions

birth defect

an abnormality of structure, function, or metabolism (body chemistry) that is evident at birth and can result in a physical or mental disability, or can cause the death of the child

As of 2004, it was calculated that in the United States, approximately 150,000 babies are born with birth defects (March of Dimes, 2005a). Schonberg and Tifft (2002) estimate that "3%–5% of births result in a child who has a birth defect or genetic disorder" (p. 27). A **birth defect** is an abnormality of structure, function, or metabolism (body chemistry) that is evident at birth and can result in a physical or mental disability, or can cause the death of the child. According to the March of Dimes, several thousand birth defects have been identified to date, but although many have been linked to genetic and environmental factors, the causes of 60–70 percent of birth defects still remain unknown. Birth defects continue to be the leading cause of death during the first year of life. Some conditions—especially the more severe ones—are recognizable at birth. Others will not be identifiable until much later. Generally, the more severe the disability, the earlier it will be detected (Howard, Williams, & Lepper, 2005).

Chromosomal Disorders

chromosomal disorders
___

individuals experience behavioral or developmental difficulties as a result of having abnormal chromosomes

Some congenital conditions stem from **chromosomal disorders**. A child can inherit a single faulty gene when one or both parents, who may or may not have the disease or syndrome, pass it along during the fertilization process. Examples include the following:

- Achondroplasia (a form of dwarfism)
- Marfan's syndrome (a connective tissue disease)
- Tay-Sachs disease (a fatal disorder)
- Cystic fibrosis (a fatal disorder of the lungs and other organs)
- Turner's syndrome (females with short stature, lack of sexual development, and other problems)
- Hemophilia (a blood-clotting disorder, passed from mothers to sons)
- Duchenne's muscular dystrophy (progressive muscle weakness, passed from mothers to sons)

Often these genetic abnormalities can be identified quite early in an infant's life by a range of observable characteristics, called a syndrome. Other times, the disease, or syndrome, is revealed only after blood tests have been conducted, or a period of time has passed and observational information reveals problems. A description of several inherited conditions follows.

Fragile X Syndrome

Fragile X syndrome is the most common inherited form of mental retardation. It affects about 1 in 1,500 boys (Shonkoff & Marshall, 2003) and 1 in 8,000 females (March of Dimes, 2005b). It occurs in all racial and ethnic groups. It is a genetic disorder that runs in families, but it is different from Down syndrome, which is caused by an extra chromosome, whereas fragile X syndrome is caused by an abnormality in a single gene.

According to the March of Dimes (2005b):

> Young children with fragile X syndrome often have delays in developmental milestones, such as learning how to sit, walk, and talk. Affected children may have frequent tantrums, be highly anxious, and have difficulties paying attention. They may have speech problems and display autistic-like behaviors such as hand flapping. While many children with fragile X syndrome do not look different from their peers, some have subtle physical signs. These include a long narrow face, prominent ears, a high-arched palate, flat feet, and overly flexible joints (especially the fingers). Girls with fragile X syndrome have fewer physical signs of the disorder; however, some affected girls with normal intelligence have learning disabilities, attention difficulties, emotional problems (such as anxiety, depression, and shyness), and poor social skills. Males tend to be more severely affected than females because, while most males with fragile X syndrome have mental retardation or serious learning disabilities, only about one-third to one-half of affected females do.

Down Syndrome

Down syndrome
___

a chromosomal abnormality characterized by distinctive facial features and intellectual deficits; also known as trisomy-21

The likelihood that a woman under 30 who becomes pregnant will have a baby with Down syndrome is less than 1 in 1,000, but the chance of having a baby with Down syndrome increases to 1 in 400 for women who become pregnant at age 35. The likelihood of Down syndrome continues to increase as a woman ages, so that by age 42, the chance is 1 in 60 that a pregnant woman will have a baby with Down syndrome, and by age 49, the chance is 1 in 12. But using maternal age alone will not detect over 75 percent of pregnancies that result in Down syndrome (National Institute of Child Health and Human Development, 2005b). **Down syndrome** is a congenital condition that results from a chromosomal abnormality. There are varying levels of severity of the syndrome. Children with Down syndrome have rounded faces and their hands have short, relatively fat, fingers. They may have heart problems and their brains may function at below-normal capacity. However, the levels of functioning vary from baby to baby. Only rarely are medical interventions necessary. An infant with Down syndrome can usually be integrated into a child care setting without difficulty. The group environment may provide the stimulation that the baby needs.

Cystic Fibrosis

Cystic fibrosis (CF), a genetically inherited condition, is most common among Caucasian people. Although infants and children with this condition experience different levels of severity, common symptoms are respiratory difficulties that include coughing, spitting, repeated lung infections, and congestion. Children with CF may also show some signs of poor growth and failure to thrive. Young children with CF will usually have salty sweat and unusually bulky and offensive-smelling stools. Depending on the individual child's symptoms, toddlers and older children can do well in small group settings. However, given their increased susceptibility to infection, exposure to large numbers of people can be undesirable. Medication is usually required for children with CF, and they need special care in hot weather to ensure that they drink sufficient fluids. These children are more likely to do well if they have a good balanced diet and if educators become familiar with the condition so that they can administer medication and perform necessary supportive functions. The impact of CF on the child's overall development is variable. Seeking good supports and professional expertise is essential to achieve optimal outcomes for each child.

Sickle-Cell Disease (Anemia)

This rare inherited disease occurs most frequently among people of Afro-Caribbean descent. It is a form of anemia that can cause tiredness, lethargy, pain in the abdomen and bones, and episodes of crisis. Ongoing medication might be necessary, as the child is susceptible to serious infection. Participation in a child care program can be successful, but there may be blocks of time when the child is absent because of the disease. Educators need to work with parents to understand the particular needs of a child with sickle-cell disease and try to develop strategies that meet the needs of each child and family.

Thalassemia

Thalassemia is another type of inherited anemia. This disease is most common among people of Mediterranean background. When both parents carry the gene, the child is more likely to be severely affected. Successful integration in a child care program depends on the severity of the disease. Some children would experience no difficulties being included in a program. For others, transfusions, medications, and the symptoms of lethargy and pain might prevent their being able to participate in parts of a child care program.

Cerebral Palsy

The condition can range from quite mild to severe, with different levels of performance as a result. Cerebral palsy can result from birth complications, motor accidents, or even child abuse. The movements of children with cerebral palsy may appear ungainly, and their posture may seem awkward. The child's motor skills may lag behind those of his peers.

Prior to a diagnosis of cerebral palsy, educators may notice that an infant's motor development is a concern, and share these observations with the parents. After the disorder has been diagnosed by a specialist, parents can work together to improve the child's motor skills. Some assistive devices might become necessary, and adults may need to learn how to position her sitting or standing to help her to become more independent. Despite the challenges of cerebral palsy, many children with the condition function well in other areas of their development.

Metabolic Disorders

metabolic disorders

disorders that impede the breakdown of food and the production of energy

About one in 3,500 babies will have a **metabolic disorder**. These disorders are not evident to the eye, but can be harmful, even fatal. Most are also genetically determined. Two of the most common disorders are described below.

Tay-Sachs

This disease is a fatal inherited disease of the central nervous system. Infants with Tay-Sachs lack an enzyme (protein) called hexosaminidase A (hex A), which is required to break down particular fatty substances in brain and nerve cells. These substances build up and gradually destroy brain and nerve cells, until the entire central nervous system stops functioning. The most common form of the disease affects babies who appear healthy for the first few months of life and seem to develop normally. Symptoms of classical Tay-Sachs disease begin to appear between 4 and 6 months of age, when an apparently healthy baby gradually stops smiling, crawling, or turning over. The child loses his ability to grasp or reach out and, eventually, becomes blind, paralyzed, and unaware of its surroundings. To date, there is no known effective treatment for these babies, and death usually occurs by age 5.

PKU

Phenylketonuria (PKU) is an inherited disorder that causes a deficiency in a particular enzyme, if untreated, causing mental retardation (Batshaw & Tuchman, 2002). About 1 baby in 14,000 is born with PKU in the United States (March of Dimes, 2005a). Currently, PKU can be detected by conducting a heel prick test during newborn screening. Following a positive test, the infant is put on a special diet. This prevents the brain damage that is a consequence of the untreated disorder. Other metabolic disorders can cause a wide variety of symptoms that can influence later development.

Structural Abnormalities

Some babies are born with defects that are present in the internal structures of their bodies.

Congenital Heart Defects

congenital heart defect

defect in the structure of the heart and great blood vessels of the newborn that impacts normal blood flow

More than 32,000 infants (one out of every 125–150) are born with a **congenital heart defect** each year in the United States (March of Dimes, 2005a). Heart defects originate in the early part of pregnancy, when the heart is forming, and can affect any of the different parts or functions of the heart. Heart defects are among the most common birth defects, and are the leading cause of birth defect–related deaths. However the death rate from congenital heart defects has been significantly reduced over the last few decades, since many defects can be repaired or helped shortly after birth by surgery, medicine, or artificial devices (Schonberg & Tifft, 2002). Almost 50 percent of children who require surgical repair of a heart defect now undergo surgery before age 2 and are able to engage in normal activities. This intervention prevents additional complications later in life. Heart defects are also often part of a wider pattern of birth defects, because approximately 10 percent of children with heart defects have other abnormalities.

Hydrocephalus and Spina Bifida

Although these are two separate conditions, they coexist in some children. Hydrocephalus is a condition in which fluid builds up in the brain. This condition may correct itself, but it is more likely to need treatment with a shunt or tube that drains the fluid. This treatment generally prevents cognitive impairments.

Spina bifida varies greatly in severity. It can be anything from a clump of hair covering a cleft at the base of the spine to a condition where part of the spinal cord protrudes from the spine in a sac. Surgery may be essential within a day or two of birth, and in many cases this will prevent later problems. Care of the infant with spina bifida may involve ensuring that the site of the surgery is protected. Some infants with the condition may experience paralysis of the legs. Medical experts can advise parents and educators on how to manage the individual child's specific needs.

Spina bifida is the most common of a group of birth defects called neural tube defects (NTDs), affecting one in every 2,000 live births (March of Dimes, 2005a) each year, making it among the most common severe birth defects in the United States. The neural tube is a structure in the embryo that eventually develops into the brain and spinal cord, and the malformation usually occurs relatively early in the fetal formation process (Liptak, 2002). Spina bifida can affect the backbone and, sometimes, the spinal cord.

Activity 4.2 in your Online Companion is a hands-on approach to finding information regarding folic acid.

Studies show that if all women in the United States took enough of the B vitamin folic acid every day before and during early pregnancy, up to 50 percent of neural tube defects (including spina bifida) could be prevented (Liptak, 2002). The key is having enough folic acid in the system before pregnancy and during the earliest weeks of pregnancy, before the neural structures close.

Genital and Urinary Tract Defects

Abnormalities of the genitals and urinary tract are among the most common birth defects, affecting as many as 1 in 10 babies. These defects can affect the kidneys (organs that filter wastes from the blood and form urine), ureters (tubes leading from the kidneys to the bladder), bladder (sac that holds urine), urethra (the tube that drains urine out of the body from the bladder), and the male and female genitals. Many urinary tract defects can be diagnosed before or after birth with an ultrasound examination, which uses sound waves to examine internal organs of the fetus. After birth, ultrasound and/or a number of other tests may be recommended to provide more information on how well the kidneys and other urinary tract structures are functioning.

Congenital Infections

Rubella (German measles)

Rubella is probably the best-known congenital infection that can cause birth defects. During the first trimester, if a pregnant woman is infected with the virus, her baby has a 90 percent risk of being born with one or more features of congenital rubella syndrome, including deafness, mental retardation, heart defects, and blindness (Hill & Haffner, 2002). Currently, most women can be tested prior to conception in order to assess immunity to the disease and can be vaccinated if such action is necessary.

Cytomegalovirus (CMV)

a common infection in child care centers; it is worth making sure that preventative health measures are followed

Cytomegalovirus (CMV)

This is the most common cause of congenital viral infection. About 1 percent (40,000 babies a year) of all newborns in this country are infected, although only about 10 percent of them (3,000–4,000) have serious consequences, including mental retardation, deafness, and microcephaly (small head size) (Hill & Haffner, 2002). Pregnant women often acquire CMV from young children, who usually have few or no symptoms, and since this is often a common infection in child care centers, it is worth making sure that preventative health measures are followed.

Hematological Disorders

The most common blood disorder, Rhesus (Rh) disease of the newborn, is caused by an incompatibility between the blood of a mother and that of her fetus. It can result in jaundice (yellowing of the skin), anemia, brain damage, and death. Rh disease usually can be prevented by giving an Rh-negative woman an injection of a blood product called RhoGAM at the 28th week of pregnancy and after the delivery, if the baby is Rh-positive (Ward & McCune, 2002).

Sexually Transmitted Infections

Infections that are sexually transmitted in the mother also can endanger the fetus and newborn. For example, "untreated syphilis can result in congenital syphilis, preterm labor and delivery, and neonatal death" (Hill & Haffner, 2002, p. 50). Other well known infections include Chlamydia, genital warts, gonorrhea, hepatitis, and herpes, although HIV and AIDS have received much attention over the last 20 years.

HIV (human immunodeficiency virus)/AIDS

In the United States, documentation on HIV infection is still confusing. Since many states still do not share their data, it remains difficult to calculate if the number of infected babies is increasing or decreasing. However, the United States has been successful in reducing perinatal transmission of HIV through counseling and voluntary testing of pregnant women, combined with treating HIV-positive pregnant women with AZT. Certain racial/ethnic populations continue to have disproportionate numbers of HIV infections (individuals from black and Hispanic groups) and females in the 13–19 age range (MMWR, 2004). The virus can be transmitted to the fetus during pregnancy or delivery, or transmitted to the infant via breast milk. It is currently estimated that 15–30 percent of HIV-infected mothers pass the virus on to their babies. Clinical trials showed that treating women with AZT during pregnancy and delivery and treating the infant with AZT after birth cut rates of perinatal transmission by two-thirds (Weaver, 2004).

Research in the field of HIV and AIDS—acquired immunodeficiency syndrome, the end stage of HIV infection, when serious illnesses appear—is expanding rapidly, and caregivers should try to keep up to date with published material on this topic. It is possible that you will become a caregiver to a baby with HIV without knowing about the presence of the virus. The practice of **universal precautions**—that is, assuming that infection is present and therefore always adopting hygiene practices to avoid transmission—will ensure that you protect yourself and other infants.

universal precautions

a principle of health and infection control that treats everyone as having the potential to transmit germs (bacteria, viruses); precautions such as handwashing and the appropriate use of gloves are used consistently with all people as infection control measures

teratogen

any substance that a pregnant woman either uses (such as smoking or alcohol consumption) or comes into contact with that has the potential to cause damage to the embryo or fetus

Teratogen Exposure

A number of other congenital conditions are related not to genetic abnormalities but to teratogens. A **teratogen** can be a drug, other chemical, or virus that causes fetal abnormalities. Exposure to environmental toxins such as PCBs or to prescription, over-the-counter, or illegal drugs taken by the mother can result in malformations of limbs, intellectual impairment, and death.

Fetal Alcohol Syndrome (FAS)

This condition is a direct result of a mother's consumption of alcohol during pregnancy. Fetal alcohol syndrome "is seen in about 2.5–4 percent of children whose mothers drink heavily, and has an estimated world wide incidence of nearly 2 per 1,000 live births" (Shonkoff & Marshall, p. 45). FAS is characterized by brain damage, facial deformities, and growth deficits. Heart, liver, and kidney defects also are common, as well as vision and hearing problems. "The most serious consequence of heavy prenatal alcohol exposure is the problem of brain development and function. Beyond diminished brain cell number and intelligence, there can be problems of malformation . . . which include faulty migration of neurons" (Jones, 1997, p. 558). Characteristics of FAS may be evident at birth, but some impairment may not show up until later, when the child experiences difficulties with learning, attention, memory, and problem-solving.

Babies Exposed to Cocaine and Other Drugs

It is not only illegal street drugs that can cause later developmental challenges. A fetus exposed to physician-prescribed and over-the-counter medications by the mother's ingestion of such substances can be damaged in some way. Advice from medical practitioners can help mothers weigh the possible benefits of particular medications against potential detrimental effects. Generally it is sensible to avoid any substance that might have an effect on the baby. The placenta acts to filter the blood passed to the unborn child, but it does not keep out all substances that are detrimental.

Exposure to cocaine and other street drugs does have a negative effect on later development, and there can be a difficult withdrawal process for babies who are born addicted to drugs taken by their mother. Some years ago the belief was that a baby born to a crack cocaine–taking mother would have severe developmental difficulties. We now know through extensive research that there is a variable effect, and it is difficult to predict exactly how the baby will be damaged. That said, there are likely to be some cognitive difficulties and a possibility of delayed motor skill development (Chasnoff, 1992). It is suggested by some pediatricians, such as Daniel Nuespiel, addressing the issue in *The New York Times*, that parents and professionals avoid the use of the term "crack babies" because the label can be a self-fulfilling prophecy, and because it is only a minority of babies who experience significant developmental difficulties.

It should be noted that babies born to drug-addicted mothers also frequently live in poverty and disadvantaged conditions. These conditions are even more likely to be detrimental to the baby than the drug exposure.

Newborn babies may need special physician-prescribed treatment soon after birth to manage their withdrawal from drug exposure. In the early months of life, the baby needs close monitoring. Babies who are born addicted to particular substances may be particularly irritable, physically sensitive, and difficult to pacify.

Infants suffering from the effects of the mother's addiction to hard drugs present particular challenges. The immediate difficulty confronting health care workers is weaning the infant off the addictive substance. The baby is likely to suffer some withdrawal difficulties because of a physical dependence on the substance taken by the mother. Babies who are born addicted to particular substances may be irritable, jittery, physically sensitive, and difficult to pacify. Later, the long-term challenges may be even harder for parents and educators to manage. The infant may have poor intellectual functioning that cannot be corrected or other developmental challenges that require significant support.

Prescription Drugs and Medications

Often not much thought is given to the drugs we ingest; however, during pregnancy, the taking of any medication must be carefully considered. Medications such as ibuprofen, Retin-A, Prozac, and tetracycline can have negative effects on a fetus. Even the use of natural products such as echinacea and Saint John's wort has to be monitored by a physician.

> All drugs are able to cross the placenta and enter the embryonic-fetal bloodstream. There exists a theoretical dose below which no effects are observed, but beyond that dose teratogenic effects are dose-dependent. For most teratogens, the threshold is unknown, but it is assumed that the threshold for a fetus is below that of the mother's. In other words, if the substance has an effect on the mother, it definitely will affect the fetus. (Berke, 1996, p. 14)

Injuries at Birth

perinatal

around the time of birth, before or after

A number of different types of injury to the infant, before, during, or after birth (the **perinatal** period), can result in minor or major health and developmental challenges. For example, the cord may wrap around the baby's neck during birth. This can stop the flow of oxygen to the baby and can cause anything from mild intellectual impairment to death.

Atypical Birth Presentations or Difficulties

atypical birth presentations

any positioning of the baby immediately prior to or during birth that is not usual—e.g., breech

Atypical birth presentations (unusual ways the baby tries to be born), prolonged labor, or pressure on the baby's head causing cerebral irritation can occur. These can cause long-term developmental challenges that may not be obvious at birth. Careful observation of the infant may produce some useful information about the infant's behavior that can alert you to the need for further assessment.

Twins and Multiples

Babies who are born one at a time are called singletons. A small number of babies, about one in 80, are born as twins. There are two types of twins: monozygotic (from a single egg that has split into two) and dizygotic (twins that develop from two separate eggs).

Twins and multiples, although born one after the other, may be very different and may also be at an increased risk for developmental delays due to preterm birth and low birth weights. It has been noted that cerebral palsy has a higher rate of incidence in twin and multiple births (National Institute of Neurological Disorder & Stroke, 2006).

There are increasing numbers of triplets and multiples being born (Kogan, Alexander, Kotelchuck, MacDorman, Buekens, Martin, & Papiernik, 2000). This is thought to be because of the increased use of fertility drugs among women experiencing fertility problems. There are several organizations in the United States that offer advice, information, emotional support, and practical support, such as the National Organization of Mothers of Twins Club. It can be very expensive to raise twins and multiples, but the greatest challenge for family members is to remain healthy and get enough sleep while simultaneously meeting the needs of the children. Parents soon come to understand that they are raising children with very different temperaments. Their patterns of sleep and wakefulness can vary to such an extent that they are never asleep at the same time. It is quite possible to breast-feed twins or even triplets, but there are a variety of demands put upon the mother, father, and other caregivers. It becomes essential to focus on the babies and try to ignore less important things such as housework!

Socioeconomic Circumstances

Poverty can cause a multitude of problems for the unborn and newborn infant. Malnutrition of the mother, poor prenatal care, unsanitary living conditions, or exposure to inappropriate environments can all affect the infant. Early maternal support can make the outcome much more positive for both mother and infant.

Keep It in Perspective

Even with all the information presented in this section about what can harm a fetus or cause developmental problems for a child at birth, it is essential to remember that generally over 70 percent of women have problem-free pregnancies. Good infant health and outcomes are directly related to the mother's overall health and prenatal care during pregnancy.

Developmental Assessment

developmental delay

the challenge facing an individual who is not developing according to the expected time frame; a classification of an individual, with or without a diagnosis, who is performing significantly behind developmental norms

All babies, regardless of their health at birth, need ongoing assessment. In 2001, the American Academy of Pediatrics (AAP) adopted a policy that all infants and young children be screened for **developmental delay** at health supervision visits, and recommended the use of valid, reliable screening tools. Information, observation, and formal screenings and assessments are essential to ensure that the developmental needs of the infant are met (Green & Palfrey, 2002).

Schedules for health and developmental checks vary from state to state. One of the most commonly used neonatal tools is the Neonatal Behavioral Assessment Scale (NBAS) (Brazelton, 1995). It requires a trained examiner and can identify a range of concerns. Other assessment tools include the NAPI (Neurobehavioral Assessment of the Preterm Infant) and the NICU Network Neurobehavioral Scale (NNNS™). The impetus for the development of the NAPI in 1977 was the need to measure the differential maturity levels of preterm infants who participated in a randomized controled study of the effectiveness of vestibular stimulation. The NAPI was published in 1990 (Korner & Thom, 1990) following more than ten years of extensive theoretical and clinical work. Lester and Tronick (2004) developed the NICU Network Neurobehavioral Scale to evaluate substance-exposed and high-risk infants, and it is a tool that can be utilized with preterm babies who are born at 30 weeks, gestation. All of these tools can help identify the need for intervention.

developmental alerts

behaviors that are atypical (significantly different from the norm) of the child's stage, or otherwise indicate cause for concern; they usually require further observation and possible referral to appropriate agencies and professionals

Many of the most serious disorders are likely to be noticed at birth. More mild, but still very significant defects may be noticed by the families and caregivers in the first weeks and months of life. Infants' responses to visual and auditory stimulation may indicate challenges in these areas. If these potential problems are observed in naturalistic, everyday situations, they may need further investigation by professionals.

 DEVELOPMENTAL ALERTS

You will see variations in each newborn. Avoid making assumptions about the causes of developmental variations or differences in appearance, but ensure that you respond to any real developmental or health concerns. Any of the following are potential causes for concern, or **developmental alerts**, in the neonatal period:

- absence of reflexive behaviors such as rooting when the cheek is stroked, sucking for milk, and swallowing
- absence of reflexive startle response where baby throws out arms and legs and opens hands
- absence of grasping a finger or small object
- absence of stepping when held upright with bare feet touching a surface

You also should notice when a baby:

asymmetrical

not straight or uniform; lacking in balance or harmonious arrangement

- has an **asymmetrical appearance**
- has asymmetrical movements

- displays prolonged jerkiness of movements
- has high-pitched crying
- does not cry
- shows no response to stimuli
- displays floppiness of the arms or legs
- has severe responses to foods or other substances
- has bulging or sunken fontanels
- has an enlarged head
- fails to feed
- shows prolonged colic/abdominal distress
- has a lack of eye engagement (after 2–3 weeks)
- displays prolonged distress and irritability

HEALTH CONCERNS

Health concerns may overlap with developmental alerts. Any of the following observations should receive medical attention:

- no breathing
- rapid respiration (over 60 breaths per minute)
- diminished breath sounds
- no pulse
- heart rate change (over 180 or under 100 per minute)
- soreness in the diaper area
- raised or lowered body temperature: normal rectal temperature is 100°F (38°C); normal armpit temperature is 97–98°F (36.1–37°C)
- choking
- skin rashes
- navel "weeping" or bleeding
- feeding difficulties
- excessive spitting up
- dehydration (diminished urination, sunken eyes, less skin firmness, quick weight loss, drowsiness, altered breathing)
- swollen or sunken fontanels
- vomiting
- unusual sleepiness or difficulty in waking
- diarrhea, unusual fecal matter, or blood in the stools
- discharge from the vagina
- swollen genitals that do not correct themselves
- unpredicted blueness around the mouth or any part of the body
- yellowing of the skin or any skin-color changes
- seizures (convulsions)
- white, furry mouth or reddened mouth
- adverse reactions to medications
- allergic responses
- breathing difficulties, congestion, or runny nose
- sticky eyes
- bleeding from any part of the body
- signs of injury, including bruising and other marks
- unusual behavior

In addition, all accidents must be documented and reported to parents. Any resultant breathing difficulty, significant bleeding, loss of consciousness, choking, convulsion, or other significant symptom should receive an immediate first aid response and referral to a qualified medical practitioner. Enrollment in a specialized infant first aid and cardiopulmonary resuscitation (CPR) course, such as those offered by the American Red Cross, is essential for anyone working with newborns.

SIGNS OF POTENTIAL NEGLECT OR ABUSE

Abuse

abuse

psychological, physical, or sexual injury inflicted on an individual

Abuse is a difficult word to define. Standards of care vary, and the perception of them is somewhat subjective. What is acceptable practice to one parent or caregiver may be thought of as abuse by another. That said, abuse can be defined as an active, aggressive act that causes physical, sexual, or emotional harm. Some believe that there must be a degree of willfulness on the part of the abuser, but this assumes that abuse can occur only when it is deliberate. In infant caregiving, it is entirely possible to abuse an infant by being careless or rough, or because of lack of skills.

Certain conditions may make abuse more likely. They include, often in combination, a lack of education and skills to meet the needs of the infant, undue stress in personal or sexual relationships, financial hardship, and social isolation. In addition, abusive adults may have a low tolerance for frustration. They may lack an attachment to the infant, see any demands by the infant as willfully intrusive, have early life experience of being abused themselves, or lack strategies to solve problems.

Parental and caregiver behavior is likely to point to problems, although it is quite unlikely that an adult will be abusive in front of others. Lack of attachment coupled with some physical sign might indicate a potential difficulty. Sometimes the adult will be overly nice to the baby in front of others. At other times, an adult's disregard for the baby might be a signal that help is needed—the adult may be trying to communicate the problem.

shaken baby syndrome

a form of inflicted head trauma. Head injury, as a form of child abuse, can be caused by direct blows to the head, dropping or throwing the child, or shaking the child. This sudden whiplash motion can cause bleeding inside the head and increased pressure on the brain, causing the brain to pull apart, resulting in injury to the baby. The vast majority of incidents occur in infants who are younger than 1 year old

The more common forms of infant abuse include shaking and bruising the infant. This usually occurs as a result of adult frustrations. As discussed in Chapter 2, **shaken baby syndrome** can lead to significant internal damage to the baby's head; it can result in brain damage and death. Marks on the infant's body can be minimal even when there has been major damage. Behavioral changes in the infant—seizures, prolonged jerkiness, floppiness, or altered awareness—may be indicators of a problem. Bruises are easier to detect; sometimes they may even correspond to the shape of the adult's hand. Abuse of very young infants can be hard to identify unless we observe the infant closely and become familiar with individual patterns. We can then notice small changes in appearance or behavior that might indicate a potential problem.

Adult Frustrations

Here we will consider why babies are sometimes the victims of adult frustrations, rather than look at the baby for signs that frustration has been taken out on her. Some adults manage their emotions better than others—this may be as a result of their own personality, the role models that they have internalized, and the frustrations that they experience. Similar sets of circumstances can lead adults to behave in opposite ways. It is likely that persons' perceptions of their life circumstances are more significant than their actual standard of living, opportunities, and relationships. That said, a person undergoing particularly difficult life transitions, such as divorce, loss of employment, change of location, breakup of relationships, and so on, is going to experience some significant stressors—how that person might respond cannot be easily predicted. Stressors are prevalent among different socioeconomic groups, and responses to those stressors may vary—people from all kinds of backgrounds express their frustrations in inappropriate ways. Lack of control of their behavior may become an issue, and is particularly damaging when directed toward a vulnerable baby.

Frustration can lead to an unhealthy emotional climate in the home—or child care center. In both settings, adults can experience frustration. The professional setting may mean that the staff members are better prepared, but they too may have challenges in their personal and/or professional lives. Fortunately the group context of child care offers some protection to the children—staff members monitor one another's behavior. But this isn't always a certainty. Staff may try to find excuses for what they see as another staff member's temporary difficulties. Friendships among staff members may also protect the staff member rather than the vulnerable infant.

Handling a baby when one is frustrated easily transmits feelings to the baby. Because physical touch is the primary path of communication, the baby may well respond to negativity before the adults even know that is what they are feeling. Frustration may show itself to the baby emotionally, physically, or both ways. Poor handling of the baby, rough management of her needs, or neglect can result from such frustration.

Neglect

neglect

the denial of an individual's basic needs; these needs can be physical, educational, or emotional

Neglect involves a passive disregard for meeting the needs of an infant. Neglect can take a variety of forms and sometimes is the result of a lack of parenting knowledge, economic hardship, mental illness, and a number of other factors. Neglect may involve negligence in providing for the infant's basic needs. It can be physical, educational, or emotional. Physical neglect can include not providing adequate food or clothing, appropriate medical care, supervision, or proper weather protection (heat or coats). Educational neglect includes failure to provide appropriate schooling or special educational needs. Psychological neglect includes the lack of any emotional support and love or total disregard of needed attention for the child. The outcome of neglect can lead to poor growth, lack of responsivity, dehydration, hypothermia, infection, developmental difficulties, and, in extreme situations, death.

Because infants require constant care and attention, it can be a real challenge for any parent or caregiver to meet all the baby's needs. However, in our society the child has the right to expect, and the parent has a duty (within reason) to provide, food, clothing, shelter, supervision, medical care, nurturance, and teaching This is especially true for very young children, since they are so dependent upon adults to meet their needs.

Premature infants are at higher risk for abuse and/or neglect, reflecting early relationship difficulties (Sullivan & Knutson, 2000). Creating a relationship between preterm infants and parents is often difficult to achieve, even though it is a critical element for building trust and attachment. According to Browne (2003), the burden of medical expenses, which foster economic hardship, stress from caregiving duties, and adjustment to a reality that was unexpected, place families in crisis and add to the difficulty of forming relationships, a problem that can last for a number of years.

baby blues

a common temporary psychological state right after childbirth when a new mother may have sudden mood swings. These emotions can range from feeling very happy to suddenly feeling very sad, which can result in crying for no apparent reason. Other moms report feeling impatient, unusually irritable, restless, anxious, or lonely. The baby blues may last only a few hours or as long as 1–2 weeks after delivery

Maternal Depression

A small percentage of mothers, rather more than might be willing to admit it, suffer from postpartum depression. This is a pathological condition that has much greater impact than the **baby blues** experienced by most women two or three days after birth.

Postpartum depression could last for only a few weeks, but it is more likely to last for months and may go on longer than that. The mother is unduly challenged to cope with her baby, other family members, domestic responsibilities, the relationship with her partner, and possibly a work situation. She is overwhelmed by feelings of negativity, poor self-worth, and apathy. She likely has sleep problems and appetite difficulties, and is unable to manage daily tasks. At times, she feels low or even suicidal. Isolation, changing family dynamics and altered roles, a diminution in sexual interest, and lack of sleep may increase the depression.

Maternal depression affects the quality and quantity of care the mother is able to offer her infant. She may not realize that her feelings are extreme, and may need supportive adults to help her address the problem and seek help. Support groups, psychotherapy, prescription drug

postpartum depression

a period of time when some mothers experience depression, low energy levels, negative moods, or other symptoms; possibly a result of chemical or hormonal changes after giving birth; moms may need medical or psychiatric assistance therapy, and a variety of other treatments are available and can be effective, given time. The problem for the infant is that he can't wait. His needs are immediate. He needs to be fed when he is hungry, changed when he is wet, and responded to rapidly and warmly so that he can start building his sense of self and trust in adults. Adults in the mother's life can help the mother–child dyad by removing pressure, by "being there" in a nonjudgmental way, providing a positive role model for quality caregiving, praising the mother's efforts at responding to her baby, and ensuring that the child is adequately protected from potential harm.

The long-term effects of maternal depression on infants can be lessened with complementary care from other adults. But the mother's role is so important throughout the child's life that early support is often essential to ensure positive outcomes for the child. Attachments between mother and child may need extra support. This may be expensive and time-consuming, but early intervention may prevent later emotional problems that would require a much larger investment.

Both adult frustration and maternal depression have the potential of contributing to the profile of the person who commits abusive behavior or neglects infants and very young children. While the majority of professionals may wonder how such terrible things occur—and no excuse should be found, only perhaps some reasons as to why it happens—some families may reflect on their experiences and wonder how they stopped themselves from going over the edge. In most of us, fortunately, there is an inner voice that stops us from committing acts that we know are wrong—but it's a voice that is silent at times for some people.

Frustration and depression are not the only reasons for victimizing infants with abuse or neglect— but they explain many of the circumstances when they might suffer.

The infant's long-term development is likely to be affected by any kind of abuse or neglect. Physically abused and neglected children have a variety of difficulties, including developmental delay, behavioral problems, and excessive hostility. Even though the infant will not have an autobiographical memory detailing the events of abuse or neglect, any negative pattern of interaction and violent events will influence every aspect of the child's later development.

Caregivers' Responsibility

Early childhood educators can play a key role in the primary prevention of child abuse and neglect and the promotion of children's healthy social and emotional development because of their collaborative role in family life. A NAEYC national survey found that 97 percent of early childhood educators wanted to join efforts to help families prevent child abuse and neglect, and that 70 percent felt it was their professional responsibility not just to report it, but to do whatever they could to prevent child abuse and neglect (Olson & Hyson, 2003). The caregiver needs to ensure that signs of abuse are documented and offered to the child protection agency for investigation. It is not the task of the caregiver to diagnose abuse or assign blame, because it is possible that the same signs and symptoms have an explanation other than neglect or abuse.

For a review of abuse and neglect, see the Additional Support section of your Online Companion.

EVERYDAY SAFETY ISSUES

Protection from all kinds of hazards is essential for any baby in the neonatal stage, because they are so small, lacking in physical control, and generally vulnerable.

The Additional Support section of your Online Companion contains a heading entitled "Everyday Safety Issues." There you can read about some of the most common and significant factors that caregivers should consider at each stage of development. Make sure that you consult these suggestions, since you will be responsible for protecting these precious lives. A newborn needs to be supervised at all times. In most instances, accidents do not happen to newborns because most incidents are preventable. The lists you will find in your Online Companion are only a start to ensuring that infants are safe. Protection involves a

A word about baby swings. Many child care facilities no longer allow the use of baby swings, both from a safety and a responsive care standpoint. Many accidents can occur while babies are in baby swings. In addition, it has been documented that often baby swings are overutilized and replace the human contact that infants require. You need to clarify the policy on baby swings in each facility where you work in order to have a clear understanding. Even if the site allows baby swings, you need to be on guard for safety issues and you need to make sure that the swings are not a substitute for loving arms and a warm and responsive person.

supportive guidance
providing the individual with appropriate encouragement, nurturance, and instruction, and reinforcing positive behavior

constant evaluation of the environment and an awareness of the child's developmental stage and particular vulnerabilities.

STARTING POINTS FOR RESPONSE

Responsive Caregiving

Newborn babies are dependent upon their caregivers in every way, although they have remarkable potential. Mother and baby usually have opportunities to get to know each other and form a bond. All caregiving strategies need to address this bonding process. The most important part of caregiving is in providing for the physical needs of the child. Parents and other caregivers have to learn the baby's cues. Through feeding, changing, holding, cuddling, dressing, bathing, and talking to the baby, and tuning in to the responses, two-way communication can be established.

Although it may seem that the baby responds to experiences more than she initiates them, it can be interesting when we pay close attention to the communications that start from her. Two-way communication is dependent upon our reading the cues—identifying the messages that the baby is deliberately, or by chance, sending to us. When we acknowledge the cue, we are trying to engage with the baby—just as she might be trying to engage with us. Engagement is the two-way connection that comes about when baby and adult enter each other's consciousness. There is a special communication that doesn't necessarily require words or sounds, but is likely to rely upon facial expression. Sound production from either the baby or adult may enhance this connection; adults may use some high-pitched words to support the engagement, or the baby may make cooing or contented noises. The neonate does not yet have a social smile, but she is programmed to seek and stare as methods of early engagement.

After a short while, the baby's engagement is likely to fade. After all, her concentration span may not be very long. Adults might be surprised at how long the sequences can last, but eventually the baby will disengage by looking away, showing another focus, drooling, or showing behaviors unrelated to the engagement.

Babies separated from their mothers can bond successfully with their caregiver, but such a process must be based on responsive physical contact and meeting needs promptly. Box 4.4 provides some suggestions to help you tune in to the newborns, read their cues, and respond in a helpful way.

 This list is not comprehensive, and many more suggestions can be found in your Online Companion under the section entitled "Getting in Tune with Infants, Toddlers, and Twos."

Supportive Guidance

The object of **supportive guidance** is to do far more than just make clear where the boundaries are. The intent is to provide a positive framework within which the baby is comfortable, feels safe, and can take small risks. She needs to learn about people in her immediate world and to learn to function effectively in society. This starts with building relationships.

To discipline a newborn baby is inappropriate, but this is the time to establish positive patterns of interaction. Being responsive to the baby's needs is the first guidance strategy that the adult must offer. Later behavior is dependent upon the social relationships that the baby makes. Time, opportunity, and shared experiences are reinforcers of behavior.

It is impossible to spoil babies. No effort to meet their needs can be too much. The reciprocal communication between baby and mother (or other adults) provides the backdrop for establishing trust. It would not be an overstatement to say that this relationship provides for the roots of character development, security, self-knowledge, moral understanding, emotional regulation, physical health, and later development.

 In Activity 4.3, in your Online Companion, the question of spoiling infants is hotly debated. Where do you stand?

BOX 4.4

GETTING IN TUNE WITH THE NEWBORN

Below are some starting points for building your **responsivity** skills with a newborn:

- Respond to crying promptly.
- Identify possible causes of discomfort (need for diaper change, hunger, gas, need for attention).
- Notice the type of cry and what that means for this baby.
- Respond to the baby's state of awareness (uptime, downtime, trance, sleep).
- Check the supply of all basic needs (warmth, protection, hunger, comfort).
- Identify the baby's temperament style and provide appropriate responses.
- Support attachments by offering responses quickly and tenderly.
- Take time for eye-gazing.
- Rock the baby in your arms or over your shoulder, whichever the baby prefers.
- Observe reactions to stimuli and respond to the baby's preferences.
- Imitate the baby's own sound production.
- Take turns sending and receiving messages.
- Protect the baby from any danger.

responsivity

the process of being responsive to the needs of each child; involves a philosophy and an attitude of mind

Facilitating Development

When newborns' emotional and physical needs are met, all domains of development are supported. Early brain development occurs rapidly, and newborns need adequate human stimulation more than toys or fancy rooms. Caregivers need to tune in to babies' responses to stimuli and withdraw when necessary. Constant bombardment is confusing rather than helpful.

Supporting parents in both their confidence and competence can be particularly important at this early time. Facilitating development is typically the responsibility of families, but most parents need practical and emotional support so that the baby–adult relationship can get off to a good start. Early relationships between adults and babies can be challenging when their knowledge of each other is insufficient to identify the baby's rhythms and responses. All relationships take time; any efforts to further the relationship provide the foundations for healthy development.

Babies need opportunities to move and to gain physical control over their bodies. They gain preliminary schemes of understanding from the actions they make. The beginnings of understanding about being a separate person arise from the responses the newborn gets from adults and the way they affect her world.

Holistic Response

Activities 4.4 and 4.5 on your CD-ROM encourage a **holistic response** to newborns. Activity 4.4 suggests different ways of responding to the changing needs of newborns in order to extend your interactions with them. Activity 4.5 helps you observe each baby and create a responsive curriculum that is targeted to individual interests and skill levels. If the baby is demonstrating engagement and interest, then utilize Activity 4.6, which offers additional information on experiences and interactions.

In each of the following chapters, you will find similar activities included in your Online Companion and CD-ROM. The intent of these activities is to provide a range of potentially useful

holistic response

any response to an individual that takes into account each interacting domain of the person's development

experiences appropriate for the age or stage of the infant, toddler, or 2-year-old. Remember, young children vary tremendously in their stages of development, styles of interaction, interests, and moods of the moment!

The concept of *See How They Grow* is to develop relationships and offer experiences that support the very young child's optimal development. The core activities that you will have with a newborn will be entirely spontaneous. Because communication is a two-way process, you'll need to merge receiving and initiating communication. The main point of all the holistic response activities in your Online Companion and CD-ROM is engagement. "Engaging babies is crucial for not only obtaining a fuller empirical picture of infant development, but also for the infant's development as well—for well-being, learning, and teaching" (Reddy & Trevarthen, 2004). As in all relationships, you need to balance sending and receiving messages. You read her messages and you try to enable her to read yours. It's a give-and-take process, and she needs to be as much in charge of it as you are.

Remember that human relationships are more important than materials, particularly at this very early stage. The experiences are starting points for joyful engagement. If the baby is not responsive to the stimulation or appears interested in something else, follow her lead rather than your own! Observe her actions, try offering the experience in a variety of different ways, check her response. If she is engaged with the experience, or anything that happens as a result of your planning, ensure that you enter the moment with her. If she is enjoying the experience, support it with language and calm encouragement. Whenever the experience is successful, try repeating it—babies often respond well to repetition. They learn what to expect, which is gratifying for them. Then, for novelty, try a variation of the activity, with only minor differences. Monitor the response you get from her. At all times focus on her rather than trying to make your activity successful. Relatively minor activity can prompt positive engagement. Enjoy your interactions!

Even as a very young infant, the baby needs an adult to support her learning about the human and concrete environment. She is not a passive receiver of information, but an active seeker. She performs actions on her world to help her learn about it and she initiates communications, but she is limited in her mobility and language, even though she has some competence at making attachments. Guiding the baby responsively requires understanding these things and providing a bridge for her between her known world and the world she has yet to learn about. Activity 4.7 in your CD-ROM offers several suggestions on responsive guidance.

Although purchasing toys is not an essential part of nurturing babies, many parents and other adults like to buy toys to express their celebration of the child's life. Having a room full of toys is more likely to impress adults than babies, but there are some purchases that are more appropriate than others. Some toys are more suitable for the home environment than for group care, but the expense of some materials can only be justified if the items will have multiple users. The baby stage is so short that some toys are only played with for a very short period in any one child's life. Always check each item for safety and clean it appropriately, especially between its use by one baby and the next. Your Online Companion contains a section entitled "Toys." It lists suggested toys for all ages and stages of infancy and toddlerhood.

THE IMPORTANCE OF FACILITATING LITERACY

literacy-rich environment

an environment containing essential components (e.g., books, daily reading, adult role models, writing materials, etc.) that help foster and support the acquisition of literacy

Although most attention on the topic of literacy has been focused on the preschool and elementary years of children's lives, it is evident that the first three years are "incredibly important in producing a nation of readers" (Rosenkoetter & Knapp-Philo, 2004, p. 5). Research documents that the more children understand about language and literacy (listening, speaking, writing, reading, and viewing), the stronger their foundation for reading success (Bardige & Segal, 2005; Bennett-Arminstead, Duke, & Moses, 2005). Exposure to language and books is essential for supporting emerging literacy skills. "Indeed, by the end of infancy, children growing up in **literacy-rich environments** can pretend to read books,

The care providers in this facility have purposefully placed a book on the edge of the baby padded ring to encourage this infant's independent engagement in a literacy experience.

make letter-like marks (in finger-paint, perhaps), and, most important, show a strong interest in reading and writing materials" (Bennett-Armistead, Duke, & Moses, 2005, p. 7). According to Jalongo (2004) and Vukelich, Christie, and Enz (2002) these environments have the following:

- children are surrounded with oral language, books, and print;
- book reading to children is an activity that occurs multiple times every day;
- reading and writing materials are available; adults model reading and writing as part of their daily routine and activities;
- TV viewing is not available to infants and toddlers, and is closely monitored for preschoolers;
- adults support literacy acquisition by answering questions through pointing out print, reading, visiting the library, and providing varied experiences rich in opportunities for learning about the world—such as trips to parks, museums, and local points of interest; and
- playing with language and linking play experiences with books and print is supported.

In these environments, print and language are seen as functional and essential. However, besides the provision of a literacy-rich environment, there are other significant elements creating an atmosphere that fosters literacy. Consider the following points:

efficacy

the knowledge that it is worth trying something because you know you will succeed, and the confidence stemming from the belief that your actions will have predictable effects

- Oral language provides the foundation for literacy skills.
- Self-motivation and **efficacy** (Bardige & Segal, 2005) are essential to the attainment of literacy success.
- Relationships lay at the heart of literacy, since it is through those relationships that infants and toddlers learn to trust the world, reach out to explore the world, and feel confident enough to take the risk to tackle all the components involved in literacy learning.
- Play supports the acquisition of literacy, since it is the perfect medium through which children can make connections between oral and written modes of expression (Howes, & Wishard, 2004; Owocki, 1999; Roskos & Christie, 2004).
- The home, community, and culture exert tremendous impact on children's attainment of literacy (Daly, 2005; Rosenkoetter & Knapp-Philo, 2004).
- Every family, in ways that respect their culture, is capable of helping infants and toddlers gain competence in language and literacy (Bardige & Segal, 2005; Rosenkoetter & Knapp-Philo, 2004).

Given that Bennett-Armistead, Duke, and Moses (2005) found that parents routinely read to only 50 percent of infants and toddlers, and that often facilities providing care for our youngest are pitifully lacking in literacy materials and experiences, "the question is not whether to weave literacy into the early childhood environments and activities, but how to do so in ways that are developmentally appropriate and productive." Rosenkoetter and Knapp-Philo (2004) identified five factors that could help caregivers share language and literacy with infants and toddlers who would support best practices in an infant and toddler setting if interpreted and carried out in sensitive and respectful manner. They termed this as helping children "read their world" (p. 6). They include: *presence, time, words, print,* and *intentionality.*

- *Presence* means that caregivers are available to children because they are physically in the same space, and therefore able to respond to children's actions and vocalizations.
- *Time* denotes the concept that caregivers take the time to notice and expand on children's experiences.
- The factor of *words* acknowledges that children need an environment steeped in words, many, many words. The Hart and Risley studies (1995, 1999) documented the importance of the amount of language heard by children from different economic backgrounds. The result is that children who initially have a wider base of vocabulary tend to keep learning words at a faster pace than children who have a smaller base (Bardige & Segal, 2005).
- *Print* implies that adults need to constantly point out the existence of printed material and convey to children the power that the printed word carries.
- Finally, and most importantly, caregivers' *intentionality* "means thoughtfully providing children with the experiences they need to achieve developmentally appropriate skills in early literacy" (Parlakian, 2004, p. 37). This intentionality includes such things as creating print-rich environments, providing culturally appropriate materials, singing songs and nursery rhymes, allowing children to access and handle books, reading stories, reading stories repeatedly, using rich descriptive vocabulary both in the context of current experiences and in decontextualized situations (language that signifies moving beyond the here and now into imaginary realms or to past and future events) and modeling and offering strategies to families in order to increase the support of literacy across the dividing boundary of home and school.

If we take these points to heart, it becomes obvious that purposeful planning to provide book reading and opportunities to play with language has to be a critical component of our interactions with infants and toddlers each and every day. To help foster the love of literacy, there is a Children's Books section in your Online Companion. It is separated into different ages, which align with the chapters of the textbook.

SUMMARY

Newborns have greater capabilities than we thought even a decade ago. Their sensory activity allows them to take in lots of information from their early experiences of life. Even more significant, infants are born with a wide range of reflexive movements that are innate and somehow allow them to acquire skills later in life. The pre-wiring for learning is present at birth.

Each birthing experience is different. A positive birthing seems to result in fewer emotional difficulties. Early physical contact is essential, helps to cement the bond with the caring adult, and fosters attachment, an essential component of emotional well-being. The transition to motherhood can present some challenges, and some mothers may need extra support, both physically and psychologically.

The demands of parenting can be considerable. Newborn babies are totally dependent on adults for every aspect of their care. Although newborns may sleep for longer than older babies, they take time to establish a pattern. They thrive on consistent handling and prompt responses to their needs. A feeding routine may not be established for some time.

Infants are unique. They are born into families with differing styles, values, and practices. There are many ways to be an effective parent, and all of them must be respected.

Although each family dreams and hopes for a healthy child, sometimes that is not the case. Each year some children in the United States are born premature, or with birth defects stemming from chromosomal, metabolic, or structural abnormalities. Some children have been exposed to teratogens in utero, and display negative consequences from that experience. Developmental assessments can help identify conditions that are not readily apparent at birth,

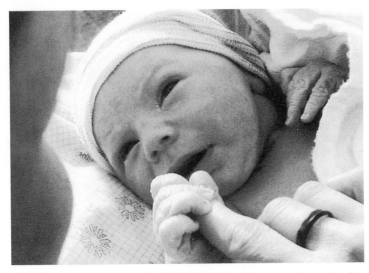

It is in the first weeks and months of life that children first try to understand and master their environment, and find those efforts encouraged—or not; first attempt to concentrate and find it possible—or not; first conclude that the world is an orderly place—or not; first learn that others are basically supportive—or not. It is in those years that the foundations for later learning are laid down. Or are not. (Beatty, 1992, p. 4)

and care providers need to be aware of developmental red flags and health conditions that signal potential problems.

Newborns are at risk for potential abuse and neglect for many reasons, including the fact that they are vulnerable and totally dependent on the adults who care for them. Adult frustration and maternal depression, including postpartum depression, can place infants at risk. One form of abuse that is sometimes seen is shaken baby syndrome. Teachers need to be vigilant and help support new families as they adjust to the new, and sometimes overwhelming, responsibility of caring for a new life. Suggestions to aid caregivers in developing responsivity skills for newborns, and additional resources for engagement activities, toys, and books are available in the Online

Companion. The chapter concludes with a focus on the importance of language and literacy, even for these very young children.

DISCUSSION QUESTIONS

1. To what extent do you think birthing experiences affect the child's later development?
2. Explain why you think that neonates are competent or incompetent.
3. How urgent is attachment? Do neonates need immediate bonding with an adult?
4. If you were caring for toddlers, what information about their neonatal period might be helpful to your understanding of their development?
5. What if a father is the primary caregiver? Do you think/feel that there would be differences in the baby?
6. Newborn babies often raise conflicting feelings in people. What are your feelings regarding newborns? Are you scared, confused, overwhelmed, in awe, confident?

ADDITIONAL RESOURCES

Further Reading

American Academy of Pediatrics. (2004). *Caring for your baby and young child: Birth to age 5.*

Armistead, V. S., Duke, N. K., & Moses, A. M. (2005). *Literacy and the youngest learners: Best practices for educators of children birth to 5.* Philadelphia: Teaching Resources.

Bardige, B. S., & Segal, M. (2005). *Building literacy with love: A guide for teachers and caregivers of children birth through age 5.* Washington, DC: ZERO TO THREE.

Brazelton, T. B. (1992). *Touchpoints the essential reference: Your child's emotional and behavioral development.* New York: Addison-Wesley Publishing Company.

Fraiberg, S. H. (1996—re-issue). *The magic years.* New York: Scribner.

Harrison, H. (1983). *The premature baby book.* New York: St. Martin's Press.

Harwood, M., & Kleinfeld. (2002). Up front and in hope: The value of early intervention for children with fetal alcohol syndrome. *Young Children, 57*(4), 86–90.

Henderson, K. (1999). *Newborn.* New York: Dial Books.

Klaus, M., Fox, N., & Keefe, M. (1998). *Amazing talents of the newborn: Emerging perspectives in perinatal care—Reference guide & video.* St. Louis, MO: Johnson & Johnson Pediatric Institute.

Klaus, M. H., & Klaus, P. H. (1999). *Your amazing newborn.* Cambridge, MA: Perseus Books.

———. (1994). *The new baby and child care: A quick reference encyclopaedia.* Toronto: Family Communications.

Lindsay, J. (2003). *Nurturing your newborn: Young parents' guide to baby's first month.* Buena Park, CA: Morning Glory Press.

Mehren, E. (1998). *Born too soon.* New York: Kensington Pub. Corp.

Rosenkoetter, S. H., & Knapp-Philo, J. (Eds.). (2006). *Learning to read the world: Language and literacy in the first three years of life.* Washington, DC: ZERO TO THREE.

Sears, J., Sears, M., Sears, R., & Sears, W. (2003). *The baby book*. New York: Little Brown

Simkin, P., Whalley, J., & Keppler, A. (2001). *Pregnancy, childbirth and the newborn: The complete guide*. Deephaven, MN: Meadowbrook/Simon and Schuster.

Skonkoff, J. P., & Marshall, P. C. (2003). The biology of developmental vulnerability. In J. P. Skonkoff & S. J. Meisels (Eds.), *Handbook of early childhood intervention* (2nd ed.), pp. 35–53. New York: Cambridge University Press.

Verny, T. R., & Weintraub, P. (2002). *Tomorrow's baby: The art and science of parenting from conception through infancy*. New York: Simon & Schuster.

WestEd Center for Child and Family Studies. (1998). *Talking points for essential connections*. Sacramento, CA: California Department of Education.

Zero to Three—Bulletins. National Center for Infants, Toddlers and Families, Washington, DC.

Useful Videos

Child Development: The First Two Years (1992**)**. Available at http://www.amazon.com

First Person: Impressions of Being a Baby (1994). 30-minute video on the first two years of a child's life. Available from http://www.childdevmedia.com/

Click on Child Development, click on First Person: Impressions of Being a Baby.

I Am Your Child Video Series. Available at http://store.parentsaction-store.org/

Click on StoreFront.

Individual videos, or sets of 7 or 11 videos on different topics.

Keys to Quality Infant and Toddler Care. Available at http://www.magnasystemsvideos.com/

Investing in Caring Relationships. Available at http://www.magnasystemsvideos.com/

NOVA: Life's First Feelings—Growing Pains (1986). Available at http://www.amazon.com

Ten Things Every Child Needs (1999). Available at http://www.amazon.com

Useful Web Sites

American Academy of Pediatrics (AAP)
www.aap.org

Association of Women's Health, Obstetrics and Neonatal Nurses
http://www.awhonn.org/
Click on News & Events, click on Press Office, click on Press Releases—General Index, click on July 29, 2003—WHAT PARENTS SHOULD KNOW ABOUT HEALTH SCREENINGS FOR NEWBORNS.

Breast-feeding
www.waba.org.br/

Child Development Institute
http://www.childdevelopmentinfo.com/

Dr. Sears—Parenting and Caregiving Issues
www.askdrsears.com

Fetal Alcohol
www.fetalalcohol.com/
Click on ENTER, click on What is FAS/E?

Indicators of Child Abuse
http://www.safekidsbc.ca/
Click on Community, click on Possible indicators of child abuse and neglect.

La Leche League—Breastfeeding
www.lalecheleague.org

March of Dimes—Birth defects
www.marchofdimes.org

Medscape
www.medscape.com

National Center for Education in Maternal and Child Health (NCEMCH)
www.ncemch.org\

National Center on Shaken Baby Syndrome
http://www.dontshake.com/

National Down Syndrome Society
www.ndss.org

National Healthy Mothers, Healthy Babies Coalition
www.hmhb.org

National Institute of Child Health and Human Development (NICHD)
www.nichd.nih.gov

National Network for Childcare
www.nmcc.org/

National Network for Childcare—ages/stages
www.nncc.org/
Click on Learn, click on Child Development, click on Infants and Toddlers, click on Programming Resources, click on Ages and Stages: Newborn to One Year.

Neonatology on the Web
www.neonatology.org/
Click on Diversions and Classics, click on Blast from the Past.

Organization of Teratology Information Services (OTIS)
www.otispregnancy.org

Premature Child
www.prematurity.org

Resources for Educarers
www.rie.org/
Click on Educarer.

Sure Baby Information
www.surebaby.com/

The Baby Center
www.babycenter.com

CHAPTER 5

Taking Notice: Infants from 6 Weeks to 3 Months

Some babies sleep much more than others. Their personal rhythms can differ, too. Many babies will soon sleep through the night, but for some parents, broken nights continue for months or even years.

LEARNING OUTCOMES

After reading and studying this chapter, you should be able to:

- identify the observable characteristics of development of infants at the 6-week to 3-month stage
- explain the significance of behaviors of infants from 6 weeks to 3 months of age in a developmental context
- recognize and respond to the developmental diversity of 6-week-old to 3-month-old infants
- assess the development of infants in the 6-week to 3-month stage
- respond to the health, safety, and development of 6-week-old to 3-month-old infants with appropriate nurturance, activities, protection, and caregiving
- develop strategies to work with parents as partners in the care and education of their young infants

SCENE

Early childhood education students are having a break for coffee and are enjoying a chat.

"I thought she would miss her mom," said an early childhood education student, **"but my 8-week-old niece was quite happy with me looking after her when my aunt went out shopping."** Like this student, you may have noticed that as long as the immediate needs of babies this age are met, they don't seem to mind who is meeting them.

This period, after the sometimes difficult adjustments to a newborn baby, can be rewarding. Said one young mother, "I remember that my son was much more like a real person by the time he was 6 or 7 weeks old. But by then I was feeling a whole lot better after a difficult delivery."

The early days and weeks are a challenging time for many parents and their babies. By about 6 to 8 weeks, there has usually been a settling period, and they may have managed to establish a pattern of sleep, feeding, and activity that suits all family members. "Baby blues," which are sometimes experienced by the mother because of hormonal changes, are likely to have passed, and the physical challenges of birthing are usually behind the mother as well.

Protecting very young babies from germs is important, but after a few weeks mothers will typically want to get out and about. Babies will be introduced to friends, extended family, and anyone else who wants to take a look. They generally will respond fairly well to seeing all these new people, actively scanning their faces. And they don't mind being fed by someone unusual, but they prefer to be comforted by their mother and the people they know best.

INITIAL SIGNS OF DEVELOPMENT AND GROWTH

separation

awareness of being without a person or object

You might be able to imagine what it is like to leave a baby with a caregiver when you are only just getting to know each other. **Separation** is two-sided: The baby separates from the mother, but the mother also has to separate from her baby. While we usually focus on one side of the challenge, we need to remember the reciprocal nature of separation. The family's emotional welfare is a significant issue for caregivers, because it directly affects the infant's security and building of trust. If separations are overly emotional, the climate will be tense and difficult for the baby. Watch for the way the separation occurs and try to support both mother and infant.

Social Relationships

Because infants at this stage are beginning to make associations between things that are pleasurable and the presence of their mother, they are likely to be more comfortable with their mother. Yet this does not mean that they cannot make a transition to multiple caregivers. If the infant's world expands to include other adults, these people must live up to the standard of reliability that exists between mother and baby.

Temperament Style

temperament

the observable traits or patterns of behavior of an individual; the way the individual behaves; the how of behavior, not the why

Some babies are slow to warm up to new people. You will see that their **temperament** shapes the patterns of interaction they have with adults (Chess & Thomas, 1996). Others are more accepting of changing surroundings and faces; these babies may appear to be easier to care for. The slow-to-warm-up infant may need a slower transition and more comforting. Watch for the kinds of reactions that babies have to new people. Although 6 weeks to 3 months may seem to be a very young age to have a baby cared for by a stranger, some parents report that the change to multiple caregivers is easier at this age than later, when the baby is attached more specifically to one adult.

Self-Regulation

self-regulation

the ability to control feelings and emotions, or the behavior that results from those emotions; the ability to modify or change behavior as a result of managing inner emotions

At this age, the ability of the baby to control herself in small ways is a major milestone. This process is called **self-regulation** (Bronson, 2000; Greenspan & Greenspan, 1994; Kopp, 2001; Lengua, 2002). During this period, the baby begins to be able to calm herself down, responds to stimuli with recognizable patterns, and tends to feed and sleep with a more discernible cycle. Recent studies have shown self-regulation emerges in the early interactions of infants with their primary caregivers (Schore, 2001; Shonkoff, Phillips, & Keilty, 2000; Keller et al., 2004). Sensitive and responsive caregiving in the first year of life, which protects children from excessive physiological stress, has been shown to significantly contribute to the development of children's capacity for self-regulation in later years (Brazelton & Greenspan, 2000;

This very young baby has learned a technique of calming himself, a very important part of self-regulation.

egocentric

from the perspective of the individual; in infancy, an inability to see from the perspective of others

McArthur, Martin, & Prairie, 2004; Ramey & Ramey, 1999). Her interest in the world remains completely **egocentric**—from her own perspective—and she sees everything through her own senses, with only a little knowledge that she is a separate human being, never mind the agent of significant emotional turmoil. So it is important to remember that when a baby appears to be driving an adult to despair, she is not doing it deliberately.

Growth Patterns

At this stage, infants grow approximately 1 inch a month (Allen & Marotz, 2007). The weight gain is more obvious than the relatively small increase in length. Weight will depend upon birth weight, maturity, nurturance, general health, activity level, and nutrition. Most babies will have a more plump appearance than they had in their first weeks. You may see some skin folds on their chubby arms and legs.

Not all babies are like this, though; others will be longer, thinner, and yet perfectly healthy. Steady weight gain and growth are more important than the baby's actual weight.

Sleep and Wakefulness

There are many variations in infants' patterns of sleep and wakefulness. According to Davis, Parker, and Montgomery (2004), sleep can be defined as quiet (sleep), active (alert), and indeterminate (neither sleep, or alert):

- Quiet sleep is characterized by minimal large or small muscle movements and rhythmic breathing cycles.
- During active sleep, sucking motions, twitches, smiles, frowns, irregular breathing, and gross limb movements (converse to the typical REM sleep paralysis seen at later ages) are seen.
- Indeterminate sleep is the period of sleep that cannot be defined as either active or quiet sleep using scientific measurements and predetermined criteria.[1]

Families may report that their infants are sleeping through the night and have been for some weeks. Other parents who look tired may be dealing with interruptions in their sleep because the baby awakens and wants feeding or other attention. Some babies may sleep only four or five hours at a time; others may sleep up to ten hours. The total amount of sleep per day will vary from infant to infant. They may take many or few naps, and be awake for short or prolonged periods.

DEVELOPMENTAL DOMAINS

Physical Development

Fine Motor Skills

By about 6 weeks, the baby can usually bring her hands to the middle of her body as she lies on her back. Your baby's hands are an endless source of fascination throughout much of the first year. She may look at her hands and appear to examine them carefully. "Her finger movements

---

[1]Reprinted from *Journal of Pediatric Health Care, 18* (2). K. F. Davis, K. Parker, & G. L. Montgomery. Sleep in infants and young children: Part I normal sleep, 65–71, 2004. With permission from The National Association of Pediatric Nurse Practitioners.

cephalocaudal/ proximodistal sequences

the development of the body follows dual sequences simultaneously—from head to foot (cephalocaudal) and from the center of the body outward to the hands (proximodistal)

myelination

the process where myelin is laid down on the nerves of the brain; when parts of the brain myelinate, it allows or improves the function of that area, such as movement or vision

are limited, since her hands are clenched in tight fists most of the time. But she can flex her arms and bring her hands to her mouth and into her line of vision "(Shelov, 1998, p. 148). She has some limited voluntary control of her hands, which she uses to grasp things, but she cannot deliberately let go. Initially, she is more likely to swipe at an object with her arm. This fine motor skill will not be very precise, but with time and practice, the swinging becomes more controlled. Until the control is established, babies usually endure many whacks in their faces from the uncontrolled movements.

Gross Motor Skills

When a young infant is placed in a sitting position, she may slide down the seat because her back is still rounded. She has not gained the back control necessary for real sitting and so extra care will be needed to ensure that she is comfortable. You may need to place some folded blankets around her to provide some extra support. Remember, this is not propping to get her sitting up faster, but rather a comfort consideration. She will usually hold her head up without a head lag, but she may not do this for prolonged periods or if she is tired. It takes a lot of physical effort and concentration to achieve the gross and fine motor skills that adults take for granted.

An infant may pull herself up on her arms for short periods if she is lying on her stomach, but she soon collapses and lays her head down again. These little press-ups show the increase in strength in her arms. So far, similar strength and control has not spread to her legs, although she may like to stretch them and kick. A random kick may become more controlled in time. At this stage, the baby may learn to kick her legs and feet deliberately, but this usually comes later.

Babies' physical skills develop gradually, with marked improvement in head control. According to the **cephalocaudal** sequence, physical skills progress from the head downward, while the **proximodistal** sequence of physical coordination is from the middle of the body outwards. This observable sequence of skills explains why young infants display gradual head control, then slowly improving chest, shoulder, arm, and hand control, but they can't sit up or even put their hand to their mouth in one smooth effort for months. In order to accomplish those tasks, they have to spend months exercising their muscles while their brains have to learn and retain the information necessary to reach those milestones. (See Figure 3.4 in Chapter 3.)

As babies gain new bodily control, they will use their skills to discover the world. Children who have cognitive challenges often have delayed physical skills. Remember, these skills are interdependent. (Review Box 3.6 in Chapter 3.) They may be less motivated to explore their environments, therefore they have fewer experiences upon which to build their knowledge.

Neurologically, physical and cognitive skills are mutually supportive. The brainstem and midbrain, which are called the subcortex, are the most developed parts of the brain of a very young baby. They regulate basic biological functions such as digestion and breathing. The outer layer of the brain, the cortex, allows for many kinds of thinking processes, but it is underdeveloped at birth. In time, the nerve cells that transmit messages from the cerebral cortex become more effective. They need a sheathing of myelin, which is a fatty substance, to do this.

The myelin serves as a type of insulation for the axon, but it also enhances the transmission of electrical signals. This process of **myelination** begins in the brain in the ninth month of gestation and continues for years. "Even when the neurons have grown all their branches and formed the synapses that complete the fundamental brain circuits, these circuits don't work very well until the axons are myelinated" (Eliot, 1999, p. 33). This helps explain why infants are not born with the ability to walk and talk. At birth, their synaptic connections are only sophisticated enough to enable them to survive. The process of myelination takes time and it progresses slowly. However, myelination eventually enables individuals to behave and think in a developmentally more mature manner. Of concern, however, is the effect that the stress hormone (cortisol) can exert on myelination. Research has documented that cortisol can interfere with the gene that regulates the insulation process and decrease the effectiveness of nerve signal transmission (Weaver, Diorio, Seckl, Szyf, & Meaney, 2004).

Reflexes

Reflexes such as stepping, sucking, and the withdrawal from painful stimulus disappear without warning during this stage (Allen & Marotz, 2007). Some of these reflexes, which were present at birth, may have triggered particular skills. For example, babies now do not need to root for food—they know where to find it. Also, their sucking is voluntary rather than reflexive, because they can choose when to suck. Researchers are divided about the purpose of the reflexes, but they are likely the outward sign of neurological pathways in the brain that allow for later development (Kotulak, 1996).

Some of the baby's actions develop from his reflexes, even when the reflexes have disappeared. Perhaps it is because the neural pathways have been formed that the baby extends reflexive actions from automatic to controlled behaviors. Early deliberate behaviors tend to be repetitious; this too reinforces new neurological connections.

The Senses and Perception

The sensory information received by the brain needs to be processed. Because this processing takes place internally, it cannot be observed. Nevertheless, we need to understand infants' cognitive processing if we want to be able to interpret subsequent behavior. Dr. Harry Chugani (1998), a pediatric neurobiologist, has studied this activity by using positron-emission tomography (PET). His exciting discoveries indicate that early experiences, not only pre-wiring, influence how the brain develops. If that is the case, then we have a challenging task to ensure that those experiences are appropriate.

Sight

maturational readiness

the notion that the child is ready for particular experiences at certain stages of growth

Visual information can be absorbed only according to the **maturational readiness** of the infant. For example, a baby who cannot yet focus on a mobile will be unable to take in information from it, but the same baby may be able to focus on an adult's face and therefore absorb that information. Research has documented that, in fact, babies are most interested in objects that present marked differences in contrasts of light and dark (Lamb, Bornstein, & Teti, 2002). From the eyes, chemical and electrical messages pass the information to the brain. The process works so fast that the baby can take in many thousands of sensory messages every minute. Visual stimulation can cause different kinds of responses. A simple reflexive response such as a blink is organized by the subcortex, while a more sophisticated response, such as recognizing what he sees and comparing it to previously understood information, is organized by a more complex part of the cortex. If the response is more complex, he might even cluster together some thoughts about what he sees; these we call visual schemes—early understandings gained through images.

What we will see is the infant's fixation on the visual stimulus and his reaction to it. If we become familiar with the baby, we may notice patterns of response and indicators of his familiarity with a particular form of stimulation. We may also notice when the baby looks away from the stimulus, or when he re-engages with it. These may be examples of habituation—that is, of the baby's becoming used to a stimulus—and may indicate the need for new stimuli. After lengthy observations of the infant, it will become increasingly clear to us that he is taking in a lot from his environment.

binocular vision

the capacity to coordinate the sensory input from both eyes; results in the ability to perceive depth

visual acuity

the degree to which the individual can see

It helps that a baby can use both eyes together to take in visual information. At this age, the eyes will usually be working together, or converging, so that the infant can begin to understand the idea of depth from his **binocular vision**—both eyes working in coordination. The brain has to process the information sent to it. If, at first, the baby has little experience of depth, it is likely that the information is not processed according to that concept. Maturational and experiential influences need to work together; in time, the baby's perception of depth increases. Generally, **visual acuity**—the ability to see—is improving throughout this stage. By about 3 months, the infant will be able to see farther away, perhaps to a mobile hanging from the ceiling or to an adult across the room.

Taste, Smell, and Hearing

The infant is likely to have a preference for sweet tastes, and might refuse water, being more satisfied by breast milk, which has a sweet taste, or formula. Not yet ready for solid foods, the baby will

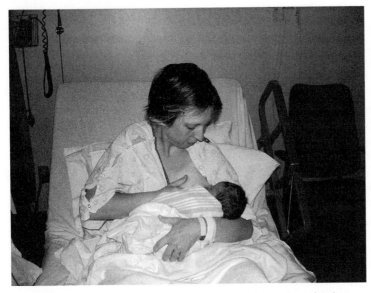

Although the child in this photo is momentarily engrossed in nursing, when he pulls back, he will gaze into his mother's face. The distance is perfectly suited for his current state of visual acuity.

At birth, a baby is only able to see figures to a distance of approximately 8 inches, which, fortuitously, is approximately the distance between a caregiver's face and the face of the child when nursing or being fed. The image is fuzzy, but soon recognizable.

probably consume more milk, but at fewer feedings. The infant can discriminate between familiar and unfamiliar smells. New smells are not necessarily disturbing to her, but familiarity tends to be more comforting. Babies soon learn to recognize familiar smells, including their mother, their blanket, and their stuffed animal, and they are more easily comforted when nestled next to that familiar scent (Mennella & Beauchamp, 2002). During this stage, an infant's hearing will be better than that of a newborn, but not as acute as an adult's. Infants tend to respond to sounds in the higher frequencies.

Touch

Touch is a part of infants' lives from the moment of birth. They leave an environment where they have been gently massaged by a warm fluid 24 hours a day and enter an environment where touch represents a new sensation. As they mature, their sensitivity to take in messages through the touch modality is refined. They learn by being touched, and by touching objects and people with their mouth, hands, and body.

Although infant massage has been a regular part of the mother–baby dyad in many cultures for centuries, it is a relatively new experience in the United States. Fredrick Leboyer, a French physician who was a natural childbirth guru in the late 1960s and early '70s (*Birth Without Violence*), initially helped people understand that the emotional environment of birth had a profound impact and lifelong effects on everyone—baby, siblings, Mom, and Dad. Because of his influence, natural childbirth became more acceptable and resulted in hospital birthing rooms being the norm, rather than women being wheeled to the operating room for delivery. He also spent time in India each year observing the art of childbirth in that country and became interested in infant massage because it was an accepted tradition practiced there. He wrote *Loving Hands: The Traditional Art of Baby Massage* (re-issued in 2002) in order to introduce Western mothers to the power and magic of infant massage. Through his influence, infant massage gained popularity in this country, although in recent years there has been a decrease in interest in both massage and natural childbirth.

Research has shown that "gently touching, stroking, and cuddling infants furthers their perceptual and sensory capabilities" (Marion, 2004, p. 69) and that premature babies, massaged from birth on, usually gain weight more quickly, improve their sleep–wake cycle, and improve their motor skills (Storm & Reese, 2005). Families can receive training in this method from certified instructors who guide them through learning the approach to massage, as well as the strokes to be used with infants. The techniques of infant massage are geared toward fostering attunement to infant cues and strengthening attachment. "Infant massage provides parents with a way to feel more competent as caregivers and nurturers to their babies" (Storm & Reese, 2005, p. 15). Modified forms of massage with older children have also been utilized in child care centers and schools with some degree of success (Berggren, 2004; Marion, 2004), although touch is a highly sensitive topic, with some centers and schools adopting "no touch" policies. Touch is also individually mediated, since temperament, culture, and comfort levels are all involved in how it is perceived. This topic is worth reflecting upon, and Box 5.1 outlines the benefits of massage for children.

As infants mature, they may have increasing sensitivity to touch. Individual responses vary with temperament and sensory sensitivity. You may observe that some infants respond erratically to the same stimulus, others respond in predictable patterns, and still others show little response to their experience of being touched. A baby who is 6 or 8 weeks old may arch his back to show you he dislikes being touched. It may be possible to find ways of communicating and stimulating without emphasis on touch, if that is what is needed.

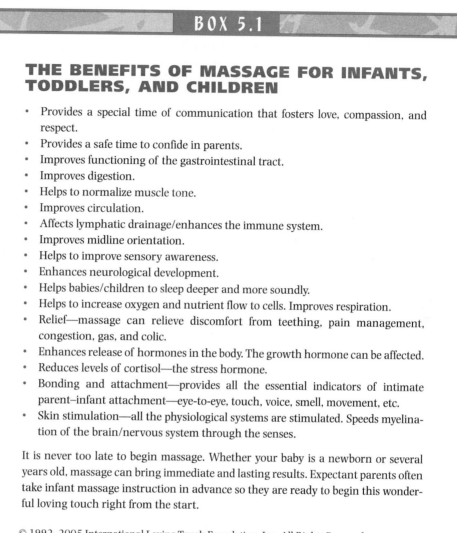

Some babies are much more cuddly than others. For some mothers, having a baby who does not want to be touched or cuddled causes profound disappointment. Adults must observe the baby's responsiveness to each type of stimulation so they can fine-tune their strategies for caregiving. It is important to acknowledge perceived differences in responses and to develop ways of working with all infants rather than ignoring those who have a negative response.

Some experts believe that a baby's face—soft, round, and so kissable—has evolved precisely to invite needed touch from loved ones (Levy & Orlans, 1998). Keep in mind, however, that our idea of what is "loveable" is culturally imprinted.

Cognitive Development

primary circular reaction

simple repetitive acts resulting from an enjoyable experience—typically observed at 1–4 months; a substage of the sensorimotor stage

When something occurs that the baby likes, such as stroking the texture of her new soft blanket, she repeats the action that caused the sensation. Piaget called this a **primary circular reaction** (Piaget, 1952). To understand this stage in the context of Piaget's series of developmental stages, review the chart on developmental stages found in the Additional Support section of your Online Companion.

Through these repetitive actions, infants build up an inner understanding of their world. They don't have the language to describe it, so they think in terms of physical things. Piaget

described this pattern of activity as the second of a series of substages of sensorimotor development, the stage of learning through action. Babies at this stage make more use of their senses and are beginning to organize information using the neurological processes available to them. This means that repeated actions are allowing infants to build up mental schemes—clusters of ideas—related to their experience. These are the exciting beginnings of learning.

Reviews of research (Branford, Brown, & Cocking, 2000; Eliot, 1999; Ramey & Ramey, 1999) demonstrate that there is new understanding about the function of the infant's brain and the child's potential. It is thought that the brain is greedy for information at a very young age, and if optimal conditions are presented to infants, they will achieve much more than if they are understimulated. Some people assume that we should provide intensive experience in subjects of learning for infants during their sensitive periods of neurological activity. David Elkind (2001b) and the National Scientific Council on the Developing Child (2005) oppose this view, pointing out that it may present a distorted analysis of brain research. Infants need to be supported in their development and nurtured in accordance with their individual needs rather than being exposed to a subject-based "curriculum," especially if the curriculum does not balance the development of cognitive and literacy skills with the fostering of social and emotional skills.

> Alarmingly, much of the popular advice about how adults should react to infants and toddlers in view of recent brain research findings is leading child care providers to focus on adult-selected and adult-driven activities. . . . In a rush to make sure that the windows of opportunity do not close before children under 3 are given the experiences they need, there have already been anxious calls for various types of early stimulation [rigid learning games and educational materials emphasizing adult-directed lessons and activities]. Many of these suggestions are shortsighted, and some are even detrimental to development. (Lally, 2001, p. 21)

This negativity toward structured curriculum is echoed in Magda Gerber's (1998b) philosophy of responsive caregiving. She argues that infant development is not a race, and that nothing of worth is achieved in the long term if babies are not allowed to be babies.

Self-Concept

The way a baby perceives and reacts to any situation or person is shaped by her emotional well-being and temperament style. Without adults who are actively engaged with the baby, there will be no opportunity for her to establish a oneness or separateness (Kaplan, 1978). In other words, the baby will not develop the notion that she is a separate and complete human being. These ideas are related to the concepts of "self" and "others," and mark the beginning of the emergence of the personhood of the baby.

To know that you are a separate person, you need to be involved in some kind of relationship. From the infant's experiences and interactions during the first year with key adult caregivers in her life—her attachment figures—"she gradually builds up pictures of relationships between herself and others" (Honig, 2002, p. 3). Your self-image develops from seeing parts of yourself reflected back in other people. If the reflection of the self is positive, you will conceptualize that part of yourself as positive. This interactive dance allows the baby to shape her world as her world shapes her. It seems a stretch to think of this as a first step of personal empowerment, but that is what it is.

Social Relationships

Because the baby makes generalized rather than specific attachments at this stage (Ainsworth et al., 1978), caregivers may fail to appreciate the baby's need for predictability and constancy. The baby may appear to be able to deal with changes in caregivers, but that positive response depends on consistency of care, if not of caregiver. This need for predictability probably means that the baby will thrive on the establishment of relationships with a few people to whom he can relate (Honig, 2002). The Additional Support section in your Online Companion has some information that debates the issue

> "People create their lives through relationships with others: development and learning take place in, through, and for relationships."
>
> (Edwards & Raikes, 2002, p. 10)

The relationship dance has begun.

resilience

the idea that an individual can be prepared or strengthened to withstand and recover from negative circumstances

of how soon is too soon for child care and also discusses the impact of multiple caregivers on child development.

Emotional Development

Emotional damage at a very young age can certainly have lasting effects, even if the infant cannot remember it. Yet not all infants brought up in emotionally deprived circumstances turn out to be emotionally troubled (Brooke & Goldstein, 2001). Nonetheless, a strong correlation exists between the two. However **resilient** some children may seem in the face of emotional deprivation, it remains a serious cause for concern. The deprivation may not be as severe as the "hospitalism" documented by Renee Spitz (1945) or as that seen, more recently, among orphans from countries around the world. But there is significant reason to believe that early emotional deprivation can lead to anything from mildly maladaptive behaviors to extreme violence, or even long-term lack of emotional responsiveness.

Happy infants are those who remain active and receptive to people and situations. Although different temperaments lead to a range of responses, babies in trusting relationships with one or more adults are most likely to be secure and are poised to develop an increasing capacity to experience, express, and regulate their emotions (Day & Parlakian, 2003).

Smiling is a wonderful way for babies to engage adults. First smiles, which occur when a baby is about 6 weeks old, are usually a response to a person—that is, they are connected to a social relationship. Although smiling isn't necessarily a sign of happiness, the social relationship in which it occurs is likely to promote a baby's security, and therefore her happiness.

As the infant grows older, she may initiate a smile as an invitation to the adult to make a social connection, or she may smile to reflect her happiness. This smile may occur without visual stimulation, such as an adult smiling at her. Blind or visually disabled babies smile without having been able to make a visual connection with a person.

The range of emotions that a baby can demonstrate at this stage is not very wide, but he can make his feelings known to the adults around him. Distress, for example, can be seen even in very young babies. Within a few weeks, the range of emotions expands. During this period, babies might show anger and delight. Social situations may cause a baby delight. This is displayed by more than a smile, and often involves whole-body squirming or slight rocking. Anger can be seen when an infant is hungry or uncomfortable, or when his needs are not met immediately. It is quite normal for this emotion to be shown, but adults must respond as quickly as possible. Box 5.2 provides some guidelines for responding to the needs of an infant at this stage. This list is not comprehensive, and many more suggestions can be found in your Online Companion under the section entitled "Getting in Tune with Infants, Toddlers, and Twos."

Language and Communication Skills

The ability to communicate and use language is pre-wired into the brain, suggested Chomsky (1968). Some recent brain research may have confirmed this, but researchers are divided on the best way to approach the infant's sensitive periods for communication development. All seem to agree, however, that various conditions must be in place before communication skills can develop. Two-way connections are essential. This is the dyad on which all communication is based. The infant needs to be heard and to hear. She also needs to know that she has an effect; for example, her cries must draw an adult response.

BOX 5.2

GETTING IN TUNE WITH INFANTS AT 6 WEEKS TO 3 MONTHS

Below are some starting points for building your responsivity skills with a 6-week-old–3-month-old infant.

- ensure that all basic needs are met: diapering, contact, feeding, protection, warmth, etc.
- identify the infant's sensory acuity: visually and through hearing, taste, smell, and responses to touch
- establish the infant's preferences, response patterns, and style, and make all responses in accordance with this style
- observe the infant's patterns of wakefulness and sleep, and try to anticipate the need for both quiet and stimulation
- take every opportunity to talk to the baby, and use a high-pitched, repetitive way of talking
- sing or talk as you perform many of the domestic tasks in relation to the infant
- allow the baby to sleep when she wants to
- feed the baby on demand and as she lies in your arms
- use infant massage techniques in a warm room
- make bath time a warm, pleasant experience with lots of caressing and talking
- talk through your actions as you change diapers
- build trust by ensuring continuity of care and attention
- respond to crying promptly and try to read the type of crying
- notice the baby's body language as cues for your responses

In communication, there must be a sender, a receiver, and a message. The baby and the adult can be both senders and receivers. The baby can send the message that he is content, hungry, in need of comfort, and so on. The adult can convey the message that the baby matters and that he is loved and will be responded to.

The infant's attachment to or relationship with one or several adults is essential for the baby to learn to communicate. Communication flourishes in a **reciprocal relationship**. Helping this relationship along is the baby's newfound ability to coo or make happy sounds (Stern, 2000). The adult enjoys the happy response of the baby, and the flow of communication is enhanced.

Although babies' first communications may not be intentional, attentive parents and other caregivers are able to interpret their meanings. For example, they can differentiate between the rhythmic, intense cry that means "I'm hungry," the sharp cry that means "I'm in pain," and the whiney cry that means "I'm uncomfortable." . . . Most important, they tune in to the baby's rhythm of interaction. They follow the baby's lead as she makes eye contact, engages in back-and-forth play, signals that she needs a break by briefly turning away, and then resumes the play when she is ready. (Bardige, 2005, p. 22)

There are some other important conditions for communication. The infant must be able to process auditory and visual stimulation to make meaning of it. In addition, he must have the ability to recognize people, to make links between actions and thoughts, and to memorize and recall pieces of information. For language, he must have the capacity to make sounds, imitate vocalizations, and control sound production.

As discussed in Box 5.3, communication becomes even more complicated when a second language is involved—a challenge for parents and practitioners, anyway. On the positive side, it may seem surprising that the infant's exposure to more than one language does not lead to

reciprocal relationship

social relationships between two people where there is a two-way exchange and mutual benefit

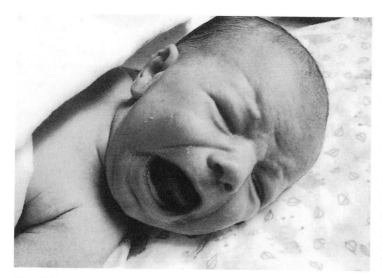

This child is communicating. We just have to figure out what she needs.

complete confusion. The baby is not pre-wired for any particular language, and her early communications are not dependent upon spoken language. When she is exposed to a second language, there are also distinct intellectual advantages—even if the two (or more) languages get a bit muddled in the short term. At this stage, the baby is still pre-verbal, but being exposed to the sounds of two or more languages may enable her to begin to babble using both sound types—because that's what she hears. Communicating this to families can be challenging, particularly when their first language is other than English—but it is worthwhile for all parties. Enhanced communication between families and practitioners, as well as directly with the baby, can make the baby's experience become more meaningful.

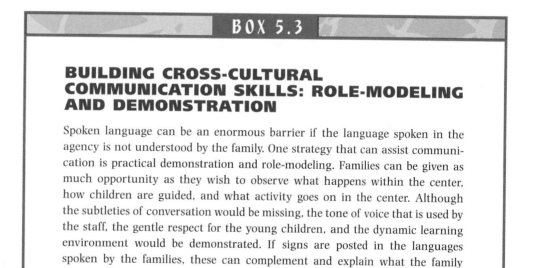

BOX 5.3

BUILDING CROSS-CULTURAL COMMUNICATION SKILLS: ROLE-MODELING AND DEMONSTRATION

Spoken language can be an enormous barrier if the language spoken in the agency is not understood by the family. One strategy that can assist communication is practical demonstration and role-modeling. Families can be given as much opportunity as they wish to observe what happens within the center, how children are guided, and what activity goes on in the center. Although the subtleties of conversation would be missing, the tone of voice that is used by the staff, the gentle respect for the young children, and the dynamic learning environment would be demonstrated. If signs are posted in the languages spoken by the families, these can complement and explain what the family member observes.

Personal Story

Many years ago, while living in Quebec, Canada, I knew a family who had young children and who spoke several languages.

The mother was an émigré from Czechoslovakia and she spoke Czech and English.

The father, although from the United States, spoke German—his first language—and English.

The first child attended child care where French was spoken.

For the first four years of this child's life, I could understand very little of what he said to me because it seemed as if he never talked completely in one language.

As he approached age 5, it was if a light bulb went off.

He would speak to his father in German, his mother in Czech, to his playmates in French, and to me in English.

I have never forgotten that incredible example of learning multiple languages.

PARTICULAR NEEDS

Babies who are 6 weeks–3 months old must have their needs understood and their cries responded to quickly. The baby is aware of the people around her, has some understanding of how to attract adults' attention, is becoming a social person, responds to stimuli, is learning from experience, and has the beginnings of some bodily control that will ultimately lead her to independence. What she needs is to have her stage of development understood as being extremely important, not just a chrysalis stage before the "real" person emerges.

The infant's potential is quite incredible, so the adult must appreciate the infant's ability to take in information and try to make sense of it. Stimulation is important, in ways that the baby can understand. Contrasting stimulation with calm helps the baby to regulate herself. The quality of relationships and their consistency are the core requirements for helping her form attachments to adults. Babies also need adults who can interpret cues. Some are obvious, others subtle. Review the information in Chapter 4, Box. 4.2, as well as the Additional Support section in your Online Companion, for a list of verbal and nonverbal cues.

DEVELOPMENTAL VARIATION

Development may vary according to the infant's gestational age at birth, the birth process, and her health in the neonatal period. Some developmental issues become apparent at 6 weeks, when most infants have established some patterns of sleep, feeding, and activity.

developmental milestones

stages in the individual's development; commonly accepted advances that mark new achievements

Progression is as important as the **developmental milestones**, which are the significant stages of development. For example, if a baby was floppy in the neonatal period, it is more important that her muscle tone improves than that she acquire particular skills. Infants who are less responsive than average at birth may show development by being more responsive to different kinds of stimulation within a few weeks. A few babies who have experienced particularly difficult births may be more settled now. So the flow of progress must be the focus for the observer of infants at this stage.

screening

the basic process of reviewing, checking, or assessing a group of individuals to determine if any meet specified criteria—e.g., hearing deficit or developmental delay; may lead to further investigation

You may see some babies who hold up their heads and have more back control than others. These advances do not necessarily indicate a lifelong advantage in gross motor skills. And the baby who begins to swipe at objects and grasp them is no more likely to become a boxer than a baby with later-developing grasping skills!

Caregivers should take notice of individual patterns. These include health indicators and developmental stages. By observing the infant and noticing her particular patterns, the parent and educator can support the infant's needs more effectively and precisely.

DEVELOPMENTAL ALERTS

Pediatric Examination

assessment

the process of gathering data (including observational data) from several sources using informal or standardized instruments and making deductions that explain behavior; child assessment is not based on a single measure

Although **screening** and **assessment** schedules will differ according to the locality, a comprehensive pediatric appraisal of the infant's development usually takes place at about 6 weeks. Pediatricians, particularly those who were involved in the infant's neonatal period or who are informed about significant developmental issues, are able to support families and infants in a variety of ways. They can provide screenings to exclude the possibility of a variety of health and developmental conditions. They can perform a detailed assessment to establish the child's health status. Other services include providing immunizations, weight checks, and nutrition advice, and assisting the family to meet the needs of the baby.

Some health providers utilize a tool provided by the American Academy of Pediatrics entitled *Bright Futures*. The "guidelines are based on the belief that health supervision requires a partnership between health professionals and families" (Green, 1994, p. xviii; Green & Palfrey, 2002). AAP recognizes that families, especially families with infants, are committed to learning how they can best contribute to their child's growth and development. Health care providers are perfectly positioned to facilitate that learning. *Bright Futures'* sections align with well-baby visits

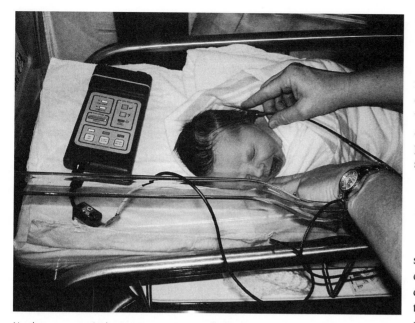

Newborns are routinely given a screening test for hearing.

and include all the pertinent information that should be covered during the visit. What is so unique about this tool is the focus on the relationship established between the family and the health care provider. The visit does not just concern the health issues of the child, but includes other topics such as anticipatory guidance for the family and promotion of constructive family relationships.

An overview of materials for visits at two different ages is included in the Additional Activities section of your Online Companion.

Some infants may show some significant signs or symptoms, or present particular challenges for their parents. The pediatrician can offer advice or refer the families to other resources. Availability of resources depends on the location. Some families may be able to access special interventions, nurse practitioners, toy libraries, drop-in centers, child welfare services, and parenting classes, although many of these services may not exist in some rural, remote, or less-advantaged areas. Although all babies with special needs should have access to special services, in reality accessibility varies. Most families will never require such services, but pediatricians and educators can be successful advocates for those who do.

Family Response to Medical/Developmental Diagnoses

A few infants face special challenges. In such cases, early identification of developmental or health concerns can lead to better understanding, improved caregiving, and, if necessary, an intervention program.

Families face an enormous hurdle in accepting that their baby is not developing as they had hoped. Frequently parental hopes remain high despite medical opinions that indicate a real or potential developmental challenge for their baby. Family resistance to such information can be very real and is entirely understandable. Yet most family members want to be as well informed as possible, even if what they hear seems negative. However, a parent who feels stressed, vulnerable, and emotionally tired may have difficulty understanding medical terms and complex discussions about the baby's future. For this reason, families may want to have someone with them at specialists' appointments.

Neurological Problems

A difficult birth increases the chance of the infant suffering some degree of neurological damage. Pressure on the head is the most obvious cause. After a birthing trauma, a doctor may pay particularly close attention to a baby's reactions to stimuli and her general progress. It is not always possible to determine the cause of a brain injury or other neurological problem. Neonates who showed little sign of a problem may demonstrate developmental differences by the time they are 6 weeks old or so.

Typically, brain-injured infants are irritable, hard to settle, and difficult to feed. They may frustrate their caregivers because they don't seem to respond well to the usual calming techniques. Their sleep is fitful and interrupted. These same signs can be seen in babies who are abused, so care should be taken to avoid making any assumptions about why a baby is extremely irritable.

HEALTH CONCERNS

Feeding and Weight Gain

Inconsistent feeding habits are common. These may relate to how frequently the baby feeds and how much she eats, which may in turn be connected to weight gain. Breast-fed babies may be test-weighed before and after a feeding to determine what they have consumed, but in practice, determining the amount of breast milk they have had is difficult. This may be a good thing: It is normal for a baby's appetite to fluctuate, and too much attention should not be paid to it. Bottle-fed babies' consumption of formula is easier to monitor, so small and large feedings are easy to detect. More important is the amount of weight the baby is gaining. The typical weight gain is fairly steady, except when she is not feeding well or has an ongoing condition that makes feeding more difficult.

Skin Care

By this stage, most of the lumps, bumps, and marks on the newborn's skin have disappeared, and the baby has clear skin. The baby's skin is delicate and needs careful attention, particularly in the diaper area. Adults need to ensure that the baby is not exposed to direct sun, since at this stage, the baby is too young to have sunscreens applied. Regardless of their skin tones, babies have skin that easily burns.

Body Temperature

Although the baby's ability to regulate his body temperature is improving, he does not have the ability to sweat or to increase his activity to keep warm. Room temperature should be maintained. Checking the baby's hands to see if he is cold is a poor way of assessing temperature. If it is necessary, checking the baby's neck and back would be more accurate. If the baby is low on the ground in a seat or lying on the floor, the surrounding temperature might be lower than you think. Also note that a comfortable room temperature for an active adult might be cooler than what is needed for a young infant. On the other hand, avoid having the room too warm or having too many clothes or blankets on the baby.

Exposure to People

There are differing views about when to introduce the baby to new people. The timing may be dictated by circumstances; if the parent has to return to work, exposure to a much wider range of people happens earlier. Personal preference may also be an issue. Some families prefer to keep their babies at home for the first few months, while others take their infants to the park, the mall, daycare centers, parties, and other gatherings. The baby's immunity to the germs of all those people may be sufficient to protect her, but the wider the range of germs, the more likely the baby is to catch something. Yet babies cannot constantly be kept in a germ-free, sterilized

Personal Story

I often consulted with families about the topic of breast-feeding, since I had nursed my four children.

Although you cannot monitor the amount of milk consumed by a breast-fed baby, the rule of thumb is to change 6–8 urine-soaked diapers daily. This indicates that the baby is consuming an adequate amount of milk.

Another issue families were often interested in was the number of feedings.

Newborn infants sometimes nurse 12 times in 24 hours.

I informed the clients that the baby's stomach was no larger than a golf ball. (See Figure 5.1.)

Since breast milk is digested more easily than formula, breast-fed babies tend to eat more often than formula-fed babies.

Figure 5.1 The Approximate Size of a Newborn's Stomach

environment. Moreover, babies need to have social contact and to make relationships, so exposure to people is essential. Hand washing, good personal hygiene, and reduced contact with people with colds, flu, and upset stomachs are common sense precautions.

Infant Seats, Car Seats, and Strollers

In both home care and group care, caregivers need to be able to move infants from place to place. Sometimes inappropriate equipment, like strollers and inadequate baby seats, are used. At this stage, the infant's back control is likely to be poor. The baby, if put in a seated position, can slump forward with a rounded back, flop sideways, or slide down in an improper seat. The infant needs to have adequate back support and protection. Most babies at this stage need a baby carriage that allows them to lie on their back or be safely propped up. Avoid premature use of strollers that have little support for the back. Similarly, the infant is probably not yet ready for a high or low infant chair unless she is wedged in with foam or pillows. If pillows are used to support a baby in an infant chair, the baby should be closely supervised, as the pillows can present suffocation hazards. A lie-back baby seat can be a good idea, enabling the baby to have a better look around. But the base of such seats can slide across a surface as the baby's motion causes the seat to move. Thus, babies in lie-back seats should never be left unsupervised, especially if the seat is resting on a table or other piece of furniture.

Extended indoor use of car seats can be inappropriate, even when the baby appears to be comfortable. This is because the baby shouldn't be left in a rounded-back position for unduly long periods. When traveling, the baby must be in a car seat that is approved for his weight and that has been securely anchored in accordance with the manufacturer's instructions. Newborns and young babies need to be placed in rear-facing carseats in the back seat of cars, preferably in the middle seat position, if possible. All infants should ride rear-facing until they have reached at least 1 year of age and weigh at least 20 pounds. That means that if your baby reaches 20 pounds before his first birthday, he should remain rear facing until he turns one.

Car travel puts a baby in danger, and every effort should be made to select, install, and use safety restraints. Take notice of the following considerations when planning to travel with a baby of this age:

- The selection of appropriate restraints should be based on the weight and height of the baby.
- If using secondhand equipment, make sure that it meets current safety standards.
- The back of the car is the safest place for all passengers.
- Although rear-facing car seats are best for younger babies, they should not be placed in front of an air bag on the front seat (Figure 5-2).
- Follow manufacturers' instructions for fitting baby restraints.
- The baby should not be held in a passenger's arms at any time.
- Straps should be fastened around the baby with room for her movement (put your finger under the straps to test).

Figure 5.2

- Blankets (if necessary) should be placed over the baby after securing him in the seat (over the straps).
- Accidents are caused by drivers attending to a baby's needs while in motion or at stop signs.

In 1997, the National Transportation Safety Board recommended that all states adopt legislation that would require all children under the age of 13 to be transported in the rear seat of a vehicle, if available. To date, only 20 states have a current provision regarding transport of children, and most regulations only address the needs of children age 6 and younger. Government research documents that during a crash, children are safest in the back seat (http://www.nhtsa.dot.gov). Each state has different requirements for transportation of children, so be sure that you are aware of the requirements in your state.

Activity 5.1 in your Online Companion focuses on car seat safety requirements.

Sudden Infant Death Syndrome

sudden infant death syndrome (SIDS)

the sudden death of any infant or young child under 1 year of age which remains unexplained after a thorough case investigation, including performance of a complete autopsy, examination of the death scene, and review of the clinical history

Unfortunately, this age range is the peak time for **sudden infant death syndrome (SIDS)**. "The occurrence of SIDS is rare during the first month of life, increases to a peak between 2 and 4 months old, and then declines" (American Academy of Pediatrics, 2000, p. 650). Caregivers must remember that, although rare, SIDS does happen. In these instances, the parent or caregiver puts the infant down to sleep and returns to find that the baby has stopped breathing. This is a parent's worst nightmare. A thorough investigation of the circumstances must follow, and an autopsy will be performed. If a diagnosis of SIDS is made, it is not a clear explanation for the death. Rather, SIDS remains an unexplained phenomenon.

The Back to Sleep campaign started in 1994 in response to The American Academy of Pediatrics recommendation in 1992 that infants be placed to sleep on their backs. Placing babies on their backs to sleep reduces the risk of SIDS, also known as "crib death." This campaign has been successful in promoting infant-back-sleeping to parents, family members, child care providers, health professionals, and all other caregivers of infants:

> The frequency of prone sleeping has decreased from >70% to ~20% of US infants, and the SIDS rate has decreased by >40%. However, SIDS remains the highest cause of infant death beyond the neonatal period, and there are still several potentially modifiable risk factors. Although some of these factors have been known for many years (e.g., maternal smoking), the importance of other hazards, such as soft bedding and covered airways, has been demonstrated only recently. (American Academy of Pediatrics, 2000, p. 650)

African-American infants are at a greater risk for SIDS. "To address this issue, the Back to Sleep campaign sponsors, the National Black Child Development Institute, and several other organizations worked together to develop materials for a new initiative to reduce sudden infant

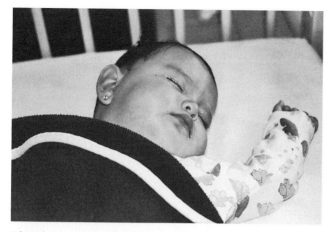

When sleeping, on the back, but . . .

when awake, on the stomach is beneficial!

death syndrome (SIDS) in African-American communities" (NICHD, 2005a). According to the National Institute of Child Health and Human Development (2005a), Native Americans are about three times more likely than whites to succumb to SIDS. To date, however, there has not been a well publicized effort to reduce that number. Interestingly, more boys than girls fall victim to SIDS, although the reason this may happen is unclear. Often male infants are born with less-developed systems, and this may contribute to the difference in statistics, but that is pure conjecture. Not surprisingly, the incidence increases during cold weather, probably due to the fact that families bundle children with extra clothing and wraps to ward off the chill and drafts.

If a parent chooses to have their baby sleep in the bed with them, they need to make sure their baby sleeps on her back. Avoid soft surfaces, pillows, and loose bed covers to prevent suffocation. There is also the danger that the baby can get trapped between the mattress and the framework of the bed (headboard or footboard), a wall, or other furniture.

Alarms that alert adults if the baby's breathing stops can be used, but opinion is divided about their usefulness, their reliability, the frequency of false alarms, and the fact that they cannot prevent the problem. Various causes of SIDS have been theorized, but as yet we have very little indication of the reason why some babies die.

SIDS is sometimes mistaken for child abuse. It is very difficult to accept the death of a young infant, and so much harder if the parent is wrongfully accused of abuse. Yet because death does occasionally result from parental abuse or caregiver abuse, we must be vigilant in looking for signs of abuse.

The American Academy of Pediatrics revised its position on SIDS in the fall of 2005. Recognizing that in spite of the major decrease in the incidence of SIDS over the last 10 years, "SIDS is still responsible for more infant deaths beyond the newborn period in the United States than any other cause of death during infancy" (AAP Web site, 2005):

- Side-sleeping is no longer recommended as a reasonable alternative to lying on the back for sleeping.
- Bed sharing is not recommended during sleep.
- However, there is growing evidence that room sharing (infant sleeping in a crib in parent's bedroom) is associated with a reduced risk of SIDS.
- An association between pacifier use and a reduced risk of SIDS was found, so the AAP recommends the use of pacifiers at nap time and bedtime throughout the first year of life.

EVERYDAY SAFETY ISSUES

The baby's complete dependence means that adults must ensure that the infant is protected. Families and educators have to think about the situations and environments into which they bring young infants and make sure that every eventuality is considered. Thinking about the infant's physical environment is the first step.

Infant Equipment

Cribs, bassinets, strollers, carriages, baby seats, and car seats (as discussed earlier) must be maintained in safe working order. Although it is a good idea to check the item for a safety tag, visual inspection of the article is always essential. It must not allow the baby's head to become wedged, or toes or fingers to become entrapped. The materials must be nontoxic, smooth, and sturdy. The item should offer firm support with no possibility of suffocating the infant or collapsing. When babies are in their cribs, they might not be supervised every moment of the day and night, so the crib must be entirely reliable.

The appropriateness of the equipment for the infant's size and stage is as important as its condition. What is safe at one stage might present considerable hazards at another. In making this judgment, it is important to remember that babies develop new skills rapidly, and sometimes unexpectedly. In addition, not all babies have the same level of activity. Some particularly boisterous babies might not be safe in seats that others take to well. Individual preferences of the infants might also shape choices: some babies like to be upright; others prefer to lie back. Although these preferences should be a central consideration, safety is of foremost importance. Always be aware of the need to strap infants into their seats and strollers; this is something both parents and educators tend to be lax about.

Change Tables

Change tables present several potential hazards. There is the issue of hygiene and cross-infection, as well as the additional risk of the baby falling from the table. Adults sometimes assume that because a baby cannot yet sit or crawl, she cannot move enough to fall from a change table. Yet such falls are a real possibility. Diaper-changing procedures need to include a "keep one hand on the baby" rule (See Personal Story above.)

On-the-Floor Protection

Babies at this stage may be laid on the floor to play or propped up to see what is going on. The floor is a very vulnerable place for the infant. Adults or older children can fall onto the baby, particularly if they are walking around the infant. Avoid stepping over an infant even if there appears to be no obvious danger. Keep equipment away from the infant so nothing can fall on top of her. Make sure that you do not hold objects over the heads of infants on the floor. It is too easy to drop items onto the baby. Rocking chairs are a particular hazard; they should not be in an area where infants are on the floor. The chairs can slide across the floor, and infants' hands or feet can easily slip under the rocker.

Why Equipment Might be Inappropriate

Besides the safety issues of some of this equipment, developmental issues must also be considered. Magda Gerber is opposed to the use of swings and walkers because she feels they put children into positions that their bodies are not ready to be in yet. Sobell (1994) notes that "the excessive use of . . . modern conveniences such as infant seats, walkers, jumpers, swings, and vertical baby carriers (back and front packs) is believed to delay normal development—not improve it" (p. 45).

Babies who are frequently restrained in braces or casts—or that favorite swing, baby seat or walker—will be unintentionally limited in their opportunity to explore their body (head, hands, feet, legs) as well as the reflex motor patterns and general motor movements necessary for good visual-spatial-motor development. As parents and care providers, it is up to us to be sure that our infants have ample opportunity to develop these basic motor abilities. These are the foundation for movement, balance, and eventually the control necessary for fine eye/hand manipulation, visualization, and cognitive achievement. (Marusich, 1999, p. 2)

Many centers overuse this equipment and, as a consequence, children are positioned in swings and walkers for long periods of time. "Fixed pieces of equipment, such as playpens, high chairs, and bouncy seats, should be used sparingly, as they provide little opportunity for varied and active experiences" (Gallagher, 2005, p.14). They may help the caregiver by providing needed time to complete tasks such as preparing bottles, changing diapers, or feeding a child. However, they may work against some of the tenets that underlie the philosophy of responsive caregiving by eliminating human-to-human physical touch and preventing children from acquiring varied sensory experiences.

Because there are so many concerns with baby swings and walkers, the overall recommendation is that they not be used.

STARTING POINTS FOR RESPONSE

Responsive Caregiving

While responding to a baby's needs and supporting her through appropriate guidance tend to merge into similar nurturance, responsive caregiving tends to focus on providing for the most basic physical needs and guidance strategies to support emotional and psychological needs.

At 6 weeks–3 months, infants are initiating social contact as well as responding to people. Through these relationships their needs are met. Adults need to read a baby's extensive cues; she uses crying, a range of sounds, body language, and facial expressions to let us know what she wants. She may want attention or need time alone. She may experience sensory overload and need to tune out. Her need for stimulation is balanced by her need for quiet times. The adults to whom she is attached will encourage the baby's repeated actions through playful sequences. They will respond to her cues and enable the baby to discover her body and its competence. Allowing time for the baby to kick and swipe at the air helps to develop physical control and supports the baby's focus on what her body can do. Neurological connections being made through this activity are vital for later development. The baby needs to build schemes of understanding and is dependent upon the adults to provide opportunities, space, and time for her development.

Supportive Guidance

The baby, who is in need of physical contact and response, will begin to "fall in love" with the adults who meet her needs. Attachment to primary caregivers is essential. The baby has the ability to make multiple attachments, but particular attachment will come about only from continuity of responses. Infants who transition to group care need to have their emotional needs met just as much as they would in a home situation. Supporting physical needs is only the beginning of meeting infants' needs so they can blossom as human beings.

Facilitating Development

Babies' emotional well-being comes from the satisfaction of their physical needs and the establishment of nurturing relationships. For some adults, meeting infants' needs is relatively easy; for others, reading infants' cues can be difficult. The challenge can lie in mismatched temperament styles and patterns of behavior, or the ill health or disability of either the adult or baby. Parents can be assisted in reading their baby's cues, but this needs to be done sensitively; it is ineffective to teach a skill if the educator undermines the parents' confidence.

A balance between stimulation and quiet time continues to be important at this stage. Babies need to make sense of their environments, and the adults in them, in a multisensory way, but too much information can be challenging to process. Enormous gains in brain development occur at this time, but the core stimulation needs to be relationship-based rather than object-based. As the baby's sensory acuity increases, his world of learning broadens. The baby will become more interested in physical experiences. The adult will learn when this happens from the dance of communication and from the baby's responses to the immediate environment.

Adult responses allow the infant to begin a process of **individuation**, where he starts to see himself as a separate person. The emergence of a sense of self needs support through responsive attention and meeting the infant's needs.

individuation

the process of working on becoming a separate person

Activities

Your CD-ROM contains activities to help you increase your skills while engaging infants in caregiving routines, play, and supportive guidance.

Activities 5.2 and 5.3 encourage a holistic response to infants. Activity 5.2 helps you develop ways of engaging in young babies' experience and extending your interactions with them. This activity always starts from the framework of observation. Activity 5.3 helps you create responsive curriculum for each infant and develop activities that are targeted to individual interests and skill levels. Activity 5.4 includes suggestions for further experiences and interactions. Activity 5.5 describes several possible scenarios for responsive guidance.

SUMMARY

Many child care centers accept infants from around 6 weeks of age, an age that corresponds to the end of some mothers' maternity leave. This may be changing in some areas, because parental leave has been extended. Separation may be a more significant issue for mothers than for infants, because babies are more interested in having their needs met than in who is meeting them. Nevertheless, infants need to be supported through this transition. The greater the continuity of care, the better they settle into their new environment. Infants are able to make attachments to several people. With a predictable pattern of care from the new caregiver, these attachments can be made successfully.

The individual style of an infant is clearly observable; his temperament may well be a fairly constant part of his individuality through the following months and years. Caregivers must identify individual patterns of behavior if they wish to provide appropriate and responsive care.

An infant's sensory abilities are the core elements of her learning about her world. Very gradually, she receives information about her immediate environment and creates schemes of understanding in relation to those experiences. Although the infant's physical skills are not yet well coordinated, she will make some deliberate attempts to repeat sequences of behavior that she finds pleasurable. This is the sensorimotor stage of cognitive development, when there is a significant step forward in creating a mental representation of the world. Practicing actions leads to increased motor control. It also expands the infant's appreciation of how things happen; the infant makes connections between actions and results, and can feel some control over the environment.

At this age, an infant begins to gain the sense that he is a separate person. He doesn't have a clear concept of self, only an understanding that he can bring about some responses in adults and with objects. Consequently, it is important for the infant to be able to build strong emotional ties with adult caregivers. He is building trust, an important element of emotional growth that will influence every other domain of development.

There are particular health and safety concerns at this stage of the infant's life, including transport in car seats, changing tables, baby swings, and positioning for sleep. A new position statement has been issued by the American Academy of Pediatrics (Fall 2005) that rescinds the recommendation for side-sleeping.

This chapter concludes by making some suggestions for responsive care, and suggests that students refer to their Online Companion to find recommendations for activities to foster engagement with infants aged 6 weeks to 3 months.

DISCUSSION QUESTIONS

1. If you had to choose between center-based care and private home care for your baby of 2 months, what would you choose, and why?
2. This chapter presented information on the importance of touch for young infants. How does touch align with a responsive caregiving approach? How would you integrate touch into the everyday care routines at a child care center? (The article by Carlson listed in Further Reading might be helpful.)
3. If the temperament of a new infant seemed "difficult," what might you do?
4. If a baby were born prematurely, what difference might it make to her development at 8 weeks?
5. How might you help a mother to provide breast milk for her baby while she is at work?

ADDITIONAL RESOURCES

Further Reading

Allen, K. E., & Marotz, L. (2001). *By the ages: Behavior and development of children pre-birth through eight*. Clifton Park, NY: Thomson Delmar Learning.

American Academy of Pediatrics, American Public Health Association, & National Resource Center for Health and Safety in Child Care—APA, APHA, and NRCHSCC. (2002). *Caring for our children: National health and safety performance standards: Guidelines for out-of-home child care programs* (2nd ed.). Elk Grove Village, IL: Authors.

American Academy of Pediatrics. (2000). Changing concepts of sudden infant death syndrome: Implications for infant sleeping environment and sleep position. *Pediatrics, 105*(3), 650–656. Back to Sleep Campaign—http://www.nichd.nih.gov/sids/

Bassett, M. (1994). *Infant and child care skills*. Clifton Park, NY: Thomson Delmar Learning.

Carlson, F. M. (2005). Significance of touch in young children's lives. *Young Children, 4* (60), 79–85.

Cassidy, J., & Shaver, P. (1999). *Handbook of attachment: Theory, research and clinical applications*. New York: Guilford Publications.

Cryer, D., & Harms, T. (Eds.). (2000). *Infants and toddlers in out-of-home care*. Chapel Hill, NC: National Center for Early Development and Learning.

Day, M., & Parlakian, R. (2004). *How culture shapes social-emotional development: Implications for practice in infant-toddler programs*. Washington, DC: ZERO TO THREE.

Day, M. & Parlakian, R. (2003). *How culture shapes social-emotional development: Implications for practice in infant-family programs*. Washington, DC: ZERO TO THREE.

Edwards, C. P., & Raikes, H. (2002). Extending the Dance: Relationship-based approaches to infant/toddler care and education. *Young Children, 57*(4), 10–17.

Gandini, L., & Edwards, C. Pope. (2003). *Bambini: The Italian approach to infant/toddler care*. St. Paul, MN: Redleaf Press.

Goldberg, S. (1997). *Parent involvement begins at birth: Collaboration between parents and teachers of children in the early years*. Needham Heights, MA: Allyn & Bacon.

Greenberg, P. (1991). Infants and toddlers away from their mothers? Is it good for their mental health? Is it good for their self-esteem? Chapter 1 in *Character development: Encouraging self-esteem and self-discipline in infants, toddlers, and two year olds*. Washington, DC: NAEYC.

Honig, A. S. (2002). *Secure relationships: Nurturing infant/toddler attachment in early care settings*. Washington, DC: NAEYC.

Kaplan, L. J. (1978). *Oneness and separateness: From infant to individual*. New York: Touchstone/Simon and Schuster.

Karp, H. (2002). *The happiest baby on the block: The new way to calm crying and help your baby sleep longer*. USA: Bantam Books.

Klaus, M. H., Kennel, J. H., & Klaus, P. H. (1995). *Bonding: Building the foundations of secure attachment and independence*. Reading, MA: Merloyd Lawrence/Addison-Wesley.

Kotulak, R. (1996). *Inside the brain: Revolutionary discoveries of how the mind works*. Kansas City, MO: Andrews and McMeel.

Leboyer, F. (2002) *Birth without violence* (2nd ed.). United States: Healing Art Press.

Leboyer, F. (2002, re-issue) *Loving hands: The traditional art of baby massage*. New York: Newmarket Press.

Miller, K. (1999). *Simple steps: Developmental activities for infants, toddlers, and two year-olds*. Beltsville, MD: Gryphon House.

Murray, L., Fiori-Cowley, A., Hooper, R., & Cooper, P. (1996). The impact of postnatal depression and associated adversity on early mother–infant interactions and later infant outcome. *Child Development, 67*(5) 2512–2526.

Nadel, J. (Ed.). (2006). *Imitation in infancy*. USA Cambridge University Press.

NAEYC. (2004). Preventing SIDS in child care: What can you do? *Young Children, 59*(2), 48.

Warner, P. (1999). *Baby play and learn: 160 games and learning activities for the first three years*. St. Paul, MN: Redleaf Press.

Weissbourd, B., & Musick, J. (Eds.). (1981). *Infants: Their social environments*. Washington, DC: NAEYC.

Useful Videos

The Happiest Baby on the Block Video. (2003) Available at http://www.amazon.com/

An automatic "off-switch" for baby's crying is the topic of this video. Dr. Karp blends modern science and ancient wisdom to prove that newborns are not fully ready for the world when they are born. His approach is based on three basic principles:

- The Missing Fourth Trimester: Babies cry is because they are born three months too soon.

- The Calming Reflex: The automatic reset switch to stop crying of any baby in the first few months of life.
- The 5 "S's": Five simple steps that trigger the calming reflex.

Infant Massage: The Power of Touch Video. Available at http://www. amazon.com/

A licensed neuromuscular therapist and nurse guide this program, teaching the steps and strokes of infant massage while offering important tips and information to help the caregiver tailor the massage to each baby's individual needs.

Useful Web Sites

Education for Change (SIDS)
  http://www.efc.co.nz/

The National Highway Traffic Safety Administration
  http://www.nhtsa.dot.gov

The National SIDS/Infant Death Resource Center (NSIDRC)
  http://www.sidscenter.org/

PBS resources
  www.pbs.org
  In box next to Search, type Whole Child, click on link for The Whole Child, click on link for For Early Care and Education Providers

Psychology resource
  www.psy.pdx.edu

CogDev-Child/The great child care debate
  www.childcarecanada.org/

CHAPTER 6

Grasping the World: Infants at 3 to 6 Months

Engaging babies is an important part of responsive care. Since babies spend a lot of their "awake" time on the floor, this provider settles into a play routine using that location.

LEARNING OUTCOMES

After reading and studying this chapter, you should be able to:
- identify the observable characteristics of development of infants at the 3- to 6-month stage
- explain the significance of behaviors of infants from 3 to 6 months in a developmental context
- recognize and respond to the developmental diversity of 3- to 6-month-old infants and discuss issues pertinent to this stage
- assess the development of infants in the 3- to 6-month stage
- respond to the health, safety, and development needs of 3- to 6-month-old infants with appropriate nurturance, activities, protection, and caregiving
- develop strategies to work with parents as partners in the care and education of their infants

SCENE

A conversation between a father and an educator at the start of a day:

"Babies seem so much more human when they smile," commented a young father as he brought his baby of 3 months into the child care center. "It's easy to love a baby, but you see the real person in there when they make this connection with you." "This is a milestone of development," explained the educator. "It is wonderful when you get a smile. It shows there is really a two-way social relationship." "I can see that you are enjoying Sam," continued the educator. "We really love him, too." "Yes . . . but during the night when Sam wants company I get quite annoyed, and I feel bad about that" disclosed Dad. "I know what it's like to do without sleep. That seems quite usual to me; try not to feel bad about it . . . babies do well if the basic relationship is good . . . none of us has to be perfect," replied the educator, as she took Sam from Dad's arms. "Any chance of you catching up on some sleep?" she asked. "No, I'm already late for work," said Dad. "After a busy night it looks as though Sam wants to sleep now," said the educator, as the baby closed his eyes. "Just my luck," said Dad, as he kissed Sam softly on the cheek.

See the Additional Support section in your Online Companion for a discussion of differences in patterns of care for young children.

At this stage, we find that babies will smile at anybody, but that won't always be the case. We particularly enjoy young babies at this stage: They get to know us well and we make strong attachments to them, as well as the other way around. But sleep patterns are not always as regular as families might wish.

Smiling signifies a change in behavior that has significance to each domain of development, but most importantly indicates an advance in social interaction. Babies respond to smiles and will show you how much they are interested in you and everything in the world around them. Even though the sleep patterns are not entirely predictable, you will notice that 3-month-old babies are awake and taking notice for longer periods. They look interested in many of the things around them. You will probably notice that the baby has become a "real person" and is happiest with people he knows. Strangers don't pose a threat, and the little person will be content to look at a new face and swipe at it with his fist.

DEVELOPMENTAL DOMAINS

Physical Development

Growth

Observing weight, height, and head circumference increases is essential when monitoring changes—these measurements are major indicators of health. Babies may double, or nearly double, their birth weight by about 6 months of age (Shelov & Hannemann, 2004). This pattern may be different for low-birth-weight infants. The outfits that were so big at birth will be outgrown within a short time. Babies' heads also grow quite rapidly. This is most noticeable between 3 and 6 months of age, when the head circumference will increase as much as $3/8$ inch per month (Allen & Marotz, 2007). This increase is important because it is an observable indicator of brain development. A baby's length will also increase as much as $1/2$ inch a month (Allen & Marotz, 2007), and this will be particularly noticeable when she is kicking and stretching. Her legs may be quite bowed, but she does not need them yet for walking, so this is usual. Her bones are still malleable, because the ossification and calcification processes have not yet hardened them. It is important to notice how well a baby's clothes fit, because any restrictions can influence growth and the formation of bones. This is especially true for shoes—which babies really do not need until they begin to walk—as well as socks and footed pajamas. If they are too small and worn for prolonged periods of time, they can interfere with foot growth (Shelov & Hannemann, 2004). Also, tight clothing around the neck, stomach, arms, or legs is uncomfortable, as well as a safety hazard.

A notable effect of having infants sleep on their backs—due to SIDS prevention—is that babies are more frequently seen as having a head that is somewhat flatter at the back. This does not appear to have any lasting effect, and because of the skull's malleability it will return to a more rounded shape in time. For the same reason, the baby may have a bald spot at the back of the head, as the head rubs against the sheet. The hair does grow back and it is not an ongoing issue.

Infants at this stage may appear more chubby or filled out than they did in their first months. Although weight gain varies, increases should be charted. Feeding patterns, activity levels, and individual differences all contribute to the baby's growth.

Physical Skills

The new physical skills of a baby of this age enable increased learning. The coordination required to see objects and learn how to hold them is a complex skill gained during this stage. The baby goes from swinging an arm or leg at a dangling object to being able to grasp items with her whole hand. Once she can grasp objects and practice this skill, she will soon discover how to pass them from hand to hand (Allen & Marotz, 2007). These actions allow her to have a small amount of control over the physical world. Play objects must be safe for the baby to explore and should be the right size to be grasped by tiny hands, but not too small. Because objects grasped by the baby will inevitably make their way to the baby's mouth, items should be kept as clean as possible. As babies progress through these months, their bodily control increases significantly.

Gross Motor Skills

The physical actions of reaching and grasping help babies find out about the world through their senses. When they are able to sit, they see the environment differently than they do when they are in a lying position. During these months, babies are likely to increase their back control and may be able to sit, supported at first and then unsupported, for short periods. Even when they can sit without some support, they can topple over because they are not yet able to rotate their upper body. Also, their high center of gravity—top-heaviness—makes this difficult. If a baby's back "collapses" and he rolls to one side, he may not be ready for real sitting. This skill will be mastered a little later. High chairs and other hard forms of seating may be uncomfortable for the baby who has not yet gained control of his back. He may grow to dislike the seated position and even slide out of a chair if he is not well supported with firm cushioning.

Gradually, the baby will be able to sit straighter and for longer periods of time. As we mentioned in previous chapters, the baby's increasing neck and then back control is an example of the cephalocaudal sequence—that is, the usual sequence of bodily control, which starts from the head and works downward. Another significant sequence of control goes from the center of the body outward. In keeping with this proximodistal sequence, you may see increasing back control followed by arm and then hand control.

When a baby of this age is placed on her front or back (with supervision), she may discover how to roll over. This often happens unexpectedly. There are some safety risks attached to the baby's increased movement, especially since, at first, rolling over is not a controlled action. After the baby learns to roll over, her range of movements begins to expand. When lying on her front, she may find a way of moving forward by "swimming" with her legs. At first this is accidental; in later months it may allow her to crawl. The "back to sleep" advice from pediatricians should be followed when babies are put in their cribs to sleep, but spending longer periods on their backs has the potential of altering the patterns of pre-crawling actions. That is why it is so important to make sure that children are purposefully placed on their stomachs when they are awake and are supervised. Otherwise, there may be an impact on developing gross motor skills, which could delay crawling, or even lead to the baby's skipping the crawling stage altogether.

Another skill babies usually obtain by 6 months of age is the ability to put their feet in their mouths and suck on their toes. From an adult perspective, this is an incredible feat and it demonstrates how flexible young children's bodies are.

Fine Motor Skills

A baby's ability to grasp objects increases her access to sensory information. Often you will see her putting objects in her mouth. This is more likely for the sensation of touch than of taste. Mouthing objects is also satisfying because, by the end of this stage, the first teeth may be nearing readiness to erupt (American Academy of Pediatrics, 2000). It is interesting that one emerging skill—such as mouthing objects—coincides with a need to gnaw objects. In many ways development is not a linear progress of skill acquisition but a process that is interdependent— each domain influencing other domains.

Through the 3-month to 6-month stage there is a big increase in the baby's hand control. His ability to perform deliberate actions is increased, and frequently he does them over and over just for enjoyment. The repetition reinforces neural pathways, so it has an important function. Early

This child has established some control over grasping objects and, of course, into her mouth it goes.

playfulness and experimentation are aided by the baby's gaining a little control of the objects he grasps. At the beginning of the stage, the baby may not yet manage to manipulate any objects: Grasping, and then letting go of the object he grasped, is challenging enough. In time, he will be able to pass items from hand to hand, but coordinating his eyes and watching his own actions prove difficult, as he doesn't know where items are in space. He may even knock himself with the object he grasps. Items are often wet from the drool from his exploration; this makes handling the item particularly tricky. You may see a whole-hand grasp—called a **palmar grasp**—so the things he can pick up have to be just the right size to fit in the palm of his hand. Letting go remains a difficulty for some—particularly if he has grabbed your hair, earlobes, or glasses! A simple game that involves grabbing and letting go may bring almost endless amusement.

Accidentally at first, the baby may knock two items together—one in each hand. Finding amusement in this may keep her occupied for a while. As it occurs to her that banging things together makes a desirable noise, this may encourage the repetition. Passing things from one hand to the other, reaching to grab things without toppling over or as she lies on her back, and modifying her actions to fit different things that she handles may be features of her fine motor control at 6 months. Lying on her tummy poses particular challenges, because her arms are not as free to reach and grasp things. Some babies enjoy this position more than others. The sitting position may be preferred because she can see around her and make more successful attempts at grabbing, but time on her back or stomach offers a different perspective.

palmar grasp

a hand grasp using the whole hand (and palm)

Cognitive Development

Senses and Perception

At this stage, babies' senses are acute. A baby prefers to hear human voices but is influenced by a wide variety of sounds (Allen & Marotz, 2007). She may find that kitchen appliances make interesting sounds, but some high-pitched sounds could be uncomfortable for her. As time goes on, the baby's ability to differentiate—or distinguish between—sounds increases.

Responses to smells may produce facial expressions similar to those of adults. Facial expressions have been found to be fairly similar across different cultures and among people of differing ages and experiences. They are not learned behaviors. Facial expressions are part of an inborn mechanism to allow for communication without benefit of language. With a continued liking for sweet tastes, most babies will reject some foods or the taste of some objects. At the age of about 4–6 months, infants are introduced to purées, their first "solid" foods. Although babies have general and personal preferences, there is a clear need to feed them nutritious foods without added sugar.

At this stage, a baby can more easily follow moving objects with her eyes, (called tracking), and by turning her head, because she is able to see a little farther away and has improved head control (Sheridan, 2001). This expands her access to visual stimulation. She has binocular vision and, consequently, some sense of spatial dimensions (Eliot, 1999). The images that she receives can be interpreted so that she can have an improved idea of where things are in relation to her.

At 5 to 6 months, babies will reach for objects that they can see and that are within their grasp. Early attempts at judging distances may be incorrect, but trial and error helps her learn to gauge how far away objects are. The baby is particularly interested in visual information as her **acuity** increases. She will appear to enjoy looking at contrasting patterns, bright colors, and particularly at faces (Gopnik, Meltzoff, & Kuhl, 1999).

acuity

the degree to which one or more of the senses is functional or effective

The visual system is basically wired into the baby's brain at birth; however, the brain needs experiences early in a child's life in order to assure refinement and the eventual achievement of adult levels of visual performance. For this to occur, a baby's eyes need to be able to form clear images, and the eyes have to be aligned in order to send simultaneous and nonconflicting images to the brain (Tychsen, 2001). "If misalignment (strabismus) is constant and persists longer than

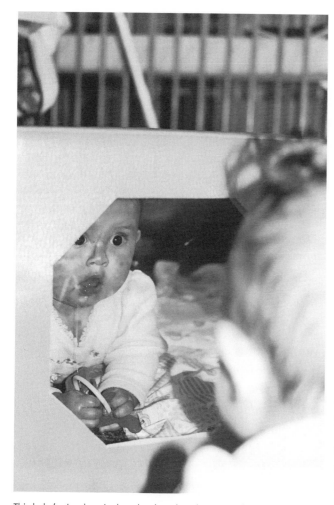

This baby's visual acuity has developed to the point where she can appreciate a reflected image. She is still a year away from recognizing that image as herself.

tracking

the ability to follow a target that moves on an imagined line in front of the face from the nose to the ear; is not present at birth

habituation

the decrease in the response to a stimulus that occurs after repeated presentations of the stimulus—e.g., looking away from a mobile after continued stimulation

scheme

an organized pattern of sensorimotor functioning; a preliminary cluster of ideas; early infant ideas

60 days during the first 9 months of life, the development of 3-D depth perception in human infants is permanently lost" (Tychsen, 2001, p. 72). Also, the visual connections in the brain, which allow for smooth eye **tracking**, are not present at birth. This ability usually stabilizes by 6 months (Trawick-Smith, 2006). Unfortunately, if there is visual impairment that impedes the process during this time, the cerebral connections needed for tracking are not established and the impairment is permanent (Horton, 2001). Trawick-Smith (2006) points out that research has revealed cultural differences in tracking efficiency. This may be due to genetic inheritance or the environments babies are raised in. Regardless, it is interesting to note that culture can affect even very minute factors in an individual's life.

The infant's sense of touch is often underestimated. The skin is the baby's largest sense organ, and it sends many messages to the brain. A baby's skin is soft and particularly sensitive to temperature, texture, pleasure, and pain. Most babies enjoy gentle touches, but some are irritated by too much touching. The infant's ability to regulate her body temperature will probably have improved, but, because she is unable to tell us if she is hot or cold, we must pay attention to such considerations. It is worth repeating that the temperature for a baby lying on the floor can be lower than for an adult moving around the room. Caregivers must be aware of this possible difference.

The process of sensory stimulation and how it promotes brain development are not fully appreciated, but it is important to understand that infants and toddlers are sensory gluttons. "Because objects and events are multifaceted, our experience of them is multimodal; that is, we experience simultaneous visual, auditory, and tactile stimulation, and sometimes olfaction and taste as well" (DeLoache, 2000, p. 12). In light of the brain research findings now, more than ever, it is recognized that early stimulation is highly desirable because the brain needs it in order to make neurological connections (Shonkoff & Phillips, 2000; Bruer, 2004). At this stage of development, sensory discovery is extremely significant, but keep in mind that there must be a balance between times of high and low stimulation. "The trick to stimulation is to stay one step ahead of a child's habituation, which is incredibly potent, even in early infancy" (Eliot, 1999, p. 448).

A decrease in responding to a repeated stimulation, known as **habituation**, demonstrates that the child has formed a mental representation, or **scheme**, of that stimulus. The stimulus could be a person, object, or event. Because of repeated exposure to the stimulus, the child will recognize it when and if it occurs again. **Dishabituation** represents an increase in responding to a stimulus because the stimulus is novel and the child has not yet created a mental representation. Habituation is an important tool; imagine how exhausting it would be if we had to pay attention to each and every stimulus we encountered, each and every time we encountered it. Continuous dishabituation would be like a permanent short-term memory loss (rather like the movies *50 First Dates* or *Memento*).

Mental Schemes

The infant will gain some understanding of her world as she experiences it. Gradually she will create a mental map of preliminary concepts connected with her firsthand experience. These are called cognitive schemes. They involve neurological activity at a level beyond previous achievements. Examples of early schemes might include how her blanket feels, the smell of

dishabituation

the increase in responsiveness after stimulation changes

sensorimotor

the first stage of the individual's cognitive development; this stage has six substages

primary circular reactions

simple repetitive acts resulting from an enjoyable experience—typically observed at 1–4 months; a substage of sensorimotor activity

secondary circular reactions

actions the child repeats as a result of his becoming interested in the external results that they produce, typically observed at 4–8 months; a substage of sensorimotor development

Mom, or, in the case of combined information, how she feels, sees, and smells her soapy bath water. These schemes reflect her understanding of her external world and consequently affect her actions. Everyday happenings and material are babies' most important stimuli. They enjoy simple things, like holding a small object and squeezing it to make a sound, or swiping at a face.

Sensorimotor Behavior and Circular Reactions

At the age of 3 months, babies are likely to take an increasing interest in their world, and can be seen playing with people and objects that are within their sight and grasp. Their behaviors will be changing from random movements to more controlled, deliberate actions. Piaget (1952) describes this as the **sensorimotor stage**. Piaget theorized that this stage of cognitive development, from birth to age 2, was comprised of six substages. This chain of substages, termed "circular" because one action prompts a reaction, which causes the action again, is marked by behavior that is repeated by the child, over and over again. The child progresses from one substage to the next substage as he gains greater gross and fine motor skills and cognitive ability. His actions help him to make sense of all the sensory stimulation he receives. Some of the things that he did by chance will now become part of his range of skilled movements. His thinking will allow him to anticipate some events, particularly if they have to do with his own needs. For example, you may notice that he becomes excited when you go to get his bottle, or displays displeasure when he sees that you are about to take him to the change table.

Babies' explorations will move into patterns when they perform actions that cause a response. This is called a **primary circular reaction**. Babies will repeat actions many times, which shows us that they have some sense of deliberation and an ability to decide to do something, even if they cannot carry it out successfully.

Later in the stage, the repetitions of action will become more complex, what we call **secondary circular reactions**. The baby's actions will be concerned with the external environment rather than with her own body. When the baby notices that something has happened by chance, she will repeat the action that brought about the result. This shows that the baby has some basic understanding of cause and effect, and knows that objects are separate from her.

 Figure 6.1 outlines Piaget's six substages of the sensorimotor developmental phase. The Additional Support section of your Online Companion also contains more information about Piaget's cognitive theory.

Concentration Span

A baby may show enjoyment by playing for longer periods during these months. He might also show happiness by his facial expressions and by making cooing sounds. The range of expressed emotions becomes wider, as does the range of his social relationships. You will probably find that his moods alter quite quickly (Allen & Marotz, 2007). Boredom with a simple activity may indicate that he needs a new source of interest. Familiarity with objects can be a source of comfort, but he may

Figure 6.1 Piaget's Substages of Sensorimotor Development

Piagetian Substage	Substage 1: Simple reflexes (Birth–1 month)	Substage 2: First habits and primary circular reactions (1–4 months)	Substage 3: Secondary circular reactions (4–8 months)
	Substage 4: Coordination of secondary circular reactions (8–12 months)	Substage 5: Tertiary circular reactions, novelty, and curiosity (12–18 months)	Substage 6: Internalization of schemes (18–24 months)

habituate from boredom and look away. Physical agitation, such as wriggling, leg-stretching, and sound changes, indicates the need for a change of scenery or a new object to handle and mouth.

The baby of 3–6 months is particularly interested in new things to look at. Her attention is drawn to novelty; anything is of interest. Her visual preferences—the things she likes to look at most—continue to be faces, which she scans in outline and in some detail. But she is also interested in patterns of high contrast. Findings from brain research document that "repetition of sensorimotor patterns may help infants and toddlers maintain important synapse linkages" (Gallagher, 2005, p. 13). Why this happens is still not known for certain. However, the following response from babies has been observed:

> Babies will turn toward complex patterns of high contrast and away from patterns with little contrast . . . . Images such as stripes, where there is a sharp contrast between the brightness and texture of two surfaces, are important because they usually indicate where objects begin and end . . . . Newborns are already imposing order on what William James called the "blooming, buzzing confusion" of their senses. They're organizing their world into a bunch of different things. (Gopnik, Meltzoff, & Kuhl, 1999, pp. 64–65)

Knowing this, adults have often responded by providing black-and-white images—particularly in mobiles that are within the baby's field of vision. However, the baby's attention to patterns can also relate to color images—so we shouldn't limit the visual discovery of the infant.

Babies have different styles that lead to different patterns of attention. Some like frequently changing things to see or pay attention to and tire quickly of what is presented; they want to be exposed to action and change. Other babies will concentrate longer on a face or picture or stay with a playful activity longer. Their calmer style does not necessarily suggest a better focusing ability that will lead to the ability to keep at a task longer. These are merely style differences and may indicate that their learning will take different paths—neither path more effective than the other.

Communication and Language

We have already looked at the baby's sensory acuity and determined that all five senses are usually working effectively at this stage. Because the senses are the primary means of learning and communicating, they are very significant. Early screening and close observation are necessary to ensure that a baby's senses are enabling her to play and communicate. The senses of sight, touch, and hearing are probably the most important. Difficulties relating to the sense of touch are rare; there is a higher incidence of visual and hearing impairments. For communication purposes we generally depend on both sight and hearing, so early intervention may be necessary for babies who show a deficit in either sense.

At this stage, babies have the ability to recognize the range of sounds that are found in speech. It will take a while before they can use language, but they soon learn that your pitch and the way you speak have meaning. A baby may begin to recognize her own name during this stage (Allen & Marotz, 2007). She will begin to understand what is happening to her by associating sounds with seeing adults do things. She may enjoy hearing your voice talking or singing. There is comfort in the human voice and the patterns of adult conversation even when they are not understood.

> One interesting study involved playing audiotapes of each vowel sound to 5-month-olds. They could tell which face went with which sound because they gazed at the face with the wide-open mouth when the *ahhh* sound was played and at the face with the pulled back lips when the *eeee* sound was heard. The authors concluded that babies "have a primitive ability to lip-read, at least vowel sounds." (Gopnik, Meltzoff, & Kuhl, 1999, p. 71)

Research into language acquisition—how babies learn to communicate verbally—indicates that exposure to the sounds that are integral parts of two or more different languages (such as English and Spanish) exposes the baby to a wider variety of sounds than would be experienced in a monolingual (one language) context. However, at 3–6 months, the baby will make the same sounds regardless of the language she hears: contented sounds, cries, and a few more differentiated noises. The sounds may have meaning attached to them. For example, a particular cry can indicate to adults that she has a particular need. This does not necessarily mean that she makes particular sounds in order to get the responses she desires. But gradually her sound production will become more controlled and deliberate. Adults also send messages that are only partly understood. When there is effective communication through body language, the way the baby is handled, and the way she is played with, there is reinforcement of shared meaning.

Sound, by way of real language, conveys meaning, but so far the baby does not have a very broad understanding of language, and depends on context for any shared understanding. For example, at around 5 months, the baby may raise her arms and make an "ah-ah" sound, which is translated by the adult as "lift me up now." Similarly, the adult may talk to the baby and emphasize key words. The sound, coupled with an action—within a context—may offer meaning. "I'm going to change you now," said repeatedly while taking the child to the change table, may have the effect of linking sounds and action that, together, have meaning for the baby.

receptive language

hearing and knowing what a sound means

There is a big difference between a baby's receptive and expressive language. The meaning or understanding that a baby associates with a particular vocal sound is **receptive language**—hearing and knowing what a sound means. Toward the end of this stage, babies may have some limited receptive language, but it will remain context-dependent for some while. The beginnings of **expressive language** are found in crying or cooing. They can tell us what the baby is feeling, but as yet she is not making the sounds deliberately. Over the next few months the baby will make vocalizations that are deliberate—she is expressing herself, even if we don't know her meaning. In time, she will use a wider range of sounds that are part of one or more languages. Simultaneously, she will make stronger associations between sounds and meanings.

expressive language

utterance of meaningful sounds, words, phrases, and sentences

How Do Infants Communicate?

Try living 24 hours without talking to anyone. This condition, I'm sure, would produce some difficult and frustrating moments for you. Now do it for a year. This is the situation infants experience in their first year of life. So how do infants communicate their needs and wants? If you take the time to really observe them, you will learn the many channels through which babies send messages, and soon be able to interpret those messages. You can see babies communicating at this stage through **body language**, facial expressions, sound production, and responses. Babies are not able to tell you what they want or even to point to it, but they have a remarkable ability to let you know when they are pleased or unhappy. Crying can indicate unhappiness, but it can also be used to get a response when attention is required. Calm or agitated movement can be another cue for adults. Facial expressions and states of awareness are still other indicators of mood and responsiveness. Many of these are not deliberate communications, but they can be interpreted and responded to as though they were (Bardige, 2005; Messinger, 2002).

body language

messages sent either deliberately or unconsciously; conveyed by the individual's posture, facial expressions, gestures, and other behavior

motherese

changes in a mother's speech that emphasize particular sounds and the use of a higher pitch than normal when communicating with infants and young children; may be culture-bound

Some of the baby's communication is not deliberate, but during this stage the baby may make deliberate attempts to communicate with adults. These attempts are called intentional communications (Greenspan & Greenspan, 1985) and involve the infant initiating connections with an adult, using sound and body language. As well, the baby is likely to respond to the adult's attempts to communicate. Early communication sets the pattern of reciprocity: the fact that communication requires give and take, or sending and receiving. It is a two-way, turn-taking process.

Babies are especially likely to respond to adult language if it is relatively high-pitched, simple, repetitive, and accompanied by eye contact and exaggerated facial expressions. This type of communication is called **motherese** (Eliot, 1999), or **parentese**, and appears to reflect an innate ability of adults to communicate successfully with infants.

parentese

speech pattern used in talking with infants and young children; refers to either male or female and utilizes the elements found in motherese—the high-pitched, sing-song tone adults use instinctively with infants

Young babies are becoming familiar with the language spoken around them. Their early babbling contains some sounds of that language. The language environment is important to language learning: Conditions that encourage language development include positive relationships, exposure to simple language, and reinforcement of the infant's sound production.

The importance of language cannot be understated. A study conducted by Hart and Risley (1995) documented the amount of language input between families identified as professional, working class, and welfare. The comparison of the number of words heard by the children at age 4 between the welfare and professional families was 35 million words. All families used approximately the same amount of language directed at accomplishing family routines, including behavior management. However, Hart and Risley (1999) found a difference in what they termed "optional" talk, the talk utilized in play interactions or in parallel task completion. In the homes where more language input was observed, the family members engaged in more playful conversations and elaborated language structures, and were more encouraging toward language production. As a result, the children in these homes not only heard more language, but had more opportunity to practice expressive language. Another researcher, Huttenlocher (1999), made a similar conclusion, stating, "children who hear complex sentences more frequently are more skilled at understanding and producing them" (p. 74). Unfortunately, it is more than likely that the differences between these two groups cannot be compensated for, no matter what type of schooling is provided at age 4, and the gap continues to widen as the years pass.

It might seem strange to be discussing vocabulary and language when children at this age are not even talking. However, it is important to remember that these early years are crucial for the foundation of learning. Many children, by 3 months of age, are placed in child care when a family member returns to work. As a care provider you need to know that the acquisition of language is impacted not only by the amount and type of language children hear, but also by the *quality* of child care:

> A significant body of research links children's language development with the quality of their child care environments and links the quality of the child care environment to the teachers' training and education, the staff/child ration and class size, and the level of compensation the staff receives. . . . In general, children who get a healthy dose of language interaction at home or in child care develop hefty vocabularies and strong functional language; children who do not get enough input or meaningful practice in either situation are likely to be at a loss for words. (Bardige, 2005, pp. 12–13)

Staff working with infants must learn how to communicate effectively with them. It does not mean that you talk nonstop to children. That type of action will certainly result in overstimulation for them. Instead, appreciating the fact that communication is building a relationship and knowing that it depends on mutual respect and understanding are essential. The communication dance, especially with young children, moves to a rhythmic and harmonious tune, with anticipated pauses and responses. Developing **reciprocal communications** depends on the adult and infant having enough relaxed time to share experiences and on the adult's attuned "sensitivity" (Erickson & Kurt-Riemer, 1999), which includes the following:

reciprocal communications

communication exchange in an equal give-and-take manner

- a recognition that even the youngest infant can signal her needs and wishes
- accurate reading and interpretation of a baby's cues and signals
- an adult's response contingent on the baby's signals (the hallmark of sensitivity)
- consistency and predictability over time

On the other hand, insensitivity can present itself in a variety of ways, including persistent and chronic failure to respond, inconsistent or erratic patterns of response, or intrusiveness that is driven by the needs of the adult rather than the child. Insensitivity does not necessarily imply "bad" parenting or caregiving, rather it could stem from lack of knowledge about child development, erroneous information, stress, or emotional issues. According to Erickson and Kurt-Riemer (1999), child care providers are often guilty of being intrusive as "we allow ourselves to be driven only by what is in our lesson plan for the day, rather than by the baby's cues, [thereby] missing a wonderful opportunity to give the child a message that his or her wishes count" (p. 66). If caregivers support language development appropriately, they are most likely ensuring a positive future for children.

Magda Gerber's philosophy has, at its heart, reciprocal relationships. Those types of relationships support affective, as well as cognitive and motor, development in children. They are part of the philosophy of care also espoused in this text.

BUILDING CROSS-CULTURAL COMMUNICATION SKILLS: USING VIDEOS

Family permission must be obtained before any videotaping can be done. It's a great way of showing family members what happened during their child's day while they were at work.

Using a video camera is relatively easy; with a little practice, the educator will gain sufficient skill to make a good image and capture significant parts of the child's day. Showing these video segments at family meetings, making them available for lending, and using them as an integral part of your assessment process will be a useful addition for all families, but for those who speak a language outside your own scope they can be invaluable.

You might have a particular intention in your recordings. You may want to highlight each baby's individual temperament, or capture behaviors that show the baby's skills.

> "Caring and trust enable teachers to understand a family's child-rearing practices and values and thus offer seamless and holistic care."
>
> (Baker & Manfredi/Petitt, 2004, p. 11)

Communicating with parents is essential for reinforcing educator–infant interactions. It helps to synchronize communication strategies to avoid confusing the baby. Parents for whom English is a second language may benefit from sharing the infant's experiences through video. (See Box 6.1)

Facial Expressions

Certainly facial expressions are part of the overall body language that allows communication of a baby's fear, joy, anger, and other primary emotions. This provides the adult with a way of reading a child's reactions to stimuli, needs, and preferences, and seeing how to further communicate. Charles Darwin initiated interest in universal emotions, but this work was extended by Izard (1977, 1993) at the University of Delaware, who developed the Maximally Discriminative Facial Movement Coding System (MAX), which codes distinct facial responses to specific emotions. An example of the MAX coding system is seen below:

- ANGER is coded when:
  1. Infants eyes are squinted and narrow.
  2. Eyebrows come together.

Others, including Campos (1970, 1983), Emde (1998), and Ekman (2004), continued to expand our knowledge base regarding the range of human emotions evidenced by infants. Future research will possibly give us insight on how to read children's emotions more effectively and even help recognize that "emotions can be a sensitive barometer of early developmental functioning in the child–parent system" (Emde, 1998, p. 40).

Facial expressions are fundamental, and appear consistent across cultures. Emotions in infants are expressed by facial reactions and, through careful observations, can be interpreted. According to Restak (1986), "eyebrows, forehead, eyes, eyelids, nose, cheeks, mouth—each of these regions assumes a distinct facial muscle pattern according to the emotion ascendant at the time" (p. 200). Thus, combining the research of Izard, Campos, Ekman, and others yields the following list of basic emotions observed from birth to age 1:

0 to 6 Months
- Distress/Crying
- Happiness/Joy/Smiling
- Interest

From 6 to 12 Months
- Anger
- Fear
- Sadness

All other feelings evolve from these basic emotions (Kostelnik, Whiren, Soderman, & Gregory, 2006). Further studies may include other emotional expressions.

"Recognition of Visual Cues" in the Additional Support section of your Online Companion also contains information on cues gained from facial expressions.

Emotional and Social Development

It is most interesting to observe babies at 3–6 months because it is then that real social relationships begin to emerge. Infants' curiosity about the world and their eagerness to have it respond to them is amazing. In addition, their increasing physical control allows for more sensory discovery. The infant is starting to take hold of the world!

Smiling

The emotional growth that babies experience at this stage is reflected in their use of smiles. A baby may initiate an interaction by making a facial expression that is similar to a smile. When the adult responds positively, the baby repeats the expression. As the interaction proceeds, the baby's enjoyment is indicated by her real smiles. The baby finds the give-and-take of the social interaction pleasurable: a clear sign of emotional growth. The **social smile** is a clear indication of the emotional well-being and sociability of the baby. Many adults relate better to babies when they have reached this stage because of their openness to social relationships. Laughter comes later—but the smile is captivating.

There is something about a smile that makes people respond to a baby—even adults wrapped up in their own business open up in response to the smiling baby. This may be another part of the baby's protective system; he seems appealing and yet vulnerable. A phenomenologist writing over 50 years ago (Buytendijk, 1947) tells of his fascination with the first smile and wonders, ". . . what is the essence and meaningful significance of a certain expression, such as a smile?" (p. 2) Answering his own question, Buytendijk speculates that perhaps the smile exists without an inner life—an animalistic response without human experience. Perhaps the smile brings a human reaction that creates a first human experience, he suggests.

Laughter, which begins at around 3 or 4 months, requires a level of cognitive development because it demonstrates that the child can recognize incongruity. What that means is that the child can recognize a pattern that deviates from the norm. For example, the sound of "raspberries" on the stomach, which is produced by the adult blowing air out of his mouth when placed against the surface of the abdomen, produces gales of laughter because it is an unusual sound—and probably sensation.

social smile

a smile, appearing at approximately 6 to 8 weeks, which clearly indicates an ability to be social because the infant smiles in response to human faces

Here is the beginning of the social smile, which is so endearing.

From a scientific perspective, it may be difficult to know what is behind the smile. "Eye-to-eye contact and smiling are inborn responses that speak of our human preparedness to become attached to other human beings," suggests Kaplan (1978, p. 75). The seemingly simple act of smiling becomes increasingly complex over time and takes on a wide variety of meanings as the infant develops and increases her social relationships. Kaplan suggests that the baby's smiles tend to be context-specific and can be "read" accurately only by the person who is engaging with the baby—this is the specific smile. The specific smile is characteristic of an attachment to an adult that can usually be observed in this 3–6-month period. Kaplan notes that at this stage the baby smiles more often as a result of hearing human voices, especially the ones she recognizes. By 3 months, she is often looking into her mother's eyes as she smiles, rather than looking through her or past her.

Attachment

Through the relationships the baby makes that are evidenced by smiles, the baby can feel secure to explore her world. As she does this, she begins to see herself as a separate, autonomous (self-directed) "person." This depends on **attachment**—babies who are unable to make such human connections will not come to see themselves as separate human beings, an enormously significant psychological step in emotional development.

At around 5 months, the baby will start moving outside what is called the **shared orbit**, her physical and emotional circle. This is a sign of strong attachment and risk taking. The baby knows through experience that when the adult goes away, she comes back, or there is certainly some continuity—her needs are being met both emotionally and socially. At the same time, that separation becomes harder. Because the bond to the **primary caregiver** (most significant attachment figure) can be counted on as being reliable, the baby appears to be fearful if separation from the primary caregiver occurs. This may seem strange, because the relationship is stronger than it has been—but so too is the emotional turmoil when the caregiver disappears.

Both Mary Ainsworth and John Bowlby have contributed significantly to the study of attachment. Their separate findings, with a common agreement on there being a secure base relationship at the root of attachment, have been reinforced over 25 years of subsequent research. Attachment theory is based on a multitude of concepts: that bonding will occur in the first months of life; that basic trust, which Erickson identified as being the first step in psycho-social development, will be established through a warm, safe, and loving relationship with a caregiver; and that gradually, over the first year of life, child and caregiver will solidify a unique and permanent connection—one to the other. Elaborating on the work undertaken on attachment over the years, Waters and Cummings (2000) are attempting to test the theory and see how it holds up to cross-cultural examination. Indications are that the broad base of attachment theory is applicable across different populations. This means that looking at how attachments happen might be less important than the fact that they do happen. This is not to imply that attachments are anything other than relationship-based, but that adults and infants may create their connections in a variety of ways. In one culture this may mean having the baby in close proximity for long periods, and in another it might include meeting the baby's needs in a reliable way. This should alert us to the fact that caregivers and parents may have different styles that contribute to making sound attachments with babies. In other words, there is more than one way to ensure **secure attachments**. Information garnered from the infant and toddler programs of Reggio Emilia have helped us understand that cultural differences do not impede the formation of attachment and relationships (Gandini & Edwards, 2001; Edwards & Raikes, 2002). Our profession is richer from having this cultural perspective become part of our over arching framework for quality care.

The challenge presented by infants who have made specific attachments—attachments to particular people—is that handling separation can be difficult. For an infant, **separation** can be a traumatic event. For very young babies, this is not usually the case, although they may be calmed more easily by those who are familiar with them. It may be that once the caregiver is out of sight, she might also be out of the baby's thoughts, so the less mature baby has less to worry about. The cries of the baby who is undergoing a separation can seem heart-wrenching; prolonging the act of separating may make matters worse.

Often a sense of **people permanence** is experienced before **object permanence**, which is at about 8 months, so people permanence may occur during the latter part of this age period—possibly at 6 months. The concept of object permanence is that when an object goes out of the baby's sight and she then seeks it, she is looking for the missed object because she can hold it in her mind. People permanence is similar—when a familiar person goes out of sight, the baby still remembers the person. So it's possible that some babies show some signs of separation anxiety because they have the concept of people permanence. Separation anxiety can show itself in several ways, depending on the stage of the baby, her ability to communicate, and her personality. Typically she might show fear or distress and cry for some period. Babies who do not cry at the time of separation have either not made a secure attachment or, more likely, are still too young to hold the person who is gone in their minds.

attachment

the positive emotional relationship that develops between two individuals—between adult and child

shared orbit

the two-way communication and shared space of two individuals

primary caregiver

the adult to whom the child has the strongest attachment

secure attachment

a positive, trusting, and reliable relationship with an adult

separation

awareness of being without a person or object

people permanence

the realization that people continue to exist when they are out of view

object permanence

the realization that objects continue to exist when they are out of sight

BOX 6.2

USEFUL STRATEGIES FOR SHARING INFORMATION

Families are often extremely distressed when the time comes to leave their young infant at a child care center. They may have wide-ranging fears about what will happen to their child while they are away. Addressing these fears may involve preparatory meetings or parental observation of the center "in action." The caregiver should take time to hear the families' concerns, explain how the child's needs will be met, give families information about the center and its philosophy, and organize processes to help share information about the child. In addition, the parent can be encouraged to stay with the infant until both parties are ready to separate. The caregiver might also arrange meetings that allow the new families to meet and chat with the family members of other children at the center.

Decades of research (Cassidy & Shaver, 1999) support the ideas that forming a secure attachment is a critical part of an infant's development, and that it is essential to later emotional adjustment. This is being revealed through many studies of children who have not been successful or who present behavior problems later in childhood (Honig, 2002; Landy, 2002; Charlesworth, 2004; Hyson, 2004). An infant's attachment to her caregivers is important, but the way it occurs in different infant–adult dyads may vary. Possibly, infants discern early in their experience that different people do other things for them, or do the same things differently; this may be the start of internalizing role models, as well as establishing various relationships with different people. Ultimately, the infant needs secure attachments with both caregivers and parents in order to build trust and a clear sense of self. Regular communication with families can help ensure that attachment occurs at care facilities. One way of facilitating communication is by establishing a process of sharing information with families, including daily information forms, which should come from the home as the child arrives, and from the school as the child leaves. Box. 6.2 describes several strategies for fostering communication between home and school. (Obtain sample forms for daily exchanges in the Additional Support section included in your Online Companion.)

Self-Concept

We have already mentioned some aspects of self-concept—the idea that the baby knows that she is a separate human being. Margaret Mahler, who had a strong influence on Louise Kaplan's work, developed a complex theory of **separation individuation** (Mahler, Pine, & Bergman, 1975) that explains how infants perceive themselves. At first, there is no dividing line between who the baby is and who the mother is. Through developing a strong and secure attachment with the mother (here Mahler's work focused on mother and child), the infant finds that she can influence her immediate world and the people in it; then the infant could see herself as a separate individual.

Social relationships help a baby to discover and assert his separateness. Only in a relationship can a baby discover that he has influence. This helps the baby understand a human cause-and-effect connection. At 3 months, the baby finds that his behavior brings a response from the adult. He smiles, and the adult smiles back. He cries, and the adult supplies what the baby wants. The baby becomes an agent of change and is empowered to take some control in his social world. The development of the baby's self-concept and self-esteem depends on the baby having a sense of control over his world. He needs to have some idea that he makes a difference and that his needs matter. Basic trust in the adult to support his needs and desires, and the

separation individuation

the process of becoming a separate and individual person

beginnings of trust in himself, form the emotional roots from which confidence and self-esteem can later grow.

Temperament

Babies are far from being all alike; we have already mentioned this in relation to making attachments. Temperament styles are clearly evident in the patterns of reaction that babies demonstrate (Chess & Thomas, 1996). Some babies are quick to respond; others take time. Some babies are more fearful than others. There are infants who accept comforting rapidly; others hold on to their moods. Some babies have a tendency to observe what is happening, while others are more inclined to initiate communications. These different temperaments are observable even in very young infants. In fact, families and caregivers should be taught how to understand temperament because it has such a determinant impact on their daily interactions with their children (Carey, 1998; Lerner & Dombro, 2004). "The essential messages for parents should be that: temperamental traits are real; they are important for both child and parent; they are best managed by accommodation, not confrontation or attempts to change them" (Carey, 1998, p. 223).

In this rhythm of a reciprocal interplay, the teacher smiles (stimulus). The message is received and the child responds.

According to Wachs (2004), since temperament styles have some biological basis such as genetic influences, biomedical influences (low birth weight), known developmental disabilities, teratogen exposure, and nutrition factors such as iron-deficiency anemia, the baby's traits tend to remain fairly consistent over time. An adult who is sensitive to the infant's patterns of behavior will find that two-way communication becomes more effective. By modifying his own patterns of response, the adult will find that they become increasingly synchronized. Repetition helps this process, which is easy because the baby tends to repeat behavior sequences.

The rhythm of the baby and her responses to stimuli may influence social relationships as well as the types of activity that the baby enjoys. Careful observation and sensitive responses will help you to determine her needs.

Given what you have learned so far, you must now consider how important it is to ensure that all children experience a secure emotional environment, whether in or out of home care. Take the time to review Erik Erickson's first four stages of psycho-social development, which are shown in Box 6.3. These are some of the social–emotional tasks children struggle with in the first eight years of their lives. Reflect on how you see these tasks being supported in the child care facilities you visit. How do the teachers foster trust? How do the toddlers gain a sense of **autonomy**?

To help you strengthen your knowledge about emotions in infants and toddlers, use the following resources:

Look at "Recognition of Visual Cues" as well as the information on temperament theory in the Additional Support section of your Online Companion.

This interactive communication influences the social relationship.

autonomy

an inner drive to become independent and meet one's own needs; a sense of independence, self-government, or self-reliance

consistency

a pattern of predictable and reliable behavior and/or uniformity in caregivers

---

BOX 6.3

FIRST FOUR STAGES OF ERICKSON'S PSYCHO-SOCIAL THEORY

NAME OF STAGE	POINT IN LIFE CYCLE	CRISIS
Trust vs. Mistrust	Infancy	Either: Gaining trust in self and others OR: Feeling mistrust and wariness of others
Autonomy vs. Shame and Doubt	Ages 1½–3	Either: Achieving a sense of autonomy OR: Having shame and doubt over one's ability to be independent
Initiative vs. Guilt	Ages 3–5½	Either: Learning how to take initiative comfortably OR: Feeling guilty over motivations and needs
Industry vs. Inferiority	Ages 5½–12	Either: Gaining a sense of industry and competence OR: Feeling inferior and inept

---

This center has established a primary caregiving system, which aids this child in forming an attachment.

Activity 6.1 on your CD-ROM contains a list of emotions and a form to document a baby's acquisition of emotional milestones.

PARTICULAR NEEDS

This section discusses issues that are of particular importance for children at this stage of development. Some of the information may be repetitious, but that is purposefully planned. Sometimes, we all need reminding about the essential components of care.

Trust and Responsiveness

Infants' relationships with adults are based mostly on trust. Babies are likely to trust adults if their needs are met in a regular and reliable way. We must be sensitive to the fact that babies need **consistency**. They need to see the same faces and be responded to in ways that allow them to predict patterns of adult behavior. This is part of their discovery of how the world works. If babies do not have a small number of adults who provide reliable, sensitive attention and with whom they can form lasting attachments, they may have difficulty later forming relationships, or suffer other social or emotional challenges.

Infants need to be responded to in ways that are positive. The cues that they give us tell us what they need; we must learn their system of communication. When hungry, they must be fed; when uncomfortable,

BOX 6.4

GETTING IN TUNE WITH INFANTS OF 3 TO 6 MONTHS

Below are some starting points for building your responsive skills with a 3–6-month-old infant. This list is not comprehensive, and many more suggestions can be found in the "Getting in Tune with Infants, Toddlers, and Twos" section of your Online Companion.

- identify the infant's temperament and work with his style in all activities and communications
- supply all the infant's basic needs: stimulation, food, diaper change, physical contact, etc.
- respond quickly to the infant's cries and other cues for attention
- build trust by being consistent and loving
- assist separation from other adults by providing continuity
- place the mother's belongings near the infant so he is comforted by their sight and/or smell
- provide visual stimulation in the form of pictures, faces, and patterns
- raise the pitch of your voice and repeat simple words for the objects and actions that the baby sees
- provide simple sensory experiences within the baby's reach (e.g., food, textures, or objects to touch and see)
- allow the infant to sleep when he wishes
- check all objects/materials for their safety
- help the baby to tune out by decreasing stimulation
- make sounds (popping, tongue clicking) to engage the baby
- imitate the infant's own vocalizations
- smile frequently and respond to the baby's smiles
- take the infant for walks outside in a stroller when she can be propped up to look around
- place the baby on his back to sleep

A technique that I used to help babies separate from families was to ask the primary caregiver in the home to bring in a piece of clothing. If I was rocking the baby I would place that clothing item over my shoulder, or if I was feeding the baby, over my chest. Since infants' sensory mechanisms are so enhanced at this point in their lives, they would often calm down when they recognized a familiar scent. It didn't always work, but in many instances it seemed to help.

they must have attention and comforting. They may also convey the need for love and physical contact. Responses to all these needs build trust. Box 6.4, "Getting in Tune with Infants,"underscores the many ways you can begin to build your responsive skills with 3–6-month-old children.

Stimulation

At this stage, infants need sensory stimulation and the opportunity to play safely, both alone and with the assistance of an adult. Without this play, much early learning will be limited and the infant's thinking skills will be affected.

Along with times of stimulation, babies also need downtime, or opportunities to be quiet and relaxed. Reading the infant's cues will tell the caregiver when to provide stimulation and when to provide a calmer environment.

Language and Communication

Careful reading of a baby's cues is the most important part of the adult's role. This leads to a reciprocal relationship, where messages are sent and received by both parties.

vocalization

any sound production

Before she can learn a language, a baby needs to hear the language spoken and have adults imitate and reshape her **vocalization**. It is essential that a baby be nurtured in a language-rich environment. At this stage, adults should speak in a very clear and direct way to the baby. Her early vocalizations will be framed within the language in which she is nurtured.

Nutrition

Infants need good nutrition, preferably breast milk, during these months. A breast-feeding mother whose baby is in group care may be able to express her milk so a caregiver can give it to the baby in a bottle. Alternatively, if the mother is nearby, she may be able to come by to feed at regular times. Some mothers maintain morning and evening breast-feeding, and the infant is bottle-fed during the main part of the day. During this stage, the infant may begin to take some solid food, but the main nutritional source remains milk. He should be held closely when fed. This is an important social time. If this opportunity for closeness is missed, it cannot be repeated as successfully at another time, because there is a strong association between physical closeness, warmth, comfort, and feeding.

Physical Contact

Most babies thrive on lots of physical contact and affection. There can be exceptions to this; a few babies are not so receptive to touch and prefer emphasis on other types of communication. Infants are supplied with warmth and a feeling of trust when they experience the adult in close proximity. Infants need physical contact, not just to have their obvious physical needs met. Caregivers need to plan for the close times and be able to create them spontaneously when the opportunity arises and the baby is responsive.

Opportunity to Move

The chance to stretch, move, and explore physical capabilities must be a regular part of the infant's day. Sometimes it is possible for the infant to go without restrictive clothing, but colder climates may make this difficult to arrange. In this case, the infant needs to wear clothing that is warm but does not limit movement. Movement is an important feature of physical skill acquisition and finding out about the body.

Accommodation of Individual Styles

In center-based care, it can be difficult to ensure that all infants' needs are met. Those who have styles that get attention rapidly are more likely to have their needs met. Educators must make sure that even the most contented babies receive the attention that is essential for their well-being.

DEVELOPMENTAL VARIATION

Many of the reasons for variations in developmental patterns have been discussed in earlier chapters. Some developmental differences may not have been identified in the first three months of life. These may be congenital, chromosomal, metabolic, or other conditions. The most severe will probably have been diagnosed. Less severe conditions may be discovered at this stage through the diligent observation of the adult caregivers.

Birth Weight

Infants who had low birth weight may have weight increases that vary from the usual pattern (Papalia, Olds, & Feldman, 2006). Premature babies may have continuing difficulties beyond those of weight. Sometimes they have long-term breathing problems. You may notice sensory deficits, and they may also show some skills a little later than other babies. Most will catch up, but it is important to observe such babies carefully. Developmental information from the adult caring for the infant can be essential, because the baby may need special support.

My first two children were girls, and I made sure that their toys ranged from doll to block, to trucks. I did dress them in frilly girl clothing, but they also got to wear jeans and flannel shirts. I always felt that I was treating them as babies, not girl babies. However, my third child was a boy and one day, when he was about 3 months old, I suddenly realized that I was pushing his arm rather forcefully through the sleeve of his t-shirt. It was at that point that I began to analyze treatment of my children. I was handling them differently. I was using much more physical oomph with my son, probably just because he was male. The lesson learned is that we constantly have to be on guard because so much of what we do is affected, not by our conscious mind, but by our subconscious attitudes and beliefs.

Male-Female Variation

There are minor differences at this stage between the development of boys and the development of girls. Girls tend to grow slightly faster and acquire vocalization skills slightly earlier than boys. The differences at this stage are extremely small and will probably be unnoticeable among a small group of infants in a child care center.

Studies have shown that adults respond in distinctly different ways to male and female infants. You may see babies as young as 3–6 months experiencing treatment according to their gender. Girls are sometimes treated more sensitively than boys. Boys' cries tend to be responded to less quickly. Ideally, you will not see this type of treatment. Caregivers may use language and display distinct expectations in accordance with the infant's gender. To treat children equitably, you must be sensitive to this issue. Avoid responding to boys and girls in ways that are directly related to whether they are girls or boys.

DEVELOPMENTAL ALERTS

You will see developmental variations in every baby. As an educator, you are responsible for supporting development and identifying possible concerns if they arise. Although your task does not involve making a diagnosis, your observations can be very helpful and lead to the appropriate supports. Avoid making assumptions about the reasons for differences, but always respond if you think there might be a developmental concern.

During or at the end of this period of development, you may observe some things that could indicate a cause for concern and the need for further assessment and referral. These include:

- uneven weight increase
- prolonged food refusal
- too rapid or slow an increase in head circumference
- lack of response to facial expressions
- no smile
- lack of interest in visual stimuli
- staring without response to stimuli
- little excitement for people
- prolonged periods of sleep without alert phases
- eyes not converging on objects
- lack of vocalizations
- prolonged periods of crying without response to comforting
- lack of crying
- not being startled by loud sounds
- not turning head toward sound
- not following moving object within expected field of vision
- not grasping small objects put into hand
- not reaching for objects
- head lolling (leaning or rolling without control)
- asymmetrical appearance
- continuing rounded back (does not sit supported)
- failure to use hand and mouth for sensory discovery
- no anticipatory behaviors (e.g., for feeding)

HEALTH CONCERNS

A few health issues apply particularly to infants of this age. Teething, ear infections, viruses, coughs, colds, and other common health concerns are usually the cause of the problem, but any significant change in behavior or health status should be documented. These changes may have a variety of causes, which can be identified by a health professional.

In the "Everyday Health and Safety" section of your Online Companion, there is a list of signs and symptoms that should be reported to families in they are observed in the infants in your care.

Licensed child care facilities and family child care homes are required by law to have forms available to record any accidents or incidents that might require attention. All accidents must be documented and reported to families. Any breathing difficulty, significant bleeding, loss of consciousness, choking, convulsion, or other significant symptom should receive an immediate first aid response and referral to a qualified medical practitioner.

Some babies at 3 months may still be experiencing colic, or tummy pain that causes them to stretch out their legs until rigid and cry angrily. There are differing medical explanations for this and many home remedies. Any treatment must be checked with the parents—frequently you will find that they have developed strategies to cope. A family member might take the baby and safely put him in a secure restraint in the car; the ride tends to be calming. You cannot do this as a center-based caregiver, but as an alternative you might try carrying the baby in a sling, walking with him on the hip, or laying him in a baby carriage and going for a walk. The rocking motion can calm the baby.

The sharp pains—from colic or other digestive problems—should be attended to by a doctor if they persist. Mention your concerns to the family promptly; they may already have experienced the problem during the night. Gently rubbing the baby's tummy and keeping him warm often seems to help. Some parents like to offer warm, rather than cold, fluids, and to burp the baby to ease the gas. You might follow the parents' strategies.

> About a million babies, and everyone around them, are affected negatively by what appears to be inconsolable crying, or colic. Although it is a distressing situation, the good news is that babies do outgrow colic.

This child is enjoying the exploration of the floor. Her care providers have ensured that the space is clean, free from safety hazards, and warm. Interesting toys are within her reach. All the conditions have been met in order to provide a great opportunity for learning!

The Floor

To most adults, the floor is simply for walking on, often in shoes that have been worn outside. Yet young infants are often put on the floor to play. There are three issues to be considered here: hygiene, temperature, and vulnerability

- *Hygiene.* Adults must not wear street shoes in rooms where infants are on the floor at any time, even on a blanket or rug. The risk of infection is too high. Slippers, socks, or "house shoes" can be worn if they are clean. Outdoor shoes should be left outside the infant rooms.
- *Temperature.* The floor can be cold, and the infant's ability to regulate his temperature is poor, so check that he is warm enough. A child care planner might consider installing under-floor heating.
- *Vulnerability.* When infants are on the floor, they should not be in a position where adults have to climb over them or pass things above them. Particularly risky are hot foods or liquids such as tea or coffee. These should not be consumed in the infant room.

SIGNS OF POTENTIAL NEGLECT OR ABUSE

Very occasionally, the caregiver might come across signs that raise real and immediate concerns for an infant. Suspected abuse or neglect is a difficult issue, and the caregiver must be aware of many considerations. Obvious symptoms can be responded to quickly, but other signs may be much harder to decipher. Be aware that a sign that seems to point to abuse or neglect could just as easily have another explanation. Inadequate levels of supervision, medical treatment, nutrition, or protection may constitute neglect, but these may be difficult to distinguish from accidents, faulty decision making, poverty, or different values.

This is not to minimize the possibility of encountering real neglect or abuse. Remember that neglect or abuse can happen in any type of family and any social or economic status. At this age, the baby is especially vulnerable to shaking, which can cause brain damage. Any behavioral changes, bruises, marks, or other concerns must be documented and responded to if unexplained.

Neglect may be more difficult to observe than some of the more obvious outward signs of physical abuse. When a baby's needs are not met, there may be no physical sign other than a lack of developmental progress. Yet, as we have seen earlier, there can be many reasons for such a lack of progress, many of which are not due to neglect.

failure to thrive

a condition where a seemingly healthy baby fails to grow and develop normally

One example is **failure to thrive** (FTT) babies. Historically, failure-to-thrive babies resulted from inadequate human contact and an absence of attachment, which then led to physical, emotional, and social decline, such as children in concentration camps or in state-run orphanages (Spitz, 1946; Sameroff & Chandler, 1975; Morison, Ames, & Chisholm, 1995). However, current research reveals that failure-to-thrive babies often have underlying physiological problems, although the syndrome does develop a significant number of children as a consequence of child neglect and abuse.

"About 25% of normal infants will shift to a lower growth percentile in the first two years of life and then follow that percentile; this should not be diagnosed as failure to thrive."

(Krugman & Dubowitz, 2003, p. 1)

If there are concerns, it is important to determine whether the failure to thrive results from medical problems with the child or from psychosocial factors in the environment, such as abuse or neglect. Failure to thrive is diagnosed when a child's weight for age is below the fifth percentile. "A more useful classification system is based on pathophysiology—inadequate caloric intake, inadequate absorption, excess metabolic demand, or defective utilization" (Krugman & Dubowitz, 2003, p. 1). One of the first actions taken is an extensive medical work up to rule out any physiological explanation. Failing this, attention then focuses on abuse or neglect, although some cases of failure to thrive come from the hypervigilance of parents, meaning they are overly attentive to the child's needs. Poverty is the greatest single risk factor for FTT worldwide and in the United States. FTT can also be unintentional, occurring with breast-feeding difficulties, errors in formula preparation, poor diet selection, or improper feeding technique. Cystic fibrosis, cerebral palsy, HIV infection or AIDS, as well as several other chronic conditions can also cause FTT.

Strong indicators of FTT outlined by the American Academy of Pediatrics (Block, Krebs, et al., 2005) include:

- intentional withholding of food from the child;
- strong beliefs in health and/or nutrition regimens that jeopardize a child's well-being; and
- family that is resistant to recommended interventions.

As noted in earlier chapters, in all cases of suspected abuse or neglect, the protocol of the individual child care center should be followed, and any cause for concern must be reported to the local child protection agency.

EVERYDAY SAFETY ISSUES

Infants at this stage must be supervised at all times when they are awake and closely monitored at sleep and rest times. Their vulnerability stems from their inability to anticipate, recognize, or move away from danger. An infant at this stage is completely dependent upon adults. He can attempt to grasp things within his reach, but this constitutes an additional potential hazard.

Since after grasping an object the baby will likely take it up to his mouth, caregivers have to exercise particular caution.

Although you might see advice on how to check the safety status of swings, walkers, and over-the-door jumpers, they are *not appropriate* for use in child care settings. Many children are injured each year in these pieces of equipment. Children have tumbled down stairs in child walkers, had head injuries from collapsing swings, and have sustained neck injuries from the bouncers. All in all no matter what piece of equipment is used with children, supervision is necessary. And remember, there is no piece of equipment as good as two arms, a cuddly embrace, loving eyes, encouraging words, and a warm smile.

Remember to check the "Everyday Health and Safety" section in your Online Companion for a list of suggestions of which caregivers need to be aware in order to safeguard children at this stage of development. Once again, make sure you review these suggestions, since you will be responsible for the care and safety of infants.

STARTING POINTS FOR RESPONSE

Responsive Caregiving

The infant looks to the adult to provide what she wants and needs, as a trusting relationship, one based on love, emerges. Social smiles may indicate secure attachments. Responding to the infant's cues remains the highest priority for caregiving. Body language and facial expressions may provide useful hints to help us understand the baby. These will have evolved into more complex patterns that adults need to be able to read. Compared with those given at earlier stages, infants' cries have a wider range of meaning. "Assume that if infants over 3 or 4 months of age cry during times when you expect them to be awake, they're *telling* you that something's the matter" (Greenberg, 1991, p. 122). Their sound production is more differentiated and therefore more likely to send messages. Their body control has increased, and their bodily responses can be linked with likes or dislikes and positive or negative responses. Entering the two-way dance of communication is essential for social interaction. The adult has to tune in to the infant as the baby tunes in to the adult. Reciprocal communication builds the foundation for later language learning and more complex social communications.

Supportive Guidance

Enter the moment with the baby and find experiences where there can be shared meanings. The baby needs to receive loving care and continuity for emotional growth attachments and the development of self. This type of care requires carefully supported transitions between the adults responsible for the baby. Multiple attachments can form if the child is exposed to several adults, but support is best offered in such a way that the same people are with the child each day. A primary caregiver model can be particularly supportive at this stage. Under such a model, the infant is in a small group of babies who receive care from the same person or people each day.

Meeting the baby's psychological needs requires supporting her through the processes of separation and individuation. She needs firm attachments to ensure that her sense of oneness develops. Continuity is essential for emotional well-being.

Facilitating Development

At this stage, babies are still entirely egocentric, and their focus is on ensuring that their own needs are met. A baby finds her place in her family and learns that she is loved when her basic needs are met and she receives the attention she craves. Adults can support her development by being there and providing what the infant needs at that time. She needs to have the opportunity to play with adults, to move, to hear voices that are directed to her, to be in an environment in which she is accepted and responded to rapidly, and to be positioned so she can see more of the world. Some sensory stimulation can be found in everyday experiences. A baby needs the time, space, reciprocal communication, and opportunity to discover people and objects. Such discovery will improve the control and influence she is beginning to have on her world.

Activities

Your CD-ROM contain activities to help you increase your skills while engaging infants in caregiving routines, play, and supportive guidance. Activity 6.2 (all activities listed here are on your CD-ROM) helps you develop ways of engaging in young babies' experience and extending your interactions with them. These activities always start from the framework of observation. Activity 6.3 helps you create a responsive curriculum for each infant, and to develop activities that are targeted to individual interests and skill levels. Activity 6.4 includes suggestions for further experiences and interactions. Activity 6.5 describes several possible scenarios for responsive guidance. *Remember*, your Online Companion also contains a section entitled "Toys." It has a listing of suggested toys for all ages and stages of infancy and toddlerhood. There is also a separate section on children's books because exposure to language and books is essential for supporting emerging literacy skills. Be sure to take the time to check out these resources.

SUMMARY

The emerging personhood of the baby is becoming obvious to all the adults in the infant's life. Individual personality, style, and response patterns are becoming evident. Adults are likely to respond positively to the social smile that emerges during this stage. When a baby realizes that her smile engages adults, she will repeat it and use it to get attention. A happy baby is one whose cries are responded to quickly. This helps to build her trust in the key adults in her life. One or more attachments to an adult will aid in emotional development through the establishment of trust and in the emergence of a basic self-concept.

The dance of communication between a caregiver and a baby in this period is interesting to watch. There is a clear process of dialogue as both partners listen, watch, and wait. The infant's vocalizations will usually be more extensive in this period; the repertoire of sound production increases to cooing, happy sounds. Exposure to real language will gradually allow the infant to pass from undifferentiated sound production to the sounds necessary to learn a particular language. Much of the infant's communication is through gestures, crying, gazing, and nonlanguage sounds. There is a marked difference between receptive and expressive communication. She will usually find that adults respond to her needs by translating her cues. It is therefore essential for adults to be able to interpret all the signs that a baby is sending, not only her deliberate communications.

For the baby to thrive, she needs lots of physical contact, along with talking, singing, and other noises. Because she is not yet mobile, or even able to sit without much support, she is likely to enjoy seats that allow her a good view or to be held in such a way that she can see around her. Physical skills development is usually evident at this stage, in increased neck and back control, which leads to sitting. The baby's fine motor skills repertoire will be increasing; she may be able to release a grasp as well as hold on tightly to something in her hand. She can bring objects to her mouth and discover parts of her own body.

Interest in the environment is particularly evident at this time, although the baby can handle only those things that are within her reach. Everything is taken to the mouth for sensory exploration, so all toys and play materials must be clean. All kinds of sensory stimulation are necessary, but infants at this stage also need times of relaxation. Reading the signs of overstimulation is just as important as interpreting signs of boredom. Increased motor control, combined with sensory discovery, allows the infant to repeat and perfect some basic actions and add to her mental schemes.

Highlights of this chapter also include the link between vision development and the brain, the first two substages of Piaget's sensorimotor stage, the use of parentese language to engage infants, the importance of establishing a primary caregiver system in order to support attachment, the influence of temperament on social and reciprocal relationships, failure-to-thrive babies, and a warning about the use of baby swings. Information about everyday health and safety concerns, developmental delays, and techniques to engage babies is touched on, and you are directed to your Online Companion for even more information and ideas to add to your repertoire of growing knowledge about caring for infants and toddlers.

DISCUSSION QUESTIONS

1. How might you handle a situation where a mother is reluctant to leave her infant with you?
2. What kind of stimulation might be appropriate for infants at 3 to 6 months if their development is fairly typical of the stage?
3. If you were to observe bruises on an infant's legs when you changed her diaper, what might you do?
4. When a mother wants you to give sugared drinks to her 5-month-old baby, what response would be appropriate?
5. How do you deliver a positive response to someone who says that your work with infants is "baby-sitting"?

ADDITIONAL RESOURCES

Further Reading

Baker, A. C., & Manfredi/Petitt, L. A. (2004). *Relationships, the heart of quality care: Creating community among adults in early care settings.* Washington, DC: NAEYC.

Bardige, B. (2005). *At a loss for words: How America is failing our children and what we can do about it.* U.S.A.: Temple University Press.

Caplan, F. (1995). *The first twelve months of life: Your baby's growth month by month.* New York: Bantam.

Edwards, C., & Raikes, H. (2002). Extending the dance: Relationship-based approaches to infant/toddler care and education. *Young Children, 57* (4), 10–17.

Fenichel, E., & Eggbeer, L. (1990). *Preparing practitioners to work with infants, toddlers and their families: Issues and recommendations.* Washington, DC: Zero to Three.

Greenberg, Polly. (1991). *Character development: Encouraging self-esteem and self-discipline in infants, toddlers, and two year olds.* Washington, DC: NAEYC.

Greenspan, S., & Greenspan, N. T. (1989). *The essential partnership: How parents and children can meet the emotional challenges of infancy and childhood.* New York: Penguin.

Hart, B., & Risley, T. (1995). *Meaningful differences in everyday experience of young American children.* Baltimore: Paul H. Brookes Publishing Company.

Hart, B., & Risley, T. (1999). *The social world of children learning to talk.* Baltimore: Paul H. Brookes Publishing Company.

Honig, A. S. (2002). *Secure relationships: Nurturing infant/toddler attachment in early care settings.* Washington, DC: NAEYC.

Hyson, M. (1994). *The emotional development of young children: Building an emotion-centered curriculum.* New York: Teachers College Press.

Kaplan, L. (1978). *Oneness and separateness.* New York: Touchstone/Simon & Schuster.

Pimento, B., & Kernested, D. (2000). *Healthy foundations in child care* (2nd ed.). Scarborough, ON: Nelson.

Raikes, H. A secure base for babies: Applying attachment concepts to the infant care setting. *Young Children, 51*(5), 59–67.

Snow, C. W. (1998). *Infant development* (2nd ed.). Englewood Cliffs, NJ: Prentice Hall.

Wilson, L. C., Douville Watson, L., & Watson, M. (1995). *Infants and Toddlers: Curriculum and Teaching* (3rd ed.). Clifton Park, NY: Thomson Delmar Learning.

Useful Videos

Getting in Tune: Creating Nurturing Relationships with Infants & Toddlers. (1992). Sacramento: California Department of Education.
Description: 24 minutes; study guide.
Series: Program for Infant/Toddler Caregivers.

Exploring First Feelings. (1985). Washington, DC: Institute for Mental Health Initiatives.
Description: 21 minutes.

The Separation-Individuation Process. Van Nuys, CA: Child Development Media.
Description: an 84-minute, 3-part video depicting the separation-individuation process:
Part I: "Symbiosis and the Differentiation Subphase: 0 to 8 Months."
Part II: "The Early Practicing Subphase Proper: 8 to15 Months."
Part III: "The Rapprochement Subphase and On the Way to Object Constancy: 13 to 36 Months."

Flexible, Fearful, or Feisty: The Temperaments of Infants and Toddlers. California Department of Education: PO Box 944272, Sacramento, CA 94244-2730

Useful Web Sites

Kids Growth—child development
   www.kidsgrowth.com
More than Just Babble—The Patterns of Language in Young Cantonese-Speaking Children
   http://www.cuhk.edu
Under Search CUHK, type More than Just Babble and click on link
   www.mayoclinic.com/
The Developmental Psychology Student Newsletter—stages of development
   http://www.mc.maricopa.edu
Type Psychology in Search MCC box, click on link for The MCC Developmental Psychology NetLetter

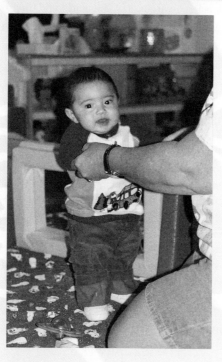

CHAPTER 7

Me and You: Infants at 6 to 9 Months

By the end of the 6- to 9-month stage of development, many children will begin to pull themselves to a standing position and usually enjoy small walks that are assisted by adults. Look at this little one's face!

LEARNING OUTCOMES

After reading and studying this chapter, you should be able to:

- identify the observable characteristics of development of infants at the 6- to 9-month stage
- explain the significance of behaviors of infants from 6 to 9 months in a developmental context
- recognize the developmental diversity of 6- to 9-month-old infants and discuss issues pertinent to this stage of development
- assess the development of infants in the 6- to 9-month stage
- respond to the health, safety, and development of 6- to 9-month-old infants with appropriate nurturance, activities, protection, and caregiving
- develop strategies to work with parents as partners in the care and education of their infants

SCENE

"They really sit up and take notice of everything going on," said a student after her first week of work with infants. "They seem to watch you all the time and are incredibly smart in how they try to get your attention," she continued. "I didn't always know what they were thinking, but they made lots of connections. When I went to the refrigerator and got out a bottle of formula, one 7-month girl would get so excited. If the bottle wasn't for her, I had to hide it."

This young child is relating to his caregivers in a very social way. His affect is one of joy and happiness.

Much of babies' learning is observational, as the student suggested. As well, their increasing awareness of the world and their part in it makes being with babies at this stage really exciting. When they are awake, they can pay attention to all sorts of things. It's important to make all those learning experiences very positive.

Students notice that being with infants at this stage is different from working with younger babies. Their personalities are more clearly observable. They seem to respond in accordance with their temperament style, and they demand that you pay attention to them.

Their capacity to learn is obvious, as they examine everything that they can reach. Their own bodies are also a source of interest, and they may spend time finding out what their bodies can do. This is an essentially physical time. Infants enjoy the effect they can have on things and people, and will repeat many actions with objects. They enjoy the surprise of a playful exchange with adults, and will do the same thing with them many times over for pure enjoyment.

Infants at this stage have adapted to their **caregivers** in a more sociable way. They like to spend a lot of time with adults. They enjoy interactions, and will imitate people in subtle ways. Particular adults become important to infants, and they may become distressed when a familiar adult leaves. Relationships are made with particular adults, so it becomes increasingly important to have the same people caring for the baby.

caregiver

a person responsible for meeting the physical (and other developmental and health) needs of an individual

DEVELOPMENTAL DOMAINS

Physical Development

Growth

At the beginning of this stage, many babies will have doubled their birth weight, although weight-gain patterns can vary considerably. Then the rate of growth slows down slightly, but the first year of life is the time of most rapid increase in size. The usual weight gain is about one pound per month (Allen & Marotz, 2007), so at this stage the baby may weigh between 15 and 21 pounds (Shelov & Hannemann, 2004), depending upon age, birth weight, sex, body type, and general health. A fairly steady gradual increase in weight is more important than reaching an "ideal" weight. Chubby babies used to be considered healthy, because they had weight to fall back on if they became sick, but we now know that overweight babies tend to retain that pattern (Lumeng, 2005). Slight chubbiness is not a reason to reduce the fat content of the baby's diet. The baby needs some fats to increase neurological functioning. The baby is likely to be making the transition to some solid but puréed foods by this stage.

Gains in length and height drop off slowly, but growth remains more significant than in later years. This may mean growth of 1/2 inch per month (Allen & Marotz, 2007). At this stage, babies may vary in height from 24 to 28 inches (Shelov & Hannemann, 2004).

The circumference of the baby's head and the chest are roughly equal (Allen & Marotz, 2007). The baby's body proportions are noticeably changing. The head becomes smaller in proportion to the body as the body grows considerably more rapidly than the head. Brain development is not dependent on significant size increase of the baby's head.

For some babies, teething is observable by a flushed appearance on the cheeks and increased drooling. The first tooth may come through at about 6 months (Berk, 2004), but this varies considerably.

Gross Motor Skills

The slow change in body proportions, along with increase in muscular control, allows the baby to gain more bodily control. At about 6 months, most babies are able to sit unsupported for short periods. The length of time the baby can sit up gradually increases over the next few months. By

This child has mastered the skill of crawling!

crawling

mobility involving propelling the body forward, backward, or sideways while on the knees; typically a stage of physical development prior to walking

9 months the baby will probably be able to remain sitting while leaning forward to pick up an object and be able to roll from a lying position to a sitting position or vice versa (Shelov & Hannemann, 2004).

Usually, rolling from front to back comes before back-to-front rolling (Sheridan, 2001). However, at 6 months, a baby lying on her back may roll over quite easily; when this happens, she may repeat it over and over for pleasure. You may also see early attempts at **crawling**. If she finds herself on her front, she may pull herself up on her extended arms, and will later attempt a "commando crawl" using her arms to move forward. Gradually her legs will gain control. She will then be able to propel herself backward or forward in a more proficient crawl (Allen & Marotz, 2007).

Currently, observational evidence suggests that some babies are crawling later and even more babies are bypassing the crawling stage entirely. As stated previously, this may be a result of the Back to Sleep campaign, so remember that children need to be placed on their stomachs when they are awake. A few babies will be ready to demonstrate some sort of crawl by 9 months, but do not imagine there is anything wrong if the baby doesn't crawl for several months—or never crawls at all. Incidentally, the peak period for SIDS is over by the 6–9-month stage, but the possibility remains for some months to come. Following the Back to Sleep policy is necessary even when babies can roll over.

Some babies do not crawl in the usual way: They may do a crab crawl, moving sideways, or they may not crawl at all, finding that they can shuffle in a sitting position to get from place to place. Toward the end of this stage, the baby may become mobile, and it is noticeable that her legs are gaining control, including strength and directioning; this comes from lots of practice at kicking.

If the baby is held in a standing position, she is likely to push her feet down and bounce, taking most of the weight on her feet. In time, her foot movements will become more controlled, and she will step on each foot alternately (Sheridan, 2001). Opinion is divided over the advisability of encouraging a child to stand before she does so independently, although the authors of this text side with the opinion that development should not be forced. No long-term advantage exists in encouraging babies to acquire skills ahead of a natural progression. Some competitive adults want their babies to be developmentally advanced, and associate early physical skills with improved all-around development. Evidence suggests that "pushing" is more likely to be detrimental. For example, families may put their child in an infant walker because they believe it will hasten walking. Actually, research demonstrates that the opposite occurs (Siegel & Burton, 1999). The researchers compared motor and cognitive results from 109 infants and found that the children in walkers actually had delayed motor skills, as well as lower cognitive scores. A specific conclusion drawn from the results is that children in walkers are denied the feedback their brains can receive from their feet because their visual line of sight is blocked by the tray on the walkers. Garrett, McElroy, and Staines (2002) also found delays, but of much less significance. However, the American Academy of Pediatrics (2001a) issued a strong warning regarding the use of walkers. They feel walkers should be banned from the United States because:

- baby walkers put children at risk for injury; and
- no clear benefits from using a baby walker have been demonstrated.

Remember, it is more important for the child to use her muscles to practice getting into the position than to actually be in the position.

At 9 months, a few infants can lower themselves from standing without dropping to the ground in an uncontrolled way. However, for many, it is still a skill to be learned. In fact, often at this stage of development, families are awakened in the middle of the night by an infant who has pulled himself up in his crib, but cannot figure out how to let go and get back down.

This child is refining his palmar grasp.

palmar grasp

a hand grasp using the whole hand and palm

intermediate grasp

a grasp that refines the palmar (whole hand) grasp; may involve scooping or some effort at thumb–forefinger opposition

pincer grasp

the use of the hand where the thumb and the forefinger work in opposition to each other

object permanence

the realization that objects continue to exist when they are out of sight

depth perception

the integration of information from both eyes in order to gauge relative size or distance; seeing the world in three dimensions

Fine Motor Skills

Much of the development of the fine motor skills of an infant at this stage is displayed in her ability to grasp objects. At 6 months, a useful but unrefined grasp is possible. This **palmar grasp** involves the whole hand. Practice and deliberate attempts to reach for smaller objects lead to an **intermediate grasp**, which uses the fingers in a more defined way (Edwards, Buckland, & McCoy-Powlen, 2002). But it is unusual for infants at this stage to be able to use a **pincer grasp**, with the fingers and thumb in true opposition. In any group of infants, we see that developmental patterns vary from one to another. By 9 months, the infant may use her fingers more precisely. In addition to developments in grasping, she may use her index finger to point.

Initially, the infant spends time looking closely at items she picks up. She will frequently play games that involve picking up objects or banging together items held in both hands. Releasing items from the hand presents greater challenges than grasping them. If a toy drops from her hand, she is likely to watch it rather than try to pick it up. This might be because she is interested in the act of dropping things, but it is more likely that when it goes out of sight it is also out of mind. Yet by 9 months, the infant will drop and pick up things if interested (Sheridan, 2001). At about 8 months, the infant may reach for an item that is partially hidden, displaying the beginning of a sense of **object permanence**. At 9 months, she may attempt to find something that has disappeared from view. It is interesting that with many infants, people permanence—remembering that people continue to exist when they are out of sight—occurs before object permanence.

Cognitive Development

Senses and Perception

Vision   Infants spend much of their early weeks and months of life learning how to see by developing such skills as focusing, teaming their eye movements, recognizing depth, developing eye–hand coordination, and making spatial judgments. Normal visual acuities, or a child's sharpness of vision, has usually developed to 20/20 by the time the child reaches 6 months (Gonzalez-Mena & Eyer, 2004). Long-distance vision and visual perception (interpreting what the child sees) continue to improve. Binocular vision, the eyes moving in unison (Tyschen, 2001), is well established, and the baby can track moving objects with just her eyes instead of having to move her head. Faces and patterns still hold a child's interest. The combination of improvements in her visual acuity allows the baby to widen her perception of her world: She gets to look at objects and people both close up and a little farther away. Having **depth perception** and generally improved vision allows the baby to see her environment and manipulate objects within it.

In this stage of development, the infant usually relates size to distance. She consequently understands that near objects look larger than the same object farther away. Depth perception has been studied using a visual cliff (Campos et al., 1970), an artificial construction involving a glass, or plexiglass, table with a surface that is split in two. On one side, the surface appears to be directly below the glass, while on the other the surface appears to drop several feet. Infants of 6–9 months will crawl across the "shallow" surface, but not the "deep" one. This indicates that they have a sense of depth.

It is speculated that although infants 6–9 months may understand that images found in books and pictures represent real objects, it is preferable that children encounter "real" three-dimensional aspects of an object (Ramey & Ramey, 1999; Fogel, 2000). This also applies to television images.

No TV viewing for children aged 2 and under!

A baby can be interested in the visual patterns that a television screen presents but it does not mean the screen provides her with significant learning. Firsthand experience is far more important. She needs the knowledge about the properties of materials that comes from interacting with concrete (real) objects. To a limited extent, babies know that images represent real objects. Adults might therefore think that babies learn through watching television or videos. However, her interest is little deeper than being engaged by staring at a television screen—interesting at first, but boring after a while. She cannot follow an abstract story line, either. Also, the baby has no control over the image and cannot remove herself from it, except by looking away from the screen. Watching television may even be damaging because of that lack of control; the baby must learn how to interact with her environment and experience the effect of her actions—TV doesn't allow this. We need to ensure that the baby doesn't experience sensory overload.

visual insatiability

the individual's unstoppable interest in looking

Another point to consider is that according to Sheridan (2001), infants at this stage can be termed **visually insatiable**, meaning they cannot have too much visual information. However, Gonzalez-Mena and Eyer (2004) warn that too much visual information can lead to what they call a "circus effect," which can result in children who become entertainment observers rather than children who actively engage in learning experiences. (See Box 7.1.)

Hearing   The 6- to 9-month infant has increasingly good auditory discrimination; that is, the ability to hear sounds and tell them apart. Human voices are preferred over any other sound, and familiar voices are listened to most carefully.

multimodal stimulation

stimulating two or more senses simultaneously

When auditory and visual stimuli are presented simultaneously, the baby will more likely pay attention to the sound than to the image. This indicates that auditory perception is the dominant sense of the two at this stage. That said, it is also clear that **multimodal stimulation**—that is, stimulation of several senses—holds greater interest than stimulation of only one sense.

No TV Viewing for Children Aged 2 and Under!

The American Academy of Pediatrics has recommended that there be no television viewing by children 2 and younger.

A recent Parent Survey (Weber & Singer, 2004) did reveal that children under 2 are television and video viewers.

This is of concern since the recommendation is no television viewing.

The Benchmark Survey (DYG, 2000) also found that adults often believe that educational TV is actually educational.

Unless there is an adult sitting next to a child to help interpret what the child is seeing, it is just visual confetti and not an educational experience.

It is in the conversation about what is being seen that meaning is constructed for children and connections can be made.

This process transforms the experience into education.

BOX 7.1

ARE YOU RAISING AN ENTERTAINMENT OBSERVER?

An entertainment observer is quite different from a scientific observer. Entertainment observers get hooked on a constant flow of novel visual stimulation. They get bored quickly and demand constant visual change. They may become television addicts. Because they experience such a strong assault on one sense (the visual), they ignore the fact that they are not involved physically or socially with the world around them. This eventual habit of observation and lack of involvement is detrimental to the development of a wide range of abilities. (Gonzalez-Mena & Eyer, 2004, p. 114)

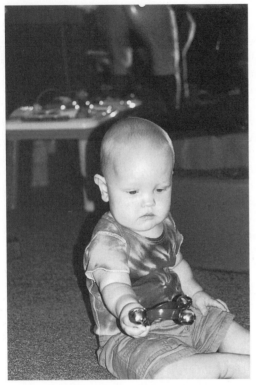

It's never too early to have music in their lives.

uni-modal stimulation

offering stimulation through one sensory channel at a time—e.g., visual material

Ongoing research into infants' multimodal sensory stimulation (Lickliter & Bahrick, 2000) suggests that the typical **uni-modal stimulation** approach to sensory stimulation that is favored by many infant caregivers may be insufficient. (This refers to stimulating the baby's vision, hearing, or other senses separately.) Although uni-modal sensory stimulation may enable the baby to focus more deliberately on one type of sensory information, it lacks the simultaneous processing possibilities of multimodal stimulation. There is some suggestion that multimodal stimulation supports learning more successfully because the dual or multiple channels reinforce one another. The brain's neurological pathways strengthen as they receive multiple sources of sensory input. As they grow up, children find themselves confronted with technologies that require multimodal processing, and may be in classrooms that are busy places, with many sources of stimulation bombarding them. Younger children might be on track to deal with this if they learn skills in excluding superfluous sensory information—learn to tune out what they don't need and focus on what is most relevant (Greata, 2006). But excluding uni-modal learning is probably a mistake, because attention to detail, conscious focus on specific sensory data, and refinement may all be necessary for particular skill acquisition. Learning to play a musical instrument or becoming a visual artist might depend on the ability to focus on the use of one sense while tuning out other sensory channels.

This might seem distant from infant experience, but early artistic expression is found in the first months and years of life, and the skills are rooted in early experience. Entering into the musical world of the infant, as well as providing materials for discovery, is important. Referring to work by Dissanayake (2000) and Gembris and Davidson (2002), Hodges (2002) stated that "critical to musical development in the earliest years is the home environment. Opportunities, not just to hear music but to interact with musical games and activities, are critical to emotional and psychological development" (p. 3). Central to all of this is the recognition that human beings are born with a biological preparedness for musical appreciation and ability, and this inborn predisposition has artistic, emotional, and social consequences (Custodero, 2002; Greata, 2006; Imberty, 2000; Trehub, 2000). Edwin Gordon contends that a child's highest musical aptitude is present at birth and begins to decline immediately (Greata, 2006). Gordon developed a music learning theory, for newborn and young children, which describes how children develop their tonal and rhythmic

Personal Comment

One recommendation from the brain research was that the results should not be used to market products for improving the brain.

In fact, the reports all acknowledged that most families already have the skills and abilities they need to help grow their children's brains.

Of course, what happened, almost immediately, was that products were produced and marketed with claims of being able to "grow a child's brain."

Some of these products are TV videos and computer games directed specifically to children 2 and under.

However, what young children need are hands-on experiences with real objects and real people, especially from birth to age 8.

Many of these products may actually deprive children of the necessary sensorimotor and interactive experiences they require.

A video or computer game is not an adequate substitute for one-on-one time spent with a caring and responsive adult!

audiation

the cognitive process that enables individuals to hear and comprehend music in their heads even with no music playing

audiation. These skills allow us to hear melody, and the rhythm of a melody, in our heads. The early childhood years are a prime time for the development of this skill. Although musical activities are not new to early childhood programs, recent research underscores the importance of purposefully planning for experiences "so that each child can be musically nurtured in an appropriate manner" (Greata, 2006, p. 47). Box 7.2 highlights some benefits gained from musical experiences.

Touch   The skin remains a very sensitive organ through which the infant absorbs new tactile information. Handling objects with increasing skill enables the infant to learn about new textures and the feel of toys and other items. He will enjoy the sensory discovery of domestic

---

BOX 7.2

Benefits of sharing music with children:

1. It aids in the acquisition of early language through the use of rhyming and rhythm.
2. It connects to the emotional domain by strengthening relationships, communicating feelings, and fostering a sense of comfort.
3. It can increase listening skills, memory, and concentration through repetition of songs and movements.
4. It develops fine and gross motor skills through finger-plays, movement, and the playing of instruments, and helps foster coordination as they follow a beat or move in unison to a song.
5. It develops imagination, invention, creative thinking, and communication skills by encouraging children to discover new sounds and make up their own versions of songs.
6. It teaches such values as self-discipline, perseverance, and responsibility as children learn to take turns and cooperate in musical experiences.
7. It can help children find their "own voice" as they explore their abilities to create unique sounds and styles of music.

Personal Comment

As a mother of four and a college professor, I frequently hear the latest "hits" in music.

I tell my students that as a teenager and young adult, I enjoyed music that spanned 50 years.

These tunes included songs sung by Frank Sinatra, Perry Como, Bing Crosby, Patsy Cline, Elvis Presley, Jerry Lee Lewis, Diana Ross and the Supremes, the Beatles, Simon and Garfunkel, John Denver, Carly Simon, Roberta Flack, etc.

I enjoyed the Big Band sounds of jazz, Motown, rock and roll, disco, country, blues, etc.

When I had my children, I could hold them in my arms and dance to music from my mother's generation, as well as music from my generation.

However, as hard as I try, I cannot imagine dancing with my grandchild to the tunes of heavy metal or most rap songs.

In doing my research for this book, I figured out why this might be so.

Research studies (Zentner & Kagan, 1998; Trainor & Heinmiller, 1998) demonstrated that babies as young as 4 months old prefer consonance in music to dissonance.

Consonance means that the music is perceived as pleasant.

To my ear, heavy metal music is often unpleasant to hear.

When 4-month-old babies perceive dissonance in combinations of two or more frequencies, they fret and turn away from the music source.

So turn off that heavy metal and replace it with some soothing tunes. Aren't those babies smart!

objects, gaining increasing knowledge of their attributes. The mouth remains an important part of the body for taking in tactile information. Most objects find their way to the baby's mouth, but for purposes of feeling rather than tasting.

Taste   Infants may be fed their first solid foods at this time, although some babies may have been **weaned** somewhat earlier. Giving babies solid food too early can be counterproductive, because their digestive systems are not ready to process anything but milk. At about 6 months, babies need more nutrients than can be supplied by mother's milk or infant formula. Cues that indicate a baby may be ready to begin solids include the following:

weaned

the process of transiting from fluids to solid food

- the ability to keep her head and neck in a steady, upright position;
- the ability to sit upright to swallow well, although she may still need extra support;
- the loss of the extrusion reflex—use of her tongue to push food out of her mouth;
- the ability to move food to the back of her mouth and swallow;
- doubled birth weight (or weight of at least 15 pounds);
- after 8–10 feedings of breast milk or formula in a day, she still appears hungry; and
- expressed curiosity about what others are eating evidenced by the baby's eye tracking or by her reaching for a bowl or plate of food.

Babies who experience a wide range of tastes early in life are more likely to accept a variety of foods. Nonetheless, adults should be cautious about offering the baby too wide a choice too quickly. Babies may dislike the taste of some foods, or react negatively to the smell of certain foods. If the baby does not like what is presented, remove the item and try it again later. Initial foods also need to be introduced gradually with enough time left between each new food in order to identify any possible food allergies (Roberts & Heyman, 2000).

Smell   Smell may play a part in establishing attachments (Mennella & Beauchamp, 2002). Clearly, babies respond positively to smells associated with the adults they know well. Infants may withdraw and turn away from unpleasant odors, but their preferences are not the same as those of adults.

sensorimotor

the first stage of the individual's cognitive development; this stage has six substages

scheme

an organized pattern of sensorimotor functioning; a preliminary cluster of ideas; early infant ideas

secondary circular reaction

actions the child repeats as a result of his becoming interested in the external results that they produce, typically observed at 4–8 months; a substage of sensorimotor development

Sensorimotor Intelligence

The baby's brain is capable of an amazing degree of acquiring, processing, and storing information. It is not surprising that babies tune out from time to time when they are in sensory overload! Much of the infant's time awake is spent taking in bits and pieces of information and trying to make sense of them with reference to what he already knows from previous experience. Increased ability to grasp, hold, and mouth objects, along with improved visual acuity, allows the baby to take some control of the sensory input.

Throughout infancy, the baby progresses through the substages of the **sensorimotor** period. (See Figure 6.1.) Piaget (1952) offers insight into the typical patterns of action and reaction that we can observe. At 6 to 9 months, the baby's abilities to see and move enlarge his world somewhat. He can see and touch more objects and has a broader experience of people. Some things in his world become predictable, and he discerns some sequences. Certain actions from the adult bring responses from the baby ahead of what is actually happening. When experiences are enjoyable, he wants them to go on and on. Sequences of playful exchange between the infant and adult provide great satisfaction when they are repeated many times. The repetition reinforces neural pathways essential for learning. It is as though practice play lays down the foundations of learning.

New information is assimilated as the baby's senses send data to the brain. As this information is processed, and the baby compares, filters, and adds new parts to his existing **schemes**, the sensory input continues. Almost simultaneously, the infant goes through the **secondary circular reaction stage** (Piaget, 1952). Review Piaget's theory in the Additional Support section in your Online Companion.

cause and effect

understanding that particular actions bring about (cause) particular reactions (effects)

assimilation

the process of incorporating new learning into existing schemes

accommodation

the process that changes existing ways of thinking in response to new experience—reorganizing or creating new schemes in response to external stimuli

The baby repeats many deliberate actions, particularly when they involve things around him. He varies his actions to bring about different responses. This recognition that particular actions bring about certain effects is called **cause-and-effect** learning.

This period is one of tremendous sensory input, as increased physical skills allow extended periods of discovery. New information is **assimilated** with previously absorbed information. The infant then goes through a process of **accommodation**, in which his existing patterns of thought change in accordance with the new information. The cycle of assimilation and accommodation is integral to his learning. Bits and pieces of information are gathered and sorted mentally to create schemes of understanding.

Although infants at this stage are remarkably open to sensory input, we must be careful not to overstimulate them. Box 7.3 deals with the issue of trying to hurry development. This is an issue that feeds into some adults' insecurities. They may want what they think is best, but their efforts backfire when they make an infant or child overly stressed. David Elkind (2001) strongly advocates for children's right to develop naturally without being harmed.

BOX 7.3

ISSUE: CAN WE HURRY DEVELOPMENT TO MAKE INFANTS SMARTER AND MORE COMPETENT?

We are more likely to slow down an infant's development than speed it up. Lack of knowledge about the infant's development and about the particular needs of infants can lead to reducing the possibility of the child reaching her potential. So it's more important that we support emerging skills and subtle changes, making sure that we don't miss something that is essential to the developmental process.

The best way of looking at this issue is to appreciate the complexities of early development and do everything possible to facilitate it. This means that we have to consider our role in supporting the process, but first we have to understand something about the child's potential.

Years ago, it was thought that a child's potential was completely determined at birth. We now know, as a result of neuroscientific research, that the child's potential is determined, to some extent, by his genetic inheritance, but this isn't an absolute. Potential can be considered to be somewhat plastic. Given the optimal circumstance for development, that potential can be stretched to some extent. For example, a child who has an average aptitude at something may do slightly better in an enriched environment. But most aspects of potential have a limit. An infant will not learn to walk at an earlier age because we encourage her to stand on her feet. These skills appear according to an inner maturational schedule.

Limited, short-term advantages have been observed in infants and toddlers who have been subjected to intensive programs, but these offer dubious benefits. In the case of toddlers who are taught to read, it has been found that advantages may be at the cost of other developmental areas. There is a fine line between providing optimal experiences and pushing the child. Sometimes putting undue pressure on a very young child, or having expectations that are very high, can have the opposite outcome.

So we have the power to limit children's development by failing to provide for all the child's needs. We have the responsibility to facilitate development and provide an optimal environment, appreciating how competent the infant and toddler really is. But we won't be successful if we try to push the child, have overly high expectations,

(continues)

BOX 7.3 (Continued)

or provide developmentally inappropriate experiences; these are more likely to be counterproductive.

A number of well-known educators have expressed their concern about pressuring young children. The most notable, David Elkind, writing in *The Hurried Child* (2001), focuses on the experience of childhood that involves a drive to ever-higher achievement, a loss of spontaneous play, and early entry into adulthood. Elkind thinks that the focus of adults in children's lives can be inappropriate: he favors an approach that is sympathetic and allows a child the freedom to enjoy childhood and develop naturally. Hirsh-Pasek and Golinkoff (2003) also recognize that teaching discrete and nonrelevant bits of information to children, outside their experience, is potentially harmful. The outcome, which produces children who are able to memorize but who end up having no real understanding of what they're learning, also creates children who do not value that learning. Ultimately, they end up frustrated and let down. Garbarino (1995) expressed it very well by stating "that we ought to view childhood as a social space in which to lay the foundation for the best that human development has to offer" (p.12).

Children are hurried from a very early age, claims Patricia Thomas (2000), a clinical counselor. In her experience, many children from infancy onward are exposed to pressure and unnecessary stress. Echoing Elkind's claims, she suggests that pressure intended to produce children who are smarter, more skilled, and better able to enter the adult world is in fact causing children to experience fear of failure, to have insufficient time to play and amuse themselves, to have chronic psychosomatic complaints, and to be unhappy, even depressed, lethargic, or unmotivated.

Infancy should be a time of discovery, happiness, little achievements, maturation, playfulness, and close relationships—along with some risk taking in everyday activities, getting over minor failures, learning to deal with other young children, learning by doing, building trust, trial and error, building preliminary concepts, recovering after short periods of unhappiness, and taking in everything they can about how the world works. Hurrying infants and toddlers does not make them smarter. Infancy should be an amazing sheltered but free experience, not a race.

memory

a complex function of the brain to recall past events and experiences; storage of and access to information previously obtained; elements of memory include recognition, recall, association, internalized scripts, control mechanisms, selection, and retrieval

information processing

the approach to cognitive development that views the brain as a sophisticated computer with memory and symbolic functioning

trial and error

learning through experimenting and mistakes, as well as experiencing success

imitation

the act of copying single actions of another person, or the copying of complex actions, as with role models

Information Processing

Infants at this stage cluster together bits of information to make sense of what they take in through their senses. By 7 months, infants tend to categorize everything they see (Horst, Oakes, & Madole, 2005), although they do not have the language to label their thoughts. They will be gaining basic schematic understanding of the properties of objects and what is linked with what. By simple association, babies may predict what will happen and find pleasure in cause-and-effect actions.

The infant's **memory** of events tends to lengthen as she gets older. "Memory is a clear indication of how much a child is noticing and actively processing" (Ramey & Ramey, 1999, p. 58). Sometimes you can observe that an infant remembers a person, object, or event, and performs an action that indicates this memory.

Memory is one component of **information processing**. Probably because her memory is relatively short, and the infant responds positively to new stimuli, she tends to be distracted relatively easily. However, her attention span may be longer than before, due in part to her increased interest in playful activity. Toward the end of this stage, the infant looks for items gone from sight, showing her concept of object permanence and, possibly, her increased memory and understanding of objects.

Other components of information processing involve external characteristics that can be observed in **trial-and-error** learning, **imitation**, cause-and-effect discoveries, and

At this point in their lives, we need to give babies the world, *not* teach them discrete bits of information about the world.

action–reaction

the link or association between one action and a reaction that it causes

egocentric

from the perspective of the individual; in infancy, an inability to see from the perspective of others

preverbal cues

the messages conveyed by means such as facial expressions, gestures, and sound production before true language is acquired

intentional communication

the third stage of emotional development— typically occurs at 3–6 months; or any deliberate attempts to convey a message.

action–reaction sequences (Tortora, 2006). When the baby is experiencing something new, or rediscovering something familiar, she will try out some actions to see what the response will be. She gains significantly through trial-and-error learning as she mouths objects, grabs, and generally discovers what she can do with the things within her reach. Similarly, many bits and pieces of learning will occur because she finds out such things as banging her hand hurts or bashing something hard makes a loud noise; she links an action or "cause" with an "effect" or result.

Play

Much of the infant's play activity is solitary—by herself. Babies familiar with a group setting do observe each other, but they treat other infants more as objects than as people. This is because babies' thinking is essentially **egocentric**—from their own perspective. Yet, although they cannot appreciate the perspectives of others, they are intrigued by the presence and actions of others.

Adults who enter into play with an infant at this stage can do much to assist the give-and-take of communication. The infant is usually delighted to have the attention. Infants will respond to simple nursery rhymes (and make attempts to imitate the adult's accompanying actions). Some infants at this stage initiate play with adults, but others are more likely merely to respond to the adult's advances. This may have as much to do with temperament as with developmental stage. Most babies certainly do interact with adults, and find much pleasure and joy in those interactions. "Play is a major factor in the development of social and emotional relationships. Much of what children learn in adult–child care and play routines is how to regulate their emotions and act in socially appropriate ways" (Bergren, Reid, & Torelli, 2001, p. 14).

Sensory play allows the infant to discover new materials, but caution must be exercised. The infant has little fear and even less ability to predict what might happen in potentially dangerous situations. Newly acquired reaching and grasping skills further complicate matters. Yet, under safe conditions, the infant learns much from repeating actions of grasping and observing material.

Increased mobility leads to more physical play activity. The 6- to 9-month-old infant enjoys practicing the movements that lead to getting from place to place, but many early movements are performed for pure joy rather than as attempts to go somewhere specific. Indeed, playful rolling or crawling can lead to the baby moving farther away from a target, rather than advancing toward it!

Communication and Language

Before they are 9 months old, babies commonly lift both arms to communicate their desire to be picked up. This is a peak time for **preverbal cues**—indicators without words—so the process of communicating depends upon adults interpreting infants' messages and responding to them. The infant needs to learn the give-and-take nature of communication. You can see this being practiced in the many "dances" the infant has with adults (Stern, 2002).

The adult needs to be able to "interpret the infant's intentions" (Fogel, 2000), because the baby will be sending out signals that are **intentional communications**—deliberate efforts to communicate—as well as signs that are unconscious. Refer to the Additional Support section in your Online Companion to refresh your memory on the recognition of visual cues.

In addition to the smiling seen at earlier stages, the baby now laughs, and laughter can be prompted by all sorts of give-and-take situations, such as playing tug of war with an object pulled on the other end by an adult (Fogel, 2000). Her smile is truly social. Social smiling indicates a

Although these young children are playing near one another, they are still egocentric in their thinking. As a result, they will crawl over each other, tug on each other's clothing and bodies, and grab toys away, but they are still not aware of each other's perspective. Playing together purposefully is still several years away.

babbling

production of consonant–vowel sounds of varying intonation, usually involving repetition of sounds in long strings, such as da-da-da-da-da, or ba-ba-ba-ba-ba, developing in an infant between the ages of 4 and 6 months

"The central players in your baby's world of cause and effect are people. Nothing can take the place of people in teaching your baby about causality. All the games you play, as well as your responses to your baby's coos and gurgles, will be among her major sources of pleasure."

Ramey & Ramey, 1999, p. 51

rich human experience—it is more complex than the reflexive or physical smile.

The 6-month-old baby's vocal apparatus is becoming more like that of an adult (Fogel, 2000). She can make several different sounds, because she is now breathing through her nose more than her mouth. She is likely to vocalize tunefully to herself (Otto, 2002). At this stage, a baby can probably make a full range of vowel sounds and may begin to make some consonant sounds, such as *r, s, z,* and *w* (Allen & Marotz, 2007). Increasing ability to vary the airflow allows the infant to make a range of sounds by varying loudness and pitch. The sounds that she makes at this stage are called **babbling**, and bear some resemblance to speech. This babbling is partly based on imitated sounds, and intonation patterns, the up-and-down flow of spoken language (Bardige, 2005). Babbling also stems from the baby's discovery of her voice potential. Initially, babies all over the world produce similar sounds, but they will eventually stop producing sounds that are not articulated in the languages they hear (Otto, 2002). Recent research credits this developmental accomplishment with the infants' innate ability to perceptually map linguistic input in their brains. "This theory emphasizes the role of linguistic input ('parentese') and the way in which it enhances speech contrasts" (Kuhl, 1999, p. 121). (This was discussed in Chapter 6.)

At 9 months, the infant's repertoire of sounds has increased, and many of the babbling sounds contain two or three syllables, such as "ma-ma" or "aga-aga-aga," which are repeated over and over again (Sheridan, 2001). The babbling produced by the child begins to take on a rhythm similar to the adults who are **modeling** language patterns to him, and is often referred to as **jargon** (Otto, 2002) The babbling may begin to have some meaning, but most babies at 9 months are not yet using words to convey a meaning. They do, however, understand some associations, such as the link between waving goodbye and the word "goodbye."

The 9-month-old baby might be observed in lengthy **dyadic** (two-way) communications. Attracting the attention of the adult, she raises both arms, interpreted by the educator as "up," and initiates a pointing-and-reaching sequence while looking toward toys, and sustaining the look until given the toy, or she pushes your hands away or shakes her head to signal that she doesn't want something. All of these cues (signals) indicate an attempt to communicate via purposeful actions, even though language production is often still months away. Family members and caregivers who interpret and respond to these important cues help children learn the importance of conversational interactions.

Imitation

Imitation of adults encourages the development of language and social skills in the infant. Lots of adult contact will, usually quite spontaneously, involve **reciprocal imitation**—the infant or child will imitate the adult and the adult will repeat the behavior. Adults can encourage this by making sounds, facial expressions, and simple actions that the baby can imitate. The baby can be encouraged with smiles and verbal cues.

Deferred imitation occurs when the baby copies someone else's action some time after the event. She might wave goodbye in a situation after she has seen others wave or she could make a stirring action after she has watched an adult bake cookies. Although deferred imitation is only just emerging at this time, it can lead to a very early indication of a type of symbolic understanding. With experience, the baby discovers that for most of her actions there comes a reaction. When she cries, she gets attention, or when she knocks a toy off her high chair, it disappears. At the same time, she is getting to know that things still exist when they go out of

the process of demonstrating a social role performance; it is required for observational learning

jargon

a type of babbling that appears to echo the rhythm and phonation of adult speech heard in the child's environment, developing when an infant is between 8 and 10 months old

dyadic

any activity or relationship involving, either an individual and an object, or two individuals

reciprocal imitation

two individuals copying each other's actions

deferred imitation

copying single behaviors or complex roles some time after the initial observation of the behavior

clear-cut attachment

the infant's attachment to a specific adult

mistrust

to regard without trust or confidence; part of first crisis stage in Erickson's psychosocial theory

stranger anxiety

anxiety, distress, or uneasiness shown by a child when an unknown person is present

separation anxiety

distress shown because of departure, or impending departure, of a person to whom the individual is attached

sight, so her action–reaction sequence may become a repeated activity that causes a humorous response.

Social Development

As we have already discussed, the infant has a wider range of physical skills involving handling things and interacting with people, an increased knowledge of his world through exploration and discovery, a broader range of communication skills, a longer memory, and an increased ability to pay attention to details. All these skills make possible more complex social relationships.

During this stage, the child's attachments to adults begin to change. Her links with particular adults become more intense, and her anxiety increases when those to whom she is attached are absent. This is the stage of **clear-cut attachment** to particular adults. It is essential that the infant have the possibility of forming these clear-cut attachments to one or more people. These attachments contribute to the infant's ability to build trusting relationships, the most important issue that underlies all social development. Erik Erikson (1987), known as the father of psychosocial development, describes the first task of infancy as the creation of trust. Without it, the infant cannot build a separation of himself from others, a positive sense of self, or lasting relationships with anyone.

If their needs are met consistently and responsively, babies will develop secure attachments and will learn to be generally more trusting. If this does not happen, **mistrust** toward people, the environment, and even themselves can result. If early attachments fail to occur, the subsequent mistrust may be very difficult to remedy later on. There are examples of babies who have been placed in institutions and who were deprived of loving care having difficulties later on with social relationships (Ames & Chisholm, 2001). Fortunately, some early interventions can be effective, and trust can be built over time. Generally, though, the older the child, the more difficult it is to make up for lost nurturing.

Several studies have looked at the quality of infants' care in relation to the quality of their attachments. There appears to be a strong link between the two: Sensitive care allows infants to develop more secure attachments (Honig, 2002). It is encouraging to know that even when there are poor attachments between parents and infants, there can be some remediation if high-quality care is provided and trusting relationships are built (Ames & Chisholm, 2001).

At 6 months, the infant may not yet be concerned about moving from the care of one adult to that of another, but this will soon change, causing the infant, and the adults, considerable stress. By 9 months, the infant may experience **stranger anxiety** if passed to an unfamiliar adult or placed in unfamiliar surroundings with adults to whom he is not attached (Thompson, 2001).

Separation anxiety tends to appear at 8 to 9 months of age (Bowlby, 1973), and varies in frequency from one culture to another, but usually reaches its peak in children, regardless of cultures, sometime between the ages of 13 to 15 months (Trawick-Smith, 2006). What is observed is an infant who becomes distressed and may protest loudly at being removed from the care of a person to whom he is attached (Cassidy & Shaver, 1999). Adults who observe the infant's distress may assume that there is something wrong with the infant, or that the adult who is rejected has done something inappropriate to the child. This is not necessarily the case. Such distress can be a sign that the infant has made a healthy attachment (Cassidy & Shaver, 1999). Although the manifestations of separation anxiety should not be a cause for great concern, the baby needs comfort and support through any transition of care.

Ainsworth's research on attachment utilized a test method called the **strange situation procedure**, and the findings resulted in four types of attachment classifications: *Secure; Insecure/Avoidant; Insecure/Resistant/Ambivalent;* and *Insecure/Disorganized/Disoriented* (Lamb, Bornstein, & Teti, 2002). There are long-term behaviors that are associated with each of the separate classifications. (See Figure 7.1.) In a follow-up to a 1978 study, Waters, Merrick, Treboux, Crowell, and Albersheim (2000) found that the individual differences in attachment security can remain fairly stable across significant portions of the lifespan, although life experience can alter the original classification. Given the positive behaviors related to securely attached children, it is of critical importance that **child care** providers work very hard to

Figure 7.1 Attachment Classifications and Later Behaviors Associated with Them

Secure Attachment

- Cooperative with parents and other adults
- Affectively positive
- Socially competent and seeks out friends
- Has good self-control
- Can problem-solve with confidence
- Easily comforted if upset/seeks if overwhelmed
- Manages well away from parents

Insecure/Avoidant Attachment

- Tends to be noncompliant and to disobey rules
- Often very angry and hostile
- Isolated from group, does not seek interaction
- Can be excessively angry but has control on nonsocial situations
- May be quite competent
- When in pain or upset, withdraws and does not seek help
- Manages well away from parents

Insecure/Resistant/Ambivalent Attachment

- May have behavioral difficulties and fluctuate between being tense and helpless
- Tends to be fearful and tense
- Has poor social skills, tends to be dependent on others
- Impulsive; low frustration tolerance
- Lacks confidence and assertiveness, and has little ability to problem-solve
- Needs sensitive caregiving; often difficult to calm down
- Often misses parents and seems helpless and tense as a result

Insecure/Disorganized/Disoriented Attachment

- Usually has behavioral difficulties and is unpredictable
- Is often both a bully and a victim
- Has poor social skills
- Low frustration tolerance and self-control without engagement
- Very disorganized and disoriented in approach to problems
- Needs specialized caregiving
- May miss parents and appear frightened when with them as well as away from them

Source: Chess, S., & Thomas, A. (1996). *Temperament theory and practice*. New York: Brunner/Mazel Publishers, p. 34.

strange situation procedure

a research method that assesses the quality of attachment of babies to their primary caregivers by creating a number of conditions, including the departure of a parent and the arrival of a stranger, and then tabulating the responses of the babies

child care

a full-time or part-time program offering care and education, usually licensed

provide secure emotional and social beginnings for the children in their care. "Babies who are securely attached to a caregiver dare to explore, play better, and interact more with others than do babies whose caregivers are ever-changing or emotionally distant" (Raikes, 1996, p. 61). A project designed by Gray (2004) (see Further Reading section), which encompassed documentation, collaboration, and a partnership with families, encouraged care providers to focus on separation and reunion experiences. Although this project started with 10-month-old infants, it could be adapted to use with younger infants too, especially since separation is often more difficult for the family members than for the children.

As always, one must evaluate research findings against the backdrop of the culture in which they are conducted. There are cultural variations in infant attachment, although many cultural groups in the world have approximately the same rates as do children in the United States (Trawick-Smith, 2006). However, Japanese children and Chinese-American children display significantly greater rates of insecure/ambivalent attachment. One explanation offered is that these children traditionally spend so little time separated from their mothers that they are almost inconsolable when the reunion occurs. Also, there are some researchers who believe that the strange situation procedure is not valid (Waters & Cummings, 2000), because long periods of crying may be the norm in cultures where the infant–mother bond is considered sacrosanct. Alternatively, is it surprising that in northern German culture, which encourage independence and discourage dependence and closeness at very early ages, children's responses at reunion reveal a higher number classified as insecure? Might that just be the norm for that cultural environment?

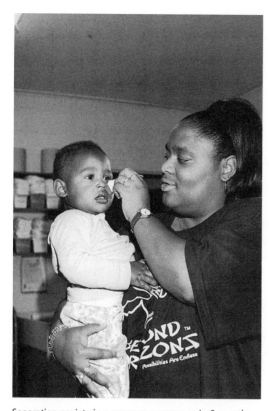

Separation anxiety is a common occurrence in 9-month-old children. The educarer comforts a child who has just parted from a family member.

Review the information on Ainsworth's Attachment Theory in the Additional Support section in your Online Companion.

As upsetting as separation anxiety may be to adults, it is a cause for celebration, because the child's behavior demonstrates that she has made an attachment. This indicates that positive social, emotional, and cognitive development is occurring.

Emotional Development

The emotions that are expressed in infants of 6–9 months tend to be ones that are easily understood by adults; they are more focused and are more likely to be related to particular experiences. Also, the baby reacts to people and events in a more clear-cut way, so adults can determine why the baby feels the way she does. The range of feelings observable through facial expressions are the basic emotions, or **proto-emotions**, that tend to be similar across all cultures.

The basic emotions, from which all other emotions emerge over time, include:

- joy;
- anger;
- sadness; and
- fear.

One of the most obvious new emotions is fear (Lamb, Bornstein, & Teti, 2002), which an infant may demonstrate in a variety of situations. Anger may also be seen in infants at this stage. Anger may result from frustration at not being able to reach something or from having to wait for a bottle that isn't produced fast enough.

As the range of emotional expression increases, so does the infant's ability to read emotions on the faces of familiar adults. By about 6 months, the infant may respond to the expressed emotions of a person in an appropriate way, matching the emotion (Lamb, Bornstein, & Teti, 2002). For example, an infant may smile back when she is smiled at, cry when someone speaks to her in a loud, angry voice, or make a face in response to one made to her (Saarni, 2000).

Activity 7.1 on your Online Companion provides an opportunity to discuss the ability to read facial expressions.

By 9 months, the infant may actively look for the expression of an adult as a sign of encouragement or discouragement. This is called **social referencing**, and may be an early indication of wanting to please and needing the security that comes from adult approval.

Frequently, the baby will look back at her caregiver and seek some eye contact that reassures her that everything is all right. It is most often observed when we see the baby confronted with something or somebody new. It is as though she were saying to the adult, "Is this okay?" or "Should I feel threatened?" Her action can tell us as much as if she had used the actual words.

A group of researchers, led by Klinnert, Emde, Butterfield, and Campos (1986), studied social referencing in early infancy and isolated a four-stage process:

1. the ability to recognize emotional expressions;
2. the ability to understand emotional expressions;
3. the ability to respond to emotional expression; and
4. the ability to alter behavior in response to emotional expressions.

Social referencing may help explain the phenomenon of stranger anxiety that begins around this age, but it also demonstrates that young children are more aware of the meanings of

proto-emotions

feelings that have not yet developed into specific emotions

social referencing

the tendency to use others' emotional expressions to help understand the situation and thus relieve uncertainty; child will look at parent or caregiver's face and monitor their expressions in order to decide how to respond

emotional expressions and how to react to them than theorists previously have been willing to acknowledge (Beebe, 2004; Striano & Rochat 2000). It also suggests that infants are capable of interpreting something as subtle as the seriousness or intention of a parental cue (Kostelnik, Whiren, Soderman, & Gregory, 2006).

Self-Concept/Self-Image

As we discussed before, social relationships with increased emotional contentment help the infant to distinguish himself from others. However, the development of a real concept of self is a slow process. The 6-month-old infant sees himself as a separate entity from his mother, the result of a process called **self-differentiation**. However, the baby still does not have a full appreciation of self. A baby of this age will look at himself in a mirror with some interest, but he does not yet appreciate that he is looking at himself.

The infant needs to discover himself and build positive elements into his concept of self. The adult can support this need by responding positively to the infant, by seeing him as a competent little person, and by encouraging small advances in development. As we saw in earlier chapters, caregivers too can help the development of a healthy self-image by ensuring that the child care environment reflects all children in their care. Keep in mind that children construct their identities from understanding their culture. They envision themselves as the perceived reflections from the eyes and actions of those who care for them. "To form a positive self-concept, children need to honor and respect their own culture and to have others honor and respect it, too" (Kaiser & Rasminsky, 2003, p. 54). Box 7.4 describes efforts a facility must make in order to ensure that cultures are honored and reflected in their environment.

See the Additional Support section in your Online Companion for information on cultural awareness.

> Socialization of emotion begins in infancy. Research indicates that when mothers interact with their infants, they demonstrate emotional displays in an exaggerated slow motion. Those deliberate and slow actions probably aid children in observing details that otherwise might be lost. Normal expression of emotions, unless you are in the arts or attempting to emphasize a feeling, usually progresses at a rapid pace. Once again, the slowing down of this behavior may be instinctual on the part of humans, and infants find the demonstrations fascinating. Furthermore, this particular process helps infants acquire cultural and social patterns for emotional display. It is significant since it teaches them how, when, and in what circumstances emotions are expressed.

self-differentiation

seeing oneself as a separate and different person

BOX 7.4

AN AGENCY WITHOUT BIAS

Everything that we do in child care has a value; we discussed this in the first chapter. A value that you want to transmit is one of respect, so for families who speak languages other than English, you will need to do this through the program you offer and the communications you have with them and their children. Respect can be considered an active as well as a passive value, but what speaks the loudest is what we do.

The child care environment should reflect the cultures of the children and families for whom it provides care. It should also mirror positive attitudes about differing family styles, cultural practices, and individual differences of ability and appearance (Derman-Sparks et al., 1989; York, 2003).

The choice of all materials must be filtered through an anti-bias review, and additions must be made that address differences. Every part of the environment, including the common parts of the building, such as hallways and waiting areas, should be considered. Pictures must represent a variety of cultures, toys must reflect appropriate positive images, photographs can create a representative picture of the diversity of the group, culturally significant artifacts can contribute to an atmosphere of inclusion, and books and scripts can be in different languages.

Be sure that inclusive representation is an ongoing focus, not just something done for effect. Making a novelty of cultural differences can be offensive. All cultural representations should be integrated, with none held up as foreign or "other."

Temperament

As adults become more familiar with the infant's personal style, they are likely to categorize the pattern of behavior into a particular type. Chess and Thomas (1996) were responsible for the New York Longitudinal Study, which researched temperament in individuals from infancy to adulthood. They identified nine temperament types and three temperament constellations— easy, slow-to-warm-up, and difficult—into which most of these types fall. (See the Additional Support section of the Online Companion for a list of all nine categories of temperament.) In their study, which used a fairly representative sample, about 40 percent of infants appeared to be easy in their style. They were mostly regular, positive, and adaptable infants who were found to be less challenging to work with than were infants of the other styles. Much more challenging were the approximately 10 percent of infants who were difficult. They were irregular in functioning, had negative responses to stimuli, and found adapting to new situations more challenging. The slow-to-warm-up category constituted 15 percent of the sample. The balance of the sample comprised mixed temperament types, and didn't fit into these constellations.

PARTICULAR NEEDS

Exploration

Infants at this stage are beginning to take control of their immediate world, and enjoy being able to affect their surroundings. Consequently, they need to be in a safe environment in which they can mouth objects and find out about everything within reach.

Physical Needs

Feeding

At this stage, the infant will usually have been introduced to baby food or puréed "adult" food to provide some nutrients not found in milk. However, breast milk or formula is still important for protein, calcium, and fat. Since fats support neurological growth, babies should not be fed low-fat milk (American Academy of Pediatrics, 2005).

Diapering

Bowel or bladder control is not yet possible, so the infant needs regular diaper checks and changed when the diaper is wet or contains feces. At this stage, babies often wriggle on the change table, which may present challenges for the caregiver. This wriggling can be a safety hazard; the increased bodily control can lead to the baby showing dislike by moving and twisting. Some educators, especially those who adhere to Magda Gerber's philosophy, focus not on the task but on the child. These educators will initiate conversation that involves the child in the process of diapering, describe the steps being taken, wait for a response from the child, and engage the child's attention through human interaction. This approach is definitely in line with the philosophy of *See How They Grow*. Other adults prefer to distract the child from the experience with mobiles, games, and rhymes. Whichever approach is taken, the diapering should be a positive experience for the infant, and adults should not be completing a task mindlessly.

Rest and Sleep

Infants vary in their sleep requirements, and their individual needs should be met. Usually, educators and parents are able to read the signs that the infant is tired. Adults need to be in tune with the infant's sleep pattern and provide an environment that is as conducive to rest and sleep as it is to stimulation. Babies in group care learn to tune out sounds that might keep other babies awake. Silence is not necessary, but most babies sleep best in relatively quiet environments with no bright lights.

Co-sleeping   Some families believe in co-sleeping—infants and adults sleeping together—but this is an emotional and debatable topic. The American Academy of Pediatrics (2005) takes a

For families who don't like sleeping apart from their baby, but who do not want to or are fearful of sharing a bed with their infant, there are some crib-like infant beds that can be attached safely next to an adult bed. Always check out the safety record of such equipment before purchasing. The U.S. Consumer Product Safety Commission (http://www.cpsc.gov/ or (301) 504-7923) tracks the safety record of the majority of equipment available for use with infants, toddlers, and older children.

strong stance against co-sleeping. The Academy says that this practice increases the risk of smothering the baby. Infants may be brought into bed for nursing or comforting, but should be returned to their own crib or bassinet when the parent is ready to return to sleep. However, there is growing evidence that room-sharing (infant's sleeping in a crib in parent's bedroom) is associated with a reduced risk of SIDS. The risk of SIDS associated with co-sleeping is significantly greater among smokers, and there are some reports of infants being suffocated by an adult, particularly when the adult is in an unnaturally depressed state of consciousness, such as from alcohol or mind-altering drugs. Scheers, Rutherford, and Kemp (2003) reported that deaths of infants who suffocated on sleep surfaces other than those designed for infants were increasing. The most conservative estimate showed that the risk of suffocation increased by twenty fold when infants were placed to sleep in adult beds rather than in cribs.

However, bed-sharing is a common practice for many families. Expecting babies to sleep alone is a Western custom of fairly recent origin. Around the world, breast-feeding mothers traditionally sleep with their babies, and it has not been proved that these babies have higher rates of SIDS. Dr William Sears, a well-known media personality, advocates co-sleeping, even in light of the AAP guidelines issued in September of 2005. Referring to his own research on the subject, Sears believes that there are numerous physical and psychological advantages for the baby, as well as for the parents. Other commentators insist that the quality of sleep and its overall benefits to the attachment process, and the engagement it encourages between parents and infants, are vastly underrated. This is usually not an issue pertinent to child care situations, although caregivers may be asked their opinion. The safe approach is to reiterate the position of the American child health experts such as the AAP, which recommends a separate but proximate sleeping environment.

DEVELOPMENTAL VARIATION

Variation in developmental stages broadens as infants get older. At 6–9 months, some infants may not yet be able to sit, even with support, while others may already be attempting to crawl. When parents are concerned about their child's development, they should check with their family doctor, pediatrician, or other appropriate specialist, even if the educator doesn't think there is a problem.

Both families and educators may be alarmed if an infant's development remains stuck in the same place for a period of time. Although the majority of infants progress smoothly and predictably, some do not. Significant concerns should be presented to specialists, although many of these developmental worries will turn out to be within the bounds of the norm.

 ## DEVELOPMENTAL ALERTS

Sensory Deficits

multiple disabilities

having two or more disabilities at the same time—e.g., having a hearing deficit and a congenital heart condition

seizures (convulsions)

uncontrolled bodily movements resulting from problems with the brain or central nervous system; they vary in severity

An infant who fails to respond in an expected way to visual or auditory (sound) stimulation should be checked by a specialist. At 6 to 9 months, hearing and visual problems may be more apparent than they were earlier. Families, parents, and educators should compare observations and discuss how to proceed. This is important for at least two reasons. First, the educator may have information that will supplement the parents' observations. Second, educators are better able to support the child's needs if they fully understand what these needs are. In many cases, hearing and sight issues can be corrected, improved, or supported in ways that prevent a **multiple disability**. If either vision or hearing challenges go undetected, the baby can miss crucial sensory information, which can have a negative impact on the child's learning.

Seizure Disorders and Febrile Convulsions

Seizure disorders or febrile convulsions may result from brain injury or other neurological difficulties. Infants may have such slight **seizures** that they appear as no more than a twitch or a

cerebral irritation

irritation of the brain caused by bacteria (or other foreign bodies) or pressure; it may result in difficulty in becoming calm; the condition may cause seizures

epilepsy

disordered brain functioning characterized by seizures (or convulsions) of varying severity

febrile convulsions

a convulsion in a child triggered by a fever; these convulsions occur without any underlying brain or spinal cord infection or other neurological cause

meningitis

inflammation of the membranes encasing the spinal cord and brain; usually caused by bacterial or viral infection

temporary detachment from attention. Other more serious seizures can also occur, sometimes resulting in a complete loss of bodily control, prolonged whole-body spasms, and a trance-like state that persists even after the seizure is over. Many things can trigger a seizure, including lights, smells, fever, fatigue, and other environmental conditions. Sometimes they occur for no apparent reason. Careful observation may help you determine what sets off a seizure; those conditions can then be avoided.

Infants who had birth injuries in the form of **cerebral irritation**—pressure on the brain—may experience seizures, so these injuries should be identified on their health history. Also, even young infants can have **epilepsy**. Educators may never witness infant seizures, but they must be able to recognize them and manage the situation in accordance with parental direction. Babies with epilepsy might not experience regular seizures, but a baby prone to seizures may need daily medication to control the condition.

Febrile convulsions, which are seizures not associated with epilepsy, are the most commonly occurring type of seizure, with approximately 2 percent to 5 percent of children in the United States under the age of 5 experiencing one of them (Stafstrom, 2001). Most of these result from a sudden high fever. Although such episodes might be alarming, they rarely lead to significant medical problems. However, because they might indicate the onset of a serious fever such as **meningitis**—inflammation of the meninges around the brain—a baby who has such a seizure should be evaluated by a physician as soon as possible.

Heart Conditions

Chapter 4 discussed congenital heart conditions that some children have when they are born. However, young children can acquire a heart condition as a result of rheumatic fever or Kawasaki disease, another illness characterized by fever. Some heart problems that haven't previously been detected by medical staff or parents might be observed by educators. Observable characteristics can include blue lips, difficulty breathing, limited growth, or weight gain from fluid retention. Infants and young children with heart conditions may be particularly susceptible to respiratory infections. This issue is significant for a child placed in a group setting. The increased exposure to infection from contact with other children could present risks to the child.

HEALTH CONCERNS

Immunizations

It is essential to ensure that infants at this stage are immunized against the most serious childhood infections. The American Academy of Pediatrics suggests immunizations against the following:

- hepatitis B (HepB)—third shot
- diphtheria, pertussis (whooping cough), tetanus (DTaP)—third shot
- poliomyelitis (IVP/polio)—third shot
- Haemophilus influenzae type b (HIB)—third shot
- pneumococcal (PVC)—third shot
- influenza—first shot

Child care centers must have a policy to ensure that young children have received their immunizations. There can be cases where parents object to immunization on religious, ethical, or other grounds. Agencies must decide how they will manage this eventuality. Although immunization programs vary, the Additional Support section in your Online Companion links you to a typical immunization schedule.

Teething

A few babies are born with teeth, but most infants will experience the soreness and eruption of their first teeth during this period. There is great variation in how this occurs. In some cases, there is very little trouble as the teeth break through the gum. Other babies might have sore gums, pink cheeks, and possibly a slightly raised body temperature and digestive upset. Sleep can be disrupted for short periods, but the most common sign of teething is that the baby gnaws on objects and drools prolifically—possibly causing some soreness on the chin.

Behavioral or symptomatic changes should be indicated to parents. Only if parents request it should any special treatment be given. In most child care centers, children will be excluded while medicated, or given only medication labeled by a pharmacist or prescribed by a doctor. Cold rings, gel toys, and other objects to mouth can be comforting. Extra cuddles and additional liquid consumption might also be needed. Gnawing on hard biscuits or vegetables may be a way for the baby to acquire new tastes and textures while easing through the discomfort caused by erupting teeth.

The Transition to Solid Food

As we mentioned at the beginning of this chapter, infants at this stage may start eating solid foods. Solid foods should be offered when the child is hungry. Although solid food may be offered, breast milk or formula remains central to the baby's diet. New foods should be introduced one at a time to see if the infant likes the taste and texture of the new food, and to ascertain whether the child has any allergic reactions to a specific food item. Small amounts of puréed food may be offered. Often parents choose to start their infants on cereals, but there is some nutritional evidence that vegetables should be tried first. The baby's sweet tooth might reveal itself in a preference for sweeter foods, but the baby should be offered several different foods of various colors, textures, and tastes over time. The best idea is to increase the baby's range of foods gradually. The baby's food does not have to be seasoned, even if it seems bland to the adult.

Introduce new foods one at a time, allowing three to four days between each new food. Choose the least allergenic foods first. These include: rice cereals; other single-grain infant cereals; carrots; bananas; squash; sweet potatoes; peaches; pears; veal; beef; lamb; and poultry.

In the early months, feed solid foods after milk as a supplement, so as not to replace milk. It is unwise to offer egg products to a baby not yet 1 year of age: allergic responses may occur, typically in response to egg white. The CDC recommends that children younger than 1 year of age should not be given honey because it often contains spores that, under the right circumstances, can turn into growing, multiplying bacteria that pump out a poison called botulinus toxin. This toxin can cause infant botulism, a sometimes fatal disease. For babies in a vegetarian or vegan family, consultation with a nutritional expert is advisable—some dietitians provide useful information, or you might consult a pediatrician. Babies who are breast-fed and weaned before 9 months should be given an iron-fortified formula. If formula-fed, it should be iron-fortified for the first 9 to 12 months of life (Green & Palfrey 2002). Formulas contain added vitamins and minerals to approximate the levels present in breast milk. The use of iron-fortified formula eliminates the need for additional mineral supplementation for full-term infants.

SIGNS OF POTENTIAL NEGLECT OR ABUSE

Following is a checklist of conditions or signs which might indicate that a child is being neglected or abused.

- poor physical growth
- poor hygiene
- inappropriate clothing
- persistent hunger
- unattended medical needs
- lack of supervision

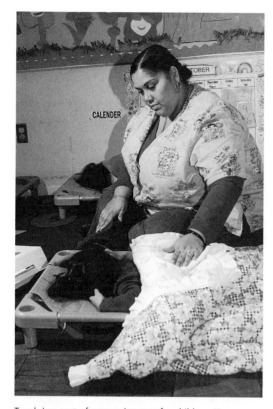

Touch is a part of responsive care for children. Here a gentle massage helps a young child settle down for her afternoon nap.

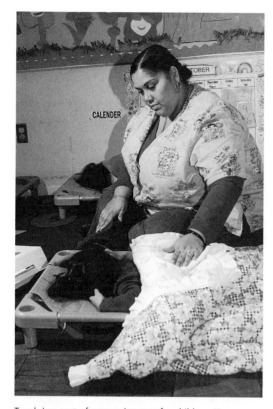

ONLINE COMPANION

"The channel of touch may be the primary mode of establishing a sense of identity in the first three years, and physical contact may be necessary for the development of satisfactory interpersonal relationships."

Kostelnik, Whiren, Soderman, & Gregory, 2006, p. 71

- frequent severe diaper rash
- unusual passive or withdrawn behavior
- repeated injuries, including cuts, bruises, burns, and broken bones

Some of those conditions might be in place for a short period; others may exist because of poverty or homelessness. The educator is required by law to report any signs, symptoms, or causes for concern to the child protection agency. The child protection agency is trained and has the legal responsibility to look into any reported neglect or abuse, without revealing the source of the concern.

As pointed out before, every child care center should have a written policy on child abuse and neglect. Staff should have annual training on how to recognize signs of abuse and neglect, and know what procedure to follow if there is a suspected case of abuse or neglect. Child care programs need to view the responsibility of being mandated reporters seriously. Unfortunately, what has occurred, in a rather knee-jerk response to well-publicized (and often unfounded) allegations of child abuse in out-of-home facilities and growing concerns about legal ramifications, is that many programs have adopted a "no touch" policy. According to NAEYC's position statement on the prevention of child abuse in early childhood programs, *"no-touch policies are misguided efforts that fail to recognize the importance of touch to children's development. Touch is especially important for infants and toddlers"* (NAEYC, 1996, p. 2). Eliminating the possibility of touching children is both senseless and potentially harmful to the emotional and social well-being of children (Honig, 2002). Every child care setting needs to formulate policies and procedures that will allow beneficial and appropriate touch to continue. Information about the contributions of touch to children's development, as well as what constitutes appropriate touching, needs to be communicated to both families and staff. This is definitely one issue that the early childhood profession must not back away from, since the consequences for children could be disastrous.

Please consult the Additional Support section in your Online Companion for *Signs of Neglect* from the National Clearinghouse on Child Abuse and Neglect, and NAEYC's *Where We Stand on Child Abuse Prevention* and *Prevention of Child Abuse in Early Childhood Programs and the Responsibility of the Early Childhood Profession to Prevent Child Abuse: A Position Statement*. There are also informative Web sites listed at the end of this chapter.

EVERYDAY SAFETY ISSUES

There should be no real separation between safety, health care, guidance, nurturance, and responsivity in practice. Adults' actions must reflect a merging of all these components of the adult role. It is necessary to be mindful of all the needs of each infant simultaneously and to do whatever is required. In being with infants, the adult protects them and ensures that they are loved and cared for—all at once. For example, there may be some safety concerns during feeding times, but this should not deflect the adult from nurturing and strengthening attachments or responding to the baby's cues during feeding. The baby's increasing mobility presents new challenges for both parents and educators. At this stage, the infant becomes better able to control his world, so that world needs to be safe. Because he can move around more and can reach, roll, and perhaps even crawl, he is able to fall off high surfaces, roll off a bed, or wriggle out of a high chair. Constant supervision is very important.

Increasing mobility provides this child with new universes to explore, but creates new challenges for his caregivers and family.

Equipment

Ensuring the high quality and safe use of items within the child care center is vitally important. Caregivers should justify the choice, use, maintenance, and appropriateness of each piece of baby equipment. Some pieces are clearly unnecessary and can even be dangerous. For example, baby walkers are of dubious developmental use. Their potential danger is too great to justify their use. In addition, over-the-door bouncer seats present hazards because they are positioned in high-traffic areas. Moreover, their benefits to the child are very limited. Too often, caregivers leave babies in them for prolonged periods.

Particular care should be taken when using secondhand or used equipment. Check to see if the equipment is old or worn. Repairs can be made as necessary, but faulty equipment should not be used. It is important to remember that equipment designed for home use may not stand up to the rigors of a group care setting. Consequently, center staff must be cautious when purchasing equipment or accepting gifts of secondhand material.

The Everyday Health and Safety Issues section in your Online Companion contains a list of equipment and furniture that should be examined on a regular basis. Be sure to review the suggestions.

> All equipment should be checked on a monthly basis. Many centers have check sheets that are kept on clipboards, and once a month, someone goes through the list. Larger centers often have a designated staff member who is the safety coordinator charged with the responsibility of checking indoor and outdoor equipment.

Interdependence of Safety and Care

The safety and caring components are not a lesser part of the caregiver role; upon them depends the possibility for supporting higher-level infant needs. An important theorist, Abraham Maslow, created a model entitled "The Hierarchy of Needs." This model explains the necessity for basic needs being met as a precondition for ensuring that more complex personal and psychological needs can be met so that an individual can become a fully actualized person. The state of self-actualization is at the pinnacle of the hierarchy, but can never be realized if basic, as well as other, needs are not met. Refer to the Additional Support section in your Online Companion for a visual and written explanation of this hierarchy.

A responsive caregiver recognizes that meeting basic needs is an essential part of the overall care and education for each child. If basic needs are not met, then the child will not grow and develop as she should. This should be of great concern for this country, since almost 1 out of every 4 children lives in poverty (Oser & Cohen, 2003). Box 7.5 has some statements that might make you think about choices being made in this country.

✂ STARTING POINTS FOR RESPONSE

Responsive Caregiving

As at earlier stages, caregivers must be able to interpret the baby's cues and respond quickly and appropriately. Box 7.6 provides some strategies for responding to infants of this age. Adults should also help to guide the baby's exploration. This is important for safety reasons and so adults can help support the baby's growing understanding of his world. Increasing communication between adults and the baby is also key at this stage. It helps the infant make secure attachments to particular adults. These attachments should be supported by continuous patterns of interactions from adults. **Separations** may be increasingly difficult times for the

separations

a series of departures and returns of a person to whom the child is attached

> "Worldwide, 40,000 children a day die of hunger-related causes. It's hard to tighten your belt when you're wearing diapers."
>
> Greenberg, 1991, p. 7

BOX 7.5

SOME STARTLING FACTS

- The United States is more than *twice* as wealthy as the nearest runner-up, Japan, and almost *four times* as wealthy as the third-ranked country, so why does the United States have the highest child poverty rate of eight industrialized Western countries?
- In 2002, an estimated 3 million children were reported as suspected victims of child abuse and close to 900,000 of them were confirmed as victims of child maltreatment.
- In 2002, infants and toddlers had the highest victimization rate, with infants representing the largest number of children victimized of any age group.
- The fastest-growing segment of people entering poverty is young children.
- About 13 million children (18 percent) lived in households that were classified as food-insecure by the USDA in 2003, unchanged from 2002. Households are classified as food-insecure based on survey reports of difficulty obtaining enough food, reduced diet quality, and anxiety about the household's food supply.

Information from the Children's Defense Fund, ZERO TO THREE, and the Report Card on America's Children 2005. These are statements to ponder.

BOX 7.6

GETTING IN TUNE WITH INFANTS AT 6 TO 9 MONTHS

Below are some starting points for building your responsive skills with a 6–9-month-old infant. This list is not comprehensive, and many more suggestions can be found in the "Getting In Tune with Infants, Toddlers, and Twos" section in your Online Companion.

- allow the baby time to observe you
- emphasize physical forms of encouragement through touch
- maintain eye contact
- enable the baby to see what is happening around him
- enjoy simple rhymes with actions together
- provide the baby with space to move on his tummy
- repeat actions and reactions over and over
- have a firm surface that the baby can kick against
- have lots of differently textured fabrics for touching, grabbing, and mouthing
- introduce toys that have a cause-and-effect function
- produce lots of objects that can be grabbed and mouthed (kitchen objects can be good)
- offer safe mirrors so the baby can see himself
- engage in communications with gestures
- blend your caregiving strategies with those of the parents
- check the baby's hearing and visual abilities through playful experiences

baby, and both parents and caregivers should think of ways to make these as smooth and easy as possible.

Supportive Guidance

The continuing development of a sense of self is important at this stage. Adults must think about how they are supporting this emerging sense of self. Providing rapid responses to requests and reading the complex cues that the baby sends out are important. The dance of communication is reciprocal: The baby enjoys the adult's interactions and tries to engage the adult in play. He may identify other children in close proximity, but his primary interest is to charm adults into communication and getting what he wants. The baby's intentional communications lead him to a pattern of trial-and-error play scenarios in which the adult can have a part. The baby has acquired the knowledge that things continue to exist even when he cannot see them. This information contributes to a new way of seeing the world, and shows that the baby has a symbolic representation of his world. Games of peek boo allow the baby to incorporate this new knowledge of object permanence into his play.

Facilitating Development

Cognitive advances are pronounced at this stage, and the infant's physical ability to sit up and pay attention makes him a much more competent person. Stimulation is particularly important at this stage. Adults will find that the infant's information-processing skills are advancing, and that his memory is increasing and new situations are better understood. The adult needs to take responsibility for the careful selection of toys and play materials. These need to be safe, and chosen on the basis of how well they support the baby's emerging development.

motherese

changes in the mother's speech that emphasize particular sounds, and the use of a higher pitch than normal when communicating with infants and young children; may be culture-bound

Language skills are not yet evident in terms of real speech, but babbling has become more complex and may take on the sounds of the language around the child. The infant needs to hear that language, and may enjoy rhymes as well as conversation. The use of **motherese** is particularly important. As mentioned in earlier chapters, in motherese the higher-pitched emphasis on sounds, coupled with exaggerated facial expressions that correspond to the sounds, is important in helping the baby figure out which sounds to pay attention to.

Activities

Your Online Companion and CD-ROM contain activities to help you increase your skills while engaging infants in caregiving routines, play, and supportive guidance.

On your CD-ROM, activities in the 7.2 section help you develop ways of engaging in the experience of babies at this stage and extending your interactions with them. These activities always start from the framework of observation. Activity 7.3 helps you create responsive curriculum for each infant at 6 to 9 months and to develop activities that are targeted to individual interests and skill levels. Activity 7.4 includes suggestions for further experiences and interactions. Activity 7.5 describes several possible scenarios for responsive guidance.

Remember to check the Book section and Toy section in your Online Companion for suggestions of materials to use with children at this stage of development.

SUMMARY

A major task of the 6- to 9-month infant is to get to know that she is a separate person, that other people respond to her, and that, together, there can be shared understanding. This can come about only if the trusting relationship remains constant between the baby and the adults with whom she is familiar. That predictability supports object permanence and people permanence, cause and effect, and action–reaction understanding. These adult–baby relationships need to be sustained, with mutual enjoyment helping the learning experience. The enjoyment is maximized if the adult can read the infant's cues and respond accordingly.

Patterns of behavior are becoming increasingly observable, and the baby's temperament style becomes more clearly evident. The adult can use this understanding of behavior and style to promote their relationship. Looking to the adult for support and encouragement, the infant finds ways of seeking and sustaining attention. She desires playful as well as domestic experiences.

Development varies between children at this and every stage, but there are common process-es for discovery learning. The sensorimotor intelligence of the infant provides a mechanism for building mental images from his sensory experience. Through the joint processes of assimila-tion and accommodation, the baby builds mental schemes. He enjoys a wide variety of materi-als from which he discovers textures, smells, and shapes. However, the baby needs adult atten-tion to thrive.

The baby's intentional communication and increased physical skills allow her to be more active in learning about her environment and in building relationships. Grasping, mouthing, and reaching are physical characteristics of this stage. She may imitate the adults around her, babble incessantly at times, and try to get adult attention through various means, including crying, gaining eye contact, and using facial expressions. Although many of the signs that she sends adults are not deliberate, she offers many cues to adults so that they can meet her needs. She is also learning to mediate her emotions through social referencing. In other words, she is learning to match her emotions to the response she observes from her caregiver.

At this age, separation anxiety and stranger anxiety may begin to appear, because object permanence has been cognitively acquired. The work of Ainsworth identified attachment categories, and those behaviors can remain stable over a lifetime. Basic emotions of joy, sadness, anger, and fear are recognizable in children this age.

Increased motor skills and locomotion abilities signal a new phase in the child's develop-ment, but also demand a raised level of caution for safety monitoring. Everything can be put into the mouth, and if children are not crawling yet, they often can roll everywhere. Equipment needs to be checked on a regular basis in order to make sure that it is maintained in good condition.

Care providers need to check the child's immunization records to ensure that they are up to date. Most children at this stage will begin to eat solid food, and careful records must be main-tained in order to determine a possible reaction to a particular food.

Some special topics raised in this chapter were the importance of music; the strongly word-ed warnings from the American Academy of Pediatrics against any television viewing for this aged child and co-sleeping with young babies; and the importance of touch for the development of children. Information about everyday health and safety concerns, developmental delays, and techniques to engage babies are mentioned, and you are directed to your Online Companion for even more information and ideas to add to your repertoire of growing knowledge about caring for infants and toddlers.

DISCUSSION QUESTIONS

1. What advantages, if any, are there for infants in try-ing to speed up their development?
2. What are the most significant concerns you might have seeing infants at this stage grasping everything around them?
3. Describe the observable elements of an anti-bias philosophy.
4. Donny, the youngest of three children, doesn't like being cuddled, and seems irritable much of the time.

When his mother tells you that she's having problems relating to his behavior, what might you do?

5. Describe a situation when touch made you comfort-able or uncomfortable. What are your personal feel-ings about touch in the early childhood setting? Do you think that it is necessary?

ADDITIONAL RESOURCES

Further Readings

Acredolo, L., & Goodwyn, S. (1992). *Baby signs: How to talk with your baby before your baby can talk.* Chicago: Contemporary Books.

Bergen, D., Reid, R., & Torelli, L. (2001). *Educating and Caring for very young children: The infant and toddler curriculum.* New York: Teachers College Press.

Carey, W. B. (2004). *Understanding your child's temperament.* New York: Xlibis Company.

Carlson, F. M. (2005). Significance of touch in young children's lives. *Young Children,* (60), 4, 79–85.

Chess, S., & Thomas, A. (1996). *Temperament: Theory and practice.* New York: Brunner/Mazel.

Cohen, G. J. (Ed.) (1999). For the American Academy of Pediatrics. *Guide to your child's sleep.* New York: Villard Books.

Dombro, A., et al., (1997). *The creative curriculum for infants & toddlers.* Washington, DC: Teaching Strategies.

Dunst, C., et al., (1996). *Supporting & strengthening families: Vol. 1: Methods, strategies and practices.* Cambridge, MA: Brookline Books.

Ekman, P. (2004). *Emotions revealed: Recognizing faces and feelings to improve communication and emotional life.* New York: Owl Books.

Elliot, E. (2003). Challenging our assumptions: Helping a baby adjust to center care. *Young Children, 58* (4), 22–28.

Godwin, A., & Schrag, L. (1996). *Setting up for infant/toddler care: Guidelines for centers and family child care homes.* Washington, DC: NAEYC.

Gray, H. (2004). You go away and you come back: Supporting separations and reunions in an infant/toddler classroom. *Young Children, 59* (5), 100–107.

Greata, J. (2006). *An introduction to music in early childhood education.* Clifton Park, NY: Thomson Delmar Learning

Hast, F., & Hollyfield, A. (1999). *Infant and toddler experiences.* St. Paul, MN: Redleaf Press.

Honig, A. S. (1998). Making music. *Scholastic Early Childhood Today,* pp. 24–26.

Honig, A. S. (2001). Comforting infants & toddlers: Secrets for teachers. *Scholastic Early Childhood Today,* pp. 35–37.

Honig, A. S., & Brophy, H. E. (1996) *Talking with your baby: Family as the first school.* Syracuse, NY: Syracuse University Press.

Honig, A. S. (2002). *Secure relationships: Nurturing infant/toddler attachment in early care settings.* Washington, DC: NAEYC.

Kaiser, B., & Rasminsky, J. S. (2003). Opening the culture door. *Young Children, 58* (4), 53–56.

Karen, R. (1998). *Becoming attached: Unfolding the mystery of the infant–mother bond and its impact on later life.* New York: Oxford University Press.

Karmiloff, K., & Karmiloff-Smith, A. (1999). *Everything your baby would ask if only he or she could talk.* New York: Golden Books/Random House.

Post, J., & Hohmann, M. (2000). *Tender care and early learning: Supporting infants and toddlers in child care settings.* Ypsilanti, MI: High/Scope Press.

Powell, D. R. (1989). *Families and early childhood programs.* Washington, DC: NAEYC.

Schiller, P. (2005). *The complete resource book for infants.* Baltimore: Gryphon House.

Segal, M. (1998). *Your child at play: Birth to one year—Discovering the senses and learning about the world.* New York: Newmarket Press.

Silberg, J. (2001). *Games to play with baby: Revised.* Baltimore: Gryphon House.

Sparling, J., & Lewis, I. (2000). *Learning games: The Abecedarian curriculum.* Tallahassee, FL: Early Learning Press, Inc.

Sroufe, L. A. (1997). *Emotional development: The organization of emotional life in the early years.* Cambridge, UK: Cambridge University Press.

Szamreta, J. M. (2003). Peek-a-boo power: To ease separation and build secure relationships. *Young Children, 58* (1), 88–94.

York, S. (2003). *Roots and wings: Affirming culture in early childhood programs* (Revised edition). St. Paul, MN: Redleaf Press.

Useful Videos

First Moves: Welcoming a Child to a New Setting. (27 minutes) Available from the Program for Infants and Toddlers at http://www.pitc.org

Learning Through Observation Video Package (2002)

This 60-minute video provides supervisors, trainers, and directors with non-narrated footage of real-life interactions between staff of infant–family programs and families in situations, including home visits in the context of Early Head Start, family support, and early intervention; and drop-offs and pick-ups at child care.

Right from the Start (60 minutes) Although this video is dated, it does have footage of Harlow's monkeys, failure-thrive babies, and T. Barry Brazelton, among others. It also has a valuable section on a child who has an attachment disorder. Available from http://www.childdevmedia.com/

First Feelings. Nova.

Description: This video outlines the stages of emotional development of infants and toddlers. It explains research and theoretical ideas in meaningful ways.

Seeing Infants with New Eyes. NAEYC.

Description: Magda Gerber's exemplary program dramatically illustrates how adult interactions with infants can make a significant difference. (26 min.)

Useful Web Sites

Caring for Kids Organization
   www.caringforkids.org/

Getting in Tune: The Magic of Music in Child Care
   http://www.zerotothree.org/

Click on: Professionals

Scroll down and Click on: Music

Legal Momentum–Advancing Women's Rights
   http://www.legalmomentum.org/

Click on: Child Care and Early Education

National Association for the Education of Young Children
   www.naeyc.org

In Search Box enter: Child Abuse

National Clearing House on Child Abuse and Neglect
   http://nccanch.acf.hhs.gov/

CHAPTER 8

Raring to Go: Infants at 9 to 12 Months

Babies at this stage of development are very keen on pulling themselves up to stand. This position offers a new and different perspective on their world. Getting back down is sometimes not accomplished with quite as much ease.

LEARNING OUTCOMES

After reading and studying this chapter, you should be able to:
* identify the observable characteristics of infants at 9 to 12 months
* explain the significance of behaviors in infants from 9 to 12 months in a developmental context
* recognize and respond to the developmental diversity of 9- to 12-month-old infants and discuss issues pertinent to this stage of development
* assess the development of infants in the 9- to 12-month stage
* respond to the health, safety, and development of 9- to 12-month-old infants with appropriate protection, caregiving, and guidance
* develop strategies to work with parents as partners in the care and education of their infants

SCENE

Parents meet the supervisor of a child care center to discuss how their whole family will be involved in their baby's transition from home care to center-based care. Although their baby, Marcia, is only 11 months old, she is to be placed with a group of toddlers, because she is mobile and has adapted to a regular routine. The family wants to be sure that Marcia's language skills are encouraged.

"Marcia jabbers away all the time," said Janet, Marcia's mother. "I'm not sure what she's talking about, but she loves the sound of her own voice." Marcia interrupted the conversation by tugging on her mother's hair and adding her own contribution, "Bada bada bada." "I think she wants to join in our chat," observed the educator. "She already knows how to make sure she's not left out!"

The educator and mother continued their talk while enabling Marcia to be part of the conversation. They talked about how infants at this stage have picked up a range of social skills by copying adults and seeking solutions to problems such as how to get noticed. Then Marcia's mother confessed, "I'm worried that Marcia's communication will be held back when she's in the center; the educators have several children to care for at one time." The educator's reply encouraged her. "We do lots of things here to help the infants let us know what their needs are. We help them to find ways of communicating and we play lots of games and sing rhymes to encourage language. Also, there is some benefit in Marcia being with toddlers who are beginning to say real words. At this stage babies copy each other as well as adults! We play many games with sounds and words, so it will be a positive place for talking." By the time she departed, Marcia's mother was feeling better about leaving her infant at the center. In subsequent days, she noticed that the educator's reassurances had been accurate. Staff did spend a lot of time talking and playing with the children.

DEVELOPMENTAL DOMAINS

Physical Development

At this stage of 9 to 12 months, infants are larger and heavier, have increased physical skills, are more interested in the world around them, play with anything within reach, and communicate with increasing effectiveness.

Growth

The infant's weight continues to increase by about one pound per month. At 9 months, the average weight (50th percentile) for girls is 15 pounds and 16.5 for boys, while at 12 months the average weight (50th percentile) is 21 pounds for girls and 23 pounds for boys (National Center for Health Statistics, 2001). If you were to examine patterns of weight gain in infants, you would likely find that at 12 months, the baby is about three times her birth weight. Boys continue to be both slightly heavier and taller than girls, but the variation is individual and depends upon birth size, ethnicity, family patterns, health status, body frame, and nutrition. Although growth patterns are useful indicators of healthy development, the infant's own pattern is more significant than his growth compared with the norm.

Pediatric examinations will usually include measurement of head circumference; what doctors are particularly interested in is whether head circumference growth is proportional to height and weight. (See Box 8.1.) Both the infant's body and head are growing, but the latter at a slower pace, so the infant is gradually becoming less top-heavy.

Gross Motor Skills

The downward, **cephalocaudal**—from head to toe—progression of physical control now allows the infant to have increased control over her legs and the lower part of her body. At 9 months, she may creep on her hands and knees (Green & Palfrey, 2002), lower herself to a sitting position from standing, and maintain good balance while sitting (Allen & Marotz, 2007). At 10 months, she will usually stand briefly (Sheridan, 2001) and may walk, or **cruise**—with a sideways shuffle—as she holds onto furniture in a standing position. Some infants find that crawling remains a faster method of getting around; most babies at this stage attempt to walk but revert frequently to their own method of crawling.

There is wide variation in the time frame for walking, and this appears to be a problem for families whose babies takes longer than the average. Yet there is no real cause for concern if the infant is not attempting to walk and shows little interest in being held in a walking position. Often, if she is mobile in other ways, the baby has little reason to struggle to her feet.

When children become walkers, they are often referred to as **toddlers**. The term comes from the characteristic wobbly gait of the early waddling walk. The term may also be

cephalocaudal (principle)

that development of the body following a sequence from head to foot

cruising

moving around by standing up and walking sideways while holding on to a stable object

toddler

the stage of the child after infancy when the child starts to walk or toddle; defined by age, a toddler may be 8 to 18 months, 12 to 24 months, etc. (variable according to practice and legislation)

The following definitions are for children who are proceeding normally in their development and do not have any physical disabilities.

- Infant—a child from birth to before he obtains the skill of walking
- Toddler—a child who has developed the ability to walk

Sometimes a toddler is defined by age, often meaning that if the child is over age 1, he is considered a toddler, even if he hasn't yet begun to walk. This definition then could result in a host of ranges—8 to 18 months; 12 months to 24 months; 18 months to 30 months. The interpretation of the definition is often reflective of policy and/or legislation. From a safety perspective, careful thought is required when making a decision on how to classify groups. The dividing line between these two stages of infancy should be the ability to walk, since walking creates a new set of care and nurturing considerations.

BOX 8.1

SENSITIVE INDICATORS OF PROGRESS

The measurements to track the growth of babies are important. The least sensitive marker is length, since that is often determined by genetics. However, weight and head circumference are fairly sensitive indicators of potential health problems. Medical personnel look first at whether there is overall continued growth of the child. Second, they note whether length, weight, and head circumference align in a reasonable pattern. A baby at the 55th percentile in length, the 45th percentile in weight, and at the 55th percentile in head circumference is probably doing fine. If the child is in the 20th percentile for length, the 95th percentile for weight, and the 60th percentile for head circumference, then this may indicate a potential problem with obesity in the future, and warrants increased monitoring. Third, they look for aberrant changes in height and head circumference measurements from one checkup to the next. If the child's weight actually decreases between well-baby checkups, there is cause to seek a reason. Another scenario could be a child who is in the 50th percentile for both length and weight and who previously was also in the 50th percentile for head circumference, but is now in the 95th percentile for head circumference. This could signal a problem such as the child's being hydrocephalic.

used to refer to children of a particular age, usually over 12 or 15 months. At this stage, the infant may be placed in the toddler room at a child care center. This move may be decided on the basis of the child's age, stage, or the number of children at a center.

Fine Motor Skills

With increased bodily control, the young child has a greater ability to move toward the objects that interest her. If her efforts are successful, she will grasp items with her thumb and fingers working in opposition. This early pincer grasp is called an intermediate, or inferior, pincer grasp (Edwards, Buckland, & McCoy-Powlen, 2002). By 12 months, the infant will probably display a more mature grasp, one that involves the thumb and index finger working in careful opposition. This is a **pincer grasp**; now even small objects can be grasped.

With this increased control of her hands, the baby will want to manipulate any objects that she can reach. When she has blocks or other items in both hands, she may bang them together, enjoying the sound that the action produces. She may hold her hand out as though offering an item to someone (Illingworth, 1990), but she finds releasing objects more challenging than grasping them. The infant is likely to be interested in putting things into and then taking them out of containers. (Figure 8.1 outlines the progression of hand grasps in young children.)

Another new skill that emerges at this stage, usually around 9 to 10 months, is the infant's ability to point with her index finger. She will also often use her hands to signal interest or to convey a message. Given the opportunity to imitate an adult, she may wave goodbye.

Motor control of the upper extremity is based on the principle of proximal and distal development. "Two distinct motor systems control the upper limbs; one, proximal, is responsible for the control of large movements of arm and hand, the other, distal, controls the subtle coordinations of hand movements" (Corbetta & Mounoud, 1990, p. 191). Thus comes the term **proximodistal**, explaining how development proceeds from the middle of the body outwards.

Figure 8.1 Progression of Hand Grasps

Reflex Squeeze

Crude Palmar

Palmar Grasp

Radial Palmar

Raking Grasp

Radial Digital

Developmental

Inferior Pincer

Three Jaw Chuck

Pincer Grasp

Neat Pincer Grasp

pincer grasp

the ability to grasp a small object between the tips of the thumb and index finger

cephalocaudal/ proximodistal sequences

the development of the body follows dual sequences simultaneously—from head to foot (cephalocaudal) and from the center of the body outward to the hands (proximodistal)

Activity 8.1 on your CD-ROM is designed to help you document the development of grasp sequence in young children.

Cognitive Development

Vision

The ability to see objects at some distance prompts the infant to want to find out what is happening. The baby has been able to identify adults from across the room for some time, but now visual acuity is improved and she is likely able to identify who adults are from their faces and their bodies.

The infant is able to see tiny objects, such as food crumbs or raisins (Sheridan, 2001), which she in turn wants to pick up. This promotes the practice of manual skills such as pointing and grasping. Having better visual acuity also means that infants at this stage may stare at moving objects some distance away. They prefer to see the three-dimensional activity of people, and are very interested in street action or any movement of people in the room. At this stage, the infant takes more notice of people and things around her when she is taken outdoors.

Hearing

differentiated hearing

the ability to simultaneously hear one's own voice and listen to other specific sounds

Differentiated hearing allows the infant to listen to his own voice and select sounds to listen to from a multitude of surrounding noises. He is particularly interested in human voices, tuning in to hear them. He experiments with his own vocalizations, which is a sign of hearing ability. When he shapes some of his sounds to resemble the language that surrounds him, he is indicating that he hears those sounds. He replicates them and makes up his own. By 12 months, the infant can usually respond to his name and understand a few single words. He may also imitate mechanical sounds (Allen & Marotz, 2007).

Touch, Taste, and Smell

It can be useful for parents and caregivers to know that infants have taste buds that differentiate among sweet, bitter, salty, and sour tastes. Babies may even have a fifth set of taste buds that are receptive to umami—monosodium glutamate (Lowry, 2001). Different parts of the tongue have taste buds receptive to different types of tastes. Coupled with the sense of taste is the textural experience associated with foods. Now that the baby is being offered a bigger range of "adult" puréed food, she will experience mouth feel, aroma, tastes, and aftertastes. Chemical receptors stimulate the taste receptors on the tongue to register a reaction at the same time that the baby experiences the texture and smell of the food. Feeding is a **multimodal stimulation** experience. Facial expressions are very good indicators of how well the baby is accepting a new food. At this stage, the introduction of foods that have a mildly bitter taste may be problematic; the baby has a more acute sense of bitterness—for instance, with some green vegetables—than she had in earlier months.

multimodal stimulation

stimulating two or more senses simultaneously

Babies who are breast-fed are exposed to a variety of tastes as they receive milk that has been filtered through the mother's digestive system into the mother's milk supply. Mothers may report babies reacting in particular ways after eating spicy foods. Mothers who continue to breast-feed for some, if not all feedings, are providing ideal nutrition and health protection for their babies. Ideally, they should be supported in child care settings so that the mother can feed her baby when necessary, or that the baby is fed mother's milk that has been previously pumped and stored. The experience of feeding is as important as the nutrients that are delivered. Closeness, cuddling, bodily warmth, and the smell of the adult all contribute to the development of attachments to adults; the senses of touch and smell are important to the bonding process. The fact that babies are able to hold a bottle and lie propped up is no reason to deprive the baby of the nurturance that a good feeding situation should provide.

Infants at this stage assimilate a tremendous amount of information from grasping, feeling, and experimenting with objects and materials. During the 9–12-month stage, the infant is less and less likely to take items to her mouth for discovery (Sheridan, 2001), although this remains a common behavior. Perhaps her increased manipulative skills allow her hands to make the discoveries instead. Although some infants are quite adventurous with new textures, tastes, and smells, most need time to accommodate totally new experiences. For this reason, new foods should be introduced gradually and all types of sensory stimulation should be balanced with quiet times.

Sensorimotor Behavior

Greater deliberation in play is observable at this time. Piaget (1952) identified characteristics of this substage of the sensorimotor stage as "coordination of secondary circular reactions." The infant is beginning to be able to solve little problems, such as how to get the

feeding bottle the right way round into his mouth, or what to do when a toy rolls away, out of easy reach. Review Piaget's substages of sensorimotor development in Figure 6.1 (Chapter 6), or go to the Additional Support section of your Online Companion.

egocentric

from the perspective of the individual; in infancy, an inability to see from the perspective of others

The infant retains an **egocentric** way of seeing things, and does not yet appreciate the perspectives of others. He does, though, observe adults closely, and is interested in the activity of other infants and older children.

object permanence

the realization that objects continue to exist when they are out of sight

After the infant understands that objects and people continue to exist even when they are out of sight, some new behaviors become evident. Mastery of the concept of **object permanence** is an indication of a new type of mental scheme that involves holding information in mind even when immediate sensory input offers no reminders of it. The infant may look for something that is hidden and enjoy games of peek boo. In both cases, the infant is excited about finding a lost item. However, the infant's memory is not very long, and he may soon become distracted. This doesn't mean that the concept of object permanence is not, at least partially, appreciated.

Awareness of object permanence demonstrates the capacity for early **symbolic thought**: To appreciate object permanence, the infant has to have a symbolic representation of the object in mind. You might observe other examples of symbolic thought at this stage. The linkage of a meaning to a word shows that the infant understands that one thing stands for another. When he lifts his arms as you say "up," he is showing you the connection. If he responds to a single word, without another prompt, he has clearly used a basic form of symbolism. The use of language relies on symbolic thought, so this is an essential cognitive skill.

Early Concept Development

The early concept development of an infant utilizes a scheme that is primarily based on sensorimotor functioning. She has a cognitive cluster of fairly primitive bits of information that have come about from her actions with objects and people. The baby's schemes at this stage are expanding but are entirely dependent upon experience. Some of her actions might lead us to think that she has a deeper appreciation of the thoughts and motives of adults than is possible, particularly when some of the actions we see her perform come from her imitation of adults. But these are surface-level imitations, and cannot reflect complexities or any real understanding of what it's like to be an adult.

The infant at this stage does not have a very long attention span. In social interactions, babies' attention can be lengthened by adults' careful intervention. Engaging in the child's own interests is particularly helpful. Also, extending experiences by increasing stimulation or making efforts to highlight what is happening can lengthen the infant's focus. Often, repeating simple play sequences can help the baby keep her focus on something. In time, the baby will use these strategies herself, but her attention span is determined as much by her **personality** as by her maturation.

Learning through **imitation** is particularly important at this stage before the child can speak. If an action has similarities to previous behaviors, the infant is more likely to imitate it (Fogel, 2000). Thus, simple actions that resemble ones imitated earlier are easier to learn. Actions that accompany nursery rhymes are soon learned because they have the added advantage of prompting memory with association of sounds.

Research has documented that mental representation, or how infants come to "think," often emerges earlier than predicted by Piaget's substages (Berk, 2002; Papalia, Olds, & Feldman, 2006). Piaget's observations led him to emphasize motor experience as the prime contributor to cognitive development. However, with the technology available to researchers today, a clearer interpretation of infants' abilities has evolved. These recent findings conclude that infants' perceptions are far ahead of their motor abilities. Object permanence, causality, and deferred imitation, just to mention a few, can often be observed in earlier time frames than Piaget predicted. Do not think this means that Piaget's theory should be ignored. His work contributed to a sustained interest in infant cognition, and still guides the early childhood profession in decisions about what constitutes developmentally appropriate environments for infants and toddlers.

Language and Communication

Body Language

With a wide repertoire of **gestures** and vocalizations, the infant may make herself understood without the use of real words. If her cues receive an appropriate response, the infant is likely to have her gestures reinforced, and so will repeat them (Kostelnick, Whiren, Soderman, & Gregory, 2006). Skillful educators and parents may extend the infant's **gesture vocabulary** by using a broader range of actions than the child would use spontaneously (Anthony & Lindert, 2005).

---

symbolic thought

the representation of reality through the use of abstract concepts such as words and gestures; generally present in most children by the age of 18 months, when signs and symbols (usually in place of language) are used reliably to refer to concrete objects, events, and behaviors

personality

the sum total of the enduring characteristics that differentiate one individual from another

imitation

the act of copying single actions of another person, or the copying of complex actions, as with role models

gesture

a deliberate action of the hands, head, or body, indicating an idea or feeling

gesture vocabulary

a range of hand and arm signs that have shared meanings

Infants can use body language so successfully that some parents become concerned that their toddlers may choose not to talk. It is true that infants whose body language is well understood may be later in gaining a spoken vocabulary. Information may be more easily conveyed and understood through gestures and facial expressions than through one-word exchanges with an infant at this stage. Use of body language enhances the infant's communication skills and encourages greater sensitivity between adult and child. The adult who uses both gestures and words simultaneously offers the child an advantage in communication skill acquisition.

Receptive and Expressive Language

The use of gestures along with the spoken word can reinforce the meaning of the words. It is likely that an infant at this stage understands several words if they are heard in context. This is her **receptive language**. Even at 9 months, an infant can usually understand a simple instruction associated with a gesture. For example, the instruction "give it to Daddy" may be understood if Daddy has his hand outstretched at the same time he utters the words (Sheridan, 2001). By 12 months, the infant may obey simple instructions given in short phrases, like "Knock down the blocks" or "Give me the soother."

The infant at this stage is beginning to reshape early vocalizations into sounds that approximate those of the language spoken around her. They are early attempts at **expressive language**. The child experiments with her ability to make sounds. She hears sounds, imitates them, and, with lots of reinforcement from adults who imitate her sounds, remodels them into word-like sounds. This sounds like a complex process, but it happens without most adults realizing what is taking place—they are just enjoying the interactions.

To express oneself using spoken language is an exciting step toward realizing one's potential. The syllabic repetitions—that is, the **babbling** repetition of long strings of consonant-vowel sounds—should be acquired by this stage (Owens, 2001). "Da-da-da" is reshaped by an adult and sounds like "dad dad." When Daddy hears this, he thinks the infant is saying his name. "Wow! Dad. Yes, come to Dad," he says. This is a simple example of the work adults do in supporting language. According to Weitzman and Greenberg (2002), techniques to use with young children include observing, waiting, and listening—the OWL method. Often adults do not utilize these techniques. If the communication is not reciprocal, then you may unintentionally teach a child not to communicate. Therefore, it is important to stop talking and concentrate your full attention on a child, signaling that you are expecting something from him. Your attention, your body language, and your facial expression all contribute to encouraging the child to take the lead in the conversation. If development progresses normally, by 12 months, the infant may speak 2–6 words in context (Sheridan, 2001).

For receptive or expressive language to occur, several conditions must already exist. If any of these conditions is compromised, the infant's language acquisition process can become difficult. The infant needs:

- adequate hearing
- vocal chords to produce sound
- a neurological system ready to process language data
- the ability to imitate
- motivation to communicate
- the understanding that words have meaning
- a memory for words
- environments where sufficient language is used
- adults who will make language accessible—appropriate for age
- relationships with adults who are caring and nurturing

In addition to these requisite conditions, many theories try to explain how children actually come to acquire language. Box 8.2 outlines several of these theories.

Two commonly observed nonverbal gestures that appear at this time are "waving bye-bye" and the back-and-forth motion of the head signaling the word "NO!"

receptive language

processing meaningful sounds, words, phrases, and sentences

expressive language

uttering meaningful sounds, words, phrases, and sentences

babbling

production of consonant–vowel sounds of varying intonation; usually involves repetition of sounds in long strings, such as da-da-da-da-da, or ba-ba-ba-ba-ba, developing in an infant between the ages of 4 and 6 months

BOX 8.2

LANGUAGE ACQUISITION THEORIES

- **Nativist**—proposes that children are prewired to learn language. Every human is born with an LAD (language acquisition device) and therefore nature, not nurture (the environment), contributes most to the learning of language. Noam Chomsky is the most well known individual associated with this theory. Currently, this theory is not widely supported.
- **Behaviorist**—suggests that children learn language through repetition and reinforcement. Specifically, this is known as classical and operant conditioning. Nurture, the family, and the environment have the most significant impact on language learning. B.F. Skinner is one of the individuals often associated with this theory.
- **Social Interactivist**—acknowledges the important contribution from both genetics (nature) and parental influence (environment) to language learning. In addition, it is the child's own intentional participation (**constructivism**) to learn the functions and forms of language. Caretakers recognize these intentions and help guide children's acquisition of language through **scaffolding** methods. Lev Vygotsky is probably the individual most associated with this theory.
- **Neuro-Biological**—based on the relatively new brain research from the last few decades, this view acknowledges the contributions of all three previous views. The brain does have designated areas dedicated to language learning [nativist]. Children do require experiences to hear language, imitate language, and be rewarded for their attempts [behaviorist]. Finally, children need caretakers who are tuned into their verbal and nonverbal cues, who respond sensitively and appropriately to their needs, and who consistently engage in conversations with children—in other words, caregivers who scaffold language learning [social interactivist]. Since the brain research has attracted so much attention, there is not one individual who is most associated with this view.

constructivism

a philosophy of learning that considers reality to be self-constructed: the child, through stages, creates an inner construction of her outer world

scaffolding

the role of the adult (or other child) to provide, and gradually remove, a support to the child's learning; providing a bridge for the child to gain a new understanding

Socio-Emotional Development

Stage of Emotional Growth

At 9 or even 12 months, infants do not understand emotions that are expressed and cannot label them. However, they are responsive to adults' facial expressions (Harrist & Waugh, 2002). They are also responsive to moods, and tend to be fussy when the adult is anxious and contented when the atmosphere seems calm. The range of emotions expressed by infants of this stage is still limited. They do not yet appear to appreciate expression of emotions such as shame, shyness, or guilt (Lamb, Bornstein, & Teti, 2002), which require a more complex understanding of self and others.

Greenspan and Greenspan (1985) assert that while this is a time of of considerable physical advancement, the infant's emotions are also taking leaps forward. The baby will begin to show specific behaviors associated with her feelings. This is significant because it helps adults interpret or "read" babies' behavior more clearly. For example, ways that she might show that she is pleased may involve sound production, smiling, and reaching out. In many other situations there will be synchronized actions and expressions. Frequently these lead to her being able to express her feelings quite effectively—particularly to the adult who takes time to read her cues. You may observe the baby making more links between things. Occasionally she may imitate an adult's action and elaborate the sequence using her own imaginative ideas. At other times, she might use one object in place of another and think that the result is funny. Whether or not she really appreciates the incongruity (things in the wrong place) is not always certain, but she'll laugh because others are laughing even if she doesn't quite get what is funny. (Review

Greenspan and Greenspan's chart of emotional milestones in the Additional Support section in your Online Companion.

A further advancement at this stage can be seen in the baby's efforts to gain greater control over things and people. She takes initiative in communication and will respond well to others' efforts to communicate with her—as long as she has established a strong bond with them. The trusting relationship is the basis of her ability to try things independently, and she needs encouragement to do this.

As her mobility increases, you may see her extend her own physical boundaries but check back for approval by way of a smile or positive facial expression. If she gets the encouragement she seeks, she may extend the circle of discovery around the adult but with regular **social referencing** as she seeks an adult's approval. Interestingly, if she gets a negative response— perhaps the adult shows mock horror at her impending action—she may be sufficiently influenced so that she stops what she is doing or returns to be closer to the adult (Moses, Baldwin, Rosicky, & Tidball, 2001). The adult's emotions influence the infant significantly at this stage, and an indication of a strong bond is that she tunes into the adult's feelings. As she reads the adult's expressions, she notices the mood that is reflected. She may take on a similar emotion to that of the adult or respond with a questioning face.

As a caregiver, it is essential to note the effect of one's own feelings. Even feelings that we think are hidden may be absorbed by infants. Earlier on in the baby's life, the effect may have related only to being unhappy if the adult was agitated, or to being easily soothed if the adult was calm and peaceful. Now the infant is more in tune with adults than we might imagine.

The emotional partnership that the infant has with adults is particularly important for emotional growth at this time. The emphasis in this partnership needs to be on building **trust** (Erikson, 1959). The adult must be physically and emotionally close and extremely consistent and responsive to the infant's needs. An increased opportunity for emotional closeness exists now that the infant can communicate a little more.

social referencing

thee tendency to use others' emotional expressions to help understand the situation and thus relieve uncertainty; the child will look at the parent or caregiver's face and monitor his expressions in order to decide how to respond

trust

confident reliance on self or others

> Trust and social referencing underscore the fact that attachment has emotional, physical, and cognitive components. Children who are securely attached (emotional component) will explore their environments utilizing motor skills (physical component). They have enough trust to feel safe in physically adventuring out some distance from their primary caregiver—"home base." Of course, the more explorative experiences children have, the more patterns or schemes are built up in their brain (cognitive component). Insecurely attached children do not venture away from "home base," which, in turn, limits their experiences and negatively impacts cognitive development.

self-regulation

the ability to control feelings and emotions, or the behaviors that result from those emotions; the ability to modify or change behavior as a result of managing inner emotions

pro-social skills

learned behavior that is intended to help or benefits others—e.g., helping, sharing, or kindness

During this stage of development, the infant begins to regulate her own emotions, gaining some degree of control over how she feels and how she behaves. The baby's awareness of her own feelings is enabling her to make these attempts to control her behavior (self-regulation). She may be able to soothe herself when unhappy, prepare herself for sleep, disengage herself from overstimulation, and amuse herself for short periods.

Early **self-regulation** leads to later **pro-social skills** (positive emotions and behaviors). Unless children have some understanding of their own feelings, and have some control over them, they will be unprepared for a much greater advance in social and emotional development later on. Emotional well-being and self-regulation are essential for happiness and relationship building through childhood and into adulthood. If they are without emotional self-regulation, it seems unlikely that young children would ever be ready to take the perspective of others and imagine others' feelings.

Supporting the infant's ability to regulate her feelings and actions requires only basic support and opportunity. She needs to be given some occasions to be alone and to comfort herself, and adults should support the child's efforts. Child care centers' programs can be so busy that the children have little time to amuse themselves. Providing opportunity for the baby to feel that she is by herself (of course, infants and toddlers are not really to be left unsupervised), to follow through with her own discoveries, or to try to calm herself when upset is advisable. Many older children find it difficult to play spontaneously or amuse themselves because they did not have the opportunity to become familiar with quiet times, talk to themselves, make "something out of nothing," become aware of their own feelings or inner voice, or use their imagination. This is not to suggest that infants at this stage should be left alone, but that a balance seems desirable between external stimulation and the opportunity for internal regulation.

Also, special consideration must be given to the physical environment and the daily routines, since they can affect how one feels. The environment and routine must be predictable for the child at this stage; disorganized patterns can be emotionally upsetting for young children and can impact their behavior. Care providers should carefully monitor the physical and social environments to ensure that they are supporting the emotional well-being of the infants.

Attachment

Infants at this stage have made specific secure attachments to the key adults in their lives, particularly their parents and caregivers, who are significant and consistent figures. It is evident that the infant, particularly at this stage, is able to make **multiple attachments** with a small group of people (Berk, 2004).

multiple attachments

having two or more secure attachment figures; having a series of important relationships involving significant bonding; typically these relationships are with parents, extended family members, and caregivers

Earlier research had emphasized the mother–infant attachment (Bowlby, 1969) rather than any bonding with other adults in the child's life. One might question the motives of some researchers at times—and this is one such time—when the outcome of their work underscored the need for mothers to stay at home to care for their children. If attachments to other people were impossible, it would seem that the mother had no other choice. Social and political motives will always influence research. However, what we now know is that because the baby can make several secure attachments, it is possible for fathers, extended-family members, and unrelated caregivers to offer adequate care to babies. Of course, for the attachment to occur, certain conditions must be present. The baby's basic needs must be met, and more importantly, so must her psychological needs. This requires emotional engagement with the baby, responsive nurturance, trust building and continuity of care.

quality of attachment

the degree to which a strong and secure bonding relationship has developed

The phrase **quality of attachment** refers to the degree of security felt by the infant in an attachment. Quality of attachment seems to be rooted early in the infant's first year (Ainsworth et al., 1978), later attachments being affected by the bonds made in the first few months. This does not necessarily mean that infants will be damaged if they make no very close attachments in their first days. Although Bowlby (1969) suggested that this was the case, later studies argue that he overstated the necessity for mother–infant bonding in the first week of life (Rutter & O'Conner, 1999). Nonetheless, attachment behaviors are essential for healthy emotional development, and later weeks and months are just as important. The quality of attachment depends on the baby's circumstances. Howes (1999) and her colleagues state that adults must be able to provide physical and emotional care and continuity, and have an emotional investment in the child's life. The sensitivity and responsiveness of the adults are critical components that also affect the quality of attachment (NICHD, 2005c). When researchers and educators observe infants, they look to see if the quality of attachment is strong—if it is what is called a **secure attachment**.

secure attachment

a positive, trusting, and reliable relationship with an adult

The construction of that secure attachment is "dependent upon particularly skilled and sensitive adult behavior" (Howes, 1999, p. 684), and infants demonstrating secure attachments are more likely to have experienced consistent and loving care. Findings on the long-term effects of securely attached children seem to indicate that overall, these children have more positive outcomes than do children who do not experience secure attachment. For example, secure attachment is one of the main conditions for later resilience. If life experiences become less desirable later on, a securely attached child is more likely to cope with the stressors.

The discussion on attachment has implications for child care because it highlights the conditions that must be available for children to form secure attachments. Once again, responsive, loving, consistent care must be provided in order for children to form attachments. The most serious problem that child care must solve is consistency of care. Because child care wages are low, turnover in staff is an ever-present problem. This turnover does affect the quality of care children receive. The United States is one of the few industrialized countries without a national plan for quality and subsidized child care for *all* children. As of the writing of this text, Canada is beginning to create a pan-Canadian system of early learning and child care. Five provinces (Manitoba, Saskatchewan, Ontario, Newfoundland, and Nova Scotia), out of a total of 13 provinces and territories, signed bilateral early learning and child care agreements with the federal government. According to government officials, negotiations are underway with all of the other jurisdictions. The overall framework includes a national vision for early learning and child care founded on principles of quality, universal inclusiveness, accessibility, and developmental appropriateness. For more information you can visit the CCCF website at www.cccf-fcsge.ca.

Self-Concept

As we discussed previously, the trust relationship and the ability to link cause and effect enable the infant to realize that he is not only a separate person but one who can influence his surroundings. These things help the infant develop a concept of an existential self—that is, that she exists on his own and has some power. If the individual is to flourish, this concept of self is crucially important.

For an infant, having control over objects and himself is part of the process of discovering what he can do. Adults have traditionally underestimated the importance of this area of development. A child's **self-concept** can either enable him to succeed or limit the realization of his potential.

self-concept

one's identity; beliefs about what one is like as a person

Some of a child's self-concept is formed by the individuals with whom the child interacts. As strange as it sounds, attachment is the tether that initially enables the child to begin to separate from his primary caregiver. For a child to find himself, he needs to separate, but this can only happen if he is attached!

Self-image also contributes to self-concept, and much of that message comes from early body awareness. Gradually, children learn what capabilities their bodies possess. In fact, most of what children know about themselves in the first years of life comes from motoric experiences. This is a fact that must be kept in mind when working with young children who have some physical delay.

Other contributors to self-concept include culture, gender, and behavior guidance. Cultures promote the criteria by which children evaluate themselves. Even though infants and toddlers have not yet reached the point of self-awareness, they are still learning about how their particular culture looks at the world. This viewpoint might include information about what foods are eaten, what social manners are expected, whether you have an inclusive view of self (meaning the group is more important than an individual), how personal body space is treated, and even a cultural interpretation of time (Miller, 2001). An awareness of gender identity happens early in life. Children learn whether they are a boy or a girl and then associate with that particular gender. All cultures have sex-role stereotyping, some to a greater degree than others. Children raised with a very rigid or narrow interpretation of their expected gender role assimilate an identity with limited capabilities because, in a sense, they fulfill the limited expectations of the adults who have prescribed those roles. Messages about gender roles can be very apparent. For example, you tell a boy that "big boys don't cry" or a girl not to play in the dirt because "girls shouldn't get dirty." Messages can also be sent in very subtle ways too. Think about some of the hidden messages that can be generated by the following:

- apparel—blue for boys and pink for girls
- toys—dolls *or* trucks rather than dolls *and* trucks
- books
- TV and other media
- movies
- greeting cards and wrapping paper
- language—fireman instead of firefighter; what image pops into your head when your hear the word "nurse"?
- role models—who takes out the garbage and who does the laundry?

Behavior guidance for young children can also affect perceptions about self. If a child is punished for normal exploration, he will soon come to believe that his curious nature is wrong. A child who is, constantly demeaned—he is stupid, worthless, a nuisance, a jerk—will come to believe that he really is, and the mantra becomes a self-fulfilling prophecy.

Activity 8.2 in your Online Companion suggests ways to evaluate gender messages in our culture.

Temperament

Sensitive adults will be able to identify the infant's temperament type among the nine sets of characteristics or three constellations suggested by Chess and Thomas (1990). It is possible that an infant's temperament may not mesh well with an adult's style. This can present a challenge to even the most responsive adult. Being aware of the goodness of fit is important. It highlights discrepancies between the expectations and interactions of adults and the infants that they care for. If a match has some troublesome aspects that challenge the caregiver, the child could be labeled difficult. This could place the child at a long-term disadvantage (Gonzalez-Mena & Eyer, 2004) that creates developmental difficulties.

How infants approach new situations, how they play, and their routine patterns are all shaped by temperament. Adults can learn to respond effectively to infants of various temperament styles, and help children recognize their own style and learn to manage that style as they mature. However, as mentioned above, not all adults' and children's styles make good combinations. In child care centers, we can alter staffing arrangements to some extent to create more effective combinations. Patterns that are either too similar or very different can present the greatest challenges. Although no adult should come to a hasty conclusion about a child in any respect, this is particularly true for temperament styles. These cannot be gauged in a short time. An analysis of consistent characteristics should be conducted over a period of weeks, not days.

PLAY

Infants **play** without having to be taught how, and this remains the core activity for learning. Play allows infants to acquire a wide range of new skills and to practice old ones.

Play becomes a little more complex for the infant as he comes to understand object permanence, uses symbolism, has greater physical skill, and uses some imitative actions. You may observe the baby playing by himself. According to Mildred Parten, the researcher who categorized six stages of play in the 1930s, this is the type of play known as **solitary play**. Babies may explore objects and repeat actions that cause a particular response. Typically, infants are intrigued by new toys and ideas, and although they want enjoyable activities repeated, they also like things that have novelty value.

This stage allows for wonderful advances in the infant's play behaviors. Until now the infant's physical ability to manipulate objects and basic schemes associated with her experience has limited the scope of her play. Leading up to this stage has been **discovery play**—which will continue in increasingly complex forms. This involves the baby's performing actions to find out about materials and objects in her world. Essentially the play has been physical. Playful activity involving the infant's actions remain at the center of her discoveries, but now her mental

---

play

spontaneous, intrinsically motivated, enjoyable activity resulting in learning; the child's work; a means of discovery, practice for adulthood; an activity to reduce stress; a means of fostering development; a route to self-discovery; a way of learning social skills; an activity for its own sake

solitary play

spontaneous activity involving only the individual, not involving others

schemes are becoming more detailed—she knows how certain things feel and finds out what happens if she tries out particular actions.

Swinging her fist around for the sheer enjoyment of physical movement, she sees that a tower of small blocks is knocked over—and she sends them flying all over the place! She enjoys the fact that she has influence—she can make something happen. Repeating the activity many times provides amusement as well as essential learning.

This kind of play involving her senses, action, and repetition is called sensorimotor play or **practice play**. The accidental discovery that certain things happen leads to activity that is more organized. Soon intentional actions are incorporated into the play. Next time she sees a tower of blocks, she takes a deliberate swipe at them and the result is the same. Repeating this is fun and she does it over and over until her dad gets tired of building the towers! The infant has found that she has some power. She has controlled the blocks to make them fall down and she has controlled Dad because, for a short time at least, he has cooperated in rebuilding the tower. Their shared experience is even more meaningful because Dad provided some key words and exclamations as the game proceeded.

Playing with objects emerges as a prime area of interest as infants' ability to grasp objects develops. (Review the sequence of grasp skills presented earlier in this chapter.) Objects may not immediately go to the mouth, but are explored in a variety of ways. "Now the baby takes note when a plaything is unfamiliar; there is more initial interest in a new object than in a familiar one, and will hold the child's interest for a longer time. In addition, the child attends to the specific features of the objects when handling them and no longer behaves as if all objects were the same" (Hughes, 1999, p. 54). This behavior indicates another significant development in the child's ability to formulate patterns in his brain.

A word of caution here. Although everyone's brain does attend to novelty—it kind of wakes our brain up—don't think that every day a young child needs a new toy or object. There is worth in repetitive experiences, especially for younger children. Caregivers need to figure out the *optimal* balance of stimulation versus over- or understimulation and the novel versus the familiar. What is optimal is dependent on a host of factors, including the child's needs, interests, temperament, developmental level, and culture, just to mention a few. In other words, it needs to be individually appropriate. Generally, however, the baby will need items she can handle—and she is often insatiable in her craving for different kinds of material, textures, and sizes of things.

This is a peak time for **sensory play** and discovery, and the baby often wants to get right into liquids and semisolids like dough, Jell-O, and safe sensory materials. She also likes less messy

objects that she can handle, bash together, throw, and bang. Materials found in the kitchen are every bit as exciting as bought toys and play material. Babies often like to play with items such as wooden spoons, plastic containers, plastic strainers, boxes, used containers (clean and checked for safety), and other items readily at hand.

Symbolic play, also known as make-believe play, pretend play, and fantasy play, starts to emerge around the 12th month of life. Before then a child may briefly imitate actions of those around her, such as quickly putting a bottle to her own mouth. However, the child doesn't yet have a full concept of the role behind the action. In other words, there is no understanding of pretending on the child's part, it is **imitation**. Between 11 and 13 months, a transition toward symbolic play becomes more apparent. The behavior will clearly signal a pretend scenario. You see this when a child lifts a cup to

These young children are involved in a sensory play experience under the close supervision of a caregiver.

Margin glossary

practice play

spontaneous activity involving repeated actions that aid discovery

sensory play

play that involves touching, smelling, tasting, hearing and/or seeing individually or simultaneously

symbolic play

activity that involves the process of using objects, actions, or words to stand for something else; may incorporate pretense or make-believe

imitation

the act of copying single actions of another person, or the copying of complex actions, as with role models

her mouth and makes drinking sounds, pretends to eat, or bakes a cake by stirring a spoon around with no cake mixture present. This is referred to as pretense play, since the action is not related to any actual needs of the child at that moment (Frost, Wortham, & Reifel, 2005). Also, the child is utilizing **observational learning**, which provides a model that she can use to internalize roles. Actual symbolic play requires the use of one object to represent another object, or the use of an action or sound to represent something else. It might be observed when a child places a block to her ear and talks on the "telephone."

observational learning

learning by watching people's behavior

Babies will usually need items that are realistic substitutes for the real thing. The infant will often use the small-sized version of the adult item in predictable and realistic ways. At times the baby may surprise us by imitating an adult's action some time after the event was first seen. This is an example of **deferred imitation**—mimicking after the action has disappeared. These may appear to be disconnected and separate actions, but they have some internalized meaning, if only the recognition that "this is what grown-up people do." We might see a baby reaching out her arm and dropping things—this might be an imitation of the educator handing out items to each toddler, but we cannot always be correct about the links that the infant makes between actions and their meanings. So far, any of these imitations tend to be short sequences. In time they will lengthen and involve stringing together a series of actions; this will be a demonstration of **role modeling**. Real objects tend to prompt role modeling for the very young child, so items like a play phone, cup, or other small object might promote acting out a role. Interestingly, infants at this stage may also copy each other in their actions—this is observational learning—but the infant is still behaving in a way that is mostly characteristic of solitary play.

deferred imitation

copying single behaviors or complex roles some time after the initial observation of the behavior

role modeling

demonstrating appropriate actions and reactions through behavior; the set of actions associated with particular roles or jobs

Adults cannot always tell the degree to which the infant is using symbolism, because she may have an idea in her mind that we cannot interpret from her actions. As the baby's first words appear—they, too, are symbols, since words stand for meanings—the infant's symbolic play may become enriched. "Both language and symbolic play require the ability to represent reality to oneself through the use of symbols, the substitution of one thing for another; it is, therefore, not surprising to see developmental parallels between the two" (Hughes, 1999, p. 62).

Children at about 1 year of age will play for increasingly long periods of time if they are engaged in the experience. In particular, they will extend the play if they have greater control over what happens—they like activities where they can control some element of the outcome, and with toys that offer a response to the baby. Although infants seem to have an innate ability to sort and organize things, the baby does not yet categorize objects according to their **attributes**. She may match two or more items that seem to belong together, but her sense of classifying may not be the same as ours. Where we might sort by shape or color, the baby might sort by what she likes or what she doesn't like, or some other criteria we cannot determine.

During this stage, the infant may be involved with object play in increasingly specific ways. In **functional play** (Berk, 2004; Charlesworth, 2004), the infant connects two or more objects. Very young infants may play with multiple items without making any obviously meaningful connection between them, but by 12 months most have made connections based on the functions of the objects. The infant might put a phone handset back on the receiver, for example, or place a small figure inside a toy car.

The infant's centeredness on herself is apparent, but she enjoys lots of adult involvement in her play. She likes the adult to repeat activities, such as partially hiding a toy and recovering it, building up towers of blocks so she can knock them down, and repeating the same short rhyme. The adult may also encourage the infant to pull himself up, stand, cruise, or, later, walk. By the end of this stage, many infants will be playing interactive games such as pat-a-cake (Sheridan, 2001; Sluss, 2005).

An example of deferred imitation is demonstrated by this child. He has been learning "patty-cake," and several times on this day he initiated the patting gesture to indicate to his caregiver that he wanted to sing the song.

Infants at this stage are not too young to enjoy books. Some books for very young children include furry, smooth, and rough textures in the illustrations; infants may enjoy exploring these with their fingers.

attributes

characteristics of a person, thing, or object, such as color, shape, or size

functional play

exploring a toy to see how it works; this begins with combination play, such as banging toys against each other or a surface, emptying containers (dumping), and knocking blocks down

consciousness

a function of the mind that is awareness of a person's self, environment, and mental activity; may choose courses of actions; there are several observable levels of consciousness; the "problem of consciousness" lies in its complexity; philosophers, neuroscientists, and many others define consciousness differently; consciousness concerns functions of the brain, behavior, mind, and soul or spirit

BOX 8.3

WAYS TO SUPPORT LANGUAGE AND LITERACY FOR INFANTS AND TODDLERS

Children need relationships with caring adults who engage in many one-to-one, face-to-face interactions with them to support their oral language development and lay the foundation for later literacy learning. Important experiences and teaching behaviors include but are not limited to:

- talking to babies and toddlers with simple language, frequent eye contact, and responsiveness to children's cues and language attempts;
- frequently playing with, talking to, singing to, and doing finger-plays with young children;
- sharing cardboard books with babies and frequently reading to toddlers on the adult's lap or together with one or two other children; and
- providing simple art materials such as crayons, markers, and large paper for toddlers to explore and manipulate. (Neuman, Copple, & Bredekamp, 2000, p. 18)

Cuddling with an infant while reading a very simple story or pointing out a few objects in a book is a positive break from other play situations. It helps to build a child's vocabulary and establish a familiarity with books as sources of learning and enjoyment. Books are also an excellent way to present culturally familiar images to children of diverse backgrounds. Box 8.3 has additional information on supporting oral language and enhancing a foundation in literacy for young children.

Reading books to children is very important, but what research documents is that it is really the discussion that ensues before, during, and after reading that enhances and supports literacy development. It is these shared moments that reveal to the child a love of language but also demonstrates the power that words can have in our lives. It offers opportunities for family members and caregivers to share beliefs, values, hopes, and dreams, and offers the child an entrée into the world of thoughts, imagination, and creativity. Don't miss the chance to give these gifts to children!

The importance of reading to children cannot be overemphasized! Look at the intense concentration on these young faces! They are entering a wonderful world.

BEING AN INFANT—A PHENOMENOLOGICAL APPROACH

Several times, we have mentioned **consciousness**. Before this stage, it is difficult to know to what extent the baby has consciousness. She obviously does in the sense of responding to stimuli, building schemes of understanding, being alert, and making relationships, but to what extent is she reacting on a biological level? True consciousness involves being aware of being aware. So, using that definition, when does the baby become conscious? Some answers come from phenomenologists, but they reframe the question. They are more likely to wonder what it's like to be a baby. They think they are most likely to get some idea about a baby's consciousness through that exploration. Several interesting studies have been conducted using a phenomenological research method. Rather than try to answer the question in relation to all children in all situations, most phenomenologists choose to focus on one area of a baby's experience.

In seeking the baby's experience, it is assumed that experience includes some level of consciousness of that experience. The following situations are some that have been explored in order to try to reach the essence of the baby's experience: finger-play, diapering, crying, and breast-feeding. The conclusions cannot be *generalized*—taken as applicable to other situations—but reading them gives a sense of how the baby experiences her world. Even casual observation conducted at the child's eye level can bring some interesting perspectives. We cannot "unknow" what we know, so this presents particularly difficult challenges for the infant phenomenologist. Our perceptions of childhood, made up of our memories of experience, being with other children, perhaps rearing our own children, and, of course, studying children from the traditional approaches of behaviorism, cognitive psychology, or other schools of thought, further compromise our ability to understand what it feels like to be an infant. One way to try, when documenting the experience of being a baby from your own perspective, is to leave aside your perceptions and analysis of the infant (called bracketing) and try to get into the moment by engaging with the infant. Being part of the dyad is more likely to enable you to reach the child's perspective.

Another way to try to understand the baby's perspective is to read sympathetic writings describing infants. Selma Fraiberg's (1959/1996) understanding of early childhood shines through in her account entitled *The Magic Years*. In particular, her description of "becoming a person" is delightfully sensitive and, although recorded from the adult's perspective, offers detail that leads us to understand who the child is, her behavior, and, most importantly, what is going on underneath her behavior. Kaplan's 1978 book *Oneness and Separateness* also attempts to view the process of a psychological birth from a young child's perspective. Only by entering her world through careful observation, reflection, and engagement can we begin to know what it is like to be a baby.

PARTICULAR NEEDS

Not only does the infant require that her basic needs are met—such as food, clothes, and diaper changes—but she also requires physical contact and emotional connection. Her psychological needs are of paramount importance because of the critical period of her socio-emotional development.

Movement and Stimulation

Mobility, whether in the form of crawling or walking, changes the child's perspective and alters the way he can take hold of the world and make it his own. Many infants continue crawling for some time. Even when they can walk, their crawling skill allows them to get where they want to go much faster. An infant needs lots of time and opportunity to move. Warm, uncluttered floor space is essential, but he also needs large pieces of furniture that he can use to cruise along when he is ready. He especially needs objects that he can safely use to pull himself to his feet.

With his improved physical control, the infant wants to explore his environment. He needs to be enabled to do this. Because the infant is able to crawl, or otherwise move toward, desired objects, he needs playthings that require the use of fine motor skills. Sensory exploration is the central theme of development at this stage, so the adult must provide a variety of safe and interesting materials. The infant may continue to mouth objects, so everything must be safe and clean.

You need to "be the baby" if you are to adopt a phenomenological approach. Getting down to the baby's eye level can be helpful, since it points out how stark the floors and walls often are.

Language

Infants at this stage are extremely receptive to what they hear and see. They copy many of the sounds that adults produce. Adult involvement in assisting language acquisition is essential. This scaffolding is needed to make links among objects, people, and actions so the baby can make meaning for herself, using simple, clear words, reinforcing them with gestures, and repeating the actions and words. This can be made fun by using action rhymes and looking at board books, but also by seeing the possibilities for learning that exist in everyday routines. Through these types of interactions, babbling and standard language can be linked.

The Additional Support section of your Online Companion has a listing of some simple finger-plays to use with children at this age.

Social Connections and Emotional Support

Infants at 9–12 months are very interested in people, and will try to get adults to join their games. Adult involvement in an infant's activities is essential to offer encouragement and stimulation and to increase the infant's comfort with such social situations. Adults need to be able to read the child's expressions and body language to interpret meanings. Shared meanings are a key part of the child's social development. Only time and attention to the infant can develop these shared meanings.

Infants at this stage search the faces of adults for familiarity and encouragement. The adults must be available to the infant for prolonged and uninterrupted periods. If the infant makes attachments with multiple adults, these need to be reinforced with ongoing, consistent caregiving.

Mealtimes can be messy, but this 1-year-old is managing to get some of the food into his mouth. The sensory experience seems to be enjoyable. Also, imagine how great he must feel to be doing this himself!

Nutrition and Mealtimes

Mealtimes can begin to be a very pleasant social occasion. It is never too early to provide a positive role model, so you spend time with the infants, modeling appropriate behavior at the table, and setting the tone for the social interactions. Babies continue to need milk as their primary source of nutrients. Of course, breast milk is best, although by age 1 many babies will begin drinking from a cup.

By this stage, infants will usually have tried a variety of different foods, and might have some clear preferences. Offer small portions of foods the child dislikes along with ones he likes. If the infant is hungry, he will eat some of each. Although balanced nutrition is most important, you want to avoid battles over eating. Mealtimes should not be associated with stress.

DEVELOPMENTAL VARIATION

Growth charts indicate that infants at this stage present a widening range of weight and height. Although many babies will triple their birth weight in 12 months, not all babies will reach this milestone as soon, and many others will surpass it. Remember that gradual progression is more important than actual measures. Professional use of growth charts can be helpful in detecting signs of nutritional or developmental issues.

A wide range of developmental stages are also evident at this age. While some babies are trying to sit unsupported, others will have control of their legs and will have been crawling for some time, or will have progressed straight to cruising and walking. Parents and educators may have concerns about these differences, but development is not a race. Those who are "ahead" have few advantages over those who develop at a slower pace.

Concerns about developmental differences might lead families to have their infant assessed by a specialist. Such an assessment may reveal a problem, but is far more likely to indicate an individual pattern that remains within the norm. Educators and families can help each other by sharing information and discussing developmental issues. If a thorough assessment is needed, both parties can contribute to this; both the family members and the educators have pertinent information to offer during the assessment process. Once the results of an assessment are known, frequently the families and educators can devise a plan together to support the infant's development.

DEVELOPMENTAL ALERTS

The American Academy of Pediatrics (AAP) stresses the importance of an ongoing screening process at each well-child visit, and recommends eliciting and valuing parental concerns regarding age-appropriate skills in each developmental domain. Some studies (Glascoe, 1997) have demonstrated that parents are often proficient at detecting developmental deficits, but they often tend to focus on behavior and emotional issues and/or speech–language skills, rather than global deficits. The administration of screening measures with monitor multiple developmental domains is the best recourse. These would include: the Ages and Stages Questionnaire; the BRIGANCE® Screens; the Child Development Inventories; the Parents' Evaluations of Developmental Status; and The Checklist for Autism in Toddlers (CHAT). With all these tools, if a concern is detected then a child can be referred for an assessment.

Autism

autism

a condition in which the individual demonstrates social isolation and communication difficulties

Autism is a little-understood syndrome that results in severe introversion or self-absorption. Autistic children are unable to form relationships, may have difficulties with speech and language, repeat behaviors for prolonged periods, and respond negatively to new circumstances. Since young children may display these kinds of behavior for a variety of reasons, the disorder can be difficult to diagnose. With the variety of symptoms, it may take time to arrive at a diagnosis of autism. By the same token, children may be assumed to be autistic when in fact they are simply slow to warm up to people or to communicate, or are onlookers rather than doers.

Approximately 1 in 500 children is diagnosed with the syndrome of autism. However, often that diagnosis is not made until or after late preschool age because appropriate tools for routine developmental screening have not been readily available, especially tools for use with very young children. Efforts for the development of tools that are valid and reliable instruments are ongoing. The designs of some of these tools include techniques for identifying the behavior markers outlined in Box 8.4. One type of behavior not included in the indicator list concerns movement milestones such as righting, sitting, crawling, and walking. According to Teitelbaum and associates (1998, 2002), analysis of movement during infancy

---

BOX 8.4

KEY INDICATORS FOR DEVELOPMENTAL DELAY

Lack of acquisition of the following milestones within known accepted and established ranges is considered abnormal:

echolalia

the infant's repetitive babbling of one sound; the repetition or echoing of verbal utterances made by another person

- no babbling by 12 months;
- no gesturing (e.g., pointing, waving bye-bye) by 12 months;
- no single words by 16 months;
- no two-word spontaneous (not just **echolalia**) phrases by 24 months; and
- loss of any language or social skills at any age.

BOX 8.5

KEY MARKERS FOR AUTISTIC BEHAVIOR IN VERY YOUNG CHILDREN—EVEN INFANTS

Zwaigenbaum et al. (2005) believe there may be at least 5–7 "flags" for identifying autism in children, even infants, including:

- Failure to respond to their name;
- A lack of solo babbling and lack of babbling in response to the speech of others;
- Difficulty tracking an object moving across the field of vision;
- Difficulty making eye contact;
- Failure to smile in response to the smiles of others;
- Difficulty changing focus from one object to another (for example, between two shaking rattles);
- Inability to imitate actions of others;
- Difficulty with nonverbal communication facial expressions, gestures; and
- A failure to point at objects in the distance (for example, if there is an airplane in the distance, the child will not point to it to share his interest with others).

might serve as an earlier indicator than any other method presently available. Designing instruments that help assess children correctly is important because the earlier that autism can be identified, the earlier treatment can begin. Early intervention improves outcomes for most children because social and communicative behaviors can be fostered or developed and autistic behaviors modified (Filipek et al., 1999; Zwaigenbaum, Bryson, Rogers, Roberts, Brian, & Szatmari, 2005).

Because there are no biological markers for autism, identification must focus on behavior. Review the information presented in Box 8.5. (You can also check out the "Autism—'red flags'" Web site listed in the Useful Web Sites section at the end of this chapter.) This information is crucial for caregivers who may be observing children during the majority of their waking hours.

Educators have to guard against a tendency to be hasty in suggesting that a child may be autistic. Some young children may have attachment difficulties or communication styles that are wrongly attributed to autism. Children may also make attachments to objects, a characteristic of autistic children, but this may simply be a phase. These children need support, but not to the degree that follows a diagnosis of autism.

The suspicion that a child is autistic may come from the observations of family members or educators, but a diagnosis can be made only after clinical assessment. Infants and young children with autism can usually be accommodated within a child care center. The typical management technique is to retain the same behavioral expectations for these children as for others of the same age. Families are likely to be concerned that caregivers and educators provide adequate care and proper strategies for the autistic child. Educators should work closely with families to carry out the directions of the specialist.

The Additional Support section of your Online Companion has some links to information about autism and the CHAT assessment.

FAMILIES AS PARTNERS IN CARE

Effective communication between families and educators is always important, but never more so than when there are development concerns about an infant, especially ones as serious and difficult to diagnose as autism. Yet educators can be so concerned about communicating important information to families that they forget that listening is also essential for two-way communication. Box 8.6 outlines strategies for developing listening skills, which are indispensable if educators are to work effectively with families in the care of children.

BOX 8.6

DEVELOP YOUR LISTENING SKILLS

It is particularly important for educators to develop their listening skills when they are communicating with family members. Such skill development can include:

- ensuring that the atmosphere is conducive to talking;
- providing the time for communication;
- encouraging the parent to share his thoughts, using verbal sounds indicating listening;
- paraphrasing what the parent said to show that you are listening and understand what's being said;
- adding "I hear you" comments to acknowledge the parent's feelings;
- mirroring body language to show sympathy;
- maintaining appropriate eye contact; and
- responding positively so that the family member feels heard.

All this can be challenging, especially while you are on duty with infants or toddlers. You might find it helpful to set aside some time for such conversations in the early evening. Alternatively, you might arrange for a telephone conversation at a mutually convenient time or have another staff person cover for you so you can talk without interruption.

As **early childhood educators** are aware, communication is not always verbal. Heightened awareness of body language and reading young children's cues can lead us to apply the same skills to adults. This can be useful, but it can also lead to some assumptions that can be particularly misleading when the family member cannot tell us, in English, that we have misunderstood. English-speaking people themselves come from various traditions and have many socially learned behaviors that are particular to their background. These behaviors include their body language. Culturally shaped behavior, for example, leads some people to indicate yes with a sign that, for others, means no. This is just one example in which gestures could be read incorrectly. You will want to become familiar with the cultural styles of your family group before jumping to any conclusion about what their body language says.

early childhood educator

a prepared individual who is qualified to meet the developmental, caregiving, health, and educational needs of infants, toddlers, and preschool-age children (and sometimes school-age children); works with parents and families, in accordance with professional and ethical practices

The Additional Support section in your Online Companion has some information regarding body language and nonverbal behavior that will be useful when interacting with adults.

As we saw in the introduction to this chapter, a few moments spent in conversation with the parent who is dropping off a child at the center can help to reassure a nervous parent that the child is receiving responsive, high-quality care. This is also a good time for the family member to inform the caregiver of particular concerns or requests. However, since at this time the caregiver may be responsible for several children, a more involved conversation might have to be rescheduled for off-hours.

HEALTH CONCERNS

Hygiene

As infants become mobile, they are increasingly able to get into everything in sight. Thus, caregivers must be extremely careful about the hygiene of the environment and the spread of infection. Steps need to be taken to ensure that all toys are washed and they are not passed from mouth to mouth. Child care centers must have enough toys that they can be washed and that more than one infant can play with the same sort of toy.

Just as the environment must be hygienic, the same concerns apply to people within the environment. The best way to limit the spread of infection is to wash hands. This includes the infant's hands, as well as your own.

This is an important issue, but a balance must be maintained, since children need to get messy. If you are constantly changing their clothing, washing their hands, and wiping their faces, they will learn that even a little bit of mess is not acceptable. Remember, at this age, they are utilizing the technique of social referencing to help mediate their behaviors and reactions. If they are messy and your body language and facial expression is sending them a clear message of "Yuck," then they will likely adjust their behavior and reaction to match yours. Besides, there is that old saying, "You have to eat a peck of dirt before you die!"

> Keeping toys clean in infant and young toddler rooms is always a challenge. One of the best methods I observed was at a site that used large rubber tubs to track the toy use. They had different tubs for each day of the week and then they would rotate them. The tubs contained similar toys, but they only used the Monday tubs on Monday. That night, the toys would be disinfected and placed back in the correct container and not used for one week. This ensured that bacteria had no chance of surviving and being passed around. It was expensive to organize the tubs initially, but the staff felt that it was worth it because of the long-term gains in reduced infections.

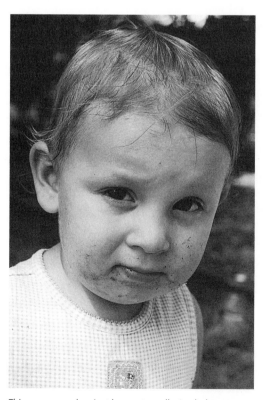

This young one has just begun to walk. A whole new world of exploration has opened up. Her caregivers are mindful that she has to be safeguarded, but they also know that some dirt on her face can remain for a while.

Dental Health

Teeth come through at different times, and by this stage many infants will have some teeth. As soon as a child has one tooth, dental hygiene becomes especially important, although babies' gums should have been wiped if they consumed something with sugar. Each child should have his own toothbrush, and brushing should occur regularly. A smear of toothpaste on a cloth or soft brush will enable you to clean the baby's teeth. The possibility of dental decay can be reduced if fruit juices or sweetened drinks are avoided, especially at sleep time. Of special note: each state has different regulations regarding the cleaning and storing of toothbrushes, so be sure to check out the requirements in your state.

SIGNS OF POTENTIAL NEGLECT OR ABUSE

Guidance and Discipline: What Is the Difference?

The early childhood profession wants to emphasize the concept of behavior guidance rather than discipline because the word "discipline" often conjures up the notion of "punishment," and that response is not developmentally appropriate (Gartrell, 2004; Miller, 2007). Guiding a child's behavior involves supporting the child's development in a positive and encouraging way. Discipline may use many of the same techniques as guidance, but it attempts to control and shape behaviors in accordance with the adult's perspective. With guidance strategies, the child learns self-control, and is empowered to operate independently; with discipline, the child learns who is boss and who holds the power in the relationship—and it's not her.

There are historical differences in the emphasis given to guidance and discipline. These differences reflect changing views of the nature of children and the role of adults. Current thinking focuses on the need to support and guide the young child rather than mold and discipline her (Gartrell, 2004; Miller, 2007). The role of the adult has changed to fit this child-centered approach. But not all people agree with this approach. Some educational circles have returned to more adult control, presumably in reaction to a perceived lack of self-discipline in older children.

In addition to historical differences, diverse cultures may emphasize guidance over discipline, or vice versa (Miller, 2007). Some cultures believe that infants and toddlers should be entirely unrestricted. Others believe that firm discipline is essential. In some families, parents from different backgrounds may not agree on the level of discipline. This may result in one parent thinking it necessary to meet every need and desire of the young child, while the other thinks the baby should be left to cry rather than be spoiled with too much attention. Experts, including T. Berry Brazelton (1992), agree that *children under the age of 6 months cannot be spoiled*. The term spoiled means damaged. Could an infant really be damaged by having her needs met? Of course not! For babies, there is no distinction between need and want. It is only adults who can distinguish the difference between those two concepts. If the child's needs are not met, then the relationship of trust is damaged. After 6 months of age, babies need support and understanding in helping them establish self-regulation skills, so adults gradually encourage self-calming techniques and wait time. A caring adult will eventually develop high expectations for behavior, but the expectations will align with the developmental age of the child. These hints can help a child develop the competencies to eventually meet his own needs.

- Learn the baby's cues and signals, because if interpreted correctly, the baby will have his needs met when required, but will also have times when he can soothe himself.
- Remember, social referencing frames a child's behavior. If you appear anxious and worried, these reactions are telegraphed to the child, who, in turn, may become more needy and anxious.
- Don't constantly rescue a child. Encounters with minor stress and frustration can actually be a great learning opportunity for the child.

As educators, we will find that our work with families continually leads us to question the values that underpin our practice. What is desirable, what is acceptable, and what is not? A useful indicator may be what we know about children from experience and from our child development study. If we use this knowledge wisely, we might realize that children develop their potential if they feel positive about themselves and their achievements, if they know who they are and can make decisions about what is right or wrong, if they internalize role models and can think critically, given the chance. If these observations are accurate, they suggest that guidance is more appropriate than discipline. Thus, we can contend that positive guidance is desirable, and that discipline, with its connotations of power and control, is not. Box 8. 7 offers some helpful hints on strategies to employ when making decisions about behavior guidance. Activity 8.3 in your Online Companion encourages you to examine the topic of behavior guidance more thoroughly.

Review "What Grown-ups Understand about Child Development" in the Additional Support section and Activity 8.3 in your Online Companion.

Is Discipline Ever Too Much?

So are families who use discipline being abusive or neglectful? Many of the classic definitions of child abuse include mention of a community standard that is commonly accepted. This standard is clear in extreme cases, but it is muddier in other situations where values conflict. To further complicate matters, child protection workers are charged with major legal and moral responsibilities, and yet agencies are often understaffed and overburdened. As a result, workers may be forced to make hasty decisions and apply personal values as well as subtle interpretations of the law. Is the parent who continually does not respond to the baby's crying continually being abusive? In light of the values in this book, yes. But this alone will probably not attract

---

BOX 8.7

BEHAVIOR GUIDANCE STRATEGIES

Remember, children are born into this world knowing nothing about expected behaviors. Adult responsibilities include guiding children in their learning about acceptable and unacceptable behavior. This means that eventually limits must be defined for children, and children actually feel more secure when limits are set. The following are some suggestions for you to think about when stymied by a child's behavior.

- Try not to judge a child by her behavior. Dorothy Briggs (1975) in her book *Your Child's Self Esteem* pointed out that "judgments are smoke screens which prevent love from coming through" (p. 88). Judgment will cloud your decision-making.
- Consider the child's age and stage of development. Would the behavior be consistent with either of them? Often children are punished for behavior that is appropriate for their age. This is termed "mistaken" behavior. This means that the adults who are caring for children need to examine their own expectations for children's behavior. Are the expectations reasonable and in line with the child's age and stage? An 18-month-old child is not a 3-year-old child.
- Carefully examine the environment in your classroom. Is it contributing to inappropriate behavior? This could include issues such as room arrangement, food and rest schedules, groupings of particular children, or equipment, either too little or too much.
- Temperaments of children and caregivers have to be considered. Is there a good match between these individuals? Obviously, accommodation by adults is easier than for a young child.
- Remember, each individual is unique, and has individual needs and abilities. Sometimes a child's unique approach is not appreciated unless an adult is willing to recalibrate her view of the "big picture."
- Assess whether a lack of prior experience in a particular area of development is contributing to inappropriate behavior. Family input could be very helpful here.
- Never use time out with infants and toddlers. This is often recommended for use with young children, but it tends to be ineffective. Children at this age do not understand why their behavior is unacceptable, nor should they ever be isolated because of safety concerns and social needs. I contend that it is usually the adult who needs the timeout, not the child.

---

the attention of child protection agencies. If the parent were poor, or on welfare, or had a history of petty crime, or lived in a place with thin walls, the child protection agency might be alerted to the crying baby. These other factors might influence people's perception of the situation, further muddying the supposed community standard.

Child abuse or neglect exists where a child is treated improperly, physically hurt, denied basic needs, emotionally manipulated, or otherwise damaged. That means that while discipline can be considered acceptable, inappropriate use of power over the child is definitely wrong. The shades of gray in between will remain a topic of discussion in later chapters.

See the section on neglect in the Additional Support section in your Online Companion.

EVERYDAY SAFETY ISSUES

The mobility of 9- to 12-month-old infants brings an ever-increasing risk of new safety concerns. Children are no longer stationary, and so their world expands. With improved fine motor skills, many more objects can be placed in their mouths. Any toy that is small enough to fit

Every child care facility should purchase a choke tube and assess the safety of the toys in the classroom.

through a 1.75-inch circle is unsafe for children under 3 years of age. If care is provided in a multi-aged group setting, additional challenges are present:

- Don't allow young children to play with toys designed for older children. Teach older children to put their toys away as soon as they finish playing so young children can't get them.
- Frequently check under furniture and between cushions for dangerous items young children could find, including:
- coins
- marbles
- watch batteries (the ones that look like buttons)
- pen or marker caps
- cars with small rubber wheels that come off
- food items such as hard candy or nuts that may have fallen to the floor

If there is a doubt, use a choke tube (see photo) to check the safety of an item. Any item that fits into the tube is a possible choking hazard. If you do not have a choke tube, substitute a toilet paper tube. Since it has approximately the same dimensions, it can also be used to help you screen any items that should not be handled by children under 3. For additional information on safety issues for this age group, consult the "Everyday Health and Safety Issues" section of your Online Companion.

STARTING POINTS FOR RESPONSE

Responsive Caregiving

Emerging skills are the focus of this period. The caregiver needs to observe each infant to determine individual patterns of development. Responses must always combine emotional and practical support. The infant still needs lots of cuddles, smiles, and playfulness. The caregiver's job is to make experiences enjoyable and to extend learning opportunities as they appear. Tuning in to the infant's needs remains important. Box 8.8 offers suggestions for getting in tune with an infant at this stage. The infant will be able to let you know whether what you are doing is right or wrong.

Supportive Guidance

The infant's developing self-concept needs support. The infant knows that he is a separate person and that he can have some effect on the people and things in his world, but he doesn't yet recognize himself in the mirror. He likes to play games where he can repeat enjoyable actions, and he is starting to solve little problems as he plays. Play opportunity is the core activity of this age. The infant needs opportunities to discover everything, with the adult's help. Transition times can be challenging, because the infant tends to be firmly attached to one adult. Caregiving strategies need to take into account his fear of strangers and possible separation anxiety.

Facilitating Development

Sensory exploration as well as body exploration is playful learning at this stage. You might remove the infant's shoes and socks so he can reach and explore his toes. Light clothing—or none at all—allows the infant to more fully experience the sensations of rolling, sitting, and looking at himself.

BOX 8.8

GETTING IN TUNE WITH INFANTS AT 9 TO 12 MONTHS

Below are some starting points for building your responsive skills with a 9- to 12-month-old infant. This list is not comprehensive, and many more suggestions can be found in your Online Companion under the section titled "Getting in Tune with Infants, Toddlers, and Twos."

- Enjoy play experiences on the baby's level.
- Imitate the baby's sound production, and assist by reshaping sounds into words.
- Respond quickly to needs and requests.
- Provide simple choices.
- Identify and accommodate the baby's level of mobility, providing space and large objects/furniture for pulling herself up into a standing position.
- Have photographs visible of the infant and family members.
- Introduce a few safe, smaller objects to test the baby's pincer grasp.
- Introduce board books and a wider range of pictures.
- Demonstrate caring behaviors with dolls.
- Use words and gestures simultaneously; repeat words and simple phrases with actions to make links.
- Provide a language-rich environment with conversation, rhymes, poems, and stories.
- Sing action rhymes.
- Slightly exaggerate your facial expressions.
- Maintain eye contact, particularly as the infant begins to move away from you.
- Acknowledge the range of the infant's feelings as they are demonstrated.
- Allow safe risk taking so the baby experiences minor consequences.
- Ensure that floor space is warm when infants are on the floor for extended periods.
- Encourage the baby to be actively involved with dressing/undressing.

External stimulation should match the infant's interests. At this stage, babies tend to be attracted to bright colors and patterns. A baby wants to engage adults in his play because he likes the attention and they provide him with increased understanding of what is happening. His language may start to emerge soon. At this stage, the baby needs lots of talking and listening to prepare for the language explosion that is about to occur.

pronation

- After initial ground contact, the foot is designed to roll inward to disperse shock
- Over-pronators roll in too much. This causes excessive movement of the foot and lower leg.
- Under-pronators have feet that don't roll enough after ground contact.

It is so important for a baby to experience sensory feedback through the bottoms of his feet. Many child care facilities are no longer allowing babies to be barefooted because of liability concerns. As professional educators, we need to balance what we give up against what is gained. The tactile feedback children receive makes connections in the brain. These connections eventually help to create children who have a stronger foundation for future learning. By the age of 2 shoes should be worn most of the time to protect against compromised **pronation**, but as they are learning to walk, let them have the occasional glorious sensation of being barefooted.

Activities

Your Online Companion and CD-ROM contain activities to help you increase your skills while engaging infants in caregiving routines, play, and supportive guidance.

On your CD-ROM, Activity 8.4 helps you develop ways of engaging in the experience of babies at this stage and extending your interactions with them. They always start from the framework of observation. Activity 8.5 helps you create responsive curriculum for each infant at 9–12 months and to develop activities that are targeted to individual interests and skill levels. Activity 8.6 includes suggestions for further experiences and interactions. Activity 8.7 describes several possible scenarios for responsive guidance.

Remember to check the Book section and Toy section in your Online Companion for suggestions of materials to use with children at this stage of development.

SUMMARY

The increased physical skills, size, and ability to handle items in her environment have led to more sophisticated activity for the infant. She tends to want to discover the properties of materials, enjoys object play, and is actively involved with everything around her. With her increasing attention to detail and longer attention span, she plays in a solitary way as well as with adults. Her play may show features of symbolism as she learns through observation and imitation of adults and older children.

When confronted with new situations or materials, she enjoys sensory discovery. When she does something by accident the first time, she may repeat the actions for fun: This also has an important neurological function. Her endless practice play can be demanding for the adult, but she enjoys being able to attract attention and have the adult play her game. She sends out messages to adults that can be read; her gestures, facial expressions, crying, and other sound productions are the adult's cues. Her babbling involves experimentation with sound and a lot of repetition, but it is influenced by the particular language sounds that she hears. She gradually increases her understanding of what adults are saying and makes deliberate attempts to use approximations of words.

Symbolism in language coincides with symbolism in the infant's play. The baby, whose thinking remains egocentric, develops new strategies for learning that are part of the sensorimotor stage. Repetitions in language, play, and other actions all have a part in her learning.

As her cognitive development advances, so does her social and emotional development. Ideally, the baby has secure attachments to adults, but because she has a clearer understanding that things, and people, continue to exist even when they are out of her sight, she is anxious when separated from those significant people. Doing things more deliberately than before is a characteristic of this stage. We see this in play, emotional situations, and social relationships. Frequently she initiates communication with adults, and those adults who are responsive find that she enjoys prolonged engagement.

She sees herself as a separate person—something that has occurred because of the trusting bond she has with adults—and realizes she does have some power over the people and objects in her environment. With increased consciousness, the baby appears to have an awareness of herself, the people around her, and the immediate environment. If she is enabled to feel secure through having reliable people around her and having all her needs met, she will be successful in passing through the first emotional challenge of her life. Our memories of our own infancy are not accessible, but we may gain insight into what it is like to be a baby if we get down on the child's level and try to see things from her perspective.

The need for careful observation and assessment of children was discussed, with key indicators for developmental delays and autism highlighted. Communicating with families remains an important factor, and enhanced listening skills help strengthen the bond between home and school. Families, as well as caregivers, still struggle with the issues of guidance and discipline, but the concept of behavior guidance is what is practiced in developmentally appropriate settings.

The need for cleanliness in the environment and with persons is crucial for controlling infections. However, this approach needs to be balanced against the experiences young children need that will result in their getting messy. Another safety factor is choking, since children at this stage of development have increased mobility and improved fine motor coordination. Every facility should have a choke tube on hand.

At this point in the reading of this text, you should revisit your philosophy, which you started to write after the first chapter. You probably have some new ideas to add, some information to take out, and many questions yet to be answered. Write down some issues and topics you hope to learn about or examine in greater depth. Share these ideas with your instructor.

DISCUSSION QUESTIONS

1. At a staff meeting, educators discuss how well they are meeting the attachment needs of the infants. "I think I'm too focused on physical needs," says one educator. How might you reply? What strategies might you suggest to improve attachments?

2. You made a mistake when you interpreted a parent's looking away as lack of interest in what you were telling her about her child. How could you repair the situation?

3. You and your colleagues can choose five new items for the infant room for the infants who are pulling themselves to standing positions. What do you buy?

4. How much of your behavior do infants imitate, and how does this influence what you do?

5. When an infant of 9 months chokes on some mashed peas, what should you do?

ADDITIONAL RESOURCES

Further Reading

Albrecht, K., & Miller, L. G. (2000). *The comprehensive infant curriculum.* Beltsville, MD: Gryphon House.

Allen, K. E., et al. (2002). *Inclusion in early childhood programs: Children with exceptionalities* (3rd Canadian ed.). Scarborough, ON: ITP Nelson.

Berk, L. E., & Winsler, A. (1995). *Scaffolding children's learning: Vygotsky and early childhood education.* Washington, DC: NAEYC.

Bos, B., & Chapman, J. (2005). *Tumbling over the edge: A rant for children's play.* Shingle Springs, CA: Finishline-Print Specialist.

Briggs, D. C. (1975). *Your child's self esteem.* USA: Main Street Books

Bronson, M. (2000). *Self-regulation in early childhood: Nature and nurture.* New York: Guilford Press.

Cassidy, J., & Shaver, P. R. (Eds.). (1999). *Handbook of attachment: Theory, research, and clinical applications.* New York: Guilford Press.

Cryer, D., Harms, T., & Bourland, B. (1987). *Active learning for infants.* New York: Addison-Wesley.

Douglas, A. (2002). *The mother of all baby books.* New York: Wiley Publishing, Inc.

Fraiberg, S. (1959/1996). *The magic years.* New York: Fireside/Simon & Schuster.

Gartrell, D. (2004). *The power of guidance: Teaching social-emotional skills in early childhood classrooms.* Clifton Park, NY: Thomson Delmar Learning. (Also available from NAEYC)

Gowen, J. W. (1995). The early development of symbolic play. *Young Children, 50* (3), 75–84.

Greenspan, S., & Greenspan, N. (1994) *First feelings* New York: Penguin Books.

Greenman, J., & Stonehouse, A. (1996). *Prime times.* St. Paul, MN: Redleaf Press

Herr, J., & Swim, T. (2003). *Making sounds, making music, and many other activities; 7–12 months.* Clifton Park, NY: Thomson Delmar Learning.

Hughes, F. P. (1999). *Children, play, and development* (3rd ed.). Boston: Allyn & Bacon.

Karen, R. (1994). *Becoming attached: Unfolding the mystery of the infant–mother bond and its impact on later life.* New York: Warner Books.

Klein, T. P., Wirth, D., & Linas, K. (2004). Play: Children's context for development. In D. Koralek (Ed.), *Spotlight on young children and play.* Washington, D.C.: NAEYC, pp. 28–35.

Lally, J., et al. (1995). *Caring for infants and toddlers in groups: Developmentally appropriate practice.* Washington, DC: ZERO TO THREE.

Miller, D. F. (2004). *Positive child guidance* (4th ed.). Clifton Park, NY: Thomson Delmar Learning.

Pimento, B., & D. Kernested. (2000). *Healthy foundations in child care* (2nd ed.). Scarborough, ON: Nelson Thomson.

Raines, S., Miller, K., & Curry-Rood, L. (2002). *Story stretchers for infants, toddlers, and twos: Experiences, activities, and games for popular children's books.* Beltsville, MD: Gryphon House.

Rimer, P., & Prager. B. (1997). *Reaching out: Working together to identify and respond to child victims of abuse.* Scarborough, ON: ITP Nelson.

Rogers, C. S., & Sawyer, J. K. (1988). *Play in the lives of children.* Washington, D.C.: NAEYC.

Shore, R. (1997). *Rethinking the brain: New insights into early development.* New York: Families and Work Institute.

Silberg, J. (2001). *Games to play with babies* (3rd ed.). Beltsville, MD: Gryphon House.

Weitzman, E., & Greenberg, J. (2002). *Learning language and loving it* (2nd ed.). Toronto, ON: Beacon Harold Fine Printing. Available from NAEYC.

Useful Videos

First Person: Impressions of Being a Baby. [30 minutes] Available from Child Development Media, Inc. http://www.childdevmedia.com/

Let Babies Be Babies: Caring For Infants and Toddlers with Love and Respect. Winnipeg, MN: The Manitoba Child Care Association (MCCA).

Understanding Special Needs Videos (Videos #31–35). #31. Caring for Infants Exposed to Crack/Cocaine and Other Drugs. (1993). Georgetown University Child Development Center and the National Maternal and Child Health Resource Center, Washington, DC

Description: This video was developed to show birth parents, foster parents, adoptive parents, grandparents, and other family members how to care for infants exposed to crack and other drugs. It is also recommended as a training tool for providers of services to these infants and their families. The video illustrates the difficult behaviors that these babies may demonstrate and identifies specific techniques to deal with these behaviors. It also identifies specific techniques that can be used to help a baby go to sleep, respond during alert times, reach and kick, and eat well. It emphasizes throughout the important role of the baby's primary caretaker.

Early Messages: Facilitating Language Development and Communication. WestEd, Center for Child and Family Studies, California Department of Ed., Child Development Division.

Together in Care: Meeting the Intimacy Needs of Infants and Toddlers in Groups.

This video presents three child care program policies that will lead to special care. Those policies include Primary Caregiver Assignment, The Use of Small Groups, and Continuity of Care. WestEd, Center for Child and Family Studies, California Department of Ed., Child Development Division.

Useful Web Sites

Affect
www.psychoanalysis.net/

Autism—"red flags"

First signs Organization
http://www.firstsigns.org
Click on Concerns About A Child, click on Red Flags

The Floortime Foundation
http://www.floortime.org/

Heimlich Maneuver
http://health.allrefer.com
Scroll to bottom, search site for 'Heimlich,' click on link for AllRefer Health – Heimlich Maneuver on Infant – Heimlich Maneuver . . .

Infant nutrition:
www.heinzbaby.com/
www.theparentreport.com/
Hover over link for Resources, click on Infant, click on Nutrition

The Interdisciplinary Council on Developmental and Learning Disorders
http://www.icdl.com/

Juvenile Product Manufacturers Association (JPMA)
www.jpma.org

Language development
National Institute on Deafness and Other Communication Disorders
http://www.nidcd.nih.gov/
also http://speech-language-therapy.com/
Click on Contents, click on Speech and Language
National Network for Child Care (U.S.):
www.nncc.org/
Click on CYFERnet, click on Early Childhood, click on Child Development

Life Seminars: Living in Families Effectively—Ask Allison—articles on a variety of issues
http://www.lifeseminars.com
Click on Ask Alison

Physical development
www.growinghealthykids.com
Click on English

Texas Women's University—Child's Play
http://www.twu.edu
Search site for Inspire, click on Adapted Physical Eduction Project INSPIRE, click on Child's Play

U.S. Consumer Product Safety Commission (CPSC)
www.cpsc.gov or 1-800-638-2772

CHAPTER 9

Becoming Toddlers: Children 12 to 18 Months

At this stage of development, this young girl's improved eye–hand coordination enables her to place a block on a structure with ease and confidence. It is likely that she will enjoy knocking over this block construction as well.

LEARNING OUTCOMES

After reading and studying this chapter, you should be able to:

- identify the observable characteristics of toddlers at the 12- to 18-months stage
- explain the significance of behaviors of toddlers between 12 and 18 months in a developmental context
- recognize and respond to the developmental diversity of 12- to 18-month-old toddlers and discuss issues pertinent to this stage of development
- assess the development of 12- to 18-month-old toddlers
- respond to the health, safety, and development needs of 12- to 18-month-old toddlers with appropriate protection, guidance, and caregiving
- develop strategies to work with parents as partners in the care and education of their toddlers

SCENE

"In the infant room we have a number of children who are up on their feet. We think of them as being mobile infants rather than toddlers," said the educator as she answered a student's question. "Sometimes we have parents visiting who ask us why they are not in the toddler room, because they are walking. I tell them that children at this age may be walking but they still have many characteristics that mean they require infant care rather than toddler care."

Parents are not the only ones who can be confused by the distinction between infants and toddlers. Back in class, a student asked, "So when does an infant become a toddler?" "That's a hard question; it depends on whether you are deciding on age or stage," responded the instructor.

"I see that some infants seek attention. Is this a sign of maturity?" asked the student. "It can be," replied the instructor. "There are many aspects to maturity: physical skills, language, cognitive advances, emotional control, and so on. But young children don't progress smoothly, they take big leaps in one domain and tiny steps in others. That's what makes the developmental process so individual, so complicated."

The student added her observations to the instructor's comments. "I've noticed that infants at this stage are trying to make sense of everything. They get into everything, and that's a safety problem. It's as though they are trying to see how everything works. But they take stuff apart, and can't put it back together." The instructor paused for a moment, and said "You've noticed an important characteristic of this stage, one that Piaget called 'the little scientist.' But every child is different and they go about things in individual patterns. Have you noticed how very young children approach things and people differently?"

Children at this age, probably more than any other, display broad variations in skill acquisition. Some children are not yet mobile; others move about rapidly. A few may be self-directed; others are more dependent. Some infants may be able to walk but still need a great deal of emotional support. Such children are probably not yet ready for a group situation in a toddler room. Other more autonomous toddlers may be striving for their independence and may fit more easily into the toddler environment. As is always the case with young children, caregivers and educators have to observe each child carefully and respond to individual differences in a supportive way.

DEVELOPMENTAL DOMAINS

Physical Development

What characterizes this period is the increased skill in the use of the body. For many young children at this stage, the most significant change is in their perspective of the world. Toddlers are beginning to see everything from a standing-up position, and they are better able to get hold of things within their reach. The toddler's new horizons present some new hazards and provide the opportunity to develop new skills.

This is the time for the big "E," suggests Fogel (2000): "expression, exploration, and experimentation." He then adds "energy" to the list!

Growth

Figure 9.1 displays growth in weight and length for female and male children in the United States, and is based on data developed by the National Center for Health Statistics (2001). Keep in mind that these growth charts may not be sensitive to cultural differences in genetic influences, but they are useful guidelines.

After an increase of about 10 inches in height in the first year, there is a slow but continual increase in weight and length, with males being, on average, slightly ahead of females. Weight continues to increase 1/4–1/2 pound per month (Allen & Marotz, 2007).

ossification

the process of converting cartilage to bone

calcification

the process of hardening, generally bone

The toddler's bones are a little less malleable, because they have **ossified** and **calcified**. The toddler's fontanels are closing after the considerable head growth during the first year of life, and will be completely closed by 18 months. Muscle mass has increased a little, and body fat has decreased (Berk, 2004). The body continues to assume more adultlike proportions, with a smaller head in relation to trunk and legs. The walking toddler takes on a more childlike appearance than that of an infant.

Obesity can become a concern at this stage. In fact, the *2002 Feeding Infants and Toddler Study* (FITS study) sponsored by Gerber interviewed over 3,000 parents and child care providers across the United States. The authors of the study gathered information about the diets and common feeding practices for infants and toddlers. The results were startling, especially in light of the new dietary guidelines issued by the U.S. Department of Health and Human Services and the Department of Agriculture in 2005. According to Dwyer, Suitor, and Hendricks (2004), the study

Figure 9.1 Weight and Length Ranges for Males and Females: 12 to 18 Months

Female Weight Ranges

Age	Low	High	50th percentile
12 Months	17 lbs	25.5 lbs	21 lbs
15 Months	19 lbs	28 lbs	23 lbs
18 Months	20 lbs	29½ lbs	24 lbs

Male Weight Ranges

Age	Low	High	50th percentile
12 Months	18.5 lbs	28 lbs	22.5 lbs
15 Months	20 lbs	30 lbs	24.5 lbs
18 Months	21 lbs	31½ lbs	25½ lbs

Female Length Ranges

Age	Low	High	50th percentile
12 Months	27 inches	31 inches	29 inches
15 Months	28 inches	32 1/2 inches	30½ inches
18 Months	29¼ inches	34 inches	31½ inches

Male Length Ranges

Age	Low	High	50th percentile
12 Months	27½ inches	32 inches	29½ inches
15 Months	29 inches	33½ inches	31 inches
18 Months	30 inches	34 3/4 inches	32¼ inches

found that by 24 months, eating patterns of toddlers look extremely similar to some of the most problematic American dietary patterns. Some of the findings included:

- Approximately one-third of the infants and toddlers consumed no separate fruit or vegetable servings in a day.
- Nine percent of 9- to 11-month-olds ate French fries once a day. For children approaching age 2, French fries or another fried potato became the most common vegetable eaten.
- After 8 months of age, the majority of infants and toddlers consumed at least one type of dessert, sweet, or sweetened beverage a day. Often this was served as a snack.
- One out of five infants ages 4 to 6 months, consumed beverages of 100 percent fruit juice. This is in direct contradiction of the American Academy of Pediatrics' recommendation that *no* juices be introduced before the age of 6 months.
- Children aged 1–2 years require 950 calories per day, but consumed, on average, 1,220 calories.
- Ten percent of children over 15 months consumed at least one soda per day.

Since approximately one in every five Americans is obese, a rate that has doubled in the last 20 years, these findings are worrisome. Research indicates that a child who is overweight at age 3 is eight times more likely to be an overweight adult (Lumeng, 2005). There is no easy solution to obesity, but ensuring that healthy snacks and meals are provided at facilities is one small step in reducing the problem. Another effort the early childhood profession can make is ensuring that physical activity and movement is part of the every day routine. Box 9.1 explains the importance of movement in greater detail.

BOX 9.1

THE IMPORTANCE OF MOVEMENT

motor development

the aspect of physical development that involves gross motor skill acquisition and mobility

Outdoor space for young children should be "gentle for crawling, kind for falling, and cool for sitting."

(Joe Frost, 1992)

active play

involves whole-body movement; requires space and simple, safe equipment

rhythmicity

the predictability or unpredictability in patterns of the child's behavior

It is a tragic commentary on our society that children are set on a path of inactivity from such an early point in their lives, especially when movement is central to their lives. Wang (2004) credits Beatty (1992) for noting "that **motor development** is so obvious and visible an aspect of children's growth that it is sometimes taken for granted" (p. 32).

In 2002, the National Association for Sport and Physical Education (NASPE) released physical activity guidelines for infants and toddlers. They warned that confining infants and young children to strollers, car seats, play pens, and swings for endless hours has the potential for delaying acquisition of gross motor and cognitive skills. This practice may also encourage sedentary behavior and predispose children to obesity. This level of inactivity, combined with fewer opportunities to play outside, and much earlier exposure to television, video games, and computers, contributes to children making recreation choices that exclude physical activity. "Software for toddlers is a rapidly growing market niche, and computer 'classes' for toddlers have parents enrolling children as young as two and a half—and many already arrive familiar with the machine" (Healy, 1998, p. 206). This seems to border on the ridiculous, since there are so many other skills, especially motor and socio-emotional, that children need to be learning.

According to Gallahue (1995), "no matter what the activity, one cannot take part successfully if the essential fundamental movement skills contained within that activity have not been mastered" (p. 25). Caregivers must carefully analyze their environment, both indoors and out, as well as their program to ensure that infants and toddlers are receiving the type of support needed to not only acquire adequate movement skills, but also to gain an appreciation of movement.

There are cultural differences regarding the importance of activity levels. Trawick-Smith's (2003) research has demonstrated that needs and preferences for activity are not only biologically inherited, but that they also reflect the values and beliefs inherent in cultures. "Puerto Rican mothers were more likely than Euro-American mothers to rate **active play** as undesirable [while] in contrast, Mexican-American and African-American parents report that action and **rhythmicity** are a central part of child-rearing and family communication" (Trawick-Smith, 2003, p. 199).

Wellhousen (2002) outlined four principles for appropriate play experiences for infants and toddlers that were recommended by Joe Frost, an expert in outdoor play:

- Allow a wide range of movement
- Stimulate the senses
- Offer novelty, variety, and challenge
- Address safety and comfort

Often, even knowing that physical activity is essential for development, teachers face challenges in regard to movement that include:

1. lack of knowledge about appropriate physical activities for indoor and outdoor settings;
2. lack of funding to purchase appropriate equipment for supporting physical activities;
3. lack of knowledge regarding adaptations in movement experiences for children with special needs; and
4. a reluctance to take children outdoors because of temperature considerations or the preparation time required for dressing children at this age.

(continues)

Early childhood educators must approach this issue with renewed commitment. Physical movement must be included and encouraged in programs on a daily basis. See the resources listed at the end of this chapter to help you figure out possible solutions to these challenges.

The organization Parents Action for Children—formerly the I Am Your Child organization—has launched a new program on raising healthy and active children. They have many materials available to help families and care givers plan nutritious meals and fitness activities. The Web address is: http://www.iamyourchild.org/. After entering, click on *Site map* to find helpful articles and resources.

Also, the Additional Support section in your Online Companion has information on the topic of obesity with strategies for how caregivers can help reduce the risks for children through appropriate physical movement activities.

Activity 9.1 will encourage you to design an indoor and outdoor play space either for an infant or a toddler class, as well as plan adaptations for special needs children.

Gross Motor Skills

The 12-month-old infant at this stage may have a variety of techniques for getting from place to place. It is likely that he is a proficient crawler, although infants have different crawling styles. Some do a crab crawl, moving in a sideways motion; others are more successful in moving backward than forward or sideways. A few infants do not crawl but become mobile using a bottom-shuffling technique. Others like to use a bear walk on all fours (Sheridan, 2001).

Usually the 12-month-old infant will be able to pull himself to a standing position and cruise around furniture, using a sideways shuffle. Independent walking may be evident at this stage, although since the muscles have not yet fine-tuned the process, the infant's early gait—the way he walks—is wobbly. After a few steps, he may collapse into a sitting position or catch his balance by holding on to someone.

Most toddlers are walking by 15 months, and those who have not yet managed their first steps are likely to be successful fairly soon. Typically, the toddler will manage to walk alone in a cumbersome way with uneven steps. She frequently bumps into things and falls down into a sitting position or onto her hands and from there twists into a sitting position. By 18 months, after a good deal of spontaneous practice, the infant will walk with improved flow of movement. She will be able to walk automatically, without having to concentrate on each separate action. Also, she will be able to start and stop more easily, although she will retain the characteristic legs-apart posture for a little longer.

At this stage, toddlers may attempt gross motor movements that they cannot yet perform successfully. For example, a toddler may walk toward a ball to kick it, even though she is not yet able to stand on one foot to kick (Miller, 2001). The ball may move as the toddler bumps it or falls against it. Although she may feel a sense of achievement because she did make the ball move, she may also be frustrated that she cannot control her body as well as she wants to.

The toddler may continue to crawl because it is faster than her slow, purposeful walk. Going down an incline or down a couple of steps may require a backward crawl, which many toddlers can do easily. Backward movements may also be displayed when the toddler learns to reverse into a chair to sit down (Sheridan, 2001).

Given the opportunity, a toddler who has been walking for a few weeks may attempt to climb stairs while holding a rail. She may look downstairs with pleasure but react to the depth with some fear (Witherington, Campos, Anderrson, Lejeune, & Seah, 2005). By this age the eyes should be working together to form one image in the brain. This is called **stereopsis**. This does not mean that children who demonstrate fear when faced with a depth perception situation have a vision problem, but if the hesitancy continues over the next year, it might be worthwhile having the child assessed. Parents and caregivers need to prepare for these new skills. Climbing is a newly discovered competence, usually appearing later in this stage. We need to watch out in

stereopsis

(or stereoscopic vision) vision wherein two separate images from two eyes are successfully combined into one image in the brain

This child displays the newly acquired ability to squat down and maintain her balance while retrieving a very tiny object off the ground. She uses a pincer grasp to pick up the object. Note the intense concentration!

hand preference

the individual's natural pattern of using the left or right hand

manipulative skills

learned behaviors involving an increasing ability to handle materials and objects successfully

pincer grasp

the ability to grasp a small object between the tips of the thumb and index finger

manual dexterity

the individual's ability to use the hands to achieve complex tasks

case toddlers try to get up onto higher levels where there is something that interests them. The toddler may also run for a few steps but have difficulty in stopping or negotiating obstacles (Sheridan, 2001).

On flat ground, the toddler might drag along a pull toy, but the coordination involved in pulling, turning to see the toy, and walking may be too challenging. Proficient walkers may manage to carry an object, such as a ball or a doll, as they walk, but they usually stop when they pay attention to the toy. Pushing is a little easier than dragging or carrying. At this stage, toddlers like to push large, lightweight boxes or toys by putting their weight behind the object. By 18 months, the toddler may be able to squat while playing or to pick up a fallen toy (Sheridan, 2001). This indicates that he has increasing control of his leg muscles. All these physical skills enable the toddler to be increasingly mobile, but using these skills can make the toddler more tired than in previous months.

Fine Motor Skills

During this period, the infant practices a variety of grasps. She can pick up small objects, hold them to examine them, and put them in the appropriate places, such as a peg in a hole (Edwards, Buckland, & McCoy-Powlen, 2002). The 15-month-old infant may stack two small blocks, pick up small toys, mark a paper with a crayon, turn a container upside down, or put items inside each other.

Although the toddler may show a **hand preference**—that is, a pattern of preferring to use either her right or left hand—it is not always consistent or permanent (Edwards et al., 2002). Her increasing skill at using her hands is significant. Feeding herself, assisting with tasks, playing, and imitating adult actions all help the toddler refine her **manipulative skills**.

During this period, a toddler will learn to hold a spoon and bring it to her mouth, hold a drink in a cup with a little adult help, carry objects using a whole-hand grasp (palmar) or holding them against her body, and pick up items using a delicate **pincer grasp** (Sheridan, 2001). She may be able to hold a crayon and scribble with a back-and-forth movement that mirrors the sway of her body.

The toddler is likely to use her finger to point at things and people. The pointing can be done in relation to books or other objects, television, or real-life action. As her interest in small things increases, she notices the details of pictures, and points and attributes names to the illustrations. She may turn the pages in a book (Jalongo, 2004), but not always in a left-to-right sequence. While the toddler may want to help with tasks in the kitchen, her **manual dexterity** is not yet up to the job. There is considerable increase in the toddler's ability to handle objects, and she does this with great care and concentration. This shows a new level of **hand–eye coordination** that allows the toddler to play in different ways and be more successful with basic toys and puzzles.

Self-Help Skills

The infant is likely to be interested in handling a spoon, but her first attempts at putting the spoon in her mouth are rarely successful as a part of feeding. Consequently, feeding time can be very messy, and educators who encourage **self-help skills** should be prepared for long mealtimes and a lot of cleaning up afterward. She is eating more adult foods and she may manage many of these with her fingers.

At this stage, the toddler may want to help as she is dressed or undressed. Her actions may not be well directed, but these efforts should be encouraged. Success is shown when she can take off items such as socks or a hat. She may also have mastered action to help with the

Personal Comment

I have always noticed that children learn to undress before they learn to dress.

This can result in some interesting moments, both in child care and in home life.

Nothing quite prepares you to see a naked child when, moments before, or so it seemed, they were fully clothed.

Our Western European culture sometimes seems schizophrenic in regards to the human body.

We use the body to sell many products thinly veiled in suggestive and sexual overtones, but at the same time we align nakedness with a concept of badness.

This sends children very mixed messages.

Some other cultures do not have the same views about the naked body.

(Read: *Fishing Naked: Nordic Early Childhood Philosophy, Policy, and Practice* by Judith Wagner—cited in Further Reading section.)

As caregivers, you need to examine your own beliefs and attitudes about the human body.

Also, if you are participating in a practicum or working at a child care site, you need to discuss their policy in regards to children undressing.

This is a very complex issue, probably because we still do not understand that "sex" does not enter into the minds of children for quite sometime.

If we could come to understand that they are children, not miniature adults, perhaps we could become more relaxed about bare bodies.

Also, families often have beliefs, attitudes, and values about the concept of nakedness.

These opinions have to be considered when dealing with this issue.

No matter what is decided, one area that should not be compromised is the use of correct terminology for children's "private parts."

A boy has a penis and a girl has a vulva and a vagina. That's it!

I have never understood the nicknames that abound for these organs.

We use all the correct terminology when we discuss other body parts, except for these.

Once again, our uncomfortable relationship with the body is revealed!

---

hand–eye coordination

the skilled connection between seeing something, reaching for it, and grasping it

self-help skills

skills that demonstrate the ability to eat, dress, keep clean, or toilet by one's self

toilet learning

the individual's gradual maturational process of understanding and acquiring skills required to use the toilet for bowel movements and urination

dressing process, raising her leg to put on pants or holding out her hands for mittens. Her actions will not always be in the correct sequence, and she may try to put on her boots before her snow pants.

During this stage, the toddler may make some connections between bowel and bladder fullness, the urge to urinate or defecate, and the feeling of evacuation and diaper soiling. This does not mean that all the signs of readiness for **toilet learning** are yet in place. However, some families may already be encouraging their toddler to use the child potty or toilet, and their choices should be respected. Although it is commonly agreed that this learning should not be stressful, there is considerable variation in how parents interpret that process.

In order for a child to learn to use the toilet, she has to be physically, socio-emotionally, and cognitively ready in order to succeed in the process. It helps if families and caregivers also:

1. view the process as learning, rather than training;
2. understand that bowel control *usually* happens before bladder control; and
3. have a consistent procedure that is followed both at home and in out-of-home care facilities.

What should not happen is a power struggle over the toilet issue. Young children have very little power in their lives. If this is the only area in which they have a real choice, they may choose not to be cooperative if they feel they are being coerced.

The Additional Support section of your Online Companion outlines the criteria for toilet learning in great detail. Also, you can read the article on toilet learning listed in the Further Reading section at the end of this chapter to find out more about this controversial topic.

Cognitive Development

Senses and Perception

Each of the five senses provides information to the toddler's brain, and she is able to process this data efficiently. Her perceptions are limited more by lack of experience than by lack of sensory **acuity**.

acuity

the degree to which one or more senses is functional or effective

Personal Story

My son was almost 3 before he learned to use the toilet.

I struggled with him for six months in an attempt to get him to use the toilet.

One day, when I was changing his diaper, I asked him, "When are you going to start using the toilet?"

His reply: "When I want to!"

Well, it hit me like a rock.

His message couldn't have been clearer. From that point on, I didn't hassle him at all.

Guess what?

Two weeks later, he was using the toilet during the day and he was dry at night.

What did I learn?

When children are ready, they will achieve the next step.

He had been trying to tell me in so many ways, but I wasn't listening.

What a humbling experience!

Taste/Oral Exploration She may have particular taste preferences and food jags, during which she refuses particular tastes. However, she is likely to try new flavors if the foods are presented one at a time with other familiar food.

A finding from the FITS study (Dwyer, Suitor, & Hendricks, 2004) was that 8–15 repeated exposures to a new food were necessary for a child to accept the new food. However, caregivers are only offering the food 3–5 times and then giving up. Most children need many experiences of smelling, feeling, touching, and crunching a food before they will even begin the exploration of taste. The bottom line is that children need to have multiple exposures to different foods in order to get to the point of trying them. Even after that, the food might have to be tasted 5–10 times before it is accepted.

The toddler now uses her hands, more than her mouth, for feeling objects, but she may still use her mouth for discovery of new textures and objects.

observational learning

learning by watching people's behavior

Smell The toddler will respond to "good" and "bad" smells. She may notice the smells of food cooking, bathroom toiletries, or play materials that she likes, and respond negatively to the smells of the contents of her diaper, the garbage bin, rotting vegetables, or fish at the market. Interestingly, the associations she makes between smells and enjoyment may last a lifetime, even though she may not remember particular incidents.

Vision Visual acuity has reached 20/20 by this age for most, although this is not the case for all toddlers. That is because visual acuity is genetically linked and can also be affected by birth disorders, nutrition, and other factors.

The infant's ability to attend to details of pictures is observable. She is likely to recognize objects if they are simple images. It is difficult, though, to know how much of an image she recognizes, because she doesn't yet have the language to tell us. If the image is in any way obscured—half-hidden behind a door, for example—the infant may not recognize that what is represented is part of a whole.

At times, he might point to a picture and make a sound, perhaps something approximating a real word, as though he is trying to identify the picture. He particularly likes to look at photographs of his immediate family members, and appears to know who they represent. Images in board, paper, or cloth books can also provide interesting things for a baby to look at; it's a good idea to display pictures around the room at the infant's eye level.

Some effort to imitate the actions he sees tells us that he is taking notice of the people's actions as well as their faces or bodies. In fact, he remains more interested in faces than bodies—his eyes move from faces to hand actions. The imitation and **observational learning** that occurs is directly related to visual acuity. However, babies whose visual acuity is not

The sense of smell remains a valuable channel for sensory information.

so good tend to rely on their other senses to make sense of what is around them. Toys and play materials need to be visually appealing to infants. If their sense of sight is below average, children may be more likely to mouth and feel objects, as well as hold them up close, to experience their attributes. Mouthing is also associated with teething, and may also be a behavioral pattern linked with some personality types—so don't immediately conclude that the baby has vision difficulties if she continues to mouth objects!

Hearing Imitating different sounds and responding to music and other domestic sounds are the clearest indications that the infant has a functional sense of hearing. Her sound production may become more like the language sounds that she hears. Early speech tells us that her hearing is likely to be adequate.

Infants at this stage are able to follow moving sounds, respond to the rhythm of music by waving their hands about or moving their bodies to the beat, and enjoy making sounds using one or more objects and banging them together or against a hard surface. Not all sounds evoke a positive reaction, however. A startled response to a loud sound indicates some fear, but the infant is usually calmed when she realizes there is no threat. Sounds that seem threatening at first may bring a different reaction when the infant finds out they are not associated with anything negative.

Sensorimotor Behavior

The 12- to 18-month-old toddler is in the tertiary circular reaction substage of the sensorimotor stage (Piaget, 1950). Please see the Additional Support section in Online Companion, or Figure 6.1, to review these substages.

During this time, the infant performs deliberate actions that bring about desirable consequences. What this means, in the very simplest terms, is that infants and toddlers will repeat an action over and over and over again. This repetitive activity sometimes drives family members and caregivers to the point of craziness. However, this is the scientist at his best. Experimenting in order to discover a pattern in the minute variances of the activity, the child separately evaluates each action and reaction. This is how he uncovers some of the mysteries of his universe.

trial and error

learning through experimenting and making mistakes, as well as experiencing success

In the first half of this stage, the infant has a particular interest in things that are new. Rather than meeting situations and objects in ways he has used before, he now tries completely new solutions. He now uses **trial and error** in a deliberate way—rather than in the random actions he would have utilized earlier to try to find solutions. His tertiary circular reactions are applicable to many situations, including problem-solving. In playing with an adult or older child, he has fun with objects. He may like to repeat actions that involve disappearing and reappearing, such as peekboo. However, rather than do this again and again in exactly the same way, he might start looking for the person out of sight, or try to cover his own face in an attempt to disappear. He can't see the adult, so he assumes that she can't see him!

discovery play

spontaneous activity that involves finding out the properties of materials and how they work

You may see him handling materials in a slightly different way. He may perform actions to gain greater understanding of the properties of materials. The toddler might, for example, press different tools into dough to make a range of shapes. He might repeat these actions because they are pleasing to him, but he is also likely to extend his discovery by finding other objects to press, whether they are appropriate or not. Lots of **discovery play** is evident as he builds increasingly complex schemes of understanding about materials. New experiences might be treated cautiously, but soon the toddler will be squeezing, pressing, prodding, lifting, and dropping things just to see what happens. After he sees the results, he may repeat his actions or modify them in some way. When sensory experiences are extended using a variation of what is familiar, the toddler is interested in the novelty but remains confident of his previous learning.

concepts

clusters of schemes (patterns, mental representations) that together create an idea

The sensory discovery of materials remains the primary way that the toddler learns. He has great fun finding out what objects and materials will do. At 12–18 months, he responds well to many new sensory activities. Through these, he extends his mental schemes, clustering together many bits and pieces of information to lead to fuller **concepts**. The toddler now knows how materials work after he performs a variety of actions on them. Extending initial discoveries happens every day, so the same materials can offer the toddler new discoveries repeatedly. Minor changes, such as making the dough a different color, or providing different-shaped pieces of paper, will extend the learning even more. Gradually he will build conceptual understandings of color, shape, and so forth. This will happen before true language has surfaced, but once language can be applied to experience, the understanding is consolidated. Every time the toddler has a new experience, or a variation of an old one, his original concept is challenged. He will take in, or assimilate, this new information, and change, or accommodate, his existing concepts accordingly. Most of the toddler's learning process involves discovery, assimilation, accommodation, and equilibration refer to Box 3.2 in Chapter 3 to review Piaget's terminology. The toddler's world has expanded because of his increased mobility and perfected manipulative skills, so concept development occurs rapidly.

Brain Development

The most important thing that we need to understand about brain development at this stage is the significance of **synaptic connections**. Within the different areas of the brain, each having different purposes, are billions of nerve cells (**neurons**) that send messages to each other across synapses. (See Figure 9.2.) These neurons and synapses, and the pathways between them (synaptic connections), are the wiring of the brain. They enable all the different areas of the brain to communicate and coordinate their functions. At the time of birth, nearly all the neurons that will be needed have already been formed. So what we think of as brain development is actually the increase in connections between the neurons. Infancy and early childhood are the prime times for synaptic growth, but they are dependent upon the child's experiences. While new synapses are being made, other neurons are being pruned or lost. The **pruning** is essential because it increases the efficiency of the brain. However, if the child is deprived of important early experiences, too much pruning can occur.

There are some areas of the brain that are less adaptable than others. These parts of the brain become less **plastic**, or less able to change, after certain time periods. This gives us the idea that there are important periods in the child's life when key experiences are essential for brain development. We can reasonably assume that when those peak times or **windows of opportunity** are over or closed, certain learning cannot easily occur. Appreciating the significance of this is especially important in the first three years of a child's life, because these windows of opportunity can be missed.

Many of the areas of the brain are responsible for different functions, such as hearing, sight, language, and so on. (See Figure 9.3.) Neuroscientists have some idea about which areas are responsible for which functions, but some skills and abilities have not yet been associated with a particular location in the brain.

synaptic connections

the connections between neurons through which nerve impulses travel

neuron

a nerve cell

pruning

a process whereby unused synapses (connections among brain cells) are shed; experience governs which synapses will be shed and which will be preserved

plasticity

the brain's ability to change (its malleability) as a result of experience or injury; particularly changeable in early life

windows of opportunity

sensitive periods of time when the brain is particularly capable of learning certain things most efficiently and thoroughly; the time when a child can benefit most from appropriate learning experiences

Figure 9.2 Synaptic Connections

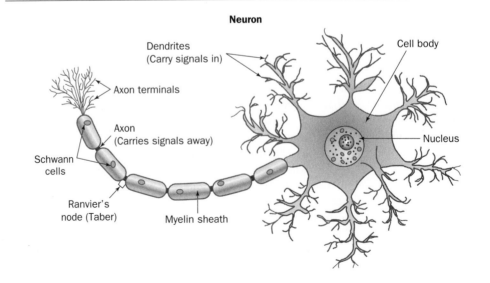

Figure 9.3 Parts of the Brain and What They Do

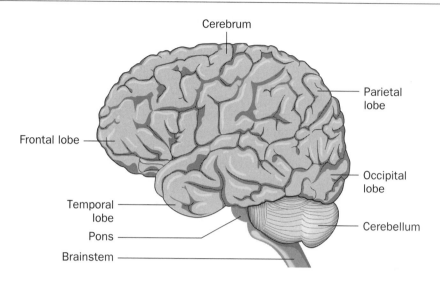

Figure 9.4 Functions Handled by the Left and Right Hemispheres of the Brain

Left Brain Functions:
- Written language
- Number skills
- Reasoning
- Spoken language
- Scientific skills
- Right-hand control

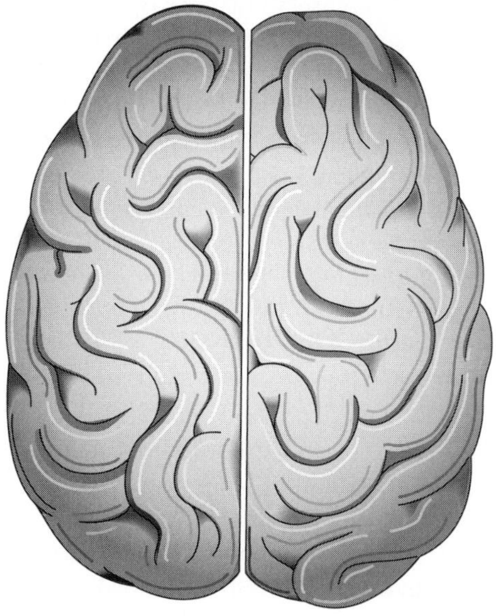

Right Brain Functions:
- Insight
- 3-D forms
- Art awareness
- Imagination
- Left-hand control
- Music awareness

We also know that the left and right hemispheres of your brain process information in different ways. (See Figure 9.4.) We tend to prefer one hemisphere over the other, but information is shared back and forth across the two spheres. Since infants' and toddlers' brains are still at their peak of development, it is important that we monitor the types of activities we offer to ensure that we are not concentrating too much on one type of learning and ignoring the other modes. Again, a balance needs to be achieved. It is like preparing a great recipe that takes a bit of this and a bit of that. For example, alternating experiences using language, music, manipulatives, movement, and sensory exploration should enhance both sides of the brain. A responsive caregiving approach, aligned with developmentally appropriate practices, should ensure that children are receiving a well-rounded set of experiences.

Do you want to discover if you are a right-brained or left-brained learner? Go to Activity 9.2 in your Online Companion to find out.

So how does this research translate into practice? We have always known that our responsibility is to protect young children. For many years, it meant protection in the physical sense—ensuring that they come to no harm. This is still true, but now we also know that we must provide protection in the neurological sense, to ensure that children are not put into any situation that could be injurious to their brain development. As mentioned before, brain development is dependent upon appropriate early experience. Neglect, trauma, abuse, institutionalization, prolonged hospitalization, inadequate parenting, lack of play opportunity, parental depression, lack of attachment and emotional well-being, along with many other negative situations, can be damaging to brain development—especially in the first three years (Hawley, 2000).

Another responsibility is to ensure that young children receive age-appropriate nurturing experiences. It is a good thing that current neuroscience has reinforced understandings about:

- the conditions for very young children to make secure attachments to adults (parents and out-of-home caregivers)
- socio-emotional development
- sensory experiences, perception, and sensorimotor intelligence
- components of quality child care
- the characteristics of age/stage-appropriate activities
- when important sensitive periods occur

sensitive period

the window of opportunity when the brain is most receptive to particular types of learning experiences

profound experiences

the emotional and social experiences that an individual must have in order for any other learning experience to be meaningful

essential experiences

experiences that are necessary for growth and development to occur at an optimal level

The **sensitive periods** of the toddler stage lead us to pay particular attention to certain parts of the child's experience. All experiences are not equally important. For example, having experiences that lead to secure attachments are more important than playing with sand. (not to imply that sensory discovery is unimportant!) The emotional experience is a profound one that enables other types of learning to occur. If the toddler does not have a secure attachment, she might be uninterested in venturing out to play with the sand, and even if placed in front of it, she might lack the motivation essential to discover its properties. The following list of key experiences differentiate between **profound experiences**, those emotional experiences that are the foundation upon which all later learning is built and the **essential experiences** that lead to optimal development. The basic needs described by Maslow are encompassed in the profound needs. Each of these experiences is based on the current understandings of toddler brain development.

Profound Experiences:

1. being loved
2. having all physical needs met
3. being respected as a separate person and having the opportunity for self-discovery and self-regulation
4. enjoying physical proximity, comforting, and cuddling
5. having consistent caregiving, based on mutual trust
6. having adults respond to toddler-initiated cries, gestures, expressions, and language
7. being in a reliable and consistent environment with regular routines
8. having adults mediate between the child and the child's world
9. being competent, successful, and enabled to be independent
10. recovering from temporary negative situations

Essential Experiences:

1. having safe space to explore her own body and the environment
2. being offered a wide range of sensory discovery and experiencing the natural world, with adult encouragement
3. enjoying the time, opportunity, and space to play—with adult facilitating
4. being immersed in spoken language, and having adults support the toddler's language acquisition through scaffolding
5. having the opportunity for social interaction with other children and being part of a group

6. being given opportunity for the discovery of music, song, story, and experimentation with sound
7. being offered a wide variety of visual stimulation
8. being offered the regular opportunity and experience to identify, sort, order, and build concepts, and to recall, organize, and solve problems
9. having the opportunity for minor risk taking and finding out the consequences of actions
10. being offered the opportunity and materials for imitative, creative, symbolic, pretend, block, object, role-play, and imaginative play

Just to reiterate. Without the critical foundation supplied by profound experiences, nothing that comes after will really make a difference. Profound experiences really are the components that create our emotional and social anchors for life. If we lack these experiences early in life, we are doomed to continually and unsuccessfully seek an oasis that offers guidance and comfort.

Also worth mentioning at this point is how the consumer market has jumped on the findings from the brain research. In recent years there have been a number of videos and toys that claim to offer brain-based activities. The manufacturers claim that their products will enhance the infant's brain functions, thus implying that they will provide superior ways of supporting brain development. Some of these are benign: they don't actually do any harm. But the claim that certain experiences are brain-based is usually a marketing tool, without significant evidence as to their effectiveness. The "Mozart effect" was behind several products claiming advanced learning—in some cases, advanced mathematical understanding—in young children. The idea was that by exposing infants to music—in particular, new recordings of Mozart's work (which doesn't seem like a bad idea in itself)—the infants' brains would somehow be advanced. This practice is unlikely to cause damage, but its supposed benefits are not supported by solid research. Play Mozart's music if you think that's a good idea, but it is not necessary to purchase materials especially marketed to parents and caregivers. Any experience that the infant has is brain-based; it is not necessary to purchase something especially for that purpose. The most effective brain development occurs when we provide developmentally appropriate experiences, offer consistent nurturing that promotes secure attachment, and engage in the infant's spontaneous play and efforts to communicate.

Information Processing

A busy room or outdoor environment may produce many noises, but the infant is able to tune out some sounds and pay increased attention to human voices or a particular sound that interests her. This is an example of the process of **habituation**. In other words, when the infant hears, feels, sees, or otherwise experiences simultaneous perceptions, she has to be able to prioritize her attention.

Learning is built on the infant's exploration, using her senses in a single or multimodal way (Allen & Marotz, 2007). She can take in information through more than one sense simultaneously and process it in complex ways (Siegler, 1991). Consequently, we need to balance stimulation with downtime. The infant requires quiet time to filter, sort, and memorize relevant features of information and forget the rest. It may be difficult for an infant to assimilate information when it is too complex and delivered by several media at once, but different babies respond differently.

Up to this point, only the senses of sight, vision, taste, touch, and smell have been discussed. However, in reality, the brain is a much more complex structure, and integrates information not only from these five senses, but from other sensory systems as well. These less-well-known senses, or process systems, are the **tactile**, **vestibular**, and **proprioceptive systems**. They are interconnected, and allow the body to experience, interpret, and respond to different stimuli in the environment. Each sense works with the others to form an over arching interpretation of:

- who we are physically;
- where we are located in space and time; and
- what is going on around us.

The collaboration of all these senses is known as **sensory integration**, and it provides a crucial foundation for later, more complex learning and behavior. For most children, sensory integration occurs automatically, unconsciously, and, perhaps most critical, effectively. For

habituation

the decrease in the response to a stimulus that occurs after repeated presentations of the stimulus—e.g., looking away from a mobile after continued stimulation

tactile system

includes nerves under the skin's surface that send information to the brain

vestibular system

controls the sense of movement and balance and, in part, is dependent on movement and changes in the position of the head

proprioceptive system

refers to components of muscles, joints, and connective tissue that provide a subconscious awareness of body position

sensory integration

the interaction of two or more sensory processes in a manner that enhances the adaptiveness of the brain

others however, sensory integration proves to be inefficient and difficult. This dysfunction known as a sensory processing disorder (SPD) or sensory integration disorder (SI disorder) can have a profound impact on learning and the ability to function on a day-to-day basis. This disorder "is not one specific disorder, as blindness or deafness is, but rather an umbrella term to cover a variety of neurological disabilities" (Kranowitz, 2005, p. 9). Initial indicators of sensory integration problems can sometimes be observed by the time children are 12 months old. According to the Sensory Integration International Web site and general knowledge gained through practice, these signals might include some of the following indicators:

- Overly sensitive or under reactive to touch, movement, sights, or sounds
- Activity level that is unusually high or unusually low
- Inability to calm self
- Refusal to eat certain "textured" foods
- Overly sensitive to certain types of clothing
- Avoiding getting hands dirty (i.e., glue, sand, mud, fingerpaint)
- Apprehensive crawling or walking on uneven or unstable surfaces

Once again, a warning must be given that children at this age still demonstrate a wide variation in development. Briefly, observing a number of these indicators may not mean that the child is having a problem with sensory integration. He may just be transitioning to a new stage of learning, may be teething, or may be coming down with a cold. Never jump to a swift conclusion. Children must be observed on a regular basis for a significant amount of time, and the observations must be documented. Only then can a pattern emerge that might be worth consideration and further assessment.

For more in-depth information on sensory integration problems, see the Additional Support section in your Online Companion.

Observational learning is particularly important at this stage. This means that the toddler learns about the world from watching it. From observation comes some imitation of what is seen. Such imitation shows that the observations are more than visual stimulation—they are processed in some way. When you see a toddler copying a parent's actions with the vacuum cleaner, you can see direct learning from imitation. Sometimes toddlers will show deferred imitation. In one memorable example, the day after a visit from her uncle, a 17-month-old toddler was seen holding a crayon to her mouth to imitate him smoking; not all observational learning turns out to be positive.

Deciding what to pay attention to is a challenge for toddlers who are bombarded with sensory information. Adults assist the process by isolating key features—pointing to a picture in a book or emphasizing a particular naming word, for example. Yet much of the toddler's attention has to be directed by herself, without adult intervention. Although the process is supported by adults, toddlers achieve the ability to attend to information independently. Selecting and **attending** to information is, to some extent, driven by the toddler's interests and motivation. Attending is a way we have of describing how the child pays attention to some aspect of what she is experiencing. She may attend to texture, for example, rather than any other perceptual information. Attending to some features of an object or experience is essential for learning. Without this ability, the child cannot single out characteristics or see how details relate to each other. Her ability to attend is variable and is shaped by her interests, maturational stage, state of alertness, sensory acuity, and skill level. Neurological (synaptic) connections are made and reinforced though attending and it is—probably the most significant skill for later success in school (Berk, 2004).

attending

paying attention to a stimulus

This child demonstrates sensitivity to the texture of grass on her bare feet.

Learning Style/Channel of Preference

Toddlers who are active, as most are for all their waking time, may display some preference in their sensory interests. Observable differences exist in

---

Personal Story

In my visits in and out of child care facilities, I am often struck by the fact that many infant rooms have music playing constantly.

Sometimes the music is pleasant, but at other times it is too loud or just consists of mind-numbing tunes.

Once again, a balance must be struck.

Lullabies for sleeping are great. Music to move to and sing along with is also beneficial.

However, opportunities that afford babies the chance to listen to environmental noises inside and outside, or enable them to have the experience of listening to the sounds of silence, should not be undervalued.

Figure 9.5 Types of Learners

- Visual Learners: *learn through seeing.*
- Auditory Learners: *learn through listening.*
- Tactile/Kinesthetic Learners: *learn through moving, doing, and touching.*

---

the way toddlers prefer to take in information. Some theorists and practitioners reduce learning modalities to three categories of learning styles—visual, motor, and auditory. Learning styles are simply different approaches or ways of learning (Figure 9.5). Learning modalities refer to the styles learners use to concentrate on, process, and remember information. Visual children tend to learn by watching and looking at visual cues and information. They may be easily distracted by movement and action in the classroom. Auditory children tend to learn listening—and retain instructions and information—best by being told. These types of learners may be easily distracted by noise. Those who have a tactile/kinesthetic learning style tend to actively explore the physical world around them and would rather do than watch, meaning they cannot sit still for long. They prefer to be involved in "hands on" projects and discovery learning.

If you look for the responses of toddlers to different stimuli, you can determine their preference. Quilliam (1994) suggests that we can detect these differences by observing the child's posture, movements, eye patterns, facial expressions, speech, skin, heart rate, and breathing. Toddlers who receive information through their **channel of preference** will tend to sit upright, move toward the source of stimulation, open their eyes wide, and smile. Their skin color may deepen and their heart rate and breathing will quicken—except in the case of hearing music, when it may synchronize with the music. A negative response may indicate that the stimulation is not through their favored channel. Negative responses include being startled, withdrawing, frowning, going blank, getting paler, whimpering or crying, closing the body by becoming stiff or shrinking inward, covering the head or ears, turning away, or shutting the eyes. The same positive or negative responses can be used to determine if a toddler is comfortable with multimodal stimulation, receiving sensory information via two or more channels at once. It can be very helpful for the adult to observe and interpret these largely involuntary responses.

channel of preference

the individual's best or preferred way of communicating and functioning—e.g., visual, auditory, or tactile

Language and Communication

Body Language

There is usually an emergence of a new type of **body language** at the beginning of this stage, and it is quite easy to read. The infant uses her finger to point. Pointing may coincide with saying a word or just a sound. The finger pointing is an effective tool because we can often understand what the infant wants more easily than before. The newfound ability may have the baby using pointing to her advantage, and have her caregivers running to get what she wants. Although this might seem a demanding stage—and she will often want an item that she can see but that is not intended for her—it is not spoiling her to respond to her requests. The meaning

body language

messages, sent either deliberately or unconsciously, that are conveyed by the individual's posture, facial expressions, gestures, or other behavior

Pointing is a gesture children learn to use rapidly. It is almost guaranteed that this child's gesture will capture the attention of adults.

Bev Bos, an early childhood specialist, states that she tells a child "no" only if any of the three following conditions exist:

- the child is hurting himself
- the child is hurting someone else
- the child is destroying property

tuneful babbling

strings of sounds that have patterns of pitch and rhythm

variegated babbling

long strings of different syllables used in the vocal experimentation of infants

she intends isn't always as obvious as we might imagine. For example, pointing at a bottle does not necessarily mean that is what she wants, and pointing to her crib may not mean that she wants to sleep.

Joseph Garcia (1994,1999) suggests that toddlers' communication can be assisted if adults add a language gesture to their actions. These gestures, he thinks, can be offered before, during, or after the specific actions. His experience with toddlers indicates that they are receptive to this communication method and can gain a repertoire of motions that can assist them to communicate their needs and ideas, and to respond to adults, while their oral language skills are still limited.

Garcia's communication enhancement is known as baby signing. It is a somewhat controversial approach to assisting infant and toddler communication. Some practitioners think that there is no long-term advantage to offering these skills to young children even if, in the short term, it enables them to express themselves and opens a channel of communication with adults. For infants and toddlers who are experiencing hearing impairments, this modification of American Sign Language (ASL) is likely to offer a very useful communication tool. There are some child care centers that accommodate both hearing and hearing-impaired children who are using this method of supporting communication, and they consider it advantageous.

Receptive and Expressive Language

This stage is an exciting time in language growth for young children. The infant, at 12 months, is on the brink of language use. From the time of the first real words, there is usually a rapid increase in receptive language. This means the child knows the meaning of some words even though he may not yet be able to articulate them. "By his first birthday, the average child understands around seventy words, mostly nouns like people's names and terms for certain objects, but also certain social expressions, like *hi* and *bye-bye*" (Eliot, 1999, p. 372). Sometimes, as toddlers concentrate on walking, language advancement seems to stagnate. However, the pause is usually only temporary. During this stage most children will acquire 5–50 words accurately, although some will talk more, and some less. The first word is usually greatly anticipated and wildly celebrated. Other language milestones include: following simple directions, pointing to familiar objects when asked, identifying several parts of the body (nose, eye) when asked, and (by 18 months) having speech that is 25 percent intelligible to anyone who hears it (Allen & Marotz, 2007). Also, she may understand the word "no" and appreciate what it means (Sheridan, 2001). Some educators avoid the word no and find it more effective to tell children what they can do, instead of telling them what they can't do. However, avoiding using the word "no" is probably not feasible, nor advisable. Children do need to hear constructive language, but they also need to understand boundaries.

Tuneful babbling continues during this stage and the infant does a lot of experimenting with her own voice. Repetition of sounds is appealing, especially the consonants of *m, p, b, t, d,* and *n,* which are made at the front of the mouth. She does something else that indicates that she is listening to language. It is called echolalia, and it is an attempt to imitate the sounds of whole phrases; it involves a parrot-like imitation of sounds, syllables, and words. If you overhear the child in her crib, you might hear a combination of babbling, echolalia, and rhythmic sounds that are like singing.

Within this time frame, babbling becomes more complex, turning into **variegated babbling**, or tuneful jabbering (Sheridan, 2001). This babbling takes on the sounds and intonations more closely associated with real language. Variegated babbling combines consonants and vowels—and often results in some wonderful words of the baby's own creation: "Gabbada" and "namana" are two examples. The meaning may change with the context, so they mean one thing during a monologue (such as talking in the crib to herself) but something else in a dialogue (as she converses with her caregiver in the playroom).

proto-words

vocal interactions that resemble real conversation but lack real words or grammatical rules

holophrase

a one-word utterance that stands for a whole phrase; the meaning depends on the context

overextension

the child's application of a language rule in a situation where it does not apply—i.e., extending it beyond the situations where it does apply

underextension

a child applies a word meaning to fewer examples than is generally accepted; restricted use of a word

scaffolding

the role of the adult (or other child) to provide, and gradually remove, a support to the child's learning; providing a bridge for the child to gain a new understanding

phonological awareness

conscious ability to detect and manipulate sound (e.g., move, combine, and delete); awareness of sounds in *spoken* words in contrast to *written* words

Now children utter **proto-words**: words that do have a particular meaning, although they are not real words with commonly understood meanings. Often when they use these proto-words, such as "bo-bo" for bottle, the infant may be trying to convey a variety of meanings. She might mean "Can I have my bottle now?" or "That's my bottle!" The use of one word to convey an entire thought, whether or not the meaning changes, is called a **holophrase**.

We may hear an infant call all animals "dog" or use the word "ba" to mean anything associated with water—not just bath time. These language errors are **overextensions**—one sound or word has a variety of meanings. In a similar misunderstanding of words and categories, the infant might also use **underextensions**—these are heard in situations where the infant uses a general word for a single object—often something that belongs to her; for instance, she may have a blanket and call it "blankie" and not be able to use the same term for other people's blankets.

Infants during this period commonly understand words in context, but the words usually have to be isolated from the flow of everyday language. From the infant's responses, you can see that she knows the meaning of some key words such as cup, bottle, bed, bath, and other domestic things. Owens (2001) suggests that this early receptive language is dependent upon perceptual abilities involving hearing and discriminating between sounds.

The acquisition of language is a complex process, although infants seem to learn language without consciousness. They have little awareness that they are moving into an adult world that involves learning about four cueing systems:

1. *phonological*—the sounds of the language (in English, usually 44 sounds)
2. *grammar/syntax*—absorbing rules of the language
3. *semantics*—gaining a vast vocabulary and appreciating meanings of words
4. *pragmatics*—learning the purposes and intents of the language

It is worth noting that worldwide, children acquire language in a similar sequence (Owen, 2001). For the most part, children "follow virtually identical schedules for speaking single words, then two-word phrases, then sentences of ever-greater complexity—all between 1 and 4 years of age. Even deaf children abide by this same sequence, effortlessly picking up sign language, provided they are immersed in it from birth (that is, their parents are deaf also)" (Eliot, 1999, p. 352). So, even with all the differences in sounds among the hundred languages spoken on earth, children demonstrate a strikingly universal pattern in acquiring a mother tongue. This is one way that children, regardless of cultural heritage, are similar.

Essentially language is a social process: It is not just hearing words spoken. Even if she listens to voices on a television or radio, an infant cannot acquire language. At this stage, and later on, she needs a mediator to help her. This is someone who will respond to her sound making, create a reciprocal communication process, help her associate words and meanings, and extend her vocabulary. These things will be done by people to whom she has made attachments. The supportive process is called **scaffolding**. In order to scaffold language with infants, adults must employ some useful strategies such as gaining and maintaining eye contact; being face-to-face with the child; imitating the child's actions and language; leaning forward and looking expectant; listening; singing songs and finger-plays; expanding on the child's language; and reading books (Weitzman & Greenberg, 2002). These are by no means the only techniques to employ, but these are strategies that have proven to be successful in helping young children progress in language acquisition.

The enriched language environment that is offered by the adult is enormously important to the toddler's language acquisition. Unlike the earlier infant stage, when it did not matter exactly what you said to the baby–it only mattered that she heard comforting adult voices and absorbed sound patterns–toddlerhood is a time to ensure that you are providing your child with a rich and varied vocabulary and experiences that foster a love of language. This actually is a critical component necessary for the attainment of literacy. Using lots of language with children strengthens their **phonological awareness**, which is the ability of "hearing and understanding the different sounds and patterns of spoken language" (Heroman & Jones, 2004). Phonological awareness abilities are actually a good predictor of reading performance (Bardige & Segal, 2005; Paulson, Noble, Jepson, & van der Pol, 2001), and include skills such as

phoneme

the smallest linguistically distinct unit of sound

phonics

a method of teaching beginners to read and pronounce words by learning to associate letters or letter groups with the sounds they make

You are a role model for your children's language. This is a time to be cognizant of the *form* of your language but also the *content* of your language. Family members are sometimes unpleasantly surprised when the toddler imitates some of their words.

One can never hear this statement too often: reading a book to a child is not so much about reading the book—it is the conversation that ensues before, during, and after the reading of a book that actually contributes most to literacy, as well as to relationships!

listening, understanding that oral language can be broken into separate sounds and syllables, rhyming (similar end parts of words), alliteration (similar initial sounds of words) and recognition of **phonemes**, the smallest unit of sound (e.g., cat is *c/a/t*). Phonological awareness lays the groundwork for later teaching of **phonics**, the ability to connect a printed symbol with a sound. The key is to play with language each and every day. Toddlers need conversation rather than the passive language of television, radio, audio tapes, or videos. The American Academy of Pediatrics strongly recommends that there be no television viewing for children under the age of 2, specifically because it recognizes the importance of children getting a strong oral language foundation from interactions with real people. Any time spent viewing or hearing is better spent on real two-way conversations. If television is watched, it has to be a shared experience offering interactive opportunities between child and adult.

Books, stories, and action rhymes provide wonderful opportunities for interaction and offer closeness and mutual enjoyment. Use music to sing and listen to and encourage the children to move with you to a variety of different musical styles: jazz, blues, classical, hip-hop, and country. Take the time to visit many places such as local museums and libraries. Create books with the children's photographs in them, as well as photos of their favorite things and people. And of course, read, read, read to children.

The toddler's attention span may not be too long, but when an adult is truly engaged with her, you may be surprised at how long she stays on task. Reading to toddlers is a pleasant experience, but the toddler will want to see the book's pictures. (See the personal comment about toddler circle time.) At bedtime or naptime, stories provide comfort as she hears the adult's voice; we cannot imagine that she is always following the story or understanding what the pictures mean, even if she seems to be staring at the book. Although there are divided opinions about reading to children as they drop off to sleep, it is the experience of most educators and families that toddlers get used to the routine of story-reading before bed. This provides a nice downtime and a ritual for sharing gentle conversation over a book.

Be sure to check out the information on strategies for supporting language acquisition in the Additional Support section of your Online Companion.

Action rhymes are a wonderful strategy to use for teaching language to toddlers. In this bilingual program, these children have just started learning about singing songs together. You might notice that in the first photo the action seems to be on the part of the teachers, but in the second photo the children gradually join in the action.

Personal Comment

I have been in many toddler classrooms where circle time for toddlers is a protracted affair, taking much too much time and ending in frustration for both children and teachers.

Remember, toddlers are egocentric and active learners.

Being required to sit quietly in a circle for 20 minutes is much too long.

This does not mean that you should never gather toddlers together.

However, since we know the most effective learning for young children happens when they have one-on-one time with adults, group gatherings (circle time) for toddlers should be very brief.

If you have a circle time, it should be with a small number of children and only last as long as it takes to sing one or two songs or complete a few finger rhymes.

I do not recommend book reading to toddlers in a circle setting.

Lap reading or cuddling close while reading is really the best choice.

Emotional Development and Self-Regulation

This time represents a stage of transition from babyhood to toddlerhood that is observable, not only in terms of mobility but also with reference to psychological change and a move toward self-help and independence.

The new emotions of shyness and contempt appear in this stage (Landy, 2002). These may indicate an increased understanding of the self and the toddler's relationship with others. These emotions may be observed when the child meets new people or attributes something she doesn't like to a particular person.

The toddler's mood can change quickly, and may be influenced more by her current activity than her ability to regulate her moods. She might calm herself and attempt to deal with a frustration, but this may not last. Caregivers who help a child recognize the emotion by labeling feelings—"You seem angry" or "You are happy"—are supplying language that is an underlying step in controlling emotions. Adults can also show toddlers how to deal with emotional situations by modeling appropriate responses themselves.

Psychosocial Stage

Shame and **guilt** are relatively new emotions for toddlers at this stage also (Izard & Malatesta, 1987). They signify the gradual emergence of an emotional conflict between **autonomy** and shame or doubt (Erikson, 1987). (Review Erikson's theory in the Additional Support section of your Online Companion.) The toddler is attempting to do things independently, but is also becoming increasingly aware of her dependence on and need for approval from adults. She feels shame (a new condition) when she doubts her ability to act independently. These feelings mark the emergence of the toddler's sense of power and her fear about having it, or losing control. She may try to exercise this power in a variety of ways. Soon she will start to say "no!" and find behavioral ways of showing us that she is an independent person with a different opinion.

One thing adults can do is to prepare an environment that supports children in their ability to make choices. In a family child care home, it might mean having a drawer or cupboard children can open and then play with the items found inside. Often this means children will be able to bang on pots and pans. In a child care facility, care providers can ensure that toys are accessible and provide furniture that is appropriately sized, thereby helping children feel autonomous.

The struggle between autonomy and doubt is such that the toddler is prone to **temper tantrums**. Some toddlers feel frustration more than others; for some, it may be that their personality style leads them to a more assertive manner and stronger emotions; for others, adult interactions might lead them to manage their emotions more effectively. A sensitive balance is needed between appropriate external controls and ones that are coercive and forceful. Although a forceful action may elicit an immediate response, in the long term there is a negative effect on internal controls (Kostelnik et al., 2006; Landy, 2002).

---

shame

a social emotion involving embarrassment or awkwardness about an imagined or real behavior; includes a level of self-consciousness

guilt

the feeling of remorse and responsibility for something that occurred, whether a real or imagined wrong; a product of conflicted feelings

autonomy

an inner drive to become independent and meet one's own needs; a sense of independence, self-government, or self-reliance

temper tantrum

a loss of control of emotions or the experience of conflicted feelings, resulting in anger, crying, stamping feet, kicking, screaming, or other extreme behaviors; frequently occurs in toddlers when they cannot regulate their feelings and actions

This room is arranged with low shelves so that toys are accessible to the children. Did you notice that there are multiples of the same toys? Why might that be helpful?

self-regulation

the ability to control feelings and emotions, or the behaviors that result from those emotions; the ability to modify or change behavior as a result of managing inner emotions

emergence of an organized sense of self

the fourth stage of emotional development; typically occurs around 9 to 18 months

Self-Regulation

Self-regulation takes a significant step as the toddler becomes more autonomous and is able to act more independently. However, much of the toddler's learning is shaped by the culture in which she is nurtured (Berk, 2004). Behaviors that are desirable in one culture may be inappropriate in another. In fact, the move toward independence is highly regarded in some cultures, while others are more comfortable with long-term dependence.

Moving toward 18 months, the toddler has an increasing sense of self, in what Greenspan and Greenspan (1985) call "the **emergence of an organized sense of self.**" The toddler is better able to take initiative in a variety of situations. It is noticeable that even toddlers who were previously considered relatively passive will start conversations with adults, extending their physical proximity from the adult, playing spontaneously, and exerting their independence. The toddler's emotions may seem extreme, but she is gaining some control over the extremes. Although she may not seem as though she wants to have her independence reined in, the toddler needs to have a clear sense of boundaries. She may not accept "no" very well, and may need to be distracted from something that is inappropriate, but she needs the feeling that there are some external controls on her overwhelming feelings. The toddler will still often use social referencing, and this checking in with the adult seems to aid his ability to control feelings. As children near 18 months, the toddler whose language was limited to object-related speech will now start to use words to label her feelings.

Stages of Emotional Growth

Greenspan and Greenspan's (1985) work in helping families recognize the key stages of children's emotional growth suggests that a number of behaviors that occur at this stage can be explained by using their ideas of emotional milestones.

1. *Emotional partnership and complex imitation*—where the child is capable of reciprocating and copying adult behavior and emotions
2. *Expressing needs and interests through taking initiative*—where the child begins to instigate activities based on her own needs and desires rather than by imitation alone
3. *Independence and distal communication*—where the child leaves the adult for a short time in order to explore; she feels connected with the adult from a distance by using her hearing and vision
4. *Originality*—where the child adds her own interpretation to things she has been taught, and uses objects or toys in ways she has not been shown
5. *Understanding function and meaning*—where the child begins to understand the uses and meanings of people and things
6. *Toddler-to-toddler relationships*—where the child can begin to develop a shared relationship with a toddler who is a regular playmate that goes beyond parallel play
7. *Recognizing emotional polarities*—where the child begins to realize that people are composed of different emotions—that even though Daddy may be mad at Mommy, he still loves her at the same time
8. *Ability to communicate with words*—where the child begins to communicate with gestures, sounds, and a few words
9. *Accepting limits and using the distal mode*—where the child begins to respond to your setting limits verbally or with a gesture

As the toddler gains a clearer sense of the fact that she exists, and achieves an emotional separation from her adult attachment figures, she is gradually accumulating some ideas about her

Personal Comment

In some of the child care sites I visit, I see many activities that are not open-ended being used with toddlers.

They are painting pre-drawn apples on dittos with red paint, they are gluing eyes on pre-drawn brown bears, or they are making some art project that the teacher really does.

When I ask the teachers why they do these things, the usual response is, "The families really like it!"

My response is that as professionals, educators need to explain to families that "product" and "process" are two different concepts.

Adults may be comfortable with products, but young children need to be immersed in process, immersed so deeply that it becomes part of who they are.

The process skills help lay the foundation for the skills children will draw on later in life—the skills that future mechanics, mathematicians, public relation managers, plumbers, scientists, and parents, to name a few, will need.

---

personal attributes. Although she is not yet ready to identify or describe what those characteristics are, she nevertheless develops a sense of how she feels about herself.

The thoughts and feelings that she has about her competence and security are created by the experiences she has and the way she is treated. At this stage, it is important for her to hear and feel encouraged about the initiatives that she takes. As she goes about trying to become more independent, the adult needs to let her go. When the toddler returns to the adult, after a little exploring in the big world, that the adult is there to greet her and praise her for her courage, the experience is enriched. The adult is largely responsible for the child's self-esteem—how she feels about herself. Whenever the toddler makes an effort, whether successful or not, she needs to know that it is okay to try things out. Also, having adult support allows her to find out that it's okay to make some small mistakes; that, too, is part of autonomous living. The toddler's **self-esteem** can be firmly established if she receives positive, but not shallow, encouragement from the adults who are special to her. There are strategies families and educators can employ to help ensure that the toddler's world is stimulating, but also one where she can have challenges while simultaneously experiencing a measure of success:

- Provide play material that is developmentally appropriate.
- Offer materials that create opportunities for problem-solving.
- Utilize *open-ended activities.**
- Observe the child's interaction and scaffold the learning by playing next to the child and modeling different methods of problem-solving techniques.

self-esteem

an individual's perception of his own overall positive or negative self-worth; the degree to which one feels positive about oneself; one's overall sense of worth, competence, and control over life

Self-Esteem

Prosocial Skills

Using positive language supports the toddler's self-esteem. It can be based on all the toddler's strengths and effort that she makes. Pointing out new achievements, pinpointing successes, remarking on the child's efforts, and commending the toddler on her **prosocial skills** build healthy self-esteem. A toddler needs to know that she is loved, and she must know that her activity is acknowledged as being important. Adults must ensure that the toddler's routine includes cuddle time, story time, and time for intimacy. It is essential that whenever her body is hurt, her feelings are recognized. As the toddler gains some idea of what is **socially acceptable behavior**—acting in accordance with prevailing social norms—her efforts to behave according to the social rules should be recognized. Such things as the toddler's natural curiosity, her interest in how things work, or her efforts to pay attention to a story are all worthy of praise. There are plenty of things the toddler does right! Adults may overlook this when they feel assaulted by the

prosocial skills

learned behavior that is intended to help others—e.g., helping or sharing; a component of social competence, comprised of acts that support, assist, or benefit others without any expectation of external reward

socially acceptable behavior

any actions or language that are generally accepted as being appropriate in a particular situation or context

---

*Open-ended activities and materials allow for children to set their own agenda. There is no intrinsic right or wrong way to experience the activity or to use the materials. Empty boxes, different-textured cloth, Play-Dough and rolling pins, sand and water play, and scarves all offer opportunities for the children to succeed at the activity.

This child is involved in an open-ended activity using colored dough that he helped to make.

This child's emotions have overwhelmed her. The teacher gently talks to her, informing her that she is angry, and then picks her up and takes her to a quiet corner of the classroom. The teacher will rock her until she regains control of herself. Toddlers often need this kind of respite in order to calm themselves down. This is not a "time out" but rather a time-together with a caring adult who can help her to recognize what she is feeling.

traits

an individual's personality characteristics

toddler's extreme feelings, challenging behavior, and frustrations. This approach to supporting the emergence of the toddler's strong self-esteem can also be helpful to the family or educator. It can remind us of all the advances that the young child is making.

Reading Emotions

As the infant enters the toddler stage, the range of emotions becomes broader. Her feelings of frustration may begin to mount as she finds that she wants to do things that are beyond her physical capabilities. Consequently, adults must be able to recognize, label, and understand the toddler's emotions. Though they are starting to do things by themselves, toddlers still have great dependence upon adults and need emotional security to launch out into the world independently. Rather than become frustrated with a child who shows anger or negative emotions, recognize her feelings in a calm manner.

As the 12- to 18-month-old moves toward greater independence, she encounters frustrations that are challenging for the adult. When she seems to be fighting adults the most, she is really trying to overcome her own conflicted feelings. To help her regulate her feelings and actions, there needs to be a place that she can go to so she can calm down—perhaps where stimulation is reduced. Learning to remove herself from frustrations can be a technique that builds on her natural disengagement when stimuli become overwhelming. In addition, she needs help to recognize what she is feeling, though it is too early for much understanding of words that describe abstract concepts. Provide comfort rather than adding to her emotions by projecting your own onto the situation. Also, read her signs of tiredness and different levels of alertness, because your response to those indicators may keep events from becoming overwhelming for the young child.

Personality and Temperament

It is important to keep in mind that temperament is a set of **traits** with relatively stable tendencies that often make an individual act or react in a particular way. Remember too, that temperament is the how of behavior—the ways in which an individual plays out encounters with the world. However, temperament is not destiny. "These propensities may be magnified, downplayed, or changed in quality in the course of development, depending on the nature of the child's encounter with the environment" (Lieberman, 1993, p. 56). Carey and McDevitt (1995) support this view because they say other factors can affect temperament, including:

- the strength and duration of the temperament characteristics
- other characteristics of the child, such as age or gender
- the environment—which can be stated as Brofrenbrenner's view of the ecological system
- the outcome—cultural, social, and political influences can result in different interpretations of the same temperament traits

In describing temperament, Lieberman (1993) points out that we often use language that represents nonverbal, kinetic actions:

> high-strung, low-keyed, bursting with energy, slow to warm up. These terms overlap with what Stern calls "vitality effects"—qualities of feeling that accompany the basic or vital processes of life, such as hunger and satiation, falling asleep and waking up, breathing in and out, moving around, experiencing different emotions surging and fading out. In this sense, emotionality and activity level are the hallmarks of temperament. (p. 56)

personality

the sum total of the enduring characteristics that differentiate one individual from another

temperament

the observable traits or patterns of behavior of an individual: the way the individual behaves; the how of behavior, not the way

Most theories of **personality** development that focus on **temperament** consider personality as something attributable to the child's nature—his genetic inheritance. This might lead us to believe that adults cannot do much to change the basic temperamental style. There may be some truth in this—we are unlikely to change an individual's personal style. And we probably don't want to tamper with what makes the person who they are. However, temperament is not destiny. We can work with the child's style to help him to function effectively, and we can also help the child grow in awareness of what that style is. This helps the child to identify his personal characteristics and to maximize his potential by developing strategies appropriate to his style.

Refer to the Additional Support section in your Online Companion for a review of temperament.

ATTACHMENT

attachment

the positive emotional relationship that develops between two individuals— between adult and child

Close observation of the behavior patterns of a toddler can tell parents and caregivers how well the toddler is attached to the adult. Susan Goldberg (2000) provides an excellent definition of **attachment** that can be used as a lens through which to observe the toddler: "Attachment is usually defined as an emotional bond between two individuals based on the expectations of one (or both) members of the pair that the other will care for and provide protection in times of need" (p. 134). Goldberg's definition is particularly helpful to us at this stage because it highlights a consciousness on the part of the toddler—as well as the adult—as though there were some kind of unwritten contract between the two parties!

Toddlers are capable of doing things in a conscious way, and it appears that they are aware of the attachment relationship even though they cannot yet articulate their thoughts in language. However, their behavior is a good indicator to adults of whether they are attached to one or more adults.

By the time the toddler has developed to this stage, it is hoped that she has made some secure attachments to the important adults in her life. As discussed in previous chapters, attachment depends upon an ongoing, reliable, consistent relationship with an adult who meets the needs of the young child. If the toddler has had some difficult life experiences involving relationships that have been damaged because of neglect, abuse, or emotional unavailability of adults, there can be significant long-term difficulties for the child. If the toddler is experiencing attachment difficulties, immediate support should be provided. Early interventions may provide the dyad of toddler and adult with some strategies to help support the formation of an attachment. At 15–18 months, families and caregivers should be concerned if the toddler is not:

- seeking the support of an adult when distressed
- showing interest in her immediate environment
- responsive to adults trying to engage her
- demonstrating a wide range of emotions
- demonstrating typical play behaviors for her age
- showing distress at the time of separation from her primary caregiver/parent
- showing anxiety in the presence of strangers
- demonstrating secure attachment behaviors (as above)

Of course, all toddlers are different in their stages of development, experiences, and personality, so any one or more of these behaviors is not necessarily cause for alarm—they are

attachment difficulties

situations that occur where the child is unable to form one or more appropriate positive relationship with adults because the child's experience is erratic or deficient

attachment disorders

situations that occur where the child is unable to form one or more appropriate positive relationship, to such an extent that there may be long-lasting implications; intervention may be successful

nature (development)

the aspects of individuals that exist because of their genetic heredity

nurture (development)

the aspects of individuals that they inherit

indicators of potential **attachment difficulties**. True **attachment disorders** require closer observation by experts; they are characterized by pathological behaviors that can be diagnosed only by a clinician. Referral to experts, such as pediatricians involved in early intervention programs, can be made through the family's general practitioner or directly, depending on local protocols/health plan. Many early interventions are successful in that they result in much healthier attachments.

Nature or Nuture?

All attachments are not equal. Many forces come into play to enable attachments to be made:

- Some forces are biological, or what is called **nature**: factors largely determined by genetic inheritance, including baseline brain wiring, potential for communication, and temperament.
- Some forces are experiences after birth, or what is called **nurture**: factors include primary care figures, family circumstances, and the ever-widening encounters and experiences a child has.

How a child makes attachments depends upon both nature and nurture, as well as the interaction of nature and nurture. So we can see there are infinite varieties of human attachments. Although attachment is most often associated with emotional development, attachment is linked to all other areas of development and is likely to shape the child's:

- *emotional development*—because through attachments, she builds a sense of security and trust, and the ability to recognize and regulate her behavior
- *cognitive development*—because she needs to be secure to play, explore, and learn
- *social development*—because secure attachments shape her ability to make positive relationships
- *personality development*—because she needs to have a secure attachment so that she can develop her own personality
- *moral and character development*—because her security and trusting relationships provide the backdrop necessary to internalize positive role models and learn what is socially acceptable
- *language development*—because language acquisition is dependent upon adults with whom she is attached
- *physical development*—because she needs to feel secure and confident to have the motivation to move, explore, and acquire skills
- *resilience*—because having a secure base allows her to cope with difficulties that she encounters

History of Attachment Research

The essential source for our understanding of attachment stems from the pioneering work of John Bowlby (1953), Mary Ainsworth (1969), and Klaus and Kennel (1976), who focused on the attachment of mother and child or parent and child. Bowlby called this monotropy, a bias to have a hierarchy of attachment preferences, with one primary attachment figure—usually the mother. Today our understanding of attachment is somewhat more broad, and there is some disagreement about applying the same theory of attachment to all attachment relationships. That said, the ways in which infants and toddlers make these attachments tend to fall into four categories. The behaviors associated with the first three were identified by Ainsworth (1973), and the behaviors in the fourth category, Insecure/Disorganized/Disoriented Attachment, were identified by Main and Hesse (1990). These attachment categories and associated behaviors are listed in Box 9.2. Be sure to also review the information in Chapter 7, Figure 7.1, on attachment categories and long-term behavior outcomes.

Effect of Primary Caregiving System on Attachment

By the time the infant becomes a toddler, it is likely that the circle of people to whom she is attached will have widened. There will be primary caregivers and possibly secondary caregivers, depending on how big the child's social world becomes. A **primary caregiving system** is advisable—that is, one specific person who is responsible for a major portion of interaction with

primary caregiving system

an approach to caregiving that values relationship-building. One specific person is responsible for a major portion of interaction with a child on a day-to-day basis, but is not entirely responsible for the care. Sensitive teamwork is essential in order for this system to be effective

BOX 9.2

AINSWORTH AND MAIN AND HESSE'S ATTACHMENT CHARACTERISTICS

SECURE ATTACHMENT

- *not overly stressed*
- *demonstrates a range of emotions*
- *attempts to self-regulate*
- *trusts that her needs will be met (relatively calm about hunger, thirst, etc.)*
- *confident in becoming independent (will move away from adult for periods of time)*
- *casual, relaxed physical contact*
- *cooperative with parents and adults*
- *can problem-solve with confidence*
- *uses regular social referencing (checking to see if the adult is there)*
- *shows curiosity*
- *lengthy attention span*
- *acquires pro social skills earlier*
- *expects support of adult*

INSECURE/AVOIDANT ATTACHMENT

- *neutral affect (emotion)*
- *does not seem happy or sad with separation or reunion*
- *unconcerned about mother/adult*
- *makes little attempt at self-help skills*
- *unresponsive to stimuli*
- *avoids social contact with others children/adults*
- *may appear distant or blank*
- *behavior erratic and unpredictable at times*
- *imitates others emotionally*
- *apathetic in play situations*
- *makes limited eye contact*
- *often angry or hostile*
- *tends to be noncompliant and disobey rules*

INSECURE/RESISTANT/ AMBIVALENT ATTACHMENT

- *overly dependent*
- *seeks attention*
- *frequent temper tantrums*
- *behavior is not socially acceptable (with reference to the norm)*
- *ignores play/exploration*
- *difficulty in settling*
- *shows no pro social skills and poor social skills*
- *fails to regulate extreme behaviors— impulsive*
- *poor attention span*
- *tests adults*
- *exhibits helpless or baby behavior*
- *tends to be fearful and tense*
- *often difficult to calm*
- *needs sensitive caregiving*

INSECURE/DISORGANIZED/ DISORIENTED ATTACHMENT

- *not easily comforted*
- *emotions/reactions unpredictable*
- *moves from one adult to the next without engagement*
- *not focused on tasks*
- *easily distracted*
- *emotions change very rapidly*
- *plays with objects without following through a play sequence*
- *short attention span*
- *picks up toys and drops them, moving on to something else*
- *low tolerance for frustration*
- *lacks self-control*
- *wanders aimlessly*
- *erratic contact with adults*
- *loses interest quickly*
- *has little curiosity*
- *acquires many skills later than average*
- *fails to categorize, organize, or put objects where they belong*
- *requires specialized caregiving*

a child on a day-to-day basis—but it does *not* mean that one person cares for an infant or toddler exclusively, all of the time. Primary caregiving *does* mean that the infant or toddler has someone special with whom to build an intimate relationship. The system is dependent on teamwork with members who communicate and collaborate well. We know that children can form multiple attachments to caregivers (Rutter & O'Connor, 1999), but transitions must be handled with sensitivity—and consistency in care is essential. This means you must: pay attention to how many individuals interact with young children daily; monitor the children's separation and stranger anxiety behaviors; and closely supervise the impact that breaks and vacation times can have on children. This should not be viewed as an inconvenience, but rather as an investment in the emotional well-being of children. Programs that value the primary caregiving system take to heart the seriousness and importance of fostering relationships. Observations of the toddler recorded by both the family members and child care staff can lead to a better understanding of a difficulty. In addition, adults might take notice of a toddler who:

- is indiscriminately friendly (makes a superficial relationship with every passing adult but is not distressed at their departure)
- shows no preference for one adult over another
- has a preferred caregiver but clings to that adult in a distorted manner
- appears disorganized/disoriented (relative to expected behavior)
- engages in reckless activity (more dangerous than is typical even at the toddler stage)
- spends long periods alone rocking herself or banging her head

Resilience

resilience

the idea that an individual can be prepared or strengthened to withstand or recover from negative circumstances

solitary play

spontaneous activity involving only one individual, not involving others

Resilience refers to the infant's ability to protect himself from unpleasant or negative experiences. Resilience is related to both autonomy and attachment. Psychological characteristics of the person (internal locus of control—autonomy) and personal skills such as competence can help offset the effects of negative experiences. Strong attachments also tend to act as a buffer against adversity. Studies (e.g., Weinfield, Sroufe, Egeland, & Carlson, 1999) have documented that securely attached children are often rated as "ego-resilient" (p. 77), meaning that these children demonstrate flexibility in their thinking—especially when encountering frustration—and a great deal of persistence in the face of difficult tasks. It is now thought that emotional IQ (Goleman, 1997), or the capacity of emotional competence such as self-regulation of one's emotions and empathy, is "related to coping and long-term resilience even in situations of great adversity. Although children need the support of a caring adult, coping skills can, nevertheless, enable them to be far more in control and flexible in adapting, even when confronted by significant problems" (Landy, 2002, p. 425). However, if negative experiences are more common, if the child is never given opportunities to be autonomous, or if the child does not have the reassurance of strong attachments, it will be almost impossible for him to sustain his resilience (Carnegie Task Force, 1994). The prognosis for the long-term outcomes is not good, as the child will be at risk for maladaptations, academic difficulties, and emotional problems (Kostelnik et al., 2006).

PLAY

Accessing a full range of sensory discoveries is the central theme of play activity at this stage. Most of this will be **solitary play**, and may last for prolonged periods of time. Improved motor control assists the toddler to perform more complex actions and move about to play more easily. Standing or sitting at a table may be possible for a few activities, but the floor is often preferred.

Toddlers at this stage will draw for short periods using chubby wax crayons. The marks they make on the paper are pleasing to them. Frequently these will be arc-like scribbles or back-and-forth or even up-and-down lines. Toddlers may also enjoy

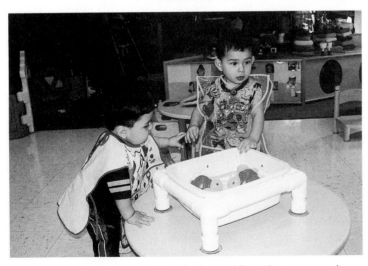

Water play is a great sensory experience for these toddlers. What are some other factors that make this an appropriate activity for these children?

object permanence

the realization that objects continue to exist when they are out of sight

block play

playful activity involving the use of manufactured or found materials to build or construct; observable stages of play behavior are evident; such play may involve imagination and creativity, but will usually contribute to mathematical concept building

parallel play

spontaneous activity occurring alongside other children, without sharing or cooperation; playing separately at the same activity at the same time and in the same space

egocentricity

the state of seeing only from the individual's perspective; in infancy, an inability to think from the perspective of others

shared meanings

communication involving eye contact, close proximity, language, play, or other ways of being at one with another person; exchanging understandings

imitative play

spontaneous activity that involves the copying of single actions of another individual, or the acting out of an internalized role; may involve deferred imitation

deferred imitation

copying single behaviors or complex roles some time after the initial observation of the behavior

making dots by repeatedly stabbing at the paper. The toddler's scribbles mostly follow her body movements, because the arm is moved as an extension of the body rather than as a flexible tool.

The toddler may display actions that relate to hiding and finding toys or other objects. These games give great satisfaction and reinforce the concept of **object permanence**. Simple hide-and-seek, played with an adult, also provides the reinforcement of people permanence.

Destruction is evident in knocking down towers of blocks or taking apart toys and domestic items. This is a natural stage toward construction, which is soon evident as the toddler builds stacks of blocks two or three high (Hughes, Elicker, & Veen, 1995). **Block play** is an important opportunity to learn some basic mathematical concepts.

The toddler may spend some time as an onlooker, particularly if there are other toddlers at play. She may play alongside them in early **parallel play**, using similar materials, but she is more likely to play in a solitary manner. Parallel play may be seen in a group situation where two or more toddlers do the same thing, such as splashing water, running, playing with dough while sitting in adjacent seats, or playing with pretend objects. **Egocentricity** prevents the toddlers from playing together, but mutual activity is common with toddlers as long as there are enough playthings. Toddlers are not capable of sharing or understanding that another toddler has her own perspective, but they do know that other children have feelings, because they hear their cries and acknowledge their laughter. They may also show a toy to a child of the same age or even invite another child to play (Hughes, Elicker, & Veen, 1995) and engage in some **shared meanings**, where there is a common understanding, whether spoken or not.

You may see some toddlers involved in **imitative play**. This can be immediate copying or a **deferred imitation**, where the toddler copies an adult some time after the initial observation. Deferred imitation is more complex than basic imitation because it involves memory and some degree of **symbolism**. It may also involve some association that the toddler makes between objects and their function. Some play sequences may involve pretend actions, but this is more typical of slightly older toddlers.

Practice play, when the toddler repeats sequences of actions, is not only important in reinforcing synaptic connections, but is also pleasurable for the toddler. Appreciating the significance of repetition, we can enter into the toddler's fun, knowing that there is a significant reason why it's important. Practice play often involves playing with objects. So **object play** is not necessarily a different type of activity; it's just defined separately by adults because they see that it has a different function. Object play is play that involves discovering the properties of the object.

In toddlerhood, object play takes on greater complexity than it did in earlier months. Now it might involve more than one object, and can involve discovering the relationship of one object to another. The toddler loves to put things inside other things. For example, she will put a toy car in a box or put a doll in its crib. In doing this, she is demonstrating some relationship between one object and another. It might be that one item is smaller and therefore will fit inside the other, or, as in the case of the doll, she may understand that dolls go in cribs. Knowing the function of objects is more sophisticated than just identifying what they are. Sometimes toddlers will be amused if objects are used wrongly. If they have built a concept in which, for example, "shoes go on your feet," they might laugh if they see you putting a shoe on your head. This shows that they understand the appropriate and inappropriate use of objects—but this involves only things that have domestic familiarity.

Sometimes you might see a mental substitution in toddler play (Hughes, 1999). The toddler might use one object to represent another. For example, you might see a toddler use a stickle brick on his face as a shaver to "shave like daddy" or pull along a telephone and say "bzzzzzzz bzzzz" to symbolize a car. So far, the toddler uses objects to represent other objects rather than indulge in flights of pure imagination. Consequently, the toddler needs plenty of objects that might strike his imagination as representative of other things. This **symbolic play** has various levels during toddlerhood. At first, the symbolism involves things in relation to himself—as his egocentricity might suggest. He might use an object as mommy's purse and carry it around. Later it might involve playing alone as he acts out the caregiver's handing around snacks to the children. He might use the stuffed animals close by and another object for a plate.

Role playing has yet to become very sophisticated, possibly because toddler language does not allow for complexity. However, you may see some imitative actions embedded in play behavior. When observing play, you might want to categorize what you see to help make sense of what is happening. Our adult interpretations of play show that several components of play happen

symbolism

the process of using objects, words, or actions to stand for something else

practice play

spontaneous activity involving repeated actions that aid discovery

object play

spontaneous activity that involves manipulating objects or materials for purposes of discovery

symbolic play

spontaneous activity that involves using objects, actions, or words to stand for something else; may incorporate pretense or make-believe

role playing

play in which children take on characters, or parts, that have personalities, motivations, and backgrounds different from their own

---

BOX 9.3

MILDRED PARTEN'S PLAY STAGES

1. **Unoccupied.** Not active object play—just observing others. No interaction. Lots of body play—gross motor.
2. **Onlooker.** Watching others play. More direct observation. May engage in conversation but not engaged in doing. Really focused on the children. Really tuning in.
3. **Solitary or independent.** Separate from other kids. No reference to what others are doing, even if they are physically close.
4. **Parallel.** Playing with similar objects clearly beside others and not with them. We have our own blocks.
5. **Associative play.** Playing with others. No organization of the play activity. No cooperating in the activity. We're not going to build the same structure—we're sharing the blocks.
6. **Cooperative play.** Everybody has a role—sense of group and of belonging. Beginning of sports team work sort of thing.

---

simultaneously. For example, a toddler might be playing in a solitary way as she pretends, with objects, to imitate an adult. This involves at least some elements of solitary play, object play, imitative play, sensorimotor play, and symbolic play—all at once!

Mildred Parten was one of the first individuals to classify types of play. Box 9.3 describes her six categories of play, some of which have been described in the previous passages.

BECOMING A TODDLER—A PHENOMENOLOGICAL APPROACH

The Toddler's Consciousness

In this chapter so far, we have looked at the behavioral characteristics of toddlers in each domain of their development. These are the things we see when we observe children and are seeking some understanding of where they are developmentally and how we might respond. But we might be in danger of forgetting to look at how the toddler perceives his world from the inside out. What is it like to be a toddler?

Looking at how the toddler responds to stimuli is the traditional way of trying to understand his experience, but there is another route that seems at once simpler and much harder—it seeks to appreciate the world of the toddler through his eyes or, rather, through his consciousness.

What is the toddler's consciousness? Of course we cannot generalize very successfully because we know that consciousness is individual. However, we can try to see the world from the toddler's general perspective. We have mentioned the toddler's understanding of trust, attachments, imitation of others, cognitive skills, and so forth. Each of these things demands a level of consciousness—not just being awake or alert. To feel trust from a toddler's viewpoint is difficult to understand. What is he feeling or knowing associated with trust? This question is of enormous importance to philosophers. They call it the "hard question." (They're right!) The easy question of consciousness is what they think science can answer—from MRI machines, PET scans, experiments, and theoretical concepts. They don't have the answers to the easy questions yet—but they are answerable, given time. However, we can attempt to look at the hard question. To the scientists, this question—"What is consciousness?"—is hard because it cannot be answered using scientific methods.

The way the phenomenologists have of trying to understand what it's like to be a toddler (or anybody else) is by making a systematic attempt "to uncover and describe the structures, the internal meaning, of lived experience" Van Manen (1994, p. 10). So what is the meaning of being a toddler as he lives his experience? We are hampered because we know the toddler doesn't have the language to tell us—that would be an easier route. For older people, we might ask them or read what they say it's like. For toddlers, what can we do to reach their lived experience?

We might try to use what knowledge we have about toddlers' development and lives to help us appreciate their structures. But these are adult ways of looking at toddlers, rather than their way of looking at us. However, some cognitive phenomenologists do use their theoretical ideas about what is happening inside children's minds to try to understand their world. Appreciating the child's egocentricity might be helpful—she see things from her own point of view most of the time. (But does she know she is doing this?—probably not) The toddler thinks in sensorimotor ways. She doesn't know the chart of substages, but she does have some consciousness of how her actions give her ideas about her world! These theoretical ideas can help us to appreciate something of the child's consciousness.

A helpful concept in understanding what it's like to be someone else—in this case a toddler—is to understand the notion of **qualia**. It's an odd term meaning "the qualitative content of mental states" (Dennett, 1991). The idea is to understand the essence of what makes the thing, or person, what it is. For example, the qualia of the color red is its redness. So the qualia of being a toddler is in being a toddler. It doesn't sound like we are much further ahead. But we are approaching an answer. The essence of being a toddler is being—it's fairly simple, if you are not a scientist! However, qualia are not the same across individuals—being Larry is not the same as being Lenny. Possibly, we can position ourselves to "be" alongside the toddlers "being"—this way we can enter the toddler's lived experience.

Following is an example from a well-loved children's book, which asks an associated question.

In the *Velveteen Rabbit* by Margery Williams, the rabbit asks the question, "What is it like to be real? Does it mean having things buzz around inside you with a stick-out-handle?" In the story, the rabbit gets this response from the skin horse: "Real isn't how you are made. It's a thing that happens to you. When a child loves you for a long, long time, not just to play with, but really loves you, then you become real." Later the skin horse elaborates. "It doesn't happen all at once. You become. It takes a long time. That is why it doesn't happen often to toys that break easily, or have sharp edges, or have to be carefully kept. Generally, by the time you are Real, most of your hair has been loved off and your eyes drop out and you get loose joints and very shabby. But these things don't matter because once you are Real, you can't be ugly except to people who don't understand."

This excerpt describes the wonderment of trying to imagine the unimaginable, which is what we do when we try to understand an experience from some other person's perspective.

PARTICULAR NEEDS

Profound and Essential Experiences

Earlier in this chapter we were introduced to the idea of the toddler requiring certain "profound experiences"—without which she cannot develop healthily—and essential experiences. Neither set of experiences is optional: Both must be provided. The profound needs have to be met as a priority at this stage because of the sensitive periods in the toddler's development. The essential experiences will be meaningful only if the profound experiences are being provided. Consider the lists of these important experiences and plan accordingly to ensure that each toddler is given experiences that fit his developmental needs.

Attachment and Emotional Needs

In discussing attachment in previous chapters, and focusing in this chapter on the attachment needs of the toddler, we have a clear idea of what the toddler needs. It is essential that we observe the toddler's attachment behaviors to see if secure attachments have been made. The details in the earlier section on attachment indicate the kinds of behaviors to watch for. How to respond to the attachment needs becomes apparent when we realize what is necessary to make secure attachments. The most important issues are to provide all the child's basic needs, consistent and loving care, and to be there in a relationship that allows the toddler to become independent because of the trust that has developed.

Greenspan and Greenspan's overview of emotional stages in their book *First Feelings* (1985) offers a good structure for examining the child's stage of emotional development and for ensuring that the toddler's emotional needs are met.

---

qualia

the qualities of experiential states; the nature of the self or ego and its relation to thoughts and sensations; the mystery of consciousness; the introspectively accessible, phenomenal aspects of our mental lives; the "what it's like" character of mental states; the way it feels to have mental states such as pain, seeing red, smelling a rose

Careful observation and documentation are essential for monitoring the child's progress. In the event that the toddler is having attachment difficulties or is displaying behaviors that are of concern, discussion with parents is vital. There may be need for a referral to an expert. Following the advice of the external agency and family and working collaboratively with them is the best way of meeting the toddler's needs.

Autonomy and Emotional Support

The toddler must be offered opportunities to try to do things for herself. Behaviors that indicate a need for autonomy are not an indication that the toddler doesn't want adults, although it may seem that way. She needs opportunities, indicate negativity, express feelings of joy and frustration, and the time to do things her way. Despite the toddler's focus on autonomy, she needs the calm and nurturing support of the adults she knows. This provides her with a sense of trust and security.

Parameters for Behavior

The toddler needs to have a clear understanding of what is acceptable behavior. While focusing on positive behavior is necessary, her limited grasp of language means she will have to hear the word "no" on occasion. Knowing the boundaries increases her security.

As she begins to learn what is socially accepted behavior, she needs to have positive role models and lots of encouragement as she learns to do the right thing.

Self-Help Skills

Toddlers learn by imitation and want to be as grown up as possible. They tend to want to please, unless they have developed a strong idea of how they want to do things their way. Provide lots of opportunity for her to help get dressed and perform domestic helping tasks (even if it's more trouble than doing them all yourself).

Sensory Materials

The toddler can rarely have too much sensory activity. Water, sand, Jell-O, cornstarch and water, foodstuffs of all sorts, dough, and so on are all wonderful opportunities for play and discovery. Try offering the same experience many times over—it is always new to the toddler. You can vary

Personal Comment

I do not know where I read or heard this story, so I cannot credit whoever thought of this and for that, I apologize.

However, I have always found it an excellent way of helping adults understand why children need limits.

Most of you reading this book have probably driven over a long bridge with guard rails.

How many of you have ever driven into the guard rails?

I imagine very few.

Well, there may be one or two of you who are now reliving what must have been a frightening experience, but we won't go there as to how that might have happened.

Suffice it to say that 99.9 percent of those reading this text have never driven into the guard rail of a bridge.

Now, close your eyes and imagine a mile-long suspension bridge that spans across a ravine that has a 300 foot drop.

Can you see it in your mind's eye?

Concentrate.

You are driving across this bridge, having a great day when, suddenly, you become conscious of the fact that there are no guard rails.

There is nothing there to protect you.

How do you start to feel inside?

Are you scared, maybe even terrified?

You have never driven into a guard rail on a bridge before, so why are you now so frightened?

When children do not have boundaries (guard rails) given to them, they probably feel the same way you did in the scenario just described.

That is why they need appropriate limits.

It helps them to feel safe and secure on the inside, even if they are protesting loudly on the outside.

Do your job of helping them learn to cope with limits.

Sometimes it is difficult, but in the long run they will be better off emotionally.

the activity by changing its color and the items that you add to the activity. Play alongside the toddlers and extend their play.

Language

Lots of talking, stories, books, pictures, and rhymes provide opportunities to extend the toddler's receptive and expressive language. Emphasize key words, and spend time with each child as you support all of their communication skills. Scaffolding is the adult's responsibility. When you provide a bridge to language acquisition, the toddler extends meanings, gains new words, and develops new ways to express himself. You might consider using toddler signing with toddlers if their parents think it is a good idea.

Entering the Toddler's World

Make sure that you spend lots of time at the same eye level as the toddlers. Let them take the lead in their games. Follow their instructions—they'll be given to you through gestures, facial expressions, and signs. Be quiet at times and mirror the mood of the toddler—except when she is overly frustrated or angry. Anticipate her actions by observing where she is looking. Take note of her observational learning and the times that she imitates others. You might extend the imitation yourself and see how the toddler enjoys having you enter the game. Be open and think in the present for as long as your responsibilities will allow.

Experimentation

The toddler needs lots of experiences and the time to explore them. She also needs to find out about materials by taking them apart, being messy, and being free to explore and experiment with them. Of course she also needs an adult present to ensure that these activities are safe. Discovery learning needs to have lots of open-ended activities so that there are many ways for the toddler to be successful.

Preferred Learning Style

Toddler styles differ. The toddler needs the adult to understand, tune in to, and provide activities that are in his preferred learning style, or channel of preference, whether auditory, visual, or some other.

Refer to the information earlier in this chapter on learning styles in order to help you begin to analyze each toddler's style. If identified, provide activities that are consistent with the child's preferred learning style or channel of preference.

 # DEVELOPMENTAL ALERTS

Chronic Illness: Hospitalization and Its Effect on Development

One emphasis in this chapter was on emotional development in toddlers. Therefore, we need to consider various situations that might compromise the child's sense of trust and well-being. Young children who have had to be hospitalized for specific treatment may appear to be behind other children of the same age in some areas of development. This is simply because they have not had the same opportunity to play, explore, or be with other children. In most cases, if hospitalization is not prolonged, the child will catch up fairly quickly. Where there has been longer-term institutionalization, the prognosis may not be as good.

For children, hospitalization can be a stressful experience. According to LeRoy, Elixson, O'Brien, Tong, Turpin, and Uzark (2003) and to Smith (2005), stressors for children undergoing hospitalization, either planned or emergency, and invasive medical procedures include:

- concerns related to injury and the accompanying discomfort of pain;
- separation from family members;

- stranger anxiety;
- fear of the unknown, including sights, smells, and sounds;
- lack of predictable structure and routines;
- lack of guidance regarding acceptable behavior; and
- loss of control and autonomy, which results in the child feeling helpless.

Stress is especially worrisome in young children because of its potential negative impact on brain development. Studies (e.g., Landy, 2002) have demonstrated that stress produces a hormone called **cortisol**, which then threatens brain development because it shrinks dendrites in the brain and also impedes the myelinization process. This ultimately results in fewer synapses, or connections, to brain cells (neurons). Infants who experience long-term stress "are more likely to suffer from anxiety, impulsivity, hyperactivity, and poor control of their emotions later in life" (Trawick-Smith, 2003, p. 116). Perry's (1997) work with abused and neglected children led him to conclude that great stress had a very negative impact on the region of the brain that controls emotions. In addition to the stressors emphasized above, other factors can affect the long-term outcomes for children who are hospitalized:

cortisol

a hormone that is released by the body while experiencing stress. Research findings indicate that too much cortisol has the potential to negatively impact synapse development in the brain

- Previous experience with doctors, illness, hospitalizations, and medical procedures;
- Temperament, personality, age, and coping style of child;
- Role of parents, such as attitude, behavior, personality, rooming in, own experiences; with the medical profession;
- Policies of the hospital;
- Attitudes of the medical staff.

Most hospitals have instituted procedures to ensure that children do not suffer psychological, emotional, behavioral, or other long-term negative effects. They realize that damage to an infant's or toddler's developmental sequence cannot be easily repaired, even with later intervention methods or support. Many hospitals treating infants and toddlers incorporate Piaget's conceptual framework by acknowledging the limited conceptual abilities of these tiny patients. As a result, the focus often shifts to preparing the families or primary caretakers. A first step is to offer as much information to families as possible. This might include welcome books, pre-admission tours, and detailed discussions with care nurses and doctors. The use of a prop, such as a doll, is often incorporated if children are old enough. Another successful technique trained hospital personnel may utilize is play therapy. After the completion of a procedure, attempts are made to minimize the separation time from the primary caregivers. This relationship, based on trust, is essential in helping to reduce fear, anxiety, and stress. The hospital staff is also usually cognizant of the importance of reducing pain as quickly as possible and reinstituting normalcy and routine for the child.

According to Smith (2005), families can help reduce psychological stressors by utilizing these approaches:

- becoming as knowledgeable as they can about any procedure;
- giving information to their child at his level of understanding so that misconceptions; can be cleared up and fear dispelled;
- remaining calm;
- utilizing nonverbal communication strategies (body language, facial expressions; and gestures);
- providing a transitional object, such as a blanket or stuffed animal, for easing separation; and
- reading books about going to the hospital.

Any circumstance that causes a child to be placed in a situation with individuals, outside the primary circle of attachments, should be planned carefully. There must be the strong presence of at least one person with whom the infant is attached, along with a supply of objects that are associated with home. It is important to accept that there will be some negative reactions associated both with being away from home and with any treatments given (particularly if they are invasive). The same parameters for behavior at home and in hospital help the child to feel that there are consistent elements in her world.

Some of the birth defects, congenital conditions, and other abnormalities discussed in Chapter 4 might require long-term hospitalization for a child. Review that information and then complete Activity 9.3 in your Online Companion.

Diabetes

Juvenile diabetes is a medical condition in which the pancreas fails to produce sufficient insulin, an essential hormone that helps the body use and store sugars. Diabetic children must have their blood-sugar levels monitored, and may need insulin injections. A good diet and exercise help to manage the condition. Symptoms of the disease include excessive hunger, thirst, urination, and weight loss, but these will be alleviated with appropriate treatment. Children with diabetes can thrive in a group child care setting and usually can participate fully. Families can provide information on how to meet their children's needs, and the caregivers should provide them with feedback on their children's progress.

Allergies

Allergic reactions vary in severity, but should always be taken seriously. Some allergens can produce anaphylactic shock, a severe reaction that can cause death. Child care agencies can take steps to exclude all signs of a known allergen, which can mean that an agency becomes a peanut-free zone or a feather-free place, depending on the allergies of its children. Allergic responses to a wide variety of materials, airborne particles, bee stings, animals, or foods can vary from a mild skin rash, itchiness, or wheeziness to a whole-body reaction that blocks the airway and stops the heart. Most of the time, children with allergies appear not to have any difficulties, but they must be kept away from their allergens. Allergies to foods must be discussed with parents and all staff. Reminders of food and other allergies should be posted in a place where they will be noticed. It's desirable for known allergens to be excluded from the agency for all children. Educators need to be informed about what to do in the event of an allergic response for each child who suffers allergies; measures may include seeking medical attention immediately and administering epinephrine.

(See the Holland [2004] article in Further Reading section for more information on allergies.)

Asthma

Asthma is a chronic breathing disorder in which the child wheezes, experiences shortness of breath, and has particular difficulty breathing out. The severity of the disorder varies, but about one in ten children is affected to some extent. The majority of children who have asthma can participate in a group child care program, and will benefit from it significantly. Child care staff can work with parents to ensure that the child avoids circumstances such as weather conditions or allergens that might trigger asthmatic responses. The child is likely to have prescribed medications, some of which might need to be administered to the child at the appropriate time in the agency.

(See Getch and Neuharth-Pritchett [2004] in Further Reading section for more information on asthma.)

HEALTH CONCERNS

Increased social contact can heighten the risk of cross-infection. Several common conditions can be prevented, or at least reduced in frequency. Simple precautions, such as hand washing, are the most effective measures to prevent cross-infection.

Toileting and Diapering

As the child takes a more active part in her diapering and toilet learning, there is increased need for hand washing. The infant might touch the potty, toilet, used diaper, or diapering materials,

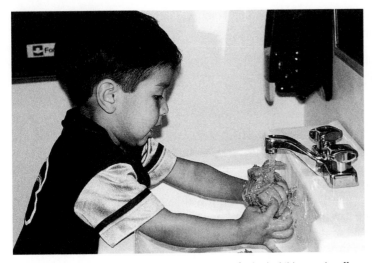
Teaching good hand washing technique is important for both children and staff.

and can easily transmit germs to her mouth and spread them to other children. Teaching hand washing as part of the procedure is a good idea. If the hand washing is fun, children are more likely to do a thorough job. Using **universal precautions** is the most effective way of controlling infection. Child care centers will follow exacting procedures to protect both the adult and child.

Ear Infections (Otitis Media)

Ear infections (**otitis media**) occur frequently, and are one of the most common reasons for families to take their child to a clinic or physician's office. Irritability is the most common sign of a problem, but the child may have other symptoms, such as those similar to the common cold. Also, the child may tug on his ear lobe or shake his head repeatedly.

Although otitis media occurs much earlier than at this stage of development, this is often a time when doctors and families consider surgically inserting tubes in children's ears if they have had severe and repeated ear infections. The tubes help drain the fluid that is collecting in the ear passages. This relieves pressure and enables children to hear clearly, a very important consideration, since this is a crucial point in their lives in regard to learning language. These children generally require little extra special attention from child care staff.

How or why these infections occur so regularly is debatable, but ear infections are extremely common. Naturopathic or medical doctors can make a diagnosis of otitis media, but only medical doctors can prescribe **antibiotics**. Physicians, naturopathic doctors, and chiropractors all have strategies to treat young children who experience frequent bouts of these infections, but many parents feel that medical intervention is essential. Among the medical community, there is divided opinion about prescribing young children antibiotics every time they have an infection. To what extent ear infections can be transmitted to other children is uncertain, but caregivers must be cautious in order to protect all the children. This is why centers might exclude a child on antibiotics. Also, children may have reactions to the antibiotic that are more effectively dealt with at home. Young children may experience side effects from the drug, as well as the misery caused by symptoms of the infection. It should be noted that many families become frustrated over the frequency of their children's ear infections. Not only do they have to manage irritable children, but they must also be absent from their workplace. Some centers do offer facilities for children who are mildly ill; they develop their own criteria for whether a child can be accommodated.

Head Lice

Head lice is of special note because it is a very common occurrence in child care and it is becoming resistant to some of the medications currently being used. Head lice are tiny insects that like the warm environment of the scalp. Their eggs, called nits, are laid on the hair shafts close to the scalp; they are hard to remove because they stick to the hair shaft and defy hair-washing. They are not caused by poor hygiene: A child may have clean hair and still have head lice. They may cause itching, but not all infected children will scratch their heads. Treatment is essential, and children should be sent home with their bedding, clothes, and soft toys. Parents are responsible for treatment and for returning the personal items after they have been washed. Meanwhile the educator should check that no other children have been infected—it is very likely that they are. All bedding, dress-up clothes, and washable items should be laundered in hot, soapy water and dried in a hot dryer. Carpets should be vacuumed thoroughly. Head lice are responsible for many lost days of work, child care, and school, even though they are relatively harmless—at least in the sense that they do not transmit any serious disease.

universal precautions

a principle of health and infection control that treats everyone as having the potential to transmit germs (bacteria, viruses); precautions such as hand washing and the appropriate use of gloves are used consistently with all people as infection-control measures

otitis media

inflammation of the middle ear

antibiotics

physician-prescribed courses of medication that target particular bacterial infections

Remember, the Everyday Health and Safety Issues section in your Online Companion has information on numerous health topics. Of special interest at this point in the development of your professional knowledge base are the topics of pinworms, diarrhea, impetigo, scabies, ringworm, and additional information on head lice.

FAMILIES AS PARTNERS IN CARE

Communication between family members and caregivers is essential, especially in cases where children have health or developmental problems, such as some of the conditions discussed above. Families and educators must be able to share initial concerns, the diagnoses and recommendations of medical professionals, and strategies for helping the children cope with the challenges they face.

Communication between family members and caregivers should not, of course, be limited to serious situations. Educators should take care to talk to parents regularly about their children's progress. At this stage, one of the rites of passage that marks a child's progress is the move from an infant room to a toddler room at the child care center. This is a hurdle for the child, families, and infant staff alike, and can best be handled as a gradual transition. At some point, it is helpful to hold a transition meeting with the toddler's parents. Although this meeting should be personalized, there can be mutual benefits if two or more sets of families who have children at the same stage meet together. They can share their concerns and apprehensions with the educator and one another. The educator can explain what happens in a toddler room, including changes in environment, routine, and staff–child ratios. Offering families access to resources that explain toddler development can have great benefits for shared care at this stage. As in so many other cases, communication and cooperation between family members and caregivers is the most effective strategy for quality care.

Another strategy that can involve both families and educators is the use of portfolios. A portfolio is a personalized collection of information about a child that celebrates that child's life and accomplishments. Family members and educators contribute items to the portfolio. These might include health records, observations, daily charts, assessment results, individual program plans, contextual questionnaires, photographs, tape and video recordings, favorite items, artwork, and any other items that tell the story of the child's development. Documenting a child's progress has both a developmental and a sentimental purpose, each equally important to families and educators. The portfolio can accompany the child as he moves from the infant room to the toddler room and can be added to as the child develops. When he leaves the center, the portfolio can be given to the families.

Some of the items in the child's portfolio may be designed to honor the culture of his family. Including such items is one way to communicate to families that you are interested in their culture. Another way is through celebrations that have cultural connections. It is important to be sensitive to family concerns when deciding what occasions to celebrate. Having some familiarity with the cultures of the families who have children at the center will be helpful. For example, families from some cultures are very happy to celebrate birthdays, but others may feel such celebrations are inappropriate on religious grounds. Although religious holidays can be another occasion for a celebration, some may think that a nonreligious observance of a religious occasion is disrespectful. In other cases, families may be uncomfortable with their children participating in a celebration of a religious holiday that is not connected to their culture. For example, Christmas is part of a Christian celebration that is not shared by everyone outside that faith or culture. Halloween, too, can have negative connotations for some people, so costumes and trick-or-treating at the child care center may not be appropriate.

These considerations shouldn't lead you to bypass all celebrations. Most centers are able to develop a strategy for deciding which occasions to highlight and for creating their own celebrations. Discussions at family and staff meetings should give some indication of which celebrations are appropriate, but be careful to solicit everyone's opinion. Involve the family members in planning the celebration and invite them to attend the actual event.

The Additional Support section in your Online Companion has some information that might aid decision-making regarding celebrations in child care facilities. Also, *The Anti-Bias Curriculum*

by Louise Derman-Sparks and *Roots and Wings* by Stacey York (see Further Reading section at end of the chapter) are excellent resources.

SIGNS OF POTENTIAL NEGLECT OR ABUSE

Infants who are making the transition to toddlerhood pose some challenges to families and care-givers who were not present earlier. Issues for both the child and adult can create conditions that potentially could lead to neglect or abuse.

For the toddler:
- Increased mobility
- Inability to appreciate a sense of danger
- Striving for independence
- Frustration as a result of wanting to do something but still lacking skills
- Self-regulation of emotions still not fully established
- Demands for attention and comfort still at a high level

For the adult:
- Overwhelmed by need to constantly monitor child's location and behavior
- Feelings of frustration in face of challenging behavior
- Feelings of failure
- Loss of patience
- Misreading cues and signals from the child and thus ignoring needs
- Unrealistic expectations for behavior
- Family, health, or financial concerns

As you can see from this list, these conditions could cause situations where adults lose control and act inappropriately toward the child. If they are unable to manage their own emotions, they may lash out at the child, causing irreparable emotional damage to the child as well as physical damage.

As practitioners, we need to do what we can to address the issue of stress in the life of individual parents and to provide both support and resources to help them cope. Parent education is extremely helpful; this includes the positive role model that the educator should present.

It should not always be assumed that family members are the only potential perpetrators of neglect or abuse. Family friends and relations may have similar problems that manifest themselves in projecting anger and damage to the child. Possibly worse than that, educators can also be the perpetrators of abuse. They, too, experience stress and can lack the skills to manage challenging and demanding situations.

Some of the most common injuries that occur to toddlers as a result of inadequate supervision (which is a form of neglect) are burns and scalds (mostly from heaters and stoves); falls from such places as kitchen counter tops and shopping carts; poisonings from household cleaning chemicals; choking on a variety of small objects; strangulations from such things as blind cords, inappropriate clothing, or ropes; and the consumption of medications. Toddlers should not be left alone at any time. They need to have their play experiences selected wisely and monitored closely. Finally, they need to be protected from their own curiosity.

The Role of the Child Protection Agency

When a child protection agency receives information from the general public, or from educators and teachers, it has a legal and moral responsibility to investigate. If the matter is urgent, it will be referred to the police. The child protection worker is trying to establish whether there is reasonable cause for concern and whether the child is at risk. Although child protection workers will work alongside the police investigation, their task is to protect the child, not to find someone guilty.

Confidentiality is an issue in these investigations; sources of information are not revealed by the worker. However, sources may become obvious if the case comes to prosecution and evidence is needed. Child protection workers are more concerned with the child's health, emotional well-being, development, family interactions, and safety than anything else. They take a holistic view rather than basing their action on single incidents.

Although people who report suspicions of abuse to protection agencies may have reasonable grounds for concern, the child protection worker does not assume that everything described by onlookers necessarily reflects what is actually happening. The worker is trained to work with families, determine what is happening, and make decisions about the child's best interests.

Uncovering what happens in a family, neighborhood, or child care agency is a complex and demanding job. Many child protection workers have a large caseload and need all the assistance they can get. Educators can be of enormous help by providing documented observations. Educators and caregivers may occasionally feel that the decisions of protection agencies seem inappropriate. However, the educator is not usually in possession of all the facts and should accept that the decisions that are made are in the best interests of the child.

EVERYDAY SAFETY ISSUES

Mobility leads to exploration, climbing, and getting into a wide variety of new difficulties. Safety is of great importance, but we do not want to spoil the toddler's chance for discovering the limits of his body or enjoying his newfound abilities.

Indoor Safety

The walking—and soon to be climbing—toddler needs to be protected from his inability to spot danger. He may have some fear of falling, but he may get on top of things without realizing there is drop. Stairs are a major hazard. Even a crawler can climb the stairs and look down to see the floor below. He does not know the risk of falling and how much he could hurt himself. Consequently, stairs must be gated.

All kinds of furniture can be used for climbing. The 12- to 18-month-old child is capable of some interesting problem-solving when it comes to reaching what he wants. Chairs can become launching pads for efforts to climb onto countertops or other unsuitable and dangerous places. Falling when climbing up or down is not the only danger. When he reaches the summit, he may find tools and materials that are potentially dangerous for him to handle. Close supervision can help prevent these dangers, but the child's skill at moving fast should not be underestimated.

Now that the infant is mobile, this is the time to take an inventory of the environment to determine potential hazards before an incident occurs. Families need to take special notice of dangers within their homes. There are many safety resources available. Some provide checklist; others offer explanations of how to handle the most common home injuries. Typically, the mobile infant needs to be protected from electricity, choking hazards, strangulation hazards, water, sharp objects, objects that can be swallowed, falling, and poisonous substances, including cleaning materials and medications. The child care center environment must address the same issues that pertain to the home, but additional care must be taken to ensure that the whole environment is suitable for groups of children.

Outdoor Play and Climbers

Small climbers can present the mobile infant with physical challenges that are developmentally appropriate, but the child may not use the equipment according to the manufacturer's instructions. She may try getting onto it with the help of a chair, climb up the slide, try to put wheeled toys inside as a garage, or any other imaginative use. All of these present dangers. The choice of suitable equipment is only the beginning of safe practice. Educators need to ensure that children are using equipment in ways that present no undue risk.

To soften falls, soft mats should be placed under all areas where the child could jump or fall. Any climbing apparatus must reach the standards set by the major safety organizations. A mobile infant must not be able to jam her head, catch her fingers, or become trapped inside the structure. The surfaces of equipment should be smooth, without splinters. Swings should be set up so that the child cannot get into or out of the swing without assistance. Always remember that as the child's physical capabilities increase, so do the situations in which there is potential danger.

The Additional Support section of your Online Companion contains safety checklists for indoor and outdoor evironments.

Stranger Danger

Stranger anxiety peaks in toddlers at around 15 months. After this time, the toddler starts to trust people in a broad sense, particularly if he has been securely attached to his parents and educators and has no reason to feel distrust. The toddler's trust marks important emotional growth, but it can bring with it new dangers.

The toddler is physically incapable of protecting herself. In addition, the trusting nature of toddlers can make them particularly vulnerable to strangers. Toddlers at this stage may begin to trust all adults. They are too young to understand why they shouldn't take candy from someone they don't know or be led by the hand of a stranger. It is too early to teach the toddler about such dangers, so families and educators must remain vigilant. Now that they are mobile, toddlers can easily stray. Concern about strangers is legitimate, but more children have bad experiences with people they know than with strangers. The National Center for Missing and Exploited Children has valuable information to help families learn about steps they can take to help safeguard their children.

Travel Safety

The growing toddler may resist sitting in his car seat. This is not the time to give in to requests for autonomy—here, the adult knows best. But you can make the car seat more fun by providing the strapped-in toddler with new playthings. His continued growth means that the adults should often check the appropriateness of the car seat size. Be sure the opening mechanism is impossible for the toddler to operate, despite his improved fine motor skills.

Anticipating Danger

Toddlers live in the here and now, and this reality presents another danger to the age group. They cannot predict what is going to happen. They might walk behind a swing, not realizing that it will hit them, pour milk from the carton and spill most of it on the floor, or fail to get out of the way of a bigger child pedaling toward them. Time and experience will help, but for now toddlers need to be in an environment where they can't get into things that are potentially harmful. In addition, they must be supervised closely so that they won't be hurt by things they can't predict.

STARTING POINTS FOR RESPONSE

Responsive Caregiving

Autonomy is something that the toddler wants and should have. Toddlers want encouragement to do things for themselves. Caregiving strategies should include making available a few choices, having activities in which the toddler can be successful, praising all efforts, making self-help skills fun, and showing the toddler you are proud of her desire for independence. Box 9.4 lists some of these strategies.

BOX 9.4

GETTING IN TUNE WITH TODDLERS AT 12 TO 18 MONTHS

 Below in are some starting points for building your responsive skills with 12- to 18-month-old toddlers. This list is not comprehensive, and many more suggestions can be found in your Online Companion under the section entitled "Getting in Tune with Infants, Toddlers, and Twos."

- Let the toddler direct the activity and make safe choices
- Encourage the toddler's natural curiosity
- Allow the child to experience some consequences
- Provide space for movement
- Encourage the baby's efforts (to walk, to do a puzzle, etc.)
- Provide lots of sensory discovery experiences
- Enable the infant to choose toys and play material
- Demonstrate practical problem-solving (e.g., putting hand in mittens)
- Provide domestic objects for play
- Provide a variety of board books and picture books
- Encourage independence and cooperation
- Add gestures to communications
- Encourage cooperation in nonfrustrating ways
- Remain in close proximity for social referencing, enabling eye contact
- Remain calm, even when he is extremely emotional

Supportive Guidance

Emotional support is the backbone of toddler autonomy, so providing consistent nurturance is important. It must be offered when the toddler wants it, not only when you have time to give it. Because the toddler learns from observation, many of your guidance strategies will involve positive role modeling. You will need to show the toddler how to eat and perform all kinds of domestic tasks; she will want to copy you and gain your approval when she tries to get it right. The internal conflict between independence and dependence may cause frustrations at times; these may need to be deflected in some way. For example, providing a new play situation may help the toddler move past an emotionally challenging situation. It's too early to talk things out, as the child doesn't yet have adequate language. The toddler does need to know how to handle emotionally difficult situations, but she may be overwhelmed by the intensity of her feelings and need adult support and distraction. There are some concerns about using distraction too often. The toddler needs to work through some of her challenges. If, for example, sharing is a problem, the adult can introduce turn taking. Having enough toys to reduce such difficulties is also effective. The toddler might copy sharing behaviors, but as soon as the child has to give up something she has, conflict is likely. The educator needs to handle this with the understanding that the toddler cannot delay her gratification. She wants what she wants now, and talking about it will help only a little. It is important for the center to have enough toys, as well as duplicates of the most popular toys, so that these conflicts are reduced.

Facilitating Development

The toddler's play behaviors show her interests and competences. She plays with materials differently now; she wants to perform little experiments to see what will happen. The trouble is that she is not aware of danger; the choice of play materials available must reflect this reality.

This teacher is aware of the egocentric nature of toddler thinking and, is helping this child to understand the concept of sharing.

Playing alongside other children can allow the toddler to mirror the actions of her peers. Opportunity for this kind of parallel play should be provided. A large enough number of playthings should be available to minimize conflict. The toddler really wants to please, so positive and helpful behaviors, as well as early demonstrations of empathy, should all be praised.

Language skills can be supported in all situations: Adults can use lots of labeling words and repeat short sentences so that the toddler can focus on the important part of what is being said. She is likely to love books, stories, pictures, rhymes, and songs, but tends to want them in a quiet moment rather than in a group circle. Toddlers love to make music with percussion instruments, so set out the instruments and have a parade!

Activities

Your Online Companion and CD-ROM contain activities to encourage a holistic response to toddlers at 12 to18 months. On your CD-ROM, Activity 9.4 suggests ways of engaging in the experience of toddlers at this stage and extending your interactions with them. These activities always start from the framework of observation. Activity 9.5 helps you observe each toddler and to develop activities that are targeted to individual interests and skill levels. Activity 9.6 includes suggestions for further experiences and interactions. Activity 9.7 describes several possible scenarios for responsive guidance.

Remember to check the Book section and Toy section in your Online Companion for suggestions of materials to use with children at this stage of development.

SUMMARY

When young children make the transition from infancy to mobility, their perspective changes enormously. Their physical skills allow them much greater movement. The enjoyment they derive from seemingly pointless running or repeating a simple action, reinforces the learning that comes from those experiences. Toddlers who are enabled to play, discover, and explore have the opportunity to find out how the world works. Some safety issues are associated with this, but there are even greater benefits.

A toddler is less likely to be playful and motivated to explore if her emotional development is hindered. This can happen if she is not experiencing secure attachments with the important people in her life. Attachment is still important at this stage of development, and the work of Ainsworth and of Main and Hesse identified behavioral characteristics associated with four different categories of attachment. Children are also seeking autonomy, and are besieged with feelings of shame and doubt accompanying that struggle. Only if the toddler's emotional needs are met can she play spontaneously and take risks and solve minor problems. There are some profound experiences that are essential for her development: Without these key experiences, she cannot develop successfully in the other domains. Once she experiences, emotional well-being, she can then get on with the business of being a toddler. This involves learning through many different types of play. Through play activity, she builds new conceptual understandings of her world. By performing many actions, she finds out the properties of materials and what she can do with them.

Her sensorimotor intelligence is taking steps forward as she thinks in ways that have greater degrees of symbolism. Knowledge about brain development, including how messages are sent and received through synaptic connections; how the plasticity of the brain allows continual learning; and the special windows of opportunity when the brain is primed for the absorption of key information; informs us that these young children's minds are at a state of heightened readiness for learning. Different parts of the brain are responsible for handling different kinds of information, and the two hemispheres of the brain are responsible for specific functions.

The toddler's ability to communicate becomes a little more refined as she manages to use a few real words. Her repertoire for communicating involves gestures, facial expressions, crying, and using some made-up words, as well as a few real ones. She has a need to connect with adults, and enjoys prolonged engagement, particularly if the adult follows her lead. If the adult uses scaffolding techniques, the child's language acquisition can be supported. In addition to using traditional language, the child may respond well to techniques that allow her to use a form of sign language.

The first words are often heard during this stage of development. Other oral language indicators include babbling, variegated babbling, overextensions, underextensions, holophrases, and proto-words. No television watching is recommended, and adults play a critical role in helping to support language development, including phonological awareness. Real conversations face-to-face, shared experiences, and book reading are authentic ways adults can foster language development and a foundation of literacy.

There is even greater evidence at this stage of differing styles of behaving. The temperament style of each child can be categorized in several ways, but each child is different. Each child's own favored channel of communication is something that the adult must discover. Using the favored channel will help the toddler to communicate more successfully. Reading the toddler's cues and behavioral signs will help the toddler and the adult to understand each other better.

Entering into the life of the toddler requires being on his level and trying to see things as might. Get down on the toddler's level, be still, listen, and follow the toddler's lead.

Increased mobility invites increased threats to health and safety. This is the opportune time to teach children about hand washing. Providers must be attuned to the toddler's whereabouts at all times. This chapter also highlights threats to children's emotional security as a result of hospitalization, and warns about the potential for abuse due to the toddler's increasing demand for independence. Becoming a toddler is an amazing journey. As the caring adults in these children's lives, we are charged with an awesome responsibility.

DISCUSSION QUESTIONS

1. Compare the play behaviors of an infant at 6 months with those of a toddler at 18 months. What developments have occurred that make the play different?

2. If the learning style (favored channel) for a toddler is auditory, how might you provide appropriate experiences for him?

3. When a mother worries that her toddler's gross motor skills are not as advanced as those of other toddlers in the room, what might you say to her?

4. How resilient are children to inappropriate child-rearing practices and traumatic events?

5. A family stops sending diapers to the center because they are insisting that their 15-month-old child start using the toilet. How should you react in this situation? What are some things you could share with the family to help them understand that their child might not be ready to undertake this step of development? The NAEYC Code of Ethics might also help guide your decision. (See the Additional Support section in your Online Companion regarding toilet-learning.)

ADDITIONAL RESOURCES

Further Reading

Allen, K. E. & Marotz, L.R. (2007). *Developmental Profiles: Pre-birth through Twelve.* 5th edition. Clifton Park, NY: Thomson Delmar Learning

Bainer, C., & Hale, L. (2000). From diapers to underpants. *Young Children,* 55(4), 80–84.

Brazelton, T. B. (1989). *Toddlers and parents: A declaration of independence.* New York: Dell Publishing.

Breslin, D. (2005). Children's capacity to develop resiliency: How to nurture it. *Young Children,* 60 (1), 47–52.

Brooks, R., & Goldstein, S. (2001). *Fostering strength, hope, and optimism in your child: Raising resilient children.* New York: McGraw-Hill Companies.

Derman-Sparks, L. (1989). *Anti-bias curriculum: Tools for empowering young children.* Washington, DC: NAEYC

Frost, J.L., Wortham, S.C., and Reifel, S. (2005). *Play and child development, 2nd edition.* Upper Saddle River, NJ: Pearson Merrill Prentice Hall.

Gallahue, D. L. (1995). Transforming physical education curriculum. In S. Bredkamp & T. Rosegrant (Eds.), *Reaching potentials: Transforming early childhood curriculum and assessment* (2nd ed., pp. 124–144). Washington, DC: NAEYC.

Garcia, J. (2002**).** *Sign with your baby: How to communicate with infants before they can speak* (Rev. ed.). Seattle: Northlight Communications.

Gardner, H. (1993). *Multiple intelligences.* New York: BasicBooks.

Gartrell, D. (2004). *The power of guidance: Teaching social-emotional skills in early childhood classrooms.* Clifton Park, NY: Thomson Delmar Learning. (Also available from NAEYC.)

Getch, Y. Q., & Neuharth-Pritchett, S. (2004). Asthma management in early care and education settings. *Young Children,* 59 (2), 34–41.

Griffey, H. *Johnson's your toddler from 1 to 2 years.* New York: DK Publishing, Inc.

Healy, J. M. (1998). *Failure to connect: How computers affect our children's minds—for better and worse.* New York: Simon & Schuster, Inc.

Herr, J., & Swim, T. (2002). *Creative resources for infants and toddlers* (2nd ed.). Clifton Park, NY: Thomson Delmar Learning.

Holland, M. (2004). "That food makes me sick!" Managing food allergies and intolerances in early childhood settings. *Young Children,* 59 (2), 42–46.

Huettig, C. I., Sanborn, C. F., DiMarco, N., Popejoy, A., & Rich, S. (2004). The O generation: Our youngest children are at risk for obesity. *Young Children,* 59 (2), 50–55.

Isbell, R., & Isbell, C. (2003). *The complete learning spaces book for infants and toddlers.* Beltsville, MD: Gryphon House, Inc.

Kersey, K. C., & Malley, C. R. (2005). Helping children develop resiliency: Providing supportive relationships. *Young Children,* 60 (1), 53–58.

Kranowitz, C. S. (2005). *The out-of-sync child: Recognizing and coping with sensory processing disorder.* New York: The Berkeley Publishing Group.

Levin, D. E. (1998). *Remote control childhood? Combating the hazards of media culture.* Washington, DC: NAEYC.

Lieberman, A. F. (1993). *The emotional life of the toddler.* New York: Free Press.

Neubert, K., & Jones, E. (1998). Creating culturally relevant holiday curriculum: A negotiation. *Young Children,* 5 (5), 14–19.

Parlakian, R. (2003). *Before the ABC's: Promoting school readiness in infants and toddlers.* Washington, DC: ZERO TO THREE.

Pica, R. (2000). *Experiences in movement with music, activities, and theory.* Clifton Park, NY: Thomson Delmar Learning.

Segal, M. (1998). *Your child at play—One to two years: Exploring, daily living, learning and making friends* (Rev. ed.) New York: Newmarket Press.

Silberg, J. (2002). *Games to play with toddlers* (Rev. ed.). Beltsville, MD: Gryphon House.

Soudy, C., & Stout, N. *(2002).* Pillow talk: Fostering the emotional and language needs of young learners. *Young Children,* 57 (2), 20–24.

Sparling, J., & Lewis, I. (2001). *Learning games 12 to 24 months.* Tallahassee, FL: Early Learning Press.

Stanford, B. H., & Yamamoto, K. (Eds.). (2001). *Children and stress: Understanding and helping.* Olney, MD: Association for Childhood Education International.

Van der Zande, I. (1995). *1, 2, 3, the toddler years.* Santa Cruz, CA: Santa Cruz Toddler Care Center.

Wagner, J. (2004). Fishing naked: Nordic early childhood philosophy, policy, and practice. *Young Children,* 59 (5), 56–62.

Weitzman, E., & Greenberg, J. (2002). *Learning language and loving it* (2nd ed.). Toronto: Beacon Harold Fine Printing.

Wellhouse, K. (2002). Chapter 2—Outdoor play for infants and toddlers. In *Outdoor play every day*. Clifton Park, NY: Thomson Delmar Learning.

York, S. (2003). *Roots and wings: Affirming culture in early childhood programs* (Rev. ed.). St. Paul, MN: Redleaf Press.

Useful Videos

The High/Scope Approach for Under Three: U.S. Addition. (1999). 68 minutes. High/Scope & Realta Productions. www.highscope.org Or 1-800-40-PRESS.

It's MINE-Responding to Problems and Conflicts. 40 minutes High/Scope & Realta Productions. www.highscope.org Or 1-800-40-PRESS.

Food & Fitness Matter: Raising Healthy, Active Kids (2006) DVD-45 minutes. Parents Action for Children http://www.iamyourchild.org/. Click on Videos/DVD's

Useful Web Sites

American Academy of Pediatrics—Parenting Corner
  http://www.aap.org
  Click on Parenting Corner

American Foundation for the Blind—Guide to Toys—Toys for children with visual challenges
  http://www.afb.org
  Search the site for Toys, click on link for articles, click on link for Toy Guide 2005

American Speech Language Hearing Association
  http://www.asha.org
  Hover over link for The Public, click on link for Speech, Language & Swallowing, click on link for Development

Baby Center—Toddlers
  http://www.babycenter.com
  Search for toddler

Brain research/neuroscience
  www.macbrain.org
  Click on link for Resources
  (You can read *Neurons to Neighborhood* online.)

Child Development Institute—language development
  http://www.childdevelopmentinfo.com

Computers and the Very Young—an article by Patricia Cantor
  http://www.acei.org
  Click on link for Journals, click on link for Professional Focus Quarterlies, click on link for Infancy, click on link for focus on Infants & Toddlers, click on link for Computers and the Very Young

Early Childhood.com—click on Reading Center for articles
  http://www.earlychildhood.com/

Early Childhood Community Development Center
  http://www.eccdc.org
  Scroll down and click on Library of Research

Emotional Development
  www.rti.org/
  Click on Research Fields; click on Family and Early Childhood

Fisher Price—play stages
  http://www.fisher-price.com
  Hover over the link for Parenting Advice, click on the link for All About Play . . . stages, toys & tips

Healthy Minds—ZERO TO THREE—language development
  http://www.zerotothree.org
  Search for healthy minds, click on the first link

Keep Kids Healthy—answers to many questions, including safety and sleep problems
  http://www.keepkidshealthy.com/

Kids Health—click on Parents—this has a great search engine; type in topic of interest
  http://kidshealth.org/

National Center for Missing and Exploited Children
  http://www.missingkids.com/

National Network for Child Care—click on Learn from our articles and resources
  http://www.nncc.org
  Also click on Articles and Resources; click on Child Development; click on Infants and Toddlers

Toddlers Today
  http://toddlerstoday.com/
  http://toddlerstoday.com
  Click on link for articles & tools, click on link for Development, click on link for When Left is Right:
  Left-Handed Toddlers (left-handedness)

University of Illinois—Dealing with toddlers
  http://www.urbanext.uiuc.edu
  Click on link for Parenting & Seniors, click on link for Dealing with Toddlers

CHAPTER 10

Feeling Around: Toddlers at 18 to 24 Months

At this stage, children still see situations from their own perspectives. As educators, we must strive to find solutions to these types of encounters that help each child become more conscious of "others."

LEARNING OUTCOMES

After reading and studying this chapter, you should be able to:

- identify the observable characteristics of toddlers at the 18- to 24-month stage
- explain the significance of the behaviors of an 18- to 24-month-old toddler in a developmental context
- recognize and respond to the developmental diversity of 18- to 24-month-old toddlers and discuss issues pertinent to this stage of development
- assess the development of 18- to 24-month-old toddlers
- respond to the 18- to 24-month-old toddler's health, safety, and development issues with appropriate protection, guidance, and caregiving
- develop strategies to work with parents as partners in the care and education of their toddler

SCENE

Outside the door of the toddler room, a staff member started to orient new students to the program.

"They leave you so tired at the end of the day," said the educator in the toddler room as she introduced two new students to the center. "But it's so rewarding. You see the toddlers developing right before your eyes. I shouldn't admit that I have a favorite age range, but this is it. I just love watching them walk, talk, and become such interesting little people!"

The educator asked the students if they had spent any time with toddlers before. "Just a bit of baby sitting," said the first student. "That was fun, but it was hard work. I couldn't guess what this little boy was going to do next." The other student added, "My experience is much the same, but the toddler I baby sit is my nephew, so I've become familiar with him. I don't know if he's like other toddlers, but he watches me all the time and has a lot of fun copying me."

"You both have some idea of what it will be like here," observed the educator. "Yes, you will find it a hectic place, because the toddlers are so busy and into everything, but try to take time for some quiet moments—that is, if you can find any! The time goes quickly when you're busy, but I find it hard to stay awake at nap time on some days when they all go off to sleep and I'm tired! But I have to stay alert. All kinds of things can happen quickly with toddlers. I think you will have to prepare yourselves by keeping well and making sure you get a good night's sleep."

In her comments, the educator gave the students confidence that they knew something about working with toddlers and agreed with them about the toddlers' activity level. But she also hinted to the students that toddlers' moods change quickly, and that they are responsive to close contact and the building of relationships. She concluded with some observations on the toddlers' curriculum: "Activities need to be fairly easy, although you might be surprised what some of the senior toddlers can do. We like to build curriculum on the toddlers' interests rather than watering down preschool ideas. We don't have themes and that sort of thing in the toddler room because the toddlers' learning comes from their interests, not ours!"

DEVELOPMENTAL DOMAINS

Physical Development

The 18-month-old toddler is extremely active and enjoys her new freedom to move about. During this stage, the toddler refines the skills that have been emerging and moves toward increasing independence. Even her appearance is different than it was just six months ago. The changes are not in size, but more in looks.

At 12 months she still looked like a baby, even though she may have been walking and saying a few words. Her head and abdomen were still the largest parts of her body, her belly stuck out when she was upright, and her buttocks, by comparison, seemed small—at least when her diaper was off! Her arms and legs were still relatively short and soft, rather than muscular, and her face had softly rounded contours. All this will change as she becomes more active, developing her muscles and trimming away some of her body fat. Her arms and legs will lengthen gradually, and her feet will start to point forward as she walks, instead of out to the sides. Her face will become more angular and her jawline better defined. By her second birthday, it will be hard to remember how she looked as an infant (Shevlov & Hannemann, 2004, p. 267).

Growth

The toddler's height continues to increase, but the rate of growth slows a little. Figure 10.1 displays the variance in weight and length for female and male children.

Some growth trends can be observed. Increased mobility tends to reduce the amount of fat storage, and the toddler's shape becomes a little slimmer. Infants and toddlers of larger parents are more likely to be large themselves. It is also likely that children who begin life somewhat larger or smaller than average will maintain that difference (Shevlov & Hannemann, 2004), but this is not always predictable. Racial differences are also observable (Trawick-Smith, 2006), with those of African-American descent tending to be slightly larger than growth chart norms and those of Southeast Asian background tending to be a little smaller. Further differences can be noted when considering the growth patterns of Native American toddlers. Refer to the growth chart information in the Additional Support section in your Online Companion.

Gross Motor Skills

The awkward walking and running motion of the 18-month-old toddler is gradually refined during this period. The toddler's movements become more polished, and she can usually maneuver around obstacles with increasing ease. By 2 years of age, the toddler can run, stop, and start

Figure 10.1 Weight and Length Ranges for Males and Females: 18–24 Months

Female Weight Ranges

Age	Low	High	50th percentile
18 months	20 lbs	29½ lbs	24 lbs
24 months	22 lbs	33 lbs	26½ lbs

Male Weight Ranges

Age	Low	High	50th percentile
18 months	21 lbs	31½ lbs	25½ lbs
24 months	23 lbs	34½ lbs	28 lbs

Female Length Ranges

Age	Low	High	50th percentile
18 months	29¼ inches	34 inches	31½ inches
24 months	31¼ inches	36½ inches	33¾ inches

Male Length Ranges

Age	Low	High	50th percentile
18 months	30 inches	34¾ inches	32¼ inches
24 months	31¾ inches	37 inches	34½ inches

trundle

movement on a sit-upon wheeled toy that requires the use of alternating or simultaneous leg or foot movement to push the vehicle forward; pre-pedaling

with no difficulty (Sheridan, 2001). She still has a wide-stance walk (Allen & Marotz, 2007), as her legs are closer together now than when she started to walk. The toddler's walking process usually involves a heel-to-toe pattern at this stage. "Their belly button is the first thing to meet the world as they walk around with their stomachs protruding" (Miller, 2001, p. 46). This unique feature of toddlers is due to weak stomach-muscle control and an uncertain center of gravity, which is still shifting as the toddler gains motor balance and weight is redistributed on his frame.

Most toddlers enjoy climbing, but don't appreciate the inherent dangers. They may climb stairs one at a time, always having both feet on one step before moving to the next one (Douville-Watson, Watson, & Wilson, 2003). They may also climb onto chairs or other furniture (Sheridan, 2001). Frequently toddlers will try to get a view of the action going on. Because adults are usually carrying out domestic tasks at a higher level, the toddler will try to reach a good viewing position. Adult awareness of this issue can lead to effective planning. Sometimes a small step stool can be provided for toddlers to stand on so they can reach the desired height. Of course, toddlers tend to forget that they need to take a step down as they return to the floor, so be careful when the toddler wants to descend. Toddlers may walk or run toward a ball to kick it, but their movement will be erratic. They will usually have to stop and ponder before coordinating her feet to kick the ball, but because balance is still difficult, they often just run into the balls (Miller, 2001).

During this stage, the toddler is likely to enjoy ride-on toys (Douville-Watson et al., 2003), but she will use her feet to **trundle** along rather than to pedal. Trundling involves the toddler propelling herself forward using alternate foot pushes as she sits astride the ride-on toy. Pedaling may take longer to learn, because it involves more complex coordination of movement.

At 2, trundling is still a preferred mode of getting around, but by 3, the trikes rule!

Although these two toddlers are the same age, they demonstrate different techniques in their grasp. Even though one grasp is representative of more complex development, both children are able to demonstrate their competence in making marks on paper.

Balancing on one foot becomes possible toward 2 years of age (Allen & Marotz, 2007), and the toddler may jump up and down or stand on tiptoes (Furuno et al., 1993b), but her balance is likely to be precarious. A typical position for a 2-year-old at play is squatting (Allen & Marotz, 2007). This posture may start at 15 months; by 24 months, the toddler may play in this position for an extended period of time.

Fine Motor Skills

With refinement of various hand movements and a more precise grasp, the toddler is able to do some things that she couldn't do before. The scribbling seen at 18 months is refined, using a more effective pincer grasp of the thumb and fingers (Edwards, Buckland, & McCoy-Powlen, 2002). Hand control and **hand–eye coordination** increase. Hand–eye coordination involves fairly complex movement and judgment as the toddler connects what she is looking at and the action she is endeavoring to take. Various different hand–eye coordination skills are emerging at this stage. They can be observed in the manipulative skill involved in undoing buttons, pouring from and filling containers, folding paper, stringing a bead, stacking objects, throwing a large ball, catching a large ball with arms outstretched, picking up small items, and holding a book and turning its pages (Allen & Marotz, 2007; Douville-Watson et al., 2003; Sheridan, 2001).

Self-Help Skills

The drive to do things independently can be frustrating for the toddler because her skills don't always match her will to do things by herself. In addition to the toddler's making attempts to do things for herself, she may say something like "Leila wanna," speaking of herself. Such phrases can be one of the toddler's earliest. She may refer to wanting to help with dressing or undressing, putting feet into shoes, using the toilet, feeding herself, delaying sleeping, or helping with household tasks (Allen & Marotz, 2007; Douville-Watson et al., 2003).

It can be time-consuming to deal with the toddler's need to try to do things herself. We can make it a little easier for her if we provide her with clothing that has relatively easy fastenings and items that are easy to put on and take off. Striving for independence is necessary at this stage, and in the long run, it leads the toddler to the management of many life skills. Acquiring self-help skills requires hand–eye coordination and determination; both are challenged when the toddler becomes frustrated.

One aspect of toddler self-help that often appears to be of greater concern to adults than to toddlers is **toilet learning**. Learning to use the potty for urination or defecation carries with it emotional overtones for adults who want to know that their child has gained the socially acceptable behaviors associated with toileting. This stage carries with it a heavy emotional load for families and toddlers. Fortunately, most adults have learned that it is not fruitful to emphasize the issue by applying any sort of pressure on the toddler. We can leave the matter until the child is ready herself to control her bowel and bladder, presuming she has the physical capacity to do so, or at least provide the opportunity for toilet success without making a fuss over it.

hand–eye coordination

the process of coordinating movements of the eyes and hand/arm system so that they both move toward the same target; the use of vision to guide arm movements

toilet learning

the individual's gradual maturational process of understanding and acquiring skills required to use the potty or toilet for bowel movements and urination

You might like to review the points made in Chapter 9 about the toddler's readiness for toilet learning, as well as the information on this topic in the Additional Support section in your Online Companion.

Cognitive Development

Senses and Perception

Interest in the world is the most clearly observable characteristic of the toddler at this stage. With insatiable curiosity the toddler explores and experiments with everything within reach and spends time studying the details of objects and actions that interest her. Although she uses her hands more than her mouth, she still uses her mouth for some tactile exploration, and particularly for comfort. Refinement of her manipulative skills allows her to touch things and find out their properties. She is particularly interested in visual stimulation involving colors, patterns, and shapes. Movement intrigues toddlers. They may watch moving images— whether real or on television, video, or film—for prolonged periods, although this isn't desirable. Usually a combination of sound and visual stimulation is the most successful at holding their interest. Games and stories that involve hearing and vision are received particularly well. Taste and smell are not the most significant channels of sensory information, but they remain important parts of multimodal perception; they tend to reinforce experiences and make them more memorable. At this stage, the toddler's sensory acuity is close to that of an adult, although her processing of the sensory material will be different because she has much less experience.

Sensorimotor Behavior

The toddler at this stage is likely to make a transition in the way he thinks and operates. He is entering the mental representational substage of the sensorimotor stage (Piaget, 1950). This means that she is making a progression from linking two objects together to making mental representations and linking them in combinations. **Mental representations** are symbolic ways of thinking about objects that are not physically present. This stage, 18–24 months, is the stage in which these mental representations help the toddler to understand reality. His mental representations are inner constructions of his real world. They allow him to think in symbolic ways such as deferred imitation—performing an action some time after he has observed it demonstrated—and in pretend ways in make-believe play. We might see the toddler solving little challenges through symbolic means, by using internal images of objects that are out of sight or of events that occurred previously. He will continue to use a trial-and-error technique to attack problems, but his new skills will involve various forms of symbolism. At this stage, a toddler can begin to think his way out of a situation that requires more than random tries at a solution. For example, imagine that a toddler's blocks keep falling over after he has stacked two or three. He may keep building, but eventually he will stop and think about the problem. Turning over the blocks, he may see a small stone on the bottom of the first block, which has caused it to rock when the others were piled on top. He will be able to make the connection, remove the stone, and then build his tower.

mental representations

the symbolic ways of thinking about objects that are not physically present

Brain Development

"Risk is not destiny," claims Rima Shore (2003, p. 59). What she means is that there is hope for children who are exposed to detrimental experiences. The brain's ability to adapt to experiences that are both good and bad leaves us with some hope for children who have suffered various forms of deprivation or negative experiences. Parents sometimes worry if their toddler is exposed to a minor trauma or upsetting experience; they might reasonably think that this will have detrimental effects on the child's development. While there is clear evidence that young children can overcome some poor experiences, similar experiences might have a greater impact on one child than on another (Landy, 2002). Children are individual in these responses, just as in every other area of their development.

One of our greatest difficulties is to determine which experience will bring about what response from each child. We can recognize some signs that one toddler is more sensitive than another, but predicting his response is impossible. The degree to which a child is damaged by negative experiences is partially explained by the plasticity of the toddler's brain, and is influenced by previous experience. It is hoped that positive early experiences will build some resilience. We do know that early intervention can ameliorate some of the damage that might be done. This can be done through **early intervention programs**, but it can also be addressed through regular classroom programming and the home experience of the toddler. Generally speaking, the earlier the intervention, the more likely it is to be effective.

Preventive measures are always better than trying to put things right after they've gone wrong. If the toddler has mostly positive stimulating experiences within a context of consistent care, she is likely to be developmentally healthy. It has been determined that the human brain doubles in weight during the first year of life—starting at approximately 1 pound and weighing 2 pounds at the second birthday. What we must appreciate is the significance of this scientific understanding. This enormous brain growth indicates the interaction of both *nature* (genetic inheritance) and *nurture* (life experience). Stanley Greenspan describes this as an ". . . elaborate dance between biology and the environment" (Greenspan, 1997). Knowing that there is an interplay between the toddler's biology—in terms of each child's intellectual potential, emotional style, and temperament—and the early experiences for which the adults are primarily responsible puts a heavy weight of responsibility on families and caregivers. In fact, many brain researchers put weight behind arguments for strong and ongoing collaboration between families and caregivers.

Start Smart (Zero to Three), *Rethinking the Brain: New Insights into Early Development (*Families and Work Institute), and *Neurons to Neighborhoods* (National Research Council and Institute of Medicine) are publications that are based on findings from the past decade, plus data from brain research. All these publications conclude that a central aspect of supporting brain development is **responsive care**. In fact, early care effects can impart long-lasting and decisive consequences on development and learning, enhance coping abilities for handling stress, and the effect self-regulation of emotions. We now know that:

- Warm and responsive care plays a vital role in healthy development.
- Individuals' capacities to self-regulate emotions appear to hinge on biological systems shaped by their early experiences and attachments.
- A strong, secure attachment to a nurturing adult can have a protective biological function, helping a growing child withstand the ordinary stresses of daily lives and even, in certain circumstances, demonstrate resilience in overcoming terrible circumstances.

We can see a strong theme running through current brain research and its applications: The cognitive and emotional aspects of development are intertwined. Earlier attempts to understand the workings of the brain tended to focus on cognitive functions rather than those associated with emotions and feelings. Indeed, it is now evident that intellectual activity is dependent on emotional security. Meeting emotional needs is a priority, laying the groundwork that allows cognitive needs to be met. In other words, mental stimulation is relatively ineffective if emotional security has not been established.

 Activity 10.1 in your Online Companion encourages you to think about why findings from brain research seem to be ignored when decisions are made regarding children.

Information Processing

Increased memory ability helps the toddler's cognitive skills; recognition and recall functions work well and are reinforced with practice. Making **mental combinations**—that is, linking one thing with another—helps memory. Mental combinations lead to the toddler's ability to make a wide variety of associations (links). Things that match or go together may be features of puzzles and games that the toddler is now beginning to appreciate. The toddler may also link people and actions, making associations between, for example, people and the jobs they do, or things belonging to different rooms in the house. Frequently games involving this sort of matching are particularly challenging, because they require that the toddler hold in mind several details—something that still poses a cognitive difficulty for the toddler. However, simple games

mental combinations

putting together two or more ideas; holding in mind two or more attributes simultaneously

of sorting and matching can be helpful, and they do assist in building memory skills. Toddlers respond well to games that involve linking things together. For example, they may enjoy a game with felt images in which they have to connect different people with the type of clothing they might wear.

Language and Communication

The toddler's communication skills are improving in both spoken language and body language. Because toddlers at 18 to 24 months are more mobile and have more experience in the world, they have more to communicate.

Body Language

We can read toddlers' needs quite quickly if we pay attention to the messages being sent. Often they communicate using several signals at the same time—a sound, a gesture, and a facial expression, for example. The total is a very effective communication process. The toddler may point and make a sound that approximates the name of the object he wants. "Dondon wan nana" may indicate that Don (talking about himself) wants a banana.

Toddlers' facial expressions can convey a lot of information. The responsive adult can identify the toddler's apprehension, boredom, tiredness, enthusiasm, or his need to be helped or reassured. Often these expressions are accompanied by body movements. You might read excitement not only in a facial expression but in the toddler's movements. The need to use the bathroom may be conveyed by a pensive stare and a dance up and down. Each child has particular body signs, but the experienced educator will notice that children have many signs in common, too.

social learning

a theory of learning that emphasizes observational learning, imitation, deferred imitation, and internalizing of roles

Imitation is a big part of being a toddler, and adults can capitalize on this by providing detailed two-way communication techniques. Toddlers pay close attention to the details of communication, and will copy them if the opportunity arises. This imitative process leads to **social learning** (Bandura, 1977).

Body language can be made more systematic if a **sign language** system is introduced. In earlier chapters we discussed the potential for introducing **signing** to assist infant communication. Garcia (1994) felt that pre-lingual children could have their communication enhanced using signing based on the **American Sign Language (ASL)**, the sign system most commonly used in North America.

sign language

a system of communication, such as ASL (American Sign Language), that enables individuals (especially those who are deaf) to communicate using gestures and hand signals

Although its usefulness for toddlers who have hearing impairments is obvious, its use with toddlers who have average auditory capacities also appears to be valid. Interestingly, communicating by means of ASL and other signing systems uses the same area of the brain that is accessed when using spoken language, even though it depends on a different sensory channel. Currently, there is little evidence of the long-term effect of early signing on those who can hear.

signing

the process of using a language of gestures and hand signals

Receptive Language

The toddler always understands much more than she can articulate. She will appreciate the meaning of many words if they are said clearly, but she may not understand the flow of adults' conversation. Toddlers listen attentively, although they can be confused about what they hear. Yet adults cannot assume that anything said in front of a toddler is confidential!

American Sign Language (ASL)

a hand-signaling system most frequently used for and by those without hearing; like other sign languages, it incorporates grammatical rules (informally called Amesian)

Toddlers will not usually assimilate talk that involves complex symbolism or concerns things beyond their experience. They are more likely to understand language if it is about concrete things and basic feelings. Understanding is also enhanced when actions accompany words. The adult might say, "We're having a story in a minute," and imitate opening a book. The toddler may now have sufficient language skills to understand and be calmed by reassurances like "Mommy will come back after play time."

Expressive Language

The language explosion at this stage is exciting to observe. Imitation assists the acquisition of new vocabulary, which typically grows very quickly. The toddler may use 50 or more words by 2 years of age (Sheridan, 2001). Some linguistic researchers think this estimate is low, and that the majority of 2-year-olds are using more like 150–300 words (Owens, 2001), but vocabulary depends upon toddlers' exposure to language, their cognitive and social skills, and their temperament. The words they use tend to be related to people and objects that are present. However, because toddlers now have some mental representations, conversation can be about things that are not immediately visible. The toddler's expression of ideas contains many mistakes. Rather than explicitly correcting the toddler with a "No, that's wrong," it is better simply to say back the words correctly, perhaps using an inquiring tone. Constant correction can inhibit toddler language development. Also, avoid laughing at the mistakes, even though they can be funny. You can seem amused, but make sure the toddler doesn't think you are ridiculing her.

At the beginning of this stage, the toddler will usually be using two-word sentences (Douville-Watson et al., 2003). These will increase to three- and four-word phrases very quickly. Commonly, she will go from saying "Daddy home" to "Daddy's home now," or from "Hally up" to "I want up." The toddler may continue to babble using mostly consonant sounds and use jargon with strings of modulating sounds. She will also begin to use that all-important word "Mine!" as she comes to recognize her personal possessions.

Songs and rhymes hold particular interest for the toddler. She may want the same ones repeated, but is usually receptive to new ones as well. She will also listen and sing along readily. Sometimes she hears the song as a flow of tuneful sounds rather than as separate words. Hence, her repetition of the lyrics may sound peculiar, even funny. "Five little dicky birds" might be sung as "My little squitty dirds."

Although imitation explains the learning of vocabulary, there is more to language acquisition than vocabulary. The toddler connects words using a set of rules. Did she learn that, too, by copying? How is it that she can use phrases that she has never heard before? Chomsky (1957) thinks that toddlers acquire language because they already have a **universal grammar**, which is biological rather than learned. In other words, their brain is **pre-wired** to learn language. (See Box 8.2.) Piaget (1954) explained the process somewhat differently, as one of assimilation and accommodation similar to other cognitive processes. We discussed these concepts in earlier chapters. Regardless of how it occurs, this stage of language acquisition is fascinating time for toddlers' caregivers because it takes a significant leap forward.

Along with the new use of a simple **grammar**, or set of rules, in her language, which we see as she attempts to string words together, there is another aspect of language that is noticeable and demanding. The toddler is likely to be asking her first real questions. Earlier she might have implied them by pointing and looking quizzical. Her first questions might be just one word, suggesting that the adult give her a name of something. For example, she may point at a fruit in the shopping bag and want to know what it is called—"Wha dat?" Soon she may demand a yes or no response to a simple question. She may ask, "Daddy gone?" and so ask if, rather than state that, Daddy has gone. She is likely to use an inflection in her voice that indicates that it is a question, and may point to the door that Daddy uses.

At this stage, she may soon be able to pull together a two- or three-word phrase. Along with a spooning gesture, she might ask, "Moma want 'ing'?" meaning, does Mommy want pudding? Frequently, early questions are accompanied by gestures and pointing to reinforce her meaning, and some words may have meanings only she understands.

Emotional Development

Stage of Emotional Growth: Challenging Behaviors

The ability to control emotions begins in the second half of the second year (Berk, 2004). The toddler faces a number of challenges that make emotional control difficult. First, the toddler has to know what he is feeling. This in itself is difficult, because the toddler's feelings swing from one extreme to the other very rapidly. Second, the toddler needs to understand the request to control his feelings or behavior, if the request for control is external. This requires understanding of the language, particularly the words for the feeling that he has. It also means compliance with the adult's request. Third, if the control is motivated from within, the toddler must listen to himself as he attempts self-regulation—the ability to control his own feelings and

universal grammar

the internalized set of rules and principles integral to all existing languages

pre-wired

the idea that the brain is prepared or structured to acquire language or other learning prior to such learning occurring

grammar

the system of rules that governs syntax in language

social emotions

feelings that exist because of relationships

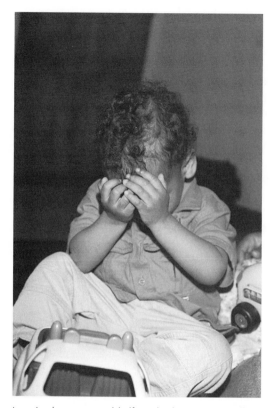

Learning how to control (self-regulate) emotions is still a difficult task at this age.

positive guidance strategies or techniques

ways that an adult can support a child's learning and behavior through encouragement, natural and logical consequences, coaching, using internal and external motivators, and rewards that avoid the use of inappropriate punishments; rely on an understanding of the child's stage of development and comprehension

temper tantrums

a loss of control of emotions or the experience of conflicted feelings resulting in anger, crying, stamping feet, kicking, screaming, or other extreme behaviors; frequently occurs in toddlers when they cannot regulate their feelings and actions

actions (Bronson, 2000). He has to know what he is trying to achieve. This requires having the memory to hold in his mind an adult's earlier request.

The complex capabilities of symbolic representation, self-awareness, and language enable the toddler to take greater control of his feelings and actions. These things lead toddlers to be "increasingly able to understand and obey external rules and restrictions and to hold themselves back from engaging in prohibited acts" (Bronson, 2000, p. 67). From this description we might think that the toddler is able to be completely self-controlled. Of course, that is not what is meant! The toddler is beginning to struggle with controlling himself, but he is frequently frustrated and needs much encouragement. For example, the toddler might see a cookie he wants, and although he has been told not to take one, he might hover over the cookie because he is tempted. His inner voice is saying something like "I want a cookie," but he knows that the educator has said that he cannot have another one. Whether or not he takes a cookie does not depend merely upon his understanding of right and wrong, or whether he wants to please this adult: He is trying to overcome the strength of feeling associated with wanting the cookie.

When lying down to sleep, he might be fearful of the shadows and cry softly for an adult. Hopefully someone will come, but perhaps nobody hears his quiet cries, so he might try to calm himself. These attempts at self-regulation occur throughout the toddler's day. Often he is successful, but frequently he is not. Sometimes the distress of the toddler, because of his inability to regulate his feelings, builds to a state of frustration. If the adult then shows disapproval of the resulting behavior, the toddler can be disheartened.

At this stage, the toddler's emotions are particularly challenging because they are becoming more complex. The toddler may show signs of pride, doubt, empathy for others, or shame about some supposed failure. These are often called **social emotions**, because they are feelings associated with the toddler's relationships. This is the time to be extremely nurturing and understanding, while building on all the toddler's positive accomplishments. Enabling the toddler to have some sense of control is helpful. Offering choices can be good, but make the choice between just two things or activities—having more choices is difficult for the toddler to hold in mind and might increase his frustration. Phrasing requests in positive ways, such as "Stir the paint like this" (while demonstrating what you mean), is more effective than saying "Don't flick the paint." Supplying a concrete model of what is right is preferable to introducing a negative idea. A variety of **positive guidance strategies or techniques** will help the toddler improve his self-regulation.

Toddlers have a reputation for being challenging. Among the toddler's negative behaviors are biting, hitting, kicking, and having temper tantrums. Toddlers do not always learn these from imitation, but when they see that another child gets attention as a result of any of these acts, this may prompt imitation. The behavior that seems most troubling to both parents and caregivers is that of biting. This may be because it appears to be a kind of animalistic and primitive antisocial behavior.

The reason behaviors occur is usually more important than what actually happens, so it is better to avoid overreaction in any situation where the adult observes challenging behaviors. When we can appreciate the inner conflicts experienced by toddlers we can see why, so frequently, their behavior is difficult to manage. **Temper tantrums** are challenging for adults, as well as toddlers. Remember that when a tantrum occurs, the toddler is not able to manage her own feelings—that is why it started. Try to remain calm, ensure her physical safety, and avoid giving in to whatever the display of feeling is focused upon. Toddlers respond in different ways to adult intervention. Some seem to want to be controlled by the adult and cuddled as this happens. Other toddlers may become increasingly angry if an adult is in any way involved with them. This may alter how you deal with the toddler, but the principle of remaining calm is essential.

Refer to the Additional Support section in your Online Companion to find more information on positive guidance techniques and strategies to use when dealing with biting and temper tantrums.

Toddlers are most likely to have an outburst of emotion at a transition time during the day. A display of anger, physical acting out, or a tantrum is most likely to occur when the toddler is tired, unwell, or stressed. Some toddlers are prone to tantrums because of their temperament type and the way they are handled by their parents and caregivers. Some combinations of adult and toddler personalities result in calmer behaviors. Rushing at the end of the day is problematic for some toddlers. They can become overwhelmed by the stress and not understand the concept of time that is associated with moving quickly. It is better to schedule extended periods of time for transitions or, preferably, reduce them to a minimum, planning around the toddler's own schedule.

A resource for parents called *Toddler's First Steps* offers some practical advice that is appropriate for both the home and child care settings (Government of British Columbia, 2002, p. 12). We have made some slight changes to fit our purposes.

Help the toddler to behave well by:

- letting each toddler know that you accept her feelings
- letting each child know that other children have needs, too
- offering solutions to problems
- being clear about behavioral limits
- offering explanations for limits
- helping toddlers see consequences of their actions
- redirecting behavior and giving them something else to do
- offering simple choices
- helping toddlers express their feelings and desires
- being consistent in your responses
- letting the toddler know what is going to happen
- making sure that your actions don't reinforce whining, tantrums, or other negative behavior
- offering a positive role model
- physically restraining the child if she is in immediate serious danger

Finally, the toddler does not yet have the language ability to express her feelings. Instead, she may act them out in apparently aggressive behavior such as hitting, biting, and pushing. It is not surprising that the toddler needs frequent reminders about appropriate behaviors and will benefit from sensitive guidance to support her attempts at inner control.

A positive factor is that toddlers at this stage are usually willing to please, so they often comply with an adult's requests. They frequently look at the adult to see if what they are doing matches the adult's expectations. This social referencing continues for a while. At the same time, although he still wants to please, the toddler has conflicting feelings of wanting to do things his way, in his own time, and on his own terms. This results in a challenge for this stage of development, where feelings of autonomy conflict with shame and doubt (Erikson, 1950).

The toddler's behavior may often seem to move between extremes. He may be quietly compliant at times and extremely negative and assertive at others (Douville-Watson et al., 2003). Adults find this frustrating. They must realize that both the positive and negative behaviors are indications of healthy toddler development. Even so, guiding the toddler to support his emotional development can be a challenge, particularly if the toddler's temperament differs from that of a family member, parent, or educator.

Personality

In a room full of toddlers, there will be as many personality types as there are children. We have already looked at some ways of classifying temperament in earlier chapters. Now we will examine another way of characterizing patterns of behavior that may be more pertinent to toddlers and older children than the temperament models we have already examined.

traits

an individual's personality characteristics

There are several models of personality that categorize the **traits** of individuals. Traits are the particular characteristics of the individual that make him unlike anyone else.

Some trait theorists use a checklist of adjectives that apply to individuals. Others have adopted a list of opposites. Some models consider core or central traits; others cluster traits to make a profile; yet others produce a map that can be compared with the norms for a particular type of individual. It seems undesirable to make lasting decisions about a toddler's personality on the basis of limited criteria, but at the same time, having model of traits can help us to know what to look for as we try to determine the core characteristics of each child. Although traits are considered characteristics that remain constant over time, the toddler's behavior patterns are influenced by many factors, such as mood, attachments, current struggles, and emotional issues. Data gathered over time are more significant than an assessment conducted on any single day. All of these models require reflection on the individual's style, or observation of responses in naturalistic not contrived settings.

Cattel's Factor Theory, one of the best-known trait theories, looked at opposite traits. The theory presents, in semantic opposites, the following traits:

What are the personality traits of this young child? One minute reserved, serious, apprehensive, conservative . . .

- reserved and outgoing
- concrete thinking and abstract thinking
- affected by feelings and emotionally stable
- submissive and dominant
- serious and happy-go-lucky
- expedient and conscientious
- shy and bold
- tough-minded and sensitive
- trusting and suspicious
- practical and imaginative
- forthright and shrewd
- self-assured and apprehensive
- conservative and experimenting
- group-dependent and self-sufficient
- undisciplined and self-controlled
- relaxed and tense (Cattell, 1951)

It is an interesting list, but you might reasonably have some difficulties with it. Do you see all the traits as true opposites? Are they all, in fact, traits? Are some of the behaviors developmental? A major problem is that personality is such a subjective issue that each of us might look for different characteristics in each trait and measure the toddler's behavior patterns differently. This subjectivity makes personalities difficult to assess, but not impossible.

Social Development

. . . The next outgoing, happy-go-lucky, self-assured, experimenting. We cannot judge on one encounter. Traits should be observed over time in order to be identified.

Toddlers' increased communication skills are part of the reason why their social competence improves. Practice with social relationships supports the acquisition of communication skills.

Attachments to adults remain close and physical. The toddler will demand lots of attention, encouragement, and cuddles. Having multiple caregivers is not a problem as long as the relationships are continuing and consistent (Shonkoff & Phillips, 2000). The challenge for educators is to ensure that the patterns of response to the toddler are similar. Although toddlers know that they may get different responses from each adult in their lives, needless conflict is avoided if the patterns are not widely different. The child experiences greater security if adults agree on the parameters for the toddler's behavior, as well as the style of interaction used by the adults.

The primary caregiving system that helps to ensure consistency in responsive care has been discussed. An example of another approach is used in the infant and toddler care centers in Italy. Many of these centers focus on continuity of care and keep the same group of children together with the same teachers until the child turns 3 (Gandini & Edwards, 2001). This arrangement enables teachers to make an "investment in relationships" with both the child and family. "Continuity makes it possible to overcome intense emotions aroused by transition into the center and to have a long period of good work based on reciprocal knowledge and mutual trust" (Mantovoni, 2001, p.32). In response to this approach, Head Start's performance standards now include a recommendation that "children should stay with the same caregivers for as much of their first 36 months of life as possible" (Lally, 2001, p. 15). Currently, Head Start has very few programs that include infants and toddlers.

The toddler is a frequent onlooker of the play of other children. She uses this as a device to know when to enter the play and how to conduct herself once engaged in it. She is also often an onlooker in her relations with adults, because she learns by imitating adults and internalizing aspects of their roles, creating an internal scheme of what adults do.

Onlooker behaviors are often considered to be a type of observational learning. As the toddler gains knowledge of the roles of adults and other children, she internalizes them as models of behavior. This primary social learning skill is needed in many ways as the toddler learns what is socially acceptable and what is inappropriate behavior. The adult models that are available to the toddler are probably the strongest influences in her social learning.

Learning to focus on one's own activity is an important step, and it must be taken before the toddler can hold in mind what she is doing and at the same time be aware of the presence of others. The gradual shift to increasing degrees of cooperation with others provides the basis for success in later social interactions. Because toddlers find it difficult to balance their own needs with those of others, frequent adult supports have to be offered. Although avoiding undue conflict is one suitable strategy, toddlers do need to learn how to deal with conflict. Taking turns, providing reasonable choices between play materials, finding alternative activities, or offering future times to access a toy might be helpful approaches. Also, labeling—using a descriptive commentary of the experience they are each having—can help them to come to terms with the conflict. Try to remember that toddlers find it hard to wait for their turn at something and are stuck in an egocentric pattern of thinking. Learning that it is possible to recover from upset is also important, but this should not be considered a primary strategy for managing conflict.

During this stage, you may begin to see signs of pro-social behaviors. These initial behaviors may be more a result of "contagion," meaning that the child resonates to behavior he observes in others (Lamb et al., 2002). However, many children demonstrate acts of kindness and caring long before we might think them capable of such selfless acts. Adults must role-model pro-social skills if we expect toddlers to learn these behaviors. Saying "please" and "thank you," sharing materials, helping another, giving a hug, and demonstrating caring and kindness are all pro-social behaviors. Labeling feelings for children and describing what others are feeling also help children understand someone else's perspective (Landry, 2002). All these strategies can help children become less egocentric and more empathetic. If you do see a child exhibit pro-social behavior, quietly tell him that you saw what he did and that it was a kind thing to do. Children need praise, but teachers need to reflect on the ways they choose to do this. Do not announce the behavior to the other children. Teachers often think that this approach will persuade others to imitate the behavior. This is usually not the best technique for having children learn pro-social skills, and the child who is show cased may be embarrassed, and often does not really understand the public announcement. One study actually found that children who were frequently praised for their generosity tended to become less interested in sharing and helping, so the praise actually reduced pro-social skills (Kohn, 2001). Remember, a trusting relationship is usually fostered in a quiet, one-on-one situation, rather than in a public arena. Why might this

An example of pro-social behavior is demonstrated when this young girl comes to the aid of a classmate after she falls down.

motivation

the reasons or incentives for human behavior, explained as basic drives

intrinsic

a drive that comes from within (rather than from external forces)

extrinsic

encouragement, inducement, or support that comes from outside the individual

locus of control

the perception of control over one's own destiny or future; the belief that's one's actions are controlled by the self

rouge-and-mirror test

an informal test to determine the child's understanding of the concept of self

type of approach be necessary? Here a brief discussion about **motivation** might be helpful.

Motivation can be **intrinsic**, coming from within, or **extrinsic**, coming from the environment. Intrinsic motivation is natural in toddlers, especially given their drive for independence and their desire to establish a **locus of control**—a place where their control is located. For any of us, being able to have the power to control our lives is important. It is the same for toddlers, although they often lack the skills necessary to actually control their lives all the time. That is why adults must guide them as they go through their day. Often adults choose to provide extrinsic motivation through activities and experiences that have built-in reinforcers, the use of artificial incentives such as stickers, stamps, stars, or words such as "Good Job," or by larger societal influences. Research (Kohn, 1999) has documented that extrinsic motivators may work in the short term, but ultimately they do not produce long-term gains. Although external rewards may be helpful, the child's intrinsic motivation is the true driving force for achievement. If the toddler becomes dependent on adults for praise, she is likely to remain focused entirely on her own interests, but not in a positive way, since rewards often breed competition, not collaboration. Kohn (1999) contends that rewards "rupture relationships" (p. 54), since they actually do nothing to promote a sense of community.

Activity 10.2 in your Online Companion will help you examine the topic of praise at a more in-depth level.

Self-Concept

The toddler has discovered that she is a separate person who can influence her environment and the people in it. At this stage, a toddler's self-recognition becomes more clear-cut, and she shows increased interest in her own face. This is an advance in the toddler's concept of self that is evident in the **rouge-and-mirror test** (Lewis & Brooks-Gunn, 1979). When the toddler sees herself in the mirror with her nose reddened by makeup, she shows embarrassment. Before this time, the young child looked into the mirror and failed to recognize herself. When she looks and recognizes herself—knowing that her nose is not usually red—she feels very uncomfortable. The toddler has gained a mental representation of her own face, along with a sense of how it ought to look.

During the 18- to 24-month stage, the toddler becomes able to name herself, apply the pronoun "I" to her image, and identify herself in a photograph (Douville-Watson et al., 2002). Soon she will be able to categorize herself by gender and as having particular attributes.

The toddler's increasing selfhood also allows her to be positive in her feelings and behavior. In her clarity of what is "you" and what is "me," she can show some signs of empathy within her social relationships. Differentiating between herself and others offers a clearer notion of the roles that people play; this is facilitated by her move away from totally egocentric thought.

PLAY

The Importance of Play

Play is a pivotal force in children's learning. It contributes to the development of every domain, encourages divergent thinking, helps children create a wonderful storehouse of memories, and is just fun! Adults suffer from childhood amnesia, and have forgotten the joy of playing. Consequently, adults often view playing as a waste of time, and this mindset is revealed when they ask "What else will my child do besides play?" However, Bos and Chapman (2005) state that "attempts to divert children from their self-directed play shuts down the drive to explore and to experiment. These two prongs, exploration and experimentation, are essential to the learning process and have been the roots of all culture—material, spiritual, written, and oral—since the beginning of mankind's time upon Earth" (p. xi). An article in a 1985 *Young Children* journal entitled "Supporting Toddler Play" by Eheart and Leavitt focused on play as the "central activity of childhood" (p. 22), and concern was expressed regarding the gradual erosion of play as the prime medium of learning for young children:

> Yet, perhaps in part because of the recent expansion of toddler group care and the criticism of education in general, we hear more and more about the lack of programs that are developmental and child-centered. For example, one mother wrote extensively about her difficulty in finding a child care center for her 2-year-old which would "let children be kids" Documenting this trend has been the important and enlightening research of Suransky. She is concerned that although childhood is a natural phase of life, we are eroding this life phase because of the social ideology of schooling which is embedded in many early childhood programs.
>
> Why has this trend toward schooling and structure in toddler programs become so widespread? . . . One mother of a 9-week old baby [said], "There is so much pressure to get into college, you have to start them young and push them toward their goal." (Eheart & Leavitt, 1985, p. 22)

Glossary Terms

deferred imitation

copying single behaviors or complex roles some time after the initial observation of the behavior

pretend play

play guided by the imagination; objects stand for something else; roles are taken on so children act "as if"

decentration

the degree to which a child is able to shift her focus of interest; e.g., from herself to external objects

egocentric thought

from the perspective of the individual; in infancy, an inability to see from the perspective of others

decontextulization

understanding something out of context, or outside of its usual setting

integration

the process of combining incoming information; one of the functions of the nervous system

make-believe (play)

spontaneous activity involving pretend and imaginative ideas

Reflect on those words from an article that is over 20 years old! Play and child-centered curriculum was an issue then and it continues to be of grave concern now. Expectations for young children have only become more unrealistic. The downward push of academics and the inappropriate measurement of "learning" have marched steadily onwards. Most of what is known about how young children learn best—and that is through play, unplanned and planned—has been tossed aside in favor of a much more structured and directed teaching approach. Hunter (2000) concluded that "brain research suggests that, at least in early childhood, direct instruction diminishes learning, [and] that the demand for children to be aware of what they know decreases what they actually do know" (p. 85). This continued assault on childhood seems to be continuing with no let-up in sight, since our country's educational policies keep eroding the critical underpinning of childhood learning—the chance to play! That is why I often say that the outcome of the *No Child Left Behind Act* will actually result in—*No Child Left!*

Play Can Inform Us about Children's Development

The toddler's play activity reveals many things about his cognitive, fine and gross motor skills, and his socio-emotional stage of development. Much of the toddler's play activity is very physical. He loves to run around, just for the feeling it creates. Climbing is characteristic of this stage (Douville-Watson et al., 2003; Miller, 2001). Toddlers like to use small climbers and slides, and may repeat the action many times.

The toddler's play activity reveals many of his cognitive skills coupled with his socio-emotional stage of development.

Imitation and **deferred imitation** lead to **pretend play**. The characteristics of this type of play include decentration, decontextualization, and integration (Bretherton, 1984), each of which is a significant developmental advance. We will discuss each of these three characteristics separately.

Decentration involves the toddler's emerging ability to gain a new perspective. He is beginning to be able to move away from total **egocentric thought** and see things from the viewpoint of another person. We might see this when another child with whom the toddler is playing becomes hurt. The toddler may show some understanding that the child is upset.

Decontextualization refers to the toddler's ability to think and to act outside the context, or surroundings, where the learning initially took place. Thus, a toddler may pretend to prepare or serve food—actions she observed at home—in a game of food court at a child care center.

Lastly, with **integration**, the toddler is better able to connect symbolic ideas. Thus, toddlers might understand that skills acquired in one area are applicable in another. For example, a toddler who has learned how to mix paints to create colors may then try to mix other substances to create colors. Or after playing a game that involves matching items, she may apply matching

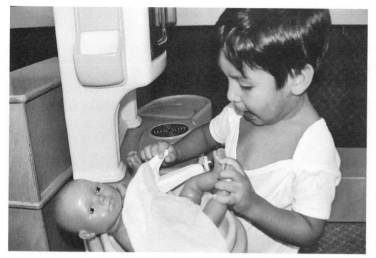

The generalization about girls demonstrating empathy in play and real-life situations before boys is just that—a generalization. Here, a young boy displays a very caring attitude towards his baby as he plays in the kitchen area.

techniques to other interests. By 2 years of age, toddlers may play **make-believe** games requiring deferred imitation of roles, skill in handling domestic items, and the acceptance of another toddler playing alongside.

A noticeable feature of toddler play is that the use of objects tends to relate to the purposes of the objects used. If the toddler uses a play telephone, she will usually use it for talking, and if she uses items from the house area, she uses them in imitation of the real actions. That said, she might use some neutral objects in a variety of ways as they arise in her imagination. For example, water might become "juice," or pieces of paper might be pretend pizzas. The symbolism used in pretend play or play with objects can be characterized by adults as being both pretend play and imaginative play.

It is noticeable that girls are somewhat earlier at displaying caring roles in their pretend play, but the reason for this is open to speculation. They may hug a bear or doll or pat a hurt child more readily than a boy would. Because they can both decenter, boys and girls may display some **empathy**, or understanding for someone else's feelings. However, in both real and pretend situations, girls show the ability to empathize earlier than boys.

empathy

a social emotion; experiencing the emotions that someone else is feeling; the ability to understand the feelings of another individual

associative play

spontaneous activity in which children play alongside each other and interact on a similar theme, but remain focused on their play

Types of Play

A wider variety of play activities can be seen at this stage. Although you may observe toddlers playing by themselves in solitary play, they will more often play alongside each other in *parallel* play. Here the toddler may perform actions similar to those of another toddler near her, but she is not influenced very much by what the other child is doing. Toddlers who have more experience playing alongside other children, and who are developing well in the complexity of their play behaviors, may show some signs of **associative play**, but if we look closely, we can see that their play remains focused on their own direction and shows very little sign of mutual activity or even sharing. (Look back at Box 9.3 to review Mildred Parten's stages of play.)

Direct and deferred imitation are both important activities that demonstrate the toddler's ability to think symbolically. Ultimately, this ability will enable him to internalize adult roles that

Personal Comment

The lovely photo of the young boy playing with his baby underscores the fact that both boys and girls need experiences with all sorts of material and equipment.

Girls should play with blocks and trucks and boys should play with dolls and paint.

All experiences for young children should be gender-neutral.

You need to evaluate your own feelings and attitudes on this topic.

Do you subconsciously direct boys away from playing with dolls?

Or girls away from the sand pit and trucks?

Another point to reflect on is family attitudes.

Many fathers are uncomfortable with their sons dressing up in frilly dresses and playing with dolls.

This is not the time to go into a psychoanalytical discussion of why that is.

However, don't we want future fathers not to have experienced the feeling of love and tenderness that is evoked when tending a baby doll?

Pretend play is an avenue that helps young children experiment with these roles in a safe and explorative fashion.

A child playing Mom or Dad, whether female or male, is acting "as if."

Hopefully, these types of experiences will give them a "window on the world," and enhance their understanding and sensitivity towards all human beings.

will lead to **socio-dramatic play**. In time, the attention to detail of the toddler's imitation is startling. Because they don't realize the significance of behaviors, the toddler can copy both undesirable, as well as desirable roles. There are times when parents and educators are taken aback when watching the imitation of their own behaviors and language that they might wish to be ignored by the toddler. Imitative learning is at its height in the toddler period, but it is a form of learning that is used throughout life.

Observing toddlers playing with blocks can lead us to think that they are more interested in destruction than construction! Toddlers do enjoy knocking over towers of blocks, but they can also build small towers of a few blocks by themselves. The destruction phase is not damaging at all, but it may be prolonged if the adult continues to build

These two children demonstrate the stage of parallel play often seen with toddlers.

socio-dramatic play

a fantasy-play scenario that involves at least one other individual

construction (constructive) play

spontaneous activity involving making, building, or creating; typically involving blocks or found materials; may involve imaginative aspects or make-believe; usually includes an end product—i.e., what is made

the towers that the toddlers then knock down. The concepts that are built during block play are important in a mathematical sense. Toddlers are learning about space, weight, distance, height, and so forth. Their buildings tend to be made in straight lines along the floor or vertical constructions. Remember that toddlers cannot yet hold several characteristics in mind at once, so building in three dimensions is not yet part of their play. At this stage, the block play remains elaborate object play rather than true **construction play**, but there is evidence of emerging understanding about building.

Constructive play is one of four types of play identified by Piaget. He described four types as follows:

1. *Functional:* Simple, repetitive muscle movements to explore and examine the functions and properties of objects. Pushing, pulling, banging, and dropping help children learn how things feel, taste, smell, and sound, and what they do.
2. *Constructive:* After gaining experience playing with materials through manipulation and exploration, children begin to construct something. For example, after exploring the properties of sand, children may begin to use the sand to make a pie or a hill.
3. *Dramatic:* Substitution of an imaginary situation or object in a pretend play situation. Pretend play emerges in the toddler years as imitation, and then transforms into make-believe play, usually from age 2 onwards. Dramatic play becomes quite elaborate for older preschool- and primary-aged children.
4. *Games with rules:* Acceptance of prearranged rules and adjustments to them in organized play. This type of play is never seen with toddlers; the younger the child, the more simple the rules need to be.

Adult's Role in Play

The adult's role in play is pivotal in ensuring that children gain the play skills they need to function in the social-emotional playscape of childhood. A word of warning though—do not spoil the spontaneous nature of play. Deciding to enter children's play depends on a multitude of factors.

For many years, the philosophy in early childhood was to never intrude upon children's play. However, children are arriving in child care facilities with fewer and fewer play skills. Several reasons could contribute to this phenomenon:

- a decrease in the amount of face-to-face engagements with adults due to overburdened lives
- the sedentary lifestyles children experience
- play experiences dominated by inanimate and noninteractive media, including television and videos

This teacher is adopting the role of parallel player. She can use this role to observe this child's play with a sensory material. It also offers her a way of assessing the child's learning style, skills, and interests.

Whatever the reasons, the reality is that teachers are discovering that they often have to plan purposeful intrusion into children's play in order to help children gain play skills. This intrusion should be minimal, but if it has to be more intense, it should only last until play skills are established. Do not dominate children's play!

You always start with a position very similar to the way a child observes other children's play—as an onlooker. Since we know that relationships with adults are so important for young children, you will play with them quite often. The role you choose will depend on what you observe. According to Van Hoorn, Nourot, Scales, and Alward (2003), these roles are called Artist, Apprentice, Peacemaker, Guardian of the Gate, Parallel Player, Spectator, Participant, Matchmaker, Storyteller, and Play Tutor. These roles are on a continuum from no intrusion to high intrusion on children's play. Often with children under 3, the roles adults choose include:

- Apprentice—supplying a needed prop at an opportune time or clearing space as needed
- Parallel Player—playing next to the child with same materials, but not with the child
- Participant—actively engaged in the play to enhance or extend the scenario

Always try to follow the lead of the child. Toddlers will invite adults to play when they are ready. Resist trying to make the play interaction a teaching episode: This will make it boring for children. Instead, take the opportunity to talk with them about what they are doing—as though you were a narrator. This can encourage their awareness of their actions and it adds language that helps strengthen the toddlers' thoughts. Also, resist any urge you may get to clean up or otherwise organize the play until near the end of its natural flow. If it becomes essential to conclude a play experience sooner than the toddlers might want to stop, give them a warning or try to guide them in a way that brings about a happy conclusion. Since play is the center of the toddler's learning, you want to ensure that you maximize its potential and demonstrate your respect for play through your own actions, language, and facial expressions.

Play and the Environment

The topic of play cannot be left before a few thoughts are shared on the environment's contributions to play. The environment sends very clear messages about what is acceptable to do and not to do. Choices must be made on how the environment is physically arranged and what materials are placed in the environment. Toddlers must be in environments that support their social and emotional stage of development and respect their natural curiosity and need for active learning and play. They also need to be in environments that are more home-like than school-like.

Physical Environment

- Does the space offer opportunity for relationship-building—are there nooks and crannies that are comfortable and beckon for adults and children to cuddle together, to explore together, to be together in smaller numbers?
- Does the physical environment have a warm, welcoming, and home-like quality?
- Is the importance of movement respected and reflected in the physical layout of the room? Are there spaces to climb on, over, under, into, and on top of?
- Are there spaces that accommodate the need to be alone safely?
- Are there spaces for pretend play, messy play, and quiet interactions?
- Are there examples of connections to home and community?

Personal Comment

Not enough can be said about the need for *softness* in the environments for infants and children.

The younger the child, the more home-like the environment needs to be.

This is what I tell the college students I teach: "Think about moving into your dorm room, or think about the first apartment you lived in."

"What did you do first?

"You started to make it your nest—you wanted it to feel like home because you were living there now.

"Well, if you work in a child care setting, you live there.

"Even more so, the children who are there, live there!

"Some children spend 10–12 hours a day in that classroom.

"Should it not feel like home?"

Softness can help create that feeling.

Softness can be derived from pillows, upholstered furniture, carpeting, material hung from walls and ceilings, plants, animals, stuffed toys, mirrors, reflected light, baskets, and natural materials such as driftwood and bamboo.

- Is there a balance between what Elizabeth Jones (1974) refers to as hard and soft, open and closed, and intrusion and seclusion elements?

Materials in the Environment

- Are there an adequate number and variety of developmentally appropriate materials available to the children?
- Are the materials accessible to the children? In other words, can children readily reach materials themselves? This aspect is critical to the development of autonomy and competence.
- Are there materials that reflect the needs of children, including sensory needs and different learning styles?
- Are there materials that offer open-ended exploration and problem-solving opportunities for the children?

All these careful considerations about the environment contribute to the opportunities for children to play. An elaborate physical environment, filled with expensive materials, will not matter if the caregivers responsible for the classroom do not interpret the space and materials from the perspective of a toddler. Needs and interests of toddlers must supercede needs and interests of adults. Toddlers require messiness and what I call "lots of lots," meaning repetitive experiences and encounters with lots of the same materials presented in an increasingly complex manner. The adults who work and play with toddlers must be able to see the environment as critical to play and learning.

BEING A TODDLER—A PHENOMENOLOGICAL APPROACH

Getting down on our knees might be a good start at trying to understand how the toddler perceives her world—but it's only a beginning. Earlier in this chapter, we tried to understand the toddler's behavior as we observed it. And we have applied various theoretical and practical ideas to help us explain or find meaning in what we see. Some of these understandings offer insight into what the toddler's world is like. For example, appreciating the toddler's physical abilities, coming to grips with her drive for independence and the consequent struggles that this imposes, trying to understand the egocentricity of her thinking and how she tries to solve problems, and observing the intricacies of the toddler's play can give us some precious gems of understanding of the toddler's own experience. Even appreciating something of her awareness that is on a conscious level, and what is lurking in her subconscious, gives us glimpses into her inner world.

You might have some other techniques for entering the toddler's world—ones that are intuitive rather than theoretical. Being able to sit quietly and listen and move into the child's activity might help.

Your Online Companion contains a phenomenological approach that may offer you a framework for being in the child's world. Activity 10.3 is entitled "What's It Like to Be a Toddler?" It is not presented as a correct model: Only toddlers could tell us if it approaches their experience, and they cannot tell us in traditional language forms.

Having tried to enter the toddler's world, you may want some ideas about what to do with your experience. Some adults interpret the toddler's consciousness of her world as something that lets us engage at the toddler's level. That might be useful, but it makes our response little more than that if another toddler! Better still might be to use the essence of the experience to enter the toddler's world as she expects us—as an adult with adult responsibilities. That way, we can maintain the adult role but with a much greater sensitivity and a new ability to be a **facilitator** in the child's work. The idea of a facilitator offers a different approach to our role (as either parent or employee); it gets away from the idea that we are simply offering care—although care in many ways must be provided. And it is removed from educator because the role is more than teaching or supporting learning activities. Being a facilitator involves:

1. being there: being alongside the toddler in a mode of respect and accepting the toddler as a competent human being
2. observing and monitoring: observing the toddler, using all the adult's senses before moving in to be her **play partner**, and monitoring the maturational unfolding of her development
3. recognizing individual interests and developmental patterns: recognizing and supporting the toddler's intrinsic motivation, pre-wiring, and instinctual drives
4. interpreting: acting as an interpreter of body language, gestures, facial expressions, and sound production, and providing a channel for successful communication
5. environmental designing: assessing, designing, refreshing, and altering the environment in accordance with her interests, needs, and capabilities
6. offering responsive support and positive guidance: determining when the toddler needs support, and providing it in whatever form is necessary—and advocating for the child's rights
7. working with (not against) and accommodating individual styles, traits, and needs: celebrating the toddler's individual characteristics and providing a consistent safe base for emotional and physical security
8. honoring autonomy: accepting the toddler's drive for autonomy and enabling her to be successful at becoming independent
9. providing exterior construction (for interior construction): providing a scaffold for any aspect of the toddler's learning as it evolves naturally, and offering a bridge from where the toddler is functioning to where she aspires
10. consistent role modeling: being a positive role model for the toddler's social learning and offering constructive strategies for successful relationship building

None of these roles might seem extraordinary, given the philosophy of *See How They Grow*, but as we observe the infant becoming a toddler, we must adapt our role accordingly.

As we have determined, in our efforts to understand the toddler, we also need to appreciate what it's like to be a toddler and have some sensitivity for what that means. This phenomenological approach offers a higher-level response to the needs of toddlers—one that leads, one hopes, to the toddler's self-actualization. This goal of self-actualization can be explained using Maslow's Hierarchy of Needs, but the toddler's needs have to be met in sequence. Like building blocks, the child's physical needs have to be met before his psychological needs can be addressed. Therefore, higher level needs, including the pinnacle self-actualization are dependent upon earlier needs being met. (See the Additional Support section in your Online Companion to review Maslow's Hierarchy.)

TODDLER CONSCIOUSNESS IN THE AGE OF THE BRAIN

The true nature of consciousness lies outside the boundaries of science because it is entirely subjective—it is always a personal experience (Frattaroli, 2001). This does not reduce the significance of recent brain research, which most scientists conclude demonstrates that all mental processes, even the most complex emotional and psychological ones, derive from the brain. However, these findings should lead us to inquire about other **ways of knowing**, or how the

facilitator

someone who makes progress easier; a person who makes it easier for learners to learn by attempting to discover what the learner is interested in knowing, and then determines the best way to make those experiences and information available to the learner

play partner

one who acts as a facilitator of child's play in such a way that the child takes the lead and the partner follows directions or performs similar actions; partnership may involve making suggestions or providing new materials, but the partnership is led by the child

ways of knowing

the different viewpoints or mental structures from which individuals construct their reality

Where would you start in order to enter the consciousness of this child?

positivism

the idea that there is an ultimate truth and unquestionable reality, rather than personal perspective or construction of reality

perspective of actually coming to know is influenced by gender, culture, or stage of development—for example, childhood.

The late Loris Malaguzzi, founder of the Reggio schools in Italy, described children has having one hundred languages to represent all their ways of knowing (Edwards, Gandini, & Forman, 1998).

By conducting many narrative recordings and informal observations, we can get some answers to the questions of toddler consciousness. However, the answers remain focused on the observation of behavior—what the child does on the outer level—rather than on the inner experience of consciousness.

Much of the thinking of the 19th and 20th centuries was based on **positivism**—the idea that there is only one objective truth and that scientific discovery requires separation between the observer and the subject, the person being observed. Phenomenologists usually take a different view, one that accepts that truth (if there is such a thing) is created by the individual involved in the experience. So his consciousness is highly individual and subjective. Frattaroli (2001), in addressing this issue, states clearly: "It should be self-evident that the only way we can possibly know anything—scientific or otherwise—about conscious experience is through observing someone's conscious experience of it!" (p. 170). True understanding of what it's like to be a toddler can come only from trying to see the toddler's perspective—and that includes getting down to her eye level and letting her take the lead in play activities. While academic learning can help us to understand behavior, for us to understand her consciousness of the world, we need to spend time with her.

With this kind of examination of the issue, we have validated the fact that experience is subjective and that there are more significant ways of approaching a toddler's consciousness than strapping her into a CT or PET scan to get a map of which centers of her brain are active during consciousness!

PARTICULAR NEEDS

Attachment and Support

Toddlers need strong relationships with adults. They need those relationships to be consistently loving and caring. Nothing is more important. Offer physical and emotional support, but respect the toddlers' own boundaries and tune in to their individual styles.

The Competent Toddler

Rather than focus on what a toddler cannot yet accomplish, we respect toddlers more and learn to meet their needs better if we see them as competent human beings. Looking at all the things that toddlers can do is amazing. They have achieved a lot in so little time.

Safety

One area that might be an exception to the last statement is that of safety. We need to plan, protect, and anticipate the toddler's actions because he is focused on his own development. The environment must offer some basic risk-taking opportunities, but this should be balanced with careful measures that match the toddler's ability to climb, examine, and get into almost everything.

Brain Work

Toddlers need stimulation and relaxation; learn to respond and initiate activities accordingly. Every experience must be positive and nurturing. Try to offer a wide variety of learning experiences, delivered in a loving and supportive manner.

Sensory Discovery

Materials that he has played with previously become completely new toys, because the toddler's skill at handling things and problem-solving behaviors are more sophisticated. Offer a range of materials that stimulate all the senses—hearing, tasting, touching, seeing, and smelling—but make sure they are safe.

Communication

It takes two to communicate, and you are the person to respond and initiate gestures, signs, and real language. Use lots of descriptive language, but emphasize significant words so that the toddler can pick up what they are in context. Using lots of books, pictures, stories, tapes, music, sound experimentation, puppets, and rhymes, as well as everyday domestic conversation, is essential.

Being a Facilitator for Toddlers

You can consider yourself the toddler's translator. Offering a bridge between what she currently knows and what she is trying to find out is your prime job. This provides a scaffold for her learning that is impossible without an adult.

Personality Style

There are several ways of looking at a toddler's temperament: You may consider her temperament style, favored channel of communication, or traits. Whichever way you go about it, make sure that you appreciate the different patterns of response from every individual toddler.

Play Partnership

Toddlers lead; you follow. Start by observing quietly and move into the circle of play very cautiously. Follow the child's lead—she'll tell you what she wants you to do. Avoid teaching, but be there to help her strategize when things get difficult. Do what you can to extend the play experience in order to maximize its usefulness and learning potential.

Role Modeling

The toddler's imitative learning puts the adult on a challenging stage since the toddler watches everything. Make sure that your language, behavior, facial expressions, and all your interactions are positive.

Self-Help

Toddlers want and need to do things themselves. Adults need to allow enough time to make this possible. Adults can also help to ensure that the toddler is successful by simplifying the task. For example, clothes that are easy to take off and put on make the task more manageable.

Taking Control

Toilet learning—as well as other kinds of learning—can easily turn into a battle of wills. It is better to deflect this by not making toilet learning an issue. The toddler is likely to want to feel grown up in this area, too, and decide for herself when to use the potty or toilet.

Toddlers need to be independent and make choices: This gives them a sense of control. They want to do everything themselves and they want to do it their way. The toddler needs opportunities to make decisions, direct her own play, and involve adults in activities directed by her.

Pretend Play

Opportunity and props for basic domestic play and simple role play are important at this stage. The toddler may like to put her doll to bed, drive a pretend car, or think up scenarios in which she can take a part. Early pretend play is not truly cooperative, so there should be enough props that several children can play at the same time.

Dealing with Emotions

The frustrations of being a toddler, the powerful emotions that well up without much warning, the joy that makes the child unable to be still, the enthusiasm she brings to so many things she does—all this can be overwhelming. Parents and educators need to work together to help the toddler to label her feelings, accept how she feels, and gain some mastery over her emotions. The toddler needs to develop calming strategies. She may have learned some self-comforting techniques as an infant, but she needs to broaden her repertoire now, with adult help. Efforts at self-regulation need to be reinforced, and toddlers need to start expressing feelings rather than demonstrating them negatively. Toddlers need to have their feelings accepted rather than being directed to feel "appropriately."

Rituals

Many toddlers find comfort in predictable sequences of events and enjoy some structure to their routines. This helps them to understand what is happening and what is likely to happen, and gives them some sense of time and sequence.

rituals

the routines and sequences of behavior linked with particular activities, relationships, or times of the day

Some children create **rituals** for themselves, or have adults participate in rituals that have some comfort. You might see this at nap time, when the toddler will not sleep if her cuddly toys are not in the preferred places. She may demand to eat and drink from a particular bowl and cup. Although the need for this seems trying to the adult, it should be understood as a developmental stage that will pass.

DEVELOPMENTAL VARIATION

Toddlers with specific developmental needs may be registered in a child care agency at this age. Those who were cared for at home in their early months may now transfer to a child care center or a home child care setting, where their individual needs can be met. Some of the more common and observable differences in development require considerable accommodation, but with some professional assistance, most children can be included in toddler programs.

Orthopedic Disabilities

orthopedic disabilities

the lack of muscular tone or mobility resulting from abnormalities in the musculoskeletal system

Orthopedic disabilities result from impairments to the bones, joints, or muscles. They can stem from a variety of conditions, including arthritis, spina bifida, cerebral palsy, or congenital malformations. The most obvious challenge that these children face is in the area of motor skills, but they may also experience debilitating pain. Moreover, their impaired motor skills might affect other areas of their development, such as language acquisition, cognitive development, and social skills.

Children with these disabilities vary considerably in the degree to which they are affected, so each child should be accommodated individually. Commonly, children with orthopedic impairments can be assisted with various devices that provide increased motor control, and they may benefit from physical positioning so that they can access toys, learn some self-help skills, and take part in the program. Toddlers with orthopedic disabilities may be helped by individually constructed structures that allow the child to play and explore in an upright position. The toddler educator can assist the child in a holistic way, not just to support her mobility or manipulative skills. Careful observation, good documentation, and individually responsive caregiving are essential.

Multiple Disabilities

Some children entering a child care program may have more than one disabling condition. One condition may have caused the other, or there may simply be coexisting conditions. Each child's needs must be assessed. Determining how the child can best be accommodated must be a priority. Children

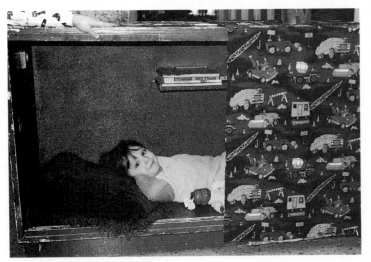

This cozy space offers toddlers the opportunity to be alone—safely.

who are multiply disabled may present challenges that can be overcome with special assistive devices, external support from community resources, training for the educators, or the addition of an assistant or specially trained resource teacher. Parental communication and shared care can help the family and the agency collaborate effectively.

DEVELOPMENTAL ALERTS

Hearing and Vision Impairments

The educator may be the first to realize that a child has a hearing problem. When observing the child, if the educator discovers any kind of perceptual impairment, it should be shared with the family. Everyday play experiences may give rise to concern. If the toddler fails to give typical responses to either hearing or visual stimuli, further observation and documentation should lead to professional assessment. It is the responsibility of the family to ensure that the child receives appropriate assessment. Children who have hearing or vision problems can usually be assimilated into the regular child care program. Educators should be aware of each child's ways of learning and should accommodate them accordingly. **Assistive devices** such as hearing aids and eyeglasses can be enormously helpful. These children need to see specialists regularly, because their conditions can change rapidly. The most useful strategy for supporting children with any sensory impairment is to build on the child's strengths in areas of their sensory capabilities. (See Box 10.1 for warning signs of potential vision or hearing problems).

assistive devices

any device, such as a machine, leg brace, or computer, that enables an individual to be as able-bodied or intellectual functional as possible

---

BOX 10.1

WARNING SIGNS OF POTENTIAL VISION OR HEARING PROBLEMS

Signs of potential vision problems include:
- Constant eye-rubbing
- Extreme light sensitivity
- Poor focusing
- Poor visual tracking (following an object)
- Abnormal alignment or movement of the eyes (after 6 months of age)
- Chronic redness of the eyes
- Chronic tearing of the eyes
- A white pupil instead of a black one

SIGNS OF POTENTIAL HEARING PROBLEMS IN INFANCY INCLUDE:

- Failure to turn the head toward familiar sounds
- A consistent ability to sleep through loud noises
- Greater responsiveness to loud noises than to voices
- A failure to babble, coo, or squeal
- Monotonal babbling

SIGNS OF POTENTIAL HEARING PROBLEMS IN TODDLERS INCLUDE:

- Failure to speak clearly by age 2
- Showing no interest in being read to or in playing word games
- Habitual yelling or shrieking when communicating or playing
- Greater responsiveness to facial expressions than to speech
- Shyness or withdrawal (often misinterpreted as inattentiveness, dreaminess, and/or stubbornness)
- Frequent confusion and puzzlement

FAMILIES AS PARTNERS IN CARE

During the period leading up to the second year of life, many toddlers are diagnosed with developmental disabilities. Some of the signs and symptoms of disability might have been detected earlier, but this is not always the case, for a variety of reasons. At this stage, many caregivers, along with the toddlers' families, observe behaviors that signal some cause for concern. Knowing that early intervention is almost always beneficial, the caregivers should share their concerns with family members and request an exchange of information. They, as well as the staff, may have started to have the same concerns. Sometimes the families do not respond to the situation until prompted by the staff. Young children who spent their infancy at home, or who were previously cared for by local baby-sitters, may not have been observed by professional caregivers. Being enrolled in a program within a child care center might offer a new opportunity for observing the toddler. Also, there may be some signs and symptoms that are new or have become more obvious during this stage. Consequently, some toddlers at 18–24 months may be referred to specialists. There must be ongoing consultation with family members, and it is usual for them to make the appointments with specialists. This generally follows an initial consultation with the family doctor. It is the place of the professional caregiver to supply families with adequate observational information, assist them in accessing resources, advocate for the toddler to ensure that her needs are met, keep appropriate relevant documentation, and make appropriate accommodations to the program in accordance with the outcome of any assessment that is made. Frequent consultation between key professionals and families is essential to support the toddler. Typically, an **individual family service plan** (IFSP) is developed for the toddler that can be implemented both at home and at the center.

It is understandable that families might resist seeking a specialist consultation that might lead to an unwelcome diagnosis. From the time of pregnancy and birth, most families anticipate a healthy child. Accepting that the child may not match their internalized image is an emotional struggle.

Again we see that communication and shared care are particularly important when a child has disabilities or other problems that may require specialized care. In such cases, families and educators can be excellent resources for each other. Families can communicate the results of assessment and information about the abilities of, and the challenges facing, their child. In turn, the educator can provide the family members with observations of the child's progress or challenges, and may be able to help with access to community resources.

Depending on the severity of the disability, families are often under an unusual amount of stress and may be nervous about placing their child in care. They can be reassured by conversations with the educator, who conveys the staff's knowledge of the child's condition and sensitivity to his needs.

The issues surrounding the special needs of children, requests by families, and demands on educators raise the general problem of boundaries. One of the goals of a child care center is to be flexible and accommodating for all families and children, not just for those with special needs. But how far can educators go, and how do they communicate limits? The Additional Support section in your Online Companion has an article that offers strategies for communicating boundaries to families.

individual family service plan

the IFSP is a written plan developed by parents or guardians with input from a multidisciplinary team. The IFSP (1) addresses the family's strengths, needs, concerns, and priorities; (2) identifies support services available to meet those needs; and (3) empowers the family to meet the developmental needs of their infant or toddler with a disability

HEALTH CONCERNS

Contact with a widening circle of people can lead a toddler to greater exposure to childhood illnesses. Only a medical doctor can diagnose specific illnesses, but educators must be knowledgeable about and watch for signs and symptoms of diseases, and be aware of how to respond to any outbreaks. Local health authorities can provide families and educators with up-to-date information on when to exclude children and what constitutes a reportable disease. Prevention of disease is an important issue—particularly early in life.

It is essential that toddlers receive immunizations in accordance with the required protocols before and during their time in child care settings. Remember to check the immunization schedule in the Additional Support section in your Online Companion.

There is also information on numerous health topics in the Everyday Health and Safety Issues section on your Online Companion. Of special note at this point is information about the common cold, influenza, and strep throat, as well as additional information on lead poisoning that is not touched on in the section below.

Lead Poisoning

Lead poisoning is one of the most common environmental child health problems in the United States, and is caused by too much lead in the body. Lead is especially harmful to children younger than 6, but anyone who is exposed to lead either through eating, drinking, or breathing something with too much lead can get lead poisoning. Currently, lead poisoning affects 3–4 million young children—one in six under age 6. Large amounts of lead in a child's blood can slow a child's development and cause learning and behavior problems. Other possible concerns are brain damage, anemia, liver and kidney damage, hearing loss, hyperactivity, other physical and mental problems, and, in extreme cases, death. Lead contamination is often found in homes, in house dust, in paint, in toys imported from outside North America, in drinking water, and in soil. A child may have lead poisoning and not feel sick. Or the child may have stomachaches, headaches, a poor appetite, or trouble sleeping, or be cranky, tired, or restless.

A blood test is the only way to find out if a child has too much lead. The Centers for Disease Control and Prevention (CDC) recommends testing every child at 12 months of age, and again at 24 months, if warranted. Screening should start at 6 months if the child is at risk for lead exposure—for example, if the child lives in an older home built before 1960 with peeling or chipping paint. Depending on the results of blood tests, further testing may be required. In some states, more frequent lead screening is required by law. Activity 10.4 in your Online Companion directs you to a site where you can print out a brochure on lead poisoning.

The professional must keep current about safety hazards and be aware of every aspect of the environment. It is not suggested that adults keep toddlers away from all potential hazards, but most materials and situations require risk management:

1. Identify the potential hazard.
2. Recognize the developmental level of the child (and what dangers she might be in because of her skills and judgment—or lack of them).
3. Assess the risk of harm:
   - Consequences too great, therefore avoid the material/situation completely
   - Consequences mild, therefore allow only careful use of material/situation
   - Consequences negligible, therefore allow open use of material/situation
4. Alter the environment in accordance with the level of risk.
5. Monitor the use of material/situation.

In general, if the adult responsible for decision-making finds it difficult to make a risk assessment of a material or situation, it is advisable to avoid its use until further information can be accessed.

EVERYDAY SAFETY ISSUES

Field Trips

Although toddlers of this age benefit from being taken out and about, excursions present some safety issues. Short walks and visits to local events are better than traveling long distances for larger events that won't be meaningful for children so young. Any outing requires extensive preparation. There must be contingency plans for a variety of mishaps. Ensure that:

- parental permission has been granted for the trip
- liability insurance coverage is in place
- the toddlers know what is going to happen
- the supervisor knows where you and the children are going

- your trip has manageable travel arrangements
- you carry all the necessary medical supplies and first aid equipment, cash, emergency plans, and phone numbers
- you take a mobile phone, if possible
- you have enough adults available
- you take changes of clothing
- you plan for toilet/potty/diaper arrangements
- you have antibacterial gel in case hand washing is impossible
- you count the number of children regularly
- if walking in convoy, you have adults at the front and back
- you use strollers that are in good repair and have safety straps over the shoulders
- strollers are taken along for any children who might become tired from walking
- you plan food and snacks, and supply drinks
- sunscreen is applied if any skin is exposed (young children should not have skin exposed to the sun)
- children wear hats in the sun
- you plan for cold, rain, or wet snow, or other extreme weather
- if the large group splits, which is better for toddlers, each adult is assigned specific children

For easy identification, you might consider clothing all the children in brightly colored t-shirts. Be prepared to cancel the trip if:

- there are not enough adults to help
- the weather is poor or threatening
- some children seem listless or show symptoms of illness
- the children don't seem interested in going

Check out more issues on safety in the Everyday Health and Safety Issues section of your Online Companion.

STARTING POINTS FOR RESPONSE

Responsive Caregiving

This is an active phase of childhood, and the adult can find it challenging to keep up with the toddler. His interests may change quickly, but when he finds something to explore, he may stay with it for a while. He will not appreciate stopping, so you may give a warning about when that is going to happen. The toddler continues to need support and will look to adults for assistance when he needs it. He may have a clearer idea of who he is but, because his thinking is still ego-centric, he is strong-willed about what he wants. The caregiver has to handle this in ways that prevent conflict with other children. Although the toddler likes to have the approval of adults and will do things to please them, his own immediate wishes are stronger. The cues he sends are blended with some conventional language, but the caregiver will do well to read his signs. The caregiver may be able to help the toddler recognize how he feels with simple questions that he can respond to with a nod or shake of the head. Box 10.2 provides strategies for building your responsivity to toddlers at this stage.

Supportive Guidance

Helping the toddler learn to control the tide of emotions that sweeps over him is an important guidance issue. The educator's calm manner and consistent approach is helpful, but clear strategies are necessary to assist this. Labeling feelings is helpful, but doesn't, in itself, provide control. Fortunately, the toddler wants to regulate himself, so praising his efforts should encourage

BOX 10.2

GETTING IN TUNE WITH TODDLERS AT 18–24 MONTHS

Below in are some starting points for building your responsivity skills with an 18–24-month-old toddlers. This list is not comprehensive, and many more suggestions can be found in your Online Companion under the section entitled "Getting in Tune with Infants and Toddlers."

* respond positively to attention-seeking—what does the toddler want or need?
* listen to the toddler before you talk to her
* plan activities based on emerging skills
* provide plenty of space for mobility
* encourage simple problem-solving play
* monitor climbing activities
* reinforce language and introduce new words and phrases
* support the toddler's initiatives to do things independently, and praise her initiatives
* sing songs, rhymes, and action verses
* follow the toddler's lead in her play
* extend play into nature and the outside world
* have materials ready for pretend play
* extend play episodes, adding new ideas
* model empathic responses, exaggerating key features of your role
* respond to invitations to play, and play along with the toddler's ideas
* offer meals at the table in small groups, encouraging conversation

further progress. There will be times when the toddler is overwhelmed with emotion and will need distraction because he cannot control himself. In such cases, the educator's empathy is particularly important. The toddler may sometimes find it difficult to make decisions. The educator can help the toddler by narrowing down the decision to a choice between two things.

Facilitating Development

Learning to play alongside others is an important social skill. The educator should ensure that the toddler has opportunities to do this. Play experiences involving basic construction, pretend play, and lots of sensory and discovery materials are starting points for supporting both cognitive and social development. Toddlers respond well to painting and to making things, but they need to be focused on the process rather than on the product. At the same time the toddler is playing, language is being learned. The adult has responsibility for supporting and extending play with lots of encouragement and the use of clear and direct words and phrases. Even when the toddler is engrossed in a chosen activity, he will look across to the adult for a supportive response.

Activities

Your CD-ROM contains activities to encourage a holistic response to toddlers at 18–24 months. Activity 10.5 suggests ways of engaging in the experience of toddlers at this stage and extending your interactions with them. Activities 10.6–10.8 are on the CD. These activities always start from the framework of observation. Activity 10.6 helps you observe each toddler and develop activities that are targeted to individual interests and skill levels. Activity 10.7 includes suggestions for further experiences and interactions. Activity 10.8 describes several possible scenarios for responsive guidance.

SUMMARY

The stage of 18 to 24 months marks significant changes in all aspects of the toddler's development. There is clear evidence that every advance within each developmental domain is paralleled by advances in all the other domains.

The physical size and mobility of the toddler shows marked changes, as she is able to run, climb, and demonstrate a variety of gross and fine motor skill advancements.

Her sensory acuity is near that of an adult, but her limited experience and sensorimotor thinking limits the processing of her perceptions. At this stage, the toddler wants to discover materials and see what they can do. She performs actions upon everything she can handle to determine the properties of the materials and objects. The toddler cannot recognize the potential hazards of a situation and cannot predict outcomes of her actions. Because her grasp is more refined, she is able to manipulate objects and carefully handle small items, demonstrating her hand–eye coordination.

The toddler's play behaviors are increasingly complex, and we see examples of imitative, pretend, role playing, symbolic play, construction, and a variety of other solitary activities, along with some social interaction linked with parallel and even associative play. The play sequences tend to be longer, and she enjoys adults playing with her; any social interactions are usually desirable. As she is in the latter stages of sensorimotor behavior, we tend to observe characteristics of this stage of thinking in her play. These include imitation, deferred imitation, some shift away from egocentric thought, and more complex ways of solving problems. Play is central to the toddler's life, and is the conduit through which she learns. Play informs us about many developmental areas in a child. Adults can adopt different roles to support play, and they need to access the environment to ensure that it is conducive to play. The toddler has intense curiosity that leads her to learn; identifying her interests is very important. Of course, every child is different in style and temperament, so we need to respond to each toddler differently. One way of looking at personality differences is to look at traits that are demonstrated fairly consistently.

Having established strong attachments to adults, and continuing to make them with new people in her life, she usually demonstrates emotional security. That said, the toddler is striving for autonomy, and we can see her trying to be independent in many different ways. She wants to do things for herself, so she helps with domestic tasks and with personal self-help activities, such as dressing and toileting. The toddler needs adults to be responsive to her changing needs. This approach is supported by findings from recent brain research.

Contrasting with the independence is the toddler's fear of being shamed. She has some idea of what is socially acceptable behavior, and tries to regulate her own feelings and actions, but she is not always successful. Temper tantrums are fairly common at this stage, but even when they are not demonstrated, many toddlers show ways of venting their frustrations. Although there is an emotional tug of war for toddlers at this age, it is not unusual to see children demonstrate pro-social skills, but we need to carefully consider how we praise children so that the positive behavior continues. There are numerous positive guidance strategies that can help the toddler to manage her behavior—overall, it is best to remain calm and to understand the developmental root of the behavior.

The toddler's communication skills often include single-word, two-word, and even three-word phrases. She tends to use actions as well as sounds to indicate meaning. Learning a signing technique may advance the toddler's communication skills even at the pre-language stage. The ability to use language with some forms of grammar indicates that the toddler's brain has been wired for language. Her brain development continues; the actual size of her brain has doubled since birth. The activity of her brain is enhanced by positive experiences. Some negative experiences may not have long-term effects, because there is some resiliency, but this should not be taken for granted. The adult's responsibility is to make the toddler's experiences as positive as possible. Brain research points to the necessity for supporting emotional development as a first concern. Other domains can develop successfully only if the toddler is emotionally secure.

Partnering with families is always of critical importance. Toddlers with specific developmental needs may be registered in a child care agency at this age. It is important that care providers be vigilant in observing children so that developmental delays can be identified and intervention can begin. Children may have multiple disabilities due to the impact of interaction between domains. Care providers should familiarize themselves with waning signs for hearing and vision delays. Lead poisoning is another important topic of which caregivers need to be aware.

DISCUSSION QUESTIONS

1. Identify all the examples of symbolism that you can infer from a toddler's behavior.
2. Compare the trait model of personality development with any other model of personality development or temperament theory.
3. Share at least five songs, five finger-plays, and five nursery rhymes you might sing with toddlers with your fellow classmates.
4. How does the rouge-and-mirror test indicate the concept of self?
5. Discuss how play contributes to the development of toddlers, and describe specific strategies you would utilize to support play in your own classroom.

ADDITIONAL RESOURCES

Further Reading

Albrecht, K., & Miller, L. G. (2000). *The comprehensive toddler curriculum.* Beltsville, MD: Gryphon House, Inc.

Caitlin, C. (1994). *Toddlers together.* Beltsville, MD: Gryphon House, Inc.

Curtis, D., & Carter, M. (2003). *Designs for living and learning: Transforming early childhood environments.* St. Paul, MN: Redleaf Press.

Douville-Watson, L., Watson, M. A., & Wilson, L. C. (2003). *Infants & toddlers: Curriculum and teaching* (5th ed.). Clifton Park, NY: Thomson Delmar Learning.

Edwards, C., Gandini, L., & Foreman, G. (1998). *The hundred languages of children: The Reggio Emilia approach to early childhood education.* Norwood, NJ: Ablex Publishing

Gandini, L., & Edwards, C. P. (2001). *Bambini: The Italian approach to infant/toddler care.* New York: Teacher College Press.

Goldberg, S. (1997). *Parent involvement begins at birth: Collaboration between parents and teachers of children in the early years.* Needham Heights, MA: Allyn & Bacon.

Greenberg, P. (1991). *Character development: Encouraging self-esteem and self-discipline in infants, toddlers, and two-year-olds.* Washington, DC: NAEYC.

Greenman, J., & Stonehouse, A. (1997). *Prime times: A handbook for excellence in infant and toddler care.* South Melbourne: Longman.

Heidemann, S., & Hewitt, D. (1992). *Pathways to play: Developing play skills in young children.* St. Paul, MN: Redleaf Press.

Hodges, S. (1998). *Toddler art: 18 months—3 years.* Torrance, CA: Totline.

Howard, V. F., Williams, B. F., & Lepper, C. (2005). *Very young children with special needs: A formative approach for today's children* (3rd ed.). Upper Saddle River, NJ: Pearson/Merrill/Prentice Hall.

Kinnell, G. (2002). *No biting: Policy and practice for toddler programs.* St. Paul MN: Redleaf Press.

Kohn, A. (1999). *Punished by rewards: The trouble with gold stars, incentive plans, A's, praise, and other bribes.* New York: Mariner.

Kohn, A. (2001). Five reasons to stop saying "Good Job!" *Young Children, 56*(5), 24–28.

Lally, J. R., Griffin, A., Fenichel, E., Segal, M., Szanton, E., & Weissbourd, B. (2003). *Caring for infants & toddlers in groups: Developmentally appropriate practice.* Washington, DC: Zero to Three.

Lowman, L. H., & Ruhmann, L. H. (1998). Simply sensational spaces: A multi-"S" approach to toddler environments. *Young Children, 53* (3), 11–17.

Miller, K. (2000). *Things to do with toddlers and twos.* West Palm Beach, FL: Telshare Publishing Co., Inc.

Moyer, I. (1983). *Responding to infants: The infant activity manual: 6 to 30 months.* Minneapolis, MN: T.S. Denison and Company, Inc.

Mulroy, M. T., Bothell, J., & Gaudio, M-M. (2004). First steps in preventing childhood lead poisoning: The role of the child care practitioners. *Young Children, 59* (2), 24–26.

Pruett, K. (1999). *Me, myself and I: How children build their sense of self.* New York: Goddard Press.

Stonehouse, A. (ed.). (1990). *Trusting toddlers.* St. Paul, MN: Redleaf Press. (Out of Print, but excellent!)

Trawick-Smith, J. (2006). *Early childhood development: A multicultural perspective* (4th ed.). Upper Saddle River, NJ: Pearson Merrill Prentice Hall.

Useful Videos

NAEYC videos
Ready for Life.
Description: This documentary follows the lives of six children and their families. It illustrates how children develop the strength and confidence to face life's challenges in emotionally healthy ways. Showing diverse family structures, the video is narrated by Ruby Dee and features the expert advice of Dr. Bruce Perry.

Dramatic Play: More Than Playing House: How Caring Relationships Support Self-Regulation, by Marie Goulet
Description: Children acquire self-regulatory skills through interaction with caregivers. The video and its 50-page video guide explore child development, including what we know from brain research, in relation to self-regulation. Wonderful footage in care settings illustrates caregiver practices that support self-regulation at different ages.

Say It with Sign (Tape 1), by L. & S. Solow
Introduction to Sign Language: Signs You Already Know.
Higher Learning Systems, Fairfield, CT 06430
Cooing, Crying, Cuddling: Infant Brain Development (1998), by Child Care Collection, is a 28-minute video that explores the process of brain development during the first 15 months of life. Additional information is available on the Web at http://www.naeyc.org/
Laughing, Learning, Loving: Toddler Brain Development (1998), by Child Care Collection, is a 28-minute video on how to promote optimal brain development. Additional information is available on the Web at http://www.naeyc.org/
Together We Can Know the World series of four videotapes (1989) These four videos demonstrate how parents can encourage their children's communication development through everyday music, reading, art, and play activities. Parents share their frustrations and successes as they apply the Hanen approach to each type of activity. These tapes have information applicable for families, students, paraprofessionals, and professionals involved in early intervention. Available at www.hanen.org/

Useful Web Sites

American Sign Language
   www.lessontutor.com/
   Click on link for American Sign Language (ASL), click on link for Using ASL Alphabet Flashcards Effectively
Brain Research
Education Commission of the States
   http://www.ecs.org/
   Click on link for Education Issues
North Carolina Smart Start
   http://www.ncsmartstart.org/
   Click on link for Parents, click on link for Brain Development
The Southern Early Childhood Association
   http://www.southernearlychildhood.org/
   Click on link for Position Statements, click on link for Brain Research and Its Implications for Early Childhood Programs
ZERO TO THREE
Healthy Minds: Nurturing Your Child's Development From 0–2 Months; From 2–6 Months; From 6–9 Months; From 9–12 Months; 12–18 Months; From 18–24 Months; From 24–36 Months.
   http://www.zerotothree.org/
   www.naeyc.org/
   Click on link for Early Childhood Issues, click on link for Early Years Are Learning Years, select 1999 in By Year pulldown, click Show List, click on link for do early childhood experiences really count?

Children with disabilities/early intervention
   http://www.centreforability.bc.ca/
   Hover over link for Programs & Services, hover over link for Early Intervention Program, click on link for Frequently Asked Questions
   http://www.atsweb.neu.edu/
   http://www.kidsource.com/
   Click on link for Preschoolers, click on link for Disabilities, click on link for What Is Early Intervention?
Families with Toddlers
   http://www.parentingtoddlers.com/
   http://www.zerotothree.org/
General Information
   http://www.families.nt.gov.au/
   Click on Babies; Toddlers
   http://www.zerotothree.org/
   http://www.investinkids.ca/
Guiding Behavior
   http://www.wccip.org/
   Click on link for Tip Sheets, click on link for Infant/Toddler, click on link for Best Practices Tips: Guiding Behavior of Toddlers
Language and communication
   www.literacytrust.org.uk/
   Click on Research and stats; Click on Early years and emergent literacy; Click on any topic of interest, i.e., Early language development
Lead Poisoning
Centers for Disease Control
   http://www.cdc.gov/
   Click on link for Environmental Health, click on link for National Center for Environmental Health (NCEH), click on link for Lead Poisoning
National Safety Council
   http://www.nsc.org/
   Hover over link for Resources, click on link for Fact Sheets, click on link for Lead poisoning
Play
   http://www.kidsource.com/
   Click on link for Recreation, click on link for Academic Studies and Play on a Collision Course
   http:/ /www.literacytrust.org.uk/
   Click on link for Talk To Your Baby, click on link for issues, click on link for Play
   www.nncc.org/
   Click on link for Articles & Resources, click on link for Child Development, click on link for Intellectual, scroll down to link for Intellectual Development of Toddlers

CHAPTER 11

The imagination and energy of 2-year-olds is astounding!

Here and Now: Toddlers from 2 to 3 Years of Age

LEARNING OUTCOMES

After reading and studying this chapter, you should be able to:

- identify the observable characteristics of toddlers from 2 to 3 years of age
- explain the significance of the behaviors of toddlers in their third year in a developmental context
- recognize and respond to the developmental diversity of 2- to 3-year-old toddlers
- assess the development of young children between 2 and 3 years of age
- discuss issues pertinent to this stage of development
- respond to the 2- to 3-year-old child's health, safety, and development issues with appropriate protection, guidance, and caregiving
- develop strategies to work with parents as partners in the care and education of their 2-year-olds

SCENE

The toddler room teachers at an infant and toddler child care center hold an evening meeting with a small group of tired parents.

"You can have a conversation with a 2-year-old," said one mother. "But such a lot of what Josh says I don't understand. And when I can make out what he's saying, I'm hearing him say 'no' and 'won't.' This feels so negative."

"I have some of the same difficulties," responded another mother, "particularly the 'no' part. I find that Adrienne wants to do everything herself and talks to herself as she does it. I feel as though Adrienne sees me as the biggest challenge in her life. I ask her to do something and she says 'no'; everything seems like a battle."

"Is it any help to hear that most 2-year-olds are like that?" asked the educator. The educator smiled sympathetically. "It can be a really demanding time when toddlers are at this stage. I try to deal with this by thinking of why the toddler is behaving this way, but it can be physically draining to keep up with the toddler and these behaviors can make you feel horrible." Several parents nodded in agreement. Adrienne's mom asked the educator what they did at the center when a toddler was appearing to be so negative.

"We try to see the 'no' part, the refusal to do things and the wanting to do everything by themselves, as an important developmental stage. But it's hard to keep that in mind when you have to manage the situation. I think it comes down to the fact that now they are able to do some things for themselves, they like to feel independent. They have changed a lot in a short time; now they can show us just how independent they can be!"

Adrienne's mom seemed a little uncomfortable, but said that she was bothered by her daughter's attitude and negative behavior when she picked her up from child care. While offering reassurance, the educator proposed a strategy to try to help matters. "You have such a challenging time because she is striving for independence and this means conflict with the people closest to her. I also think that when you pick her up she is tired. Adrienne, like the others her age, is so active that she gets cranky by early evening even when she's had a nap. Would it be a good idea if we made snack time a bit later in the afternoon, so she's not going home hungry, too?"

Mom didn't reply immediately, then said, "I feel silly, but Adrienne can ruin the evening. When I need to come home from work and have a few minutes of quiet, I feel that she assaults me with 'I want dinner' and 'No, not macaroni' and so on. Yes, it might be an idea to give a later snack. Or perhaps I could bring her a snack in the car to keep her going."

Josh's mom had another idea: "I can imagine how you feel, I get tired, too! But, you know, it wouldn't be a bad idea if you collected Adrienne just a few minutes later, after you've had some down time and collected your thoughts. Having a few minutes to yourself might help." Adrienne's mother looked relieved, and responded, "Let's try those two ideas."

A family night at a child care can provide an excellent opportunity for families to discuss their fears, problems, and frustration with early childhood educators. This meeting wasn't ideal—everyone was tired—but real issues were addressed. The educator should listen, sympathize, and respond with sensitivity. If possible, make practical suggestions that alleviate problems.

DEVELOPMENTAL DOMAINS

The age range discussed in this chapter is broader than those in earlier parts of this book because the rate of change slows somewhat in the third year of life. Consolidation of development is apparent, skills are refined, conceptual understanding is gained through lots of hands-on learning, the notion of self becomes categorized, language becomes more complex, and the 2-year-old maintains a keen interest in everything around him.

Physical Development

Growth

The growth rate is never again going to be as rapid as in the first two years, but the toddler continues to make gains in height and weight. Figure 11.1 displays the variance in weight and length for female and male children between 24 and 36 months of age.

As children mature, the range of height and weight becomes greater. As a rough guide, weight at 2 years of age is approximately four times that at birth (Patrick, Spears, Holt & Sofka, 2001) and height is about twice that at birth. Boys continue to be larger than girls (Allen & Marotz, 2007). Refer to the growth chart information in the Additional Support section in your Online Companion for more information on expected growth rates.

The child's proportions continue to alter, with a more elongated body that is larger in proportion to the head. The toddler will continue to have a protruding tummy because the abdominal muscles have not yet developed fully. The toddler will likely have his first full set of teeth—twenty deciduous, or milk, teeth.

Figure 11.1 Variance in Weight and Length for Female and Male Children

Female Weight Ranges

Age	Low	High	50th percentile
24 Months	22 lbs	33 lbs	26½ lbs
36 Months	25 lbs	39½ lbs	30½ lbs

Male Weight Ranges

Age	Low	High	50th percentile
24 Months	23 lbs	34½ lbs	28 lbs
36 Months	26 lbs	39½ lbs	31½ lbs

Female Length Ranges

Age	Low	High	50th percentile
24 Months	31¼ inches	36½ inches	33¾ inches
36 Months	34¼ inches	40¼ inches	37¼ inches

Male Length Ranges

Age	Low	High	50th percentile
24 Months	31¾ inches	37 inches	37½ inches
36 Months	35 inches	40½ inches	37¾ inches

lymphatic system

the tissues of the body that screen out harmful substances and manage infection control

brain maturation

the biological process of growth and development of the structure and function of the brain

myelination

the process where myelin is laid down on the nerves of the brain; when parts of the brain myelinate, it allows or improves the function of that area, such as movement or vision

axons

the part of the neuron (brain cell) that transmits messages to other neurons, muscles, or glands of the body

glial cells

supporting cells that form a protective coating and nourishment for neurons; they provide scaffolding for growing and developing neurons

Internal changes to the bones and muscles continue. The child's bones are less malleable because they have hardened by calcifying and ossifying. Muscles are increasingly defined, but this is not really apparent through casual observation.

Breathing occurs through the mouth and nose, and is a little slower than in previous months. Body temperature can fluctuate in accordance with activity level and emotion, but the body is better at regulating itself than it was in infancy. The **lymphatic system**, which provides the child with the ability to fight infection, is in a stage of fairly rapid growth.

Brain Maturation

The process of **brain maturation** is important for all learning, as well as all types of physical, perceptual, social, and emotional competence (Shonkoff & Phillips, 2000). Babies are born with approximately 100 billion brain cells, and this number remains fairly stable throughout a lifetime. However, it has been determined that the human brain doubles in weight during the first year of life, and the 2-year-old brain is approximately 70–80 percent of its adult size (Allen & Marotz, 2007). This weight gain is due to a number of different changes that are occurring simultaneously. See Figure 11.2 to help clarify some of the following information.

- First, each neuron, or brain cell, has one axon, which transmits messages. The nerve cell gains mass through a process referred to as **myelination**. The myelin sheath is a protective layer that forms around **axons** and speeds transmission of impulses through the brain cells (Berk, 2004).
- Second, there is an increase in the number and size of **glial cells**. Glial cells provide support and protection for neurons. They are known as the supporting cells of the nervous system. The four main functions of glial cells are: to surround neurons and hold them in place; to supply nutrients and oxygen to neurons; to insulate one neuron from another; and to destroy and remove the carcasses of dead neurons.

Figure 11.2 Brain Primer

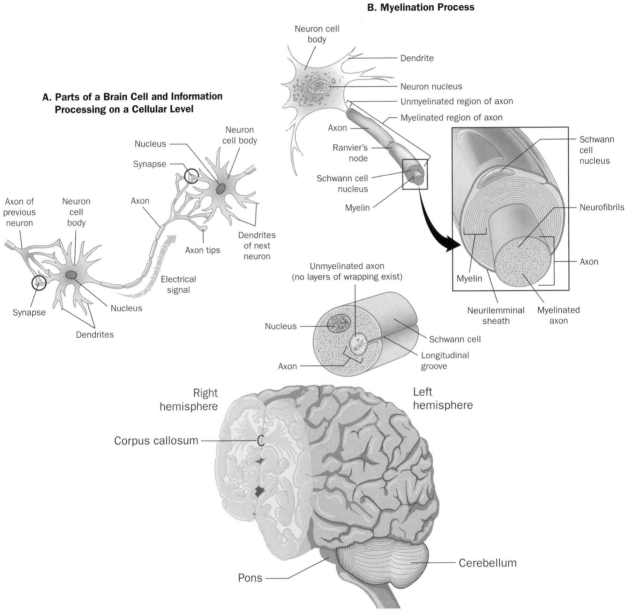

B. Myelination Process

Neuron cell body

Dendrite

Neuron nucleus

Unmyelinated region of axon

Myelinated region of axon

Axon

Ranvier's node

Schwann cell nucleus

Myelin

Schwann cell nucleus

Neurofibrils

Axon

A. Parts of a Brain Cell and Information Processing on a Cellular Level

Nucleus

Synapse

Neuron cell body

Axon of previous neuron

Neuron cell body

Axon

Axon tips

Dendrites of next neuron

Electrical signal

Synapse

Nucleus

Dendrites

Unmyelinated axon (no layers of wrapping exist)

Nucleus

Axon

Schwann cell

Longitudinal groove

Myelin

Neurilemminal sheath

Myelinated axon

Right hemisphere

Left hemisphere

Corpus callosum

C

Cerebellum

Pons

C. A View of the Cerebellum and Corpus Callosum

dendrite

the neuron branch that is the major receptive surface of the neuron; it receives and processes signals from other neurons (brain cells)

synapse

the connection between neurons through which nerve impulses travel

- Third, each neuron has many **dendrites** (hairlike fibers) that receive messages from other neurons. The experiences children have cause the axon to transmit messages that are received by the dendrites of other nerve cells across a space known as a **synapse**. These messages are sent via an electrical chemical impulse, which is aided by a neurotransmitter, such as serotonin or an endorphin. Learning involves making these synaptic connections, and as connections are repeatedly made over and over, the dendric (or synaptic) mass increases, thus adding weight to the baby's brain:

By the age of 2, the number of synapses reaches adult levels; by age 3, a child's brain has 1,000 trillion synapses—about twice as many as her pediatrician's. This number holds steady throughout the first decade of the child's life. In this way a young child's brain becomes super-dense. (Shore, 2003, p. 19)

Neurons, the nerve cells in the brain, have undergone an explosion of new connections. The axons that send signals and the dendrites that receive signals have made these connections as a result of all the child's sensory experiences. If those experiences hadn't occurred, the brain's potential would have been limited.

So, as the brain grows, other changes enhance the child's learning capabilities. The myelination process also accounts for the child's increasing motor skills, improved coordination, and enhanced body control, since messages can be transmitted more rapidly. This results in increased efficiency of message transfer to and from the brain (Berk, 2004).

cerebellum

the part of the brain that uses sensory inputs to guide motor activity

corpus callosum

the area of the brain that contains the largest bundle of nerve fibers and connects to the two hemispheres of the brain; allows the two hemispheres of the brain to communicate

ambidextrous

hand activity without hand dominance (right or left)

The part of the brain called the **cerebellum**, which aids in balance and control, is in an important stage of development that peaks at 4 years of age (Barlow, 2002). (See Figure 11.2 C.) You can see evidence of this growth as the toddler gains motor control and ability to balance and maneuver around things.

Developments in the brain affect the child's level of alertness. You may notice that the toddler's concentration now can be relatively long, depending upon his interest in an activity. The **corpus callosum** has the largest bundle of nerve fibers and connects the brain's two hemispheres (sides), and enables the child to perform more complex tasks. (See Figure 11.2 C.) The 24–36-month-old toddler is usually at a stage of thinking that gradually involves more problem-solving behaviors. Children develop hand preference by 2 or 3 years of age (Berk, 2004). Right or left-handedness is determined by the child's dominant cerebral hemisphere. It is inappropriate to force a child to be right-handed. Although many 2-year-olds are **ambidextrous**—that is, able to use both hands equally well—they should be allowed to play and use implements with the hand of their choice (Fogel, 2000).

The profusion of advances in brain science should drive educators to consider the quality of the programs that they offer young children. We need to appreciate that there are significant consequences of this growth in terms of the child's learning potential—and our role in maximizing this potential is critical. We now know that the early years of a child's life are windows of opportunity that, if not utilized, will severely limit the child's potential. After brain functions

 have atrophied from lack of use, they cannot be regenerated with much success. Go to Activity 11.1 in your Online Companion to find out all sorts of amazing things about your brain!

Many 2- and 3-year-olds are ambidextrous, since hand preference is still not established.

Gross Motor Skills

Gross motor skills can be identified in three different ways: locomotor—which includes walking, running, skipping, and galloping; stability—which includes balancing, jumping, hopping, and twirling; and manipulative—which includes throwing, catching, and batting. The 2-year-old will run, walk, jump, squat, and climb (Miller, 2001). From the time of her second birthday, she will increase her skills so that she can run faster and with more maneuverability, walk forward with less knocking into things, walk backward, jump down from stairs or other heights with better control, jump higher in the air, walk upstairs and downstairs taking one step at a time, squat for periods of time, and climb up onto chairs, climbers, and any other available structure. With her improved sense of balance, she may be able to walk for a few steps on a beam. Through all these actions, the child gradually extends her competence and increases her confidence (Allen & Marotz, 2007; Fogel, 2000).

Her response to music allows the 2-year-old to move with rhythm, moving parts of her body while staying in one spot, or moving around the floor (Pica, 2004). Arm and leg movements are not usually coordinated. Later in the third year, the child will probably have better physical control, and might learn to move her arms and legs simultaneously.

Kicking a ball can pose some difficulties for the 2-year-old, but soon she will be able to coordinate her actions so that she doesn't have to run, stop, and then kick, but can flow from the run into the kick. Catching a large ball requires concentration for the 2-year-old as she extends her arms (Miller, 2001). Coordinating the body and judging speed and

A monumental motor accomplishment is being able to pedal a tricycle!

direction are the challenges that face the child in her third year. By 3 years of age, the child may manage both kicking and catching with greater ease and alignment.

Some 2-year-olds find that the pedals of some tricycles are hard to use because they are positioned in front of the body rather than underneath, where the child can push down using her weight to pedal successfully. By 3 years old, children who have had experience with pedal vehicles can usually operate them.

Since children this age are active learners, it is important to plan for and support physical activities. *The Future of Children* organization (http://www.futureofchildren.org/) recently published a complete online journal focusing on childhood obesity, while the *Parents Action for Children* organization (http://www.iamyourchild.org/) has dedicated resources to produce materials and a DVD focusing on fitness. Also, the May 2006 issue of *Young Children* (NAEYC journal) took on the timely topic of *Healthy Young Children: Encouraging Good Nutrition and Physical Fitness.* Also, you can access the NAEYC website and search for "Beyond the Journal" to access additional information about physical fitness. Story, Kaphingst, & French (2006) have argued that child care settings have the potential to significantly impact children's dietary intake and physical activity, so this topic is important for care providers to research. Box 11.1 has some information about the importance of physical activity for young children. It also includes some suggestions for ways of monitoring and increasing physical activity for infants and toddlers.

BOX 11.1

THE IMPORTANCE OF PHYSICAL ACTIVITY

As of August 2005, one out of every six children is medically obese. One-third of all adult Americans are obese. Obesity continues to outpace all other medical concerns in this country.

The American Academy of Pediatrics recommends no more than two hours of television viewing per day, and that includes video games, computer time, and movies. "Early childhood is a key time for the development of motor skills and physical activity behaviors" (Patrick et al., 2001, p. 34). The human body was designed to move, so early childhood programs must plan to include movement in the daily plans for children.

In child care centers, 40 percent (plus or minus 10 percent) of the time children are awake, they should be moving. All facilities should monitor the proportion of time children spend moving at their site. This can be done with a Time Sample Tool. The Additional Support section of your Online Companion contains just such a tool in the Observation Tools section.

You should monitor the program for at least two weeks to see what is planned and what actually occurs. If you approach the benchmark of 40 percent, your program is doing the children a service by contributing to their physical well-being. If your program doesn't meet the goal, you need to brainstorm to come up with ideas about what can be changed or put in place to improve the opportunity for movement. The benefit of such an undertaking is that the staff will also be moving, which will improve their physical well-being also.

(continues)

Do not make the mistake of thinking that *large motor activities* have to be planned for 40 percent of the day. What this percentage of time means is that:

- children have large blocks of free play time;
- they spend less time waiting for everyone to be ready before an experience is undertaken; and
- they experience alternating active and passive activities.

Suggestions

1. In toddler classrooms, large blocks of time for free play should be the norm.
2. Do not make toddlers wait for everyone:
   - It should not be an expectation that everyone has to participate in a planned experience offered in the classroom.
   - Divide the children into smaller groups when getting dressed to go outside and then go outside as soon as the first group is ready.
   - Do not have circle times that last for more than five minutes.
3. I have been in so many toddler classrooms where they children eat a snack, have circle time (long), and then participate in a large group art experience—much too much passive time.
4. Provide space for children to move.
5. Provide equipment for children to crawl over, into, through, on top off, around, behind, and under.

Of course, nutrition is another important part of the equation that has to be examined. In most instances the solution to obesity is simple: calories in, calories out. Do not fill children up on empty calories—so, less sugar and fats, more fruits and vegetables.

Fine Motor Skills

Fine motor control is further refined in the third year of life. The 2-year-old can hold things using one hand in a careful pincer grasp, reach, grasp, manipulate a crayon or paintbrush, and operate a computer mouse. She will often attempt to dress and undress, putting her arms into sleeves, legs into pants, and feet into shoes. You may see the child using zippers and Velcro, and trying to use buttons (Allen & Marotz, 2007). She may increasingly like copying basic shapes onto paper, but the drawings reflect motor skills rather than thoughts and emotions (Freeman, 1980). Opening doors using handles, turning book pages, constructing simple objects, gluing items onto paper, and knocking down and rebuilding towers of blocks are other fine motor accomplishments of the third year. Putting together puzzles of increasing complexity is an enjoyable pastime and a chance to increase manual dexterity (Fogel, 2000). Playing with a variety of sensory materials such as dough, clay, and water gives the child the opportunity to develop the skills required for those materials, such as pouring, rolling, stamping, pressing, and squeezing. Matching-and-sorting activities, appropriate in the third year, also refine fine motor control. In particular, the child likes to scribble and draw on paper or with chalks. As yet, her actions generally follow her body movement, but some marks she makes are considered.

Eating is a little less messy than at earlier stages, but the 2-year-old may have difficulty using a spoon or fork. By 3, the child can usually manage a child-sized knife, fork, spoon, chopsticks, or whatever implement is familiar. Still, accuracy is likely to be imperfect, and the child may prefer to eat with her fingers.

Cognitive Development

From Sensorimotor to Pre-Operational Thinking

There is a gradual, rather than abrupt, change in the 2-year-old's thinking. According to Piaget's model of development, he is moving from the sensorimotor stage to the **pre-operational stage**, in which the child uses greater symbolism and mental representation.

pre-operational stage

the stage of thought following the sensorimotor stage—typically 2–7 years—during which the child has some conceptual understanding but is limited because he hasn't acquired the means and "operations" to transform and manipulate ideas

preconceptual thinking

basic thoughts or consciousness—usually based on sensorimotor activity—that exists prior to true conceptual thinking

The **preconceptual thinking** of the 2-year-old—according to the Piagetian model—occurs because the child is not yet able to classify objects in a consistent way. See the Additional Support section of your Online Companion for a chart of Piaget's cognitive stages of development. This semi-logical thinking suggests that the child's understanding of concepts is only beginning to emerge. However, the 2- to 3-year-old child makes many attempts at ordering his world in ways that may be particular to his individual way of thinking, even though they may not conform to adult views of conceptualization. Piaget tended to focus on what a child cannot yet accomplish, but there are other ways of viewing what he can do and how he does think. The emerging ability to make connections between ideas is particularly important, and his ability to understand some number concepts is also evident. Neo-Piagetians emphasize these abilities rather than focus on supposed deficits.

The cognitive advances can be seen in several ways. The child's language is not rooted only in the moment: He can speak about what he remembers and what he wants. Deferred imitation is increasingly evident in play, demonstrating that children can internalize what they see and act it out later. Sociodramatic play generally appears at about 2 years, showing how the child's mental representations have become increasingly complex. This kind of play reinforces several different kinds of mental functioning, including memory, language, reasoning, imagination, problem-solving, and creativity (Sluss, 2005; Van Hoorn et al., 2003).

Although educators often look to Piaget for the most significant explanation of children's process of cognition, many child development experts (e.g., Berk 2004; Flavell, 2001) think that his views underestimated some cognitive activity of young children, particularly in the areas of **egocentricity**, **symbolism**, and **logic**. These experts argue that some of these abilities actually appear earlier in children than Piaget theorized. Although Piaget tended to emphasize what the child could not do, rather than what he could do (Berk, 2004), we can learn from his model of cognition and apply it to what we see children doing.

egocentricity

the state of seeing only from the individual's perspective; in infancy, an inability to think from the perspective of others

symbolism

the process of using language, character, or objects to stand for something else

logic

the aspect of the ability to think that involves reason and drawing conclusions

It is important to acknowledge that culture also determines what is important to know and mediates the manner in which knowledge is demonstrated. The Western European influence on our perspectives in education and child development may constrict our thinking. However, Trawick-Smith (2006) points out that some scholars have argued that "Piaget's view of cognitive development is more sensitive to cultural diversity than other theories of human development. . . . Piaget's framework focuses on universal thought processes, such as causal thinking and object permanence, rather than emphasizing the content of knowledge, which is shaped by culture" (p. 133).

This pre-operational thinking means the young children are capable of mental representations, but do not have a system for organizing this thinking. Therefore, their thinking is intuitive rather than logical. You might want to look for some of the characteristics of this pre-operational stage by observing some of the things children say and do. This stage is framed by some of the following behaviors and mental constructs:

- The child's thinking is from his own perspective.
- Egocentricity does not allow him to know how another child thinks or feels.
- The child may respond with sympathy, which has been fostered by modeled behavior.
- **Cooperative activity** is still limited.
- The child thinks from event to event, often without making connections.
- The child has inaccurate understandings of cause and effect.
- The child demonstrates an inability to conserve—he has no appreciation that a change in form or appearance does not change the number, quantity, or length of objects or material.
- The child lacks the ability of reverse thinking.
- The child believes in animism—the nonliving are living.
- The child cannot perceive different attributes simultaneously; he will become completely fixed on one point, which is called centration.

cooperative activity

an endeavor that is accomplished by working together or playing with at least one other person

Read the following examples to see how this pre-operational thinking translates into action.

Inaccurate Understandings of Cause and Effect He may have inaccurate understandings of cause and effect. For example, he may think that having fish sticks for lunch means

A child needs many experiences with manipulating materials before he is able to perform mental operations such as conservation.

conservation

the understanding that physical attributes stay the same even when their appearance is altered

concepts

clusters of schemes that together create an idea

temporal concepts

the collection of ideas that makes up the individual's understanding of time

the music man is coming, because he came the last time they had fish sticks. This is a type of semi-logical reasoning that shows the child's ability to make associations, even though they may be incorrect.

Lack of Reversibility His inability to think through a series of actions means that a toddler cannot reverse his thought process. He may, for example, be confused about the route when returning from a walk to the park, even if the same route was taken on the way to the destination. This could also be a memory problem or a difficulty with perspective—things look different when you turn around and see them from another angle. Because he focuses on only one aspect of something, he can neglect important details when listening to a story or telling someone what happened. His thinking is bound by perception. He makes judgments on the basis of what he sees in his immediate world.

Belief in Animism At this stage a child may attribute personal qualities to objects. He might, for example, talk to objects and expect that they understand. This is most noticeable when he talks to his stuffed toys or dolls. Of course, we see older children doing this, too, but they know it is only pretend.

Inability to Conserve **(Conservation)** The young child tends to focus on what he sees. For example, he may be fooled into thinking that there are fewer vegetables on a plate because they are all heaped together, or he might think there is more juice in his cup because the level is higher than it is in another child's cup that is wider. Similarly, the young child may think that he hasn't been given the same amount of Play-Doh because his takes on a different shape—even if he sees the shape being transformed. The child may not understand that quantity remains the same even when transformed in how it looks. Similarly, the child may not hold in mind—or conserve—one category as he sorts out several different objects. When sorting a mixture of peas and beans, within a short time he is likely to forget which type he has been separating.

These apparent problems seem to be of little importance to the child at this stage; as long as he gets whatever quantity he thinks is more or best! Because he does not hold in mind that weight, number, and so forth remain constant, he is more interested in how things appear.

Partial Conceptual Understanding

Even though the child's thinking is likely to be incomplete and often inaccurate, her increasing ability to differentiate, categorize, organize, and try to understand the world provides us with ample evidence of early conceptual understandings. You will see evidence of several new cognitive skills as a young child progresses through her third year. She is developing **concepts** in her early conceptual understanding.

You may see her developing **temporal concepts**, or concepts about time. She may understand the use of terms such as "before," "after," or "wait a minute," and expect that things will happen in a particular sequence. The toddler's spatial concept might be revealed in her use of space when playing, or in her use of words such as "near" and "far" or "up" and "down." The concept of speed is harder to observe, but you might see the child estimating how fast another child is going on a tricycle as she moves across its path, or she may talk about a car "going fast." *Color concepts* are relatively easy to observe. The first stage involves color differentiation and identification.

The *concept of number* may be evident at this stage in the child's use of words such as "lots" or "hundreds," which may be used as a broad descriptor rather than as an actual number. Songs may help the child learn counting sequences—for example, "one two three four five / Once I caught a fish alive"—but they do not contribute to a real number concept. A toddler may count in sequence but not understand the correspondence between the spoken numbers and the number of objects in front of her. She may understand the difference between number shapes (what the numeral looks like) and even recognize these by 3 years of age. True number concepts come from handling materials, experiencing quantities, and having an adult supply relevant language to assist understanding.

Many other conceptual advances can be observed in 2–3-year-olds. Listen to what they are talking about. They may use language that they don't understand, but this misuse and the way that children play with materials can give us insight into their conceptual thinking. Their understanding of the properties of materials parallels their experience of them, so observe carefully during these play times. You will notice some understanding of textures, temperatures, how things pour, and so on.

The way the adult can assist in the child's learning involves a number of different strategies, each dependent upon the type of play and learning as well as the child herself. Lev Vygotsky offers a useful model in what he called the **zone of proximal development (ZPD)**. (Refer to Figure 3.1 for a graphic depiction of this concept.)

As adults provide a support system for learning—scaffolding—they might employ some of the following strategies:

- engaging in collaborative activity
- creating a shared understanding about the task or activity
- providing the appropriate emotional tone for learning
- helping the child stay focused on the task
- promoting self-regulation
- relinquishing adult control of the activity
- gauging the level of effective problem-solving necessary for the task
- assessing the level of problem-solving skill on the part of the child
- devising strategies to assist the child
- supplying appropriate language to support the learning

Senses and Perception

Although sensory acuity is now close to that of the adult, the way the child processes the information is dictated by the cognitive processes of this stage. The toddler now has greater **sensory integration**, making better links between thought and action.

Information Processing

We can see evidence of a 2-year-old's memory when she recalls events, uses deferred imitation, or applies the same strategies that she used before to solve a problem. The child's memory is increasing, but still tends to be contextualized. Something is more likely to be memorable if it occurred in a particular situation, marked by sound, smell, or visual perceptions.

Persistence at a task usually lengthens during the third year (Fogel, 2000), and the child's attention span typically gets longer, depending on her motivation and interest. Toward the end of this stage, there is usually a surge in organizational skills. The child wants to sort, order, and classify objects. She can now do this according to several criteria, but she may not hold in mind the attributes as the activity continues. Tasks that involve matching items, sequencing a series of pictures, or classifying by one attribute often make pleasing games. (Figure 11.2 A demonstrates how information-processing occurs on a cellular level.)

Multiple Intelligences

How young children come to know what they know is an important part of understanding this stage of development. We have discussed various theories regarding this topic, including Piaget's cognitive theory, Erikson's psycho-social theory, brain research, play, and learning styles, or channels of preference, just to mention a few. A relatively new theory that looks at intelligence and learning is called the **multiple intelligences (MI) theory**. Howard Gardner (1993) has offered this model, which is markedly different than previous explanations of intelligence. His theory requires us to regard intelligence as multifaceted, meaning there are many different types of intelligence. These various intelligences (at least eight) affect the

---

zone of proximal development (ZPD)

behaviors that are on the edge of emergence; the gap between the child's actual performance when operating alone and the child's potential performance when assisted by more knowledgeable adults or children

sensory integration

making meaning out of information received through two or more of the five senses

multiple intelligences theory

the idea that there are many ways of being smart—a theory that identifies at least eight or more ways of being intelligent

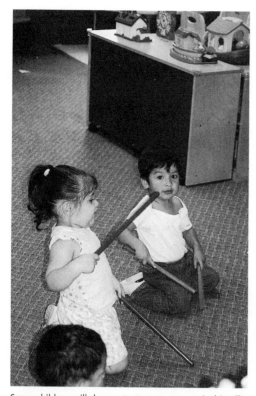

Some children will demonstrate a strong musical intelligence, but all children should have music in their lives.

way each person learns by affecting how an individual encounters, interprets, and reacts to experiences. These include:

- Linguistic intelligence ("word smart")
- Logical–mathematical intelligence ("number/reasoning smart")
- Spatial intelligence ("picture smart")
- Body–kinesthetic intelligence ("body smart")
- Musical intelligence ("music smart")
- Interpersonal intelligence ("people smart")
- Intrapersonal intelligence ("self smart")
- Naturalist intelligence ("nature smart")

Gardner's theory is not limited to these—it is likely that he will identify further ways of being smart!

Children at this stage are establishing their patterns of functioning, their favored channels of communicating, and their particular interests. Because of these things, we can use Gardner's model to identify and promote dominant intelligences and find ways of supporting the less-visible intelligences through the stronger ones. We might identify that a child has a particularly pronounced interpersonal intelligence, and support her developing musical intelligence by providing activity bridges between the two. This support might mean encouraging the child to use her interpersonal skills to have older children help her with a musical skill. Alternatively, she might transfer her interpersonal intelligence to musical games that have the same give-and-take of the conversational style she has adopted—clapping rhythms between adult and child might do this. Gardner's model helps us to see the child's learning in a different light and to provide experience for the child that is not only developmentally appropriate, but also individually and culturally fitting.

Rather than being a static theory, Gardner's model demands that educators, and others in the lives of young children, pay attention to the "individualization of intelligence" (p. 228). His ideal is to have an education system that can be tailored to the intelligence of each child

> Hand-in-glove with an accurate and accurately evolving description of each person's intelligence is the need for an educational regimen that helps every person achieve his or her maximal potential across the range of disciplines and crafts. (Gardner, 1993, p. 229)

Perhaps the toddler educator is better-placed to do this, at a time when the adult–child ratio is more favorable for children than in later years. Gardner's view is in accord with brain research, and is sufficiently flexible to incorporate new neuroscientific findings; he thinks this ongoing work will uncover further understanding about the brain and behavior.

By the age of about 2 years, there is usually an observable pattern of the child's play and learning that indicates her style preferences and modes of thinking. Several publications claim to further the concept of multiple intelligences through supplying specific activities and prescribed curricula; these may not be consistent with Gardner's premise. Many of the practical published resources suggest completing a personal inventory of intelligences that you yourself possess before attempting to understand the intelligences of each of the children—and this does seem like an excellent idea. Discover your intelligences by completing Activity 11.2 in your Online Companion.

The open-ended nature of a portfolio system captures the multidimensional aspects of each child's progress. Using this approach provides assessment coupled with individual learning profiles for each child. You may want to develop a portfolio system that focuses on each child's strengths or talents as a starting point for implementing a MI-based program.

Box 11.2 suggests one way child care facilities can enhance the naturalistic intelligence in children.

Do not overlook the importance of incorporating music into the daily lives and routines of children. "Music helps us learn by heart. Rhymes and songs are powerful in that they usually filter into memory through the beat of the heart, the body, the hands, and the feet."

(Bos & Chapman, 2005)

BOX 11.2

ENHANCING NATURALIST INTELLIGENCE

The naturalist intelligence, added to the original seven intelligences, refers to the ability to recognize and classify plants, minerals, and animals, including rocks and grass and all variety of flora and fauna. Some child care facilities, especially those located in a metropolitan area, need to provide a respite for children from the constant noise of the environment. A wonderful way to do that is by putting in a children's garden. This can be done gradually, over a period of years. Local nurseries may be willing to donate

a perennial plant or a tree or bush, especially if it is only one or two a year. The Additional Support section in your Online Companion has some good references to help you start thinking about gardening with children. We need to ensure that the children in our care reconnect with nature because many of us are losing touch with Mother Earth.

"The quiet wisdom of nature does not try to mislead you like the landscape of the city does, with billboards and ads everywhere. It just doesn't make you feel like you have to conform to any image. It's just there, and it accepts everyone." (Louv, 2005, p. 83).

Language and Communication

Body Language and Reading Emotions

Reading the child's body language and translating her cues remain important ways of understanding the child's thoughts, feelings, levels of awareness, and personal interests. First, remember that body language can be conscious or unconscious. The 2-year-old may be able to present some conscious body language, which sometimes even contradicts the truth, but on the whole the child will send clear and honest messages. Body language can also be innate or learned. In innate body language, the message comes from bodily functions, feelings, and reactions that are automatic. Learned body language involves shaping the language in accordance with a family, setting, culture, or context. Much of what we observe combines innate and learned behaviors, and we generally don't distinguish between the two.

On the whole, *needs* are communicated through innate means, and *desires* are communicated via learned methods. Body language and other signs can offer adults insight into what the

Figure 11.3 Body Language Cues

EYES AND EYEBROWS
shape/gaze/openess/flickering/reddening/
puffiness/eye contact/squinting/
observing/looking away/focus

MOUTH
open/closed/down turned/jaw dropped/
lips pushed forward/smile/laugh

BODY POSITION
inward/pulled-back/symmetry/shoulders
up or down/social space/frozen

GESTURES
use of learned signs/pointing/
language and gestures together/
symbolic actions

FACIAL EXPRESSIONS
innate emotions/affect—bland
or expressive

NOSE
wrinkled/flared

BREATHING
rapid/deep or shallow

SKIN COLOR
pale/changing in color/
rash/blotchy

Other considerations

1. *Physical proximity*—space between child and another child/space between child and adult/ Watches at what distance?

3. *Play behaviors*—actions/activity levels/ interest/concentration span/type of play

5. *Congruity*—action and language matching/ action and expression matching/congruity between aspects of body language

2. *What the child says*—thoughts/feelings/ pace of speech/ability to articulate/sound production/imitation/deferred imitation/role playing

4. *Mistakes*—errors in thinking/language mistakes/memory function/incorrect associations

6. *Stimuli*—alertness/consciousness/awareness/ speed of response/lack of response/delayed response/appropriateness of response

young child is thinking or feeling. See Figure 11.3 (adapted from Quilliams, 1994) for some suggestions on reading body language cues. These cues send us subtle messages, and we need to learn how to interpret them. The Additional Support section of your Online Companion has some helpful suggestions for translating these cues. Keep in mind however, children's individual styles, as well as their exposure to culture, shape how body language should be read. Studies of children offer several alternative interpretations for most behaviors. (See, for example, Kostelnik et al., 2006.)

Language

Two-year-olds are at the beginning of a period marked by lots of questions. They ask questions as an invitation to converse, to understand the world better, and to get a response. "Where" and "what" questions usually come first. Then come the "who," "how," and "why" questions. A few children, at the end of this stage, will extend their questioning to "which," "whose," and "when" (Bloom, Merkin, & Wootten, 1982).

Although the child's questioning seems endless at times, he is using language in a variety of other ways. The child is likely to have quite a large vocabulary. However, there is tremendous variation; some children will be much earlier or later to talk. Studies estimate that, at 30 months, children know upward of 200 words (Sheridan, 2001).

consonants

speech sounds, or letters of the alphabet, that are not vowels

The early use of new words may present some pronunciation difficulties. Commonly, children at this stage have trouble making the sounds for "r" or "l," and they tend to make them sound like "w." Other **consonants** present the same challenge. This is a temporary articulation difficulty that exists because of either hearing differentiation impediments or physiological immaturity. Although children struggle with consonant sounds and blend sounds for years, most children by age 3 are able to produce all the vowel sounds.

There is more to language acquisition than the ability to use simple vocabulary. Language development is often looked at in terms of the increasing **mean length of utterance (MLU)**. This measures the average number of **morphemes**, or smallest units of meaning in language (these units include prefixes and suffixes as well as roots). Another consideration is the type of words used by the child. In his first, simple utterances, he generally uses nouns, or words that label things. Next he uses verbs, action words that indicate a relation between things. The MLU gradually becomes longer and begins to display rules of language. At the same time, sentence structure becomes more complex.

Children gain an understanding of language rules by hearing adults and other children speak, by hearing television and other media, and by trying to piece together communication in a meaningful way. Frequently toddlers create **overextensions**, or the incorrect application of a rule. For example, a child might say, "I goed" instead of "I went." or, "my foots" instead of "my feet." Although their early attempts may be full of errors, toddlers are quite successful at making themselves understood.

This stage is the time for **private speech**—talking out loud to himself for self-regulation. Children may talk about what they are doing as they do it. Private speech might involve playing with sounds, practicing saying something correctly, and even singing some lyrics. Sometimes children utter their private speech as if they were narrating their own activity. Private speech can also include the unheard voice of the child, as he uses language to structure his thinking.

During the third year of life, there is evidence of a combination of aspects of language development. Consider each of these, as they occur simultaneously:

- practice with sound production associated with language (**phonemes**, consonants, and vowels)
- listening with greater acuity and attention to language-specific sounds
- increase in length of utterance—*mean length of utterance (MLU)*
- gains in labeling objects, people, ideas, and feelings—vocabulary (*receptive* and *expressive*)
- increased appreciation of links between language and meaning—*semantics*
- use of language that has symbolic function—a word represents an object, idea, etc.
- increase in private inner speech
- internalization of organizational rules of language—*syntax*
- acquisition of the basic rules of language—*grammar*
- use of language to communicate needs, wants, and ideas
- questions increase
- follows commands—puts understanding into action

In earlier chapters we discussed theories that explain these amazing leaps forward in understanding and using language. The brain may be wired for language, but the amount of language learning that happens at this stage is staggering; never again will there be such great gains in the child's vocabulary and the understanding of meaning and structure in language.

During the explosion of language that can occur at this time, we need to remember that adults are the facilitators and mediators of the process. The adults' responsibility is to support the child's language learning—not only in increasing his vocabulary but in all the other aspects of his language that we just mentioned. A wide variety of strategies for language support are articulated by Weitzman and Greenberg (2002). They suggest addressing every aspect of the child's program, including the environment and how it is structured to support talking and learning, the adult's role in promoting conversation, supporting social interaction between children, and encouraging a variety of play activities, especially pretend play and play that encourages the use of the child's imagination. Box 11.3 explains

---

mean length of utterance (MLU)

the average length of the sentence the child produces; average number of morphemes per utterance

morphemes

the smallest unit of meaning within language—a word, a prefix, a suffix

overextensions

the child's application of a language rule in a situation where it does not apply—i.e., extending it beyond the situations where it does apply

private speech

self-directed speech or utterances that children use to guide their own behavior or use as commentary on their actions—speech that is turned inward and may support self-regulation

phonemes

the smallest linquistically distinct unit of sound, e.g., the word cat has three phonemes—c/a/t

BOX 11.3

STRATEGIES TO ENCOURAGE LANGUAGE

- speaking in sentences so that children hear correct models, *expansions*, and *extensions* (See below.)
- labeling objects, people, actions, and events
- telling children what is going to happen in the near future
- providing simple explanations
- offering intensive repetition
- timing responses to correspond to the child's focus of attention
- being slow and clear in everything you say
- positioning words that you want them to notice at the beginning or end of a sentence—and emphasizing them
- using real-life situations in which the child has a real interest
- supporting simultaneous first- and second-language learning—recognize that there are stages of second-language learning that might show themselves in a silent phase, code mixing, loss of first language, and lots of grammatical errors
- comforting the child in his first language, if possible
- using correct forms but avoiding correcting mistakes
- using music and rhymes to help with language acquisition
- introducing books, writing, and literacy materials into play situations
- helping children use language to identify and solve problems
- using literal language rather than abstract ideas and metaphors
- extending the topic of interest to the child
- imagining and pretending along with the child

Between 2 and 2½, children are:

- producing more words than jargon
- understanding approximately 500 words
- 65–70 percent intelligible
- speaking 50–200 words clearly
- perhaps omitting final consonants, simplifying consonant blends, substituting one consonant for another

By age 3, children are:

- producing all the vowels sounds
- pronouncing the sounds p/m/h/n/w/b/k/g/d
- understanding approximately 900 words
- 80 percent intelligible

Source: Owens (2001)

---

some of Weitzman and Greenberg's strategies that adults can utilize to encourage language in young children.[1]

Specific expansion and extension strategies are demonstrated by the following examples:

Expansion—adult repeats words of a child, but models correct form.

Child: Me eat.

Adult: Yes, you are eating.

Extension—adult restates the telegraphic, or short message but adds new information.

Child: Me eat.

Adult: Yes, you are eating your sandwich.

Child: Me eat.

Adult: Yes, you are very hungry.

Clearly the child's acquisition of language occurs alongside his increasing understanding about his world. Language assists in the labeling, understanding, and categorization of objects and ideas. It also enables the child to convey his thoughts and feelings and respond to others as he hears what they say. The give-and-take of language helps build social relationships. Most importantly, the child's language supports his ability to think, and his increasing experience provides opportunities for language growth.

Bilingual and Multilingual Learning

Children exposed to two or more languages have the opportunity to grow up speaking those languages. Although there can be some challenges for the child learning two or more sets of language sounds and rules, children's receptivity to language is wide open at this time. Of

---

1. Adapted from E. Weitzman & J. Greenberg (2002), *Learning Language and Loving It: A Guide to Promoting Children's Social and Language Development in Early Childhood Settings* (2nd ed.). (Toronto: Hanen Centre).

course, the child can become confused, use words incorrectly, and switch from one language to the other in mid-sentence. Yet these difficulties are relatively trivial compared with the cognitive and social advantages experienced if literacy is obtained in two languages (Freire & Bernhard, 1997; Hudelson, & Serna, 2002b).

Supporting the child's first language is absolutely essential in order to safeguard the relationship between the child and his family members. Among other benefits, such support demonstrates respect for the language and culture of the child and his family. Where possible, the educator might learn some words in the child's first language to try to provide a bridge to English. This can also have benefits for the educator's relations with family members. It is important for the child to make connections between his heritage and the language he speaks (Hudelson & Serna, 2002a), so we need to find practical ways of supporting that language learning.

Some families may want their child to learn English while at the child care center and another language at home. Family wishes must be respected, but the child's emotional well-being must be considered, too. Language acquisition is tied to profound emotions and has the potential for making a child feel either lost or well integrated.

The Additional Support section of your Online Companion has further suggestions on how to communicate with families who do not speak English.

Emotional Development

self-esteem

an individual's perception of her own overall positive or negative self-worth; the degree to which one feels positive about oneself

unconditional love

love that exists without conditions or dependence on particular behaviors or situations

Most educators and parents would agree that it is essential that young children have a positive sense of themselves (**self-esteem**). Recently the notion of self-esteem was revisited. It is now understood that esteem must result from the child's efforts and achievements, rather than for just existing. (This is not the same as being loved unconditionally.) Self-esteem does not focus on what she is, but on what she does. Experiencing **unconditional love**, which involves a sense of trust and well-being, is important, but it is separate from self-esteem. Unconditional love requires the adult to accept, support, nurture, and love the child whatever her behavior, whatever her mood—without any condition. To build self-esteem in the child, the adult offers plenty of opportunities for the child to feel good about herself because she tries to do things herself and meets with success. At times, her self-esteem will protect her from feeling a sense of failure if she doesn't measure up to her own expectations. It will also build a resilience that makes her want to try even harder. Adults may express their adulation, praise, and encouragement for the child's slightest efforts. She knows when she has made a real effort and may find the adult lacks authenticity if she receives praise that is not truly in line with the effort she has expended. Self-esteem results from genuine personal achievement and effort made for a purpose. Although children may be naturally competitive, and it may be culturally supported, competition is not appropriate in early childhood classrooms. Being first is a singularly lonely position, since only one individual can have that place. Doing things through cooperation and collaboration has a more significant impact on a child's development than focusing on being first. The early years should focus on building the skills and abilities of all children and fostering a sense of community; more of a "together we're better" and less of "alone, I'm the greatest" attitude.

EMOTIONAL INTELLIGENCE

emotional intelligence

skills that can be applied in social situations; emotional maturity; ways of being emotionally "smart"; involves emotional development

Daniel Goleman's work on emotion has led him to believe that there is such a thing as **emotional intelligence**. Goleman (1997) theorizes that children learn to control the raging emotions inside them through a variety of methods, many of which are learned from modeling behavior, or in reaction to experiences. Children who exhibit tremendous out-of-control behavior have a brain that is bypassing the slow path to the amygdala (pronounced—ə-mˇɪg'də-lə).

According to brain researchers, the amygdala is essential for decoding emotions. It can be reached by two pathways. The fast pathway is the brain's early warning system, and leads to physical manifestations of fear, anger, hate—in other words, out-of-control behavior. The second pathway, the slower pathway, has information diverted to other parts of the brain first for purposes of emotional evaluation. This slower neural pathway, acting as an emotional gatekeeper, can then override the first pathway and lead to conscious recognitions of feelings.

Figure 11.4 The Effect of Adult Responses on Toddlers' Emotional IQ

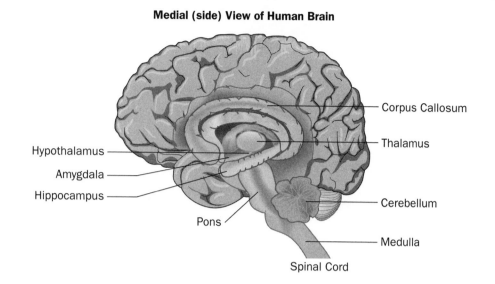

Medial (side) View of Human Brain

Corpus Callosum
Thalamus
Hypothalamus
Amygdala
Hippocampus
Pons
Cerebellum
Medulla
Spinal Cord

Essential Domains of EI

1. *Knowing one's emotions.* The root of emotional understanding is in knowing that she is a separate person, being in touch with how she feels, and having that echoed by the people she is attached to.

2. *Managing emotions.* Having some positive feedback about herself, knowing that she is loved, and having a consistent attachment figure provides the child with a base for being able to manage her emotions.

3. *Motivating oneself.* Internal motivators lead the child to be curious about things, people, and herself. She is propelled forward with a natural motivation to strive and be successful.

4. *Recognizing emotions in others.* Early attachment to adults provides the first two-way relationship in which the child finds that she has a sense of self and others. From this, she builds the relationship and mirrors the emotions of the other. In time, she becomes able to think less egocentrically and begins to know that others have feelings. With later appreciation of the perspectives of others, she is able to recognize and read their emotions. Gaining in social skills and emotional awareness, she gains a conscience. With internal and external supports and encouragement, she finds that recognizing the feelings of others is rewarding.

5. *Handling relationships.* Relationships that are built on trust in the early years provide the foundation for building mature relationships later on. The child's security in being loved and feeling positive about herself allows mistakes to happen. The child can continue to take small risks without her world caving in.

Effects of Responses on EI

Effect of Adult Response. Having her cues read and having her feelings acknowledged, not ignored, helps the young child to know her emotions.

Effect of Adult Response. When her efforts to manage her feelings are rewarded externally, and with a sense of pride, the child feels success in managing her emotions. If she does not receive the support she needs, and is shamed by her actions, her emotional regulation will be less effective, and she will lack confidence in her ability to be in control.

Effect of Adult Response. When adults interfere with that process and lead the child to doubt herself and her competence, challenge her interests, or undermine her successes, then the motivation is spoiled. Adults need to allow the child to experience success and provide external encouragement until the child can motivate herself independently.

Effect of Adult Response. Adults can spoil this process in many ways: by failing to meet the child's needs; by not providing a consistent, caring adult figure that the child can attach to; and by ignoring the need to reinforce emotional learning.

Effect of Adult Response. The young child needs opportunities to launch into her social world from a secure base. If the conditions for healthy emotional growth are not provided, the child will not have the sense of security to manage social relationships.

Children can learn to reign in their emotions and build their emotional IQ. That accomplishment is directly correlated to the experiences they have and the relationships they build with the significant individuals who are part of the fabric of their daily lives.

Emotional Intelligence Support

competent

having sufficient skill and aptitude

coach

the role of an adult or more mature child to encourage, support, and provide strategies for success

As we become aware of Goleman's five domains of emotional intelligence, it becomes apparent that some degree of that intelligence is likely to have developed in the early years of life. Figure 11.4 illustrates the location of the amydala and explains the five essential domains for emotional intelligence, along with adult responses that can either help or hinder that development. It is evident, once again, that the early years sets the standard for all that follows.

As the 2-year-old becomes better at articulating her feelings and regulating her actions, she becomes increasingly **competent** in what are now her life skills. Adults must understand that she needs to be independent but function in a social setting. As the adult appreciates her style, he can provide support as her social/emotional **coach**.

Learning that other people have different opinions is difficult.

Opportunity and Risk Taking

Learning to recover from emotional situations as well as learning from practical mistakes is essential to the child at this stage. She needs opportunities to play and discover, and her environment needs to be safe, but also offer plenty of risk-taking learning. This does not mean playing with dangerous materials, but ones that can be dealt with in open-ended way. These risk-taking experiences provide opportunities for success, but at times may provoke emotional challenges. It is under just these types of circumstances that a caring, nurturing adult helps the young child build emotional intelligence.

Social Situations

The child in her third year needs plenty of opportunity to play with other children in a safe environment. During play situations, conflicts will arise; the child needs to have these to learn that other people have different points of view. She needs the adult to act as mediator to help her bridge the gap between the two children, and for each child to have a positive learning experience as a result.

parallel play

spontaneous activity occurring alongside other children, without sharing or cooperation; playing separately at the same activity at the same time and in the same space

creative play

spontaneous activity that involves understanding how to use objects or represent ideas, making something, and using innovative or new ideas

PLAY

Types of Play at This Stage

The symbolism, imitation, and memory aspects of the child's cognitive development show themselves in the play patterns of 2- to 3-year-olds. The toddler becomes more involved in imitative play (copying the actions of adults) and pretend play (using his growing imagination). His social skills development comes from prolonged periods of social interaction. He is able to engage in **parallel play** and with increasing association, including some sharing and mutual interest. The give-and-take of social interaction provides opportunities for some sociodramatic play involving other children, but the ability of the child is not usually up to sustained conversation or developing joint goals.

Play still involves a lot of physical activity of various types. Climbers and other outdoor apparatus and lots of sensory activity support physical, exploratory, and sensory play. Fantasy play may also be seen in the latter part of this year. At that point, children's imaginations allow them to escape reality and indulge in fanciful and creative explorations in dress-up and other kinds of make-believe, some of which may be shaped by television, videos, or books. The 2–3-year-old is interested in many aspects of the real world, including other people, discovering how things are made, what everything does, and how his body works.

Puzzles, games, and sorting and matching activities (table play) allow the child to play in a more structured way than other totally spontaneous play activities do, but he will use these playthings in the way he wishes, and may not be tied to their conventional or expected uses. Games with rules are not easily played without adult guidance, but some sharing and turn taking can be observed in spontaneous play if the children are familiar with one another and have had the opportunity to play together.

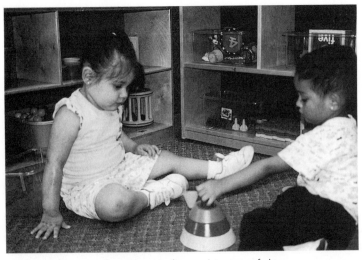

Children at this stage often engage in the associate stage of play

Creative play can incorporate a very wide variety of activities. Some of these are social, but the child in her third year is more likely to engage in associate-play except in some short episodes of **sociodramatic play** if roles are clearly differentiated. The 2-year-old sees no problem with there being two mommies or daddies in the playhouse at the same time, and children are not usually dependent upon each other for the play sequence to progress.

Creative Play

As we observe the 2-year-old's play, we can see many activities that we can categorize in a variety of ways. Some of these things that he does can be considered **creative play**—inasmuch as the ideas that go into his play are novel to him and he uses his imagination to develop play sequences. Sometimes he might share these with other children. As he approaches his third birthday, you might notice more complex sociodramatic play that involves shared imagination and some fantasy. You might also notice the child's incorporation of ideas that have come from television, videos, or books. Although there are videos produced for this age group, they do not always promote improved play; the ideas and characters tend to be imitated rather than developed in more imaginative ways.

Creativity involves a thought process that is in some way new to its creator. In the case of the young child, he makes things, uses language, expresses himself in music or sound, or imagines and plays within a wide range of creative activities. In the same way that play has its therapeutic purpose, so do all types of **creative thought**. Creativity allows children—and us—to combine logic and imagination, using both **convergent** and **divergent thinking**. It is most likely that divergent thinking produces the most creative ways of solving problems and making objects. This is why open-ended activities are most important at this stage of creative thinking. The child needs to be presented with materials for which there are no right or wrong ways of doing things. Open-ended activity allows the child to explore, discover, and then to create, motivated by his interests and needs.

Curriculum

Often educators speak about offering a creative curriculum, so a word about **curriculum** might be appropriate here. This is not a time for well-meaning adults to superimpose a set of learning objectives on young children. These might include colors, letters, shapes, and numbers, often taught on a weekly basis. If these objectives are taught using such an approach, it is inappropriate for young children. Two and three-year-olds, coloring on dittos or using flashcards, does not constitute an appropriate curriculum either. The curriculum for young children should be based on play and on the interests of the children. This type of curriculum will support the child's natural inclination for exploration and creative problem-solving.

Often educators label what is done in classroom as creative efforts, when in fact the results are little more than craft products. At this age, the emphasis should be on the process and not the product. Our job as educators is not to fulfill a family member's need for some product to come home, but to explain the importance of the creative process.

What we supply for children should be the opportunity, space, time, and materials to develop their creative thinking processes. This is why it's essential to allow the child to make things his way rather than imitate the "correct" way of doing things. In society, we tend to honor representational art—images that look like the real thing—rather than expressions of thoughts and emotions relating to the child's imagination. Because of the adult need for understanding, we may want to encourage representational picture making and be enthusiastic when the child draws a picture that we can see depicts something "real." But

sociodramatic play

a fantasy play scenario that involves at least one other individual

creativity

an individual's capacity to produce new ideas, inventions, or objects of value; the process of creating and making things

creative thought

activity of the mind that involves creativity; may involve divergent thought, problem solving, trial-and-error, or a combination of other thinking skills

convergent thinking

thinking that requires a specific correct response

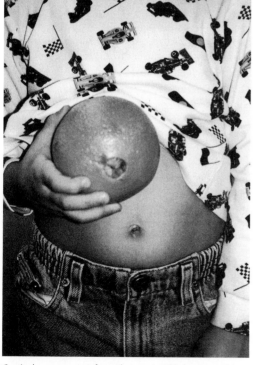

Curriculum can come from the most unlikely sources! In this care facility, the children were learning about their bodies. This child noticed that the navel orange bore a strikingly similar resemblance to his own belly button. Connections!!

Personal Comment

So often when I visit centers, curriculum plans are in place for weeks and even months ahead of time.

These predetermined curricula do not reflect the particular needs, interests, or skills of a child, or a group of children.

Many times, the curriculum plans come from directors or educational curriculum developers who are not in the classroom, have no relationship with the children or families, and often have theoretical, not practical, experience with teaching children.

Sometimes, the curriculum specialists do not even live in the state where the curriculum will be implemented.

These types of curricula are disrespectful to children, families, and teachers, since they do not take into consideration the needs of a specific group of children.

Children living on the seashore have a very different frame of reference than children living in a desert.

Curriculum must start with the children's lived experiences, since we know that learning for young children is more meaningful when it grows out of the familiar.

This also helps children make connections from what is known to what is unknown.

These connections and integration of information are what give children in-depth learning, as opposed to surface learning—the rote memory of discrete and unrelated pieces of information.

Curriculum for young children must be considered to comprise all that occurs during the day, both planned and unplanned, and it must be collaborative in nature, or as the Reggio approach has taught us, negotiated between children, families, and teachers.

---

divergent thinking

thinking involving unusual responses; associated with creativity and "thinking outside the box"

curriculum

everything that happens in a classroom, both the planned and unplanned; traditionally refers to the prescribed content of what is to be learned within a designated time period; the philosophy of *See How They Grow* uses the term to mean every aspect of a child's experience, whether it is designed or not

it is far better to allow the young child to make images that express her thoughts and feelings—frequently they can be an opening to conversation with her. This has the effect of supporting her language development, alongside her thinking skills.

The Reggio approach has demonstrated that young children are capable of representative art work, but it results from a deep involvement with a project that is supported by adult effort and knowledge (Gandini et al., 2005; Wurm, 2005). The children are allowed the great luxury of time: time spent in observation, exploration, and creation. Projects often take months, not a few minutes.

This is the stage when children's thinking can be spoiled by zealous educators who want the whole group of children to make identical objects, or the adult who draws a model to show the child what an object is meant to look like. Offering these prompts not only stunts the child's creativity, but sends the message to the child that her own efforts have failed. We need to show that we value genuine attempts at creative thinking and making things. (Activity 11.3 on your CD-ROM provides suggestions of activities and experiences that promote creative thinking.)

Aggressive Play

When the child is involved in play that allows him to express his strong feelings, he is most likely to be in a solitary play activity. Although some anger is played out in pretend play, sometimes expressed anger is imitating adults. If we hear ourselves reflected in the child's pretend play, it can be a wake-up call for us to ensure that our behavior is always appropriate.

How well will the young child be prepared to deal with situations that we cannot yet anticipate? Frequently we are shocked because we see young children expressing anger as they play. Some of this may come from within them—resulting from the natural frustrations of their stage—but other aggressive play comes as a result of the images that they see and the adult conversation that they hear. While it is undesirable to offer children weapons with which to act out their fears and aggression, it is highly likely that some acting out is beneficial. We tend to think of all play as offering both a learning purpose and a therapeutic purpose, so we must provide opportunities for safe play that concerns children's fears and ways of coming to understand the warlike images they see. Much conversation and reassurance is needed, but we must first listen to what the children are telling us in both their language and in their play.

Some **aggressive play** is an unfortunate, if inevitable, offshoot of the times we live in—but we must provide the child with peaceful methods of communicating and ensure that nobody is

aggressive play

play behavior involving actions that cause harm to other people or to objects physically or emotionally hurt. Acting out fears and concerns should be channeled into productive activity as much as possible. Above all, emotional support must be provided to ensure that the child does not feel he is under any immediate threat and knows that the adults will always be there to protect him.

It is possible that children's play has changed as a result of recent world conflicts. With September 11th, terrorist activities around the world, and the Afghanistan and Iraq wars, as well as global conflicts that may affect families in our classrooms, we all have concerns about how our children will manage both the social conflicts that are everyday parts of their lives and the larger conflicts in their world.

Part of the reality of our times is that the world contains extreme political regimes and terrorist acts; these facts cannot escape young children. Given this, we need to be particularly attentive to the fact that young children should not be exposed to the images that are presented in graphic form on television and in other media. However, no matter how much we try to protect our children, they do overhear our concerns and experience our anxieties secondhand. Play can have a positive role in helping children come to terms with a range of difficult emotions. While we do not want to promote play that is warlike, terrifying, or fear-inducing, there may be times when the children need an avenue of play to deal with ideas that might otherwise overwhelm them. The Additional Support section of your Online Companion contains resources that may help you understand how to deal with these issues in a positive way.

Purposes of Play

Play behaviors, like every other aspect of the young child's development, are highly individual. There are many factors that shape how the child plays. To some extent, the child's nature, or biological makeup, will be a factor, but his experience too will shape the way he plays. At this stage, play serves various purposes that you can observe if you look carefully. These are some of the purposes that play provides during the third year of life:

- learning about the properties of materials and how things work
- getting to know other people and how to communicate with them
- building concepts about weight, time, size, number, color, etc.
- imitating and internalizing social roles and learning what is and is not socially acceptable behavior
- improving memory and information-processing functions
- organizing the world by sorting, classifying, sequencing, striating, and ordering
- refining gross and fine motor skills
- exploring emotions and gaining insight into why people behave the way they do
- acting out some of the anxieties, concerns, and issues that trouble the child
- escaping the real world and fantasizing, using her imagination
- discovering right and wrong and the consequences of actions
- regulating feelings and actions
- increasing pro-social skills
- increasing communication and language skills

It is often during play sequences that we observe the child's particular interests and talents. Alejandro may be interested in how machines work, and Nadia may be interested in social relationships. Michael observes closely before he moves into a sociodramatic activity involving shopping, and Dulce spends long periods pouring and sifting lumpy sand. These may represent particular interests; if they become regular patterns of behavior, they are even more noteworthy.

fantasy play

spontaneous activity involving suspension of reality, imagination, pretending, and/or make-believe

Fantasy Play

The purpose of **fantasy play** is a challenge to figure out. It might be that the child is temporarily escaping the extreme feelings and demands of reality. It can also provide a pleasurable interlude from other types of play. Fantasy play hardly exists at the age of 2, but some children, at

Personal Comment

When my son was a little over 2½, my stepmother made him a red "Superman" cape for the holidays.

It became a favorite embellishment for his fantasies that he played day-in and day-out.

My stepmother died three years later and it is one of the few memories that my son has of her.

Don't ever underestimate the little flourishes that you add to children's lives to fuel their imaginations.

That piece of cloth was no longer than a foot and a half, and she spent 30 minutes putting it together.

However, the memory will last a lifetime for my son.

That red cape still hangs in a clothes closet in our home, waiting, just waiting for the next bright-eyed, full-of-energy, ready-to-fly superhero(ine)!!!

---

about 3 years of age, get stuck in a role-playing fantasy that takes up much of their waking time. Many parents become concerned, and some try to stop the child's imagination from running away with itself. This prolonged play is not a problem, but some adults worry that the fantasy has too strong a pull on the child. Actuality, the child may have greater difficulty sorting out fantasy and reality if he is denied the possibilities of fantasy than if he is encouraged. Therefore, it is likely to be more productive if the child is allowed to act out his fantasy, even if it is prolonged.

Some philosophers, like Bettelheim (1989), consider fantasy a magical experience for children—one in which the usual laws of nature and society do not apply. Educators like Levin (2003) sometimes feel that fantasy play—particularly fantasy that involves **superheroes** such as Superman, or whoever is publicized today as a character with extraordinary powers—provides an opportunity for the child to empower himself in a world where he is disempowered, or controlled by adults. Other educators, such as Paley (2004) and Bergen (2002), believe that there is a link between fantasy play and each domain of development. This is confirmed in the statement "Self-directed fantasy play . . . is an essential feature in young children's cognitive and psycho-social development" (Perry, 2001). Fantasy play remains more of a mystery to adults than other types of play, but it is obviously an important part of learning, even if we cannot easily analyze it.

superheroes

human-like figures in play and stories that have extraordinary powers; children involved in superhero play may feel especially empowered

Factors That Might Hamper the Development of Play

As stated previously, it used to be that children did not have to be taught how to play. However, the number of children who need play intervention is steadily increasing due to a host of reasons, including reduced opportunities to engage in playful activities. Children with developmental delays are apt to need support while engaging in play, although Guralnik and Hammond (1999) found that children with mild disabilities exhibit typical play-pattern sequence (e.g., from solitary to parallel to associate), even if the emergence of these stages may occur slightly later than normally developing children. Children with more global development issues require more intensive intervention in order to negotiate play scenarios. Teachers may have to adapt the environment and the toys in order to ensure their engagement in play. Also, techniques such as partnering with one other child, turn taking and creating a buffer zone (Klein, Cook, & Richardson-Gibbs, 2001) may be useful. Of special note are children with autism whose behaviors may decrease the likelihood of encounters with other children, and who often lack the language competencies and mental representations needed for social play.

Other children may have their play experiences extended or promoted because a perceptive educator picks up on the children's interests. Do be concerned if a child seems apathetic or uninterested in play. However, there might be any of the following reasons for a child demonstrating atypical play behaviors:

- illness
- tiredness
- intense shyness
- self-consciousness
- English as a second language
- cultural issues

- abuse
- neglect
- poor infant experience
- prolonged hospitalization or institutionalization
- communicative disorder
- sensory deficit
- some other disability

Children who are identified as experiencing these difficulties might benefit from a more direct play intervention by the teacher, and may need closer monitoring in case a referral is necessary.

Many developmental psychologists tend to view the young children in terms of what they cannot yet accomplish, or how their thinking limits their abilities; we might find this a negative perception of the child. Watching children at play, increasing competence in all domains of development can often be seen. Rather than focus on what children cannot yet do, the most effective means of supporting learning is to provide experiences and activities that build on existing skills and motivations. Knowing when to be involved in the children's play is something of an art. As with younger children, it is best to start with close observation and take your cue from there. The 2- to 3-year-olds will want you to be part of their play, and will realize how much you value their play activity through your respect for it, your sensitive involvement, and because you follow their lead. If you notice that play behaviors are not evolving or progressing, a review of the adult roles in play discussed in Chapter 10 might be helpful.

It should be stressed that the majority of 2-year-olds are extremely active, curious, motivated, and playful, ask plenty of questions, are messy, play for prolonged periods alone and alongside others, are strong-minded, want to please, explore everything within their reach, and show little thought for safety. Their physical exuberance can be both a challenge and a joy to the adults in the children's lives.

PARTICULAR NEEDS

Maturational changes underpin the developmental advances of the 2-year-old. She is now larger, stronger, and better able to help herself and think about her world. She has come a long way since birth. From now on, almost all skill development is a refinement of what has already emerged. To assist the 2-year-old's development, several important needs must be met.

Emotional Security

Emotional security continues to be a core issue. It constitutes the foundation on which all the other domains are dependent. Security for the child at this stage means constancy, knowing what is expected, having clear parameters of behavior, being understood and accepted, and knowing that he is loved and that what he does is important. Being sensitive to the child's fears is essential. Some planning might help avoid troubling images, but the child needs to act out and talk about his fears.

Conversation

Toddlers need to listen and to talk. They need to be reminded that conversation is a two-way process. Vocabulary can be extended only by exposure to language, so all types of language activities are important. The child needs to listen to stories, hear rhymes, talk about activities and feelings, have conversations over mealtimes, and use fantasy and reality in play. She also needs to have the opportunity to talk with adults and other children.

Even though they are now pre-operational thinkers, sensory learning is still important for children at this age.

Space

Children at this age are larger and more active, and need an increased amount of indoor and outdoor play space. In this space, they need equipment that encourages safe gross motor activity. Climbers, bikes, hoops, and balls of all sizes are appropriate. The children also need space to respond to music. At this stage, they love to move to music in a free, unrestricted way.

Hands-on Learning

Children learn by doing. They need to touch, feel, explore, experiment, and find out how everything works, how it can be taken apart, what properties it possesses, and what they can create from it. Thus children at this stage need a wide range of sensory, art, discovery, and construction materials.

Sorting Out the World

The 2-year-old's ability to sort and match starts a quest to organize and sort everything in the world. He needs some help classifying dogs or sheep, for example, but soon gets the idea and wants to cluster together everything of the same kind. The child can now handle smaller objects, so he can sort things and put them away, matching them to picture labels on the containers. Play material with sets of animals, colored items, and natural objects are needed for sorting.

Fine Motor Activities

Children at this stage like to complete puzzles with a few pieces, play with table toys, paint and do other creative activities, and build things with construction blocks. They need the opportunity to repeat puzzles, even when they have done them successfully. New games also have interesting challenges. These activities assist fine motor skill development, but they also help develop concepts of size, shape, color, and so on.

The Involvement of Adults and Other Children

Two-year-olds like to play alone and sometimes alongside other children, but they flourish when they get adult attention. The child feels empowered when he can drive the play activity. Adult involvement is needed to enhance or assist in elaborating the play, help the child attend to details, prolong his concentration, offer appropriate language, and provide strategies to assist in social skills. The adult should be a play partner, not a director.

Before the age of 2, the toddler usually does little more than acknowledge, tolerate, and play alongside other children. After 2 years, he is in a transition stage where his understanding of others increases. He is still egocentric, but he needs other children to help him become more socially competent.

Imagination

Changes in the play behavior of children this age happen because they are able to think symbolically. This enables them to play in both imitative and imaginary ways. Props and stories might encourage imaginative thinking. Fears are very real at this stage, and imaginative play can help the 2-year-old act out some of them.

Personal and Intellectual Style

The 2-year-old has a need to be understood. Adults can show that they respect a child when they take time to be with him and observe his patterns of responses. Part of the need is for adults to know how best to reach or engage a child. The child will have a favored channel of communication, a leaning toward one or more multiple intelligences, a temperament style, and particular personality traits that make him an individual. The child needs to have adults recognize all these characteristics and respond in an appropriate and supportive manner.

Shared Moments

Above all the play and social situations that are essential for learning and development, the child needs adults to share moments with her. These may involve happiness or sadness, activity or passivity; but they all involve having a mutual understanding that transcends words. She needs you to be there.

DEVELOPMENTAL ALERTS

Particularly notable at this stage are the patterns of behavior and communication in a few children that present challenges for the educator, family and, of course, for the child herself. These patterns may be the result of nurturing, inherited characteristics, life experiences, or medical conditions. Frequently the causes are multiple. These conditions are usually rare, but worth consideration.

Attention-Deficit Disorder (ADD) and Attention-Deficit Hyperactivity Disorder (ADHD)

hyperactivity

levels of physical activity that are higher than normal, sometimes associated with a disorder

Attention-deficit disorders are mentioned frequently by the media and by families who are trying to explain the behavior of their young children. Attention-deficit disorders concern the child's inability to focus on tasks, organize herself in a way that is developmentally appropriate, or think in patterns that are generally accepted as normal. **Hyperactivity** is a term used to describe the child's inability to slow down or remain seated. Hyperactive children move around a lot and tend to be excitable. A diagnosis can be made only by a pediatrician, physician, psychiatrist, psychologist, or other specialist.

Children with attention-deficit or hyperactivity disorders present challenges for educators. They may appear to do poorly in some educational settings, which is surprising because children with these disorders may have above-average intelligence. Although ADD can be treated with Ritalin and other drugs, such treatment is controversial. Some people feel that children on Ritalin are being drugged out of difficult behaviors to make the educator's job easier; others feel that Ritalin is the only way for some children to be calm, focused, and successful.

The whole subject of identification and treatment of ADD and ADHD is a controversy that cannot be resolved quickly or easily. As future educators, you need to inform yourself more fully on these topics. An easy place to start is LDOnline (http://www.ldonline.org/), which has many articles on this topic. You can read Box 11.4 to examine some of the authors' thoughts on the increase in ADD and ADHD identification.

BOX 11.4

ADD, ADHD, OR NORMAL BEHAVIOR?

According to Howard, Williams, and Lepper (2005), "the overall incidence of ADHD has increased markedly in the past decade. Furthermore, increasing numbers of very young children with ADHD are being identified" (p. 303). I am disturbed by this trend. Attention-deficit disorder is characterized by impulsivity, hyperactivity, and inattention, but this may describe most 2-year-olds. You have learned about the developing cognitive capacities of children at this age. Although so much has occurred in their development to this point, they are still children. They move without thinking, examine without weighing consequences, focus from their perspective, tune out adult voices, and often act impulsively. This is *normal* development. Children under 5 should not be receiving this label. If they are, we might need to think about some of the reasons why this is occurring.

(continues)

BOX 11.4 (Continued)

Bruce Perry, speaking at a conference on early brain development, outlined what life used to be like for children growing up during the days of hunters and gatherers and even as recently as 60 years ago. Paraphrasing his words: We lived in tribes, then extended families, and then unified neighborhoods. Our brain for hundreds of thousands of years, has been genetically coded to live in a tribe. Back then, when a new baby was born, there were at least four adults around to help take care of and nurture the infant. Today, many of us live in isolated communities, not seeing relatives for months on end, and not knowing our neighbors. Now, a baby goes to child care and there is one adult taking care of four children. We have flipped the adult–child ratio.

Perry's point is that our brains are genetically wired to receive input from adults on a regular and constant basis.

Extrapolating from Perry's words, it is evident that in the new world of much less adult input, children will nonetheless continue to seek input. In the past, adult influence might have affected the child's self-calming techniques, as well as their insatiable curiosity. With fewer adults to help, our frantic pace of life may be contributing to the fact that children are not able to find a safe haven, either in their lives or their brains, that feels safe and secure. ADD and ADHD may represent a search for a place of protection. Children cannot raise themselves. They require the attention of adults who have fallen madly in love with them and who are willing to nurture them with patience and unconditional love.

Other best guesses as to why more and more children are being diagnosed with these conditions:

- Children are living in a world that is demanding ever-increasing adult-like behavior from them, so it is not surprising that more children are failing to meet the unrealistic criteria of what adults may think is "normal" behavior;
- Children are spending more time with inanimate entertainment sources such as the television, computers, and hand-held devices that may effect their visual stimulation baseline; and
- Children may be in environments that are actually hindering them or contributing to the problem—e.g., a classroom that is controlling, highly structured, with too many children and large-group instruction.

Please note, this is not to discount the reality that there are children who do have ADD and ADHD. If it is correctly diagnosed, Attention-deficit disorder and Attention-deficit hyperactivity disorder are neurologically based conditions. There are precursors, or symptoms, even from infancy. Babies who develop these disorders were often "difficult" babies, evidencing behavior that included irregular sleep patterns, an inability to adjust to change, a tendency for perseveration, and high levels of activity once mobile (Howard et al., 2005). However, ADD and ADHD conditions should not diagnosed until the key symptoms have been present for six months to one year.

So, if you have concerns about a child's behavior, begin documenting observations in a planned and consistent manner. Ask: Is this child *more* impulsive, *more* active, *less* able to handle transitions than average? Unless the behavior is extreme and needs immediate attention, you may find that within three months, the child is a different person.

anxiety

a troubled feeling or state of emotional unrest—the state might be caused by something occurring within the individual or by particular circumstances

nightmare

a particularly vivid and scary dream—tends to occur towards the end of the night

night terrors

occur during a phase of deep non-REM sleep, usually within an hour after the subject goes to bed; symptoms include sudden awakening from sleep, screaming, sweating, confusion, rapid heart rate, inability to explain what happened, eyes open but child not awake, difficult to rouse from sleep

anxiety disorder

a feeling of emotional unrest that cannot be attributed to "real" concerns; may be associated with any one of several neurotic conditions involving irrational fears

comfort object

any object that the child finds particularly comforting; the object takes on particular significance—e.g., blanket, teddy bear a "lovie"

attachment disorders

situations that occur where the child is unable to form one or more appropriate positive relationship, to such an extent that there may be long-lasting implications; intervention may be successful

Anxiety Disorder

Life events, abuse, traumas, styles of parenting, or temperament types, in any combination, can result in a young child suffering **anxiety**. Although the specific cause is sometimes very hard to determine, it may be particularly relevant to the solution of the problem. Two-year-olds normally experience a wide range of emotions, and fears normally take up a significant part of their emotional energy. Sometimes these show up as nighttime problems, including **nightmares** and fears, and also something called **night terrors**. The Additional Support section in your Online Companion has links to more information on the difference between nightmares and night terrors.

But if the fears take over, the result can be a pattern of anxiety that is difficult to break. An extreme form of this is an **anxiety disorder**. Anxiety disorders can manifest themselves in a variety of ways, including self-comforting behaviors. The child may stroke her body or masturbate, rock, or gnaw at her own hand or arm. She may have sleep problems, experience panic, or display prolonged or obsessive attachment to **comfort objects**. She may withdraw, be unable to interact with others, and be unwilling to interact with unfamiliar places or people. Treatment may be required from a pediatrician, early interventionist, or psychiatrist.

Attachment Disorder

When infants fail to make secure attachments because their style differs from their caregiver's, or they make attachments that are later damaged or broken by significant changes in their lives, they may display **attachment disorders**. Children suffering from abuse are most likely to suffer attachment disorders, because the faulty dynamic of an important relationship has broken their trust. Even if the child does not seem particularly distressed, she can have an attachment problem if the normal boundaries of relationships concerning love and trust are distorted. In extreme circumstances, where infants have not had the opportunity to make attachments—in cases of extreme neglect, for example, or when infants have been placed in unresponsive care in orphanages—they may lose the ability to form attachments.

Many attachment difficulties respond to intervention. Parents and educators can be taught how to tune in to the child and improve the goodness of fit between themselves and the child. More severe forms of attachment disorder may be ameliorated, but it may not be possible to completely mend them. Those children can grow up unable to make or sustain normal adult relationships.

Aggressive Behavior

Children become aggressive for a variety of reasons. They may have learned this behavior from others, they may not have learned any self-calming skills or self-control techniques, they may lack adequate problem-solving skills, they may be unable to use language to articulate their feelings, or they may be showing off their power. Children who display **aggressive behavior** may simply be seeking attention and not know how to do so positively. Some aggressive behavior may stem from pain, neurological damage, or intense frustration that overwhelms the child. The child who displays aggressive behavior may feel very vulnerable or unable to take control. This child needs a lot of love and support. In many cases, particularly if the issue is addressed when the child is young, the behavior can be modified by using behavioristic techniques, by providing positive role models and strategies for overcoming frustration, and by deflecting the child's energies into activities where she feels successful. Aggressive behavior is not a behavior that can be ignored, so if it occurs, it must be dealt with as soon as possible. Make sure to involve families in any plan of action that is formulated.

Children under Stress

Children who live in an environment that stresses their families are not necessarily stressed themselves. Yet they may experience the effect of the stressors, either directly or indirectly. In the latter case, they may view a family member's stressful reaction, or receive less than ideal

aggressive behavior

any action that is motivated to cause harm—socially unacceptable behavior resulting from anger

stress

the sum of the biological reactions to any adverse stimulus—physical, mental, or emotional, internal or external— that tends to disturb a person's normal state of well-being

language delay

later-than-average acquisition of language

support from an adult. Stressors include major issues such as poverty, unemployment or under-employment, family illness, domestic violence, housing inadequacies, and separation or divorce. (Review Bronfenbrenner's Ecological System—Figure 3.3 in Chapter 3.) Families who are able to cope with their circumstances and who have support systems may be able to protect their children from their direct stressors, but it is harder for them to protect the children from their own frustrations and worries. A child experiences this **stress** and can show it in many ways, including withdrawal, disengagement from play, slowed growth and development, temper tantrums and other behavioral problems, and communication difficulties. Removal from the source of stress may be helpful, but it doesn't guarantee that the child's stress is banished, partly because it has become a pattern and partly because removal from the source is likely to mean removal from the people to whom she is attached. Interventionists can help families and children deal constructively with stress.

Language Delay

Delayed language does not always reflect a real problem. As we have seen, the range of language skills is very wide in children at this stage. However, educators may notice that a child is not progressing in speech and language acquisition within a reasonable time frame. The first step is to check hearing ability and acuity. If the delay is caused by a hearing deficit, the child might be helped by a hearing aid, tubes in the ears, or therapy to help the child feel vibrations. The physical components of sound production also need to be checked. If the **language delay** is linked to a cognitive deficit, the mode of treating the child might differ. Many educators work well with speech and language pathologists, reinforcing on a daily basis the efforts that the specialist makes. Consult the Additional Support section in your Online Companion for information on warning signs for language delays.

Communication Disorders

communication disorder

a broad term used to describe a structural or functional difficulty or deficit that impedes effective communication— may be a diagnosed disorder such as aphasia or hearing impairment

aphasia

a language impairment that may have resulted from damage to the central nervous system

Communication disorders can take a variety of forms. Generally, "communication difficulties of one type or another are universally present in individuals with autism" (Koegel, 2003, p. 17). Other communication difficulties include **aphasia** (a neurological condition that affects the ability to communicate), articulation difficulties, voice disorders, dysfluency (such as stuttering), and orofacial defects (such as cleft palate). In addition, culture shock can cause communication difficulties that have to do with an inability to speak English or emotional challenges in integrating into a new environment.

Support for children's language difficulties is best done when the child is young. A speech/language clinician or pathologist can diagnose and treat communication disorders. This person can also help parents and educators to use various techniques to assist language and communication (Koegel, 2003).

The Additional Support section in your Online Companion has links to more information on these topics.

Two- to three-year-olds are very interested and capable of being involved. Their self-help skills gradually improve during this time period. Hand washing and toileting are two very important areas of interest and involvement. Other areas include eating, environmental awareness, dental hygiene, sleep, exercise, and labeling feelings. They are covered briefly here, and can be considered an important part of the curriculum for children. Remember to check your Online Companion under the Health Concerns section for additional information.

Two-year-olds are very interested and capable of being involved in their own self-help in the area of health. The reader can view this section as the two-year-old's health curriculum.

Toilet-learning usually becomes a significant accomplishment during the third year of life.

Hand Washing

Handwashing should be a matter of routine before meals and snacks and after diapering or the use of the toilet or potty. Two-year-olds need encouragement and positive role models so that they will do this routinely. They need sinks they can reach, liquid soap they can pump, taps that they can turn on and off, and paper towels or single-use cloth towels that are washed and sanitized. Take care that young children are supervised when they use water. There is always some potential for drowning, even in a few inches of water. They can also scald themselves if the hot tap is too hot, or soak themselves completely within seconds.

Toileting

Two-year-olds may have the bowel and bladder control to use the potty or toilet. Some want to take a long time sitting on the potty, as though it were a regular social situation. There is little harm in this as long as they don't get cold. Other children will observe those using the toilet but will continue to prefer diapers. There should be no fuss about this. The atmosphere in the bathroom should be positive and noncontrolling. Telling the children stories about bathrooms can be a good strategy to encourage the children to think of toileting in positive ways.

Eating

Most toddlers at this stage feed themselves with finger food but may want some help cutting up large pieces. They can usually use their fingers, and some can use a fork, spoon, or chopsticks. Children come to child care with various mealtime experiences. They need to make a gentle transition to self-help and feeling comfortable in the social situation of sitting at a table. Children usually look forward to lunch time or snack time and enjoy the adult conversation that occurs. Mealtimes should be associated with pleasantness. Children should not be forced to eat, nor should food be used to manipulate their behavior. Appetites vary, and children should be encouraged to think about whether they are hungry, and to eat accordingly. A variety of foods should be served on a regular basis. Encouragement, but not force, is desirable. Food not eaten should be removed without fuss. Children should hear positive messages about food making them strong or giving them energy.

Learning about food can be great fun. Matching picture cards and pretend food can be good ideas, but handling real food is best. Two-year-olds love to participate in food preparation. In doing so, they find out about color and texture, about how food is prepared, and about basic rules of hygiene.

Environmental Awareness

Children at this age can be shown how to sort items for garbage or recycling. This sense of order appeals to them. While they cannot appreciate global environmental issues, they do learn from example. If we waste paper, we send the message that this is acceptable. We need to send good messages. If we make messes, we need to take responsibility to help with cleanup. If we keep a recycling bin for scraps, we are sending a message that it's good to reuse things and not be wasteful.

Dental Hygiene

Children's toothpaste and personal toothbrushes should be provided by parents for use after eating. Two-year-olds may not do a very good job and may chew the brush, but the effort is worthwhile. Adults need to monitor and help with tooth brushing to make sure it is effective. Because the child will have her first set of teeth, they need to be protected from decay. The health of first teeth influences later dental health. Sugary foods and candy should be avoided for the sake of the child's teeth and dietary needs.

The following are some general suggestions for tooth-brushing procedures in child care. Always check with your facility to ensure that you are following current state regulations.

- Make sure that each child has his own toothbrush clearly labeled with his name. Do not allow children to share or borrow toothbrushes.
- Apply (or have child apply) a pea-sized amount of fluoride toothpaste to a dry toothbrush.
- Instruct each child to brush his teeth and then spit out the toothpaste.
- Using a paper cup, each child should rinse his mouth out with water. Dispose of the cup.
- Store each toothbrush so it cannot touch any other toothbrush, and allow it to air-dry.
- Never "disinfect" toothbrushes. If a child uses another child's toothbrush, or if two toothbrushes come in contact, throw them away and give the children new toothbrushes.
- Replace toothbrushes every 3 to 4 months, or sooner if bristles have lost their tone.

Sleep

A schedule that includes quiet times and a mat or cot to sleep on are appropriate for children at this stage. They welcome the predictable routines and rituals associated with sleep. Most children welcome snuggling into their favorite cuddly toy or holding a soft piece of blanket. The pattern for naps should be similar every day, so that the child becomes used to the sequence of activities that lead to sleep. Back rubbing or playing soft music may be part of this, but whatever the educator offers on one day has to be available every day.

Exercise

Two-year-olds do not need structured activities or sports. They need to run, climb, explore, and have fun outdoors spontaneously. The adult should provide space and opportunity for this. If the weather is really bad, children will need to run around in an indoor play space. Two-year-olds need to hear that running and stretching their bodies is healthy. Refer to Box 11.1 to refresh your memory about the importance of physical activity.

Labeling Feelings

Young children will sometimes point to the part of their body that hurts, but it is useful for them to acquire a vocabulary related to how their body feels and functions. "It hurts" can help a family or educator to know what is wrong. "I feel ucky" can let the adult know that a child doesn't feel well. Sometimes it helps to ask children to point with just one finger to where it hurts.

A positive rather than shameful attitude towards bodies is essential, but children can be taught about being private. Although privacy is a socially learned behavior, many children feel more comfortable if given their own private space when needed.

sexual abuse

any abuse or maltreatment of an individual that involves the sexual organs of the perpetrator or victim, and/or unwanted or inappropriate touching, and/or damage to sexual identity, privacy, or feelings of the victim

SIGNS OF POTENTIAL NEGLECT OR ABUSE

Sexual Abuse

Of all the types of abuse, child **sexual abuse** brings out the most emotionally charged response. Realistically, educators and families are the people closest to the child on a daily basis and thus best positioned to recognize behavioral changes and signs and symptoms of abuse. As in any other type of abuse or neglect, the educator must follow the agency's child abuse protocols, pass information to the local child protection agency, consider how medical advice can be sought, and ensure that the situation is kept confidential. Signs of sexual abuse may be evident in infants, toddlers, and 2-year-olds. These may include:

- any of the signs attributable to other forms of abuse
- behavioral changes
- withdrawal
- sleep problems
- fears
- body flaunting
- masturbating or rubbing the genitals
- hiding the body
- refusing to remove clothes
- soreness of the vagina
- soreness of the penis
- anal soreness, bleeding, or itching
- bleeding or infected genitals (i.e., showing a discharge)
- soreness around the mouth
- bruises around the genitals or on the insides of the legs
- hand marks on the legs

Remember, it is not the responsibility of educators to determine whether abuse, sexual or otherwise, has occurred. However, it is their responsibility to document any observations that are pertinent and follow reporting procedures. Educators must contact the child protection agency if there is cause for concern. Extensive investigation is likely. It is essential that all concerned cooperate with staff from the child protection agency and the police. Remember to check the Additional Support section in your Online Companion to refresh your knowledge about abuse and neglect.

EVERYDAY SAFETY ISSUES

Two-year-olds can begin to take small steps toward increasing their own safety. They should be learning about what is expected behavior in a social group through observation of modeled behavior and through daily conversations. Try to always frame the behavior in positive terms, telling the children what they are able or should do, not what they cannot do or shouldn't do. It is very hard for children to remember "Rules," so expect that you will spend this year repeating many of the same things. (See Personal Comment box below.) Since children are living together for many hours a day, the approach caregivers should take is creating a family atmosphere. All families have certain ways of looking out for each other, and the classroom should be no different. Some examples of how to frame expectations in positive language could include:

We are kind to each other	Take turns
NOT	NOT
Don't hurt each other	Don't push and shove
Paint stays at the easel	Use words
NOT	NOT
Don't take the paint across the room	Don't hit each other
Forks are for eating	Go down the slide one at a time
NOT	NOT
Forks aren't for jabbing each other	Don't go down the slide together
Messes need to be wiped up	Walk around the swing
NOT	NOT
Don't step in that	Don't walk in front of the swing
Hold hands when we walk	Wait your turn
NOT	NOT
Don't run	Don't fight over the turn
Scissors go point-down	Wait for a grownup
NOT	NOT
Don't hold the scissors like that	We don't go outside without a grownup

Personal Comment

During a family class, someone asked me how many times she was going to have to ask her 2 ½-year-old to do something.

She had already told him 50 times. My reply was, "At least 51, since he still hasn't learned that behavior yet."

Then I reminded the group that toddlers don't forget rules, they just can't remember them yet.

This period of repeating yourself can be exhausting, but you must do it.

This does not mean that you yell at a child from across the room or count to ten, or forty, or whatever.

It means that you must get down at eye level with the child, establish eye contact, and talk to him in a controlled manner.

You might have to give yourself an occasional count of ten before you do this to make sure your emotions are in check.

The educator also needs to comment on the efforts children are making.

Say, "I noticed you waiting Gianni.

It's very hard, but you are doing it."

Or, "You are remembering how to keep safe.

You are holding hands."

Try not to put a value judgment on any behavior by saying "good job" or "I like."

These are overused phrases and end up not being very meaningful.

If children are demonstrating positive behavior, describe their positive behavior.

Say "I see," or "I noticed."

This approach can move us away from the "good job" mantra, which is ingrained in our heads and often ends up just being reflexive, empty praise.

Here a teacher gets down to eye level, establishes eye contact, and talks to the child in a controlled and comforting manner.

If these are offered in context, they are positive statements that are easily understood. But children at this age cannot hold two things in mind at once, so expect a lot of forgetting. Repeat the rule as necessary.

Two-year-olds can acquire some personal-safety techniques by learning to say things like:

- "No."
- "I don't like you hurting me."
- "I'll wait for Mommy at the window."
- "Don't touch me."
- "I don't want that."
- "I'll tell Mary that you did that to me."
- "Go away."

Although these statements may sound forceful, the child is beginning to exercise her right to freedom and personal safety, which is part of her need for personal empowerment.

✗ STARTING POINTS FOR RESPONSE

Responsive Caregiving

Two-year-olds are leaving behind their infancy and joining the wider world, where they are keen to become independent. But along the way, they feel vulnerable or need emotional support because things can seem overwhelming. The educator needs to read the child's signs and respond to them accordingly. Sometimes the child needs approval, at other times,

BOX 11.5

GETTING IN TUNE WITH THE 2- TO 3-YEAR-OLD CHILD

Below in are some starting points for building your responsivity skills with 2- to 3-year-old children. This list is not comprehensive, and many more suggestions can be found in your Online Companion under the section entitled "Getting in Tune with Infants, Toddlers, and Twos."

- Accept repetitive/ritual behaviors.
- Assist self-awareness and competence in labelling characteristics.
- Offer creative modes of expression, such as paint, clay, music, and movement.
- Enable the child's world to be safely enlarged.
- Support the emergence of self-help skills.
- Offer many sensory discovery experiences, including ones that challenge the child's experience of the properties of materials.
- Offer quiet spaces for the child to be alone.
- Enable the toddler to accept and help control his own feelings and recognize others' feelings.
- Introduce small-group activities to increase social exposure and cooperation.
- Acknowledge the toddler's demonstration of empathy, taking turns, following practical directions, and working together.
- Provide plenty of indoor and outdoor play space.
- Use stories and books for close one-to-one contact and to extend the child's experience.
- Use domestic objects as playthings: e.g., chairs with large cloths can become tents.
- Offer a full dramatic play center, including culturally familiar home objects.
- Identify the toddler's individual intelligences and build on those preferences.
- Use a conversational, give-and-take style in body language, talking, dance, and other activities.
- Offer achievable physical challenges in climbing, running, balancing, etc.
- Offer clear parameters of behavior and simple consequences.
- Support dual-language learning.

protection. Her feelings change so rapidly she's not always aware of how she feels. The caregiver needs to help the child to understand her feelings and how to control them so that she can use them to her advantage. Box 11.5 provides some strategies for responding to the needs of a child at this age.

Supportive Guidance

There's so much to learn, and the 2-year-old wants to do it all, right now! She needs assistance in making choices, following through with an activity, and knowing the sequence of planning, action, and cleanup. These are the socially acceptable behaviors of the toddler room. She needs to know what is expected, and she may need many reminders because she can't always remember. Everything should have a set routine. Consistent schedules help the child make sense of things.

Facilitating Development

The 2-year-old's need for order makes her interested in sorting and matching everything in sight. She starts to classify things, but forgets or changes the criteria for sorting partway through, so her activities may seem disjointed. Her imagination leads to more complex forms of play that might involve other children. With some signs of cooperation, she might be involved, too, in sociodramatic play, but the sequences will not be very long or complex. It is helpful if the adult provides lots of starting points and "why don't you . . ." suggestions. Conceptual understanding increases tremendously during this year, and language learning complements all the new understandings. The child likes lots of familiar stories and may sit for a while in a small group to listen. Creative music activities are usually well received. Children are stretching their capabilities to broaden their repertoire and refinement of motor skills. They enjoy practicing them as they paint, draw, glue, construct, and play with sensory materials and a variety of games and puzzles. The caregiver will facilitate all these learning experiences but gradually, through this stage, the toddler will demonstrate increasing autonomy.

Activities

Your Online Companion and CD-ROM contain activities to encourage a holistic response to young children 24–36 months. On your CD-ROM, Activity 11.4 suggest ways of engaging in the experience of toddlers at this stage and extending your interactions with them. These activities always start from the framework of observation. Activity 11.5 helps you observe each toddler and to develop activities that are targeted to individual interests and skill levels. Activity 11.6 includes suggestions for further experiences and interactions. Activity 11.7 describes several possible scenarios for responsive guidance.

SUMMARY

During the young child's third year, there are increased confidence, curiosity, and independence in the child, as we see that she wants to do things for herself. As her fine and gross motor skills are refined, she is able to increase her self-help skills involving dressing, toileting, mealtimes, and other everyday competencies. Now the child can improve the range of mobility skills and is able to climb, jump down from small heights, and become active inside and outside. Improving hand coordination allows the child to play with a variety of materials, including paint and crayons. Her grasp is more refined, and she uses this skill to help her with eating and dressing. These gains in skills are also directly related to the increased synaptic connections that are formed in the brain.

The child usually enjoys a predictable routine, and may demand that certain domestic actions be undertaken in a ritualistic manner. She may want to have things done in a certain way, or may be adamant that she drink from a particular cup or wear particular clothes. Frequently we may see that the child has strong emotions that might change rapidly. Although she is able to regulate her feelings and behavior to some extent, she often seeks the assistance of adults to help her manage situations. Having a small range of trusted adults is important as the child balances independence and dependence.

The child's increasing cognitive skills can be attributed to her brain development, but they also depend upon her having appropriate learning experiences. Usually the 2-year-old will be moving from the sensorimotor stage of thought to the pre-operational stage, according to Piaget's model of cognition. At this stage, it is evident that the child has increasing abilities to categorize her world, even though her thinking is not yet constant. She has some difficulty holding ideas in mind, which can make her thinking appear semi-logical. She may also make some incorrect associations between ideas. Her attention span, when engrossed in an activity, increases over time. Children have different ways of being smart. The multiple intelligence theory explains how we can recognize each child's strengths and use these favored channels to expand the child's learning.

It is very noticeable that during the third year, the child's language expands tremendously. Not only does her vocabulary grow, but so does her use of the rules of language. This enables the child's communication skills to be increasingly refined. She manages to convey and understand many more ideas. The link between language, social development, and cognition is evident within language development. When a child is acquiring one or more languages at a time, it is necessary to support both languages, even if some temporary confusion arises.

It is important at this stage that the child be given the tools to become emotionally intelligent. Many aspects of her increased self-regulation indicate an understanding of herself and others. Increasing this understanding can come about in a variety of ways, but it is predicated on solid relationships with adults and the opportunity for her to socialize with other children. She has some empathy for others but needs this reinforced. Having adults act as coaches assists her to become socially and emotionally competent.

At this stage, the child's play becomes broader and more complex. We may see a number of pretend games, but she remains interested in sensory play of various kinds as she becomes more sophisticated in how she handles the materials. Through play, the child increases her knowledge about the world, what it's made of, and how it works. In particular, she learns about the properties of materials, along with many preconceptual ideas. Her social relationships include others in her play behaviors, but her play tends to be parallel or associative rather than cooperative. Imitation continues to be important to her learning, particularly in understanding social roles. In her play we frequently see situations that are imitated or adapted from what she has seen in other situations. This deferred imitation is one signal of her symbolic thinking ability. We may see evidence of a more vigorous imagination in a variety of ways—particularly in her fantasy play. All children may require adults to take on play roles occasionally, but this is especially important if play is not evolving in a particular child.

Having an imagination and fluctuating emotions, along with an incomplete understanding of the realities of life, the child may experience a range of fears. Sometimes these are evident when she has nighttime problems, including nightmares or night terrors.

Opportunity for physical activity is essential, since children continue to learn about the world through their motor skills. Teachers must ensure that this need, along with the continued need for sensory experiences, is met. Improved self-help skills and physical skills, along with increased interactions with other children, helps fuel competence levels but also results in conflicts. An effective strategy to employ when conflicts arise between children, or a child is struggling with emotional control, is to get down to eye level, establish eye contact, and talk to the child or children in a controlled and comforting manner. Children can begin to learn about expected behaviors, especially if teachers frame the expectations in terms that tell children what they can do.

The child's parents are the most important adults in the life of their child. Working in partnership with parents can assist us to define what our role is in the lives of young children. Observing children, acting as their coach, providing scaffolding for their learning, acting as mediator, and enjoying their company are each essential elements of our role to support every part of the child's development. We must see the child as a competent human being. However, children cannot raise themselves. They still require the attention of adults who have fallen madly in love with them and who are willing to nurture them. The most important point that we must learn is to be there with them.

DISCUSSION QUESTIONS

1. A mother and father tell you they are considering taking their child out of center-based care, to put her in private home care, because of a recent incident in which their child was bitten by another child. What might you say and do?

2. Recent advances in brain science have improved our understanding of children's behavior. How does this understanding translate into a change in the educator's role?

3. How could you organize your day with under-3-year-olds so that you can enjoy more shared moments with them?

4. What strategies might you use to assist a child of 30 months to integrate into your child care setting when he has had no previous exposure to other children and speaks only Farsi?

5. What have you learned from this book that can help you advocate for higher standards of child care?

No Way—The Hundred Is There.

The child
is made of one hundred.
The child has
a hundred languages
a hundred hands
a hundred thoughts
a hundred ways of thinking
of playing, of speaking.
A hundred, always a hundred
ways of listening
of marveling, of loving
a hundred joys
for singing and understanding
a hundred worlds
to discover
a hundred worlds
to invent
a hundred worlds
to dream.
The child has
one hundred languages
(and a hundred hundred hundred more)
but they steal ninety-nine.
The school and the culture
separate the head from the body.

They tell the child:
to think without hands
to do without head
to listen and not to speak
to understand without joy
to love and marvel
only at Easter and Christmas.
They tell the child:
to discover the world already there
and of the hundred
they steal ninety-nine.
They tell the child:
that work and play
reality and fantasy
science and imagination
sky and earth
reason and dream
are things
that do not belong together.

And they tell the child
that the hundred is not there.
The child says:
"No way. The hundred is there."

Loris Malaguzzi (translated by Lella Gandini). Source: From *The Hundred Languages of Children Exhibit Catalogue*, Copyright Infant–Toddler Centers and Preschools-Instituzione of the Municipality of Reggio Emilia, published by Reggio Children, 1996. Reprinted with permission from Reggio Children.

ADDITIONAL RESOURCES

Further Readings

Berger, D., Reid, R., & Torelli, L. (2000). *Educating and caring for very young children: The infant/toddler curriculum.* New York: Teachers College Press.

Burton, L., & Kudo, T. (2000). *SoundPlay: Understanding music through creative movement.* Reston, VA: National Association for Music Education.

Caitlin, C. 1996). *More toddlers together.* Beltsville, MD: Gryphon House, Inc.

Gardner, H. (1993). *Multiple intelligences: The theory in practice.* New York: Basic Books/HarperCollins.

Goleman, D. (2000). *Working with emotional intelligence.* New York: Bantam Doubleday Dell.

Gottman, J. (1998). *Raising an emotionally intelligent child.* New York: Fireside Books/Simon & Schuster.

Greenspan, S., & Wieder, S. (1997). *Infancy and early childhood: The practice of clinical assessment and intervention with emotional and developmental challenges.* Washington, DC: Zero to Three.

Hirsh-Pasek, K., & Golinkoff, R. M. (2003). *Einstein never used flash-cards: How our children really learn—and why they need to play more and memorize less.* New York: Rodale, Inc.

Kohl, M. (2002). *First art: Art experiences for toddlers and twos.* Beltsville, MD: Gryphon House, Inc.

Lerner, C., & Dombro, A. (2000). *Learning and growing together: Understanding and supporting your child's development.* Washington, DC: Zero to Three.

Levin, D. (2003). Beyond banning war and superhero play: Meeting children's needs in violent times. *Young Children, 58*(3), 60–64

Lieberman, A. F. (1993). *The emotional life of the toddler.* New York: Free Press.

Louv, R. (2005). *The last child in the woods: Saving our children from a nature deficit disorder.* Chapel Hill, NC: Algonquin Books of Chapel Hill

Owens, R. E. (2001). *Language development* (5th ed.). Boston: Allyn & Bacon.

Paley, V. (2004). *A child's work: The importance of fantasy play.* Chicago: The University of Chicago Press.

Pawl, J., & St. John, M. (1998). *How you are is as important as what you do.* Washington, DC: Zero to Three.

Pawl, J., & St. John, M. (1998). *Learning & growing together: Understanding and supporting your child's development.* Washington, DC: Zero to Three.

Pruett, K. (1999). *Me, myself and I: How children build their sense of self—18 to 36 months.* New York: Goddard Press.

Saracho, O., & Spodek, B. (1998). *Multiple perspectives in play in early childhood education.* Albany, NY: SUNY Press.

Sparling, J., & Lewis, I. (2001). *Learning games: The Abecedarian curriculum.* Tallahassee, FL: Early Learning Press.

Weitzman, E., & Greenberg, J. (2002). *Learning language and loving it* (2nd ed.). Toronto: Beacon Harold Fine Printing.

Useful Videos

Life's First Feelings: Growing Pains. NOVA. Closed captioned; 60 minutes (VHS).

Description: This video provides a close look at babies' emotional responses, clues about developing personality traits, and how parents help with socialization.

Ready for Life. KERA. 60 minutes.

Description: This intimate story of six children and their families—depicting the joys and sorrows they face as they begin to explore the world—displays how children begin to develop the strength and confidence to face life's challenges in emotionally healthy ways.

Nourishing Language Development in Early Childhood. Davidson Films. 31 minutes.

Description: Using vignettes filmed at an exemplary children's center, students are introduced to the vocabulary of language studies. Dr. Honig describes the development of spoken language in infancy, toddlerhood, and early childhood.

Childhood Development: A Cognitive Approach to Developmental Psychology. Films for the Humanities. Five-part series; 25 minutes each.

Description: From the earliest stages of mental representation to advanced acquisition of language and social skills, this series presents various research methods, theories, and concepts of developmental psychology to promote understanding of a crucial period of development.

Babywatching. Films for the Humanities. Color; 50 minutes.

Description: Featured zoologist and peoplewatcher Desmond Morris sets out, not merely to watch babies, but to watch, think, and see the world like a baby.

Learning Language and Loving It. Two tapes, total running time 3 hours 40 minutes.

This two-part video demonstrates how teachers use strategies in play and daily activities to create enriched, interactive language-learning environments that include all children. Examples include teachers interacting with children who have special needs and language delays and children who are second-language learners, as well as children who are typically developing. The video has onscreen time codes and comes with a detailed User's Guide for easy reference. Bringing to life the *Learning Language and Loving It* guidebook (2nd Edition, NAEYC Order #210), this program addresses the vital role of preschool teachers in facilitating children's social, language, and literacy development. From the Hanen Centre.

Toddler Curriculum: Making Connections. 20 min.

This video examines how toddlers 12–36 months of age develop and learn. It depicts developmentally appropriate curriculum in the toddler classroom. Produced by South Carolina Educational Television.

Videos available from NAEYC.

Time for Toddlers. Training for Caregivers. 22 minutes. Available from Redleaf Press

Toddlers rush headlong into life. Here is help for the exasperated caregiver. Time with Toddlers is a captivating video that looks at toddler development. Sequences capture typical toddler behavior and recommended caregiver actions, with simple explanations of their behavior by Margie Carter. A useful training guide offers suggestions for follow-up discussions and activities.

Young Children in Action. Teachers College Press. Companion video to Educating and Caring for Very Young Children: The Infant/Toddler Curriculum. 56 min.

Vignettes of many different children at different stages of development, ages newborn to 3.

Useful Web Sites

Brain development
www.sparrowlake.org/

Child abuse
http://www.jimhopper.com
Click on link for Child Abuse: Statistics, Research, and Resources
www.sc.gc.ca/
www.childhelpusa.org/

Emotional development
www.athealth.com/
Click on link for (consumer), click on link for Important Issues, click on link for Common Ways

Families
www.vifamily.ca/
www.nafcc.org/

Language and cognition
http://speech-language-therapy.com/
Click on link for Ages and Stages
www.cal.org/
www.ooaq.qc.ca/
Click on link for English (under Archives), click on link for Information cards on communication disorders

Movement and music
www.cfc-efc.ca/
Click on link for Come and see our library of over 1300 documents!, search for 'creative movement,' click on link for Creative Movement and Dance in Early Childhood Education
www.menc.org/
Click on link for Index, click on link for Position Statements, MENC, click on link for Early Childhood

National Clearing House on Child Abuse
http://nccanch.acf.hhs.gov/

Play
www.cfc-efc.ca/
Click on link for Come and see our library of over 1300 documents!, pull pulldown menu down to Play
www.unbf.ca/
Click on link for UNB A to Z, click on link for the letter E, click on link for Education, Faculty of, click on link for Centres, click on link for Early Childhood Centre, click on link for The Gallery, click on link for Children Learning Through Play

Various ECE Topics
www.voice4children.org Click on Reports
www.educationworld.com/
Click on link for Early Childhood (under Specialties)
www.unicef.org/

References

Acredolo, L., Goodwyn, S., & Abrams, D. (2002). *Baby signs: How to talk with your baby before your baby can talk* (New edition). New York: McGraw-Hill.

Adamson, L. (1996). *Communication development during infancy.* Boulder, CO: Westview/HarperCollins.

Ahnert, L., Gunnar, M., Lamb, M., & Barthel, M. (2004). Transition to child care: Associations with infant-mother attachment, infant negative emotion, and cortisol elevations. *Child Development, 75* (3): 639–650.

Ahnert, L., & Lamb, M. E. (2004). Childcare and its impact on young children (2–5). In R. E. Tremblay, R. G. Barr, & R. Peters (Eds.), *Encyclopedia on early childhood development.* [online] Montreal, Quebec: Centre of Excellence for Early Childhood Development; 2004: 1–6. Retrieved July 19, 2005 from http://www.excellence-earlychildhood.ca/documents/Ahnert-LambANGxp.pdf.

Ainsworth, M. (1969). Object relations, dependency, and attachment: A theoretical review of the infant–mother relationship. *Child Development, 40:* 969–1025.

———. (1973). The development of infant–mother attachment. In B. M. Caldwell & H. N. Ricciuti (Eds.), *Review of Child Development Research, 3:* 1–94. Chicago: University of Chicago.

———. (1979). Attachment as related to mother–infant interaction. *Advances in the Study of Behavior, 9:* 2–51.

Ainsworth, M., Salter, D., & Wittig, B. (1967). Attachment and exploratory behavior of one-year-olds in a strange situation. In B. M. Foss (Ed.), *Determinants of infant behavior* (Vol. 4). New York: Wiley.

Ainsworth, M., et al. (1978). *Patterns of attachment: A psychological study of the strange situation.* Hillsdale, NJ: Erlbaum.

Allen, K. E., & Martoz, L.R. (2000). *By the ages: Behavior and development of children pre-birth through eight.* Clifton Park, NY: Thomson Delmar Learning.

Allen, K. E., & Martoz, L. R. (2007). *Developmental profiles: Pre-birth through twelve* (5th ed.). Clifton Park, NY: Thomson Delmar Learning.

Allen, K., Paasche, C., Cornell, A., & Engel, M. (1994). *Exceptional children: Inclusion in early childhood programs.* Scarborough, ON: Nelson.

Allport, G., & Odbert, H. (1936). Trait-names: A psycho-lexical study. *Psychological Monographs, 47*(211).

Amacher, N. (1973). Touch is a way of caring. *American Journal of Nursing, 73*(5): 852–854.

American Academy of Pediatrics. (2005). Breastfeeding and the use of human milk. *Pediatrics, 115* (2): 496–506.

American Academy of Pediatrics. (2001). Injuries associated with infant walkers. *Pediatrics, 108*(3): 790–792.

American Academy of Pediatrics. (2001). Physicians and breast-feeding promotion in the United States: A call for action. *Pediatrics, 107*(3): 584–589.

American Academy of Pediatrics. (2000). Changing concepts of sudden infant death syndrome: Implications for infant sleeping environment and sleep position. *Pediatrics, 105* (3): 650–656.

Ames, E. W., & Chisholm, K. (2001). Social and emotional development in children adopted from institutions. In D. B. Bailey, J. T. Bruer, F. Symons, & J. W. Lichtman, (Eds.) *Critical thinking about critical periods* (pp. 129–148). Baltimore: Paul H. Brookes.

Anthony, M., & Lindert, R. (2005). *Signing smart with babies and toddlers.* New York: St. Martins Griffin.

Apgar, V. (1953). A proposal for a new method of evaluation of the newborn infant. *Current Research in Anesthesia and Analgesia, 32:* 360–367.

Aronson, D. (Ed.). (2002). *Healthy young children: A manual for programs.* Washington, DC: NAEYC.

Avard, D., & Hanvey, L. (Eds.). (1989). *The health of Canada's children: A CICH profile.* Ottawa, ON: Canadian Institute of Child Health.

Bailey, D., & Wolery, M. (1989). *Assessing infants and preschoolers with handicaps.* Columbus, OH: Merrill.

Bailey, D. B., & Symons, F. J. W. (2001). Critical periods: Reflections and future directions. In D. B. Bailey, J. T. Bruer, F. Symons, & J. W. Lichtman (Eds.), *Critical thinking about critical periods* (pp. 289–292). Baltimore: Paul H. Brookes.

Baker, A. C., & Manfredi/Petitt, L. A. (2004). *Relationships, the heart of quality care: Creating community among adults in early care settings.* Washington, DC: NAEYC.

Bandura, A. (1977). *Social learning theory.* Englewood Cliffs, NJ: Prentice Hall.

Baptiste, N. & Reyes, L.V. (2005). *Understanding ethics in early care and education.* Upper Saddle River, NJ: Pearson/Merrill/Prentice Hall.

Bardige, B. (2005). *At a loss for words: How America is failing our children and what we can do about it.* Philadelphia: Temple University Press.

Bardige, B. S., & Segal, M. (2005). *Building literacy with love: A guide for teachers and caregivers of children birth through age 5.* Washington, DC: ZERO TO THREE.

Barnhorst, R., & Johnson, L. (Eds.). (1991). *The state of the child in Ontario.* Toronto: Oxford University Press.

Barlow, J. S. (2002). *The cerebellum and adaptive control.* New York: Cambridge Press.

Barnat, S. B., Klein, P. J., & Meltzoff, P. J. (1996). Deferred imitation across changes in context and object: Memory and generalization in 14-month-old infants. *Infant Behavior and Development, 19,* 241–251.

Batshaw, M. L., & Tuchman, M. (2002). PKU and other inborn errors of metabolism. In M. L. Batshaw (Ed.), *Children with disabilities* (5th ed., pp. 333–345). Baltimore: Paul H. Brookes Publishing Co., Inc.

Bauer, P., & Hertsgaard, L. (1993). Increasing steps in recall of events: Factors facilitating immediate and long-term in 13.5- and 16.5-month-old children. *Child Development, 64:* 1204–1223.

Bayley, N. (1969). *Bayley Scales of infant development.* New York: Psychological Corporation.

Beauchamp, G., Cowart, B., & Morgan, M. (1986). Developmental changes in salt acceptability in human infants. *Developmental Psychology, 19:* 17–25.

Beach, J., Bertrand, J., & Cleveland, G. (1998). *Our child care workforce: From recognition to remuneration: A human resource study of child care in Canada.* Ottawa, ON: Child Care Human Resources Steering Committee.

Beatty, N. (1992). *Heart start: The emotional foundations of school readiness.* Washington, DC: ZERO TO THREE.

Beebe, B. (2004). Co-constructing mother-infant distress in face-to-face interactions: Contributions of microanalysis. *ZERO TO THREE, 24*(5), 40–48.

Begley, S., et al. (1992). Mapping the brain. *Newsweek,* April 20: 66–72.

Belsky, J. (1980). Child maltreatment: An ecological integration. *American Psychologist, 35:* 320–335.

———. (1986). Infant child care: A cause for concern? *ZERO TO THREE, 6*(5): 1–9.

Belsky, J. (2001). Developmental risks (still) associated with early child care. *Journal of Child Psychology and Psychiatry and Allied Disciplines, 42,* (7), 845–859.

———. (2003). Child care and its impact on young children (0–2). In: R. E. Tremblay, R. G. Barr, and R. DeV Peters (Eds.), *Encyclopedia on early childhood development* (pp. 1–6). Montreal, Quebec: Centre of Excellence for Early Childhood Development. Retrieved June 27, 2005 from http://www.excellence-earlychildhood.ca/documents/BelskyANGxp.pdf.

Belsky, J., & Kelly, J. (1994). *The transition to parenthood.* New York: Delacorte Press.

Belsky, J., & Most, R. (1981). From exploration to play: A cross-sectional study of infant free play behavior. *Developmental Psychology, 17:* 630–639.

Bennett-Armistead, V. S., Duke, N. K., & Moses, A. M. (2005). *Literacy and the youngest learner.* New York: Scholastic.

Bentzen, W. (2005). *Seeing young children: A guide to observing and recording behavior* (5th ed.). Clifton Park, NY: Thomson Delmar Learning.

Bergen, D. (2002). The role of pretend play in children's cognitive development. *Early Childhood Research and Practice, 4*(1),

Bergen, D., & Coscia, J. (2001). *Brain research and childhood education: Implications for educators.* Olney, MD: ACEI.

Bergen, D., Reid, R., & Torelli, L. (2000). *Educating and caring for very young children: The infant/toddler curriculum.* New York: Teachers College Press.

Berger, M. (1982). Personality development and temperament. In R. Porter & G. Collins (Eds.), *Temperamental differences in infants and young children.* Ciba Foundation Symposium 89. London: Pitman.

Berggren, S. (2004). Massage in schools reduces stress and anxiety. *Young Children, 59*(5), 67–68.

Berk, L. (1994). Vygotsky's theory: The importance of make-believe play. *Young Children, 50*(1): 30–39.

———. (2002). *Child development* (6th ed.). Boston: Allyn & Bacon.

———. (2004). *Infants, children and adolescents* (5th ed.). Needham Heights, MA: Allyn & Bacon.

Berk, L., & Winsler, A. (1995). *Scaffolding children's learning: Vygotsky and early childhood education.* Washington, DC: NAEYC.

Berke, J. E. (1996). The effect of prenatal and postnatal cigarette smoke exposure on the developmental readiness of preschool children. SUNY at Buffalo, Ph.D. Thesis.

Berman, P. (1980). Are women more responsive than men to the young? A review of developmental and situational variables. *Psychological Bulletin 88:* 668–695.

Bernhard, J. K., & Gonzalez-Mena, J. (2000). The cultural context of infant and toddler care. In D. Cryer & T. Helms (Eds.), *Infants and toddlers in out-of-home care* (pp. 237–267). Baltimore: Paul H. Brookes Publishing Co.

Bertrand, J., et al. (2001). *Nourish, nurture, neurodevelopment resource kit.* Ottawa, ON: Canadian Child Care Federation.

Bettleheim, B. (1989, Reissue). *The uses of enchantment: The meaning and importance of fairy tales.* New York: Vintage.

Biasella, S. (1996). The first year of life: A lot happens in the first 365 days. *Lamazebaby Magazine, 23:* 30–40.

Birckmayer, J., et al. (1990). *Teens as parents of babies and toddlers.* Ithaca, NY: Cornell University Press.

Blackwell, P. (2004). The idea of temperament: Does it help parents understand their babies? *ZERO TO THREE, 24* (4), 37–41.

Blau, D., & Currie, J. (2003). *Preschool, child care, and after school care: Who's minding the kids?* (NBIR Working Paper No. 10610) National Bureau of Economic Research. (RePEc.nbr.nberwo:10670). Retrieved May 11, 2005, from http://ideas.repec.org/p/nbr/nberwo/10670.html#provider. Specific file: http://www.econ.ucla.edu/people/papers/Currie/Currie291.pdf.

Blaxall, J., et al. (1996). *Children at the centre.* Toronto: Harcourt Brace.

Block, R. W., Krebs, N. F., & the Committee on Child Abuse and Neglect and the Committee on Nutrition. (2005) Failure to thrive as a manifestation of child neglect. *Pediatrics, 116*(5), 1234–1237.

Bloom, L., Rocissano, L., & Hood, L. (1976). Adult–child discourse: Developmental interaction between information processing and linguistic knowledge. *Cognitive Psychology, 8:* 521–552.

Bloom, L., Merkin, S., & Wootten, J. (1982). Wh-questions: Linguistic factors that contribute to the sequence of acquisition. *Child Development, 53:* 1084–1092.

Boothe, R., et al. (1985). Postnatal development of vision in human and nonhuman primates. *Annual Review of Neuroscience, 8:* 495–545.

Bos, B., & Chapman, J. (2005). *Tumbling over the edge: A rant for children's play.* Roseville, CA: Turn the Page Press, Inc.

Bouwstra, H., Boersma, E. R., Boehm, G., Dijck-Brouwer, D. A. J., Muskiet, F. A. J., & Hadders-Algra, M. (2003). Exclusive breast-feeding of healthy term infants for at least 6 weeks improves neurological condition. *Journal of Nutrition* (133), 4243–4245. Retrieved June 13, 2005 from http://www.nutrition.org/cgi/content/133/12/4343?maxtosh.

Bower, T. (1997). *The perceptual world of the child.* London: Fontana.

Bowlby, J. (1953). *Child care and the growth of love*. London: Penguin.

———. (1965). *Child care and the growth of love* (2nd ed.). Harmondsworth, England: Penguin.

———. (1969). *Attachment and loss* (Vol. 1: Attachment). New York: Basic Books.

———. (1973). *Separation: Anxiety and anger*. New York: Basic Books.

Branford, J.D., Brown, A.L., & Cocking, R.R. (Eds.). (2000). *How people learn: Brain, mind, experience, and school*. Washington, DC: National Academy Press.

Brazelton, T. (1992). *Touchpoints: Your child's emotional and behavioral development*. New York: Addison-Wesley.

———. (1995). *Neonatal Behavioral Assessment Scale No. 137*. Cambridge, England: Cambridge University Press.

Brazelton, T., & Cramer, B. (1990). *The earliest relationship: Parents, infants and the drama of early relationship*. New York: Addison-Wesley.

Brazelton, T., & Greenspan, S. (2000). *The irreducible needs of children: What every child must have to grow, learn, and flourish*. Cambridge, MA: Perseus Publishing.

Bredekamp, S. (Ed.). (1987). *Developmentally appropriate practice in early childhood programs serving children from birth through age 8: Expanded edition*. Washington, DC: NAEYC.

Bredekamp, S., & Copple, C. (Eds.). (1997). *Developmentally appropriate practice in early childhood programs* (Rev. ed.). Washington, DC: NAEYC.

Bretherton, I. (ed.). (1984). *Symbolic play: The development of social understanding*. Orlando, FL: Academic.

Briant, M. (2004). *Baby sign language basics: Early communication for hearing babies and toddlers*. Carlsbad, CA: Hay House.

Brigance, A., & Glascoe, F. (2002). *Brigance Infant & Toddler Screen*. North Billerica, MA: Curriculum Associates.

Briggs, D. (1975). *Your child's self esteem*. Garden City, NY: Dolphin Books/Doubleday & Co.

Bronfenbrenner, U. (1979). *The ecology of human development*. Cambridge, MA: Harvard University Press.

Bronson, M. (2000). Recognizing and supporting the development of self-regulation in young children. *Young Children, 55*(2): 32–37 (March).

Brookhart, J., & Hock, E. (1976). The effects of experimental context and experiential background on infants' behavior towards their mothers and a stranger. *Child Development, 47*: 333–340.

Brooks-Gunn, J., & Lewis, M. (1982). Affective exchanges between normal and handicapped infants and their mothers. In T. Field & A. Foel (Eds.), *Emotion and early interaction*. Hillsdale, NJ: Erlbaum.

Browne, J. V. (2003). New perspectives on premature infants and their parents. *ZERO TO THREE, 24*(2): 4–12.

Bruer, J. T. (1998). Brain science, brain fiction. *Educational Leadership, 56* (3).

———. (2001). A critical and sensitive period primer. In D. B. Bailey, J. T. Bruer, F. Symons, & J. W. Lichtman (Eds.), *Critical thinking about critical periods* (pp. 3–26). Baltimore: Paul H. Brookes.

———. (2004). The brain and child development: Time for some critical thinking. In E. Zeigler & S. J. Styfco (Eds.), *The Head Start debates* (pp. 423–434). Baltimore: Paul H. Brookes Publishing Co.

Bruner, J. (1978). *Learning the mother tongue*. Boston: Allyn & Bacon.

———. (1983). *Child's talk: Learning to use language*. New York: Norton.

Budden, S. (1996). *Intrauterine exposure to drugs and alcohol: How do children fare?* Retrieved June 19, 2005 from www.medscape.com/viewarticle/409922?src=search.

Buss, A., & Plomin, R. (1984). *Temperament: Early developing personality traits*. Hillsdale, NJ: Erlbaum.

Buytendijk, F. (1947). The first smile of the child (Trans. M. van Manen, 2000). *Phenomenology & Pedagogy 6* (1): 15–24.

Campbell, J. B., & Hawley, C. W. (1982). Study habits and Eysenck's theory of extroversion–introversion. *Journal of Research in Personality, 16*: 139–146.

Campbell, L., Campbell, B., & Dickinson, D. (1996). *Teaching & learning through multiple intelligences*. Needham Heights, MA: Allyn & Bacon.

Campbell, N. D., Appelbaum, J. C., Martinson, K., & Martin, E. (2000) *Be all that we can be: Lessons from the military for improving our nation's child care system*. Washington DC: National Women's Law Center.

Campos, J., et al. (1970). Cardiac response on the visual cliff in prelocomotor human infants. *Science, 170*: 196–197.

———, et al. (1983). Socioemotional development. In P. Mussen (Ed.), *Handbook of child psychology* (Vol. 2: Infancy and Developmental Psychology, 4th ed.). New York: Wiley.

Canadian Child Care Federation. (2001). *Supporting breast feeding in child care*. Resource Sheet #57. At www.cfc-efc.ca/docs/cccf/rs057_en.htm

———. (25 March 2002). Draft Child Care Practitioner Occupational Standards. 4 March 2003. At www.cccf-fcsge.ca/subsites/training/pdf/draftoccs_en.pdf

Canadian Child Care Federation and the Canadian Child Care Advocacy Association. (1993). *Caring for a living: Final report*. Ottawa, ON: Canadian Child Care Federation/Canadian Child Care Advocacy Association.

Canadian Child Care Federation and the Canadian Institute for Child Health. (2001). *Nourish, nurture, neurodevelopment: Neurodevelopmental research—Implications for caregiver practice*. Ottawa, ON: Canadian Child Care Federation/Canadian Institute for Child Health.

Canadian Council on Social Development. (1996). *The progress of Canada's children, 1996*. Ottawa, ON: Canadian Council on Social Development.

Canadian Paediatric Society. (1991). Meeting the Iron Needs of Infants and Young Children: An Update. CPS Statement N91-01. *Canadian Medical Association Journal, 144*(11): 1451–1454.

———. (1992). *Well beings: A guide to promote the physical health, safety and emotional well-being of children in child care centres and family child care homes* (Vols. 1 and 2). Toronto: Creative Premises.

———. (1999). *A guide to promote the physical health, safety and emotional well being of children in child care centres and family child care homes* (2nd ed.). Ottawa, ON: Canadian Paediatric Society.

Canahuati, J., & de Suarez, M. J. J. (2001). Supporting breastfeeding: Current status and future challenges. *Child Welfare, 80*(5), 551–563.

Canfield, J., et al. (1997). *A 4th course of chicken soup for the soul*. Deerfield Beach, FL: Health Communications.

Cannella, G. (1997/2002). *Deconstructing early childhood education: Social justice & revolution*. New York: Peter Lang.

Caplan, F. (1973). *The first twelve months of life.* New York: Bantam.

Cappe, M., & Felligi, I. (1996). *Growing up in Canada—NLSCY study.* Ottawa, ON: HRDC/Statistics Canada.

Carey, W. B. (1998). Teaching parents about infant temperament. In J. G. Warhol (Ed.), *New perspectives in early emotional development* (pp. 225–238). United States of America: Johnson & Johnson Pediatric Institute, Ltd.

Carey, W. B., & McDevitt, S. C. (1995) *Coping with children's temperament: A guide for professionals.* New York: Basic Books.

Carnegie Task Force. (1994) *Starting points: Meeting the needs of our youngest children.* New York: Carnegie Corporation of New York.

Caron, R., et al. (1982). Abstraction of invariant face expressions in infancy. *Child Development, 53:* 1008–1015.

Carter, A. (1975). The transformation of sensorimotor morphemes into words: A case study of the development of "here" and "there." *Papers and Reports on Child Language Development 10:* 31–48.

Cassidy, J., & Shaver, P. R. (Eds.). (1999). *Handbook of attachment: Theory, research, and clinical applications.* New York: The Guilford Press.

Catlin, C. (1994). *Toddlers together.* Beltsville, MD: Gryphon House.

Cattell, P. (1940). *The measurement of intelligence of infants and young children.* New York: Psychological Corp.

Cattell, R. B. (1951). A factorization of tests of personality source traits. *British Journal of Psychology* (Stats. Sect.) 4: 165–178.

———. (1980). *Handbook for the sixteen personality factor questionnaire.* Champaign, IL: Institute for Personality and Ability Testing.

Chalmers, D. (2002). The puzzle of conscious experience. *Scientific American Special, 12* (1): 90–100.

Charlesworth, R. (2004). *Understanding child development* (6th ed.). Clifton Park, NY: Thomson Delmar Learning.

Chasnoff, I. J., Lewis, D. E., Griffith, D. R., & Wiley, S. (1989). Cocaine and pregnancy: Clinical and toxicological implications for the neonate. *Clinical Chemistry, 35* (7), 1276–1278.

Chattin-McNichols, J. (1992). *The Montessori controversy.* Clifton Park, NY: Thomson Delmar Learning.

Chess, S., & Thomas, A. (1977). Temperamental individuality from childhood to adolescence. *Journal of Child Psychiatry, 16:* 218–226.

———. (1990). The New York Longitudinal Study (NYLS): The young adult periods. *Canadian Journal of Psychiatry, 35:* 557–561.

———. (1996). *Temperament: Theory and practice.* New York: Brunner/Mazel.

Childcare Resource and Research Unit. (1995). *Child care in Canada: Provinces and territories 1995.* Toronto: University of Toronto. At www.childcarecanada.org/resources/prov_terr/prvtrrtoc.html

———. (2000). *You bet I care! Reports 1, 2, 3, and 4: A Canada-wide study on wages, working conditions, and practices in child-care centres.* Guelph, ON: University of Guelph.

Chisholm, K. (1998). A three-year follow-up of attachment and indiscriminate friendliness in children adopted from Romanian orphanages. *Child Development,* 69 (4), 1092–1106.

Chomsky, N. (1957). *Syntactic structures.* The Hague: Mouton.

———. (1968). *Language and mind.* New York: Harcourt Brace and World.

Chud, G., et al. (1985). *Early childhood education for a multi-cultural society.* Vancouver: Pacific Educational Press.

Chugani, H. T. (1998). Biological basis of emotions: Brain systems and brain development In J. G. Warhol (Ed.), *New perspectives in early emotional development* (pp. 5–16). United States of America: Johnson & Johnson Pediatric Institute, Ltd.

Clarke-Stewart, A. (1982). *Child care.* New York: Fontana Paperbacks.

———. (1989). Infant day-care: Maligned or malignant? *American Psychologist, 44:* 266–273.

Click, P. (2004). *Administration of programs for young children* (6th ed.). Clifton Park, NY: Thomson Delmar Learning.

Cohen, L., & Strauss, M. (1979). Concept acquisition in the human infant. *Child Development, 50:* 419–424.

Coll, C. M., & Magnuson, K. (2000). Cultural differences as sources of developmental vulnerabilities and resources. In J. P. Skonkoff & S. J. Meisels (Eds.), *Handbook of early childhood intervention* (7th ed., pp. 94–114). New York: Cambridge University Press.

Cook, R. E., Klein, M. D., & Tessler, A. (2004). *Adapting early childhood curricula for children in inclusive settings* (6th ed.). Upper Saddle River, NJ: Pearson/Merrill Prentice Hall.

Coon, D. (1992). *Introduction of psychology: Exploration and application* (6th ed.). St. Paul, MN: West.

Corbetta, D., & Mounoud, P. (1990). Early development of grasping and manipulation.

Bard, M. Fleury, & L. Hay (Eds.), *Development of eye-hand coordination across the life span* (pp. 188–213). Columbia, SC: University of South Carolina Press.

Coll, C. M. & Magnuson, K. (2000). Cultural differences as sources of developmental vulnerabilities and resources. In Skonkoff, J.P. and Meisels, S.J. (Eds.), *Handbook of Early childhood intervention, seventh edition* (pp. 94–114). New York: Cambridge University Press.

Cook, R.E., Klein, M.D., & Tessler, A. (2004). *Adapting early childhood curricula for children in inclusive settings, 6th edition.* Upper Saddle River, NJ: Pearson/Merill Prentice Hall.

Corbetta, D. & Mounoud, P. (1990). Early development of grasping and manipulation. *In:* C. Bard, M, Fleury, & L. Hay (Eds.) *Development of eye-hand coordination across the life Span* (pp. 188–213). Columbia, SC: University of South Carolina Press.

Craft, M., & Denehy, J. (1990). *Nursing interventions for infants and children.* Philadelphia: W.B. Saunders.

Crick, F. (1994). *The astonishing hypothesis: The scientific search for the soul.* New York: Simon & Schuster.

Cryer, D., Harms, T., & Bourland, B. (1987). *Active learning for infants.* Menlo Park, CA: Addison-Wesley.

———. (1987). *Active learning for ones.* Menlo Park, CA: Addison-Wesley.

———. (1988). *Active learning for twos.* Menlo Park, CA: Addison-Wesley.

Curtis, D., & Carter, M. (2000). *The art of awareness: How observation can transform your teaching.* St. Paul, MN: Redleaf Press.

Custodero, L. A. (2002). The musical lives of young children: Inviting, seeking, and initiating. *ZERO TO THREE, 23*(1), 4–9.

Daly, T. C. (2005). Reading enrichment: Creating a love of books that lasts a lifetime. *ZERO TO THREE, 26*(1), 19–25.

Davis, K. (1996). Learning to move, moving to learn. *ACEI Focus on Infancy, 9* (2).

Davis, K. F., Parker, K., & Montgomery, G. L. (2004.) Sleep in infants and young children: Part I, normal sleep. *Journal of Pediatric Health Care, 18* (2), 65–71. Retrieved June 26, 2005 from http://www.medscape.com/viewarticle/471909_1

Day, M., & Parlakian, R. (2003). *How culture shapes social-emotional development: Implications for practice in infant-family programs.* Washington, DC: ZERO TO THREE.

DeBoysson-Bardies, B., et al. (1984). Discernible differences in the babbling of infants according to target language. *Journal of Child Language, 11*, 1–15.

Deiner, P. (1997). *Infants and toddlers: Development and program planning.* Fort Worth: Harcourt Brace.

DeLoache, J. S. (2000). Cognitive development in infants: Looking, listening, and learning. In D. Cryer & T. Harms (Eds.), *Infants and toddlers in out-of-home car* (pp. 7–47). Baltimore: Paul H. Brookes Publishing Co.

Dennett, D. (1991). *Consciousness explained.* New York: Little, Brown.

Derman-Sparks, L., et al. (1989). *Anti-bias curriculum.* Washington, DC: NAEYC.

Derman-Sparks, L., & Phillips C. B. (1997). *Teaching/learning anti-racism.* New York: Teachers College Press.

Derman-Sparks, L., & Ramsey, P. G. (2006). *What if all the kids are white? Anti-bias multicultural education with young children and families.* New York: Teachers College Press.

Dewey, J. (1963). *Experience and education.* New York: Collier Books.

Dias, M., & Harris, P. (1990). The influence of imagination on reasoning by young children. *British Journal of Developmental Psychology, 8*, 305–318.

Dichtelmiller, M. L., & Ensier, L. (2004). Infant/toddler assessment: One program's experience. *Young Children, 59* (1), 30–33.

Digman, J. (1990). Personality structure: An emergence of the five-factor model. *The Annual Review of Psychology, 41*, 417–440.

Dissanayake, E. (2000). Antecedents of the temporal arts in early mother-infant interaction. In N. Wallin, B. Merker, & S. Brown (Eds.), *The origins of music* (pp. 389–410). Cambridge, MA: The MIT Press.

Dittmann, L. (Ed.). (1984). *The infants we care for.* Washington, DC: NAEYC.

Doering, P. L., Davidson, C. L., LaFauce, L., & Williams, C. A. (1989). Effects of cocaine on the human fetus: A review of clinical studies. *DICP, The Annals of Pharmcotherapy, 23*, 639–645.

Doherty, G., & Stuart, B. (1996). *A profile of quality in Canadian child care centres.* Ottawa, ON: Human Resources Development Canada.

Doherty-Derkowski, G. (1995). *Quality matters: Excellence in early childhood programs.* Don Mills, ON: Addison-Wesley.

Dombro, A. L., Colker, L. J., & Dodge, D. T. (1997). *The creative curriculum for infants and toddlers.* Washington, DC: Teaching Strategies.

Donatelle, R., & Davis, L. (1997). *Health: The basics* (2nd ed.). Needham Heights, MA: Allyn & Bacon.

Donatelle, R. (2004). *Health: The basics* (6th ed.). San Francisco: Pearson/Benjamin Cummings.

Douville-Watson, L., Watson, M. A., & Wilson, L. C. (2003). *Infants & toddlers: Curriculum and teaching* (5th ed.). Clifton Park, NY: Thomson Delmar Learning.

Doxey, I. (Ed.). (1990). *Child care and education: Canadian dimensions.* Scarborough, ON: Nelson.

Dwyer, J. T., Suitor, C. W., & Hendricks, K. (2004). FITS: new insights and lessons learned. *Journal of the American Dietetic Association, 104* (Supplement 1), 5–7.

DYG, Inc. (2000). *What grown-ups understand about child development: A benchmark survey.* Washington, DC: ZERO TO THREE.

Edelstein, S. (1995). *The healthy young child.* St. Paul, MN: West.

Edwards, C, Gandini, L, & Forman, G. (1998). *The hundred languages of children: The Reggio Emilia approach to early childhood education.* Norwood, N J: Ablex Publishing Corporation.

Edwards, C. P., & Raikes, H. (2002). Extending the dance: Relationship-based approaches to infant/toddler care and education. *Young Children, 57*(4), 10–17.

Edwards, S. J., Buckland, D., & McCoy-Powlen, J. (2002). *Developmental and functional hand grasps.* Thorofare, NJ: C. B. Slack, Inc.

Eheart, B. K., & Leavitt, R. L. (1985). Supporting toddler play. *Young Children, 40* (3), 18–22.

Ehrensaft, D. (1997). *Spoiling childhood: How well-meaning parents are giving children too much—But not what they need.* New York: Guildford. (ERIC Document No. ED413111)

Ehrle, J., Adams, G., & Tout, T. (2001). *Who's caring for our youngest children: Child care patterns of infants and toddlers.* Washington, DC: The Urban League.

Ehrlich, E. *Child care: Quality is the issue.* Washington, DC: NAEYC.

Eisenberg, A., Murkoff, H. E., & Hathaway, S. E. (1996). *What to expect: The toddler years.* New York: Workman Publishing.

Eisenberg, N. (2003). Prosocial behavior, empathy, and sympathy. In M. H. Bornstein, L. Davidson, C. L. M. Keyes, & K. A. Moore (Eds.) *Well-being: Positive development across the life course* (pp. 253–267). Mahwah, NJ: Lawrence Erlbaum Associates.

Ekman, P. (2004). *Emotions revealed: Recognizing faces and feelings to improve communication and emotional life.* New York: Owl Books/ Henry Holt Publishing.

Eliason, C., & Jenkins, L. (2002) *A practical guide to early childhood curriculum* (7th ed.). Upper Saddle River, NJ: Prentice Hall.

Eliot, L. (1999). *What's going on in there? How the brain and mind develop in the first five years of life.* New York: Bantam Books.

Elkind, D. (1994). *A sympathetic understanding of the child: Birth to sixteen* (3rd ed.). Needham Heights, MA: Allyn & Bacon.

———. (2001a). *The hurried child: Growing up too fast, too soon* (3rd ed.). Cambridge, MA: Perseus Publishing.

———. (2001b). Much too early. *Education Next* (Summer).

———. (2005). Reaffirming children's needs for developmentally appropriate programs. *Young Children 60* (4), 38–40.

Emde, R. N. (1998). Early emotional development: New modes of thinking for research and intervention. In J. G. Warhol (Ed.), *New perspectives in early emotional development* (pp. 29–46). United States of America: Johnson & Johnson Pediatric Institute, Ltd.

Emmet. E. (1968). *Learning to philosophize.* Harmondsworth, UK: Pelican.

Erikson, E. (1950). *Childhood and society.* New York: Norton.

———. (1963). *Childhood and society* (2nd ed.). New York: Wiley.

———. (1959). *Identity and the life cycle: Selected papers.* New York: International University Press.

———. (1987). The human life cycle. In S. P. Schlein (ed.), *A way of looking at things: Selected papers from 1930–1985* (pp. 595–610). New York: Norton.

Erickson, M. F., & Kurz-Riemer, K. (1999). *Infants, toddlers, and families: A framework for support and intervention.* New York: The Guilford Press.

Eysenck, H., & Eysenck, M. (1989). *Mind watching.* Scarborough, ON: McGraw-Hill Ryerson.

Fantz, R. (1963). Pattern vision in newborn infants. *Science, 140*, 296–297.

———. (1965). Visual perception from birth as shown by pattern selectivity. In H. W. Whipple (Ed.), New issues in infant development. *Annals of the New York Academy of Science, 118*, 793–814.

Farrell Erikson, M., & Kurz-Riemer, K. (1999). *Infants, toddlers and families: A framework for support and intervention.* New York: Guilford.

Feldman, R. (1997). *Development across the life span.* Upper Saddle River, NJ: Prentice Hall.

Fenson, C., et al. (1976). The developmental progression of manipulative play in the first two years. *Child Development, 47*, 232–236.

Fernald, A. (1989). Intonation and communicative intent in mothers' speech to infants: Is melody the message? *Child Development, 60*, 1497–1510.

Filipek, P. A., Accardo, P. J., Baranek, G. T., Cook, E. H. Jr., Dawson, G., Gordon, B., et al. (1999). The screening and diagnosis of autistic spectrum disorders. *Journal of Autism Developmental Disorders, 29*, 439–484.

Flavell, J. H. (2000). *Cognitive development* (4th ed.). Englewood Cliffs, NJ: Prentice-Hall.

Fogel, A. (2000) *Infancy: Infant, family, and society* (4th ed.). Belmont, CA: Wadsworth Publishing.

Fowler, W. (1990). *Talking from infancy.* Cambridge, MA: Brookline.

Fox, M. K., Pac, S., Devaney, B., & Jankowski, L. (2004). Feeding infants and toddlers study: What foods are infants and toddlers eating? *Journal of the American Dietetic Association, 104* (Supplement 1), 22–30.

Fraiberg, S. (1959/1996). *The magic years.* New York: Fireside/Simon & Schuster.

Fraser, S., & Gestwicki, C. (2002). *Authentic childhood: Exploring Reggio Emilia in the classroom.* Clifton Park, NY: Thomson Delmar Learning.

Frattaroli, E. (2001). *Healing the soul in the age of the brain: Becoming conscious in an unconscious world.* New York: Viking.

Freeman, N. (1980). *Strategies of representation in young children: Analysis of spatialskill and drawing processes.* London: Academic.

Freeman, R. & Swim, T. J. (2003) A critical reflection on using food as learning materials. *Journal of Early Childhood Teacher Education. 24* (1), 83–88.

Freire, M., & Bernhard, J. (1997). Caring for and teaching children who speak other languages. In K. M. Kilbride (Ed.), *Include me too! Human diversity in early childhood.* Toronto: Harcourt Brace.

Freud, S. (1940). *An outline of psychoanalysis.* New York: Norton.

Friendly, M., et al. (1998). Early *Childhood care and education in Canada: Provinces and territories: 1998.* Toronto: Childcare Resource & Research Unit.

Froebel, F. (1967). *Friedrich Froebel: A selection from his writings.* Cambridge, England: Cambridge University Press.

Frost, J. (1992). *Play and playscapes.* Clifton Park, NY: Thomson Delmar Learning.

Frost, J. L., Wortham, S. C., & Reifel, S. (2005). *Play and child development* (2nd ed.). Upper Saddle River, NJ: Pearson Merrill Prentice Hall.

Fu, V. R., Stremmel, A. J., & Hill, L. T. (2002). *Teaching and learning: Collaborative exploration of the Reggio Emilia approach.* Upper Saddle River, NJ: Merrill/Prentice Hall.

Furuno, S., et al. (1987). *The Hawaii early learning profile.* Palo Alto, CA: VORT.

———, et al. (1993a). *The Hawaii developmental charts.* Tucson: Communications Skill Builders, the Psychological Corporation.

———, et al. (1993b). *Helping babies learn: Developmental profiles and activities for infants and toddlers.* San Antonio: Communication Skill Builders.

Gable, S. (2000). Nature, nurture and early brain development. University Extension, University of Missouri-Columbia, pub. GH6115.

Gable, S., & Hunting, M. (2001). *Nature, nurture and early brain development.* At muextension.Missouri.edu/ xplor/hesguide/ humanrel/gh6115.htm.

Gabriel, H. P., & Wool, R. (1990). *The inner child.* New York: Ballantine Books.

Galinsky, E. (1987). *Six stages of parenthood.* New York: Addison Wesley Publishing Company.

Gallagher, K. C. (2005). Brain research and early childhood development: A primer for developmentally appropriate practice. *Young Children, 60* (4), 12–20.

Gallahue, D. L. (1995). Transforming physical education curriculum. In S. Bredkamp & T. Rosegrant (Eds.), *Reaching potentials: Transforming early childhood curriculum and assessment* (2nd ed., pp. 124–144). Washington, DC: NAEYC.

Galton, F. (1875). History of twins. In *Inquiries into human faculty and its development, 155–173.*

Gandini, L., & Edwards, C. P. (2001). *Bambini: The Italian approach to infant/toddler care.* New York: Teachers College Press.

Gandini, L., Hill, L., Cadwell, L., & Schwall (Eds.). (2005). *In the spirit of the studio: Learning from the Atelier of Reggio Emilia.* New York: Teachers College Press.

Garbarino, J. (1995). *Raising children in a socially toxic environment.* San Francisco: Jossey- Bass, Inc. Publishers.

Garber, S., Garber, M., & Spizman, R. (1987). *Good behavior.* New York: St. Martin's Press.

———. (1993). *Monsters under the bed and other childhood fears: Helping your child overcome anxieties, fears, and phobias.* New York: Villard Books.

Garcia, J. (1994). *Toddler talk.* Port Angeles, WA: Stratton-Kehl Publications.

———. (1999). *Sign with baby: How to communicate with infants before they can speak.* Seattle: Northlight Communications and Stratton-Kehl Publications.

———. (2002). *Sign with baby: How to communicate with infants before they can speak* (Rev. ed.). Seattle: Northlight Communications.

Gardner, H. (1993). *Multiple intelligences: The theory in practice.* New York: Basic Books/HarperCollins.

Garrett M., McElroy, A. M., & Staines, A. (2002). Locomotor milestones and babywalkers: cross sectional study. *British Medical Journal, 324*, 1494.

Gartrell, D. (2004). *The power of guidance: Teaching social-emotional skills in early childhood classrooms.* Clifton Park, NY: Thomson Delmar Learning. (Also available from NAEYC.)

Gee, R. (1985). *Babies: Understanding conception, birth and the first years.* London: Usborne.

Gembris, H., & Davidson, J. (2002). Environmental influences. In R. Parncutt & G. McPherson (Eds.), *The science and psychology of music performance* (pp. 17–30). New York: Oxford.

Gerber, M. (1998a). *Dear parent: Caring for infants with respect.* Los Angeles: Resources for Infant Educarers.

———. (1998b). *Your self-confident baby: Raising your child the right way*. Toronto: John Wiley & Sons.

Gesell, A. (1928). *Infancy and human growth*. New York: Macmillan.

Gestwicki, C. (2007). *Developmentally appropriate practice: Curriculum and development in early education* (3rd ed.). Clifton Park, NY: Thomson Delmar Learning.

Gilfoyle, E. (1980). Caring: A philosophy for practice. *American Journal of Occupational Therapy, 34* (8), 517–521.

Gilligan, C. (1982). *In a different voice: Psychological theory and women's development*. Cambridge, MA: Harvard University Press.

Giudici, C., Rinaldi, C., & Krechevsky, M. (2001). *Making learning visible: Children as individual and group learners*. Reggio Emilia, Italy: Reggio Children srl.

Glascoe, F. P. (1997). Parents' concerns about children's development: prescreening technique or screening test? *Pediatrics, 99* (4), 522–528.

Godwin, A., & Schrag, L. (1988). *Setting up for infant care: Guidelines for centers and family child care homes*. Washington, DC: NAEYC.

Goldberg, S. (2000). *Attachment and development. Texts in developmental psychology series*. London: Arnold.

Goldsmith, H. H., Lemery, K. S., Aksan, N., & Buss, K. A. (2000). Temperamental substrates of personality development. In V. J. Molfese & D. L. Molfese (Eds.), *Temperament and personality development across the life span* (pp. 1–32). Mahwah, NJ: Lawrence Erlbaum Associates.

Goldstein, S. (1992). Young children at risk: The early signs of attention-deficit hyperactivity disorder. *CH.A.D.D.er Box 5* (January), 7.

Goleman, D. (1997). *Emotional intelligence*. New York: Bantam.

Gonzalez-Mena, J., & Widmeyer Eyer, D. (1989). *Infants, toddlers, and caregivers*. Mountain View, CA: Mayfield.

Gonzalez-Mena, J., & Eyer, D. E. (2004). *Infants, toddlers and caregivers: A curriculum of respectful, responsive care and education*. New York: McGraw Hill.

Gopnik, A., Meltzoff, A. N., & Kuhl, P. K. (1999). *The scientist in the crib: What early learning tells us about the mind*. New York: Perennial.

Gordon, A., & Browne, K. W. (1995) *Guiding young children in a diverse society*. Boston: Allyn & Bacon.

Gottman, J., Declaire, J., & Goleman, D. (1998). *Raising an emotionally intelligent child*. New York: Fireside/Simon and Schuster.

Goulet, M. (2000). *How caring relationships support self-regulation. Video and video guide*. Spring 2000. Washington, DC: NAEYC.

Government of British Columbia. (2002). *Toddler's first steps: A best chance guide to parenting your six-month to three-year-old. Best chance series*. Toronto: Macmillan Canada.

Gowan, J. W. (1995). The early development of symbolic play. *Young Children, 50* (3), 75–84.

Gray, H. (2001). Initiation into documentation: A fishing trip with toddlers. *Young Children, 56* (6), 84–91.

———. (2004). "You go away and you come back": Supporting separations and reunions in an infant/toddler classroom. *Young Children, 59* (5), 100–107.

Greata, J. (2006). *An introduction to music in early childhood education*. Clifton Park, NY: Thomson Delmar Learning.

Green, M. (1994). *Bright futures: Guidelines for health supervision of infants, children, and adolescents*. Arlington, VA: National Center for Education in Maternal and Child Health.

Green, M., & Palfrey, J. S. (Eds.). (2002). *Bright futures: Guidelines for health supervision of infants, children, and adolescents* (2nd ed., rev.). Arlington, VA: National Center for Education in Maternal and Child Health.

Greenberg, P. (1991). *Character development: Encouraging self-esteem and self-discipline in infants, toddlers, and two-year-olds*. Washington, DC: NAEYC.

———. (2001). The irreducible needs of children: An interview with T. Berry Brazelton, M.D. and Stanley I. Greenspan, M.D. *Young Children, 56* (2): 6–14.

Greenspan, S. (1997). *The growth of the mind and the endangered origins of intelligence*. Reading, MA: Addison-Wesley.

Greenspan, S., & Greenspan, N. T. (1989). *The essential partnership: How parents and children can meet the emotional challenges of infancy and childhood*. New York: Penguin.

Greenspan, S., & Greenspan, N. T. (1994). *First feelings: Milestones in the emotional development of your baby and child*. New York: Penguin Books.

Grisham-Brown, J., Hemmeter, M. L., & Pretti-Frontczak, K. (2005). *Blended practices for teaching young children in inclusive settings*. Baltimore: Paul H. Brookes Publishing Co.

Gunnar, M. R., & Donzella, B. (2002). Social regulation of the cortisol levels in early human development. *Psychoneuroendocrinology, 27*(1–2), 199–220.

Guralnik, M. J., & Hammond, M. A. (1999). Sequential analysis of the social play of young children with mild developmental delays. *Journal of Early Intervention, 22* (3), 243–256.

Guy, K. A. (1997). *Our promise to children*. Ottawa: Canadian Institute of Child Health.

Hall, N., Saderman, & Rhomberg, V. (1995). *The affective curriculum*. Scarborough, ON: Nelson.

Hamner, T., & Turner, P. (1996). *Parenting in contemporary society* (3rd ed.). Boston: Allyn & Bacon.

Hancox, R. J., Milne, B. J., & Poulton, R. (2005). Association of television viewing during childhood with poor educational achievement. *Archives of Pediatric and Adolescent Medicine. 159*, 614–618.

Harden, B., & Harden, C. (1997). *Alternative health care: The Canadian directory*. Toronto: Noble Ages.

Harding, J., & Meldon-Smith, L. (1996). *How to make observations and assessments*. London: Hodder and Stoughton.

Harms, T., & Clifford, R. (1980). *Early childhood environmental rating scale*. New York: Teachers College Press.

Harms, T., Cryer, D., & Clifford, R. (1990). *Infant/toddler environment rating scale*. New York: Teachers College Press.

Harrist, A. W., & Waugh, R. M. (2002). Dyadic synchrony: its structure and function in children's development. *Development, 61*, 347–362.

Hart, B., & Risley, T. (1995). *Meaningful differences in everyday experience of young American children*. Baltimore: Paul H. Brookes Publishing Company.

———. (1999). *The social world of children learning to talk*. Baltimore: Paul H. Brookes Publishing Company.

Harter, S. (1983). Developmental perspectives on the self-esteem. In E. M. Hetherington (Ed.), *Handbook of child psychology: Socialization, personality, and social development* (Vol. 4.). New York: Wiley.

Harvey, J. M., O'Callaghan, M. J., & Mohay, H. (1999). Executive functioning of children with extremely low birthweight: A case control study. *Developmental Medicine and Child Neurology, 41*(5), 292–297.

Hawaii Early Learning Profile. (1994). *Revised HELP checklist*. Palo Alto, CA: VORT.

———. (1997). *HELP activity guide*. Palo Alto, CA: VORT.

Hawley, T. (2000). *Starting smart: How early experiences affect brain development* (2nd ed.). Washington, DC: ZERO TO THREE.

Health Canada. (1998). Infection Control Guidelines: Hand Washing, Cleaning, Disinfection and Sterilization in Health Care. *Canada Communicable Disease Report* (Vol. 24S8).

Healy, J. M. (1998). *Failure to connect: How computers affect our children's minds-for better and worse.* New York: Simon and Schuster.

Heidemann, S., & Hewitt, D. (1992). *Pathways to play: Developing play skills in young children.* St. Paul, MN: Redleaf Press.

Helm, J., Beneke, S., & Steinheimer, K. (1997). Documenting children's learning. *Childhood Education, 73*(4) (Summer), 200–205.

Hendrick, J. (Ed.). (2004). *Next steps toward teaching the Reggio way: Accepting the challenge to change.* Upper Saddle River, NJ: Pearson Merrill Prentice Hall.

Heroman, C., & Jones, C. (2004). *Literacy: The creative curriculum approach.* Washington, DC: Teaching Strategies.

Hewat, R. (2000). Living with an Incessantly Crying Infant. *Phenomenology Online*, at phenomenologyonline.com/articles/template.cfm?ID=286.

Hickok, G., Bellugi, U., & Klima, E. S. (1998). What's right about the neural organization of sign language? A perspective on recent neuroimaging results. *Trends in Cognitive Sciences, 2*: 465–468.

Hill, J. B., & Haffner, H. J. (2002). Growth before birth. In M. L. Batshaw (Ed.), *Children with disabilities* (5th ed., pp. 43–53). Baltimore: Paul H. Brookes Publishing Co., Inc.

Hirsh-Pasek, K., & Golinkoff, R. M. (2003). *Einstein never used flashcards: How our children really learn-and why they need to play more and memorize less.* New York: Rodale, Inc.

Hodges, D. A. (2002) Musicality from birth to five. *International Foundation for Music Research (IMFR) News, 1* (1). http://www.music-research.org/Publications/V01N1_musicality.html

Holt, B. (1985). Ideas that work with young children: Food as art. *Young Children, 40* (4), 18–19.

Holzmann, C. A., Perez, C. A., Held, C. M., San Martin, M., Pizarro, F., Perez, J. P., Garrido, M., & Peirano, P. (1999). Expert-system classification of sleep/waking states in infants. *Medical Biological Engineering & Computing, 37* (4), 466–476.

Honig, A. (1983). Meeting the needs of infants. *Dimensions* (January), 81–84.

———. (1995). Singing with infants and toddlers. *Young Children* (July), 72–78.

Honig, A., & Brophy, H. (1996). *Talking with your baby.* Syracuse, NY: Syracuse University Press.

Honig, A., & Lally, J. (1981). *Infant caregiving: A design for training.* Syracuse, NY: Syracuse University Press.

Honig, A. S. (2002). *Secure relationships: Nurturing infant/toddler attachment in early care settings.* Washington, DC: NAEYC.

Hooper, S. R., & Umansky, W. (2004). *Young children with special needs.* Upper Saddle River, NJ: Pearson/Merrill/Prentice Hall.

Horst, J. S., Oakes, L. M., & Madole, K. L. (2005). What does it look like and what can it do? Category structure influences how infants categorize. *Child Development, 76* (3), 614–617.

Horton, J. C. (2001). Critical periods in the development of the visual system. In D. B. Bailey, J. T. Bruer, F. Symons, and J. W. Lichtman (Eds.), *Critical thinking about critical periods* (pp. 45–65). Baltimore: Paul H. Brookes.

Howard, V. F., Williams, B. F., & Lepper, C. (2005). *Very young children with special needs: A formative approach for today's children* (3rd ed.). Upper Saddle River, N.J.: Pearson/Merrill/Prentice Hall.

Howes, C. (1999). Attachment relationships in the context of multiple caregivers. In J. Cassidy and P.R. Phillips (Eds.), *Handbook of attachment: Theory, research, and clinical applications* (pp. 671–687). New York: Guilford Press.

Howes, C. (2003). The impact of care on young children (0–2). In R. E. Tremblay, R. G. Barr, & R. DeV Peters (Eds.). *Encyclopedia on early childhood development* [online]. Montreal, Quebec: Centre of Excellence for Early Childhood Development, pp. 1–4. Retrieved June 15, 2005 from http://www.excellence-earlychildhood.ca/documents/HowesANGxp.pdf.

Howes, C., et al. (1988). Attachment and child care: Relationships with mother and caregiver. *Early Childhood Research Quarterly, 3,* 403–416.

Howes, C., & Wishard, A. G. (2004). Linking shared meaning to emergent literacy: Looking through the lens of culture. *ZERO TO THREE, 25* (1), 10–14.

Howes, P., & Markman, H. (1989). Marital quality and child functioning: A longitudinal investigation. *Child Development, 60,* 1044–1051.

Hudelson, S., & Serna, I. A. (2002a). Optimizing oral-language learning experiences for bilingual and second language learners. In C. Vukelich, J. Christie, & B. Enz, *Helping young children learn language and literacy* (pp. 57–60). Boston: Allyn & Bacon.

Hudelson, S., & Serna, I. A. (2002b).Young children's second language development. In C. Vukelich, J. Christie, & B. Enz, *Helping young children learn language and literacy* (pp. 35–37). Boston: Allyn & Bacon.

Hughes, F. (1999). *Children, play, and development* (3rd ed.). Boston: Allyn & Bacon.

Hughes, F., Elicker, J., & Veen, L. (1995). A program of play for infants and their caregivers. *Young Children* (January), 52–58.

Hujala, E. (Ed.). (1996). *Childhood education: International perspectives.* Oulu, Finland: University of Oulu Early Education Center.

Hulit, L., & Howard, M. (1997). *Born to talk: An introduction to speech and language development.* Needham Heights, MA: Allyn & Bacon.

Hunt, C. H., Burts, D. C., & Charlesworth, R. (Eds.). (1997). *Integrated curriculum and developmentally appropriate practice.* Albany, NY: State University of New York Press.

Hunter, T. (2000). Knowing things before we know them. *Young Children, 55* (4), 85.

Huttenlocher, J. (1999). Language input and language growth. In N. A. Fox, L. A. Leavitt, & J. G. Warhol (Eds.), *The role of early experience in infant development* (pp. 69–82). United States of America: Johnson & Johnson Consumer Companies, Inc.

Hyde, A. (1977). The phenomenon of caring: Part VI. *American Nurses' Foundation, 12* (1), 2.

Hyson, M. (2004). *The emotional development of young children: Building an emotion-centered curriculum* (2nd ed.). New York: Teachers College Press.

Illingworth, R. (1990). *Basic developmental screening: 0–5 years* (5th ed.). Oxford, England: Blackwell Scientific Publications.

———. (1992). *The development of the infant and young child.* London: Churchill Livingstone.

Imberty, M. (2000). The question of innate competencies in musical communication. In N. Wallin, B. Merker, & S. Brown (Eds.), *The origins of music* (pp. 449–462). Cambridge, MA: The MIT Press.

International Loving Touch Foundation (1992–2005). www.lovingtouch.com/

Intersex Society of North America. (2005). Retrieved June 22, 2005 from www.isna.org/

Isaacs, S. (1929). *The nursery years*. London: Routledge and Kegan Paul.

Izard, C. (1971). *The face of emotion*. New York: Appleton-Century-Crofts.

———. (1977). *Human emotions*. New York: Plenum.

———. (1993). Four systems for emotion activation: Cognitive and noncognitive processes. *Psychological Review, 100*, 68–90.

Izard, C., & Malatesta, C. (1987). Perspectives on emotional development I: Differential emotions theory of early emotional development. In J. Osofsky (Ed.), *Handbook of infant development* (2nd ed.). New York: Wiley.

Jablon, J. R., Dombro, A. L., & Dichtelmiller, M. L.(1999). *The power of observation*. Washington, DC: Teaching Strategies.

Jacob, S. (1992). *Your baby's mind*. Holbrook, MA: Adams.

Jacobson, A. (1994). Starting with infant development: A window to planning curriculum. *ACEI Focus on Infancy 6* (4).

Jalongo, M. R. (2002). *Early childhood language arts* (3rd ed.). Boston: Allyn & Bacon.

Jalongo, M. R. (2004) *Young children and picture books*. Washington, DC: NAEYC.

Jalongo, M. R., & Stamp, L. N. (2003). *The arts in children's lives: Aesthetic education in early childhood*. Needham Heights, MA: Allyn & Bacon.

Jones, E. (1974). *Dimensions of teaching learning environments: A handbook for teachers*. Pacific Oaks, CA: Pacific Oaks Bookstore.

Jones, K.L. (1997). *Smith's recognizable patterns of human malformations*. Philadelphia: W.B. Saunders Company.

Josephson, W. (1995). *Television violence: A review of the effects on children of different ages*. Ottawa, ON: Canadian Heritage.

Kaiser, B., & Rasminsky, J. S. (1995). *HIV/AIDS and child care*. Ottawa, ON: Canadian Child Care Federation/ Health Canada.

———. (2003). Opening the culture door. *Young Children, 58* (4), 53–56.

Kandel, E. (1998). A new intellectual framework for psychiatry. *American Journal of Psychiatry, 155*(4).

Kansas Stakeholders Advisory Committee, Early Childhood Education. (1996). *Quality standards for early childhood education for children birth through eight*. Topeka, KA: Kansas State Board of Education.

Kaplan, L. J. (1978). *Oneness and separateness: From infant to individual*. New York: Touchstone/Simon and Schuster.

Kast, V. (1992). *The dynamics of symbols: Fundamentals of Jungian psychotherapy* (Trans. S. A. Schwartz). New York: Fromm International.

Kaye, C. (2000). Evaluation of the newborn with developmental anomalies of the external genitalia. *Pediatrics 106* (1), 138–142.

Keller, H., Yovsi, R., Borke, J., Kartner, J., Jensen, H., & Papalgoura, Z. (2004). Developmental consequences of early parenting experiences: Self-recognition and self-regulation in three cultural communities. *Child Development 75* (6), 1745–1760.

Kelley, S. A., Brownell, C. A., & Campbell, S. B. (2000). Mastery motivation and self-evaluative affect in toddlers: Longitudinal relations with maternal behavior. *Child Development, 71* (4), 1061–1071.

Kelly, P. (Ed.). (1989). *First-year baby care*. Deephaven, MN: Meadowbrook Press.

Kendrick, A., Kaufmann, R., & Messenger, K. (Eds.). (1988). *Healthy young children: A manual for programs*. Washington, DC: NAEYC.

Kessenich, M. (2003). *Developmental outcomes of premature, low birth weight, and medically fragile infants*. Retrieved on June 18, 2005 from www.medscape.com/viewarticle/461571_1.

Kessler, S., & Swader, B. B. (Eds.). (1994). *Reconceptualizing the early childhood curriculum: Beginning the dialogue*. New York: Teachers College Press.

Kholberg, L., et al. (1987). *Child psychology and childhood education: A cognitive developmental view*. New York: Longman.

Kilbride, K. M. (Ed.). (1997). *Include me too! Human diversity in early childhood*. Toronto: Harcourt Brace.

Kimura, D. (2002). Sex differences in the brain. *Scientific American Special, 12* (1): 32–37.

Kitzinger, S. (1989). *The crying baby*. London: Penguin.

Klaus, M., & Kennell, J. (1976). *Maternal–infant bonding*. St. Louis: Mosby.

———. (1982). *Parent–infant bonding* (2nd ed.). St. Louis: Mosby.

Klaus, M. H., Kennell, J. H., & Klaus, P. H. (1995). *Bonding: Building the foundations of secure attachment and independence*. Reading, MA: Merloyd Lawrence/Addison-Wesley.

Klaus, M. H., Kennell, J. H., & Klaus, P. H. (2000). *Bonding: Building the foundations of secure attachment and independence*. Reading, MA: Addison-Wesley.

Klein, M. D., Cook, R. E., & Richardson-Gibbs. (2001). *Strategies for including children with special needs in early childhood settings*. Clifton Park, NY: Thomson Delmar Learning.

Klein, T. P., Wirth, D., & Linas, K. (2004). Play: Children's context for development. In D. Koralek (Ed.), *Spotlight on young children and play* (pp. 28–35). Washington, DC: NAEYC.

Klinnert M., Campos, J. J., Source, J., et al. (1983). Emotions as behavior regulators: Social referencing in infancy. In R. Plutchik & H. Kellerman (Eds.), *Emotions in early development* (pp. 57–86). New York: Academic Press.

Klinnert, M., Emde, R. N., Butterfield, P., & Campos, J. J. (1986). Social referencing: The infants use of emotional signals from a friendly adult with mother present. *Developmental Psychology, 22*(4), 427–432.

Knudsen, E. I. (2004). Sensitive periods in the development of the brain and behavior. *Journal of Cognitive Neuroscience, 16* (8), 1412–1425.

Koegel, L. K. (2003). Communication and language intervention. In R. L. Koegel & L. K. Koegel, *Teaching children with autism: Strategies for initiating positive interactions and improving learning opportunities* (pp. 17–32). Baltimore: Paul H. Brookes Publishing Co.

Kogan, M. D., Alexander, G. R., Kotelchuck, M., MacDorman, M. F, Buekens, P., Martin, J. A., & Papiernik, E. (2000). Trends in twin birth outcomes and prenatal care utilization in the United States, 1981–1997. *JAMA, 284*, 335–341.

Kohn, A. (1999). *Punished by rewards: The trouble with gold stars, incentive plans, A's, praise, and other bribes*. New York: Mariner.

———. (2001). Five reasons to stop saying "Good job!" *Young Children, 56* (5), 24–28.

Kolb, B., & Whishaw, I. Q. (2005). *An introduction to brain and behavior*. New York: Worth Publishers.

Kopp, C. B. (2001). Self-regulation in childhood. In N. J. Smelser & P. B. Baltes (Eds.), *International encyclopedia of the social and behavioral sciences* (pp. 13862–13866). Oxford, England: Elsevier Science.

Korner, A. F., & Thom, V. A. (1990). *Neurobehavioral assessment of the preterm infant.* New York: The Psychological Corporation.

Kosteck, C. (2005). *Resiliency in children: Attitude shift from deficits to recognizing and building strengths.* Retrieved June 22, 2005 from http://www.stfrancis.edu/srsymposium/projects/swrk/ckosteck_swrk.pdf

Kostelnik, M. J., Whiren, A. P., Soderman, A. K., & Gregory, K. (2006) *Guiding children's social development: Theory to practice* (5th ed.). Clifton Park, NY: Thomson Delmar Learning.

Kotulak, R. (1996). Children's brains greedy for words from infancy. *Toronto Star.*

Kranowitz, C. S. (2005). *The out-of-sync child: Recognizing and coping with sensory processing disorder.* U.S.A.: The Berkley Publishing Group.

Kratcoski, A. M., & Katz, K. B. (1998). Conversing with young language learners in the classroom. *Young Children, 53* (3), 30–33.

Krugman, S., & Dubowitz, H. (2003). Failure to thrive. *American Family Physician, 68* (5). Retrieved on July 10, 2005 from http://www.aafp.org/afp/20030901/879.html

Kuhl, P. K.(1999). The role of experience in early language development: Linguistic experience alters the perception and production of speech. In N. A. Fox, L. A. Leavitt, & J. G. Warhol (Eds.), *The role of early experience in infant development* (pp. 101–125). United States of America: Johnson & Johnson Consumer Companies, Inc.

Lally, J., et al. (1995). *Caring for infants and toddlers in groups.* Washington, DC: ZERO TO THREE.

Lally, J. R. (2001). Infant care in the United States and how the Italian experience can help. In L. Gandini & C. Pope Edwards (Eds.), *Bambini: The Italian approach to infant/toddler care* (pp. 15–22). New York: Teachers College Press.

Lamb, M., et al. (1985). Infant–mother attachment: The origins and developmental significance of individual differences in the strange situations: Its study and biological interpretation. *Behavioral and Brain Sciences, 7*: 127–147.

Lamb, M. E., Bornstein, M. H., & Teti, D. (2002). *Development in infancy* (4th ed.). NJ: Lawrence Erlbaum Associates.

Lamb, M., & Campos, J. (1982). *Development in infancy.* New York: Random House.

Lamb, M., Sternberg, K., & Prodromidis, M. (1992). Nonmaternal care and the security of infant–mother attachment: A reanalysis of the data. *Infant Behavior and Development, 15*: 71–83.

Lammi-Keefe, C. J., et al. (2000). Higher maternal Docosahexaenoic Acid (DHA) is associated with more mature neonatal sleep state patterning. Kansas City, MO: PUFA in Maternal and Child Health Meeting, September 10–13.

Landy, S. (2002). *Pathways to competence: Encouraging healthy social and emotional development in young children.* Baltimore: Paul H. Brooks Publishing.

Langeveld, M. (1983). The "secret place" in the life of the child. *Phenomenology & Pedagogy, 1* (2), 181–189.

———. (1984). How does the child experience the world of things? *Phenomenology & Pedagogy, 2* (3), 215–223.

Leach, P. (1997). *Your baby and child: From birth to age five.* New York: Knopf.

Lear, R. (1990). *More play helps: Play ideas for children with special needs.* Oxford, England: Butterworth-Heinemann.

Leavitt, R., & Eheart, B. (1985). *Toddler child care: A guide to responsive caregiving.* Lexington, MA: Lexington Books/D.C. Heath.

LeDoux, J. (1996). *The emotional brain.* New York: Touchstone/Simon and Schuster.

Lengua, L.J. (2002). The contribution of emotionality and self-regulation to the understanding of children's response to multiple risk. *Child Development 73*(1), pp. 144–161.

Leonard, M. (1977). *Nearly one year old.* Princes Risborough, UK: Shire Publications.

Lepper, M. R. (1983). Social control processes and the internalization of social values: An attributional Perspective. In E. T. Higgins, D. N. Ruble, & W. W. Hartup (Eds.), *Social cognition and social development*, 294–330. New York: Cambridge University Press.

Lerner, C., & Dombro, A. (2004). Finding your fit: Some temperament tips for parents. *ZERO TO THREE, 24* (4), 42–44.

LeRoy, S., Elixson, M., O'Brien, P., Tong, E., Turpin, S., & Uzark, K. (2003). *Recommendations for preparing children and adolescents for invasive cardiac procedures: Position Statement for the American Heart Association, Inc.* http://circ.ahajournals.org/cgi/content/full/108/20/2550#TBL2

Lester, B. M., & Tronick, E. Z. (2004). *NICU Network Neurobehavioral Scale (NNNS™).* New York: Brookes.

Levin, D. E. (2003). *Teaching young children in violent times: Building a peaceable classroom* (2nd ed.). Cambridge, MA: Educators for Social Responsibility.

Levy, T. M., & Orlans, M. (1998). *Attachment, trauma, and healing.* Washington, DC: Child Welfare League.

Lewis, M., & Brooks-Gunn, J. (1978). Self-knowledge in emotional development. In M. Lewis & L. Rosenblum (Eds.), *The development of affect.* New York: Plenum.

———. (1979). *Self cognition and the acquisition of self.* New York: Plenum.

Lickliter, R., & Bahrick, L. E. (2000). The development of infant intersensory perception: Advantages of a comparative convergent-operations approach. *Psychological Bulletin, 126*: 260–280.

Lieberman, A. F. (1993). *The emotional life of the toddler.* New York: Free Press.

Liptak, G. S. (2002). Neural tube defects. In M. L. Batshaw (Ed.), *Children with disabilities* (5th ed., pp. 467–492). Baltimore: Paul H. Brookes Publishing Co., Inc.

Louge, M. (2000). *Implications for brain development research for Even Start family literacy programs.* Washington, DC: U.S. Department of Education.

Louv, R. (2005). *The last child in the woods: Saving our children from a nature deficit disorder.* Chapel Hill: Algonquin Books of Chapel Hill.

Lowry, L. (2001). *The development of taste during infancy.* At www.heinzbaby.com/HINI/taste.htm

Lubeck, S. (1996). Deconstructing "child development knowledge" and teacher preparation. *Early Childhood Research Quarterly, 11,*147–167.

Lucas, M. A. (2001). The military child connection. In R. E. Behrman (Ed.), *The future of children: Caring for infants and toddlers, 11* (1) 129–133. Los Altos, CA: The David and Lucile Packard Foundation.

Lumeng, J. (2005). What can we do to prevent childhood obesity? *ZERO TO THREE, 25* (3), 13–19.

Maccoby, E. (1980). *Social development: Psychological growth and the parent–child relationship.* New York: Harcourt Brace Jovanovich.

Maccoby, E., & Feldman, S. (1972). Mother-attachment and stranger-reaction patterns in the third year of life. *Monographs of the Society for Research in Child Development, 37* (1) (serial no. 146).

Main, M., & Hesse, E. (1990). Parent's unresolved traumatic experiences are related to infant disorganized status: Is frightened and/or frightening parental behavior the linking mechanism? In M. T. Greenberg, D. Cicchetti, and E. M. Cummings (Eds.), *Attachment in the preschool years: Theory, research, and intervention* (161–182). Chicago: University of Chicago.

Mahler, M. (1968). *On human symbiosis and the vicissitudes of individuation.* New York: International Universities Press.

Mahler, M. S., Pine, F., & Bergman, A. (1975). *The psychological birth of the human infant.* New York: Basic Books.

Mallory, B. C., & New, R.,S. (Eds.). (1994). *Diversity and developmentally appropriate practice.* New York: Teachers College Press.

Mantovani, S. (2001). Infant-toddler centers in Italy today: Tradition and innovation. In L. Gandini & C. Pope Edwards (Eds.), *Bambini: The Italian approach to infant/toddler care* (pp. 23–37). New York: Teachers College Press.

March of Dimes. (2005a). Birth defects. *http://www.marchofdimes.com/pnhec/4439.asp*

———. (2005b). Search Fragile X. *http://www.marchofdimes.com/*

Marion, M. (2004). Would you use massage in your program? *Young Children, 59* (4), 69.

Marotz, L., Cross, M., & Rush, J. (2003). *Health, safety, and nutrition for the young child* (6th ed.). Clifton Park, NY: Thomson Delmar Learning.

———. (1999). *Take a look: Observation and portfolio assessment in early childhood* (2nd ed.). Don Mills, ON: Addison-Wesley.

Marshall, H. H. (2001). Cultural influences on the development of self-concept: Updating our thinking. *Young Children, 56* (6), 19–25.

Marusich, C. (1999). *Foundations for learning laid in infancy.* Birth to Three Organization, www.birthto3.org Article: http://thelane.communityos.org/local/os009/clientkb/handouts/18Foundations.pdf

Mayesky, M. (2005). *Creative activities for young children* (8th ed.). Clifton Park, NY: Thomson Delmar Learning.

McAfee, O., & Leong, D. (1994). *Assessing and guiding young children's development and learning.* Needham Heights, MA: Allyn & Bacon.

McAfee, O., Leong, D. J., & Bodrova, E. (2004). *Basics of assessment.* Washington, DC: NAEYC.

McArthur, P., Martin, C. A., & Prairie, A. P. (2004). *Emotional connections: How relationships guide early learning.* Washington, DC: ZERO TO THREE.

McCain, M., & Mustard, J. F. (1999). Early Years Study: Reversing the real brain drain. From *The Early Years Study: Three years later—Early child development to human development: Enabling communities* (2002). Toronto: The Founders Network.

McCormick Tribune Foundation. (1997). *Ten things every child needs.* [Brochure]. Chicago: McCormick Tribune Foundation's Education Program.

McKenna, J. (1997). Bedtime story: Co-sleeping research. *Human Nature,* October 1997, and at www.naturalchild.com/james_mckenna/bedtime_story.html

Maslow, A. (1970). *Motivation and personality* (2nd ed.). New York: Harper and Row.

Meisels, S. (2001). Fusing assessment and intervention: Changing parents' and providers' views of young children. *ZERO TO THREE, 21* (4), 4–10.

Melmed, M. E. (1998). Talking with parents about emotional development. In J. G. Warhol (Ed.), *New perspectives in early emotional development* (pp. 29–46). United States of America: Johnson & Johnson Pediatric Institute, Ltd.

Mennella, J. A. & Beauchamp, G. K. (2002). Flavor experiences during formula feeding are related to preferences during childhood. *Early Human Development, 68,* 75–78.

Messinger, D. S. (2002). Positive and negative: Infant facial expressions and emotions. *Current Directions in Psychological Science, 11* (1), 1–6.

Michalson, L., & Lewis, M. (1985). What do children know about emotions and when do they know it? In M. Lewis & C. Saarni (Eds.), *The socialization of emotions.* New York: Plenum.

Miller, D. F. (2004). *Positive child guidance* (4th ed.). Clifton Park, NY: Thomson Delmar Learning.

Miller, K. (1992). *Things to do with toddlers and twos.* Chelsea, MA: Telshare Publishing.

Miller, K. (2001). *Ages and stages: Developmental descriptions and activities birth through eight years.* Chelsea, MA: Telshare Publishing Company.

Montessori, Maria. (1914/1965). *Dr. Montessori's own handbook.* New York: Schocken Books.

Morbidity and Mortality Weekly Report (MMWR). (2004). *Diagnosis of HIV/AIDS-32 States 2000–2003, 53* (47), 1106–1110, CDC. Retrieved November 14, 2005 at http://www.cdc.gov/mmwr/preview/mmwrhtml/mm5347a3.htm.

Morison, S. J., Ames, E. W., & Chisholm, K. (1995). The development of children adopted from Romanian orphanages. *Merrill-Palmer Quarterly, l41* (4), 411–430.

Morris, D. (1977). *Manwatching: A field guide to human behaviour.* St. Albans, UK: Triad Panther.

———. (1999). *Babywatching.* London: Vintage/Ebury.

Morrison, G. (1997). *Fundamentals of early childhood education.* Upper Saddle River, NJ: Merrill/Prentice Hall.

Moses, L. J., Baldwin, D. A., Rosicky, J. G., & Tidball, G. (2001). Evidence for referential understanding in the emotion domains at 12 and 18 months. *Child Development, 72,* 718–735.

Mott, S., James, S., & Sperhac, A. (1990). *Nursing care of children and families.* Redwood City, CA: Addison-Wesley.

Moyer, I. (1983). *Responding to infants: The infant activity manual.* Minneapolis: T.S. Denison.

Moyles, J. (1994). *The excellence of play.* New York: Open University Press/McGraw Hill.

Nakamura, S., Wind, M., & Danello, M. (1999). Review of hazards associated with children placed in adult beds. *Archives of Pediatric and Adolescent Medicine, 153,* 1019–1023.

Nash, J. M. (1997). Fertile minds. *Time,* June 9.

National Association for the Education of Young Children (NAEYC). (1996). *Prevention of child abuse in early childhood programs and the responsibility of the early childhood profession to prevent child abuse: A position statement.* Washington, DC: NAEYC.

NAEYC code of ethical conduct and commitment (Rev. 2005). Washington, DC: NAEYC.

National Center for Health Statistics. (1982). *Infant development growth charts.* Washington, DC: U.S. Public Health Services.

———. (2001). Retrieved June 15, 2005 from *Growth charts.* http://www.cdc.gov/growthcharts/

National Crime Prevention Council (now known as the National Crime Prevention Centre). (1995). Retrieved July 16, 2005 from http://www.publicsafety.gc.ca/prg/cp/index-en.asp

National Institute of Child Health and Human Development. (2005a). *SIDS—The back to sleep campaign.* http://www.nichd.nih.gov/sids/

———. (2005b). *The occurrence of down syndrome.* http://www.nichd.nih.gov/publications/pubs/downsyndrome/down.htm

———. (2005c). The study of early child care and youth development: Summary. Retrieved July 14, 2005. http://secc.rti.org/summary.cfm

National Institute of Neurological Disorder & Stroke. (2006). Retrieved April 21, 2006. http://www.ninds.nih.gov/disorders/cerebral_palsy/detail_cerebral_palsy.htm

National Scientific Council on the Developing Child. (2005). *Excessive stress disrupts the architecture of the developing brain.* Working Paper No. 3. Retrieved [October, 2005] from http://www.developingchild.net/reports.shtml

Nesheim, S., Dennis, R., Grimes, V., Shouse, R. L., Dominguez, K., Ali, Z., Beck-Sague, C. M., & Asamoa, K. (2004). Assessment of increase in perinatal exposure to HIV among Hispanics—20 Counties, Georgia, 1994–2002. *MMWR, 53* (40), 944–946.

Neuman, S. B., Copple, C., & Bredekamp, S. (2000). *Learning to read and write: Developmentally appropriate practices for young children.* Washington, DC: NAEYC.

Neuman, S. B., & Roskos, K. (2005). Whatever happened to developmentally appropriate practice in literacy? *Young Children 60* (4), 22–26.

Newberger, J. J. (1997). New brain development research—A wonderful window of opportunity to build public support for early childhood education. *Young Children, 52* (4), 4–9.

Newman, L. F., & Buka, S. L. (1991) Clipped wings: The fullest look yet at how prenatal exposure to drugs, alcohol and nicotine hobbles children's learning. *American Federation of Teachers,* 27–32.

Newman, N. (1987). *Small beginnings.* Newton Abbot, UK: David and Charles.

O'Hagan, M., & Smith, M. (1993). *Special issues in child care.* London: Bailliere Tindall.

Olfman, S. (2005). What about play? *Rethinking Schools, 19* (3), 31–33.

Olson, M., & Hyson, M. (2003). Supporting teachers, strengthening families: A new NAEYC initiative. *Young Children, 58* (3), 74–75.

Oser, C., & Cohen, J. (2003). *America's babies: The ZERO TO THREE policy center data book.* Washington, DC: ZERO TO THREE.

Otto, B. (2002). *Language development in early childhood.* Upper Saddle River, NJ: Pearson Education, Inc.

Ounce of Prevention Fund. (1996). *Starting smart: How early experiences affect brain development.* Chicago: Ounce of Prevention Fund.

Owens, R. E. (2001). *Language development* (5th ed.). Boston: Allyn & Bacon.

Owocki, G. (1999). *Literacy through play.* Portsmouth, NH: Heinemann

Owocki, G., & Goodman, Y. (2002). *Kidwatching: Documenting children's literacy development.* Portsmouth, NH: Heinemann.

Paley, V. (2004). *A child's work: The importance of fantasy play.* Chicago: The University of Chicago Press.

Palta, M., Sadik-Badai, M., Evans, M., Weinstein, M., & McGuinness, G. (2000). Assessment of a multicenter very low-birth weight cohort at age 5. *Archives of Pediatric and Adolescent Medicine, 154* (1), 23–30.

Papalia, D. E., Olds, S. W., & Feldman, R. D. (2006). *A child's world: Infancy through adolescence* (10th ed.). New York: McGraw Hill.

Parlakian, R. (2003). *Before the ABC's: Promoting school readiness in infants and toddlers.* Washington, DC: ZERO TO THREE.

———. (2004). Early literacy and very young children. *ZERO TO THREE, 25* (10), 37–43.

Parten, M. (1932). Social participating among pre-school children. *Journal of Abnormal and Social Psychology, 27,* 243–269.

Patrick, K., Soear, B., Holt, K., & Sofka, D. (2001). *Bright futures in practice: Physical activity.* Arlington, VA: National Center for Education in Maternal and Child Health.

Paulson, L. H., Noble, L. A., Jepson, S., & van der Pol, R. (2001). *Building early literacy skills and language skills.* Longmont, CO: Sopris West.

Pawl, J., & St. John, M. (1998). *How you are is as important as what you do in making a positive difference for infants, toddlers, and their families.* Washington, DC: ZERO TO THREE.

Penn, H. (1999). *How should we care for babies and toddlers? An analysis of practice in out-of-home care for children under three.* Toronto: Childcare Resource and Research Unit.

Perry, B. D. (1997). Incubated in terror: Neurodevelopmental factors in the "cycle of violence." In J. Osofsky (Ed), *Children in a violent society* (pp. 124–149). New York: Guilford Press.

Perry, B. D., & Pollard, D. (1997) *Altered brain development following global neglect in early childhood.* Society for Neuroscience: Proceedings from Annual Meeting, New Orleans, 1997. Retrieved June 22, 2005 from http://www.childtrauma.org/CTAMATERIALS/neuros~1.asp

Perry, J. P. (2001). *Outdoor play: Teaching strategies with young children.* New York: Teachers College Press.

Phillips, D. (ed.). (1987). *Quality in child care: What does research tell us?* Washington, DC: NAEYC.

Phillips, D., & Adams, G. (2001). Child care and our youngest children. In R. E. Behrman (Ed.), *The future of children: Caring for infants and toddlers, 11* (1), 34–51.

Piaget, J. (1950). *The psychology of intelligence.* New York: International Universities Press.

———. (1952). *The origins of intelligence in Children.* New York: International Universities Press.

———. (1954). *The construction of reality in the child.* New York: Basic Books.

Piaget, J., & Inhelder, B. (1967). *The child's conception of space.* New York: Norton.

Pica, R. (2004). *Experiences in movement: Birth to age eight.* Clifton Park, NY: Thomson Delmar Learning.

Pimento, B., & Kernested, D. (2000). *Healthy foundations in child care* (2nd ed.). Scarborough, ON: Nelson.

Poisson, S., & DeGangi, G. (1992). *Emotional and sensory processing problems: Assessment and treatment approaches for young children and their families.* Rockville, MD: Reginald S. Lourie Center for Infants and Young Children.

Pomper, K., Blank, H., Campbell, N. D., & Schulman, K. (2005). *Be all that we can be: Lessons from the military for improving our nation's child care system.* Washington, DC: National Women's Law Center.

Project Zero. (2001) *Making learning visible: Children as individual and group learners.* Reggio Emilia, Italy: Reggio Children.

Pruett, K. (1999). *Me, myself and I: How children build their sense of self (18–36 months).* New York: Goddard Press.

Puckett, M. B., & Black, J. K. (2005). *The young child: Development from prebirth through age eight* (4th ed.). Upper Saddle River, NJ: Pearson Merrill/Prentice Hall.

Pugmire-Stoy, M. (1992). *Spontaneous play in early childhood.* Clifton Park: Thomson Delmar Learning.

Quilliam, S. (1994). *Child watching: A parent's guide to children's body language.* London: Ward Lock.

Raikes, H. (1996). A secure base for babies: Applying attachment concepts to the infant care setting. *Young Children, 51* (5), 59–67.

Ramey, C., Campbell, E., & Blair, C. (1998). Enhancing the life course for high-risk children. In J. Crane (Ed.), *Social programs that work* (pp. 184–199). New York: Russell Sage Foundation.

Ramey, C. T., & Ramey, S. L. (1999). *Right from birth: Building your child's foundation for life, birth to 18 months.* New York: Goddard Press.

———. (2004). Early educational intervention and intelligence: Implications for Head Start. In E. Zigler & S. J. Styfco (Eds.), *The Head Start debates* (pp. 3–17). Baltimore: Paul H Brookes Publishing Co.

Ramsey, D. (1980). Onset of unimanual handedness in infants. *Infant Behavior and Development, 3,* 377–386.

Raver, S. (1991). *Strategies for teaching at-risk and handicapped infants and toddlers.* New York: Merrill.

Reddy, V., & Trevarthen, C. (2004). What we learn about babies from engaging with their emotions. *ZERO TO THREE, 24* (3), 9–15.

Reents, J. (2001). Safe co-sleeping. *Geoparent.* At www.geoparent.com/family/techniques/safecosleeping.htm

Restak, R. M. (1986). *The infant mind.* Garden City, NJ: Doubleday & Company Inc.

———. (1991). *The evolution of consciousness: The origins of the way we think.* New York: Simon & Schuster.

Rimer, P., & Prager, B. (1998). *Reaching out.* Scarborough, ON: Nelson.

Roberts, S. B., & Heyman, M. B. (2000). How to feed babies and toddlers in the 21st century. *ZERO TO THREE, 21* (1), 24–28.

Roberts-Fiati, G. (1997). Observing and assessing young children. In K. M. Kilbride (Ed.), *Include me too! Human diversity in early childhood.* Toronto: Harcourt Brace.

Roberston, J., & Robertson, J. (1989). *Separation and the very young.* London: Free Association.

Rolfes, S., & DeBruyne, L. (1990). *Life span nutrition: Conception through life.* St. Paul, MN: West.

Rose, V. (1985). Detecting problems with growth development charts. *Nursery World,* Nov. 28, 6–7.

Rosenkoetter, S. E., & Knapp-Philo, J. (2004). Learning to read the world: Literacy in the first 3 years. *ZERO TO THREE, 25* (1), 4–9.

Roskos, K. A., & Christie, J. F. (2002). Knowing in the doing: Observing literacy learning in play. *Young Children, 57* (2), 46–54.

Rowland, S., & Lawhon, T. (1994). How do I love thee: Enhancing intimacy in children. *Childhood Education* (Fall), 38–41.

Russell, B. (1960). *On education.* London: George Allen and Unwin.

Rutter, M. (1979). Maternal deprivation, 1972–1978: New findings, new concepts, new approaches. *Child Development, 50,* 283–305.

Rutter, M., & the English and Romanian Adoptees (ERA) Study Team. (1998). Developmental catch-up, and deficit following adoption after severe global early privation. *Journal of Child Psychology and Psychiatry, 39* (4), 465–476.

Rutter, M., & O'Connor, T. G. (1999). Implications of attachment theory for child care policies. In J. Cassidy & P. R. Shaver (Eds.), *Handbook of attachment: Theory, research and clinical Applications* (pp. 823–844). New York: The Guilford Press.

Ryan, S., & Grieshaber, S. (2004). It's more than child development: Critical theories, research, and teaching young children. *Young Children, 59* (6), 44–52.

Saarni, C. (2000). The social context of emotional development. In M. Lewis & J. M. Haviland-Jones (Eds.), *Handbook of emotions* (2nd ed., pp. 306–322). New York: Guilford.

Sagi, A., et al. (1994). Sleeping out of home in a kibbutz communal arrangement: It makes a difference for infant–mother attachment. *Child Development, 65,* 992–1004.

Salkind, N. (1994). *Child development* (7th ed.). Fort Worth: Harcourt Brace.

Sameroff, A., & Chandler, M. (1975). Reproductive risk and the continuum of caretaking casualty. In F. Horowitz (Ed.), *Review of child development research.* Chicago: University of Chicago Press.

Sanger, S. (1991). *Baby talk/parent talk: Understanding your baby's body language.* New York: Doubleday.

Scheers, N. J., Rutherford, G. W., & Kemp, J. S. (2003). Where should infants sleep? A comparison of risk for suffocation of infants sleeping in cribs, adult beds, and other sleeping locations. *Pediatrics, 112* (4), 883–889.

Schirrmacher, R. (2005). *Art and creative development for young children* (5th ed.). Clifton Park, NY: Thomson Delmar Learning.

Schmitt, B., & Krugman, R. (1992). Abuse and neglect of children. In R. E. Behrman (Ed.), *Nelson Textbook of Pediatrics* (14th ed.). Philadelphia: W.B. Saunders.

Schonberg, R. L., & Tifft, C. J. (2002). Birth defects, prenatal diagnosis, and fetal therapy. In M. L. Batshaw (Ed.), *Children with disabilities* (5th ed., pp. 27–41). Baltimore: Paul H. Brookes Publishing Co., Inc.

Schore, A. (2001) The effects of a secure attachment relationship on right brain development, affect regulation, and infant mental health. *Infant Mental Health Journal, 22,* 7–66. (www.trauma-pages.com/schore-2001a.htm)

Schweinhardt, L. J. (2005). *The High/Scope Perry preschool project and frequently asked questions through age 40: Summary, conclusions.* Retrieved May 11, 2005, www.highscope/Research/PerryProject/PerryAge40Sumweb.pdf

Scientific American. (1998). Exploring intelligence: A search in the human, animal, machine and extraterrestrial domains. *Scientific American Presents, 9*(4).

Searle, J. (1995). The mystery of consciousness. *New York Review of Books,* Nov. 2, 60.

Secker, D. (2001). *Interpreting growth and growth standards.* At www.heinzbaby.com/HINI/growth.htm

Seefeldt, C. (1990). *Continuing issues in early childhood education.* Columbus, OH: Merrill.

Seimens, H.W. (1924). *Die zwillingspathologie.* Berlin: Springer.

Sensory Integration International, http://home.earthlink.net/~sensoryint/

Shaffer, D. (1993). *Developmental psychology: Childhood and adolescence* (3rd ed.). Belmont, CA: Brooks/Cole.

Shatz, M., & O'Reilly, A. (1990). Conversational or communicative skill? A reassessment of two-year-olds' behavior in miscommunication episodes. *Journal of Child Language, 17,* 131–146.

Sheldon, S. H. (2002). Sleep in infants and children. In Lee-Chiong, Sateia, M. J., & Carskadon, M. A. (Eds.), *Sleep medicine* (pp. 99–103). Philadelphia: Hanley and Belfus, Inc.

Shelov, S. P., & Hannemann, R. E. (2004). *American Academy of Pediatrics: The complete and authoritative guide for caring for your baby and young child.* New York: Bantam Books.

Sheridan, M. (2001). *Birth to five years: Children's developmental progress.* London: Routledge (Taylor Francis Group).

———. (2004). *From birth to five years: Children's developmental progress.* London: Routledge. Brunner Routledge.

Shimoni, R., Baxter, J., & Kugelmass, J. (1992). *Every child is special.* Don Mills, ON: Addison-Wesley.

Shonkoff, J. P., & Marshall, P. C. (2003). The biology of developmental vulnerabilities. In J. P. Skonkoff & S. J. Meisels (Eds.), *Handbook of early childhood intervention* (2nd ed., pp. 35–53). New York: Cambridge University Press.

Shonkoff, J. P., & Phillips, D. A. (Eds.). (2000). *From neurons to neighborhoods: The science of early childhood development.* Washington, DC: National Academic Press.

Shonkoff, J. P., Phillips, D. A., & Keilty, B. (Eds.). (2000). *Early childhood intervention: Views from the field.* Washington, DC: National Academy Press.

Shore, R. (2003). *Rethinking the brain: New insights into early development.* New York: Families and Work Institute.

Siegel, A. C., & Burton, R. V. (1999). Effects of baby walkers on motor and mental development in human infants. *Journal of Developmental and Behavioral Pediatrics, 20,* 355–361.

Siegler, R. (1991). *Children's thinking* (2nd ed.). Englewood Cliffs, NJ: Prentice Hall.

Silberg, J. (1993). *Games to play with babies.* Mt. Rainier, MD: Gryphon House.

———. (1996). *More games to play with toddlers.* Belville, MD: Gryphon House.

Simkin, P., Whalley, J., & Keppler, A. (1991). *Pregnancy, childbirth and the newborn.* Deephaven, MN: Meadowbrook Press.

Singer, D., & Revenson, T. (1996). *A Piaget primer: How a child thinks.* New York: Plume/Penguin.

Sluss, D.J. (2005). *Supporting play: Birth through age eight.* Clifton Park, NY: Thomson Delmar Learning.

Smilansky, S., & Shefatya, L. (1990). *Facilitating play: A medium for promoting cognitive, socio-emotional and academic development in young children.* Gaithersburg, MD: Psychosocial & Educational Publications.

Smith, L. A. (2005). *Preparing your child for surgery: Article for Erlanger Health System.* Retrieved October 6, 2005 from www.erlanger.org/childrens/prep_for_surgery.asp

Snow, C. W. (1998). *Infant development* (2nd ed.). Upper Saddle River, NJ: Prentice Hall.

Sobell, 1994. *Save your baby: Throw out your equipment.* Santa Barbara, CA: Whole Family Press.

Sonosky, C. (Ed.). (2004). *The state of America's children, 2004.* Washington, DC: Children's Defense Fund.

Spitz, R. (1945). Hospitalism: An inquiry into the genesis of psychiatric conditions in early childhood. *Psychoanalytic Study of the Child, 1,* 53–74.

———. (1946). Hospitalism: A follow-up report on investigation described in volume 1. *Psychoanalytic Study of the Child, 2,* 113–117.

Springgate, K. W., & Staglin, D. A. (1999). Adjusting to a child with special needs. *Building school and community partnerships through parent involvement.*

Spock, B. (1996). Mommy, don't go! *Parenting* (June/July), 86–91.

Sroufe, L. (1977). Wariness of strangers and the study of infant development. *Child Development, 48,* 731–746.

———. (1979). Socioemotional development. In J. Osofsky (Ed.), *Handbook of infant development.* New York: Wiley.

———. (1988). A developmental perspective on child care. *Early Childhood Research Quarterly, 3,* 283–292.

Sroufe, L., Cooper, R., & DeHart, G. (1996). *Child development: Its nature and course* (3rd ed.). New York: McGraw-Hill.

Sroufe, L. A., Fox, N., & Pancake, V. (1983). Attachment and dependency in developmental perspective. *Child development, 54,* 1615–1627.

Stafstrom, C. E. (2001). The incidence and prevalence of febrile seizures. In T. Z. Baram & S. Shinnar (Eds.), *Febrile seizures* (pp. 1–26). San Diego: Academic Press.

Stahmer, A., & Carter, C. (2005). An empirical examination of toddler development in inclusive childcare. *Early Child Development & Care, 175* (4), 321.

Statistics Canada. (1995). *National longitudinal survey of children and youth.* Ottawa, ON: Statistics Canada.

———. (1996). *1996 Census.* Ottawa, ON: Statistics Canada.

Steiner, R. (1982). *The roots of education.* London: Rudolph Steiner Press.

Stephens, K. (1999). Primed for learning: The young child's mind. *Child Care Information Exchange, 3,* 43–48.

Stern, D. N. (1985). *The interpersonal world of the infant.* New York: Basic Books.

———. (2000). *The interpersonal world of the infant: A view from psychoanalysis and developmental psychology* (2nd ed.). New York: Basic Books.

———. (2002). *The first relationship.* Cambridge, MA: Harvard University Press.

Stonehouse, A. (Ed.). (1990). *Trusting toddlers.* St. Paul, MN: Toys 'n' Things Press.

Stoppard, M. (1983). *Baby care book: A practice guide to the first three years.* London: Dorling Kindersley.

Storm, L., & Reese, S. P. (2005). Better beginnings through nurturing touch. *ZERO TO THREE, 26* (1), 14–18.

Story, M., Kaphingst, K., & French, S. (2006). The role of child care settings in obesity prevention. *Childhood Obesity, 16* (1). Retrieved April 28, 2006 from http://www.futureofchildren.org/information2826/information_show.htm?doc_id=355663

Striano, T., & Rochat, P. (2000). Emergence of selective social referencing in infancy. *Infancy, 1*(2), 253–264.

Sturm, L. (2004). Temperament in early childhood: A primer for the perplexed. *ZERO TO THREE, 24* (4), 4–11.

Sullivan, P. M., & Knutson, J. F. (2002). Maltreatment and disabilities: A population-based epidemiological study. *Child Abuse & Neglect, 24* (10), 1257–1273.

Sutton-Smith, B. (1997). *The ambiguity of play.* Cambridge, MA: Harvard University Press.

Sylvester, K. (2001). Caring for our youngest: Public attitudes in the United States. *Caring for Infants and Toddlers, 11* (1), 53–61

Teitelbaum P., Teitelbaum, O., Fryman, J., & Maurer, R. (2002). Infantile reflexes gone astray in autism in infants. *Journal of Developmental and Learning Disorders 6,* 15–22.

Teitelbaum P., Teitelbaum, O., Nye, J., Fryman, J., & Maurer, R. (1998). Movement analysis in infancy may be useful for early diagnosis of autism. *Proceedings of the National Academy of Sciences of the United States of America, 95* (23), 13982–13987.

Thoman, E., & Browder, S. (1987). *Born dancing: How intuitive parents understand their baby's unspoken language.* New York: Harper Row.

Thomas, A., & Chess, S. (1977). *Temperament and development.* New York: Brunner/Mazel.

————. (1985). The behavioral study of temperament. In J. Strelau, et al., *The biological bases of personality and behavior, Vol. 1: Theories, measurement, techniques and development.* Washington, DC: Hemisphere.

Thomas, P. (2000). Children and stress: "The hurried child." Taconic Counselling Group. At www.taconicnet.com/childstress.htm

Thompson, R. A. (2001). Sensitive periods in attachment? In D. B. Bailey, J. T. Bruer, F. J. Symms, & J. W. Lichtman (Eds.), *Critical thinking about critical periods* (Chapter 5). Baltimore: Paul H. Brookes Publishing Co.

Tice, J. (2004). *Reflective teaching: Exploring our own classroom practice.* Retrieved May 6, 2005, from http://www.teachingenglish.org.uk/think/methodology/reflection.shtml.

Tortora, S. (2006). *The dancing dialogue: Using the communicative power of movement with children.* Baltimore: Paul H. Brookes Publishing Co.

Trad, P. (1993). *Short-term parent–infant psychotherapy.* New York: Basic Books/HarperCollins.

Trainor, L. J., & Heinmiller, B. B. (1998). The development of evaluative responses to music: Infants prefer to listen to consonance over dissonance. *Infant Behavior and Development, 21*(1), 77–88.

Trawick-Smith, J. (2003). *Early childhood development: A multicultural perspective* (3rd ed.). Upper Saddle River, NJ: Pearson Merrill Prentice Hall.

————. (2006). *Early childhood development: A multicultural perspective* (4th ed.). Upper Saddle River, NJ: Pearson Merrill Prentice Hall.

Trehub, S. (2000). Human processing predispositions and musical universals In N. Wallin, B. Merker, & S. Brown (Eds.), *The origins of music* (pp. 427–448). Cambridge, MA: The MIT Press.

Trehub, S., Bull, D., & Thorp, L. (1984). Infants' perception of melodies: The role of melodic contour. *Child Development, 55,* 821–830.

Tremblay, R., et al. (1994). Predicting early onset of male antisocial behavior from preschool behavior. *Archives of General Psychiatry, 51,* 732–738.

Tronick, E. (1989). Emotions and emotional communication in infants. *American Psychologist, 44*(2), 112–119.

Turnbull, A., & Turnbull, H. (1997). *Families, professionals, and exceptionality* (3rd ed.). Upper Saddle River, NJ: Merrill/Prentice Hall.

Tychsen, L. (2001). Critical periods for development of visual acuity, depth perception, and eye tracking. In D. B. Bailey, J. T. Bruer, F. Symons, & J. W. Lichtman (Eds.), *Critical thinking about critical periods* (pp. 67–80). Baltimore: Paul H. Brookes.

United Nations. (1991). *Convention on the rights of the child.* New York: United Nations Dept. of Public Information.

Van, Hoorn, J. Nourot, P. M., Scales, B., & Alward, K. R. (2003). *Play at the center of the curriculum* (3rd ed.). Upper Saddle River, NJ: Merrill Prentice Hall.

Van Manen, M. (Ed.). (1994). Writing in the dark: Phenomenological studies in interpretive inquiry. In *Researching lived experience: Human science for an action-sensitive pedagogy.* London, ON: Althouse Press.

Voices for Children. (2002). *Promoting children's healthy development.* At www.voices4children.org.

Vukelich, C., Christie, J. F., & Enz, B. (2002). *Helping young children learn language and literacy.* Boston: Allyn and Bacon.

Vygotsky, L. S. (1978). *Mind and society: The development of higher mental processes.* Cambridge, MA: Harvard University Press.

————. (1934/1962). *Thought and language.* Cambridge, MA: MIT Press.

Wachs, T. D. Temperament and development: The role of context in a biologically based system. *ZERO TO THREE, 24* (4), 12–21.

Wainright, G. (1985). *Body language.* Sevenoaks, UK: Teach Yourself Books/Hodder and Stoughton.

Walk, R., & Gibson, E. (1961). A comparative and analytical study of visual depth perception. *Psychology Monographs, 75* (15).

Walker-Andrews, A. S. (1998). Emotions and social development: Infants' recognition of emotions in others. In J. G. Warhol (Ed.), *New perspectives in early emotional development* (pp. 109–118). United States of America: Johnson & Johnson Pediatric Institute, Ltd.

Wang, J. H-T. (2004). A study of gross motor skills of preschoolers. *Journal of Research in Childhood Education, 19* (1), 32–41.

Ward, L. P., & McCune, S. K. (2002). The first weeks of life. In M. L. Batshaw (Ed.), *Children with disabilities* (5th ed., pp. 69–83). Baltimore: Paul H. Brookes Publishing Co., Inc.

Watamura, S. E., Donzella, B., Alwin, J., & Gunnar, M. R. (2003). Morning-to-afternoon increases in cortisol concentrations for infants and toddlers at child care: Age differences and behavioral correlates. *Child Development, 74,* 16–102.

Waters, E., & Cummings, E. M. (2000). A secure base from which to explore close relationships. *Child Development,* Special Millennium, Issue, Feb.

Waters, E., Merrick, S, Treboux, D., Crowell, J., & Albersheim, L. (2000). Attachment security in infancy and early adulthood: A twenty-year longitudinal study. *Child Development, 71* (3), 684–689.

Watkinson, M. (1987). Examination of the Neonate. *Update,* November 1, 949–958.

Weaver, B. (2004). Pertinent topics on HIV infection among women: Prevention, lipodystrophy, and drug-drug interactions. *Infectious Diseases in Corrections Report, 7* (5). Retrieved April 21, 2006 from http://www.idcronline.org/archives/may04/article.html

Weaver, I. C., Diorio, J., Seckl, J. R., Szyf, M., & Meaney, M. J. (2004). Early environmental regulation of hippocampal glucocorticoid receptor gene expression: characterization of intracellular mediators and potential genomic target sites. *Annals of the N Y Academy of Science, 1024,* 182–212.

Weber, D. S., & Singer, D. G. (2004). The media habits of infants and toddlers: Findings from a parent survey. *ZERO TO THREE 25*(1), 30–36.

Weinfield, N. S., Sroufe, L. A., Egeland, B., & Carlson, E. A. (1999). The nature of individual differences in infant-caregiver attachment. In J. Cassidy & P. R. Shaver (Eds.), *Handbook of attachment: Theory, research and clinical applications* (pp. 68–88). New York: The Guilford Press.

Weiser, M. (1991). *Infant/Toddler Care and Education.* 2nd ed. New York: Merrill/Macmillan Publishing.

Weissbourd, B., and J. Musick (eds.). (1981). *Infants: Their Social Environments.* Washington, DC: NAEYC.

Weitzman, E., & Greenberg, J. (2002). *Learning language and loving it* (2nd ed.). Toronto: Beacon Harold Fine Printing.

Wellhousen, K. (2002). Chapter 2—Outdoor play for infants and toddlers. In *Outdoor play every day.* Clifton Park, NY: Thomson Delmar Learning.

Werner, E., & Smith, R. (1992). *Overcoming the odds: High risk children from birth to adulthood.* Ithaca, NY: Cornell University Press.

Weston, P. (1998). *Friedrich Froebel: His life, times and significance.* London: Roehampton Institute.

White, B. (1988). *Educating the infant and toddler*. Lexington, MA: Lexington/D.C. Heath.

White, B. (1995). *The new first three years of life*. New York: Fireside/Simon and Schuster.

Whitebrook, M., Howes, C., & Phillips, D. (1990). *Who cares? Child care teachers and the quality of care in America*. Final Report of the National Child Care Staffing Study. Oakland, CA: Child Care Employee Project.

Widerstrom, A., Mowder, B., & Sandall, S. (1991). *At-risk and handicapped newborns and infants: Development, assessment, and intervention*. Englewood Cliffs, NJ: Prentice-Hall.

———. (1997). *Infant development and risk* (2nd ed.). Baltimore: Paul H. Brookes.

Wilson, L. (1997). *Partnerships: Families and communities in Canadian early childhood education*. Scarborough, ON: Nelson.

Wilson, L. C., Douville-Watson, L., & Watson, M. (2003). *Infants and toddlers: Curriculum and teaching* (5th ed.). Clifton Park, NY: Thomson Delmar Learning.

Winter, S. (1995). *Outdoor play and learning for infants and toddlers*. Little Rock, AR: Southern Early Childhood Association.

Witherington, D. C., Campos, J. J., Anderson, D. I., Lejeune, L., & Seah, E. (2005). Avoidance of heights on the visual cliff in newly walking infants. *Infancy, 7* (3), 285–298.

Wolff, P. (1966). The causes, controls and organization of behavior in the neonate. *Issues, 5* (7).

Woolfson, R. (1995). *A to Z of child development from birth to five years*. Toronto: Stoddart.

Wurm, J. P. (2005). *Working in the Reggio way: A beginner's guide for American teachers*. St. Paul, MN: Redleaf Press.

Yeates, M., et al. (1990). *Administering early childhood settings: The Canadian perspective*. Columbus, OH: Merrill.

Yonas, A., et al. (1987). Four months old infants' sensitivity to binocular and kinetic information for three-dimensional object shape. *Child Development, 58,* 910–917.

York, S. (2003). *Roots and wings: Affirming culture in early childhood programs, revised edition*. St. Paul, MN: Redleaf Press.

Younger, B., & Gotleib, S. (1988). Development of tract and primitive syllabification in infancy: The first six months. *Purdue University Contributed Paper* (Fall).

———. Categorization skills: Changes in the nature or structure of infant form categories? *Development Psychology, 24,* 611–619.

Zeichner, K. M., & Liston, D. P. (1996). *Reflective teaching: An introduction*. Mahwah, NJ: Lawrence Erlbaum Associates, Publishers.

Zentner, M. R., & Kagan, J. (1998). Infant's perception of consonance and dissonance in music. *Infant Behavior and Development, 21* (3), 483–492

Zlatin, M. (1973). Explorative mapping of the vocal tract and primitive syllabification in infancy: The first six months. *Purdue University Contributed Papers* (Fall).

Zwaigenbaum L., Bryson, S., Rogers, T., Roberts, W., Brian, J., & Szatmari, P. (2005). Behavioral manifestations of autism in the first year of life. *International Journal of Developmental Neuroscience, 23* (2–3), 143–152.

Glossary

A

abuse psychological, physical, or sexual injury inflicted on an individual

accommodation the process that changes existing ways of thinking in response to new experience—reorganizing or creating new schemes in response to external stimuli (*refer* to Piaget)

action–reaction the link or association between one action and a reaction that it causes

active play involves whole-body movement; requires space and simple, safe equipment

activity level the motor component in a child's functioning; the degree of activity

acuity the degree to which one or more of the senses is functional or effective

adaptation the process of change within the individual—involves complementary processes of accommodation and assimilation (*refer* to Piaget)

aggressive behavior any action that is motivated to cause harm—socially unacceptable behavior resulting from anger

aggressive play play behavior involving actions that cause harm to other people or to objects

ambidextrous hand activity without hand dominance (left or right)

ambivalent attachment an ineffective and unreliable relationship with an adult characterized by distress at separation and anger on return of the attachment figure (*refer* to Ainsworth)

American Sign Language (ASL) a hand signaling system used for and by those without hearing; like other sign languages, it incorporates grammatical rules (informally called Ameslan)

anal stage the second stage of personality development, during which the superego takes form, toilet-learning usually occurs during this stage (*refer* to Freud)

analysis the process of organizing or summarizing data and then making inferences that assist in creating meaning

analysis of observation a method of documentation that separates observations into inference and validation sections and also includes specific references to theory, theorists, research, etc., in order to support conclusions

anecdotal records short, narrative observations describing significant events, recorded after they have occurred

anti-bias curriculum the curriculum and experience of the child that is designed and delivered in ways that address potential biases related to gender, race, culture, poverty, and other social issues (*refer* to Derman-Sparks, York)

antibiotics physician-prescribed courses of medication that target particular bacterial infections

antivirals physician-prescribed medications that target specific viral infections

anxiety a troubled feeling or state of emotional unrest—the state might be caused by something occurring within the individual or by particular circumstances

anxiety disorder a feeling of emotional unrest that cannot be attributed to "real" concerns; may be associated with any one of several neurotic conditions involving irrational fears

Apgar a standardized measurement instrument used to assess health indicators in the newborn infant

aphasia a language impairment that may have resulted from damage to the central nervous system

a priori a term used to identify a type of knowledge that is obtained independently of experience; a priorism is a philosophical position maintaining that our minds gain knowledge independently of experience through innate ideas or mental faculties

assessment the process of gathering data (including observational information) from several sources using informal or standardized instruments and making deductions that explain behavior; child assessment is not based on a single measure

assimilation the process of incorporating new learning into existing schemes (*refer* to Piaget)

assistive device any device, such as a machine, leg brace, or computer, that enables an individual to be as able-bodied or intellectually functional as possible

associative play spontaneous activity in which children play alongside each other and interact on a similar theme, but they remain focused on their play

asymmetrical not straight or uniform; lacking in balance or harmonious arrangement

attachment the positive emotional relationship that develops between two individuals—between adult and child (*refer* to Bowlby, Ainsworth)

attachment difficulties situations where the child is unable to form one or more appropriate positive relationships with adults because the child's experience is erratic or deficient (*refer* to Ainsworth, Greenspan)

attachment disorders situations where the child is unable to make one or more appropriate positive relationships, to such an extent that there may be long-lasting implications; intervention may be successful

attachment figure the adult or older child with whom the child makes the affectional tie

attending paying attention to a stimulus

attention-deficit disorders any disorder, in infancy or later in life, that impedes the ability to focus on tasks; ADD and ADHD are commonly known attention-deficit disorders; most attention deficits impede learning; various interventions may be helpful

attributes characteristics of a person, thing, or object such as color, shape, or size

atypical development   patterns of human development that lie outside the range of the norm or average

atypical birth presentations   any positioning of the baby immediately prior to or during birth that is not usual—e.g., breech

audiation   the cognitive process that enables individuals to hear and comprehend music in their heads even with no music playing

authentic assessment   gathering of data—including naturalistic observational material—that is reviewed in a contextualized, sensitive, and individual manner (*refer* to Wortham, Martin)

autism   a condition in which the individual demonstrates social isolation and communication difficulties

autobiographical memory   memories of one's own life (limited by infant amnesia)

autonomous   independent; self-directed; not controlled by others or by outside forces

autonomy   an inner drive to become independent and meet one's own needs; a sense of independence, self-government, or self-reliance

autonomy versus shame and doubt   the second stage of the life cycle, in which the psychological conflicts of toddlerhood can lead to healthy independence (*refer* to Erikson)

avoidant attachment   an inadequate relationship with an adult, characterized by a lack of protest under stress (*refer* to Ainsworth)

axon   the part of the neuron (brain cell) that transmits messages to other neurons, muscles, or glands of the body

B

babbling   production of consonant–vowel sounds of varying intonation; usually involves repetition of sounds in long strings, such as da-da-da-da-da, or ba-ba-ba-ba-ba, developing in an infant between the ages of 4 and 6 months

baby blues   a common temporary psychological state right after childbirth when a new mother may have sudden mood swings. These emotions can range from feeling very happy to suddenly feeling very sad, which can result in crying for no apparent reason. Other moms report feeling impatient, unusually irritable, restless, anxious, or lonely. The baby blues may last only a few hours or as long as 1 to 2 weeks after delivery

baby signing   the use of hand signals, gestures, expressions, and bodily movements that have shared meaning (*refer* to Garcia)

baseline observation   a quick and efficient overview of the child's behavior and health indicators (usually made at the start of each day) that provides a benchmark for change

basic emotions   emotions that can be inferred from facial expressions; may be universally understood (*refer* to Izard)

basic trust versus mistrust   the psychological conflict in infancy that can be resolved given appropriate support (*refer* to Erikson)

behavior   any demonstrated action, whether deliberate or not

behaviorism   the perspective that development occurs primarily because of external influences in the environment (nurture) (*refer* to Pavlov, Watson, Skinner)

behavior modification   the process of trying to change behavior by using rewards or negative consequences

best practices   ways of working (with children) that are accepted within the profession as exemplary

bias   any distorted perception of other people or social groups that is used to justify mistreatment; a preference, such as a visual preference

bilingual   fluent in two languages

binocular vision   the capacity to coordinate the sensory input from both eyes; results in the ability to perceive depth

biological clock   one of the three clocks of life-span development—the influence of heredity and maturation

birth defect   an abnormality of structure, function, or metabolism (body chemistry) that is evident at birth and can result in a physical or mental disability, or can cause the death of the child

block play   playful activity involving the use of manufactured or found materials to build or construct; observable stages of play behavior are evident; such play may involve imagination and creativity, but will usually contribute to mathematical concept building

body language   messages sent either deliberately or unconsciously; conveyed by the individual's posture, facial expressions, gestures, or other behavior

bonding   the close physical and emotional relationship (affectional tie) between an adult and a child, which is established in the early weeks after birth—usually between mother and child; bonding sets the stage for later attachment; Bowlby proposed that one key figure must provide the bonding relationship (*refer* to Bowlby; Klaus & Kendall; Rutter; Ainsworth)

bottom shuffling   a method of infant mobility involving sitting on the buttocks and using leg (and arm) movements to propel the body forward, backward, or sideways; sometimes preferred to crawling

brain   the part of the central nervous system that is encased by the skull; has approximately 100 billion nerve cells (neurons), which are responsible for every type of bodily and mental function

brain maturation   the biological process of growth and development of the structure and function of the brain

C

calcification   the process of hardening, generally bone

caregiver   a person responsible for meeting the physical (and other developmental and health) needs of an individual

catch-up   the idea that, given certain remedial experiences, the child can resume a typical stage of development

cause and effect   particular actions bring about (cause) particular reactions (effects)

categorical self   the aspect of the self that is self-descriptive (of its own characteristics)—e.g., "I'm a boy" or "I can jump"

center of gravity   concerning physical growth, the weight difference between the upper and lower parts of the body; the infant is top-heavy, and thus has a high center of gravity

cephalocaudal (principle)   that development of the body following a sequence from head to foot

cephalocaudal/proximodistal sequences   the development of the body follows dual sequences simultaneously—from head to foot and from the center of the body outward to the hands

cerebellum   the part of the brain that uses sensory inputs to guide motor activity

cerebral irritation   irritation of the brain caused by bacteria (or other foreign bodies) or pressure; it may result in difficulty in becoming calm; the condition may cause seizures

channel of preference   the individual's best or preferred way of communicating and functioning—e.g., visual , auditory, or tactile

character   the combination of traits that distinguishes an individual; the behavior of the individual that demonstrates his moral understanding

charts   prepared documents that are completed after specified behaviors or functions have been demonstrated and observed—e.g., infant feeding charts

checklist   a method of recording observational information that documents the presence or absence of predetermined criteria

child care   a full-time or part-time program offering care and education, usually licensed

child care provider   any person who meets the developmental needs of the child

child-centeredness   a philosophical approach to programming for children that focuses on the child's interests, motivations, needs, and developmental stage

children at risk   infants or children who are vulnerable in some way that may result in academic or social challenges

chronic condition   a health concern that continues and must be managed over time

chromosomes   rod-shaped portions of DNA organized into 23 pairs within each cell; they are responsible for the transmission of hereditary characteristics

chromosomal disorders   individuals who experience behavioral or developmental difficulties as a result of having abnormal chromosomes

chronological age   the actual age of the child (as opposed to the individual's performance level)

clear-cut attachment   the infant's attachment to a specific adult

CNS—central nervous system   the brain and spinal column

coach   the role of an adult or more mature child to encourage, support, and provide strategies for success

Code of Ethics   a document that delineates a common basis for resolving situations that involve ethical decision-making and presents guidelines for responsible behavior (*refer* to Online Companion)

cognition   the process of thinking, knowing, reasoning, and other mental functioning

cognitive development   changes in the individual over time that result from increased intellectual functioning; may be considered within a framework of stages; depends on interplay of heredity and experience; includes aspects of the mind, brain growth, and behavioral changes

cognitive needs   the specific experiences necessary for intellectual functioning

colic   a condition in the newborn characterized by acute abdominal pain, knees drawn up to the chest, and a high-pitched cry

colostrum   the first fluid secreted by the mother's breasts soon after birth, before true milk comes through

comfort object   any object that the child finds particularly comforting; the object takes on particular significance—e.g., blanket, teddy bear; a "lovie"

communication (skills)   the ability to share meaning with others; typically involves a shared language or signing system; includes ability to exchange ideas involving a sender and a receiver of a message

communication disorder   a broad term used to describe a structural or functional difficulty or deficit that impedes effective communication—may be a diagnosed disorder, such as aphasia, or a hearing impediment

community   a geographical area or neighborhood; one or more cultural groups within a certain proximity; a group of people with a shared economic status; a system of people with overlapping or shared needs or desires; a group of people such as family members and friends

competencies   the level of observable functioning of the individual and/or the specified knowledge and skills that are to be acquired; a view of the child that assumes that the individual has sufficient skill and aptitude (rather than a deficit model that views the child as helpless and waiting to become competent)

competent   having sufficient skill and aptitude

concept   clusters of schemes (patterns, mental representations) that together create an idea

confidentiality   the professional and ethical performance of a role that includes keeping information private and sharing information appropriately as the role demands

congenital cardiac condition   a condition that was present from birth involving the structure or function of the heart

congenital condition   a condition that was present from birth

congenital heart defect   defect in the structure of the heart and great blood vessels of the newborn that impacts normal blood flow and was present from birth

consciousness   a function of the mind that is awareness of a person's self, environment, and mental activity; may choose courses of actions; there are several observable levels of consciousness; the "problem of consciousness" lies in its complexity; philosophers, neuroscientists, and many others define consciousness differently; consciousness concerns functions of the brain, behavior, mind, and soul or spirit (*refer* to Dennett)

conservation   the understanding that physical attributes stay the same even when their appearance is altered (*refer* to Piaget)

consistency   a pattern of predictable and reliable relationships with an adult

consonants   speech sounds, or letters of the alphabet, that are not vowels (*see* vowels)

constancy   the idea that things remain the same in some respect, despite perceptual information to the contrary

construct of reality   the inner representation of the outer world; creating an understanding of what is real

construction (constructive) play   spontaneous activity involving making, building, or creating; typically involving blocks or found materials; may involve imaginative aspects or make-believe; usually includes an end product—i.e., what is made

constructivism   a philosophy of learning that considers reality to be self-constructed: the child, through stages, creates an inner construction of her outer world (*refer* to Piaget)

continuity (developmental)   the notion that the process of human growth and development follows a gradual progression

continuity of care   the design and delivery of child care programs in ways that enable particular adults to maintain special and continuing relationships with particular children, ensuring that the routines and patterns of care remain the same

continuity/discontinuity (developmental)   the opposing notions that the process of human growth and development follows either a gradual progression or a step-by-step pattern

convergent thinking   thinking that requires a specific correct response

cooing   the squealing–gurgling, happy sounds made by babies from around 6 weeks to 4 months; nonspeech sounds

cooperative activity   an endeavor that is accomplished by working together or playing with at least one other person

corpus callosum   the area of the brain that contains the largest bundle of nerve fibers and connects the two hemispheres of the brain; allows the two hemispheres of the brain to communicate

cortisol   a hormone that is released by the body while experiencing stress. Research findings indicate that too much cortisol has the potential to negatively impact synapse development in the brain

crawling   mobility involving propelling the body forward, backward, or sideways while on the knees; typically a stage of physical development prior to walking

creating emotional ideas   the fifth stage of emotional development, which typically occurs at 18–36 months (*refer* to Greenspan)

creative play   spontaneous activity with materials or ideas that involves understanding how to use objects or represent ideas, making something, and using innovative or new ideas

creative thought   activity of the mind that involves creativity (*see below*); may involve divergent thought, problem solving, trial and error, or a combination of other thinking skills

creativity   an individual's capacity to produce new ideas, inventions, or artistic objects of value; the process of creating and making things

critical period   the time when the child must be exposed to appropriate experiences for development to occur (*see also* "sensitive periods" and "windows of opportunity")

cruising   moving around by standing up and walking sideways while holding on to a stable object

cues   any indicator or message sent (deliberately or not) by an infant or young child that is read and interpreted by an adult or older child; may include facial expressions, sound productions, gestures, and bodily movements

culturally diverse   an environment that includes people of various cultures; an organization that welcomes people from different heritages; may also include individuals from various ethnic backgrounds, people of different religions, people from a range of geographic locations, people who speak different languages, and people living in different subcultures (groups within groups)

curriculum   everything that happens in a classroom, both the planned and unplanned; traditionally refers to the prescribed content of what is to be learned within a designated time period; the philosophy of *See How They Grow* uses the term to mean every aspect of a child's experience, whether it is designed or not

CVS—chorionic villi sampling   a prenatal examination of the fetus to screen for developmental abnormalities

cycles of sleep   the patterns of sleep—repeated every 90 minutes or so—that involve up to five different types or levels of sleep

cytomegalovirus (CMV)   a common infection in child care centers; it is worth making sure that preventive health measures are followed

D

dance of communication   the two-way intentional communication that goes back and forth between two individuals

decentered   the ability to alter perspectives; seeing from the perspective of others

decentration   the degree to which a child is able to shift her focus of interest; e.g., from herself to external objects

decontextualization   understanding something out of context, or outside its usual setting

deferred imitation   copying single behaviors or complex roles sometime after the initial observation of the behavior

dendrite   the neuron branch that is the major receptive surface of the neuron; it receives and processes signals from other neurons (brain cells)

depth perception   the integration of information from both eyes in order to gauge relative size or distance; seeing the world in three dimensions

deprivation   the state in which essential experiences, basic needs, or relationships are denied, absent, or inaccessible

development   the dynamic process of growth and change within a individual that occurs over time; also refers to an increase in complexity, a change that proceeds from the simple to the more complex

developmental alerts   behaviors that are atypical (significantly different from the norm) of the child's stage, or otherwise indicate cause for concern; they usually require further observation and possible referral to appropriate agencies and professionals

developmental delay   a term referring to a classification for an individual who is not developing according to the expected time frame; a classification of an individual, with or without a diagnosis, who is performing significantly behind developmental norms

developmental diversity   evidence of a variety of developmental levels, abilities, and stages

developmental domains   areas of individual growth and development, including the physical, intellectual, emotional, and social

developmental milestones   stages in the individual's development; commonly accepted advances that mark new achievements

developmental outcomes   increases in individual performance measured over a period of time; the results of a program or intervention that demonstrate its success or failure

developmental profile   an overview of an individual's development that may include written components and examples that illustrate his level of performance, or a chart indicating average performance levels at each age group

developmental psychology   the study of human behavior and the reasons for its manifestation; identification of discernable stages of change within the individual (*refer* to Piaget, Kholberg)

developmentally appropriate practice (DAP)   all aspects of children's programs and practices that are designed and implemented in ways that demonstrate that the needs of a group of children are met, that the different needs and developmental levels of individual students are considered and met, and that the needs of the family, including cultural and linguistic needs, are respected and included (*refer* to Bredekamp/NAEYC/Online Companion)

diary records   a series of anecdotal records recorded in sequential order; may provide a teacher with information about individual children or a group of children

difficult child   the categorization of a child's temperamental style as being challenging (*refer* to Chess & Thomas)

differentiated hearing   the ability to simultaneously hear one's own voice and listen to other specific sounds

direct instruction   a method of teaching where the adult takes responsibility for structuring learning experiences; adult may use demonstration and other strategies

discontinuity   the notion that human growth and development follow a fluctuating pathway of progression and regression, rather than a gradual progression

discovery play spontaneous activity that involves finding out the properties of materials and how they work

discriminate attachment the second stage of attachment, in which the infant makes an attachment to a specific person who meets her needs

disengagement when the individual takes her attention away from a stimulus; may be deliberate or not

dishabituation the increase in responsiveness after stimulation changes

disorganized/disoriented attachment an inadequate relationship with an adult, characterized by the child showing inconsistent patterns of responding to stress (*refer* to Ainsworth)

divergent thinking thinking involving unusual responses; associated with creativity and "thinking outside the box"

DNA—deoxyribonucleic acid the substance in genes that contains information

domain (of development) an aspect of human development; includes physical, emotional, cognitive

Down syndrome a chromosomal abnormality characterized by distinctive facial features and intellectual deficits; also known as trisomy-21

downtime the state of consciousness where the individual is at a low level of response to stimulation

dream mental activity, usually involving imaginary events, that occurs during sleep (REM sleep); may be open to interpretation (*refer* to Jung)

dyadic any activity or relationship involving two, either an individual and an object or two individuals

E

early childhood assistant (ECA) a person prepared to work with young children; may hold a certificate

early childhood care and education (ECCE) programs and services for young children and their families

early childhood educator (ECE) a prepared individual who is qualified to meet the developmental, caregiving, health, and educational needs of infants, toddlers, and preschool children (and sometimes school-age children); works with parents and families, in accordance with professional and ethical practices

ECE preparation (training) any program of study and practice leading to qualification for working with young children— e.g., ECE diploma, Bachelor of Applied Arts in Early Childhood Education, Specialist post-diploma in working with infants, Family Child Care Provider Certificate, B. Ed. in Early Years Education (note that such preparation varies enormously)

early intervention the practice of offering compensatory or other experiences to an infant or young child (birth to age 5) and his family with the intention of ameliorating any deficit or at-risk condition, developing strategies for success, or addressing potential problems

early intervention programs comprehensive programs designed for infants or young children and their families to support the specific needs of those children/families

easy child a characterization of the child's temperament (*refer* to Chess & Thomas)

echolalia the infant's repetitive babbling of one sound; the repetition or echoing of verbal utterances made by another person

eclectic (approach) a philosophical approach to working with children that takes elements of various different philosophies and combines them into a meaningful whole

ecological system the idea that human development occurs within and is influenced by complex social systems; involves concentric circles indicating differing social levels (*refer* to Bronfenbrenner)

educare the term that states there is no difference between care and education for young children, since you accomplish both simultaneously

educarer a prepared individual who is qualified to meet the developmental, educational, and caregiving needs of infants, toddlers, and 3-year-olds (*refer* to Gerber)

educating the process of facilitating learning—assisting in the learner's acquisition of knowledge, skills, and dispositions (attitudes)

efficacy the knowledge that it is worth trying something because you know you will succeed, and the confidence stemming from the belief that your actions will have predictable effects

ego the part of the individual that is rational and reasonable (*refer* to Freud)

egocentric from the perspective of the individual; in infancy, unable to see from the perspective of others

egocentric thought thinking that does not take into account the perspectives of others; in infancy, an inability to see from the perspective of others (*refer* to Piaget)

egocentricity the state of seeing only from the individual's perspective; in infancy, an inability to think from the perspective of others (*refer* to Piaget)

emergence of an organized sense of self the fourth stage of emotional development; typically occurs around 9–18 months (*refer* to Greenspan)

emotional development changes in the individual over time that involve understanding the self and feelings, and regulating behavior; occurs within stages (*refer* to Erikson, Greenspan)

emotional intelligence skills that can be applied in social situations; becoming emotional maturity; ways of being emotionally "smart"; involves emotional development (*refer* to Goleman)

emotions feelings; complex internal states (not directly observable, except through the interpretation of expressions and body language)

empathy a social emotion; experiencing the emotions that someone else is feeling; the ability to understand the feelings of another individual

engagement when an individual spends time paying attention to someone or something

entry-to-practice standards a set of minimum requirements for work in a particular context or of a particular type— e.g., education; standards typically set out the knowledge and skills required for the role

epilepsy disordered brain functioning characterized by seizures (or convulsions) of varying severity

equilibration the process of human adaptation in which there is a drive to balance assimilation and accommodation (*refer* to Piaget)

essence the core element of what makes individual people who they are; the phenomenon of discovering what makes another person different

essential experiences experiences that are necessary for growth and development to occur at an optimal level

ethics the values associated with good conduct; professional standards of behavior; includes levels of practice, reliability, confidentiality

event sampling   a series of observational recordings focused on a specified category of behavior; used to determine patterns and causes of behavior; may be used for behavior modification

experience   anything that produces a response, consciously or unconsciously; what happens around or to an individual; a planned or unplanned event (*refer* to Dewey)

exosystem   the parts of the ecological system that influence experience (but young children have little direct contact)—e.g., the parent's workplace (*refer* to Bronfenbrenner)

exploratory play   any spontaneous activity that involves finding out the properties of materials—e.g., water play

existential self   the individual knowing that she exists

expressive language   uttering meaningful sounds, words, phrases, and sentences

expressive volume   the level of loudness used in language

extrinsic (motivation)   encouragement, inducement, or support that comes from outside the individual

F

facilitating development   the role of the adult in organizing, observing, interacting, and supporting another individual's growth, adaptation, and change

facilitator   someone who makes progress easier; a person who makes it easier for learners to learn by attempting to discover what the learner is interested in knowing, and then determines the best way to make those experiences and information available to the learner

factor analysis   a statistical method of managing large amounts of information that reduces the data to a limited number of core themes; commonly associated with research into temperament and personality

failure to thrive   a condition where a seemingly healthy baby fails to grow and develop normally

falling in love   the second stage of emotional development—typically occurs at 2–7 months (*refer* to Greenspan)—or the process of establishing a special relationship

family   a group of individuals who share living space; a natural group in which members are related by birth, marriage, or other criteria, and share a household

family child care   child care that is offered within a home environment, typically licensed with a trained adult and the supervision of a child care agency; usually a multi-age program

family systems   the idea that groups of people who share living experiences create structures and function within them

fantasy   imagination unrestricted by reality; being whimsical; a creation of the imagination

fantasy play   spontaneous activity involving suspension of reality, imagination, pretending, and/or make-believe

febrile convulsions   a convulsion in a child triggered by a fever; these convulsions occur without any underlying brain or spinal cord infection or other neurological cause

fine motor skills   learned behaviors involving the small muscles of the body—e.g., the hands manipulating an object

fontanels   the soft spots (anterior and posterior), front and back, on the infant's head, over which unconnected bones are lined with a protective material

functional play   exploring a toy to see how it works; this begins with combination play, such as banging toys against each other or a surface, emptying containers (dumping), and knocking blocks down

G

genetics   the study of heredity; family patterns of disease; evolutionary patterns of behavior (*refer* to Darwin, Vogel)

genetic counseling   offering advice to parents and others seeking information about heredity and patterns of genetically determined conditions

germs   microorganisms that might produce disease—e.g., bacteria, viruses, molds

gesture   a deliberate action of the hands, head, or body, indicating an idea or feeling

gesture vocabulary   a range of hand and arm signs that have shared meanings

glial cells   supporting cells that form a protective coating and nourishment for neurons; they provide scaffolding for growing and developing neurons

goal-directed activity   an activity that results from an individual's efforts to do something deliberately

goodness-of-fit   the extent to which the caregiving style of the parent meshes with the temperament of the infant

grammar   the system of rules that governs syntax in language

gross motor skills   learned behaviors involving the large muscles of the body—e.g., walking

growth   increase in size of the individual; in infancy and early childhood, it is typically assessed through measurement of height/length, weight, and head circumference; often growth can be easier to observe and measure than development

guidance strategies   techniques of discipline and instruction used in order to help children gain personal competence and self-discipline

guided instruction   a method of instruction that includes strategies on a continuum ranging from less to more direction offered by the teacher

guilt   the feeling of remorse and responsibility for something that occurred, whether a real or imagined wrong; a product of conflicted feelings (*refer* to Erikson)

H

habituation   the decrease in the response to a stimulus that occurs after repeated presentations of the stimulus—e.g., looking away from a mobile after continued stimulation

hand preference   the individual's natural pattern of using the left or right hand

hand–eye coordination   the process of coordinating movements of the eyes and hand/arm system so that they both move toward the same target; the use of vision to guide arm movements

health   a state of well-being in which individuals attain their own state of optimal activity and absence of disease, show positive mental functioning and a positive sense of self, have the opportunity to realize their physical potential, and are able to function effectively within social groups, while being emotionally stable and reasonably content

health professionals   physicians, nurses, paramedics, physiotherapists, specialists, and other personnel who contribute to managing health, emergencies, illnesses, conditions, and diseases

healthy development   a desirable level of human development in which the individual becomes a fully functioning person

HIV (human immunodeficiency virus)   a virus that attacks the immune system; can be transmitted when bodily fluids are transferred from one person to another

holistic development   an approach to development that visualizes a wider concept of a child, including history, relationships, experiences, culture, present status, health, and gender, as well as the interdependence of these parts

holistic response   any response to an individual that takes into account each interacting domain of the person's development

holophrase   one-word utterance that stands for a whole phrase; the meaning depends on the context

homemade checklist   a list of behaviors or other criteria developed by a teacher or parent, used for recording the presence or absence of each item

humanistic theory   a theory of development that concerns meeting the individual's needs; based on humanism (*refer* to Maslow)

hyperactivity   levels of physical activity that are higher than normal, sometimes associated with a disorder

I

I   reference to the self; the concept of being a separate person; a symbol identifying understanding of the self

id   the part of the psyche that is the seat of instinctual processes or passions (the ego and superego manage the impulses of the id) (*refer* to Freud)

imitation   the act of copying single actions of another person, or the copying of complex actions, as with role models

imitative play   spontaneous activity that involves the copying of single actions of another individual, or the acting out of an internalized role; may involve deferred imitation

imprinting   a response to a stimulus that continues long after the stimulus has disappeared

inclusion   integrating all children into a program, regardless of their ability levels or background

indiscriminate attachment   the infant can be comforted and have his needs met by any adult; he has no special responsiveness to the primary caregiver he has; typically observed during the first three months

individual   a separate human being

Individual Family Service Plan (IFSP)   The IFSP is a written plan developed by parents or guardians with input from a multidisciplinary team. The IFSP (1) identifies the family's strengths, needs, concerns, and priorities; (2) identifies support services available to meet those needs; and (3) empowers the family to meet the developmental needs of their infant or toddler with a disability

individual program plan (IPP)   a curriculum or intervention plan created especially for one child on the basis of her assessed needs

individuation   the process of working on becoming a separate person

infantile amnesia   the phenomenon by which early experiences, typically from before 2 years of age, are not remembered later

inference   the process of drawing a conclusion from given evidence; to reach a decision by reasoning

informal observation   casual or unrecorded observation

information processing   the approach to cognitive development that views the brain as a sophisticated computer with memory and symbolic functions

initiative versus guilt   the third stage of the life cycle, in which the young child needs to resolve the conflict of powerfulness against social pressures to behave well (*refer* to Erikson)

innate (behavior)   characteristics that are inborn, pre-programmed, acquired but not learned

instinct   what is known or done without learning; feelings or thought based on knowledge without experience; behavior emanating from pre-wiring

instinctual   concerned with innate capacities or drives

instinctual drives   innate motivations

institutionalization   placing an individual into an institution; typically refers to subjecting the individual to inflexible routines and lack of nurturing and physical contact; a rigid program detrimental to the individual's development

integration   the process of combining incoming information; one of the functions of the nervous system

intentional action   the emergence of goal-directed activity, typically seen at 8–12 months; one of the substages of sensorimotor development (*refer* to Piaget)

intentional communication   the third stage of emotional development—which typically occurs at 3–6 months (*refer* to Greenspan)—or any deliberate attempts to convey a message

intentional variation   the emergence of deliberate varying of actions; typically observed at 12–18 months (*refer* to Piaget)

intermediate grasp   a grasp that refines the palmar (whole-hand) grasp; may involve scooping or some effort at thumb–forefinger opposition

internalization   the process of learning at a level where the tools used are mental, and their use is not visible to others; understanding and accepting an idea

internal world   the function of the mind; the conscious and unconscious workings of thought; awareness of one's own thinking; inner speech and emotion (*refer* to Greenspan)

intrinsic (motivation)   a drive that comes from within (rather than from external forces)

irreducible needs   the child's basic and essential needs that must be met for healthy development (*refer* to Greenspan & Brazelton)

J

jargon   a type of babbling that appears to echo the rhythm and phonation of adult speech heard in the child's environment, typically developing when an infant is between 8 and 10 months old

K

kindergarten   literally, "the children's garden"; a program for young children; a philosophy of education involving respect for the natural unfolding development of young children and the adult's role as nurturer, educator, and facilitator (*refer* to Froebel)

L

lactating   the physiological process of producing milk (as in breast-feeding)

language acquisition   the process of becoming able to use a shared code or communication system involving rule-governed combinations of symbols

language acquisition device (LAD)   an innate mechanism that allows language to occur—involves pre-wiring (*refer* to Chomsky)

language delay   later-than-average acquisition of language

lanugo   soft hair that covers the fetus and newborn and helps the vernix stick to the skin

life cycle   the natural and ongoing sequence of birth, life, and death; life-cycle theory proposed by Erikson

literacy-rich environment   an environment containing essential components (e.g., books, daily reading, adult role models, writing materials) that help foster and support the acquisition of literacy

locus of control   the perception of control over one's own destiny or future; the belief that one's actions are controlled by the self

logic   the aspect of the ability to think that involves reason and drawing conclusions

lymphatic system   the tissues of the body that screen out harmful substances and manage infection control

M

macrosystem   the part of the ecological system from which broad ideologies emanate; values and cultural patterns are transmitted through the institutions of the macrosystem (e.g., nations, governments, religious systems) (*refer* to Bronfenbrenner)

make-believe play   spontaneous activity involving pretend and imaginative ideas

mandated reporters   those individuals who by law must report suspicion of child abuse to specific agencies

manipulative play   similar to object play—spontaneous activity involving handling materials and discovering what they will do

manipulative skills   learned behaviors involving an increasing ability to handle materials and objects successfully

manual dexterity   the individual's ability to use the hands to achieve complex tasks

maturation   the biologically shaped, naturally unfolding course of growth and development (*refer* to Gesell, Illingworth)

maturational readiness   the notion that the child is ready for particular experiences at certain stages of growth

mean length of utterance (MLU)   the average length of the sentence the child produces; average number of morphemes per utterance

meconium   fetal feces, usually expelled after birth

mediator   a person or structure that acts as an intermediary between the child and the environment; provides supports for learning

memory   a complex function of the brain to recall past events and experiences; storage and access to information previously obtained; elements of memory include recognition, recall, association, internalized scripts, control mechanisms, selection, and retrieval

meningitis   inflammation of the membranes encasing the spinal cord and brain; usually caused by bacterial or viral infection

mental combinations   putting together two or more ideas; holding in mind two or more attributes simultaneously

mental operations   the ability to think about actions that were previously done physically

mental representations   the symbolic ways of thinking about objects that are not physically present

mental schemes   (*see* schemes)

mesosystem   a system of several microsystems within which the individual functions; for young children, this might mean home and child care

metabolic disorders   disorders that impede the breakdown of food and the production of energy

microsystem   the smallest unit of the ecological system; the immediate environment (*refer* to Bronfenbrenner)

milia   small white spots, mainly on the nose or the face, caused by blocked sebaceous glands; require no treatment

mind   the entity responsible for thought, feelings, and speech; the seat of consciousness; the function of the brain

mistrust   to regard without trust or confidence; part of first crisis stage in Erickson's psychosocial theory

modeling   the process of demonstrating a social role performance; it is required for observational learning (*refer* to Bandura)

moral development   the gradual increases and changes in understanding of right and wrong and the acquisition of values; acceptance of socially acceptable behaviors and moral reasoning, and appreciating societal attitudes and beliefs; stages of moral judgment (*refer* to Kholberg)

morpheme   the smallest unit of meaning within language—a word, a prefix, or a suffix

motherese   changes in the mother's speech that emphasize particular sounds and the use of a higher pitch than normal when communicating with infants and young children; may be culture-bound

motivation   the reasons or incentives for human behavior, explained as basic drives in psychoanalytic theory

motor development   the aspect of physical development that involves gross motor skill acquisition and mobility

multi-age programs   a program for young children that is designed for and delivered to a mixed group of toddlers, preschool children, and/or infants and school-age children

multimodal (senses)   involving two or more of the modes of sensory input (hearing, sight, touch, taste, and smell)

multimodal stimulation   stimulating two or more senses simultaneously

multiple attachments   having two or more secure attachment figures; having a series of important relationships involving significant bonding; typically these relationships are with parents, extended family members, and caregivers

multiple disabilities   having two or more disabilities at the same time—e.g., having a hearing deficit and a congenital heart condition

multiple intelligences (MI)   the idea that there are many ways of being smart—a theory that identifies at least eight ways of being intelligent (*refer* to Gardner)

mutual interactions   two-way communications and actions that involve both individuals in meaningful exchanges

myelin   a coating around the nerves (axons) that conducts electrical impulses from one brain area to another

myelination   the process where myelin is laid down on the nerves of the brain; when parts of the brain myelinate, it allows or improves the function of that area, such as movement or vision

N

narratives   written observations that conform to one of the standard methods of recording (running record, specimen record, anecdotal record, or diary record)

naturalistic setting   a child's normal, everyday setting that enables an observer to see how an individual lives, plays, and interacts

nature (development)   the aspects of individuals that exist because of their genetic heredity (*see* nurture and nature/nurture)

nature/nurture (development)   the interaction of genetic inheritance and life experience that contributes to making individuals who and what they are

neglect   the denial of an individual's basic needs; these needs can be physical, educational, or emotional

neural plasticity   the brain's ability to reorganize neural pathways based on new experiences

neonatal   the period of time around the birth of the infant—usually the first six weeks of life

neonate   the infant at birth and for the first few weeks of life

neuron   brain cells that store and send information; there are about 25 different types, each with a cell body, dendrites, and an axon

neuroscience   interdisciplinary study of the brain and behavior

nightmares   a particularly vivid and scary dream—tends to occur towards the end of the night

night terrors   occur during a phase of deep non-REM sleep, usually within an hour after the subject goes to bed; symptoms include sudden awakening from sleep, screaming, sweating, confusion, rapid heart rate, inability to explain what happened; eyes may be open but the child not awake; difficult to rouse from sleep

nonparticipant observation   an observation conducted from a distance without direct involvement in events or responsibility for what occurs

norms   the average performance of a large sample of children at designated ages

normative profiles   charts and tables indicting the typical patterns of growth and development at designated ages of a particular population of children considered to represent the "norm"; often presented as percentiles (*refer* to Sheridan; Illingworth; Allen & Marotz)

numerical scale   a form of rating scale that uses numbers to indicate the degree to which a behavior is present or a characteristic is evident

nurture (development)   the aspects of individuals that exist because of their experience of life (*see* nature and nature/nurture)

O

object permanence   the realization that objects continue to exist when they are out of sight (*refer* to Piaget)

object play   spontaneous activity that involves manipulating objects or materials for purposes of discovery

observation   watching behavior and activities of children in a controlled, informed, educated, purposeful manner, often with specific goals, questions, or concerns in mind; usually involves recording data utilizing a variety of methods

observation documentation   the professional written accounts of behavior, development, and significant change; may form part of a portfolio; can be used as official documents in legal proceedings

observational learning   learning by watching people's behavior

obstetrics   the branch of medicine concerned with childbirth and the care of the mother before, during, and after birth

onlooker play   spontaneous activity in which the child watches another child or children at play; may ask questions or converse with those at play but does not get actively engaged with their play

open-ended activities   learning activities that do not have built-in correct or incorrect ways of handling materials or doing things

optimal conditions   the best possible situation; exemplary environment

optimal development   the best possible development; the realization of the child's potential

oral stage   the first of a series of developmental stages characterized by the infant's drive to mouth objects and gain oral satisfaction (*refer* to Freud)

oral gratification   the emotional satisfaction gained from mouthing objects or feeding (*refer* to Freud)

orthopedic disabilities   the lack of muscular tone or mobility resulting from abnormalities in the musculoskeletal system

ossification   the process of converting cartilage to bone

otitis media   inflammation of the middle ear

overextension   the child's application of a language rule in a situation where it does not apply—i.e., extending it beyond situations where it does apply

overstimulation   a situation in which the infant or older individual is unable to process sensory information because it has become overwhelming

P

palmar grasp   a hand grasp using the whole hand (and palm)

paradigm   a way of looking at a situation; a perspective

parallel play   spontaneous activity occurring alongside other children, without sharing or cooperation; playing separately at the same activity at the same time and in the same space

parentese   speech pattern used in talking with infants and young children; refers to either male or female parent and utilizes the elements found in motherese—the high-pitched, sing-song jargon adults use instinctively with infants

participant observation   an observation made while the observer is engaged in activity or communication with the individual being observed

patterns of development   the predictable stages and changes that are observable within each individual; may involve frequent progressions and some regressions; may be continuous or discontinuous

pediatrician   medical doctor specializing in work with infants and children

people permanence   the realization that people continue to exist even when they are out of view

percentile   any value defined by dividing the group into 100 equal parts; a band that indicates the scores associated within that numerical range; commonly used in developmental profiles to indicate average performance levels and where a particular individual falls within the range

perception   the process of taking in, processing, and interpreting sensory information, through one or more sensory channels

perinatal   around the time of birth, before or after

permission   the professional requirement to ask parents if it is acceptable to observe, record, or conduct an activity

personal health   the factors that contribute to the individual's overall health and well-being—e.g., diet, exercise, nurturance, growth, development, and absence or presence of disease

PET scan   positron emission tomography; an imaging technique that uses a radioactive tracer to show the chemical activity of the brain

personality   the sum total of the enduring characteristics that differentiate one individual from another

phenomenological approach   a philosophical approach to being and working with others that respects the consciousness of the other person and endeavors to enter into the person's life-world (*refer* to van Manen); a special technique of introspection involving becoming acquainted with the objects of conscious experience (*refer* to Husserl)

phenomenology   the systematic study of conscious experience; entering into the life-world of another person (*refer* to Dennett)

phenomenon (plural: phenomena)   a thing as it appears; anything that can be perceived as a fact or occurrence (*refer* to Kant); experiences of the external world, experiences of the internal world, or experiences of emotion (*refer* to Dennett)

phenomenon of consciousness   awareness of the conscious world of oneself and others

philosophy   the investigation of knowledge and being; the perspectives and values that underpin practice

philosophy statement   the critical analysis of fundamental assumptions or beliefs

phonemes   the smallest linguistically distinct unit of sound; e.g., the word cat has three phonemes—c/a/t

phonological awareness   conscious ability to detect and manipulate sound (e.g., move, combine, and delete); awareness of sounds in *spoken* words in contrast to *written* words

physical development   growth and change of the individual over time; involves the individual's body, gross motor skills (large body movement and mobility), and fine motor skills (small muscles, such as hand control)

physical needs   the individual's basic requirements—including food, clothing, and protection—without which the individual would fail to grow and develop

pincer grasp   the ability to grasp a small object between the tips of the thumb and index finger

placental insufficiency   the situation where the placenta is unable to deliver the essential nutrients to the fetus for its growth, health, and development

plasticity   the brain's ability to change (its malleability) as a result of experience or injury; particularly changeable in early life

play   spontaneous, intrinsically motivated, enjoyable activity resulting in learning; the child's work; a means of discovery; practice for adulthood; an activity to reduce stress; a means of fostering development; a route to self-discovery; a way of learning social skills; an activity for its own sake (*refer* to Hughes)

play partner   one who acts as a facilitator of child's play in such a way that the child takes the lead and the partner follows directions or performs similar actions; partnership may involve making suggestions or providing new materials, but the partnership is led by the child

play therapy   experiences that are structured to support emerging skills and competencies; especially designed activities that prompt the child to play in ways that address her psychological, physical, or other challenges

play therapist   a prepared individual who is qualified to assess the developmental needs of a child and/or provide appropriate play experiences that address a child's particular or special needs

plaything   any manufactured or found object used to promote and facilitate play

portfolio   a systematic collection of documentation on a child's growth and development, along with information on health, family background, and other relevant material

positive guidance strategies   ways that an adult can support a child's learning and behavior through encouragement, natural and logical consequences, and coaching, using internal and external motivators and rewards that avoid the use of inap-

propriate punishments; relies on an understanding of the child's stage of development and understanding

positivism   the idea that there is an ultimate truth and unquestionable reality, rather than personal perspective or construction of reality

postpartum depression   a period of time when some mothers experience depression, low energy levels, negative moods, or other symptoms; possibly a result of chemical or hormonal changes after giving birth; may need medical or psychiatric assistance

practice play   spontaneous activity involving repeated actions that aid discovery

pragmatics   the understanding of the use of language in communication; language use within a communication context

pragmatism/functionalism   an approach to education that focuses on practicality, usefulness, social responsibility; focuses on child-centered learning (*refer* to Dewey)

preconceptual thinking   basic thoughts or consciousness—usually based on sensorimotor activity—that exists prior to true conceptual development

preferences   the individual's deliberate choice or the individual's most effective mode or channel

pre-lingual   the stage before true language emerges

premature   an infant who is born before full gestation; may be small and may experience health and developmental difficulties

prenatal   the period before birth; the time from conception to birth; the three trimesters of pregnancy

pre-operational stage   the stage of thought following the sensorimotor stage—typically 2–7 years—during which the child has some conceptual understanding but is limited because she hasn't acquired the means and "operations" to transform and manipulate ideas (*refer* to Piaget)

prepared checklists   valid and reliable instruments that include lists of behaviors or other attributes; used as guides to observe and record information about a child's development

pretend play   play guided by the imagination; objects stand for something else; roles are taken on so children act "as if"

preverbal cues   the messages conveyed by means such as facial expressions, gestures, and sound production before true language is acquired

preverbal dialogue   interactive communication between adult and infant involving intentional communication

pre-wired   the idea that the brain is prepared or structured to acquire language or other learning prior to such learning occurring

primary caregiver   the adult to whom the child has the strongest attachment

primary caregiving system   an approach to caregiving that values relationship building. One specific person is responsible for a major portion of interaction with a child on a day-to-day basis, but is not entirely responsible for the care. Sensitive teamwork is essential in order for this system to be effective

primary circular reaction   simple repetitive acts resulting from an enjoyable experience—typically observed at 1–4 months; a substage of the sensorimotor stage (*refer* to Piaget)

principles of development   the commonly agreed-upon ideas that explain human development—e.g., stage progression

private speech   self-directed speech or utterances that children use to guide their own behavior or use as a commentary on their own actions—speech that is turned inward and may support self-regulation (*refer* to Vygotsky)

problem-based play   spontaneous activity that involves solving challenges presented by the play materials, by the child, or by a play partner; a method of informal action-based discovery learning

professional development   ongoing education, training, study, or experience that contributes to the increase and updating of proficiency within a professional field—e.g., education

professional   any person who is qualified to provide health services, social services, or child care and education, and who is committed to upholding the ethical standards associated with those roles and responsibilities

profound experiences   the emotional and social experiences that an individual must have in order for any other learning experience to be meaningful

program (early childhood)   any environment and curriculum designed for and delivered to young children—e.g., an infant program in a child care center or a family home child care program for young children of various ages

program standards (exit standards)   the knowledge, skills, and dispositions (competencies) required for successful completion of a program—e.g., early childhood education

progression   steps forward in development

pronation   after initial ground contact, the foot is designed to roll inward to disperse shock. Over-pronators roll in too much. This causes excessive movement of the foot and lower leg. Under-pronators have feet that don't roll enough after ground contact

proprioceptive system   refers to components of muscles, joints, and connective tissue that provide a subconscious awareness of body position

pro-social skill   learned behavior that is intended to help others—e.g., helping, sharing, or kindness

pro-social skills   a component of social competence, comprised of acts that support, assist, or benefit others without any expectation of external reward

proto-emotions   feelings that have not yet developed into specific emotions

proto-words   vocal interactions that resemble real conversation but lack real words or grammatical rules

proximodistal   the principle that physical skill development goes in a series of stages from the center of the body outward to the hands

pruning   a process whereby unused synapses (connections among brain cells) are shed; experience governs which synapses will be shed and which will be preserved

psychoanalytic school   children undergo a series of stages of development in which they experience difficulties in dealing with biological drives and social expectations; psychological well-being depends on successful management of these conflicts (*refer to* Freud; Mahler; Erikson; Winnicott)

psychological clock   one of the three clocks of life-span development; the influence of inner needs and drives

psychological needs   the conditions necessary for the development of a healthy psyche, soul, mind, or self—e.g., love

psychosocial theory   individuals develop a personality through undergoing a series of inner conflicts—these can be resolved with appropriate supports (*refer to* Erikson)

Q

qualia   the qualities of experiential states; the nature of the self or ego and its relation to thoughts and sensations; the mystery of consciousness; the introspectively accessible, phenomenal aspects of our mental lives; the "what it's like" character of mental states; the way it feels to have mental states such as pain, seeing red, smelling a rose

quality care   the concept of exemplary services that meet the needs of children and families; indicators of quality include child–caregiver ratios and staff training

quality care indicators   (in the early childhood field) these are generally agreed-upon measures that contribute to quality in caregiving

quality of attachment   the degree to which a strong and secure bonding relationship has developed

R

rating scales   measurement devices used to record the degree to which an attribute or behavior is present or absent (may involve semantic differentials or numerical scales)

readiness   the idea that there is a state of being when a child is ready to acquire a skill or experience something meaningfully

receptive language   uttering meaningful sounds, words, phrases, and sentences

receptive volume   the level of sound at which the individual can hear best

reciprocal communications   communication exchange in an equal give-and-take manner

reciprocal imitation   two individuals copying each other's actions

reciprocal relationships   social relationships between two people where there is a two-way exchange and mutual benefit

reciprocity   the process of giving and receiving in a meaningful manner

reflection   a learning method that engages an individual in a process of self-observation and self-examination

reflective practice   professional practice that includes regular evaluation of the program and one's effectiveness within it

reflex   an inborn, automatic response to stimulation

regression   steps backward in development (opposite of progression)

REM sleep   a stage of sleep characterized by rapid eye movement, especially during dreaming

resilience   the idea that an individual can withstand and recover from negative circumstances

resource teachers   adults who are prepared to meet the needs of children with disabilities and special needs

responsive care   a philosophy of care, education, and nurturance that meets the changing needs of the developing infant and young child and is sensitive to the individual differences of each child

responsivity   the process of being responsive to the needs of each child; involves a philosophy and an attitude of mind

rhythmicity (regularity)   the predictability or unpredictability in patterns of the child's behavior (*refer to* Chess & Thomas)

risk management   the careful and thoughtful assessment of risks associated with an activity or circumstance; decision-making on the basis of risk/benefit analysis

rituals   the routines and sequences of behavior linked with particular activities, relationships, or times of day

role modeling   demonstrating appropriate actions and reactions through behavior; the set of actions associated with particular roles or jobs

role playing   play in which children take on characters, or parts, that have personalities, motivations, and backgrounds different from their own

rouge-and-mirror test   an informal test to determine the child's understanding of the concept of self (*refer* to Gibson)

rough-and-tumble play   spontaneous activity involving play-fighting, chasing, and close physical interactions such as tickling; may include adult–child interactions

routine   the regular and predictable sequence of mealtimes, sleep times, and activity during each day

running records   observational recordings that include everything the child does, everything the child utters, and the way all behaviors are demonstrated; the recordings are detailed, sequential, and as objective as possible

S

scaffolding   the role of the adult (or other child) to provide, and gradually remove, a support to the child's learning; providing a bridge for the child to gain a new understanding (*refer* to Bruner, Vygotsky)

scheme   an organized pattern of sensorimotor functioning; a preliminary cluster of ideas; early infant ideas (*refer* to Piaget)

screening   the basic process of reviewing, checking, or assessing a group of individuals to determine if any meet specified criteria—e.g., hearing deficit, developmental delay; may lead to further investigation

script   series of sequential steps to perform a task; a set of words and/or actions adopted within a particular situation

secondary circular reaction   actions the child repeats as a result of his becoming interested in the external results that they produce; typically observed at 4–8 months; a substage of sensorimotor development (*refer* to Piaget)

second birth   the idea that individuals undergo a psychological rebirth during infancy (*refer* to Mahler)

secure attachment   a positive, trusting, and reliable relationship with an adult

seizures (convulsions)   uncontrolled bodily movements resulting from problems with the brain or central nervous system; they vary in severity

self   the distinct and separate individual; conscious awareness of being

self-actualization   when the highest level of the individual's needs are met, it is possible for the person to experience actualization; includes positive self-regard and productivity (*refer* to Maslow)

self-awareness   having a sense of self as being distinct and separate from others

self-concept   the mental image, perception, or opinion that one has of oneself; in young children, self-concept evolves as they interact with the objects and people in their environment; often self-concept is affected by what is reflected back to individuals about their worth and capabilities from the significant people in their lives

self-differentiation   seeing oneself as a separate and different person

self-efficacy   the feeling that one can act, do, and achieve success using one's own abilities

self-esteem   an individual's perception of one's own overall positive or negative self-worth; the degree to which one feels positive about oneself; one's overall sense of worth, competence, and control over life

self-help skills   skills that demonstrate the ability to eat, dress, keep clean, and toilet by one's self

self-permanence   understanding that one continues to exist over time

self-recognition   the ability to recognize your image in a mirror, reflection, or photograph, or through some other representation

self-regulation   the ability to control feelings and emotions, or the behavior that results from those emotions; the ability to modify or change behavior as a result of managing inner emotions

semantics   the meanings represented by language

sensation   stimulation of one or more sense organs (sight, touch, taste, hearing, or smell)

senses   the five faculties for taking in information (sight, touch, taste, hearing, and smell)

sensitive period   the window of opportunity (*see below*) when the brain is most receptive to particular types of learning experiences

sensory   concerning the senses

sensory acuity   the degree to which one or more of the five senses can perceive stimulation

sensory integration   interaction of two or more sensory processes in a manner that enhances the adaptiveness of the brain

sensorimotor   the first stage of the individual's cognitive development; this stage has six substages (*refer* to Piaget)

sensorimotor play   spontaneous activity demonstrating the characteristics of the substages of the first stage of cognitive development (*refer* to Piaget)

sensory play   play that involves touching, smelling, tasting, hearing, or seeing, individually or simultaneously

sensory overload   receiving too much stimulation or information from one or more of the five senses; inability to make meaning from sensory input

sensory stimulation   providing auditory, olfactory, visual, taste, or touch information through one or more senses

separateness   the need to become, or the process of becoming, a separate person

separation   awareness of being without a person or object

separation–individuation   the process of becoming a separate and individual person

separation anxiety   distress shown because of the departure, or impending departure, of a person to whom the individual is attached

separations   a series of departures and returns of a person to whom the child is attached

sexual abuse   any abuse or maltreatment of an individual that involves the sexual organs of the perpetrator or victim, and/or unwanted or inappropriate touching, and/or damage to the sexual identity, privacy, or feelings of the victim

shaken baby syndrome   a form of inflicted head trauma. Head injury, as a form of child abuse, can be caused by direct blows to the head, dropping or throwing the child, or shaking the child. This sudden whiplash motion can cause bleeding inside the head and increased pressure on the brain, causing the brain to pull apart, resulting in injury to the baby. The vast majority of incidents occur in infants who are younger than 1 year old

shame   a social emotion involving embarrassment or awkwardness about an imagined or real behavior; includes a level of self-consciousness

shared meanings   communication involving eye contact, close proximity, language, play, or other ways of being at one with another person; exchanging understandings

shared orbit   the two-way communication and shared space of two individuals

siblings   children who share the same parents; brothers and sisters

sign language   a system of communication, such as ASL (American Sign Language), that enables individuals who are deaf to communicate using gestures and hand signals

signing   the process of using a language of gestures and hand signals

skills   learned behaviors; require deliberate action and practice

sleep   a state of temporary loss of consciousness in which there are discernable cycles of approximately 90 minutes; characterized by five levels, measured by an electroencephalograph; a periodic state of physiological rest during which consciousness is suspended

slow-to-warm-up child   a characterization of the temperament of a child (*refer* to Chess & Thomas)

small for dates   an infant who is smaller than average for that age; may have health and developmental difficulties

social clock   one of the three clocks of life-span development; the influence of culture and society

social context   every element of an environment that influences an individual's development, including the people, institutions, and values to which the individual is exposed on a daily basis (*refer* to Bronfenbrenner)

social development   development of one's social capabilities, including identity, relationships with others, and understanding of one's place within a social environment

social emotions   feelings that exist because of relationships—e.g., shame, empathy

social learning   a theory of learning that emphasizes observational learning, imitation and deferred imitation, and internalizing of roles (*refer* to Bandura)

social referencing   the tendency to use others' emotional expressions to help understand the situation and thus relieve uncertainty; child will look at parent or caregiver's face and monitor their expressions in order to decide how to respond

social smile   a smile, appearing at approximately 6–8 weeks, that clearly indicates an ability to be social because the infant smiles in response to human faces

socialization   the process of learning social rules and adapting to social expectations; becoming part of a social group

socially acceptable behavior   any actions or language that are generally accepted as being appropriate in a particular situation or context

sociodramatic play   a fantasy-play scenario that involves at least one other individual

solitary play   spontaneous activity involving only one individual, not involving others

soul   the spirit or essence of the immaterial, nonobservable part of the individual; the fundamental nature of the person

special needs (exceptional needs)   needs that have been identified as requiring help or intervention beyond the scope of ordinary adult interactions or normal classroom interactions and routines

specific attachments   attachment to a particular person

spirit   the essence of an individual; elements of experience that transcend everyday reality; meaning found in experience; a person's own inner energy

spiritual development   the stages of human change that involve finding increasing understanding of personal meaning and values; finding the sacredness of life; having awareness of forces within and outside the self; sharing higher-order experiences

stage   a period of time when the individual demonstrates behavior associated with a labeled explanation—e.g., sensorimotor stage

stereopsis (or stereoscopic vision)   vision wherein two separate images from two eyes are successfully combined into one image in the brain

stranger anxiety   anxiety, distress, or uneasiness shown by a child when an unknown person is present

strange situation   a sequence of staged episodes that indicate the strength of attachment between a parent (or other adult) and young child (*refer* to Ainsworth)

strange situation procedure   a laboratory procedure used to assess infant attachment style

stress   the sum of the biological reactions to any adverse stimulus—physical, mental, or emotional, internal or external—that tend to disturb a person's normal state of well-being

sudden infant death syndrome (SIDS)   the sudden death of any child under 1 year of age that remains unexplained after a thorough case investigation, including performance of a complete autopsy, examination of the death scene, and review of the clinical history

superego   the aspect of the individual's personality that represents a person's conscience; knows right and wrong (*refer* to Freud)

superheroes   human-like figures in play and stories that have extraordinary powers; children involved in superhero play may feel especially empowered

supportive guidance   providing the individual with appropriate encouragement, nurturance, and instruction, and reinforcing positive behavior

syllabic repetitions   repeating sounds that have language-like characteristics

symbiosis   a close association between two individuals where each needs the other (the needs may differ in kind); interdependence

symbol   something that represents something else

symbolic thought   ability to mentally represent an object that is not present

symbolic play   activity that involves the process of using objects, actions, or words to stand for something else; may incorporate pretense or make-believe

symbolism   the process of using objects, words, or actions to stand for something else

symbolization   the emergence of symbolic activity—typically observed at ages over 18 months; the last of the sensorimotor substages (*refer* to Piaget)

synapses   the connections between neurons through which nerve impulses travel

synaptic connection   (*see* synapses, above)

syndrome   a group of combined symptoms or signs that characterize a disorder

syntax   the rules for combining words to form phrases and sentences

T

tactile system   includes nerves under the skin's surface that send information to the brain

teaching   the process of facilitating learning, involving direct instruction, demonstration, encouraging the learner's motivation, and offering information

telegraphic speech   sentences spoken by very young children that leave out the less significant words and include only the words that carry the most meaning

temper tantrum　a loss of control of emotions or the experience of conflicted feelings resulting in anger, crying, stamping feet, kicking, screaming, or other extreme behaviors; frequently occurs in toddlers when they cannot regulate their feelings and actions

temperament　the observable traits or patterns of behavior of an individual; the way the individual behaves; the how of behavior, not the why

temperament styles　the general or predictable way of responding to stimuli or going about a task that is particular to the individual

temporal concepts　the collection of ideas that makes up the individual's understanding of time

teratogen　any substance that an individual, during pregnancy, either uses (such as smoking or alcohol consumption) or comes into contact with that has the potential to cause damage to the embryo or fetus

tertiary circular reactions　varying the repetitive actions to prolong and change the result—typically observed at 12–18 months; one of the sensorimotor substages (*refer* to Piaget)

toddler　the stage of the child after infancy when the child starts to walk or toddle; defined by age, a toddler may be 8 to 18 months, 12 to 24 months, etc. (variable according to practice and legislation)

toilet learning　the individual's gradual maturational process of understanding and acquiring skills required to use the potty or toilet for bowel movements and urination (contrast with toilet training, a more regimented approach)

tracking　the ability to follow a target that moves along an imagined line in front of the face from the nose to the ear; is not present at birth

traits　an individual's personality characteristics

trance　a level of consciousness similar to a hypnotic state; lack of awareness of the environment; loss of voluntary movement and lack of sensitivity to external stimuli

transductive reasoning　reasoning that relies on preconcepts; may attribute incorrect cause and effect

transitions　parts of the child's experience that involve a change of activity, people, or place

trial and error　learning through experimenting and making mistakes, as well as experiencing success

trundling　movement on a sit-upon wheeled toy that requires the use of alternating or simultaneous leg or foot movement to push the vehicle forward; pre-pedaling

trust　confident reliance on self or others

trust versus mistrust　the first of the stages of the life cycle, in which the infant needs to establish basic trust (*refer* to Erikson)

tuneful babbling　strings of sounds that have patterns of pitch and rhythm

twins　two individuals developing side by side during prenatal development; may be fraternal (developing from two separate zygotes, or dizygotic) or identical (developing from one divided zygote, or monozygotic)

typical development　human development that lies within the range of the norm or average

U

unconditional love　love that exists without conditions or dependence on particular behaviors or situations

unconscious　a level of mental experience not available to normal awareness

underextension　a child applies a word meaning to fewer examples than are generally accepted; restricted use of a word

uni-modal stimulation　stimulation through one sensory channel at a time—e.g., visual material

universal grammar　the internalized set of rules and principles integral to all existing languages (*refer* to Chomsky)

universal precautions　a principle of health and infection control that treats everyone as having the potential to transmit germs (bacteria, viruses); precautions such as hand washing and the appropriate use of gloves are used consistently with all people as infection-control measures (*refer* to Pimento & Kernested)

uptime　a level of consciousness characterized by an individual's high sensitivity and responsiveness to stimuli

urticaria　a hypersensitive reaction; showing large spots with a red center; typically appears during the first week of life; not an infection

V

validation　being able to justify or defend a statement

values　beliefs of a person or social group in which they have an emotional investment (either for or against)

variegated babbling　long strings of different syllables used in the vocal experimentation of infants

vernix　a protective, creamy white, waxy substance that covers some of the skin of the newborn baby

vestibular system　controls the sense of movement and balance, and is dependent in part on information received from structures within the inner ear (the semi circular canals) that detect movement and changes in the position of the head

visual acuity　the degree to which the individual can see

visual cliff　an experimental apparatus intended to test depth perception in infants and toddlers (*refer* to Gibson & Walk)

visual insatiability　the individual's unstoppable interest in looking

vocabulary　the bank of available words

vocalization　any sound production

voluntary grasping　grasping that is deliberate

vowel　a speech sound or letter of the alphabet, characterized by the absence of obstruction in the vocal tract—e.g., A, E, I, O, or U

vulnerable　susceptible to physical or emotional injury, especially at an early age

vulnerability　particular sensitivities to which the individual can succumb in adverse circumstances

W

ways of knowing　the notion that there are different viewpoints or mental structures from which individuals construct their reality—e.g., women's ways of knowing (*refer* to Gilligan)

weaning　the process of transiting from fluid to solid food

windows of opportunity　sensitive periods of time when the brain is particularly capable of learning certain things most efficiently and thoroughly; the time when a child can benefit most from appropriate learning experiences

Z

zone of proximal development (ZPD)　behaviors that are on the edge of emergence; the gap between the child's actual performance when operating alone and the child's potential performance when assisted by more knowledgeable adults or children (*refer* to Vygotsky)

Index